European
MUSEUM
Guide Volume Western Europe

9697

Publisher
Museum Media Publishers

Editorial director
A.B. van der Lans

Cover design & lay-out
Marc Heymans

Translation
TODO Talenservice

Print
Drukkerij Dröge

Binding
In Otabind by Binderij Hexspoor

Museum Media Publishers
Stationsstraat 28
Postbus 318
5260 AH Vught
The Netherlands
Telephone +31 73 657 91 47
Telefax +31 73 656 96 34

GW00371027

Although this guide has been compiled with the greatest care and attention, Museum Media Publishers cannot accept responsibility for the consequences of any error or inaccuracy appearing in the European Museum Guide.

MUSEUM MEDIA PUBLISHERS

We are proud to present the European Museum Guide '96|'97
- Volume Western Europe. This Guide is special:
it describes both the permanent collections and the
temporary exhibitions of museums in nine western European
countries.

Details are conveniently listed according to country.
The entry for each country begins with a map showing the
cities where the museums are situated. The information
regarding each museum follows under the names of the cities,
arranged in alphabetical order.

If you are interested in a particular exhibition, we suggest you
contact the museum to verify, as details may change at short
notice.

Museum Media Publishers operates independently and
guarantees the editorial neutrality of the European Museum
Guide.

We wish you plenty of enjoyment with the European Museum
Guide, and we hope it puts you on the track of interesting
museum visits.

Museum Media Publishers

A.B. van der Lans
Editorial director

Contents

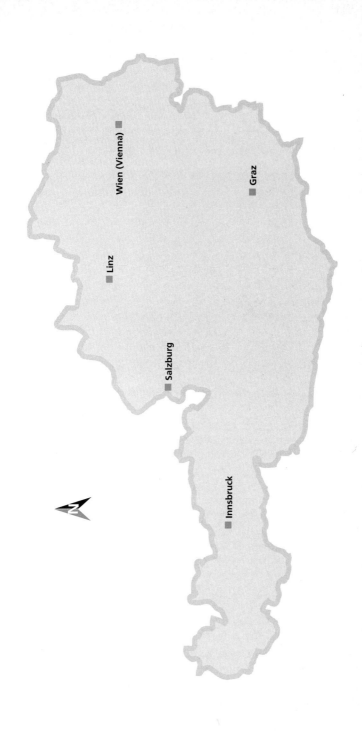

Graz

ALTE GALERIE DES STEIERMÄRKISCHEN LANDESMUSEUMS JOANNEUM
Neutorgasse 45 8010 Graz Director: G. Biedermann
☎ +43 316 80174770 🖷 +43 316 80174800
Open: Tuesday-Friday 09.00-17.00 Saturday and Sunday 10.00-13.00
Closed: Monday

COLLECTION

The Middle Ages The collection focuses on Styrian art and includes the `Procession Cross', `Madonna of Admont', `Reicheneck Epitaph Picture', pietàs from Admont, `Madonna with Corona', `Votive Tablet of St. Lambrecht', `Martyrdom of Thomas Becket' and the `Small and Large Miraculous Altar of Mariazell'.

Pieter Brueghel the Younger (1564-1638)
The fairground, detail

Landesmuseum Joanneum, Abteilung Alte Galerie, Graz

Renaissance, Mannerism and Baroque Dutch and Flemish masters: Herri met de Bles, Jan and Pieter Brueghel, Hendrik de Clerck, Josse de Momper, Bartholomäus Spranger, Cornelis de Vos and Philips Wouwerman.
Italian masters: Sofonisba Anguissola, Luca Cambiaso, Giacomo Francesco Cipper, Dosso and Battista Dossi, Teodoro Ghisi, Giambologna, Giovanni Pietro de Pomis and Rosa da Tivoli.
German and Austrian masters: Lucas and Hans Cranach, Franz Christoph Janneck, Veit Königer, Franz Anton Maulbertsch, Johann Georg Platzer, Johann Michael Rottmayr, Kremser Schmidt, Johann Heinrich Schönfeld, Josef Thaddäus Stammel, Paul Troger and Hans Adam Weissenkircher.

EXHIBITION
01·06·96–30·09·96

Treasures and Visions

Graz

LANDESMUSEUM JOANNEUM, BILD- UND TONARCHIV
Sackstraße 17/II 8010 Graz   Director: Armgard Schiffer-Ekhart
☎ +43 316 830335 🖷 +43 316 844797
Open: Monday Tuesday Thursday 08.00-16.00 Wednesday Friday 08.00-13.00
Closed: Saturday and Sunday

COLLECTION

Photography The main themes of this collection are (local) art, architecture and landscape. The archive contains more than half a million negatives and 60 000 positives, as well as 50 000 slides on various subjects. The earliest photographs date back to 1840.

Documentations of cultural manifestations and political events are present, and various material on the history of photography.
Sound recordings The collection includes gramophone records, tapes, cassettes and CD's; for the most part the recordings cover regional events and persons.
Moving images Though small (150 films), the film collection contains a number of productions which are of great local importance, such as documentation of a prisoner-of-war camp in Styria in 1914-1915 and films of the reconstruction of Graz between the world wars. There is also a video collection consisting mainly of recordings from local television.

EXHIBITIONS | No exhibitions planned.

Innsbruck

TIROLER VOLKSKUNSTMUSEUM
Universitätsstraße 2 6020 Innsbruck Director: Hans Gschnitzer
☎ **+43 512 584302** 📠 **+43 512 582682**
Open: Monday-Saturday 09.00-17.00 Sunday 09.00-12.00

COLLECTION | *Arts and crafts, popular art* The museum is situated in an old monastery building next to the Court Church (Hofkirche) that includes the tomb monument of Emperor Maximilian I.
The Tyrol Museum of Popular Art houses a large collection of popular arts and crafts representing everyday life and customs in the German and Romance speaking regions of Tirol from the close of the Middle Ages to present times.
The most memorable parts of the permanent exhibition are the Gothic, Renaissance and Baroque parlours that illustrate the lifestyles of the aristocrats, the middle-class and the peasants. Other exhibits include rustic furniture with rich carving and colourful painting, models of old Tyrol farmhouses, original costumes from the valleys and an impressive collection of cribs.

EXHIBITIONS
20·06·96–end Sep 96 | *Human Images in Folk Art*

Winter 96/97 | *Sledges and Toboggans* An exhibition to coincide with the Toboggan World Championships.

Linz

NEUE GALERIE DER STADT LINZ/WOLFGANG-GURLITT-MUSEUM
Blütenstraße 15 4040 Linz Director: Peter Baum
☎ **+43 732 70703600 +43 732 236190**
Open: Monday-Saturday10.00-18.00 Thursday 10.00-22.00
During summer Saturday 10.00-13.00
Closed: Sunday

COLLECTION | The New Gallery in the city of Linz is one of the most important museums of modern and contemporary art in Austria. The museum possesses a collection of 1170 paintings, sculptures and objects, nearly 8000 drawings, watercolours and works of graphic art, as well as a catalogue and poster collection.
The collection also includes 600 original pen drawings of the artist Kubin, who died in 1959. This 'Kubin Cabinett' is the third largest collection of his works in the world.
In the Central European Art Collection a special emphasis has been placed on the landscape paintings of the 19th century, as well as the German and Austrian Expressionists.
The most important works of the collection include paintings by

Liebermann, Corinth, Thöny, Kokoschka, Klimt, Schiele, Hofer, Mueller, Pechstein, Kolig, and Nolde, among others.
The Gallery's collection also includes works of Informal and Pop Art, Concrete Art, and Geometrical Abstraction. In addition, Austrian contemporary art and examples of international avant-garde art are represented, with works by many prominent artists.

Oskar Kokoschka
(1886- 1980)
Linz (Landscape around Linz), 1955

Neue Galerie der
Stadt Linz

EXHIBITIONS

14·03·96–09·06·96   ***Gaston Chaissac (1910-1964)***   This exhibition will draw together about 50 paintings, 62 drawings and gouaches, and 32 sculptures and totems borrowed from private and public collections throughout the world. Linz is the first site for this revealing exhibition, which introduces one of the most interesting 'outsiders' of 20th-century European art.

20·06·96–24·08·96   ***Masterpieces of International Graphic Art***   The collection of the Neue Galerie der Stadt Linz includes graphic works by Baselitz, Beuys, Dine, Hartung, Kirkeby, Lichtenstein, Miró, Oldenburg, Picasso, Rauschenberg, Rosenquist, Tàpies and Warhol.

05·09·96–13·10·96   ***Jack Ox***   A hommage to Anton Bruckner - series of paintings.

17·10·96–15·01·97   ***Ernst Haas*** *Photographs*   A major retrospective of the work of the famous Magnum photographer.

Salzburg

RESIDENZGALERIE SALZBURG
Residenzplatz 1 5010 Salzburg Director: Roswitha Juffinger
☎ +43 662 840451   📠 +43 662 840451-16
Open: Daily 10.00-17.00

COLLECTION   The current collection of Old Masters continues the tradition of the Episcopal art collection in the historical setting of the Residence Palace. It was founded in 1789, but was short-lived due to political causes. In 1923 the Residenzgalerie Salzburg was newly founded in the form of a county gallery. 41 paintings of the Austrian collection of Count Rudolf Czernin were purchased by the county of Salzburg in 1980. In 1994 the 70th painting of this collection was bought, meaning that the main bulk of the Czernin collection is now in the Residenzgalerie. In addition, 28 of the best paintings from the Schönborn-Buchheim Collection have been on loan to the museum since 1956.
The main focus of the Residenzgalerie Salzburg is the exhibition of Austrian and German painters, together with a range of Italian, Flemish, Dutch and French masters offering a good selection of European painting of the 16th, 17th and 18th centuries.
Austrian 19th-century landscape works provide a better

understanding of a famous period in Austrian painting.
Special attention is devoted to the fact that Salzburg played a
significant role as a meeting point for many painters of the
Romantic period.

EXHIBITIONS

Apr 96–Jul 96   ***Grünspan & Schildlaus***   Old Masters in the Residenzgalerie
Salzburg and their techniques

Jul 96–Sep 96   ***My Life, let me shake your hand***   An invitation to a Baroque
festivity.

Aug 96–Dec 96   ***Jacopo Borges in the Residenzgalerie Salzburg***   Historical and
Contemporary Art on the subject `The Flood'.

Salzburg

RUPERTINUM
Wiener-Philharmoniker-Gasse 9 5010 Salzburg Director: Otto Breicha
☎ +43 662 80422541 📠 +43 662 80422542
Open: Tuesday-Sunday 10.00-17.00 Wednesday 10.00-21.00; during summer
exhibitions: Tuesday-Sunday 09.00-17.00 Wednesday 09.00-17.00
Closed: Monday

COLLECTION   The focus of the collection (paintings, sculptures, works on paper,
mainly graphics) concentrates on the European art of the turn of
the century (Kollwitz, Barlach, Kubin, Dix) down to the Austrian
avantgarde (Arnulf Rainer, Günter Brus, Ch.L. Attersee). The
'Österreichische Fotogalerie' is in possession of stocks of over 10 000
works in the field of contemporary Austrian photography.
An intensive range of changing and special exhibitions focuses on
artists and tendencies of European contemporary and recent art
developments. Two floors, a sculpture hall on the ground floor and
the 'studio' continuously present special exhibitions, the first floor
of the house is dedicated to the presentation of its own collection
stocks.

EXHIBITIONS

05·04·96–09·06·96   ***Paul Strand***   The World On My Doorstep - Photographs

09·05·96–07·07·96   ***Karl Schleinkofer***   Drawings

09·05·96–14·07·96   ***Lun Tuchnowski***   Sculptures

18·05·96–07·07·96   ***Alberto di Fabio***   Works On Paper

18·05·96–07·07·96   ***Cy Twombly***   Drawings

13·06·96–14·07·96   ***Erich Lessing***   Black & White Photographs Of The 50s

11·07·96–20·10·96   ***Richard Gerstl***   The Landscapes

20·07·96–13·10·96   ***Oskar Kokoschka***   Paintings, Drawings, Watercolours
The collection of the Vevey Museum.

Jul 96–Aug 96   ***Georg Eisler***   Pictures On The Theme Of Jazz

24·07·96–27·10·96   ***Louise Bourgeois***   Objects

17·10·96–01·12·96   ***Karl Schmidt-Rotluff***   The Ink-Brush Drawings

24·10·96–15·12·96   ***Ulrich Waibel***   New Drawings

24·10·96–15·12·96	*Franz Ringel* Pictures 1970-1990
04·11·96–01·12·96	*Creative Children's Exhibition*
04·12·96–Feb 97	*Annemarie Avramidis* Marble And Bronze Sculptures
05·12·96–Feb 97	*Adolf Wolfli* Works On Paper
19·12·96–Feb 97	*The Wolfgang Graninger Collection*

Wien - Vienna

GEMÄLDEGALERIE DER AKADEMIE DER BILDENDEN KÜNSTE
Schillerplatz 3 1010 Wien Director: Renate Trnek
☎ +43 1 58816225 📠 +43 1 5863346
Open: Tuesday-Friday 10.00-14.00 Saturday-Sunday 09.00-13.00
Closed: Monday and 1 Jan, 1 May, 1-2 Nov, 24-25 Dec, 31 Dec,
Good Friday, Easter Sunday, Whit Sunday, Corpus Christi

COLLECTION

Old Masters Part of this collection is formed by the works of 14th to 18th-century Italian masters, including Botticelli, Titian, Testa, Giordano, Tiepolo and Guardi. A number of Spanish and French artists from the same period are also represented, among which Murillo, Subleyra and Hubert Robert. The main core of the collection, however, consists of works from Northern European painting schools, including Early Netherlandish and German paintings such as Bosch's 'Last Judgement' and Baldung Grien's 'Rest on the Flight'. A large part of the collection is made up of 17th-century Dutch paintings: Rembrandt's 'Portrait of a Young Woman' and Pieter de Hoogh's 'Family Group in a Courtyard' are just two examples. Works by Jacob van Ruisdael, Asselijn, Both and Berchem are also on display. The academic tradition of the gallery is expressed through its 18th and 19th-century collection, consisting primarily of works by Austrian artists, such as Meytens, Brand, Wutky, Quadal, Waldmüller, Füger and Führich.

Hieronymus Bosch
The last Judgement,
Tryptich detail

Gemäldegalerie der
Akademie der
bildenden Künste,
Wien

Modern Art The range of 20th-century Austrian art is mainly reflected in the works of teachers of the academy, among which Böckl, Wotruba, Avramidis, Mikl, Hundertwasser and Rainer.

EXHIBITIONS

No details available..

Wien · Vienna

GRAPHISCHE SAMMLUNG ALBERTINA
Augustinerstrasse 1 1010 Wien Director: Konrad Oberhuber
☎ +43 1 53483 📠 +43 1 6376977
Open: Monday-Thursday 10.00-16.00 Friday-Sunday 10.00-13.00

COLLECTION

Situated in the centre of Vienna, the Albertina Collection is one of the most important collections of prints and drawings in the world. The most valuable treasures are shown in changing exhibitions, sometimes in combination with loans from all over the world.
50 000 drawings and approximately 1.5 million prints represent the cultural heritage of our past, constantly enriched with works by contemporary artists.
At the Albertina, visitors can view a great number of masterpieces by Raphael, Dürer, Rembrandt and Rubens, as well as drawings from other European artists spanning the centuries.
Since 1920, the collection has comprised the former collection of Duke Albert of Saxe-Teschen and his wife the Archduchess Mary-Christine and the collection of the former imperial library. Together they represent one of the largest collections of prints in the world, with materials dating back to the beginning of printmaking in the 15th century. Special collections are Architectural Drawings, Posters, Miniatures and Illustrated Books.

Albrecht Dürer
(1471-1528)
Self-portrait at the
age of 13

Graphische
Sammlung Albertina,
Wien

EXHIBITIONS

Jan 96–Dec 96 ***Master Drawings of the Albertina*** *(In Facsimile Reproductions)*

04·06·96–04·08·96 ***Between the times*** *(Kunstforum, Freyung 8, Wien)*

Wien · Vienna

ÖSTERREICHISCHE GALERIE BELVEDERE AUSTRIAN GALLERY BELVEDERE
Prinz Eugenstraße 27 1030 Wien Director: Gerbert Frodl
☎ +43 1 79557 📠 +43 1 7984337
Open: Tuesday-Sunday 10.00-17.00
Closed: Monday and 1 Jan, 1 May, 1 Nov, 24-25 Dec

COLLECTION

Due to the general renovation of the Belvedere Castle the permanent collection of the Austrian Gallery in the Upper Belvedere is only partially exhibited (till autumn 1996). Since October 1995 the collection 'Vienna 1900 and Avantgarde' is reopened (Klimt, Schiele,

Kokoschka, Van Gogh, Léger, a.o.). A selection of masterpieces of Austrian and international painting of the 20th century (Kokoschka, Boeckl, Corinth, Beckmann) is on display from April 1996 to February 1997. The department of painting of the 19th century (Romantic Art and Biedermeier: C.D. Friedrich, Waldmüller, Amerling) will be reopened in May 1996.
In the Lower Belvedere the Museum of Medieval Art and the new display of the Museum of Baroque Art are opened.

Gustav Klimt
Adele Bloch-Bauer I,
1907

Österreichische
Galerie Belvedere,
Wien

EXHIBITIONS	[Upper Belvedere]
14·03·96–16·06·96	*Claude Monet*
18·12·96–02·03·97	*Oskar Kokoschka and Dresden*
Spring 97	*Rudolf Hoflehner*

Wien · Vienna

KUNSTFORUM BANK AUSTRIA
Freyung 8 1010 Wien Director: Klaus Albrecht Schröder
☎ +43 1 71191 5730 📠 +43 1 71191 5747
Open: Daily 10.00-18.00 Wednesday 10.00-21.00

COLLECTION | No permanent collection.

EXHIBITIONS
01·03·96–27·05·96 *Early Van Gogh* The beginnings, breakthrough and triumph of the 'Hague School' was experienced first hand by Van Gogh during his apprenticeship in the art dealing business. The exhibition 'Early Van Gogh' will be pursuing the links between Van Gogh's early work and the artistic works of the Hague School. 90 works by Van Gogh (45 paintings and 45 works on paper) will be placed in juxtaposition to about 80 early works by artists of the Hague School. The exhibition 'Early Van Gogh' will be shown exclusively in this museum.

05·06·96–04·08·96 *Drawing In Austria 1908-1938* *From Schiele To Wortuba* For the first time a comprehensive exhibition of Austrian drawings will highlight works from the period from 1908 until 1938. The Bank Austria Kunstforum, in cooperation with the Albertina Collection of Graphics and the Frankfurt Kunstverein, will be showing 130 works on paper - in part from hitherto inaccessible private collections and lesser known public collections - by 58 artists, including Gustav Klimt, Egon Schiele, Oskar Kokoschka, Alfred Kubin, Max Oppenheimer, Herbert Boeckl, Albert Paris Gütersloh, Max Weber and Fritz Wotruba.

29·08·96–24·11·96　*Art of the Mentally Ill*　This exhibition focuses on the phenomenon and effects of art created by the mentally ill on 20th-century art. It features 200 oil paintings, graphics and sculptures by artists including Paul Klee, Max Ernst, Wölfli and Jean Dubuffet, demonstrating that the art created by the mentally ill, in its spontaneity, roughness and anti-academic quality, is just as influential on 20th-century art as are the artworks of 'primitive cultures'.

Wien · Vienna

KUNSTHALLE WIEN
Karlsplatz Treitlstraße 2 1040 Wien Director: Toni Stooss
☎ **+43 1 5869776** 📠 **+43 1 586977620**
Open: Wednesday-Monday 10.00-18.00 Thursday 10.00-20.00
Closed: Tuesday

COLLECTION | No permanent collection.

EXHIBITIONS | [Karlsplatz]

30·08·96–03·11·96　*Illusion - Emotion - Reality*　The seventh Art on a Quest for the Six Others

[Museumquartier]

15·05·96–16·06·96　*Mail Art*

15·05·96–23·06·96　*Magnum Cinema*

Sep 96–Nov 96　*Gottfried Bechthold*

Wien · Vienna

KUNSTHAUSWIEN
Untere Weißgerberstraße 13 1030 Wien Director: Joram Harel
☎ **+43 1 7120495** 📠 **+43 1 7120496**
Open: Daily 10.00-19.00

COLLECTION | The Hundertwasser collection of the KunstHausWien provides a retrospective of works by the painter, architect and ecologist, Friedensreich Hundertwasser (born Vienna, 1928). Early works, watercolours, oils and recent mixed media paintings are exhibited. His graphics include the Rotaprint portfolio of 1951, Japanese woodcuts, etchings, lithographs and silk screens.
The tapestries, based on works by Hundertwasser, were made by weavers in Mexico and Vienna. 'Pissing Boy with Sky-Scraper' was handwoven by the artist in 1952.
Hundertwasser's concern for architecture is manifested in a collection of scale models such as the 'Hundertwasserhaus' in Vienna and 'In the Meadow Hills', which demonstrates the 'Pit houses' and 'Eye-Slit houses', the 'St. Barbara Church' in Bärnbach, Styria, the 'Incinerator Spittelau' in Vienna, and the Day-Care Centre in Frankfurt.

EXHIBITION
15·05·96–01·09·96 | *Raoul Dufy*　This first-ever Dufy presentation in Austria will include a selection of the most important paintings from many French museums, as well fabric and ceramic objects, woodcuts and Gobelin tapestries.

Wien · Vienna

KUNSTHISTORISCHES MUSEUM
Maria Theresien Platz 1010 Wien Director: Wilfried Seipel
☎ +43 1 521770 📠 +43 1 932770
Open: Tuesday-Sunday 10.00-18.00 Thursday 10.00-21.00
Closed: Monday

COLLECTION

Many of the treasures of the collections of the Kunsthistorisches Museum were assembled by members of the Habsburg Imperial Family, enthusiastic patrons and collectors over many centuries. The exhibits range from ancient Egyptian, Greek and Roman art to Medieval art and Renaissance and Baroque collections. On show are paintings, sculptures, tapestries, goldsmith work, jewellery, musical instruments, carriages, sleighs, armour and other items. The museum is divided into eight collections, some of which are housed in the Hofburg and in Schönbrunn Palace. On display in the Schönbrunn Palace are the collection of Ancient Egyptian art, the Greek and Roman exhibits, the decorative-art sculptures, the historical musical instruments, the arms and armour, the historical carriages and the coins and medals, as well as the picture gallery, which includes many paintings by Pieter Brueghel the Elder, Dürer, Titian and Rubens. The highlights of the Treasury are the Austrian imperial crown and the insignia and coronation robes of the Holy Roman Empire.

Jan van Huysum
(1682-1749)
Flowers in a vase

Kunsthistorisches
Museum, Wien

EXHIBITIONS

20·05·96–26·08·96

Auguste Rodin 1840-1917   The planned exhibition of a representative selection of Auguste Rodin's sculptures and drawings at the Palais Harrach will present not only an artistic and aesthetic perspective on the French master's work, but will also focus on the human aspects of his epoch.

24·05·96–22·09·96

Treasures from the Land of the Bible. [Hall VIII]

Autumn 1996

The Restored Pictures. [Hall VIII]

27·10·96–Feb 97

The Message of Music *1000 Years of Music in Austria*
An exhibition organised by the Kunsthistorisches Museum in conjunction with the Archiv der Gesellschaft der Musikfreunde at the Palais Harrach. This exhibition attempts to give an impression of Austrian musical history and at the same time to demonstrate the connection between the production of music and international music over a period of 1000 years.

Wien · Vienna

MUSEUM MODERNER KUNST STIFTUNG LUDWIG WIEN
20er Haus Schweizer Garten 1030 Wien Director: Lóránd Hegyi
☎ +43 1 7996900 📠 +43 1 7996901
Open: Tuesday-Sunday 10.00-18.00
Closed: Monday

COLLECTION

The 20er Haus at the Schweizergarten, a pavilion building originally constructed for the world exhibition in Brussels in 1958, is one of two buildings occupied by the Museum moderner Kunst Stiftung Ludwig Wien. On the first floor of 20er Haus, large alternating exhibitions are presented. The museum's international collection, which was expanded in 1991, is exhibited on the second floor, and features Concept Art, Minimal Art and Land Art from approximately 1950 to the present. Along with work by Joseph Beuys, works by artists such as Peter Halley, Mario Merz, Richard Serra, Sol Le Witt, Jannis Kounellius, Donald Judd, Lawrence Weiner, Hanne Darboven, Bertrand Lavier and Günther Förg can be seen. The Austrian avant-garde is represented by Franz West, Heimo Zobernig, Hartmut Skerbisch, Gerwald Rockenschaub and others. In the sculpture garden, works by Henry Moore, Fritz Wotruba, Alberto Giacometti and others are on display.

EXHIBITIONS

16·03·96–19·05·96

Franz West   In his work this Vienna-based sculptor deals with the transformation of materials. In calling attention to their utility, his 'fitting pieces', furniture objects and spatial installations reveal new dimensions of functionalism and extend perception. This retrospective shows West's oeuvre spanning the period from 1970 until today and will be presented by the artist as a large-scale installation.

05·06·96–15·10·96

Coming Up   Young Art In Austria   'Coming Up' will highlight the works of about 25 young Austrian artists dealing with media-controlled and regulated communication and information serving as the basis of an interconnected society.

26·10·96–10·11·96

Abstract/Real   This exhibition will present international examples of contemporary object and installation art devoted to the transformation of objects, with references operating simultaneously on many different levels.

21·11·96–12·01·97

Ákos Birkás   The painter Ákos Birkás (born Budapest, 1941) has been dealing with the theme of the human figure since the early 80s, reducing it to the oval shape of the head. In relation to the temporal aspects involved in artistic activities, the incessantly repeated shaping process has a highly meditative and self-reflective quality.

Wien · Vienna

MUSEUM MODERNER KUNST STIFTUNG LUDWIG WIEN
Palais Liechtenstein Fürstengasse 1 1090 Wien Director: Lóránd Hegyi
☎ +43 1 3176900 📠 +43 1 3176901
Open: Tuesday-Sunday 10.00-18.00
Closed: Monday

COLLECTION

The Palais Liechtenstein has been used as an exhibition space by the Museum moderner Kunst Stiftung Ludwig Wien since 1979. Formerly housing the Liechtenstein Galerie, it was added to accommodate growth in the museum's collection when parts of the important Ludwig Collection were brought from Aachen to Vienna and the Hahn Collection of Cologne was acquired. The building is used for the display of a cross-section of 20th-century international art. Special rooms are dedicated to various art movements including Expressionism, Cubism, Futurism, Constructivism, Surrealism, Nouveau Realism, Vienna Actionism, Pop Art and Photorealism. International painting of the 80s and 90s is also exhibited.

EXHIBITIONS

30·03·96–27·05·96

Susana Solano   Susana Solano's oeuvre forms one of the most important contributions to contemporary Spanish art. With her metal sculptures and installations she addresses issues relating to materiality, perception and remembrance, binding a formal idiom greatly reduced with regard to its design and materials to a content rich in associations.

14·06·96–08·09·96

Errò   Errò, one of the legendary figures of European Pop Art, object art and action painting, will be the subject of a retrospective of creations spanning the last 30 years. His political commitment and his reflections on the media are introduced, by means of vivid painterly imagination, into a collage-like pictorial cosmos. The exhibition will feature about 90 large-format paintings.

Wien · Vienna

MUSEUM FÜR VÖLKERKUNDE
Neue Hofburg Heldenplatz 1014 Wien Director: Peter Kann
☎ +43 1 534300 📠 +43 1 5355320
Open: Wednesday-Monday 10.00-16.00
Closed: Tuesday

COLLECTION

The Museum for Ethnography possesses a collection of about 250 000 ethnographical and archaeological objects from Asia, Africa, Oceania-Australia and America, primarily from tribal societies but also from more advanced civilisations. The most outstanding and oldest collection consists of the 'Mexican Treasures', including the unique Quetzal feather headdress, the only featherwork shield with a figural image, and the feather fan of the Aztec culture. The museum's collection also includes a portion of James Cook's famous collection of 18th-century objects from Polynesia and Northwest Coast Indians, the collection of K.A.Freiherr von Hügel (1830-1836) from India, Southeast Asia, and China, and a collection acquired by the frigate 'Novara' during the circumnavigation of the globe between 1857 and 1859. The collection was significantly broadened by contributions during the second half of the 19th century of objects from South Africa, New Guinea, Southeast Asia, Japan, New Zealand, the Caucasus and Siberia. More than 14 000 objects, primarily from India and other Asian cultures, were collected during the world tour of Archduke Franz Ferdinand during 1892 and 1893.

EXHIBITIONS

21·03·96–01·09·96

Foreign Vienna *Xenographic Perspectives*   Photographs by Lisl Ponger.

21·06·96–06·01·97

Shining South Seas *The World of the Micronesian Islands*

Nov 96–Jan 97

Erotic Art of Ancient Peru

Wien · Vienna

ÖSTERREICHISCHES MUSEUM FÜR VOLKSKUNDE
Laudongasse 15-19 1080 Wien Director: Mr. Beitl, Mr. Grieshofer
☎ +43 1 4068905 📠 +43 1 4085342
Open: Tuesday-Friday 9.00-17.00 Saturday 9.00-12.00 Sunday 9.00-13.00
Closed: Monday

COLLECTION

The Austrian Folklore Museum, founded in 1895 and located in the Palais Schönborn in the Josefstadt quarter of Vienna, houses a diverse collection of items reflecting the cultures of Austria and its neighbours. The building has been renovated and the permanent collection redesigned to give an overview of traditional folklife through the medium of the museum's folk art collection.

The exhibitions depict people in their relationship to nature and the environment, show them striving for economic survival, and offer insights into the prevailing social order. The selection and arrangement of the exhibits, as well as the design of the displays, aims to help visitors appreciate the objects in their real-life contexts. Objects from the 17th to the 19th century give the visitor a picture of everyday life and everyday needs, vernacular architecture, work and religious faith, poverty and rural pride.
Special emphasis is placed on the folk art of countries that were once part of the Austro-Hungarian Empire, but the museum also possesses an extensive collection of objects from Alpine regions.

Rupert Griessl
(1854-1924)
Chessboard

*Österreichischses
Museum für
Volkskunde, Wien*

EXHIBITIONS

Apr 96–Jun 96   *Iron Handicraft*

May 96–Sep 96   *Lace from Pag (Croatia)*

Oct 96–Feb 97   *Filigree Jewellery*

Wien · Vienna

WIENER SECESSION
Friedrichstraße 12 1010 Wien Director: Ms. Hillebrandt
☎ +43 1 5875307 📠 +43 1 587530734
Open: Tuesday-Friday 10.00-18.00 Saturday and Sunday 10.00-16.00
Closed: Monday

COLLECTION

Gustav Klimt The Beethoven Frieze This frieze was created for the XIVth Secession exhibition in 1902. The monumental wall painting is one of the most significant works of this Art Nouveau painter. Since its restoration it has once again been on display at the Secession building since 1986.

[Hauptraum]

15·05·96–30·06·96 **Carsten Höller** *Installation*

12·07·96–01·09·96 **Young Scene**

11·09·96–18·10·96 **Martin Walde** *Storyboard, Object, Installation*

31·10·96–01·12·96 **Philip Taaffe** *Paintings*

13·12·96–19·01·97 **James Coleman** *Multimedia*

[Galerie]

15·05·96–30·06·96 **Manfred Erjautz** *Project Installation*

12·07·96–01·09·96 **Marijke van Warmerdam** *Multimedia*

11·09·96–27·10·96 **Nobuyoshi Araki/Larry Clark** *Photography*

31·10·96–08·12·96 **Dorothee Golz** *Objects*

[Grafisches Kabinett]

12·07·96–01·09·96 **Alexander Braun** *Writing Pictures*

11·09·96–27·10·96 **Zoe Leonhard** *Photography, Objects*

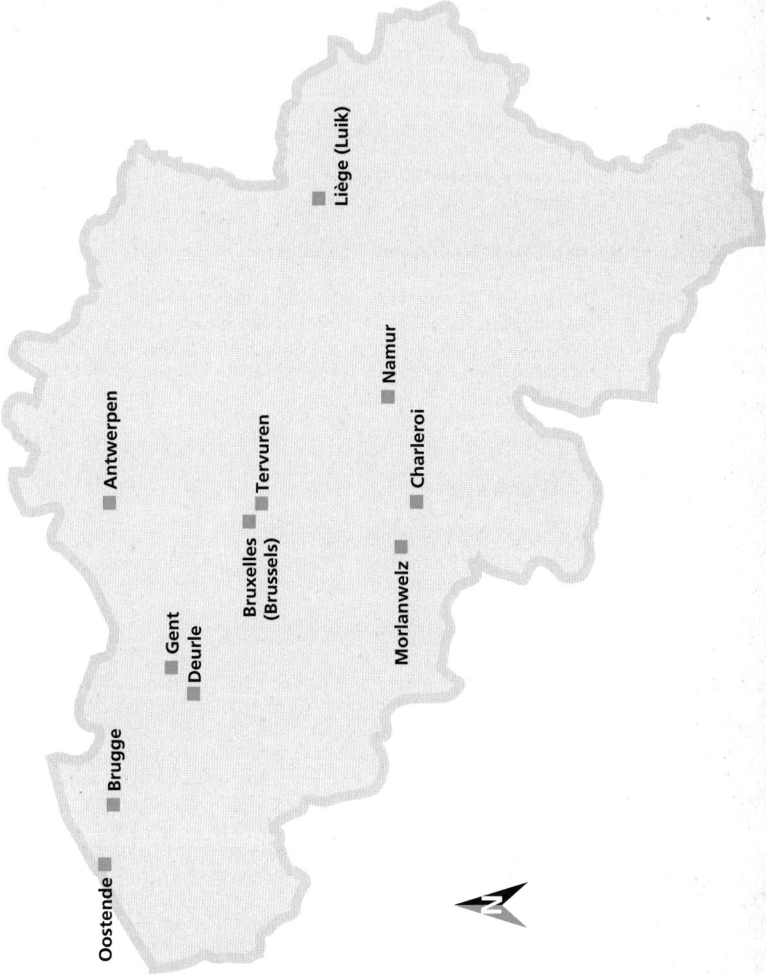

Oostende
Brugge
Gent
Deurle
Antwerpen
Bruxelles (Brussels)
Tervuren
Morlanwelz
Charleroi
Namur
Liège (Luik)

Antwerpen - Antwerp

MUSEUM VAN HEDENDAAGSE KUNST ANTWERPEN
Leuvenstraat 32 2000 Antwerpen Director: Florent Bex
☎ +32 3 2385960 Fax +32 3 2162486
Open: Tuesday-Sunday 10.00-17.00
Closed: Monday and public holidays

COLLECTION

No permanent collection.

EXHIBITIONS

12·04·96-02·06·96 ***Guillaume Bijl*** *The Collection* A selection.

21·06·96-15·09·96 ***Power/Powerlessness (Summer of Photography)*** *The Collection* A selection.

06·09·96-03·11·96 ***David Nash, Max Couper*** *The Collection* A selection.

22·11·96-12·01·97 ***Marijke van Warmerdam*** *Acquisitions from the Flemish Community 1994-1995: Above-Below the Surface* Bert De Beul, Berlinde De Bruyckere, Paul De Vylder, Ria Pacquée (Dutch-speaking Belgium) / Kari Cavén, Ulla Jokisalo, Markku Kivinen, Nina Roos (Finland).

Antwerpen - Antwerp

KONINKLIJK MUSEUM VOOR SCHONE KUNSTEN
Leopold de Waelplaats 2000 Antwerpen Director a.i.: Erik Vandamme
☎ +32 3 2387809 Fax +32 3 2480810
Open: Tuesday-Sunday 10.00-17.00
Closed: Monday, 1 - 2 Jan, 1 May, Ascension Day, 25 Dec

COLLECTION

Old Masters The museum contains a fine collection of Old Masters. It provides an interesting survey of South Netherlandish art dating from the 14th to the 18th century. Masterpieces by Jan van Eyck, Rogier van der Weyden and Hans Memling are witnesses of the artistic flowering in the 15th-century Burgundian Netherlands. Paintings by Quinten Metsys, Frans Floris, the Brueghel family, Peter Paul Rubens, Jacob Jordaens and Anthony van Dijck illustrate the prominent role of Antwerp as a leading art centre in West-Europe during the 16th and 17th century. The museum owns 21 paintings and oilsketches by Rubens.
The collection also includes work by French, Italian, German and Dutch artists. Highlights are, to name but a few, the 'Orsini-quadritych' by Simone Martini, 'Madonna surrounded by angels' by Jean Fouquet, Titiano's 'Jacopo Pesaro' and the famous 'Portrait of Stephanus Geraerdts' by Frans Hals.

Rubens Hall

Koninklijk museum voor schone Kunsten, Antwerpen

Modern Art   The collection of Modern Masters shows the Belgian art production covering the 19th century until the present. The museum, till the end of the 19th century strongly tied to the Antwerp Royal Academy of Fine Arts, contains many works by local academic artists. Besides those 'avant-garde' artists, followers of Realism, Impressionism and Post-Impressionism, are represented with various paintings. World famous is the rich collection of paintings and drawings by James Ensor. The 20th-century art collection contains representative works from the different currents ranging from Futurism to Neo-Realism. Of special interest are the Flemish Expressionists, and the Belgian Surrealists René Magritte and Paul Delvaux. Also a small number of foreign modern artists is represented such as Appel, Breitner, Chagall, David, Degas, Fontana, Modigliani, Rodin, Willink and Zadkine.

EXHIBITIONS
24·11·96–16·02·97

Naturalism in Belgium and Europe, 1880-1910

15·12·96–02·03·97

From a different World.   Unknown Icons and Byzantine Objects of Art

Antwerpen · Antwerp

MUSEUM MAYER VAN DEN BERGH
Lange Gasthuisstraat 19 2000 Antwerpen Director: Hans Nieuwdorp
☎ +32 3 2324237 ▥⊩ +32 3 2319387
Open: Tuesday-Sunday 10.00-17.00
Closed: Monday and 1-2 Jan, 1 May, Ascension Day, 1-2 Nov, 25-26 Dec

COLLECTION

The museum contains the former collection of Fritz Mayer van den Bergh, who died in 1901. Its core consists of Western European paintings and sculptures, ranging from the 6th to the 18th century, with particular emphasis on Medieval art from the 14th to early 16th century. The collection includes examples of all genres of painting and of various schools. There are works by Pieter Brueghel the Elder: the famous 'Dulle Griet' and the 'Twelve Proverbs'. Works by Pieter Brueghel the Younger and Jan Brueghel are also exhibited. Flemish painting of the 15th and 16th century is on show as well, with some unique Dutch works such as the 'Antwerp-Baltimore' panels (c. 1400).

Meester Heinrich te
Konstanz
*St. John resting on
the bosom of Christ,
early 14th century*

Museum Mayer van
den Bergh,
Antwerpen

Medieval sculptures are well-represented in the museum, with works in marble, alabaster and polychromed wood of the Gothic

period are on display. The sculpture section contains works such as the monumental group of 'Christ and St. John' (c. 1300) and carved altar-pieces from Brabant as well as French 14th-century ivory sculptures and work by Jean de Liège.

The museum has a wide range of Medieval decorative art, in the form of enamels, tapestries, furniture, silver and ceramics, in addition to selected examples from the smaller collections of drawings, textiles, plaquettes, numismatics, miniatures and manuscripts.

EXHIBITION

Autumn 96–Winter 96

The Mayer van den Bergh Breviary   A Flemish Illumination Manuscript (approx. 1510).

Antwerpen - Antwerp

NATIONAAL SCHEEPVAARTMUSEUM - NATIONAL MARITIME MUSEUM
Steenplein 1 2000 Antwerpen 1 Director: W. Johnson
☎ +32 3 2320850 📠 +32 3 2262516
Open: Tuesday-Sunday 10.00-16.45
Closed: Monday and 1 - 2 Jan, 1 May, Ascension Day, 1 - 2 Nov, 25 - 26 Dec

COLLECTION

The National Maritime Museum is the only museum of its kind in Belgium and is located in 'Het Steen', an old castle on the Schelde. The collection is displayed in 12 halls, each devoted to a different aspect of the shipping trade. It is didactically arranged and accompanied by captions in 4 languages. Model ships, paintings and ships' instruments help trace the history of shipping. The museum owns a unique collection of maritime paintings behind glass. Antique harbour equipment, ships and cranes are displayed in the department of maritime industry and harbour archaeology alongside 'Het Steen'. The highlights of this department are the barge 'Lauranda' and the steam-tugboat 'Amical'.

River Barge
'Lauranda' 1928

Nationaal
Scheepvaart Museum
Antwerpen

EXHIBITION

07·06·96–31·10·96

The History of the Belgian Navy (1831-1996)   This exhibition commemorates the 50th anniversary of the re-establishment of the Belgian Navy.

Antwerpen - Antwerp

OPENLUCHTMUSEUM VOOR BEELDHOUWKUNST MIDDELHEIM
OPEN AIR MUSEUM OF SCULPTURE MIDDELHEIM
Middelheimlaan 61 2020 Antwerpen Director: Menno Meewis
☎ +32 3 8271534 📠 +32 3 8252835
Open: Oct-Mar Daily 10.00-17.00; Apr and Sep Daily 10.00-19.00;
May and Aug Daily 10.00-20.00; Jun and Jul Daily 10.00-21.00

COLLECTION

In the summer of 1950, the late Burgomaster Lode Craeybeckx first suggested the idea of an international open-air sculpture exhibition at Middelheim Park. After deciding to permanently exhibit sculptures in the park, the Antwerp City Council founded the Open Air Museum of Sculpture Middelheim. Today, after more than 40 years of collecting, the historical sculpture collection endeavours to offer a broad international view of the development of modern sculpture.

In 1993 a rejuvenation programme was launched. The museum now spans the entire park, and acquisitions are no longer made just to fill historical gaps. On the occasion of Antwerp being named Cultural Capital of Europe for 1993, the permanent collection was enriched with works by Deacon, Genzken, Kirkeby, Klingelhöller, Lohaus, Mullican, Munoz, Panamarenko, Schütte and Vermeiren. These were exhibited in Lower Middelheim, where the Biennials used to be held, and which is now reserved for contemporary sculpture. In 1994 the museum acquired Guillaume Bijl's 'Roman Street' and Luciano Fabro's 'Bathers'.

EXHIBITIONS

Spring 96

Henk Visch   This Dutch artist (born Eindhoven, 1950) creates poetical sculptures, the origin of which can be found in dreams, memories, the subconscious and in the artist's impressions of his surroundings. In addition to sculpture, his drawings constitute an equally important part of his work: three examples include a fish with feathers instead of scales, a man who becomes a tree and a flower which is also sea.

Summer 96

Tony Cragg   The acquisition of an open-air work by Tony Cragg, acquired with the support of 'Middelheim Promotors', is the occasion of this exhibition.
This British artist (born Liverpool, 1949) collects, assorts and arranges objects to form a structure, drawing first on nature and then on the products of our consumer society. The empirical, pragmatic sensitivity to specific qualities of the materials he uses has always been a feature of his work. Often, materials which are too readily designated as waste are given a new identity.

Antwerpen - Antwerp

MUSEUM PLANTIN-MORETUS
Vrijdagmarkt 22 2000 Antwerpen Director: F. de Nave
☎ **+32 3 2330294** ▨ **+32 3 2262516**
Open: Tuesday-Sunday 10.00-16.45
Closed: Monday

COLLECTION

The Plantin-Moretus Museum is the only one of its kind. It traces its origins back to the leading printer of the second half of the 16th century, Christopher Plantin (Saint-Avertin, Tours c. 1520 - Antwerp 1589). In 1576 he installed his famous Golden Compasses on the Vrijdagmarkt, which was to remain the 'Officina Plantiniana' for the rest of his life. Plantin's descendants and successors, the Moretus family, kept the firm in the forefront of the printers' trade for almost three centuries and the Golden Compasses remained their home.

Today, the Plantin Moretus Museum is a harmonious combination of stately patrician dwelling and authentic business. The rooms, with their priceless works of art, tapestries, gilded leather, paintings (including 18 by Rubens), clocks, ceramics and porcelain still exude the atmosphere of refined luxury which the Moretus family imparted to their home.

The original workshops of the 'Officina Plantiniana' give the museum its unique personality. The type foundry, workshop, with the two oldest presses in the world (from c. 1600), type store, corrector's room, bookshop and office of the master of the house are still intact and preserved as they were in the 16th and 17th centuries.

The collections brought together here in their original historical setting are imposing and of considerable importance as the fruits of three hundred years of typographic work and art collecting.

EXHIBITIONS

29·06·96–29·09·96   *Music Books printed in Antwerp   Vocal and Instrumental Polyphony, 16th-18th Century*   This exhibition has been organised in conjunction with the 'Festival van Vlaanderen 1996'. It features music books published by Christopher Plantin and other Antwerp printers. In the 16th century, Antwerp was regarded as a centre of music publishing on a par with other cities such as Lyon, Munich and Venice. The editions published in Antwerp were unique in that they were not limited to just the compositions of local artists, a phenomenon that was of considerable influence on public taste.

18·10·96–17·01·97   *The Illustrations of Books Published by the Moretuses*
1996 marks the 400th anniversary of the year in which Jan Moretus I began to publish works solely under his own name. His descendants maintained the activities of the Press into the 19th century.
Jan Moretus I devoted increasing attention to high qualitative standards in terms of illustration and design. This evolution reached a high point under his successor, Balthasar Moretus I, thanks to Peter Paul Rubens' contribution to the design of title pages and illustrations. This cooperation between typographer and artist resulted in the development of a new style in book illustration that was widely imitated throughout Europe.

Antwerpen - Antwerp

RUBENSHUIS
Wapper 9-11 2000 Antwerpen Director: Paul Huvenne
☎ +32 3 2324747 📠 +32 3 2319387
Open: Tuesday-Sunday 10.00-17.00
Closed: Monday and 1-2 Jan, 1 May, Ascension Day, 1-2 Nov, 25-26 Dec

COLLECTION   *The Rubens House*   Antwerp is renowned as the city of Sir Peter Paul Rubens. In 1610, one year after his marriage to Isabella Brant, Rubens bought an estate in the Wapper where he had his house and studio built. The imposing portico separating the inner court from the garden and pavilion was depicted many times in his paintings and were undoubtedly built from his own designs.
The collection   The collection includes several works by Rubens and focuses on Rubens' own collection, his studio, his work as a humanist and diplomat, his family and his daily life in Antwerp. The historical garden was one of the winning projects of the European Community in 1993.

EXHIBITIONS   No exhibitions planned.

Antwerpen - Antwerp

STEDELIJK PRENTENKABINET
Vrijdagmarkt 22-23 2000 Antwerpen Director: F. de Nave
☎ +32 3 2322455 📠 +32 3 2262516
Open: Daily 10.00-16.00 Exhibitions: Daily 10.00 - 16.45
Closed: Saturday and Sunday Exhibitions: Monday

COLLECTION

The collection of drawings and engravings in the Municipal Print Room originated in the private collection of Max Rooses (1838-1914), the first director of the Museum Plantin-Moretus. The collection was systematically enlarged, and now contains 45 000 antique and modern prints, 2 240 drawings by Old Masters and 20 000 modern drawings, 1 200 antique and modern print books, copper plates, woodblocks, etc. The library contains about 14 000 volumes on graphic arts.

EXHIBITIONS
24·02·96–02·06·96

Focus on Paul van Ostaijen *Graphic Work by Contemporaries*
This exhibition, based primarily on a selection of graphic work from the museum's own collection, presents the works of artists from Paul van Ostaijen's circle of friends, such as Floris Jespers (1889-1965), Jos Léonard (1892-1957), Henri van Straten (1862-1944) and Josef Cantré (1890-1957). This selection will be grouped around themes from Van Ostaijen's poetry collections, including the Music Hall, women, the city and port, anti-clericalism, pacifism and war.

Front façade
Stedelijk
Prentenkabinet,
Antwerpen

21·09·96–20·01·97

Jan Cox This exhibition is planned in cooperation with the De Zwarte Panter Gallery in Antwerp and focuses on the graphic work of the artist Jan Cox (The Hague, 1919-Antwerp, 1980). The selection of his works will be drawn from the collection of the De Zwarte Panter Gallery and will include unique prints.

Brugge - Bruges

ARENTSHUIS (THE BRANGWYN MUSEUM)
Dijver 16 8000 Brugge Director: V. Vermeersch
☎ **+32 50 448711 📠 +32 50 448778**
Open: Wednesday-Monday Apr - Sep 09.30-17.00;
Oct-Mar 09.30-12.30/14.00-17.00
Closed: Tuesday

COLLECTION

The Brangwyn museum or Arenthuis was originally purchased by the City of Bruges at the beginning of this century and has since evolved into a museum with two very different permanent collections.
Frank Brangwyn The collection of the Pre-Modernist all-round artist Frank Brangwyn includes 40 easel paintings, 500 etchings (preferred by the author for city views and travel impressions) and examples of his interior and decorative art demonstrating both the Art Nouveau and Art Deco movements.

Lace 'At Its Best' The lace collection contains lace from the 16th to the 20th century with three sections dedicated to needlepoint lace, bobbin lace (more common in Flanders) and some remarkable examples of 'mixed lace'.

EXHIBITIONS No exhibitions planned.

Brugge - Bruges

GROENINGE MUSEUM
Dijver 12 8000 Brugge Director: V. Vermeersch
☎ +32 50 448711 📠 +32 50 448778
Open: Wednesday-Monday Apr-Sep 09.30-17.00;
Oct-Mar 09.30-12.30 / 14.00-17.00
Closed: Tuesday

COLLECTION The Groeninge Museum is a traditional Fine Art museum that collects and displays work purely on the basis of its quality. Flemish Primitives 15th century The 'Gallery of the Flemish Primitives' contains 30 works from the 15th and the beginning of the 16th century painted by masters from the Southern Netherlands who include Jan van Eyck, Rogier van der Weyden, Petrus Christus, Hugo van der Goes, Hans Memling, Gerard David and Hieronymus Bosch.

Jan van Eyck (ca. 1390-1441)
Madonna with Kanunnik Joris Vander Paele, 1436

Groeninge museum, Brugge

Southern Netherlands 16th century The collection from the Southern Netherlands in the 16th century includes Jan van Hemessen, Cornelis van Cleve, Adriaan Key and Pieter Brueghel the Younger, with particular focus on Jan Provoost and Lanceloot Blondeel.
Bruges Painting in the second half of the 16th century in Bruges is represented by Pieter Pourbus and the 17th century by Jacob van Oost.
Modern Art The aim of this collection is to build a historically founded and comprehensive survey of modern Belgian art with the accent on the 'most original moments' and limited to the most important artists.

Other collections include: Flemish and Dutch history and cabinet pieces from the 17th and 18th centuries, Jan Garemijn, Bruges Classicists, Romanticism and Realism, Symbolism, and landscape painting in the 19th century.

EXHIBITIONS No exhibitions planned.

Brugge - Bruges

GRUUTHUSE MUSEUM
Dijver 17 8000 Brugge Director: V. Vermeersch
☎ +32 50 448711 📠 +32 50 448778
Open: Wednesday-Monday Apr-Sep 09.30-17.00;
Oct-Mar 09.30-12.30 / 14.00-17.00
Closed: Tuesday

COLLECTION

The municipal Gruuthuse Museum is located in a local 15th-century patrician palace of the same name.
The sculpture department includes works in stone, wood and alabaster and carvings in ivory. One of the most important works in the museum is the fired polychrome earthenware bust of Charles V. The museum's furniture is mostly 17th and 18th-century local Baroque, with the exception of a number of Gothic items.
Silver and non-precious metalwork is well represented. The silver collection features religious and secular artefacts and an important collection of 16th to 19th-century 'guild silver'.

Konrad Meit (ca. 1480-1551)
Bust of Charlemagne, c. 1520

Gruuthuse museum, Brugge

The monumental 15th-century fireplace in the Gruuthuse kitchen is used to display the collection of copper, pewter, bronze and iron work. Other metalwork includes ecclesiastical objects and secular artefacts such as snuffboxes.
The large collection of ceramics offers a fairly comprehensive survey of all historical types and centres of production.
Tapestries are the main attraction in the textile collection.
The numismatic collection features clocks and mechanical objects and instruments of punishment as well as coins. The collection of early musical instruments is permanently on display.

EXHIBITIONS

No exhibitions planned.

Brugge - Bruges

MEMLING MUSEUM
Mariastraat 38 8000 Brugge Director: V. Vermeersch
☎ +32 50 448711 📠 +32 50 448778
Open: Wednesday-Monday Apr-Sep 09.30-17.00;
Oct-Mar 09.30-12.30 / 14.00-17.00
Closed: Wednesday

COLLECTION

Hans Memling The heart of the collection is based on six masterpieces by Hans Memling, the Medieval Bruges painter. The museum is housed in the Bruges 12th century hospital.
Hospital wards Are temporarily closed.

The church   The church is part of the hospital and the 'Memling panels' were moved there in 1985. The church was chosen for their permanent exhibition as four of the panels were originally designed for the church and it is spacious enough to house all the panels together. The only other work in this area is the statue of Cornelius.
The pharmacy   In 1971 the hospital chemists were rehoused so that the 17th- century pharmacy, established in a part of the old monastery, could became part of the museum. Much of the pharmacy inventory and attributes from the 17th and 18th century are on exhibit.

EXHIBITIONS | No exhibitions planned.

Bruxelles · Brussels

BRUSSELS MUSEUM OF MUSICAL INSTRUMENTS
17, Petit-Sablon 1000 Bruxelles Director: Malou Haine
☎ +32 2 5113595 📠 +32 2 5128575
Open: Tuesday-Saturday 09.30-16.45
Closed: Sunday and Monday

COLLECTION | The Brussels Museum of Musical Instruments has its origin in the collection of ancient and ethnic instruments of François-Joseph Fétis (1784-1871), the first director of the Brussels Conservatoire, and in a collection of Hindu instruments presented in 1876 by King Leopold II. The instrument maker and organ expert Victor-Charles Mahillon (1841-1924) became the museum's first director in 1877. He was responsible for a rapid growth of the collection (up to 3300 pieces in 1924) and for its international reputation as a research centre. The collection of over 7000 instruments remains one of the largest in the world today. Only about 10% is on permanent display, but it is hoped that the museum will be housed in new accommodation before the end of the century. The exhibition is divided into four main topics: wind instruments from the 16th to the 19th century, keyboard instruments, stringed instruments and European folk instruments.

EXHIBITIONS | No exhibitions planned.

Bruxelles · Brussels

FONDATION POUR L'ARCHITECTURE
55, Rue de l'Ermitage 1050 Bruxelles Director: Diane Hennebert
☎ +32 2 6490259 📠 +32 2 6404623
Open: Tuesday-Friday 12.30-19.00 Saturday and Sunday 11.00-19.00
Closed: Monday

COLLECTION | No permanent collection.

EXHIBITIONS
23·04·96–09·06·96 | *In Praise of Simplicity*   *Aspects of Contemporary Architecture in Flanders*   A selection of works by young architects which display a genuine quest for simplicity in terms of form, materials and urban integration.

25·06·96–31·12·96 | *The 10th Anniversary of the Fondation pour l'Architecture*
Art Deco Architecture in Brussels   A prestigious celebration presenting four exhibitions on the subject of Art Deco architecture in Brussels and its sources of inspiration, conferences, a signposted tour of the city, a major publication and many other interesting events.

Bruxelles - Brussels

MUSÉE D'ART ANCIEN
Musées Royaux des Beaux-Arts de Belgigue
3, Rue de la Régence 1000 Bruxelles Director: Eliane de Wilde
☎ +32 2 5083211 📠 +32 2 5083232
Open: Tuesday-Sunday 10.00-12.00 / 13.00-17.00
Closed: Monday

COLLECTION

The Museum of Ancient Art (the building itself was designed by Balat, 1880) displays interesting works from the end of the 14th century through to the 19th century.
It is the most important museum in its genre in Belgium. Its collection of Primitives is comparable with collections in Berlin, Madrid and Antwerp.
Schools of European art are very well represented, predominantly by masterpieces, the most important of which are Flemish.

The huge collection is divided into 'routes':
The Blue Route (15th-16th centuries) and *the Brown Route* (17th-18th centuries) include paintings by Flemish, Dutch, German, Italian and French schools. Artists include Van der Weyden, Memling, Brueghel the Elder, Massys, Rubens, Van Dyck, Cranach, Frans Hals, Rembrandt, Claude Lorrain, Guardi, Le Guerchin, Ribera, Jan Steen and Murillo, etc.

The Blue Route also takes the visitor to the Delporte Bequest, a collection donated by Dr Franz Delporte who died in 1973. This collection includes paintings, sculpture, ceramics and objects of art from the 13th to the 18th century.

The Brown Route includes the greatest attraction in this part of the museum: the famous collection of works by Pieter Paul Rubens.

The Yellow Route (19th century) features works from important Belgian Schools and some Impressionists: Ensor, Evenepoel, Meunier, Knopff, Gauguin, Seurat, Signac and others.

Brueghel, Pieter I the Elder
The census in Bethlehem, 1566

Musées Royaux des Beaux-Arts de Belgique, Musée d'Art Ancien, Bruxelles

EXHIBITIONS

26·03·96–26·05·96   ***In the Margins of the Book - the Unusual Book.*** *In conjunction with the Royal Library.*

15·06·96–29·09·96   ***The Dog, a friend through thick and thin***

04·10·96–08·12·96   ***S.O.S. Panel Paintings.*** *In conjunction with the King Boudewijn Foundation.*

15·10·96–15·12·96   ***Léon Spilliaert (1881-1946).*** *Works from the museum collection.*

Bruxelles - Brussels

MUSÉE D'ART MODERNE
Musées Royaux des Beaux-Arts de Belgigue
1-2, Place Royale 1000 Bruxelles Director: Eliane de Wilde
☎+32 2 5083211 🖷 +32 2 5083232
Open: Tuesday-Sunday 10.00-12.00 / 14.00-17.00
Closed: Monday

COLLECTION

The museum displays around 11 000 works of art, all of which are from the 20th century. Included in the exhibition are paintings, sculpture, collages and assemblages made from wood, metal, plastic and other materials. The most important works of art are lighted in such a way that the visitor automatically focuses on them.
The scope is international but with an emphasis on Belgian art. Chronologically, the work begins with Fauvism and includes works by Rik Wouters, Spilliaert, etc. Other art movements include Expressionism, Futurism, Surrealism, and Dada. Artists represented include Permeke, Chagall, Delvaux, Magritte, Braque, Bacon, Calder, De Chirico, Miro, Cragg, Segal, Paik, Broodthaers, MacCracken, Flavin, Kounellis, and Pistoletto.
The works by artists from countries other than Belgium (Miro, Picasso, Dali, Boltanski, Allen Jones, Appel, Asgar Jorn, Pierre Alechinsky and others) are arranged according to movement. Sculpture is displayed in various rooms and includes work by Wouters, George Segal, Tony Cragg, and Richard Long.

Paul Delvaux
Winter, or the hidden city, 1958

Musées Royaux des Beaux Arts de Belgique, Musée d'Art Moderne, Bruxelles

EXHIBITION
13·09·96–15·12·96

From Magritte to Magritte (provisional title).   Exhibition of the Irène Scutenaire-Hamoir legacy.

Bruxelles - Brussels

PALAIS DES BEAUX-ARTS
10, Rue Royale 1000 Bruxelles Director: Piet Coessens
☎ +32 2 5078466 🖷 +32 2 5110589
Open: Opening hours vary
Closed: Monday

COLLECTION

No permanent collection.

EXHIBITIONS
07·06·96–08·09·96

Art in Resistance *German Painters between the Wars*   This selection from the collection of Marvin and Janet Fishman offers a survey of German Expressionism and the 'Neue Sachlichkeit', with works by Max Beckmann, Otto Dix and Georges Grosz, among others. The exhibition chronicles Weimar Germany, bringing to the fore just those artistic positions that stood apart from Modernism's dominating current.

07·06·96–08·09·96   *Ilya Kabakov*   *On the Roof*   Ilya Kabakov, a Russo-Ukrainian artist, has conceived a project occupying around 800 square metres along the central exhibition circuit of the Palais des Beaux-Arts. From a footbridge above an imaginary city, images of everyday Russian life, sometimes seeming more real than the real thing, are portrayed by means of projected slides and a soundtrack of popular Russian music.

Bruxelles - Brussels

MUSEUM VAN HET KONINKLIJK BELGISCH INSTITUUT VOOR NATUURWETENSCHAPPEN
29, Rue Vautier 1040 Bruxelles Director: Daniel Cahen
☎ +32 2 6274211 📠 +32 2 6464432
Open: Tuesday-Saturday 09.30-16.45 Sunday 09.30-18.00
Closed: Monday and 25 Dec, 1 Jan and election days

COLLECTION   *Palaeontology*   The highlight of the museum's collection is a group of 29 iguanodons, the largest single dinosaur discovery ever made. They were found in a colliery in the border village of Bernissart in 1878 and are now displayed together with animated models of other dinosaurs in a splendid Victorian hall. A wide diorama portrays the sea that covered what is now Belgium during the Cretaceous and Jurassic periods. Strolling along the bottom of the 'sea' you meet unique skeletons of mosasaurs and turtles. The evolution of vertebrate animals and of man is also portrayed.
Mineralogy   This exhibition provides a systematic survey of minerals, explaining characteristics such as growth, forms, optical qualities, mechanical features, density, magnetism and radioactivity. A separate section deals with mineralisations of Belgian stone and clay quarries, both still functioning or closed down.
Zoology   This systematic display of all terrestrial mammal families is of great scientific and educational value. Some of the more familiar groups such as primates, predators and hoofed animals are displayed separately. The collection of cavicorns is one of the most comprehensive in the world.
The marine mammals collection is very large and includes recent whale skeletons, seals, walruses. Penguins and polar bears can be seen in two dioramas of the North and South Poles. The shell and insect halls contain a unique collection of unicellular animals, sponges, corals, anemones, worms, molluscs and arthropods. Other exhibits include a 'living' termite hill and dangerous insects. The Belgian fauna is illustrated in a fine series of dioramas.

EXHIBITION
Autumn 96–Spring 97   *Bats*   *Masters of the Night*   This exhibition brings the mystery surrounding these nocturnal creatures out of the dark. It gives the real story behind these fascinating animals and their unique appearance. It dispels common misconceptions about bats, reveals their ecological importance and offers visitors an appreciation of the true wonders of the bat world. The exhibition includes an animated bat scene, several spectacular scenarios and interactive stations.

Charleroi

MUSÉE DES BEAUX-ARTS
Hôtel de Ville Place Charles II 6000 Charleroi Director: C. Lemal-Mengeot
☎ +32 71 230294 ▨ +32 71 317005
Open: Tuesday-Saturday 9.00-17.00
Closed: Sunday and Monday

COLLECTION

The Fine Arts Museum of Charleroi is located on the second floor of the Town Hall, which was constructed in 1936. The museum's permanent collection includes Walloon paintings from the 19th and 20th century, representative of a range of styles including Neo-Classicism, Realism, Neo-Impressionism, Surrealism, and constructed and abstract art.

The foundation of the collections is the work of F.-J. Navez. Navez was a pupil and emulator of the Neo-Classical painter David. The works of a leading painter of the Social Realist style, Constantin Meunier, are representative of artists who stressed the importance of social values.

A variety of other Walloon movements are included, but the majority of the collection consists of six works by René Magritte, by important local representatives of Surrealism, and by Surrealist Paul Delvaux.

EXHIBITIONS

27·04·96–08·06·96

The Liège School of Engraving Collections of the Verviers Museum of Fine Art

06·09·96–05·10·96

50th Anniversary of the Academy A collaboration of the Academy of Fine Art with the Museum of Fine Art.

09·11·96–12·01·97

Vasarely This exhibition, a collaboration with the A.S.B.L. 'Antécédence', deals with the integration of art in architecture; the main streams of optical art.

Charleroi

MUSÉE DE LA PHOTOGRAPHIE
11, Avenue Paul Pastur 6032 Charleroi (Mont-sur-Marchienne)
Director: George Vercheval
☎ +32 71 435810 ▨ +32 71 364645
Open: Tuesday-Sunday 10.00-18.00
Closed: Monday

COLLECTION

The permanent collection of the museum comprises fine photographic images starting with the very beginnings of photography and continuing up to the present day. Photogenic drawing, daguerreotypes, salt prints, albumen prints and autochromes are all employed to show the technology and aesthetics of photography. Included are the pioneers, such as Poitevin, Fenton, Du Camp and Baldus; pictorialists such as Misonne, Dubreuil and Marissiaux; and the 'moderns' such as Kertesz, Florence Henri and Ueda, as well as Sander, Arbus, Dieter Appelt, Klein and others.

The museum also possesses a rich collection of original cameras covering all periods, as well as modern facsimiles of the box cameras used by Niépce, Daguerre and Talbot. There are explanatory displays, and displays of a variety of cameras ranging from huge wooden cameras up to the contemporary reflex camera, including models from Voigtlander, Ernemann, Leica, Rollei, Kodak, Agfa, Polaroid and other manufacturers.

There is also a learning area area where the visitor can experience the mysteries of light and the darkroom, review the history of

cameras and images up to their use in newspaper, or see a turn-of-the century laboratory and reconstructed portrait studion.
Archives of Wallonia   Housed in the museum but independent of it, the foundation 'Archives de Wallonie' records the region's past, bringing together images relating to daily life, work and local customs, and offering an ambitious series of documentary programmes.
Library - Documentation Centre   The museum also includes a library with 3 000 books, supplemented by photography magazines and documentary files on individual photographers.

EXHIBITIONS

12·05·96-01·09·96	**The Three Grand Egyptians** *The Piramids of Gizeh straight through the History of Photography*
12·05·96-01·09·96	**The 40th Anniversary of the Catastrophe of Bois du Cazier**
07·09·96-08·12·96	**Arno Minkinnen, Edouart Boubat, François Tuefferd**
13·12·96-02·03·97	**Stefan De Jaeger** (Retrospective), **Larry Fink**

Deurle

MUSEUM DHONDT-DHAENENS
Museumlaan 14 9831 Deurle Director: Frank Benijts
☎ +32 9 2825123 🖷 +32 9 2810853
Open: Wednesday-Friday 14.00-17.00/18.00 Saturday, Sunday and public holidays 10.00-12.00 / 14.00-17.00/18.00
Closed: Monday and Tuesday

COLLECTION   The Dhondt-Dhaenens Museum, which was founded in 1968, owns an extensive collection of paintings by internationally known painters such as G. and L. De Smet, J. Ensor, C. Permeke, A. Servaes, A. Van Den Abeele, F. Van Den Berghe, G. Van De Woestijne and many others.
The works of art were collected by Jules and Irma Dhondt-Dhaenens and the museum has now become a cultural meeting place. Regular exhibitions are organised by contemporary artists from both Belgium and abroad.

EXHIBITIONS

12·05·96-23·06·96	**Philippe Van Snick, Manfred Jade**
30·06·96-15·09·96	**Paul Robbrecht and Hilde Daem** *More Light: An Architectural Concept*
22·09·96-27·10·96	**Rik Moens,** *Logos (Moniek Darge)*
03·11·96-08·12·96	**Ria Pacquée, Jon Thompson**

Gent - Ghent

BIJLOKEMUSEUM
Godshuizenlaan 2 9000 Gent Director: A. van den Kerkhove
☎ +32 9 2251106 🖷 +32 9 2333459
Open: Tuesday-Sunday 09.00-17.00
Closed: Monday

COLLECTION   The Bijloke Museum is located in Bijloke Abbey, a former convent for Cistercian nuns, which was founded in the 13th century. The oldest abbey buildings, including the cloister, refectory and dormitory, are constructed in Gothic style and date back to the 14th century. They now house the rich and varied collections of the former Archaeological Museum of Ghent.

The interiors of the abbey buildings are one of the treasures of the Bijloke Museum. They reveal not only a succession of styles but also the power and wealth of a number of civil and religious instititutions in Ghent. Paintings, including the 'Panoramic View of Ghent in 1534', watercolours, prints and tapestries provide a picture of historical events in Ghent, the Ghent monuments and religious scenes. Sculptures and liturgical objects of abolished Ghent convents and charitable institutions complete the collection.

Various exhibits of applied art are on display in the section devoted to silver, pottery, brass and bronze, iron and pewter. These exhibits give an idea of everyday life over the centuries and reveal the creativity and craftsmanship of the Ghent artisans. The power and wealth of the Ghent merchants is evoked by numerous works of art, including, for example, a unique collection of 18th-century processional torches.

The 'House of the Abbess', 1613-1616 Bijlokemuseum , Gent

EXHIBITIONS
03·05·96–02·06·96

Agnes van den Bossche   A 15th-century Ghent Artist   In medieval archives, names of female artists are frequently mentioned, but identifying their works remains extremely difficult. The 15th-century banner painted by Agnes van den Bossche is a unique exception, and is the centrepiece of this small but charming exhibition on the artist, her entourage and the artistic community in which she lived.

30·11·96–30·03·97

Religious Art in Ghent from the Early Middle Ages up to the Late 18th Century   This exhibition of works of art created for liturgical practice or used for private worship takes place in the 14th-century refectory famous for its architectural grandeur and authentic wall paintings. Pictures, sculptures, funeral and memorial statues, glass roundels, textiles, altarpieces and church furniture dating from the early Middle Ages up to the 18th century evoke liturgy in the many Ghent churches and cloisters.

Gent - Ghent

MUSEUM VAN HEDENDAAGSE KUNST
Hofboulaan 28 9000 Gent Director: Jan Hoet
☎ +32 9 2211703 📠 +32 9 2217109
Open: Tuesday-Sunday 09.30-17.00
Closed: Monday

COLLECTION

The Museum of Contemporary Art in Ghent focuses on national and international art movements from the Second World War to the present. The museum's collection was enlarged by a substantial

inheritance from the Museum of Fine Arts - including works by
Magritte, Delvaux, Bacon and Poliakoff - and is continually enriched
by loans from private collectors, the state and the Friends of the
Museum. The collection includes work by the Cobra group
(P. Alechinsky, K. Appel, Corneille, A. Jorn and Lucebert) and
Belgian Lyrical and Geometrical Abstract painters such as A. Mortier,
A. Cortier, G. Bertrand and A. Bonnet. Pop Art and French Nouveau
Realism are represented by the likes of Warhol, Christo, Arman and
Villeglé. Pop Art's counterpart in Belgium, New Figuration, with its
everyday reality, is best seen in the work of R. Raveel and
R. De Keyzer. Works by D. Judd, S. Lewitt, C. Andre, D. Flavin and
B. Nauman illustrate Minimal Art, while the work of artists such as
J. Kosuth, D. Huebler and L. Weiner clarify conceptual Art. Arte
Povera and Land Art are represented by the work of M. Merz,
J. Kounellis, L. Fabro, R. Long and B. Flannagan. The museum also
owns an important selection of works by such artists as Beuys,
Marcel Broodthaers, Panamarenko, M. Buthe and Royden
Rabinowitch. Recent developments in art are captured in specific
works by artists such as I. Kabakov, Th. Schütte, D. Hammons,
M. Kelly, R. Gober, C. Noland and H. Steinbach. The latest crop of
Belgian artists such as J. Vercruysse, Th. De Cordier, L. Tuymans and
M. François are also included in the collection.

EXHIBITIONS

30·03·96–12·05·96   **Carl de Keyzer**   *East of Eden / Historical Paintings*

20·04·96–26·05·96   **Dan Graham**   *Pavilions*

Gent - Ghent

MIAT (MUSEUM FOR INDUSTRIAL ARCHAEOLOGY AND TEXTILES)
Minnemeers 9 9000 Gent Director: René De Herdt
☎ +32 9 2235969 📠 +32 9 2330739
Open: Tuesday-Sunday 09.30-17.00
Closed: Monday

COLLECTION

The MIAT is a young, developing museum, which aims at illustrating
and evoking the evolution of industrial society. This is realised in a
former cotton mill in the centre of Ghent.
Besides the first permanent exhibition, 'Our Industrial Past
1750-1900', the public may visit the exhibition on 'Child Labour
from about 1800 up to 1914'.
There is also a project for the last three years of primary school:
'From Raw Material to Clothing'.
In collaboration with the Taptoe Theatre and the Museum of
Scientific History, attention will be paid to 'Two Ghent Gents':
Lieven Bauwens and Leo Baekeland.

EXHIBITIONS

15·06·96–29·09·96   **Industrious and Picturesque Belgium**   Belgium became highly
industrialised at the beginning of the 19th century. The colour
lithographs from the book 'La Belgique Industrielle' (1840) offer a
representative image of the industrial activity around the middle of
the century. In addition, a selection of lithographs from the Leuven
University Library displays the man-made landscape and natural
landscape of the 19th century.

15·06·96–29·09·96   **Man and Machine**   This exhibition throws light on the various
aspects of the relationship between man and machine: the machine
as an art object, the machine as a source of inspiration, the machine
designed by artists, the machine made by artists and design and
machine.

14·12·96–01·06·97

This is How Great-Grandmother Lived *Domestic Comfort in the 19th and Early 20th Century* This exhibition explores the many changes that took place in the homemaker's world as a result of new appliances and machines. The use of new appliances (sewing machine, the introduction of radio and television), new materials (steel, bakelite), and new consumables (preserved foods, margarine) gave the domestic life of both the rich and the poor a totally different dimension.

Gent · Ghent

MUSEUM VOOR SCHONE KUNSTEN
Citadelpark 9000 Gent Curator: Robert Hoozee
☎ +32 9 2221703 📠 +32 9 2217109
Open: Tuesday-Sunday 09.30-17.00
Closed: Monday

COLLECTION

The collection of the Ghent Museum of Fine Arts consists of mainly Flemish art from the 14th century to the present. In the hall there are a series of Brussels tapestries from the 17th century, depicting the story of Darius, and an 18th-century series depicting the Glorification of the Gods. The first room contains a 13th-century French 'Sedes Sapientiae' and 15th-century paintings from the schools of Hugo van der Goes and the Master of Flemalle. Among the other 15th-century works are 'Madonna with the Carnation', attributed to Rogier van der Weyden, a Spanish 'Adoration of the Magi' and 'The Coronation of Maria', part of a polyptych by Puccio di Simone. The museum also has 'The Bearing of the Cross' and 'St.Jerome at Prayer' two important paintings by Hieronymus Bosch. One room has 14th-century bas reliefs from Italy and the Nottingham school. The 16th century is represented by Mostaert's 'Village Feast', Gheeraert Hoorenbaut's 'Triptych of St. Anne with the portraits of the donors, Lieven van Pottelsberghe and his wife and 'Calvary' by Heemskerk. There are large 17th-century works by Jacob Jordaens, Gaspard de Crayer and Peter-Paul Rubens ('Stigmata of St. Frances of Assisi'), as well as 'The Village Lawyer' by Pieter Brueghel the Younger, 'The Scourging of Christ' by Rubens, 'Jupiter and Antiope' by Van Dyck, landscapes by Roelant Savery, seascapes and animal paintings by Snyders, still lifes by Cornelis Gysbrecht, portraits by Frans Hals and works by Nicholas Maes, Jan van Goyen, Tintoretto and others.

Hieronymus Bosch
(c. 1450-1516)
Bearing of the cross

Museum voor Schone
Kunsten, Gent

The collection of Belgian and foreign art from the 19th and 20th century includes Impressionist work by Emile Claus, 'Village Fair' by Gustave de Smet, 'Young Peasant Woman' by Gustave van der Woestyne, 'The Poet E. Verhaeren Reading to his Friends' by

Theo van Rijsselberghe and 'Old Woman with Masks' and charcoal drawings by James Ensor. Foreign artists include Rodin, Kokoschka, Courbet, Daumier and others. Several contemporary streams are represented, such as Cobra, Pop Art and Minimal Art.

EXHIBITIONS | No exhibitions planned.

Gent - Ghent

MUSEUM VOOR SIERKUNST EN VORMGEVING
Jan Breydelstraat 5 9000 Gent Director: Lieven Daenens
☎ +32 9 2256676 📠 +32 9 2244522
Open: Tuesday-Sunday 09.30-17.00
Closed: Monday

COLLECTION | The Museum of Decorative Arts, established in 1903, contains 17th and 18th century furniture displayed in the Hotel de Coninck (built 1755). Its main highlight is the original dining room with a wooden chandelier made by the Ghent sculptor Jan Allaert. There are also 18th-century paintings, silk wall coverings, more than twenty 18th-century chandeliers and portraits, including one of the French King Louis XVIII which is placed amidst a collection of French furniture. The Art Nouveau exhibit contains artefacts by Belgian and other artists. Art Deco and Interbellum styles are represented by Albert van Huffel, Le Corbusier and others. Belgian and Italian designers predominate in furniture, glassware and pottery from the 60s, 70s and 80s. Work by leading Post-Modernists is also on display, including furniture, glassware, pottery, a collection of jewellery made by leading Belgian designers and Belgian carpets and upholstery materials.

EXHIBITIONS

15·03·96–05·05·96 | *Danish ceramics from the collection of the Boymans-van Beuningen Museum and the Koster and Quist collection.*
Survey of Danish ceramics from 1970-1995. Glass from the new EEC countries: Austria, Finland and Sweden - from 1900 to today.

22·06·96–15·09·96 | *Jan Eisenloeffel (1876-1957) Overview exhibition*

Autumn 96 | *Murano Glass 1900 to today*

Liège - Luik

MUSÉE D'ANSEMBOURG
114, Rue Feronstrée 4000 Liège Directors: A. Chevalier and M.-C. Gueury
☎ +32 41 219402
Open: Tuesday-Sunday 13.00-18.00 also on Ascension Day, 21 Jul and 27 Sep
Closed: Monday and 1 Jan, 1 May, 8 May, 1-2 Nov, 11 Nov, 15 Nov,
24-26 Dec, 31 Dec

COLLECTION | The collection of decorative arts is housed in an 18th-century mansion built in transitional Louis XIV-XV style for the 'haute bourgeoisie'. Much of the original decor has been preserved, including mythological motifs in stucco and elegant woodwork and wainscotting. Chandeliers, porcelain, tapestries, tiles from Delft and Liège and furniture in the styles Louis XIV, Liège Regency, Louis XV and Louis XVI can all be seen in their original setting. The house is listed as one of Liège's historical monuments.

EXHIBITIONS | No exhibitions planned.

Morlanwelz

MUSÉE ROYAL DE MARIEMONT
Chaussée de Mariemont 7140 Morlanwelz-Mariemont
Director: Patrice Dartevelle
☎ +32 64 212193 📠 +32 64 262924
Open: Tuesday-Sunday 10.00-18.00
Closed: Monday (except holidays) and 1 Jan, 25 Dec

COLLECTION

The museum is situated in a park, conceived as an English garden, with lawns and centuries-old trees encompassing monumental sculptures and castle ruins. The architectural structure of glass, steel and concrete is reminiscent of Le Corbusier. Classical civilisations (Egypt, Greece and Rome) and Chinese art are displayed side by side with European decorative arts, local archaeology and history.
In both the Classical world and Eastern Asia, cultural evolution can be defined by ceramics and bronzes. Egypt adds granite and alabaster, Greece the whiteness of marble, Rome the magnificent display of colour of the Pompeian frescoes. China completes the pattern with its lacquer, enamel and jade.

Neolithic artifacts, Gallo-Roman vases and coins, and Merovingian jewellery illustrate the Archaeology of Hainaut. The gallery devoted to the History of Mariemont depicts the old royal domain and its successive castles, the industrial revolution and the flourishing of the Centre-region.
The Tournai Porcelain collection bears witness to the aristocratic refinement of the Age of Enlightenment. The collection of precious books in the library contains thousands of antique and modern volumes, including incunabula, bookbindings and bibliophile editions. This enables regular exhibitions with renewed themes.

Bronze statuette of horse
Greece, ancien art,
6th century B.C.

*Musée Royal de Mariemont,
Morlanwelz*

EXHIBITIONS
22·03·96–16·06·96

D'une Oeuvre l'Autre   *The Artist's Book in Contemporary Art*
Christian Boltanski, Daniel Buren, James Lee Byars, Mirtha Dermisache, Peter Downsbrough, Sol LeWitt, Richard Long, Jacques Louis Nyst, Dieter Roth, Bernard Villers
In this exhibition, books created by the participating artists are displayed together with another work (painting, sculpture, installation, video) by each artist. Analogies can be discovered between the books and the other works, which are mainly examples of conceptual and minimal art.

20·09·96–08·12·96

Colours for the Four Seasons   *Korean Costumes and Pojagi of the Choson Dynasty*   This exhibition presents 9 costumes and 53 pojagi or 'wrapping cloths' lent by the Museum of Korean Embroidery (Seoul). The embroidered or patchwork pojagi, symbols of happiness reflecting Confucian values, are shown together with objects and photographs illustrating their use.

Namur

MUSÉE DES ARTS ANCIENS DU NAMUROIS
24, Rue de Fer 5000 Namur Director: Jacques Toussaint
☎ +32 81 220065 🖷 +32 81 227251
Open: Tuesday-Sunday 10.00-18.00 (17.00 between 1 Nov and Easter)
Closed: Monday

COLLECTION | The museum is housed in the 18th-century Gaiffier d'Hestroy Mansion, a listed monument. Noteworthy objects in the main building of this patrician residence, which has been renovated to accommodate the museum, are a Gothic kitchen chimney decorated with plantain leaves and an Empire double staircase with Ionic columns.
The museum's collection of Medieval and Renaissance art includes numerous wood and stone sculptures, religious paintings (Henri Blès) stained-glass windows, gold and silver objects, glassware and embroidery.

EXHIBITIONS

Jun 96–Sep 96 | ***Enamels from Limousin***   Following the exhibit held in the Louvre from November 1995 until January 1996, the Museum of Ancient Namur Arts features enamels from Limoges dating from the Middle Ages (12th to 14th century). In addition to the examples from the collection of the Namur Museum, the exhibition includes some works from other Belgian museums and private collections.

Oct 96–Jan 97 | ***Tins from the Meuse Area***   While the tins from Liège and Huy have a considerable reputation, the same is not true for those of Dinant and Namur. This exhibition highlights the production in the Meuse area during the 17th and 18th centuries. Everyday examples are displayed along with sumptuous tins, pharmacy tins, and examples intended for religious purposes.

Oostende · Ostend

PMMK - MUSEUM VOOR MODERNE KUNST
Romestraat 11 8400 Oostende Director: Willy van den Bussche
☎ +32 59 508118 🖷 +32 59 805626
Open: Tuesday-Sunday 10.00-18.00
Closed: Monday

COLLECTION | The PMMK collection provides a survey of Modern art in Belgium, starting from the origins of Modern art through to works of the present day. The collection can be chronologically divided into three parts: the oldest part, represented chiefly by Expressionism; the following part, from around the time of the Second World War and shortly thereafter; and Contemporary art.
The exhibition policy is international. Belgian art, and especially the most contemporary Belgian art, is constantly being confronted by developments abroad. The museum also strives to promote Belgian art abroad and to display special exhibitions centred around various themes and historical periods.

EXHIBITIONS
04·05·96–16·06·96 | ***Raoul de Keyzer***

29·06·96–15·09·96 | ***Pol Bury*** Retrospective Exhibition

29·06·96–15·09·96 | ***Emiel Claus*** Retrospective Exhibition

29·06·96–15·09·96 | ***Walter Leblanc***

05·10·96–02·02·97 | ***From Ensor to Delvaux*** Featuring works by J. Ensor, L. Spilliaert, C. Permeke, R. Magritte, P. Delvaux.

*Exhibition logo
'Van Ensor tot
Delvaux'*

PMMK, Museum voor
Moderne Kunst,
Oostende

Exhibition from Ensor to Delvaux
5/10/96 - 2/2/97

PMMK
Museum for Modern Art
Ostend

05·10·96–02·02·97 | ***Etienne Elias*** *Retrospective Exhibition*

Tervuren

KONINKLIJK MUSEUM VOOR MIDDEN-AFRIKA
Leuvensesteenweg 13 3080 Tervuren Director: Thijs Van den Audenaerde
☎ +32 2 7695211 📠 +32 2 7670242
Open: 16 Mar-15 Oct Tuesday-Sunday 09.00-17.30; 16 Oct-15 Mar
Tuesday-Sunday 10.00-16.30. Special opening times during the exhibition.
Closed: Monday

COLLECTION | A collection of sculptures, masks, utensils and musical instruments illustrates the wealth of African traditional culture and its artistic expression, and allows the visitor to view all aspects of the African continent. There is a Geology & Mineralogy room for those interested in minerals, rocks, the development of the earth's crust, erosion, weathering and vulcanism. A great variety of insects, fishes, amphibians, reptiles, birds and mammals are shown in a reconstruction of their natural environment. The museum also provides a historical account of the explorations of Central Africa and of the work of the Belgians in the former Belgian Congo, now Zaire. Those who wish to go further back in time may view the evolution of the material cultures from the Palaeolithic up to the Iron Age.

EXHIBITION
21·03·96-21·09·96 | ***ÆTHIOPIA*** This exhibition allows the visitor to become further acquainted with the history, customs and material cultures of the ethnic groups which inhabit this vast African country. For a better understanding of the hopes and needs of the Ethiopians, too often only viewed in terms of famine and wars, it is necessary to consider their identity and culture. The exhibition is divided into a number of sections, among which pottery, ornaments, weapons, neck supports and chairs, wickerwork and weaving, and clothing and jewellery.

Cherbourg

Rouen

Honfleur

Caen

Alençon

Rennes

Sceaux

Angers

Nantes

Tours

Angoulême

Périgueux

Bordeaux

Agen

Montauban

Bayonne

Pau

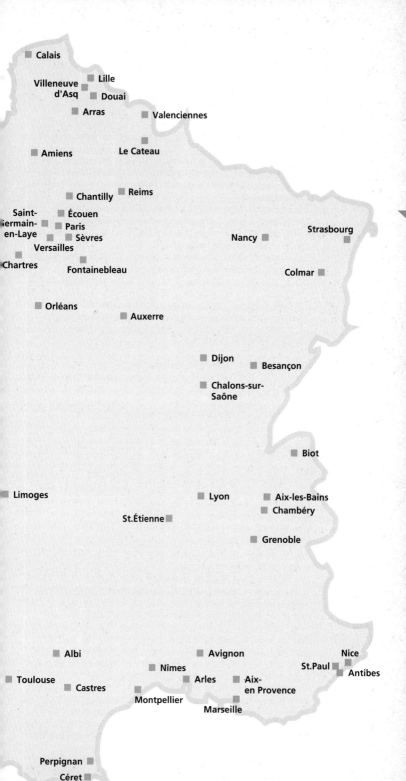

Agen

MUSÉE DES BEAUX-ARTS
Place du Docteur Pierre-Esquirol 47916 Agen Cédex 9 Curator: Y. Lintz
☎ +33 53694723 📠 +33 53662561
Open: Wednesday-Monday 11.00-18.00
Closed: Tuesday

COLLECTION

Archaeology, Painting, Decorative Art The museum of Agen has a collection of archaeological material ranging from prehistory to the Middle Ages, with the emphasis on Celtic and Roman times. Noteworthy is the famous collection of Celtic helmets and arms. Many of the finds will be restored by 1996. From the Roman period is the famous Hellenistic sculpture the 'Venus of the Mas d'Agenais' (1st century A.D.).
The museum's most important paintings are by Goya, Maella and Lucas. There is a fine collection of French paintings, including works by Philippe de Champaigne, Pierre Subleyras, Greuze, Jean-Baptiste Oudry, Corot, Sisley and others.
The museum's decorative arts include French, Italian and Spanish crockery and a collection of glass paperweights.

EXHIBITIONS
02·03·96-01·09·96

F.R.A.M. Regional Project As part of the Aquitaine festival, the Agen Museum presents pottery and Japanese drawings by the decorative artist Vieillard from the collection of the Bordeaux Museum of Decorative Art.

08·06·96-28·10·96

Dreams of Light This international exhibition of over 400 pieces of unique 19th-century encrusted glass is part of the celebration of the Jacobins of Agen.

15·11·96-31·01·97

Julio Villani An exhibition by the Brazilian artist.

Aix-en-Provence

MUSÉE GRANET
Place Saint Jean de Malte 13100 Aix-en-Provence Director: Denis Coutagne
☎ +33 42381470
Open: Wednesday-Monday 10.00-12.00 / 14.00-18.00
Closed: Tuesday

COLLECTION

The Priory of the Knights of Malta, built in 1675, now houses the museum's collection of archaeological finds and art from the 14th to the 20th century. Celto-Ligurian sculptures (3rd to 2nd century B.C.) from the sanctuary of Entremont in Sales, including groups of armed warriors, death masks and bas reliefs, are displayed in the section devoted to the archaeology of Arles in the museum's basement. Everyday life in the Roman city Aquae Sextiae has been reconstructed here. There are also Celtic heads, perhaps sculpted models of real ones that the Celts kept as oracles. The collection also contains Greek and Egyptian finds, including the statue of a Gallic Warrior (200 B.C.) from the school of Pergamon, as well as a 5th-century Christian sarcophagus sculpted in Arles.
The collection of French paintings on the first floor begins with primitive works from Avignon such as two panels of the 'Triptyque de la reine Sanche' (1340-1345) by Matteo Giovanetti de Viterbe. There are also 16th and 17th-century works attributed to Carpassin and Le Nain. 18th-century paintings include 'Madame de Gueidan en Flore' by Largillière; 'Portrait de jeune garçon' by David; 'Jupiter et Thétis' and 'Portrait de Granet' by Ingres; 'L'Oriental assis sur un roche' by Géricault; 'Étude de paysage d'Ile-de-France, fin du jour' by Corot (1874); and a collection of works by the Neo-Classical

Aix artist Granet (1775-1849) and other artists from Provence including Cézanne.
The Flemish and Dutch schools are represented by Frans Hals, Joos van Cleve, 'Portrait of the artist Rickaert' by Van Dyck and two portraits by Rubens. There are early Italian paintings by Luca Signorelli, Albani, Pietro da Cortone, Luca Giordano and Rosalba Carriera. There are more modern works by Matisse, Masson, Prassinos, Vasarely and others, and sculptures by Puget, Laurana, Houdon and d'Angers.
The museum is currently undergoing major renovation and most of the exhibits are closed. The Ingres, Granet and Cézanne collections are still open to the public.

EXHIBITIONS | No details available.

Aix-les-Bains

MUSÉE FAURE
10, Boulevard des Côtes 73100 Aix-les-Bains Director: Françoise Guichon
☎ **+33 79610657** 📠 **+33 79882748**
Open: Monday-Friday 09.30-12.00 / 13.30-18.00; Saturday-Sunday 14.00-19.00

COLLECTION | The museum contains the collection bequeathed to the city by Dr.Faure which, together with other donations, is presently housed in the mansion 'Les Chimères'. The attractively displayed works include two pastels and two bronzes of ballet dancers by Degas, and a Rodin collection of 13 watercolours and 28 sculptures in bronze and plaster, among which are 'Faunesse debout', 'Frère et soeur', 'Les Sirènes' and 'Amour et Psyche'. There are landscapes by Corot and Jongkind and Impressionist paintings by Pisarro, Renoir, Sisley, Cézanne and Boudin. The 20th century is represented by Vuillard, Bonnard, Maillol and others.

EXHIBITIONS | No details available.

Albi

MUSÉE TOULOUSE-LAUTREC
Palais de la Berbie 81003 Albi Director: Danièle Devynck
☎ **+33 63494870** 📠 **+33 63494888**
Open: Wednesday-Monday 1 Apr-1 Jun 10.00-12.00 / 14.00-18.00;
1 Jun-1 Oct 9.00-12.00 / 14.00-18.00; 1 Oct-1 Apr 10.00-12.00 / 14.00-17.00
Closed: Tuesday

Henri de
Toulouse-Lautrec
*Aristide Bruant in his
cabinet theatre*

*Musée Toulouse
Lautrec, Albi*

COLLECTION

The museum owns an exceptional collection of works by Henri de Toulouse-Lautrec (b. Albi 1864), spanning his career and covering his preferred subjects: horses, the theatre, brothels, cafe-concerts, and portraits.
Also on view are works by Bonnard, Vuillard, Valadon, and Sérusier among others. The first half of the 20th century and the Paris school are represented by Rouault, Utrillo, De Vlaminck, Dufy and Matisse, etc.

EXHIBITIONS
23·03·96-19·05·96

Bazaine and Poetry   This exhibition deals with the permanent dialogue that took place between Bazaine and poets who were his contemporaries. Bazaine's relationship with poetry sometimes included poetry editions for which he provided the illustrations, as well as other artistic works dealing with the poetic subjects, in a variety of media such as watercolours, drawings, engravings and paintings.

30·06·96-29·09·96   *From Picasso to Barcelo*

Alençon

MUSÉE DES BEAUX-ARTS ET DE LA DENTELLE
12, Rue Charles Aveline 61000 Alençon Director: Aude Pessey-Lux
☎ +33 33324007 📠 +33 33265166
Open: Tuesday-Sunday 10.00-12.00 / 14.00-18.00
Closed: Monday

COLLECTION

The Museum of Fine Arts and Lace has a joint collection of paintings and lace works on display in a specially renovated (1981) section of a 17th-century Jesuit College.
The painting collection includes drawings, prints and paintings from the 15th to the 19th century, with particular emphasis on French and Dutch painters of the 17th century (Champaigne, Jouvenet Macs, Ryckaert) and 19th-century French painting (Boudin, Courbet, Fantin-Latour, Legros, Lacombe).
The major attraction is the unique collection of lace created with various techniques (needle, bobbin, machine) from most of the European schools: Bruges, Brussels, Chantilly, Malines, Milan, Le Puy, Valenciennes, Venice, etc.
A highlight of this panorama of lace from the 12th century to the present is the display of Point d'Alençon, the unique lace of Alençon.

Jacob Ferdinand Voet
(1639-1700)
Young man from the Chigi family

Musée des Beaux Arts et de la Dentelle, Alençon

A collection of Cambodian objects and artefacts provides an unexpected finale to the exhibits on display.

EXHIBITIONS

16·02·96–12·05·96   ***Tribute to Michel Macréau***   Following the retrospectives on Chaissac and Boix-Vives, the Art and Lace Museum has brought together more than 80 works by Michel Macréau. The artist is noted for work which anticipated free figures and urban graphism.

15·06·96–15·09·96   ***Lace***   *Wedding Dresses And Gowns Of Haute Couture*
In 1993 the museum organised a collection of gowns for evening wear. This year, the art of the couturiers and designers is coupled with the use of lace, with examples by Lacroix, Nina Ricci, Balenciaga, Paca Rabanne, Lecoanet Heman, Saint Laurent and others.

Oct 96–Jan 97   ***Cambodia***   *Living Memory, Ethnological Souvenirs*   Adhémar Leclèrc (1853-1917), born in Alençon, was the last colonial governor in Cambodia (1886). While in residence, he collected everyday objects and took many photographs. This exhibition presents a contrast between contemporary and traditional Cambodia.

Amiens

MUSÉE DE PICARDIE
48, Rue de la République 80000 Amiens Director: Mathieu Pinette
☎ +33 22913644 📠 +33 22925188
Open: Tuesday-Sunday 10.00-12.30 / 14.00-18.00
Closed: Monday and 1 Jan, 8 May, 14 Jul, 1 and 11 Nov, 25 Dec

COLLECTION   ***The Paintings***   The collection of works from the 15th to 20th century includes the Puy d'Amiens from the Cathedral, 'Portrait of a Man' by El Greco, 'The Miracle of Saint Donat d'Arezzo' by Ribera, 'Portrait of the Pastor Langelius' by Frans Hals and a self-portrait by Quentin de la Tour. The 18th century is represented by Chardin, Fragonard, Hubert Robert, Guardi, Tiepolo, Subleyras, Vien, Regnault and the series 'Hunting in Foreign Lands' painted for Louis XV's 'Petits Apartements' at Versailles. There are also French landscapes mainly from the Barbizon School (Isabey, Diaz, Millet, Courbet, Corot, Th. Rousseau and Daubigny) and 20th-century paintings by Vuillard, Masson, Manessier, Hélion, Jorn, Dubuffet, Fautrier and Picabia.
The Medieval Collection   This section displays enamels, ivories, objets d'art, sculptures, lapidary work, statues and religious architecture from Picardy in the 12th century and at the end of the Gothic period.
The Archaeological Collections   The collection contains tools from Palaeolithic sites in Saint-Acheul and Cagny-la-Garenne, weapons and objects from the Bronze Age, and vestiges of a Roman forum, thermal baths and other items from the Gallo-Roman period.

EXHIBITIONS

until 19·05·96   ***Anne and Patrick Poirier***   *Fragility*

11·05·96–23·06·96   ***Bizarre Objects***   The museum exhibits its reserves at the Guynemer Cultural Centre, rue Georges Guynemer in Amiens.

21·06·96–29·09·96   ***Russian Romanticism***   A selection of paintings and drawings from the Tver Museum.

15·11·96–15·02·97   ***The Marionettes of Picardy***

Angers

MUSÉE DES BEAUX-ARTS
10, Rue du Musée 49100 Angers Director: Patrick Le Nouëne
☎ +33 41886465 📠 +33 41860638
Open: Tuesday-Sunday 1 Jun-30 Sep 09.00-18.30
1 Oct-31 May 10.00-12.00 / 14.00-18.00
Closed: Monday

COLLECTION

The museum's first-floor displays include a remarkable selection of art objects from the medieval and Renaissance periods (ivories, enamels, goldsmiths' crafts, furniture).

The great galleries, built in the middle of the 19th century, house the painting collection. The Livois collection, acquired in 1799, is the nucleus from which the collection has grown. This connoisseur had assembled a fine collection of 18th-century French paintings, as well as an outstanding ensemble of works by 17th-century Dutch and Flemish painters.

Medieval works include fine examples from Italy and a rare Swiss panel.

17th-century examples include paintings by Jordaens, Teniers, Poslenburgh, and Van Thulden of the Northern School, and French artists Mignard, Champaigne and Corneille. The Italian 'Allegory of Simulation' of the Florentine Filippo Lippi is one of the masterpieces of the museum.

The French 18th-century painting collection is particularly rich, with masterpieces by Watteau, Chardin, Boucher, Fragonard and other significant works by artists such as Hubert Robert Oudry and Greuze.

The collection of 19th-century paintings, comprised largely of portraits and landscapes, including Ingres' 'Paolo et Francesca' and Jongkind's 'L'Estacade', reveals the evolution of French art during the first half of the century, from Neo-classicism to Romanticism.

David d'Angers
Niccolo Paganini
Bronze

*Musée des Beaux-
Arts, Angers*

EXHIBITIONS

12·03·96–16·06·96

A Wallpaper Adventure   The Mauny Collection   200 pieces of wallpaper from the end of the 18th century through to the end of the 19th century recapture this golden age of French decorative art. They come from a collection of André Mauny, a French decorator of the 1930s.

29·06·96–26·10·96

Anthony Caro   Sculpture and Drawings from 1945 to the Present

Born in 1924, Anthony Caro is considered to be one of the great British sculptors of the second half of the 20th century. After a collaboration with Henry Moore in the mid-50s, he became famous as one of the great 'Constructivist' sculptors of the 60s. This exhibition will focus on his figure studies throughout his career.

Angoulême

MUSÉE DES BEAUX-ARTS
1, Rue Friedland 16000 Angoulême Director: Monique Bussac
☎ +33 45950769 📠 +33 45959826
Open: Monday-Friday 12.00-18.00 Saturday and Sunday 14.00-18.00
Closed: Public holidays

COLLECTION

The Museum of Fine Arts presents a wide collection, spanning 500 000 years of Charente prehistory from the first human habitation to the Casque d'Agris, including a masterpiece of Celtic goldwork from the 4th century B.C., precious stones from medieval Charente, 16th to 20th-century paintings from the French and foreign schools, painting and sculpture from Charente, an extensive collection of art from Eastern and Central Africa, New Caledonia, New Guinea and the Marquise Islands, ceramics from Charente, Rouen, Moustiers and Marseilles and a collection of weapons from the 15th to the 19th century.

EXHIBITION
29·03·92-Sep 96

Theodore Monod *The Spirit of the Desert*   This exhibition from the museum's Africa collection follows the travels of Monod through the Sahara, presenting its fauna and flora, geography, geology, archaeology and ethnology as seen through the eyes of the researcher and communicating his passion for the desert.

Antibes

MUSÉE PICASSO
Château Grimaldi 06600 Antibes Curator: Maurice Frechuret
☎ +33 92905420 📠 +33 92905421
Open: Tuesday-Sunday Jun-Sep 10.00-18.00
Oct-May 10.00-12.00 / 14.00-18.00
Closed: Monday and public holidays

COLLECTION

Picasso   During his stay at the Château Grimaldi in 1946, Picasso produced numerous works which he then donated to the museum.

Pablo Picassso
La joie de vivre, 1945
(detail)

Musée Picasso,
Antibes

Since then, this initial collection has been considerably enriched and includes ceramics, engravings, sculptures and paintings. The materials Picasso used clearly reflect the hardships of the post-war period, but at the same time Picasso captures the joy of living in a newly liberated country in the images he created.

Modern Art   The collection includes works from artists belonging to the main movement of 20th-century art: Adami, Alechinsky, Arman, Atlan, Bioulès, Boisrand, César, Combas, Dezeuze, Di Rosa brothers, Equipo Crónica, Ernst, Erro, Gleizes, Hartung, Klein, Magnelli, Messagier, Picabia, Pignon, Raysse, Saura, Spoerri and Viallat.

EXHIBITION
28·06·96-30·09·96

1946   This exhibition of French post-war art commemorates the 50th anniversary of Picasso's presence at the Château Grimaldi in Antibes. It is devoted to works created in the course of a single year, 1946, by major artists working in France. This was the only year in which no war took place, and it was especially rich in works of art.

Arles

MUSÉE RÉATTU
10, Rue du Grand-Prieuré 13200 Arles Director: Jean Maurice Rouquette
☎ +33 90493758
Open: Daily 9.30-12.30 / 14.00-19.00

COLLECTION

The museum is housed in the Priory of St. Gilles, built in the 15th to 16th century and bought by the Arles painter Jacques Réattu (1760-1833). Réattu's own works on display include 'Autoportrait', 'La Mort de Tatius', 'La Vision de Jacob', 'La Mort d'Alcibiade' and 'Le Peintre et sa famille au parapluie rouge'. Among the works by his contemporaries are 'Le Peintre et sa famille' and 'Atelier de couturières à Arles' by Antoine Raspal, 'Autoportrait' by Simon Vouet, 'Nature morte à l'aiguière' and 'Jeune Femme au miroir' by Meiffren Compte. There are three Flemish tapestries from the 17th century, 18th and 19th-century paintings from the school of Provence and contemporary works from Arles, including 'Les Alpilles'(1970) by Prassinos and a polyptych 'N.E.W.S.' (1987) by Pierre Mercier. In 1972 Pablo Picasso donated 57 of his drawings to the museum, and his widow Jacqueline later donated a portrait of his mother, Maria Picasso Lopez, from 1923. There is also a statue by Picasso of a woman with a violin.

The museum has a photography collection with works by Nadar, Vigneau, Man Ray, Weston, Cecil Beaton, Cartier-Bresson, Gisèle Freund and many others.

EXHIBITIONS

No exhibitions planned.

Arras

MUSÉE D'ARRAS ANCIENNE ABBAYE SAINT-VAAST
22, Rue Paul-Doumer 62000 Arras Director: Mrs. Notter
☎ +33 27712643 ▤ +33 21231926
**Open: 1 Apr-30 Sep Wednesday-Monday 10.00-12.00 / 14.00-17.30;
1 Oct-31 Mar Monday, Wednesday-Saturday 10.00-12.00 / 14.00-17.00
Sunday 10.00-12.00 / 15.00-17.00 (summer 17.30)
Closed: Tuesday**

COLLECTION

The museum is located in the centre of the Benedictine Abbey of Saint-Vaast. The ground floor houses an archaeological section and a collection of Medieval sculpture. The most important of the medieval works are funerary sculptures, among which are the tombstone of Bishop Frumauld (late 12th century), several engraved tombstones, wall stelae and the tomb of Guille Lefrançois from 1446. There are also capitals in Tournai stone from the 12th-century cathedral, 13th-century baptismal fonts and a maquette of the city in 1716. In the Alabaster Hall is a 14th-century marble sculpture of the Virgin and Child from Gosnay, a 14th-century St.John the Baptist in English alabaster and the marble funerary mask of a young woman from the early 14th century. There is also a room with wood sculptures from the 12th, 15th and 16th centuries. Also featured are a series of 6 paintings of the Muses by Baglioni, Flemish and Dutch works by Brueghel, Maes and Rubens, French decorative and religious art and paintings by Delacroix, Dutilleux and Corot.

EXHIBITIONS

10·05·96–15·07·96   *Paysages Anglais*   This exhibition focuses on the Ipswich Collection. Several major paintings from the collection by Gainsborough and Constable are being exhibited for the first time in Arras.

20·09·96–25·11·96   *La Tenture de la 'Vie de la Vièrge'*   The exhibition of French 17th-century artists sheds light on the history of this tapestry, which was commissioned in 1636 for Notre-Dame de Paris. Many tapestries, paintings, drawings and etchings are shown, including works by Philippe de Champaigne, Jacques Stella and Charles Poerson.

Fondation
Vincent van Gogh - Arles

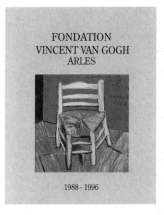

FONDATION
VINCENT VAN GOGH
ARLES

1988 - 1996

24 bis, Rond-Point des Arènes
13200 Arles
Tél. 90 49 94 04 - Tél. et Fax: 90 49 55 49

Open: Tues-Sunday 10.00-12.30, 14.00-17.30 from November through March.
From April 1st through November 1st 10.00-19.00, open every day.
Closed: Monday, Saturday morning from November through March.

Collection

Since 1988, Centennial of the arrival of Van Gogh in Arles, the Vincent van Gogh Foundation-Arles welcomes artists who have paid a tribute to Van Gogh. These artists are painters (Francis Bacon, David Hockney, Fernando Botero), sculptors (Arman, Cesar), photographers (Mary Ellen Mark, Lucien Clergue) writers and poets, music composers, and fashion designers with Christian Lacroix. All of these artists, around 120 have made their own homage to the famous painter. The Vincent van Gogh Foundation aims to recreate in Arles the House of Artists that Vincent himself wished for when he lived here.

The Palais de Luppé dating from the 18th Century is located in front of the Roman arena.

Exhibitions: Summer exhibitions July, August, Riera i Arago.

Auxerre

ABBAYE SAINT GERMAIN
2bis, Place Saint Germain 89000 Auxerre Director: Micheline Durand
☎ +33 86510974 📠 +33 86427050
Open: Wednesday-Monday Jun-Oct 10.00-18.30 Nov-May 10.00-12.00 /
14.00-17.30
Closed: Tuesday and 1 Jan, 8 Apr, 1, 8, 16 and 27 May, 1 and 11 Nov, 25 Dec

COLLECTION

The Benedictine abbey of Saint-Germain encompasses 15 centuries of Auxerre history. Overlooking the Yonne River, it includes a crypt containing the tomb of St. Germain, from the time of Charlemagne in the 9th century, adorned by highly-regarded frescoes The original monastery buildings still exist and have been restored. They are now used to house the permanent collections and for special exhibitions. On the grounds are a number of notable sites, including the church (13th century), the cellar (14th century), and the scriptorium and chapter house (12th century). The monks' old dormitory (17th century), has been converted into exhibition space for the local archaeological collections, which consist of prehistoric objects and reconstructions, and artefacts dating to the Gallo-Roman era, including sculptures, tombstones, and murals.

EXHIBITION
26·05·96-09·09·96

Jean-Pierre Risos   Paintings by local artist Jean-Pierre Risos (1934-1992).

Avignon

MUSÉE DU PETIT PALAIS
Place du Palais des Papes 84000 Avignon Director: Esther Moench-Scherer
☎ +33 90864458 📠 +33 90866121
Open: Wednesday-Monday Sep-Jun 09.30-12.00 / 14.00-18.00
Jul-Aug 10.20-18.00
Closed: Tuesday

COLLECTION

After many vicissitudes, the collection of paintings acquired by the Marquis Gian Pietro Campana (part of which was bought by Napoleon III in the 19th century) was re-united and came to rest in the 'Petit Palais' in 1976. The collection consists of 300 Italian Primitive paintings. The works of Botticelli, Carpaccio and Giovanni di Paolo are surrounded by Medieval sculptures and rare examples

Sandro Botticelli
Virgin and Child, late 15th century

Musée du Petit Palais, Avignon

of the Avignon School of Painting (Enguerrand Quarton, Josse Lieferinxe) on loan from the Calvet Museum.

EXHIBITION
15·05·96–14·08·96

Architectural Drawings by Rodin   The exhibition presents 30 drawings of medieval and Renaissance architecture by the great French sculptor Rodin. The studies in his book 'The Cathedrals of France' show the artist's love of Gothic architecture "which speaks the grand, simple language of masterpieces".

Bayonne

MUSÉE BONNAT
5, Rue Jacques Laffitte 64100 Bayonne Director: Vincent Ducourat
☎ +33 59590852
Open: 15 Jun-10 Sep Daily except Tuesday 10.00-12.00 / 15.00-19.00 Friday 15.00-21.00; 11 Sep-14 Jun Monday, Wednesday, Thursday 13.00-19.00 Friday 15.00-21.00 Saturday-Sunday 10.00-12.00 / 15.00-19.00
Closed: Tuesday and public holidays

COLLECTION

Louis Bonnat, an academician and painter of many official and society portraits, also collected paintings and over 2 000 drawings which he left to his native city. The museum has since acquired other collections and donations. An archaeological section contains Greek and Roman sculptures, bronze and terracotta statuettes, Phoenician glass and Egyptian amulets. There are 16th-century ivory sculptures, early Spanish paintings including a 15th-century Adoration of the Magi from Valencia, Brussels tapestries, 15 works by Rubens, two portraits by Van Dyck, and works by Murillo, Goya ('Self-Portrait'), Ribera and El Greco. Among the English portraits are Bonaparte by Thomas Phillips and Col. Tarleton by Reynolds. Bonnat also collected sketches by David and several studies and paintings by Ingres, including 'La Bagneuse à mi-corps'. On the first floor there are animal sculptures by Barye and Romantic paintings by Vernet, Corot, Courbet, Delacroix, de Chavannes and Géricault, as well as a portrait by Degas of Léon Bonnat Jr. A room is devoted to the works of Bonnat and a gallery contains his society portraits.

EXHIBITIONS
11·05·96-16·06·96

By Invitation: Eric Decelle, Private Collector

Summer 96

A Selection of Works from the Regional Fund for Contemporary Art

Jul 96-Sep 96

Treasures of English Painting from the collections of Aquitaine

Besançon

MUSÉE DES BEAUX-ARTS ET D'ARCHÉOLOGIE
1, Place de la Révolution 25000 Besançon Director: Françoise Soulier-François
☎ +33 81823989 📠 +33 81818109
Open: Wednesday-Monday 9.30-12.00 / 14.00-18.00
Closed: Tuesday

COLLECTION

The Museum of Fine Arts and Archaeology occupies a former grain market adapted to serve as a museum by Miquel, a follower of LeCorbusier. The museum's varied collections include archaeological finds (local, Egyptian, Greek and Roman), Medieval art, paintings ranging from the primitive to the 20th-century, ceramics, sculpture, and objets d'art. Some of the highlights of the collection are a sculpted bull with 3 horns, a number of Egyptian sarcophagi and paintings by such famous masters as Tintoretto, Cranach, Rubens, Boucher, Courbet, Renoir, Bonnard, Matisse and Marquet.

Luc Breton
(1731-1800)
*The sublime
Albertoni, after
le Bernin*

Musée des
Beaux-Arts et
d'Archéologie,
Besançon

EXHIBITIONS

24·04·96–29·07·96 · *François-Marius Granet's Drawings (1775-1849)*

29·07·96–02·12·96 · *Homage to four forgotten sculptors:* Marguerite Syamour (1857-1945), Anne de Chardonnet (1869-1926), René de Chateaubrun (1875-1942), Georges Laëthier (1875-1955)

07·08·96–04·11·96 · *Drawings of the Barbizon School*

Biot

MUSÉE NATIONAL FERNAND LÉGER
Chemin du Val de Pome 06410 Biot Curator: Brigitte Hedel-Samson
☎ +33 92915030 📠 +33 92915031
Open: Wednesday-Monday Summer 10.00-18.00
Winter 10.00-12.30 / 14.00-17.30
Closed: Tuesday

COLLECTION

The museum has been specially designed to display the 348 works by Léger. There are paintings, tapestries, ceramics and mosaics, including one that is reflected in a mirror, arranged in chronological order. Some of the early works are 'Portrait de l'oncle', 'Le Jardin de ma mère' (1905) and 'Toits de Paris' (1912). The study 'La Femme en bleu' is in Cubist style. Paintings from his 'mechanical' period include 'La Joconde aux clés' (1930) and 'L'Avion dans le ciel'. Among the other works on display are 'Les Belles Cyclistes', 'Les Loisirs' and 'La Grande Parade sur fond rouge' (1953).

EXHIBITIONS

22·06·96–15·09·96 · **'Jean Fautrier, the hothead'** The exhibition presents paintings, drawings, engravings and sculptures by Jean Fautrier, an artist who studied in England and was influenced by Turner and Old Masters such as Chardin and Rembrandt.

Nov 96 · **Drawings from the Collection of the Fernand Léger Museum** These drawings, executed with pencil or pen and then painted in gouache or watercolour, are studies for later paintings. The exhibition includes Léger's Cubist studies from the period 1919–1929.

Bordeaux

MUSÉE DES BEAUX-ARTS
20, Cours d'Albret 33000 Bordeaux Director: Francis Ribemont
☎ +33 56101749 📠 +33 56449816
Open: Wednesday-Monday 10.00-18.00
Closed: Tuesday

COLLECTION

The museum is housed in the Palais Rohan, built in the late 18th century by Prince Archbishop Mériadeck de Rohan, a part of which is the Town Hall of Bordeaux. Its collection of paintings from the Quattrocento and the Renaissance include 'Magdalen' and 'Tarquin and Lucretia' by Titian, 'Virgin and Child with St. Jerome and St. Augustine' by Perugino, 'Holy Family and Donor' by Veronese, 'The Four Ages of Man' by Lionello Spada, 'Embarkation of the Galley Slaves' and 'Galley Slaves' Arrival at the Genua Prison' by Alessandro Magnasco, 'Portrait of a Senator' by Lavinia and 'The Ecstasy of St. Anthony of Padua' by Murillo.

The Flemish paintings include 'The Martyrdom of St. George' by Rubens, 'Magdalen' by Van Dyck, 'Wedding Dance' by Jan Brueghel de Velours and paintings by Pieter van Mol, Gerard Seghers, Otto Venius, Joos de Momper, Frans Snyders and Jan Silberechts. The Dutch school is represented by Salomon and Jacob Ruysdael, Cornelis Verbeck, Claes Molenaer, 'The Lute Player' by Terbrugghen, 'Wheat Field' and 'Lute Player' by Van Goyen, still lifes by David Heem and 'Man with his hand on his heart' by Frans Hals. French portraits include the 'Duc d'Orléans, frère de Louis XIV' by Pierre Mignard, 'La Marquise du Châtelet' by Marianne Loir and 'Joueuse de mandoline' by Grimou. Among the English portraits are 'Baron Rockeby' by Reynolds and 'Mrs Arden' by Gilbert Stuart.

Among the paintings from the Romantic period are 'La Grèce expirant sur les ruines de Misselonghi' by Delacroix, 'l'Incendie du steamer l'Austria' by Isabey, 'Le Bain de Diane' by Corot, 'Les Fraises' by Renoir and eight paintings and other works by the Bordeaux artist Odilon Redon. There is an original plaster work by Rodin. Two other Bordeaux artists are Albert Marquet (1875-1947), represented by 'Portrait de mes parents', 'Nu fauve', 'Le port de Bordeaux' and other works, and André Lhote (1885-1962), a Neo-Cubist whose works include 'Baigneuses' and 'Paysage méridional'. There are also works by Braque, Kokoschka and Matisse.

EXHIBITION

15·06·96–08·09·96

Greece in Revolt Delacroix and the French Painters (1815-1848) *(in the Galerie des Beaux-Arts, Place du Colonel Raynal)* This exhibition commemorates the efforts made by French artists and intellectuals to help Greece achieve independence from the Ottoman Empire. Works by Delacroix and lesser-known artists are presented and a catalogue tells how the artists' efforts were able to influence public opinion and the course of the political situation.

Bordeaux

CAPCMUSÉE D'ART CONTEMPORAIN
3, Rue Ferrère 33000 Bordeaux Director: Jean-Louis Froment
☎ +33 56441635 📠 +33 56441207
Open: Tuesday-Sunday 11.00-19.00 Wednesday 11.00-22.00
Closed: Monday

COLLECTION

The collection, which the museum has been building since the beginning of the '80s, includes representatives of the major international movements from the end of the '60s and the beginning of the '70s, Minimal art, Conceptual art, Land art, Arte Povera, Support Surface, the Nouvelle Figuration artists from the 1980s and the Post-Minimalists.
The collection is periodically enriched with new works acquired from current exhibitions, keeping the museum in touch with the latest developments in contemporary art.
At the present time, the museum's collection includes some 500 works of reference by 50 international artists.

EXHIBITIONS

12·04·96–12·06·96	*The Grande Lande Farm*
12·04·96–12·06·96	*Jean-Paul Thibeau* 'Outside himself in his I don't know what'
12·04·96–12·06·96	*'Johannesburg: As in School'*
12·04·96–12·06·96	*For Hiroshima*
28·06·96–29·09·96	*Annette Messager*
28·06·96–29·09·96	*Cindy Sherman* Works 1985-1995
28·06·96–29·09·96	*Tony Oursler* Video Installations
25·10·96–Jan 97	*Jean-Charles Blais* Retrospective

Bordeaux

MUSÉE DES ARTS DÉCORATIFS
Hôtel de Lalande 39, Rue Bouffard 33000 Bordeaux Director: J. du Pasquier
☎ +33 56007250 📠 +33 56816967
Open: Wednesday-Monday 14.00-18.00
Closed: Tuesday and public holidays

COLLECTION

The museum occupies the Hôtel de Lalande, built in 1780 by the Bordeaux architect Étienne Laclotte. The museum's collections of furniture, miniature paintings, metalwork, ceramics, porcelain and glass, locks, keys and weapons, mainly from the 18th century, are displayed in the panelled rooms of the ground floor and the floor above.

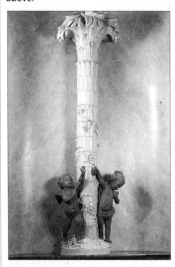

Stacking set of pans
Tin-plated faience
and terracotta,
c. 1780

*Musée des Arts
Décoratifs, Bordeaux*

The furniture includes a divan and chairs in Louis XV style, a Louis XVI spinet and Chinese vases. Among the paintings are landscapes, portraits and 500 miniatures, most of them by the Bordeaux artist Dagoty. There is a bronze statue of Louis XV on horseback, a bust of Montesquieu by Jean-Baptiste Lemoyne and a bust of 'Young America' from the house of the first American consul in Bordeaux. Silver and goldwork includes teapots, coffeepots and sugar bowls.

There is a collection of French Venetian style glass from the 16th to

18th century, an important collection of French 18th-century faience, a 12th-century gilded and enamelled copper cross and a 13th-century gemellion. The stairway to the first floor has a fine Bordeaux wrought-iron bannister.

EXHIBITION
28·10·96–06·01·97

A Glance at the Basque Region   This exhibition is organised as part of the Association of Public Collections of the Aquitaine Region (A.C.M.A.) and brings together paintings, drawings and decorative projects by Basque painter Ramiro Arrue (1892-1971) and illustrated Ciboure stoneware pottery dating from the 1930s. This is a collection that shapes the image of the Basque region, its beauty and its picturesque customs.

Caen

MUSÉE DES BEAUX-ARTS MUSEUM OF FINE ARTS
Le Château 14000 Caen Director: Alain Tapié
☎ +33 31852863 📠 +33 31791647
Open: Wednesday-Monday 10.00-18.00
Closed: Tuesday and 1 Jan, 1 May, 25 Dec

COLLECTION

The Museum of Fine Arts of Caen is known for its large collection of paintings, and in particular for its 16th and 17th-century Italian, French and Dutch collection, which is considered to be one of the finest in France. This includes works by Le Pérugin, Véronèse, Le Guerchin, Tiepolo, Poussin, Philippe de Champaigne and Rubens, among others.
The museum also possesses a fine collection of paintings relating to Normandy during the 19th century, and a modern and contemporary collection based on themes of light and space, by artists such as Gleizes, Villon, Joan Mitchell, Vieira da Silva, Tobey, Olivier Debré and Rebeyrolles.
In addition, the museum has a highly-regarded collection of more than 50 000 prints, including works by Dürer, Callot, Rembrandt, Tiepolo and Piranese. The printroom regularly presents exhibitions of works from the collection, as well as exhibitions of modern and contemporary artists. There is also a public library of art numbering some 20 000 books.

EXHIBITIONS
03·03·96-05·06·96

Normandy Paintings   Normandy during the 19th century; works from the collection of the Museum of Fine Arts of Caen.

01·06·96-05·08·96

Barry Flanagan Engravings 1970-1995   This exhibition is organised in cooperation with the Bibliothèque Nationale de France.

Nov 96-Feb 97

Italian Contemporary Painting   Recent work by Carlo Guarienti.

Caen

MUSÉE DE NORMANDIE
Logis des Gouverneurs, Château 14000 Caen Director: Jean-Jacques Bertaux
☎ +33 31069898 📠 +33 31437517
Open: 1 Apr-30 Sep Wednesday-Friday 10.00-12.30 / 13.30-18.00
Saturday-Monday and public holidays 9.30-12.30 / 14.00-18.00; 1 Oct-31 Mar
Wednesday-Monday 9.30-12.30 / 14.00-18.00
Closed: Tuesday

COLLECTION

Founded in Caen in 1946 on the initiative of G.H. Rivière, the Museum of Normandy aims, through archaeological and ethnographical collections, to show the cultural evolution of man within the historical boundaries of Normandy from its very beginnings up to the present day.

The Museum of Normandy collected the first of its ethnographical specimens during investigations undertaken in collaboration with the National Museum of Folk Arts and Traditions. These and other collections were significantly enriched when the museum acquired the collections of the Normandy Antiquarian Society in 1984.

The museum's Archaeological Service organises systemic excavations on the original religious sites in the city of Caen whenever urban development projects are undertaken.

The museum has established a conservation workshop particularly suited to the restoration of metallic objects and ceramics. After the establishment of the workshop, a survey of the entire museum collection was undertaken, which revealed that it was just as important to restore the ethnographical items as it was to maintain the archaeological collections.

In the mid-80s the permanent exhibition was completely renovated. It is now divided along three principal themes: settlement, techniques, and religious beliefs. These themes are explored in the three sections of the museum: 'From Prehistory to the Vikings', 'Man and the Land', and 'Man and Materials'.

EXHIBITIONS

Jun 96-Oct 96

Voyagers and Hermits *Popular Evangelist Saints from Normandy, 4th-8th Century* [in the Saint-Georges du Château Church]
Little is known about how Christianity came to the region now known as Normandy. A collection of manuscripts, statues, reliquaries and articles of worship sheds some light on the spread of Christianity from the cities to the countryside by saints from Ireland and Gaul, among them St. Martin and St. Colomban.

22·06·96-25·08·96

Dragons and Drakkars *The Viking Myth from Scandinavia to Normandy, 18th-20th Century* [in the Abbaye aux Dames, Caen]
In the 19th and 20th century, Normandy experienced a revival of interest in its ancestors, the Vikings, and the Scandinavians took an interest in their own Nordic heritage. The 'dragon style' was developed among Scandinavian artists but long remained unknown outside Scandinavia. The exhibition is a collaboration between the Normandy Museum and the Museums of Stockholm.

Calais

MUSÉE DES BEAUX ARTS ET DE LA DENTELLE
25, Rue Richelieu 62100 Calais Conservator: Annette Haudiquet
☎ +33 21466200 📠 +33 21466209
Open: Wednesday-Monday 10.00-12.00 / 14.00-17.30
Closed: Tuesday and public holidays

COLLECTION

The 19th-Century Sculpture Gallery The sculpture collection of the Fine Arts Museum in Calais is based on studies and maquettes realised by the sculptor Auguste Rodin for the 'Monument to the Citizens of Calais'. The works of other 19th-century French sculptors are represented, as well as works marking the transition from the 19th to the 20th century, and contemporary sculptures.

The Painting Gallery The collection includes Flemish and Dutch paintings from the 15th and 16th century, Italian paintings and French paintings, including a 16th-century nude in the form of a Memento Mori and works with maritime subject matter.

Lace Calais has been a centre of industrial lace since the mid-19th century. The museum has a collection of about 300 000 pieces from Calais and other important lace centres which includes hand-crafted as well as industrial products. There are also designer dresses illustrating the use of lace, a collection of looms, tools, plans and maquettes of tulle factories.

Contemporary Art The museum has acquired works by Jean Dubuffet, Andy Warhol and Pablo Picasso, amongst others, and displays works by regional artists.

EXHIBITIONS
23·03·96–26·05·96

Diller & Scofidio *Investments*   The various meanings of the term 'investment' are explored by two American artists, Elizabeth Diller and Ricardo Scofidio, in four video installations showing how social codes directly concern the body.

May 96–31·12· 96

The Adventure of Lace in Calais   The development of Calais lace is traced from the arrival of the first English tulle makers in 1817 up to now. On display are lingerie from the 19th century to the present, designer dresses and everyday wear, machines, tools, sample books and samples of machine-made lace from 1845 to 1930.

14·06·96–08·09·96

Alison Wilding *Sculptures*   The selected works created by Alison Wilding since 1989 make use of contrasting materials and include monumental sculptures as well as small pieces.

20·09·96–30·11·96

Felix Del Marle   Felix Del Marle, originally from Pont-sur-Sambre, is known as the first French Futurist. The exhibition of work from his last period contains abstract geometrical compositions combining different materials as well as coloured, rhythmic architecture.

14·12·96–end Feb 97

The Hand-Made Lace Collection of the Musée de Calais   The exhibition, put together by the French specialist in the field of hand-made lace, Anne Kraatz, contains nearly 400 pieces, including hand-made lace (16th to 19th century) from the original collection of the first museum of lace as well as recently acquired pieces.

Castres

MUSÉE GOYA
Hôtel de Ville 81100 Castres Director: Jean Louis Augé .
☎ +33 63715858 📠 +33 63715999
Open: Tuesday-Sunday 09.00-12.00 / 14.00-17.00
Closed: Monday

COLLECTION

The museum's Spanish paintings, displayed in the former bishop's palace built in 1666, were collected by Marcel Briguiboul (1837-1892), a local painter. The four paintings by Goya are 'Self-Portrait Wearing Spectacles', 'Portrait of Francisco del Maza', 'Portrait of Mathias Allué' and the 'Junta of the Philippines' (c. 1814) There is also a series of his engravings. The paintings are displayed in a room containing works by Domingo and father and son Lucas, Hispano-Moorish faience, pharmaceutical vases from the 15th century and Flemish tapestries. The États diocésains room contains a 16th-century Flemish tapestry and paintings from the Dutch, French and Italian schools, as well as a portrait of Lord Ligonier by Saura and a helmet which belonged to George II of England. One room is devoted to archaeological finds in the area of Castres and Celtic and Cathar objects. The Spanish works date from the 14th century to the present, including works by Borassa, Juan Rexach (panels from a retable), Luis de Morales ('Adoration of the Magi'), Velásquez and Osona, and 20th-century works by Bueno, Mateo-Hernandez and Picasso (drawing).

EXHIBITIONS
23·03·96·28·05·96

José Subira-Puig   The internationally known sculptor, born in Barcelona in 1926, has used wood, stone and metal to produce complex and highly structured forms. The exhibition presents a selection of his best work from 1988 onwards.

05·07·96-06·10·96   **Jumel de Noireterre**   To celebrate the Centenary of the Jumel de Noireterre donation, the Goya Museum presents this artist's military paintings, fantastic works and unique collection of Mexican artefacts. The exhibition also traces his political career.

Le Cateau-Cambrésis

MUSÉE MATISSE
Palais Fénelon   59360 Le Cateau-Cambrésis   Curator: D. Szymusiak
☎ +33 27841315   📠 +33 27840878
Open: Wednesday-Monday 10.00-12.00 / 14.00-18.00
Sunday and public holidays 10.00-12.30 / 14.30-18.00
Closed: Tuesday and 1 Jan, 1 Nov, 25 Dec

COLLECTION   Established by Matisse in his native city in 1952, the museum offers a wide selection of this important artist's works. The collection contains 100 paintings, drawings and sculptures by Matisse, as well as works by Auguste Herbin, a master of geometrical abstraction, and Geneviève Claisse. It is situated in a small 18th-century palace facing a romantic park.

EXHIBITIONS
11·05·96-01·09·96   **Del Marle**   *Les Années des Réalités Nouvelles*   Born in Pont sur Sambre, Del Marle is renowned for being the first French Futurist and for having fought for the integration of art into everyday life. This exhibition of his later works contains abstract geometric works combining different materials.

Nov 96-Dec 96   Illuminated drawings from the 15th century and illustrations by Matisse of poems by Charles d'Orléans.

M U S É E   M A T I S S E

Musée Départemental
Palais Fénelon
59360 Le Cateau-Cambrésis
tél: 27 84 13 15
fax: 27 84 08 78

Ouvert tous les jours (sauf le mardi, le 01/01,
01/11, 25/12) de 10h à 12h et de 14h à 18h
le dimanche de 10h à 12h30 et de 14h30 à 18h

Visites-animations,
Stages, PAE, Classes patrimoine
(programme sur demande)

Ceret

MUSÉE D'ART MODERNE
8, Boulevard Maréchal Joffre 66400 Ceret Director: Joséphine Matamoros
☎ +33 68872776 📠 +33 68873192
Open: Jul-Sep 10.00-19.00; Oct-Jun 10.00-18.00; May-Sep open daily
Closed: Oct-Apr Tuesday and 1 Jan, 1 May, 1 Nov, 25 Dec

COLLECTION	The collection has been built up with gifts from artists who have stayed in Ceret since the beginning of the century, in particularly Picasso and Matisse, who contributed 53 works and 14 drawings respectively.
	20th Century Historical Art These schools are represented by the works of Brune, Chagall, Cocteau, Coutaud, Dalí, Dufy, Apel-les Fenosa, Gris, Gargallo, Haviland, Herbin, Hugué, Jacob, Kisling, Krémègne, Lhote, Maillol, André Marchand, Jean Marchand, Marquet, Masson, Matisse, Miró, Picasso, Pignon, St. Saëns, Survage.
	Contemporary Art The museum has significant works by Arnaudiès, Ben, Bertrand, Bordarier, Brossa, Capdeville, Dolla, Eulry, Fauchier, Fischer, Fourquet, Jaccard, Jude, Martin, Messager, Rebeyrolle, Rossell, Tàpies, Viallat, Vila.
	The collection is completed by works of New Realism, including works by Arman, Bellegarde, Bertini and Gérard Deschamps. In years to come the museum will complete the collection of 20th-century Historical Art and will build up collections consistent with contemporary art by encouraging artists to think and work around the area.
EXHIBITIONS	No exhibitions planned.

Chalon-sur-Saône

MUSÉE NICÉPHORE NIÉPCE
28, Quai des Messageries 71100 Chalon-sur-Saône Director: Paul Jay
☎ +33 85484198 📠 +33 85486320
Open: Wednesday-Monday 14.30-17.30
Closed: Tuesday

COLLECTION	The museum focuses on the history of photography and is most renowned for the original equipment used by Joseph Nicéphore Niépce, who invented photography in May 1816. The route through the museum starts with the first heliographs, the first photo-landscape, the first photo-engraving, calotypes and the paper printing processes. One notable item acquired by the museum is the 'Pencil of Nature' by William Henry Fox Talbot published in six parts between 1844 and 1846. The museum also acquired the collection of calotypes from M. Le Prévost d'Iray containing works by Stephane Geoffray, Julien Vallou de Villeneuve and Louis Adolphe Humbert de Molard, three names regularly associated with the origins of photography and the calotype.
	Photographs are on display from a complete range of photographers, from the very first to the very latest, and on a wide range of support mediums including wood, canvas, photographic enamel and porcelain. The collection of photographic equipment ranges from the Camera Obscura to Hasselblad's lunar camera, from the 3D table to the 3D camera, from the daguerreotype camera to the Number I Kodak camera and from Niépce's first camera to ferrotyping.
EXHIBITIONS	No details available.

Chambéry

MUSÉE DES BEAUX-ARTS
Place du Palais-de-Justice 73000 Chambéry Director: Armand Amann
☎ +33 79337503 ⏦ +33 79750779
Open: Wednesday-Monday 10.00-12.00 / 14.00-18.00
Closed: Tuesday and public holidays

COLLECTION

The museum is situated in the former grain market opposite the Palais de Justice. Thanks to the Daille and Garrod donations, the museum has a collection of works ranging from the 14th to 20th century. The earliest work is the 'Retable de la Trinité' (1396) by Bartolo di Fredi. 15th-century works include the 'Passion Triptych' (c. 1440) attributed to Domenico di Michelino and 'Portrait of a Young Man' by Paolo Uccello. Among the 16th-century artists are Jan van Dornicke, Anton von Worms, Joos van Cleve, Bassano and Naldini. The 17th century is represented by, among others, Nicolaes Moyaert, Abraham Storck, Luca Giordano and Claudio Francesco Beaumont, and the 18th-century Neo-Classicists by Langlois and Isabey.

EXHIBITIONS

No exhibitions planned.

Chantilly

MUSÉE CONDÉ
Château de Chantilly 60631 Chantilly Director: Amélie Lefébure
☎ +33 44570800 ⏦ +33 44577031
Open: 1 Mar-31 Oct Wednesday-Monday 10.00-18.00; 1 Nov-29 Feb Tuesday-Friday 10.30-12.45 / 14.00-17.00 Saturday and Sunday 10.30-17.00
Closed: Tuesday

COLLECTION

The collection of the Musée Condé is housed in Chantilly Castle, parts of which date back to the 14th century. Its last private owner, the Duke d'Aumale, bequeathed the castle and its extensive art collection to the French Institute and restored the building to its present condition.
Manuscripts, books, and archives The collection includes approximately 800 manuscripts, books and book bindings.
European paintings European paintings from the 14th to the 19th century are displayed in the Great Gallery. The wide-ranging collection includes representative works of the Italian, Northern, and French Schools, as well as examples of French Orientalism.
Furnishings Fine examples of furniture, oriental porcelain, and Chantilly lace are on display in the museum.
Sculpture Sculpture in the classical style, commissioned by the Duke d'Aumale, is on display alongside other works of sculpture pre-dating the French Revolution.
Building and grounds In addition to the castle itself, the surrounding grounds include a park, commissioned in 1666 and designed by Le Nôtre and his nephew Gittard, a pond, five thatched cottages dating from 1774, an English garden, and an 18th-century Jeu de Paume (tennis court) which is used for concerts and other events.

EXHIBITIONS

24·05·96–26·08·96

Clouet in Chantilly The Portraits of King François I Paintings, drawings and miniatures of King François attributed to Jean Clouet (died 1540), or to his son François (died 1572). This exhibition is organised in collaboration with the Louvre Museum.

Sep 96-Jan 97

Watteau and his circle in the Collections of the Institute of France
An exhibition of paintings and drawings by Jean-Antoine Watteau (1684-1722), J.B. Pater, Nicolas Lancret, etc.

Chartres

MUSÉE DES BEAUX-ARTS
29, Cloître Notre-Dame 28000 Chartres Director: Naithe Valles-Bled
☎ +33 37364139 📠 +33 37234199
Open: Wednesday-Monday 1 Apr-31 Oct 10.00-18.00 1 Nov-31 Mar
10.00-12.00 / 14.00-17.00
Closed: Tuesday and 1 Jan, 1 May, 11 Nov, 25 Dec

COLLECTION

The collections include paintings from the 16th to the 19th century, an extensive series of Medieval polychrome woodcarvings, 16th and 18th-century tapestries, enamel work, harpsichords and spinets dating from the 17th and 18th centuries. A number of paintings by Vlaminck and a collection on French overseas territories are also on display. In addition to the collections, the architecture of the museum itself includes an 18th-century hall with a horseshoe-shaped staircase, an 18th-century chapel and a room in Italian fashion which is used for the annual 'Mai du Clavecin' (spring concerts).

Limosin Léonard
(c. 1505- c. 1575)
Saint Paul, 1547

Musée des Beaux-Arts, Chartres

EXHIBITIONS

mid Apr 96–12·06·96　***Jacques Le Brusq***　*From Landscape to Exile*　The exhibition contains about 90 paintings and drawings of the Chartres countryside by Jacques Le Brusq, professor of Fine Art at Nantes.

28·06·96–28·10·96　***Pinchus Kremegne***　Born in Lithuania in 1890, Kremegne emigrated to France between 1910 and 1920 and took part in the artistic life of Montparnasse. The exhibition contains works from his early and Provencal periods, as well as late still-lifes and landscapes.

Sep 96–Nov 96　***Marceau***　The exhibition commemorates the 200th anniversary of Marceau's death.

Oct 96–Nov 96　***Robert Nicoidsky***　The exhibition presents 40 of the least figurative pastel drawings by the Paris artist, who combines abstract and figurative elements in depicting the human figure.

Nov 96–Jan 97　***Ofer Lellouche***　Born in 1947, the artist studied at the Paris School of Fine Art and now lives in Israel. The landscapes, nudes and self-portraits recreate pleasure, anguish, sadness, joy and life itself.

Dec 96–Feb 97　***An Italian Autumn***　The exhibition presents collections of Italian paintings from the 18th century.

Cherbourg

MUSÉE THOMAS HENRY
Rue Vastel 50100 Cherbourg Director: Jean-Luc Dufresne
☎ +33 33230223 📠 +33 33230227
Open: Tuesday-Sunday 9.00-12.00 / 14.00-18.00 Closed: Monday

COLLECTION | The Thomas Henry Museum owns 300 paintings and sculptures from the 15th to the 19th century, with masterpieces from the Italian, French and Northern schools. These include a famous Fra Angelico, Romantic sculptures by Le Veel, numerous portraits and sketches by J.F. Millet and a superb collection of works by Guillaume Fouace.

EXHIBITION
20·06·96–03·11·96

Fra Angelico (1387-1455)
The conversion of St.Augustine

Musée Thomas Henry, Cherbourg

Ceramics in Normandy during the 18th and 19th century.

Colmar

MUSÉE D'UNTERLINDEN
1, Rue d'Unterlinden 68000 Colmar Conservator: Sylvie Lecoq-Ramond
☎ +33 89201550 📠 +33 89412622
Open: 1 Apr-31 Oct Wednesday-Monday 09.00-16.00; 1 Nov-31 Mar
Wednesday-Monday 09.00-12.00 / 14.00-17.00
Closed: Tuesday, 1 Jan, 1 May, 1 Nov, 25 Dec

COLLECTION | The museum is housed in what was once a Dominican convent dating from the 13th century, dedicated to St. John the Baptist. It contains fine examples of Rhenish art from the late medieval and Renaissance period. The Issenheim altarpiece, composed of sculptures by Nicolas Haguenau (c. 1490) and paintings by Grünewald (c. 1512-1516), is the masterpiece of the collection. The basement and ground floor contain the following sections: archaeology, the minor arts, decorative and popular arts from Alsace and contemporary art. Works by artists ranging from Lucas Cranach and Holbein the Elder to Bonnard, Picasso and Bazaine have been added to the Unterlinden Museum's collection.

EXHIBITIONS
16·03·96–02·06·96

Celtic and Gallic Treasures (Archaeology) *The Upper Rhine between 800 and 50 B.C.*

07·09·96–01·12·96

Otto Dix and the Old Masters (Contemporary Art)

Dijon

MUSÉE ARCHÉOLOGIQUE DE DIJON
5, Rue Docteur Maret 21000 Dijon Curator: Monique Jannet
☎ +33 80308854 📠 +33 80745299
Open: Wednesday-Monday Jun-Sep 09.30-18.00; Oct-May 09.00-12.00 /
14.00-18.00
Closed: Tuesday and public holidays

COLLECTION

The museum occupies the so-called 'dormitory of the Benedictines', dating from the 13th century, of the Abbey of Saint-Bénigne and another smaller 11th-century room. Its collection ranges from prehistoric times to the Middle Ages. The exhibit begins with monumental Gallo-Roman sculpture, including funerary figures of a wine merchant, butcher and Saône boatman. There is a collection of votive figures in wood, bronze and stone from the source of the Seine, including two rare anatomical examples, and a bronze figure of the goddess Sequana standing on a beaked boat.

Medieval and Renaissance stone sculpture includes the Bust of Christ (c. 1400) by Claus Sluter, two Romanesque tympana from the old Saint-Benigne church, the Head of Christ by Claus de Werve and two 12th-century capitals.

The prehistoric collection includes artefacts confirming the presence of Neanderthal man on the Côte-d'Or, such as a reconstructed skull fragment (70 000 years old), silex knives and arrowheads. There is a Paleolithic fragment of a laurel-leaf solutrean implement (c. 18 000 years old), a Merovingian gold bracelet and other funerary articles.

EXHIBITIONS

06·04·96–27·05·96

A Story of Pot *The Gallo-Roman potters in Burgundy*
This exhibition, presented in the dormitory of the former Abbey of St. Bénigne, depicts the rural and urban pottery workshops as they existed in the Gallo-Roman Age. Constituting an overall survey of Gallo-Roman ceramics in Burgundy, the exhibition includes displays on the technologies of the era, trade, and land and sea routes utilised for trade. A catalogue will be produced in conjunction with the exhibition.

28·06·96–04·11·96

Registered Designs *Bronze treasures in Burgundy*
The development and transformation of bronze craftsmanship in Europe, and the uses of bronze objects, between 1900 B.C. and 700 B.C. The exhibition takes place in the dormitory of the former Abbey St. Bénigne.

Dijon

MUSÉE DES BEAUX-ARTS
Palais des Etats de Bourgogne 21000 Dijon Director: Emmanuel Starcky
☎ +33 80745270   📠 +33 80745344
Open: Wednesday-Monday 10.00-18.00
Closed: Tuesday and 1 Jan, 1 and 8 May, 14 Jul, 1 and 11 Nov, 25 Dec

COLLECTION

Housed in the medieval palace of the Dukes of Burgundy, which served as the seat of regional political power almost continuously from the 15th to the 18th century, the Dijon Museum of Fine Arts has one of the largest and finest collections in France. Relics of the Burgundian dynasty itself include the tombs of Philippe le Hardi and Jean Sans Peur, several altarpieces from the neighbouring necropolis, Chartreuse de Champmol, and a series of paintings from the Flemish School, including the 'Adoration of the Shepherds' by the Master of Flémalle.

Remnants of the Medieval era include the Chapter House, the Philippe le Bon Tower and the Ducal Palace kitchen.

One of the oldest institutions of its kind in France, the museum was originally intended to serve educational purposes and was formally associated with the School of Drawing in 1766. At that time, the museum consisted of two rooms decorated in lavish 18th-century style, both of which can still be visited today. In the 'Salle des Statues', sculptures and copies from ancient originals produced by 18th-century art students are on display, while the 'Salon Condé' exhibits 18th-century paintings, sculpture and furniture, as well as some Louis XVI wood panelling.

Donations, bequests and loans have steadily enriched the museum over the years, permitting a number of extensive and varied collections to be created, including medieval weapons, Swiss and Rhenish Old Masters (unique in France), paintings from the Northern and Italian Schools, drawings and prints, French Renaissance art from the School of Fontainbleu, etc.

The 19th century is represented by James Tissot, Eugène Boudin and Edouard Manet, as well as local sculptors such as François Rude and his pupil Emmanuel Fremiet.

The collection of contemporary art has been enlarged by a series of donations from Pierre and Kathleen Granville, including works by Lapicque, Messay Bertbolle, Vieira da Silva and others.

Melchior Broederlam
(documented at
Ypres between 1381
and 1401)
Details from the back
of the panels of the
Scene of the
Cruxifixion.
Left panel:
*The Annunciation
and the Visitation*

*Musée des
Beaux- Arts, Dijon*

EXHIBITIONS

09·03·96-13·05·96   ***Claudio Parmiggiani***   *Drawings*   100 drawings by this Italian artist, also a sculptor and poet, show the evolution of his work since the 60s. The exhibition contains small sketches, 3-dimensional works, large drawings contrasting light and dark on a lightly sketched human form, as well as two sculptures and a video.

22·06·96-28·10·96   ***Ages and Faces of Asia***   From the past century to the 50s, many Frenchmen set out to explore the Far East. The exhibition, based on the collections of the Guimet Museum in Paris (liturgical objects, manuscripts, ceramics) traces their explorations of the Silk Route, the Levant and the mountains of the land of the Dalai Lama.

13·12·96-17·03·97   ***Bernard Plossu***   *Photographer*   The photographer, who works in black and white, has travelled to Mexico, India, California and Africa, stopping a moment at Mont-Afrique in Burgundy and the Combes around Dijon to take 'photographs of silence'.

Dijon

LE CONSORTIUM
16, Rue Quentin 21000 Dijon Directors: Douroux & Gautherot
☎ +33 80307523   ⅢⅢ +33 80305974
Open: Tuesday-Saturday 14.30-18.30
Closed: Sunday and Monday

COLLECTION   The collection of Le Consortium recalls the art centre's past exhibition activities, consisting of almost 150 works, predominantly from the 1980s. Largely comprised of new geometric works (Armleder, Mosset, Federle, Diao, Parrino, etc.), the painting section also includes more 'conceptual' canvasses by artists such as Kawara, Zaugg, G. Merz and others.

The sculpture collection is characterised by large pieces, including works by Graham, Genzken, Stockholder and Knoebel. Lavier, Burkhard and DiBenedetto are especially well represented in the collection.

The international range of the collection is notable (from McCollum to Ruthenbeck and from Vermeiren to Nordman), as is the particularly good representation of recent French art, including works by Boltarski, Morellet, Verjux, Messager, Vieille and Rutault. Labels such as minimal, conceptual, post-modern and especially expressionist and decorative are not applicable; the collection is nevertheless testimony to contemporary artistic approaches. Exhibits organised by Le Consortium take place at the principal exhibition space as well as at l'Usine, a secondary exhibition space.

EXHIBITIONS

26·04·96-15·06·96	*Rirkrit Tiravanija (USA)*
22·06·96-05·09·96	*Dan van Golden (NL)*
15·09·96-Oct 96	*Liam Gillick (GB)*
Nov 96-Dec 96	*Pierre Huyghe (F)*

Dijon

MUSÉE MAGNIN
4, Rue des Bons Enfants 21000 Dijon Director: Emmanuel Starcky
☎ +33 80671110 📠 +33 80664375
Open: Tuesday-Sunday Jun-Sep 10.00-18.00 Oct-May 10.00-12.00 / 14.00-18.00
Closed: Monday and 25 Dec, 1 Jan

COLLECTION

A visit to the Magnin Museum is a visit to the home of two extraordinary collectors. The museum, located in the heart of Dijon, houses the collection of over 2000 paintings, drawings and art objects assembled by Jeanne and Maurice Magnin at the turn of the century. The collection is displayed in their 17th-century mansion, the Hôtel Lantin, which was bequeathed to the state in 1937. In addition to the collection, the furnishings assembled by the Magnins are on display. While the collection includes some important works, the Magnins rarely made expensive acquisitions and thus much of the collection is comprised of paintings and drawings by minor masters.

Giovani Cariani
*Christ and the
adulterous woman*

Musée Magnin, Dijon

The collectors continuously sought out rare works, and the museum's rooms, taken together, present a brief history of painting. Northern European artists are especially well represented, including works by Lastman (Rembrandt's master), Bijlert, Janssens, Van der Helst, Lairesse, Van Bloemen and Mengs. The collection also includes a large number of paintings by relatively unknown Italian painters from Venice, Rome and Lombardy.

The major painters of the French school are represented, including Sébastien Bourdon, Laurent de La Hyre, Eustache Le Sueur, Jean-Baptiste de Champaigne, and others. The collection extends to the 19th century, with works by David, Girodet, Isabey, and Delaroche. Drawing and tracings, which are too fragile to be permanently displayed, are exhibited on a rotating basis. The Magnins also purchased furniture and original or unusual objects including a combined desk and chest of drawers by Carel, a double-sided lady's desk, and many faience pieces.

EXHIBITIONS | No exhibitions planned.

Douai

MUSÉE DE LA CHARTREUSE
130, Rue des Chartreux 59500 Douai Director: Mrs. Baligand
☎ +33 27871782 📠 +33 27910981
Open: Monday-Saturday 10.00-12.00 / 14.00-17.00 Sunday 10.00-12.00 /
15.00-18.00
Closed: Tuesday and Bank Holidays

COLLECTION | The Musée de la Chartreuse consists of a town hall and a Carthusian convent dating from the 16th and 17th century, where visitors can view the former cloister and refectory.
The collection itself includes works from *the Northern Schools* dating from the 15th, 16th and 17th century. One example is the impressive Anchin's Polyptych by the Flemish artist, Jean Bellegambe, which is exhibited in the Carthusian refectory. Dutch works include paintings by the Master of Manna, Van Scorel, Saenredam, Van Ruisdael and Balthazar van der Ast.
From *the Italian Schools* of the Renaissance Period and the 17th century come works by Maestro di Desco Da Parto, Cavaliero d'Arpino, Vasari, Veronese, Carrache and the sculpture of Jean de Bologne. The masterpiece entitled 'The Denial of Saint Peter' by Pensionante de Saraceni is the only work belonging to a French public collection.
The *French Schools* of the 18th and 19th century include masters such as Chardin, Nattier, Lebrun, Corot, Isabey and Boudin. Impressionism is represented by works of Sisley, Pissaro and Renoir. The Modern Art collection boasts paintings by Cross, Maurice Denis and Bonnard. The Musée de la Chartreuse is one of the few French museums owning the relief map of a town. The map representing the town of Douai was commissioned by Louis XIV in 1709.

Alfred Sisley (1839-1899)
The haystack

Musée de la
Chartreuse, Douai

EXHIBITIONS
May 96-Jul 96 | ***Georges Demeny and the Invention of Cinema*** Georges Demeny, a physiologist born in Douai in 1850, collaborated with his colleague Marey to set up a laboratory in which they could study motion frames. Employing the phonoscope, Demeny was able to

reconstitute motion in successive frames. In this exhibition, undertaken in collaboration with the French Film Library and Cinema Museum, the Chartreuse Museum presents Demeny's inventions and the movies that he produced.

Autumn 96

Henri Edmond Cross (Douai, 1856 - Saint-Clair, Var, 1910)
Influenced by the Impressionists, Cross befriended the Neo-Impressionists, who were utilising small dots of pure colour or colour mixed only with white, the size of which they varied depending on the size of the work and the distance from which it was to be seen. Between 1895 and 1900, Cross developed a style utilizing pure colour to intensify the light, setting the standard for Fauvist painting.

Écouen

MUSÉE NATIONAL DE LA RENAISSANCE
Château d'Écouen 95440 Écouen Director: Hervé Oursel
☎ +33 1 39900404 📠 +33 1 39949337
Open: Wednesday-Monday 09.45-12.30 / 14.00-17.15
Closed: Tuesday

COLLECTION

The National Renaissance Museum occupies one of France's most beautiful 16th-century châteaux. Spectacularly overlooking the Plaine-de-France, this lavish residence was built between 1538 and 1555 for Anne de Montmorency, High Constable of France. Some of the most famous artists of the era were engaged, and the château epitomises French architecture towards the middle of the 16th century, including innovations such as the portico on the south wing built to house Michelangelo's 'Slaves', which had been given to the High Constable by King Henri II. The château has retained much of its original painted décor, including a dozen monumental fireplaces reflecting the influence of King Francis I's gallery in Fontainebleau, and it remains a unique example of mid-16th-century French decorative painting.

Chateau d'Ecouen
North gate (16th
century)

Musée National de la
Renaissance, Ecouen

This setting serves to display one of the most important collections of artwork of the period, illustrating the extraordinary luxury and refinement of the European Renaissance. It includes tapestries, furniture, painted enamels, sculpture, arms and armour, leather wall hangings, goldsmith's work, glasswork, ceramics and stained glass. Notable amongst these treaures are the automaton-cum-clock once know as 'Charles V's Nef', and 'The Story of David and Bathsheba', a 245-foot long tapestry of silk and silver threads. The château is surrounded by 42 acres of park and woodland accessible to museum visitors.

EXHIBITIONS

No exhibitions planned.

Fontainebleau

MUSEE NATIONAL DU CHÂTEAU DE FONTAINEBLEAU
Château de Fontainebleau 77300 Fontainebleau Director: Amaury Lefébure
☎ +33 1 60715070 📠 +33 1 60715071
Open: Wednesday-Monday Nov-May 09.30-12.30 / 14.00-17.00;
Jun 09.30-17.00; Jul-Aug 09.30-18.00; Sep-Oct 09.30-17.00
Closed: Tuesday and 1 Jan, 1 May, 25 Dec

COLLECTION

Eight centuries of art and history The epithet of 'House of the centuries, true residence of Kings' given to the Château de Fontainebleau by Napoleon reflects the memory of more than 700 years of sovereigns in France, from the enthronement of Louis VII in 1137 to the fall of the Second Empire in 1870. Much of the interior appearance of the Château as it appears today is due to Napoleon Bonaparte.

Napoleon I Museum The Napoleon I Museum is devoted to the Emperor and his family. The decision to create this museum was taken in 1979 when Prince Napoleon, his wife the Princess and Countess de Witt made an arrangement with the state involving the donation and transfer of a part of the imperial family's collections. The museum is located in the Louis XV wing, constructed between 1738 and 1774, and divided thematically between the rooms of the first and ground floors. The themes include: Napoleon, Emperor of the French and King of Italy; the splendour surrounding imperial power; everyday life in the palaces and on campaigns; the tireless worker; Empress Marie-Louise; the birth of his son 'the Little King'. There are also several rooms each depicting one of the members of the Bonaparte family.

The Chinese Museum The Chinese collections of Empress Eugénie are exceptional due to both their origin and their sheer number. The Napoleon III salons that house these pieces have been restored. Almost 400 objects were seized as war trophies from the Chinese Emperors' Summer Palace in 1860, mainly jades, porcelains, silks, candelabra, vases, perfume burners in enamelwork and a great 'stupa' in gilded copper decorated with turquoises.

Apartments, Courts, Gardens and the Park The Château has many other places of interest, including the Private Apartments situated on the ground floor below the Great Apartments, the various courts, gardens and lakes as well as The Great Border, The Great Park and The Grand Canal.

EXHIBITION

May 96-Jul 96   Porcelain, Earthware and Enamel of Sèvres at Fontainebleau

Grenoble

MUSÉE DE GRENOBLE
5, Place de Lavalette 38000 Grenoble Director: Serge Lemoine
☎ +33 76634444 📠 +33 46634410
Open: Thursday-Monday 11.00-19.00 Wednesday 11.00-22.00
Closed: Tuesday and 1 Jan, 1 May, 25 Dec

COLLECTION

The Musée de Grenoble houses a fine collection with a remarkable range of Old Masters and many modern and contemporary works. The collection includes many Flemish, Dutch, Italian, Spanish and French artists from the 16th to the 18th century. Highlights are 'Saint Jérôme' by Georges de la Tour, 'Saint Grégoire' by Rubens, 'L'adoration des bergers' by Francisco de Zurbarán and 'Roger délivrant Angélique' by Delacroix. The 19th century is also well represented, but the museum's main strength is its 20th-century collection, with works by Matisse, Marquet, Derain, Vlaminck, Van Dongen, Picasso, Matisse, Léger, Bonnard and leading figures of Surrealism including Magritte, Tanguy, Miró and Max Ernst.

The various trends in geometric or informal abstract art are represented by artists such as Van Doesburg, Kupka, Arp, Bill Lohse, Gorin and Soulages. In the contemporary art collection, a great diversity of themes are explored, with works by Sol LeWitt, Kenneth Noland, Ellsworth Kelly, Carl André, Imi Knoebel, François Morellet, Niele Toroni, Allan MacCollum, Christian Boltanski and Bertrand Lavier, among others.

EXHIBITIONS

Spring 96–Summer 96

Black and White Stories   Black and white works by Frank Kupka, Piet Mondrian, Aurélie Nemours, Marcelle Cahn, Julije Knifer, François and Vera Molnar, Christian Floquet, François Perrodin and Dominique Dehais.

28·09·96–16·12·96

Morris Louis   The first retrospective in France of this American artist who was a precursor of Minimalism.

In 1997

Signac and the Liberation of Colour

Honfleur

MUSÉE EUGÈNE BOUDIN
Place Erik-Satie 14602 Honfleur Cedex Director: Anne-Marie Bergeret
☎ +33 31895400 📠 +33 31891876
Open: 15 Mar-30 Sep Wednesday-Monday 10.00-12.00/14.00-18.00; 1 Oct-14 Mar
Monday, Wednesday-Friday 14.30-17.00 Saturday-Sunday 10.00-12.00/14.30-17.00
Closed: Tuesday and 1 May, 14 Jul, 25 Dec and 1 Jan-15 Feb

COLLECTION

The museum was officially founded as a municipal museum in 1868 by two painters and natural sons of Honfleur, Louis-Alexandre Dubourg and Eugène Boudin. Renamed the 'Eugène Boudin Museum' on the occasion of significant expansion in 1974, the museum was further enlarged by the addition of a neighbouring building in 1988. Today, the museum offers 1200 sq.m. of permanent exhibition space on six different levels.

Eugène Boudin
(1824-1898)
Trouvaille, the entrance to the jetties at low tide

Musée Eugène Boudin, Honfleur

The Désirée-Louveau Hall. An extensive ethnographic collection including costumes, accessories, lace, furniture, dolls and headgear from various regions of Normandy.
Dries, Gernez, Herbo, Saint-Delis and Bigot. Works by five contemporary artists who have lived in Honfleur.
The Katia-Granoff Hall. Works by contemporary artists who have lived or worked in Honfleur and Normandy: Vallotton, Dufy, Marquet, Friesz, Ozenfant, Villon, de Belay, Souverbie, Cappiello, Lagar, Grau-Sala, Oudot and the painters of the Rouen School.

The Chapel. Temporary exhibitions (2-3 times a year) devoted to artists who have worked in Normandy or to ethnographic and historic themes. When no temporary exhibitions are planned, the Chapel is used to display works kept in reserve.

The Eugène Boudin Hall. 19th-century painters, including Jongkind, Huet, Isabey, Cals, Courbet, Dupré, Pécrus, Hamelin, Dubourg, Boudin, Monet, Gagnery, Lebourg, Georges-Michel, etc. The Hambourg-Rachet Donation. Works by Boudin, Dubourg, Cals, Saint-Delis, Gernez, Carrière, Gen-Paul and André Hambourg.

The Hall of Drawings. Some hundred drawings classified according to theme and artist. New drawings are selected for exhibition each year.

EXHIBITION

06·07·96–28·10·96   ***Still-Life Evolution in the 19th Century***   An exhibition culled from E. Boudin Museum collections, other museum collections and private collections.

Lille

MUSÉE DES BEAUX-ARTS
Place de la République 59000 Lille Director: Arnauld Brejon de Lavergnée
☎ +33 20570184 📠 +33 20546948
Closed: The museum is closed for renovation.
Reopening end 1996 - begin 1997.

Limoges

MUSÉE NATIONAL ADRIEN DUBOUCHÉ
Place Winston Churchill 87000 Limoges Director: Chantal Meslin
☎ +33 55774558 📠 33 55796439
Open: Wednesday-Monday Sep-Jun 10.00-12.00/13.30-17.15; Jul-Aug 10.00-17.15
Closed: Tuesday

COLLECTION

The permanent collection contains more than 12 000 items of porcelain, earthenware, stoneware, pottery and glass.

The pottery section displays works from as far back as the 7th century B.C., proving that pottery is undoubtedly one of the oldest crafts practised by man. This section also features Graeco-Roman, Medieval and 19th-century terracotta works.

Faience is produced by steeping modelled clay in a bath of enamel with a tin base. First developed in the Middle East during medieval times, this technique later spread across Europe. The collection includes outstanding examples of faience from various countries. Made from clay with a high silica content, stoneware was developed in China. In use in Germany since the Middle Ages, it was only used in France on a large scale during the 19th century by such artists as Delaherche, Chaplet and Decoeur.

Porcelain is made from a mixture of quartz, felspar and kaolin. When fired at 1400 C, the material becomes white, hard and translucent. The museum owns an astonishing collection of Chinese porcelain and an unrivalled collection of Limoges porcelain from around 1771 right up to the present. The museum also houses a collection of 16th to 19th-century European glassware.

EXHIBITIONS

No exhibitions planned.

Limoges

FRAC LIMOUSIN
Impasse de Charentes 87100 Limoges Director: Frédéric Paul
☎ +33 55770898 📠 +33 55779070
Open: Tuesday-Friday 12.00-19.00 Saturday 14.00-19.00
Closed: Sunday, Monday, and public holidays

COLLECTION

The 'Fonds Régional d'Art Contemporain' (FRAC) has the largest collection of contemporary art in the Limousin region. The sculpture collection features works by Duprat, Toni Grand, Monnier, Muñoz, Séchas, Schütte and Whiteread. The museum also focuses on the various ways in which artists use photography: as a document (work by Acconci, Bas Jan Ader, Burden, Cohen, Dimitrijevic, Huebler, Matta-Clark, Wegman); in its relationship to text (Aballéa, Calle, Kruger, Messager, Mogarra) and as a substitute for sculpture (Culbert, Cumming, Raetz, Webb). The FRAC collection also includes work by the French Supports-Surfaces movement of the late 60s and early 70s.

One-man exhibitions alternate with displays culled from the museum's collection, supplemented by loans from private collectors.

EXHIBITIONS

04·04·96-25·05·96   **Joseph Grigley**, *FRAC Limousin, Les Coopérateurs, Limoges*

21·06·96-28·09·96   **Michel François**, *FRAC Limousin, Les Coopérateurs, Limoges*

03·10·96-03·11·96   **Martine Aballéa**, *Chapelle saint Libéral, Brive*

Lyon

MUSÉE DES BEAUX-ARTS
20, Place des Terreaux 69001 Lyon Director: Philippe Durey
☎ +33 72101740 📠 +33 78281245
Open: Wednesday-Sunday 10:30-18.00
Closed: Monday and Tuesday

COLLECTION

Founded in 1801 and located in the former Benedictine Abbey of the Dames de Saint-Pierre, which was built in 1659, the Museum of Fine Arts houses a collection which includes paintings of the French, Flemish, Dutch, Italian and Spanish Schools, and has sections devoted to local painters, Impressionists, and modern art. There are also displays of ancient, medieval and modern sculpture; French, Italian Oriental and Hispano-Moorish ceramics; and drawings, prints and furniture. The museum has an Islamic collection and a numismatic collection.

EXHIBITIONS

01·06·96–16·02·97   **The treasure of the Place des Terreaux**   Presentation of the medieval monetary treasure discovered during excavation work on the Place des Terreaux in December 1993.

19·09·96–01·12·96   **New acquisitions and restored works (1990-1995)**   A review of six years of enhancement of the museum's collections, through purchases (Houdon, Stella, Blanchard), donations and bequests (Bonnard, Appian), together with loans (Matisse, Chagall, Picasso) and a number of spectacular restorations.

23·01·97–06·04·97   **Kees van Dongen**   *Drawings 1895-1914*

Lyon

MUSÉE DES ARTS DÉCORATIFS
30, Rue de la Charité 69002 Lyon Director: Guy Blazy
☎ +33 78371505 📠 +33 72402512
Open: Tuesday-Sunday 10.00-12.00 / 14.00-17.30
Closed: Monday and public holidays

<table>
<tr><td>COLLECTION</td><td>The Decorative Arts Museum was opened to the public in 1925 and is designed to complement the neighbouring Textile Museum. The museum is housed in the Hôtel Lacroix Laval and displays the use of textiles and tapestries in a 17th and 18th century interior setting. This is one of France's rare 'ambiance' museums with the objects and furniture fitting in perfectly with the décor of a typical town mansion of the classical age. Visitors will also enjoy discovering fine collections of pottery, old watches and clocks, jewellery, enamels and furniture.</td></tr>
<tr><td>EXHIBITIONS</td><td>No exhibitions planned.</td></tr>
</table>

Lyon

MUSÉE DES TISSUS
34, Rue de la Charité 69002 Lyon Director: Guy Blazy
☎ +33 78371505   📠 +33 72402512
Open: Tuesday-Sunday 10.00-17.30
Closed: Monday and public holidays

COLLECTION

The Textile Museum is closely associated with the history of silk and is housed in the 18th-century Hotel de Villeroy. The collections are divided into two categories, Eastern and Western. The visitor can trace the development of weaving and textile décor, with a special focus given to the Lyon silk industry between the 17th and 20th centuries and to the various uses of the silk produced in Lyon, from high-quality interior decoration to 18th-century costumes through to 20th-century haute couture.

Embellished robe made in a silk factory in the style of Jean Revel, c. 1730

Musée des Tissus, Lyon

EXHIBITIONS

11·05·96–25·05·96   ***The Art of Quilt, Treasury of Silk***   This exhibition will present about 40 ancient and modern 'crazy quilts', mostly made of silk, showing irregular patterns and bright colours.

22·06·96–31·08·96   ***Kimonos of the Hata Family***   The exhibition will present 50 kimonos created by Tokio Hata. In 1989 Hata received the title of National Living Treasure in recognition of his work and constant research on the Yuzen technique. The museum will also show kimonos created by Tokio Hata's son and granddaughter.

Autumn 96   ***Church Vestments of the 19th Century***   The Textile Museum will present a large part of its 19th- century church vestment collection.

Marseille

MUSÉE DES BEAUX-ARTS
Palais Longchamp 13004 Marseille Director: Marie-Paul Vial
☎ +33 91622117 📠 +33 91906307
Open: Tuesday-Sunday 1 Oct-31 May 10.00-17.00 1Jun-30 Sep 11.00-18.00
Closed: Monday

COLLECTION

The museum is housed in a wing of the Palais Longchamp, built by Espérandieu in 1870. The collection includes two 19th-century works by Puvis de Chavannes: 'Marseille colonie grecque' and 'Marseille porte de l'Orient' and earlier views of Marseille by Michel Serre (1658-1733), one depicting the plague of 1720-1723.

The ground floor contains 15th to 17th-century paintings from the Flemish, Dutch, Italian and German schools, and French works mainly from Provence. Among them are a 'Crucifixion' in the style of Van der Weyden, 'Virgin and Child with donors' by the Master of the Death of the Virgin, two anonymous German panels, 'Noah Building the Ark' by Bassano, 'Gypsy Camp' by Jean de Venne, 'Adoration of the Shepherds' and 'Boar Hunt' by Rubens, 'Village Wedding' by Annibal Carrache, 'The Tears of St. Peter' by Zurbarán, and works by Joos van Cleve, Pieter Brueghel the Elder, Teniers, Snyder, and Ruysdael. Provençal works include 'The Ecstasy of St.Catherine' by Barthélemy Chasse, 'Samson and Delilah' by Louis Finson and 'Virgin and Child' by Nicolas Mignard.

Two rooms are devoted to the works of the Marseille artist Pierre Puget (1671-1745). Among his paintings are 'St. Cécile' and 'The Baptism of Constantine'. His sculptures include 'Perseus and Andromeda' and 'Immaculate Conception'. There are also works by Vannini and Tiepolo, 18th-century paintings of the port of Marseille by Joseph Vernet, and busts and lithographs by Daumier (1808–1897), including 'Don Quixote and Sancho Panza'.

EXHIBITIONS

26·04·96–30·06·96 | ***Philippe de Champaigne*** The Kidnapping of Madeleine, A Rediscovery

30·09·96–30·01·97 | ***Rodin*** La Méditation, Photographs, Sculptures, Drawings

Marseille

MUSÉE CANTINI D'ART MODERNE ET CONTEMPORAIN
19, Rue Grignan 13006 Marseille Curator: Nicolas Cendo
☎ +33 91547775 📠 +33 91550361
Open: Tuesday-Sunday 10.00-17.00
Closed: Monday

COLLECTION

The museum is housed in the Hôtel Montgrand, which was bequeathed to the city together with the collections by Jules Cantini. It contains Modern and contemporary art from the beginning of the 20th century up to the present. Among the important earlier works are 'Arcades à l'Estaque' by Dufy; 'Le Tramway' by Vuillard; 'A tire-d'aile by Braque; 'Les Lutteurs' by Kandinsky; 'Self-Portrait' by Bacon; and works by Miró, Dubuffet, Chabaud, Kupka and others. Later works include 'Colère de violon' by Alechinsky; 'Le Verre vert' by Honegger; 'Pretextat' by Picabia; an untitled work by Sam Francis from 1971; 'Peinture' by Yves Klein; 'Ritva dans un fauteuil' by Saura; 'La Fête à Seillans' and other works by Max Ernst; and 'King of the Zulus' by J-M. Basquiat. There are sculptures by Arp, 'Genèse' and 'Ptolémée III'; Christo, 'Empaquetage'; and works by Gonzalez, Brauner, Pons and others. The photography collection includes work by Clergue, Giordan,

Mulher Pohle, Pham Viet-Si, Martine Franck, Ralph Gibson and others as well as photographs of Marseille taken in the period 1930 to 1935.

EXHIBITIONS

22·03·96–02·06·96 | *Pierre Girieud and the Experience of Modernity 1900-1912*

05·07·96–end Sep 96 | *Auguste Chabaud*

Montauban

MUSÉE INGRES
19, Rue de l'Hôtel-de-Ville 82000 Montauban Director: Georges Vigne
☎ +33 63221292   📠 +33 63221353
Open: Tuesday-Saturday 10.00-12.00 / 14.00-18.00
Closed: Monday, Sunday morning

COLLECTION

The museum is housed in the 12th-century episcopal palace which became the Town Hall of Montauban after the French Revolution. In 1843, a legacy from Baron and former Mayor Vialètes Mortarieu formed the basis for the museum's collection. Subsequently, by means of an initial donation in 1851 and a legacy in 1867, Ingres considerably enriched the museum of his native city with collections of antiquities and Classical paintings as well as more than 4 000 drawings and 20 paintings from his own hand, numerous personal belongings (including the famous violin), and his entire collection of documentation, including engravings, photographs, calques and copies.

In addition to the great Montauban artist, a general survey of painting in France and other countries since the 14th century is provided. The collection features works by renowned artists from Daddi to Delacroix, including Masolino, Lesueur, Mignard, Boucher and David. A hall devoted to the sculpture of Bourdelle provides the link with the 20th century, represented by Olivier Debre, Zao Wou-Ki, Vieira da Silva and others.

Jean-Auguste-
Dominique-Ingres
(1780-1867)
*The song of Ossian,
1812-1813*

*Musée Ingres,
Montauban*

EXHIBITIONS

end Apr 96–mid Jun 96 | *A la Lisière du Trouble*   This year the exhibition 'Encounters with Art' presents a collection of works by artists whose world seems 'normal' at first, but surreptitiously transgresses the borders of the strange (Fred Deux, Poumeyrol, etc.).

Summer 1996	***Robert Lapoujade (1921-1993)*** Retrospective of the works of this painter and director, born in Montauban in the first quarter of this century.
mid Sep 96–Jan 97	***Xavier Krebs & Jean Suzanne*** A retrospective exhibition of the works of these artists, one a painter and the other a sculptor.

Montpellier

MUSÉE FABRE
39, Boulevard Bonne Nouvelle 34000 Montpellier Curator: Michel Hilaire
☎ +33 67148300 📠 +33 67660920
Open: Tuesday-Friday 09.30-17.30 Saturday, Sunday 09.30-17.00
Closed: Monday

COLLECTION

The museum's collection, housed in a former Jesuit College and the adjacent Hôtel de Massilian where Molière once performed, is based on the donations of François-Xavier Fabre, Antoine Valedau and Alfred Bruyas, a friend of Delacroix and Courbet. The basement houses works by Rubens, Brueghel, Teniers, Ruysdael, Jan Steen, Albert Cuyp, M. van de Velde, Van Goyen and Gérard Dou. There is a display of ceramics and faience from Montpellier in the former kitchen. Fabre's collection includes 'Infant Samuel in Prayer' by Joshua Reynolds, 'Virgin and Child with St. John' by Botticelli, 'The Mystic Marriage of St. Catherine' by Paolo Veronese, 'St.Agatha' and the 'Angel Gabriel' by Zurbarán, English landscapes by Richard Parkes Bonington, 'Fontenelle' and 'Louis XIV' by Rigaud, portraits by the Montpellier artist Sébastien Bourdon, 18th-century sculptures by Pajou, Roland, d'Antoine and Houdon, including his 'Voltaire' in terracotta, portraits by Fabre of the Countess of Albany, Alfieri, Canova and Allen Smith, and a self-portrait.
The Bruyas collection contains portraits of Bruyas by Delacroix, Courbet, Glaize and Tassaert, 'St. Jerome in the Desert' by Vincent (1777), 'Portrait of Dr Leroy' by David, 'Solitude paysage franc-comtois' and 'Bonjour Monsieur Courbet' by Courbet, 'The Tempest' by Isabey, 'Portrait of Lord Byron' and sketches by Géricault, 'Stratonice ou la maladie d'Antiochus' and studies by Ingres, 'Matinée' and other works by Corot, and works by Cabanel, Degas, Berthe Morisot and Monet.

EXHIBITION
mid Jul 96-end Oct 96

On Nature *The Landscape in the Fabre Museum's Collection of Paintings and Drawings from the 17th to the 19th Century*
The collection includes classical French, Italian and North European landscapes (Poussin, Dughet, Rosa, Van Bloemen, Moucheron), native and Italianesque North European works (Ruysdael, Berchem), Neoclassical paintings and drawings (Clerisseau, Fabre, Roguet, Michallon, Gauffier), realistic and Romantic works (Corot, Rousseau, Courbet) and late 19th-century works (Bazille, Guillamin, Maufra, Didier-Fouget).

Nancy

MUSÉE DES BEAUX-ARTS
3, Place Stanislas 5400 Nancy Curator: Béatrice Salmon
☎+33 83376501 📠+33 83853076
Open: Wednesday-Monday 10.30-18.00
Closed: Monday morning, Tuesday

COLLECTION

The museum occupies one of four pavilions built by the architect Héré in 1755. The exhibit opens with Cubist and Post-Cubist sculptures by Arp, Duchamp-Villon, Henri Laurens and Zadkine

('Vénus accroupie'). Among the 19th and 20th-century French paintings are 'Portrait of Zélie' by Courbet, 'Autumn' by Manet, 'Sunset at Étretat' by Monet, 'Portrait of Germaine Survage' by Modigliani, and works by Suzanne Valadon, Matisse, Utrillo, Vlaminck, Vuillard and others. A section is devoted to decorative art by the Maison Daum from 1878 to the present.

The first floor contains early Italian, Flemish, Dutch and Spanish works, including 'The Tomb of Christ' by Tintoretto, 'The Annunciation' by Caravaggio, 'The Cumaean Sibyl' by Pietro da Cortana, 'Transfiguration' by Rubens, 'The Baptism of Christ' by Ribera and works by Perugino, Palmerucci, Stetter, Van Goyen and others.

Among the French paintings are Claude Lorrain's 'Pastoral Landscape'(1635), Philippe de Champaigne's 'Charity' and Boucher's 'Aurora and Cephalus'. The graphics collection contains drawings by the Nancy artist Grandville, 'La Bataille de Nancy' by Delacroix, and works by Isabey, Friant, Ingres and others.

EXHIBITIONS

13·05·96–30·07·96   *Around Clodion*   Thirty terracottas from the Paul Cailleux Collection (Museum Bonnat - Bayonne).

16·09·96–18·11·96   *Henri-Leopold Lévy (1840-1904)*   The Symbolist Temptation

Nantes

MUSÉE DES BEAUX ARTS
10, Rue Georges Clemenceau 44000 Nantes Director: Henry-Claude Cosneau
☎+33 40416565 ▥ +33 40416790
Open: Monday, Wednesday, Thursday and Saturday 10.00-18.00
Friday 10.00-21.00 Sunday 11.00-18.00
Closed: Tuesday

COLLECTION

Established in 1801 by consular decree, the restored Museum of Fine Arts presents a chronology of western painting from 13th-century Italy up to the present day. Each period is represented by works of art of exceptional quality, displayed in galleries surrounding a large central courtyard.

Old Masters   Less than ten years after its foundation, the museum's collection was enriched when the city of Nantes purchased the private collection of François Cacault which included, among other works, three masterpieces by Georges de La Tour. In the period following this acquisition, the museum focused primarily on acquiring contemporary art. As a result, it made important purchases including 'Portrait of Madame de Senonnes' by Ingres, 'The Winnowers' by Courbet and 'The Kaïd' by Delacroix.

Modern Art   Donations from the 'société des Amis du Musée', created in 1911, have permitted continuous expansion of the collection by acquisition. For example, works by Monet, Signac and Dufy were first exhibited at the museum and then later acquired by the society. The Modern Art section also contains works by Sonia Delaunay, Max Ernst, Marc Chagall, Jean Hélion and Pablo Picasso. There is, in addition, an entire room devoted to Vassily Kandinsky.

Contemporary Art   The works of numerous contemporary artists, including Pierre Soulages, François Morellet, Martin Barré, Claude Viallat, Toni Grand and Rosemarie Trockel are on display in the museum to provide an impression of contemporary art trends. The museum's focus on contemporary art has been further underscored by the creation of 'La Salle Blanche' (The White Room), where the work of younger artists is on display.

EXHIBITIONS

02·03·96–27·05·96	*Olav Christopher Jenssen*　 *Once*
11·04·96–24·06·96	*Yves d'Ans, Alain Guillard, Hervé Lemasson, Philippe Ruault* *Photographs*
03·05·96–02·09·96	*Henry Moore*　 *From the Inside Out*　 An exhibition featuring examples of his plasters, carvings and drawings.
14·06·96–09·09·96	*Philippe Cognée*
20·09·96–10·01·97	*Troels Wörsel*
25·10·96–15·02·97	*Paul-Armand Gette*

Nice

MUSÉE ARCHEOLOGIQUE DE CIMIEZ ET SITÉ ARCHEOLOGIQUE
160, Avenue des Arènes 06000 Nice Director: Danièle Mouchot
☎ +33 93815957 ▥ +33 93810800
Open: 1 Oct-1 May Tuesday-Saturday 10.00-12.00 / 14.00-17.00
Sunday 14.00-17.00; 2 May-30 Sep Tuesday-Saturday 10.00-12.00 /
14.00-18.00 Sunday 14.00-18.00
Closed: Monday and certain public holidays and 1-20 Nov

COLLECTION

The museum, inaugurated in January 1989, exhibits glassware, ceramic and bronze objects, jewellery and documents - discovered during excavations - from Cemenelum and the Alpes Maritimae province, together with Greek and Italic ceramic vases from the 5th to the 2nd century B.C. Artefacts, inscriptions, scale models and plans are thematically arranged with explanatory notes in a contemporary setting on two levels. The architectural site includes three complete Roman thermal complexes dating from the 2nd to the 3rd century A.D. and a Paleochristian cathedral and baptistry from the 5th century A.D.

EXHIBITION

Jul-Oct 96

Life and handicraft in Thysdrus/El Djem (Tunisia), an African town (2nd to 3rd century A.D.)

Nice

MUSÉE DES BEAUX-ARTS
33, Avenue des Baumettes 06000 Nice Directors: B. Debrabandère / J. Forneris
☎ +33 93445072 ▥ +33 93976707
Open: Tuesday-Sunday May-Sep 10.00-12.00 / 15.00-18.00;
Oct-Apr 10.00-12.00 / 14.00-17.00
Closed: Monday

COLLECTION

The 17th-century collection is mainly Italian and includes works by artists including Tassi, Cozza, Guarino, Keil.
The Vanloo dynasty, Natoire, Hubert Robert, Fragonard and Vien (France), Zuccarelli, Creti, Trevisani and Batoni (Italy) form the core of the 18th-century section.
19th and early 20th-century (French) art is well represented from Neo-classicism to Impressionism and beyond. There are works by Besnard, Benjamin Constant, Cabanel, Carolus-Duran, Flameng, Dinet, Degas, Boudin, Monet, Sisley, Guillaumin, Ziem, Bonnard, Vuillard and Van Dongen, ceramics by Picasso and the glass works of Maurice Marinot.
The museum also houses the collections of Jules Chéret, J.B. Carpeaux, Bastien-Lepage, Marie Bashkirtseff and Marcellin Desboutin.

The Raoul Dufy collection and the Symbolist works of Gustav Adolf Mossa are now exhibited at 77 and 59 quai des Etats-Unis at Galerie-Musée Dufy and Galerie-Musée Mossa.

Alfred Sisley (1839-1899)
Road with poplars near Moret

Musée des Beaux-Arts, Nice

EXHIBITION
05·10·96–05·01·97

Wine, vineyards, drunkenness and wine-growers in French Painting 1600-1900 A thematic exhibition on a subject which combines realism and symbolism.

Nice

MUSÉE MATISSE
164, Avenue des Arènes de Cimiez 06000 Nice Curator: Xavier Girard
☎ +33 93534053 📠 +33 93530022
Open: Wednesday-Monday 1 Oct-31 Mar 10.00-17.00; 1 Apr-30 Sep 11.00-19.00
Closed: Tuesday

COLLECTION

The museum's permanent collection is composed of works donated by the painter and his heirs supplemented with works on permanent loan from the State. The artist lived in Nice from 1917 to 1954.

Musée Matisse, Nice
Entrance hall, new section of the museum

The collection includes 68 oil paintings and paper collages, 236 drawings, 218 engravings, 57 sculptures, 14 illustrated books, 95 photographs, as well as 187 objects from Matisse's personal collection of silk screen prints, tapestries, ceramics, stained glass windows and documents. The comprehensive nature of the collection provides an insight into Matisse's creativity, sensitivity and tireless labour.

Included here are works from all periods of Matisse's career, from his very 'first' painting, 'Nature morte aux livres' (1890) to the paper collages of 1952: 'Nu bleu IV', 'La Vague' and 'Fleurs et Fruits'. The museum also boasts masterpieces from the artist's Neo-Impressionist and Fauve periods: 'Jeune Femme à l'ombrelle' (1904) and 'Portrait of Madame Matisse' (1905), as well as an ensemble of Matisse's best-known works: 'Interieur à l'harmonium' (1890), 'Tempête à Nice' (1919), 'Fenêtre à Tahiti' (1935-1936), 'Nu au fauteuil plante verte' (1936-1937), and 'Nymphe dans la fôret' (1935-1943). The Vence period, displayed in the familiar context of the artist's furniture and personal belongings, is represented with 'Liseuse à la table jaune' (1944), 'Fauteuil rocaille' (1946), 'Nature morte aux grenades' (1947).

EXHIBITIONS

12·04·96–17·06·96　　　　*La Ceramique Fauve*　　An exhibition of 80 ceramics created by André Metthey in cooperation with the 'Fauve' artists between 1907 and 1911: Matisse, Derain, Vlaminck, Van Dongen, Rouault, Puy etc.

28·06·96–07·10·96　　　　*Matisse et Bonnard*　　Oil paintings, drawings and photographs as well as correspondence between Matisse and Bonnard will cast light on the friendship between the two artists from the 1920s to 1947.

06·11·96–08·01·97　　　　*Trois Oeuvres à l'Étude*　　A series of exhibitions with a strong educational purpose which will take place every year, focusing on the museum's collection. The three works to be studied this year are: 'Le serf' 1900-1903 (bronze); 'Fauteuil rocaille', 1947 (oil on canvas); 'Le platane', 1952 (Indian ink on paper).

In 1997　　　　*La Côte d'Azur et la Modernité*　　This large-scale multidisciplinary exhibition brings together 16 museums and sites in La Côte d'Azur in order to present aspects of the art of this region between 1918 and 1958. The Matisse Museum in Nice together with the Picasso Museum in Antibes present the subject of leisure and 'joie de vivre' and the other side of the coin - personal tragedy - with works by Matisse, Picasso, Soutine, Stael and others.

Nice

MUSEUM OF MODERN AND CONTEMPORARY ART
Promenade des Arts 06300 Nice Director: Pierre Chaigneau
☎ +33 93626162 📠 +33 93130901
Open: Wednesday-Monday 11.00-18.00 Friday 11.00-22.00
Closed: Tuesday and Bank Holidays

COLLECTION　　　　The collection contains works by all major artists of the New Realism movement: Arman, César, Martial Raysse, Yves Klein, Niki de Saint-Phalle, Tinguely, Rotella, Deschamps, Villeglé, Raymond Hains, Christo, etc. Each of these artists is represented by at least two works from various periods. Works donated by M. and Mme. Moquay made it possible to create an Yves Klein Room and install the 'Wall of Fire' on the terraces.
American Pop Art is well represented by artists as Andy Warhol, Robert Rauschenberg, Tom Wesselman, Roy Lichtenstein, Claes Oldenburg and James Rosenquist.
Works of the most recent New York abstract school, by artists as Morris Louis, Olitski, Larry Poons and Kenneth Noland are also part of the collection.
The museum also exhibits an important collection of Minimalist art, including works by Viallat, Pagès, Dolla, Flexner, Bioulès and Cane. Works by Groupe 70 artists such as Charvolen, Chacallis, Miguel and Maccaferri are set off against works by Sol Lewitt, Richard Serra and others.
Artists related to these movements, such as Bernard Venet, Gilli, Malaval, Sosno, Verdet and many others are also featured. A special place is reserved for Ben, a tireless driving force, and other artists

connected with Fluxus, such as Filliou, Manzoni, Serge III, etc. A number of works by young artists complete the collection, justifying the double title of the Museum of Modern and Contemporary Art.

EXHIBITIONS

23·03·96–16·06·96 ***Giovanni Anselmo***

29·06·96–18·09·96 ***'Chimériques Polymères'*** *Plastics in Contemporary Art*

28·09·96–09·12·96 ***Tom Wesselmann***

Nîmes

CARRÉ D'ART-MUSÉE D'ART CONTEMPORAIN
Place de la Maison Carrée 30000 Nîmes Director: Guy Tosatto
☎ +33 66763570 Fax +33 66763585
Open: Tuesday-Sunday 10.00-18.00
Closed: Monday

COLLECTION

The permanent collection is comprised of about three hundred sculptures, paintings, photographs and works on paper of mainly European art from 1960 to the present day. Important streams of contemporary art originating from the Mediterranean countries are represented, such as the Nouveaux-Réalistes, Arte Povera and Support-Surface. Work from outstanding personalities can also be found, for instance J.P. Bertrand, C. Boltanski, B. Lavier, R. Long, J. Munoz, S. Polke, G. Richter, T. Schütte and S. Solano. A selection of American art is on display with work from R. Artschwager, D. Flavin and J. Schnabel.

EXHIBITIONS

23·02·96–27·05·96 ***Jean-Pierre Bertrand***

15·06·96–22·09·96 ***Gerhard Richter***

25·10·96–02·02·97 ***Nîmes in the Mirror of its Museums***

Orléans

MUSÉE DES BEAUX-ARTS
1, Rue Fernand Rabier 45000 Orléans Curator: Eric Moinet
☎ +33 38533922 Fax +33 38792008
Open: Wednesday-Monday 10.00-12.00 / 14.00-18.00
Closed: Tuesday and 1 Jan, 1 and 8 May, 1 Nov, 25 Dec

COLLECTION

The Museum of Fine Arts occupies a relatively new five-floor building. The collection ranges from the 16th to 20th century, with an emphasis on 17th and 18th-century French painting. Among the foreign paintings are 'Portrait of a Venetian' by Tintoretto, 'Holy Family' by Correggio, 'St. Thomas, Apostle' (1602) by Velásquez and works by Lambert Doomer, Van Goyen, and Ruysdael. The French paintings begin with 16th and 17th-century works including 'Four Evangelists' by Martin Fréminet, 'St. Carlo Borromeo' by Philippe de Champaigne and 'Triumph of St. Ignatius' by Vignon. Later works include Le Nain, 'Bacchus et Ariane'; Baugin, 'Christ mort'; and portraits by Nonotte, Subleyras, Perroneau, Boucher and others. There are early 19th-century works by Scherrer ('Entrée de Jeanne d'Arc)', Etty, Glaize, Courbet ('La Vague') and Boudin, and later works by Gauguin, ('Fête Gloanec'), Sérusier ('Tricoteuse au bas rouge'), Rouault ('Le Député'), Soutine ('La Raie'), Kupka ('En forme de bulbe'), and Dufy. The section dedicated to Max Jacob contains a portrait of him from 1928 by Picasso. The sculptures include works by Pilon, Houdon, Rodin ('L'Ombre'), Maillol ('Figure centrale des trois Nymphes'), Zadkine ('Le Compositeur') and Gaudier-Brzeska. There is also a collection of 5 000 drawings and 35 000 prints.

Matthieu (?)le Nain
(1602-1610 (?)- 1648)
Bacchus discovering
Ariane on Naxos,
dating from before
1635

Musée des Beaux-
Arts, Orléans

21·03·96–30·06·96   **Mémoire du Nord**   Flemish and Dutch Paintings from the Museums of Orléans

Oct 96–Mar 97   **Un Automne Italien**   Italian Paintings from the Museums of the Région Centre

Dec 96–Apr 97   **Romanticism**   Paintings, Sculptures and Romantic Designs from the Orléans Museum.

Paris

ARC-MUSÉE D'ART MODERNE DE LA VILLE DE PARIS
11, Avenue du Président Wilson 75116 Paris Director: Suzanne Pagé
☎ **+33 1 53674000 📠 +33 1 47233598**
Open: Tuesday-Friday 10.00-17.30 Saturday-Sunday 10.00-18.45
Closed: Monday

COLLECTION   Inaugurated in 1961, the Museum of Modern Art of the City of Paris is located in the left wing of the Palais de Tokyo, designed by the architects Dondel, Aubert, Viard and Dastugue for the International Exposition of 1938. The museum owns a large part of its distinctively Parisian image to the generosity of numerous donors, as well as artists from Matisse to Boltanski.
Since 1988 the museum has dedicated itself primarily to specifically European art, an identity which is affirmed in its acquisition and exhibition policies. The priority of the current purchasing policy is to compile a coherent and representative collection of contemporary works from the 1960s to the present. The programme of 'historic' exhibitions alternates between presentations of the work of major figures such as Fautrier, Kupka, Van Dongen, Manzoni, Lissitzky, Giacometti, Sima, Pougny and Derain, and critiques of the European scene organised by the departments of historic and contemporary art ('20th-Century Art in Belgium, Flanders and the Walloon Region', 'German Expressionism 1905-1914', 'Holland in the 20th Century', etc.)
The ARC provides up-to-date information on current national and international artistic events and developments and supports young talent and innovative artistic research. The museum organises regular complementary events (cinema programmes, readings, contemporary music and jazz concerts, discussions).

Hall of the
permanent
collections

ARC-Musée d'Art
Moderne de la Ville
de Paris

EXHIBITIONS

05·04·96–23·06·96	***Pierre Soulages*** *Restrospective*
18·04·96–16·06·96	***Felix Gonzales-Torres***
18·04·96–16·06·96	***Willie Doherty***
18·04·96–16·06·96	***Nigel Rolfe***
mid Jul 96–mid Oct 96	***Alexander Calder***
mid Oct 96–08·01·97	***Georg Baselitz***
Jan 97–Apr 97	***The 1930s in Europe***

Paris

MUSÉE DES ARTS DÉCORATIFS
107, Rue de Rivoli 75001 Paris Curator: Pierre Arizzoli-Clémentel
☎ +33 1 44555750   📠 +33 1 44555784
Open: Wednesday-Saturday 12.30-18.00 Sunday 12.00-18.00
Closed: Monday and Tuesday. Due to renovation works the permanent
displays will be closed, temporary exhibitions remain open.

COLLECTION

The Decorative Arts Museum was created through the initiative of
the Central Union of Decorative Arts in the 19th century and has
been housed in a wing of the Louvre Palace and the Marsan
pavilion since 1905. It also englobes the Nissim de Camondo
museum, and the museums of Publicity, Fashion and Textiles. The
museum's collections are very rich and form a reconstitution of the
stages of the `art of living' from the Middle Ages up to present day.
Some 220 000 works are milestones in the collection: from ceramics
to glassware, silverware to jewellery, from furniture to wallpapers
and drawings, not forgetting toys and posters. And a large number
of these pieces were realized by such reputed creators as Lalique,
Vever, Vever, Gallé, Majorelle, Riesener, Jacob, Oudry among others.

EXHIBITIONS

07·02·96–30·06·96 ***Les Dubuffet de J. Dubuffet*** *The Donation of Jean Dubuffet*
Following the first retrospective in the Decorative Arts Museum in
1960, Jean Dubuffet donated a large number of works to the
museum. The works were created between 1942 and 1966 and
include 135 drawings, 21 paintings and 6 sculptures.

23·10·96-23·02·97 ***A Vision of the City in Toys*** Monuments, schools, post-offices, fire
stations, markets, shops, the metro, railway and taxis - all are part
of the everyday urban landscape. This exhibition includes some 600
toys, ranging from the beginning of the 19th century up to today's
contemporary toys.

Paris

MUSÉE NATIONAL DES ARTS ET TRADITIONS POPULAIRES
6, Avenue du Mahatma Gandhi 75116 Paris Director: Michel Colardelle
☎ +33 1 44176000 📠 +33 1 44176060
Open: Wednesday-Monday 09.45-17.15
Closed: Tuesday and 1 Jan, 1 May, 25 Dec

COLLECTION | The collection of the Museum of Folk Art and Tradition is a testimonial honouring French peasant and craft culture. Dating from the Middle Ages to contemporary times, the works primarily concern aspects of rural life (crafts and occupations) and of social life (festivities, celebratory art, customs and beliefs). The museum also houses a documentary and research studies centre, including a book and record library, text and photography archives and an iconography department. In addition, the museum includes two exhibit halls: reconstructions of past times can be visited in the cultural gallery of the museum, while the study gallery offers a more systematic approach to various themes.

EXHIBITIONS | No details available.

Paris

MUSÉE NATIONAL DES ARTS ASIATIQUES - GUIMET
6 and 19, Place d'Iéna 75116 Paris Director: Jean-François Jarrige
☎ +33 1 47236165 📠 +33 1 47205750
Open: Wednesday-Monday 9.45-18.00
Closed: Tuesday The museum on nr. 6 will be closed for renovation until beginning of 1999

COLLECTION | The Guimet Museum is one of the largest museums of Asian art in the world. During the renovation of number 6 the original collections of Guimet are for viewing in the nearby superb neo-baroque mansion that encloses a Japanese garden. The galleries tell the Chinese and Japanese religious history from the 4th to the 19th century. In 1876 Emile Guimet brought from Japan this unique collection that depicts all types of divinities regarded by the various Schools and Sects of the selected ones. If the majority among Buddhists practises Jôdo, the Imperial family's devotion is the Tendai, the nobility's the Shingon and the samurais' the Zen. On display are paintings and sculptures of Buddhas and Saints, serene or fierce gods, historical Masters, and the largest Mandala in the western museums. Plus some exceptional images of kamis, divinities of prebuddhic religion, the Shinto.

Mandala, Right-hand group
The five Kings of Science with Fudô Myôô in the centre and the two Guardian Kings of the West and the South

Musée Guimet, Paris

EXHIBITIONS | No exhibitions planned.

Paris

MUSÉE CARNAVALET
23, Rue de Sévigné 75003 Paris Curator: Jean Marc Léri
☎ +33 1 42722113 📠 +33 1 42720161
Open: Tuesday-Sunday 10.00-17.40
Closed: Monday and public holidays

COLLECTION

Although several wings of the hotel Carnavalet are currently undergoing restoration, visitors still have access to the archaeological rooms; the Café Militaire and the reception room of the hotel d'Uzès; and portions of the Louis XV and Louis XVI period rooms, where most of the Bouvier and Debray collections are on display. The great staircase, with its mural paintings by Brunetti, and the drawing room of the engraver Demarteau, whose paintings were executed in 1765 by Boucher, Fragonard and Huet, are especially impressive. Noteworthy in the hotel Le Peletier are the Room of Mirrors, the souvenir collection of the Royal family at the Temple, the gouaches by Le Sueur, the cradle of the Imperial Prince, and works by Jean Beraud depicting Paris during the 'Belle Epoque'. Also noteworthy are the restored settings, including the private room of the Café de Paris, in the Art Nouveau style; Fouguet's jewellery shop by Mucha; and the Art Deco ballroom of the hotel de Wendel.

The hotel garden
Carnavalet, Paris

EXHIBITIONS
02·04·96–30·06·96

The Russians in Paris A humoristic portrait of the Russian community in Paris in the 19th century, seen from a French point of view.
Works from the collections of the many Russians who had settled in Paris between 1814 and 1896, supplemented by works from museums in Russia and France, present a picture of the Russian community as seen from a French point of view: benevolent and with a good sense of humour, but maintaining a harsh attitude towards Russian politics. The portraits by Winterhalter, the busts by Carpeaux, the manuscripts, humoristic etchings, documentaries and historical accounts put each person and each event into context. Works on loan from the Tretiakov Gallery in Moscow show Paris from the point of view of Russians visiting the capital or studying at the School of Fine Arts.

Mid May 96–18·08·96

Georges Aerni *Parisian Façades - Boulevards and Streets*
Georges Aerni photographs Parisian façades in the tradition of the great serial works of Atget, Sander, etc. capturing architectural panoramas and rhythms at a glance. His works will be shown alongside panoramic engravings from earlier centuries, presenting an idealised vision of the same locations.

15·10·96–12·01·97

Madame de Sévigné A celebration of the famous writer who lived in the Hotel Carnavalet for about twenty years, from 1677 to 1696, on the occasion of the third centenary of her death.

The exhibition centres upon the personality of Madame de Sévigné, whose interests included medicine, the battles of Louis XIV, religion and the literary world, as well as her family, friends and entourage. An attempt is made to analyse the reasons for her fame and popularity.

28·10·96–28·01·97　**_Mois de la Photo 96_**　_Frank Horvat: Paris-London, a confrontation between two worlds_　A journey through Paris and London of the 50s and 60s. The 110 black and white photographs taken by Frank Horvat between 1950 and 1960 give a new perspective on the work of this photographer, mainly known for his fashion photographs.

Paris

COGNACQ-JAY MUSEUM
8, Rue Elzévir 75003 Paris Director: Pascal de Lavaissière
☎ +33 1 40270721 📠 +33 1 40278944
Open: Tuesday-Sunday 10.00-17.40
Closed: Monday and public holidays

COLLECTION

During the course of his long life, the businessman, philanthropist and collector Ernest Cognacq (1839-1928) managed to assemble an impressive painting collection.

The Great Hall 'Marie
Leczinska'

Musée Cognacq-Jay,
Paris

To accommodate his treasures he built his own museum on the boulevard des Capucines, which was opened in 1929. In 1986 the museum was transferred to the 16th-century Hôtel Donon, which provides a rare example of the Philibert de L'Orme's style as applied to a modestly proportioned mansion. It was restored by the City of Paris and the garden, which stretches as far as the rue Payenne, has been reinstated.

The house comprises some 20 cabinets, galleries, salons, a spacious loft used for temporary exhibitions, and a research library. The aim is to recreate a museum which appears lived in.

The eclectic collection reflects Cognacq's wide range of interests. While paintings predominate, the display also includes wood panelling, tapestries, china figures (Meissen), terracotta busts, furniture (Louis V, Louis XVI), porcelain (Sèvres), marbles (Houdon, Falconet) and precious objects made of gold, enamel and ivory. There are also drawings by Boucher, Fragonard, Watteau, Ingres and many more. The painting collection, including a wealth of portraits, comprises mostly 18th-century works by a range of renowned French artists: Watteau, Chardin, Fragonard, Greuze, Quentin de la Tour and Robert. Other European artists are also represented, such as Rembrandt, Ruysdael, Canaletto, Guardi, Tiepolo and Reynolds.

30·01·96-12·05·96   **The Animal, Mirror of Man**   *The little Bestiary of the 18th Century*
Wild boars of the forests, wild beasts of the Menagerie, sheep of
the fields, the wolf of the Fables, salon monkey cages, lap-dogs and
a world of birds are depicted in almost 70 works (paintings,
drawings, sculptures, prints, porcelain and faience).

Paris

GALERIES NATIONALES DU GRAND PALAIS
3, Avenue du Général Eisenhower 75008 Paris Director: Gaïta le Boissetier
☎ +33 1 44131730 📠 +33 1 45635433
Open: Thursday-Monday 10.00-19.00 Wednesday 10.00-22.00
Closed: Tuesday

COLLECTION   No permanent collection.

EXHIBITIONS
28·02·96-27·05·96   **Corot (1796-1875)**

16·04·96-15·07·96   **The Romantic Years, 1815-1850**

17·09·96-09·12·96   **Nara**

24·09·96-01·01·97   **Manet, Van Gogh, Gauguin, Matisse**   *Masterworks from a Collection*

15·10·96-20·01·97   **Portraits by Picasso**

11·02·97-02·06·97   **Khmer Art**

05·03·97-08·07·97   **'Masterpieces' of the MNATP? or Saura?**

18·03·97-01·07·97   **France-Belgium**

Paris

MUSÉE DU LOUVRE
34-36, Quai du Louvre 75058 Paris Cédex 01 Director: Pierre Rosenberg
☎ +33 1 40205050 📠 +33 1 40205442
General information for visitors: ☎ +33 1 40205151 (answering machine)
Reception office: ☎ +33 1 40205357
Main entrance: Pyramid. Minitel 3615 Louvre /Internet: http:// www.louvre.fr
Entrance for groups and visitors with free access: Passage Richelieu.
Open: Entrance Pyramid: Daily except Tuesday 09.00-18.00 evening opening
hours on Monday (Richelieu Wing) and Wednesday (entire museum) till 21.45.
The Hall Napoleon (under the Pyramid): 09.00-22.00 Temporary exhibitions
under the Pyramid: 10.00-21.45 Closing of the galleries starts 30 minutes
before closing of the museum.
Closed: Tuesday and certain public holidays.

COLLECTION   The Musée de Louvre is one of the most comprehensive museums in
the world. Its collections present western art from the Middle Ages
to the mid-19th century and the antique civilisations. They are
divided into seven departments: Oriental Antiquities; Egyptian
Antiquities; Greek, Etruscan and Roman Antiquities; Paintings;
Sculptures; Objets d'Art; Prints and Drawings. For curatorial reasons,
this last department does not exhibit its collections permanently,
but presents them either by temporary display in other
departments, or by temporary exhibitions or by giving access to its
consultation room for individual visitors after prior request at
+33 1 40205251.

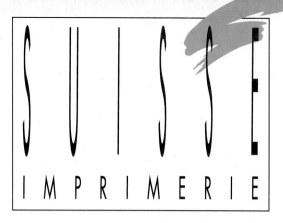

IMPRIMERIE

4 CITE DE PHALSBOURG - 75011 PARIS
TEL: +33 1 43707474 - FAX: +33 1 43705633

N°1

Dans le domaine de l'Art

Artistes - Galeries - Musées - Associations

Trophée Compas
des Imprimeurs

Further renovations within the Grand Louvre Project will take place until 1998. This may cause temporary closure of the museum galleries. However, masterpieces from these galleries will be on show in other parts of the museum.

Louvre-Richelieu
Wing, view from the
Pyramid

*Musée du Louvre,
Paris*

EXHIBITIONS
10·05·96–05·08·96

[Hall Napoléon]
Pisanello   Pisanello (1395-1450), the painter of the seven virtues, was one of the last great painters of the international Gothic style and stood at the cradle of Renaissance art in Italy. He is particularly famous for his portraits and animals. The exhibition will include 350 works, among which 250 paintings, four of his five paintings known in the world, fragments of frescoes and around 50 miniatures and medailles. Works from the Louvre Museum will be accompanied by works from other museums in France, Europe and the United States.

21·10·96–20·01·97

Recent Acquisitions of the Department of Paintings   This exhibition presents 71 works which the Department of Paintings purchased during the last four years (1992-1995). In addition to paintings that illustrate the history of the Louvre, the visitor will discover, among other things, the 'Christ à la Colonne' by the Italian Antonello da Messina, the little 'Angel with Olive Branch' by the Flemish Memling, 'Mr. Levett and Miss Glavani in Turkish Costume' by the Swiss Liotard and 'The Colonel Lee Harvey' by the Briton Henry Raeburn.

21·04·97–21·07·97

Centenary of the Friends of the Louvre Society

[Richelieu Wing]
05·04·96–08·07·96
Recent Acquisitions from the Department of Sculptures
This exhibition presents 36 works which the Department of Sculptures purchased during the last four years (1992-1995). The works cover a period of 6 centuries and include an Italian relief dating from the High Middle Ages and the wax model of a statue of Napoléon III by the 19th-century artist Antoine Louis Barye.

04·10·96–06·01·97

Barye   The French Romantic sculptor Antoine Louis Barye (1795–1875) is notably famous for his statues of animals in action. The theme of this exhibition is, so to speak, the 'claws and teeth' of all kinds of wild animals. Two large lions will overlook the entrance to the exhibition, which will include some 80 statues of rather small size. One interesting feature of the exhibition, offering a special perspective on the work of an artist, is a collection of different bronze casts of one and the same sculpture.

[Sully/Cour Carrée]
24·05·96–26·08·96
Clouet at the Louvre   Two famous portraits of François I from the Louvre Museum are originally attributed to Clouet. The question is

this: to which one? Jean Clouet, who died in 1540, or his son François, who died in 1572? Perhaps they both worked on this painting together. And what can be said about Paul Clouet, his brother? This exhibition, in part displayed in the Musée du Louvre and in part in the Musée de Chantilly, attempts to find an answer to these questions.

Paris

MUSÉE DE LA MARINE
Palais de Chaillot Place du Trocadéro 75116 Paris Director: François Bellec
☎ +33 1 45533170 📠 +33 1 47274967
Open: Wednesday-Monday 10.00-18.00
Closed: Tuesday and 1 May

COLLECTION

The Musée de la Marine is housed in the Palais de Chaillot, opposite the Eiffel Tower and the Champ de Mars. Its long glass-roofed main gallery retraces the history of the French Navy, beginning in the 17th century.

Anonymous, late 17th century
The great royal galley

Musée de la Marine, Paris

The Musée de la Marine contains an important collection of original scale models of warships dating from the 17th century and onwards, including large-scale models. The collections include models of famous ships from the last years of sailing ships and inventions by French engineers from the early years of steam - the archetypes for contemporary naval fleets. These models, along with those of merchantmen, make the Musée de la Marine the guardian of three centuries of naval construction.

A depository for prestigious paintings from the Louvre, the Musée de la Marine exhibits numerous works from various French schools. Among dozens of figureheads, caryatids and atlantes, the museum contains the original sculptures of the galley Réale which sing the praises of the Sun King.

EXHIBITIONS

Sep 96-Nov 96

The Clippers   For the centenary of the Belem, the Musée de la Marine tells the epic story of the clippers, those fabulous long and fast sailing ships, which were the finest achievement of the age of sail. Their faraway sea voyages, their cargo, the life on board and in the harbours are evoked in this exhibition.

Dec 96-Feb 97

The Salon de la Marine   This exhibition presents the recent works of the official Navy Painters and of many amateur or professional artists. Watercolourists, sculptors or photographers all share the same devotion to the sea, and have captured with their art the moving spirit of seascapes and seamen.

Paris

MUSÉE MARMOTTAN
2, Rue Louis-Boilly 75016 Paris Director: Arnaud d'Hauterives
☎ +33 1 42240702 fax +33 1 40506584
Open: Tuesday-Sunday 10.00-17.30
Closed: Monday

COLLECTION

The collection assembled by Jules Marmottan, founder of the Mines de Bruay and Treasury Paymaster in the Gironde Region, reflects a particular interest in the German, Flemish and Italian Primitives. In contrast, his son Paul concentrated on the history and art of the Napoleonic period, acquiring paintings, sculptures and Empire furniture created most often for the Emperor and his family, including bronzes by Thomire, settees by Georges Jacob and paintings by Carle Vernet and Louis Boilly.
A collection was also donated by Henri Duhem (born 1860), containing paintings, pastels and sculptures by Boudin, Carrière, Corot, Gauguin, Guillaumin, Monet, Pissarro, Renoir, Rodin, Lebourg and Le Sidaner.
The donation made by Madame Donop de Monchy includes works by Monet, Pissarro, Renoir and Sisley collected by her father, Geroges de Bellio, doctor and friend to the Impressionist painters.
Michel Monet, second son of Claude Monet and Camille Doncieux, bequeathed to the museum an important collection of paintings which he had inherited from his father. This not only contained eighty oils, four pastels and three drawings by Monet, but also works by the painter's friends, including Boudin, Caillebotte, Guillaumin, Jongkind, Manet, Morisot, Pissarro, Renoir and Rodin.
The Daniel Wildenstein donation consists of his father's extraordinary collection of 228 illuminated miniatures taken over the centuries from French, Italian, German, English, Flemish and Dutch antiphonaries, missals and books of hours.

EXHIBITIONS

No exhibitions planned.

Paris

MUSÉE NATIONAL DU MOYEN AGE THERMES DE CLUNY
6, Place Paul-Painlevé 75005 Paris Director: Viviane Huchard
☎ +33 1 43256200 fax +33 1 43258527
Open: Wednesday-Monday 09.15-17.45
Closed: Tuesday

COLLECTION

Medieval Art The National Museum of the Middle Ages, founded in 1843 by the French state, combines two edifices: the ruins of the Gallo-Roman baths and the Hotel of the Abbots of Cluny, housing a substantial collection of Medieval art assembled by Alexandre Du Sommerard. This ranges through sculpture, stained glass, tapestries, textiles, furniture, caskets, metalwork and paintings. The museum is situated in the heart of the Latin Quarter near the Sorbonne.
The Paris residence of the Abbots of Cluny was reconstructed by Jacques d'Amboise. The U-shaped building enclosing an inner courtyard was surrounded by a stone wall and overlooked a garden on the north side. The well-preserved inner lay-out of the Hotel has been maintained. The chapel has a vaulted ceiling in the Flamboyant Gothic style.
According to tradition, the Gallo-Roman baths consisted of three large rooms, one for hot steam baths, another for tepid baths and the frigidarium for cold-water baths, with additional common and service rooms. The greater part of these ruins still remain, including the 15-metre high vaulted cold room.

The museum's varied collection evokes all aspects of medieval life and activities. The tapestries, including the magnificent series of the 'Lady and the Unicorn', and stained glass windows conjure up the colourful decoration of Medieval buildings.

The lady and the unicorn

Tapestry, wool and silk

Musée national du Moyen Age, Paris

EXHIBITION

13·03·96–10·06·96

A Gothic Treasure   *The Shrine of Nivelles*   In 1272, the Nivelles chapter commissioned a silversmith to produce a shrine to receive the relics of its first abbess, St. Gertrude. This monumental reliquary, one of the biggest ever realised, resembled a miniature cathedral and reflected in its magnificence the influence of the Parisian art characteristic of the court at the end of the 13th century. The Shrine of Nivelles was destroyed during an air raid in 1940, but it has now been restored and is presented to the public as part of this special exhibition.

Paris

MUSÉUM NATIONAL D'HISTOIRE NATURELLE
57, Rue Cuvier 75005 Paris Director: Henry de Lumley
☎ +33 1 40793000 ⅢⅢ +33 1 40793855
Open: Opening hours vary
Closed: Tuesday

COLLECTION

Established in 1635, the Royal Garden of Medicinal Plants, which became the Museum of Natural History in 1793, is today still devoted to the conservation and enrichment of collections in the field of the natural and human sciences, basic and applied research, education and the dissemination of knowledge to the general public.
The collection contains meteorites, giant crystals, butterflies, dinosaur skeletons, plants and a herbarium, stuffed animals, shells and prehistoric and cultural objects from all over the world, as well as an arboretum, greenhouses and parks with animal figures. It is one of the three largest in the world which are capable of displaying the biodiversity of our planet.
The museum's staff of 1800 geologists, palaeontologists, mineralogists, botanists, zoologists, entomologists, physiologists, chemists, biologists, ethnologists, gardeners, animal trainers and administrators work in 26 research laboratories and service centres towards a better understanding of the history of life, the mechanisms of evolution, the origin of man and his relationship to nature.

EXHIBITIONS

31·01·96–15·06·96 **Fantasy of Precious Stones** *[in the Gallery of Mineralogy and Geology, Garden of Plants]* This exhibition displays 2500 gems and jewels, including the obsidian divinatory mirror of the Aztec Emperor Montezuma and a large sapphire that belonged to Louis XIV, and examples of donations to the museum. The Art of Contemporary Jewellery is illustrated by the houses Gianmaria Buccellati, Van Cleef & Arpels and others.

22·05·96–08·01·97 **Exhibition of Meteorites** *[in the Garden of Plants, Grand Gallery of Evolution]* This exhibition explores the origin, structure and mysteries surrounding meteorites in three sections: 'meteorites and man', 'meteorite showers' and 'reading meteorites'. Bilingual information (French and English) is provided for young and old.

15·06·96–1998 **Natural History of Radioactivity** *[in the Garden of Plants, Gallery of Mineralogy]* The exhibition retraces the discovery of radioactivity by Henry Becquerel in 1896 and the research done by Pierre and Marie Curie. On display are documents by Becquerel, original laboratory equipment, historical minerals and products offered to the museum by Marie and Pierre Curie.

Paris

MUSÉE NATIONAL DE L'ORANGERIE
Jardin des Tuileries 75001 Paris Director: Pierre Georgel
☎ +33 1 42974816 ▥ +33 1 42613082
Open: Wednesday-Monday 09.45-17.00
Closed: Tuesday

COLLECTION | Installed in an old orangery in 1852, the Musée de l'Orangerie des Tuileries is devoted entirely to the presentation of two collections of pictures. The first is Claude Monet's 'Water Lilies', which were painted in the period from 1918 until the artist's death in 1926. Here one may view this collection in a presentation designed by the artist himself. The second is the Jean Walter and Paul Guillaume Collection, which consists of 143 pictures dating from the Impressionist period until 1930. Examples of artists included in this collection are: Renoir (24 works), Cézanne (14 works), Matisse (11 works), Rousseau (9 works), Derain (28 works), Picasso (12 works), Soutine (22 works) and Utrillo (10 works). The collection was compiled with no particular regard for systematics and is above all a reflection of the taste and preferences of its creators. It represents fifty years of artistic creation in Paris.

EXHIBITIONS | No exhibitions planned.

Paris

MUSÉE D'ORSAY
1, Rue de Bellechasse 75007 Paris Director: Henri Loyrette
☎ +33 1 40494814 ⅢⒻ +33 1 45485660
Open: Tuesday, Wednesday, Friday, Saturday 10.00-18.00 Sunday 09.00-18.00
Thursday 10.00-21.45; 20 Jun-20 Sep Museum opens at 09.00
Closed: Monday

COLLECTION

A splendid turn-of-the-century edifice on the banks of the Seine, the Gare d'Orsay originally served as the major rail terminus for the Southwest of France. Classified as a national monument in the 1970s, the arching iron and glass structure of this defunct railway station has since been transformed into an important art museum. The museum houses a magnificent collection of thousands of diverse works of 19th-century (1818-1914) art, including numerous representatives of Impressionism, Realism, Post-Impressionism and Art Nouveau, in some 80 galleries on three exhibition floors. Masterpieces on display on the ground floor include Ingres' 'LaSource', Millet's 'L'Angelus', Whistler's 'Mother', Manet's 'l'Olympia', as well as works from the Barbizon School and other early Impressionists.

On the top floor, more Impressionist works are exhibited, including Manet's 'le Dejeuner sur l'herbe', Renoir's 'le Moulin de la Galette', Degas' 'l'Absinthe', Van Gogh's 'Self Portrait', as well as works by Sisley, Pissarro, Cézanne, Seurat, Gaugin (including a new acquisition, 'Portrait au Christ Jaune') and the Pont-Aven School. The middle floor is devoted to Symbolism, Naturalism and Art Nouveau, along with sculptures by Rodin, Pompon and Maillol.

Edouard Manet
The balcony,
c. 1868-1869

Musée d'Orsay, Paris

EXHIBITIONS

05·02·96–19·05·96

From Beirut to Damascus *Photographs*

19·02·96–19·05·96

Offenbach

19·02·96–19·05·96

The Halévy Family (1760-1960)   Between Theatre and History

15·04·96–28·07·96

Menzel (1815-1905)   *The Neurosis of Reality*   The exhibition, organised by the Washington National Gallery and the Berlin Nationalgalerie, presents 50 paintings and several drawings by the 19th–century Berlin artist Adolf von Menzel. This important and original artist was soon recognised by Degas, who collected and copied his work. One painting is a precursor of Impressionism, other works show Menzel's curious view of the world around him.

17·06·96–15·09·96	*Landscapes* Photographs
17·06·96–15·09·96	*Drawings by Fantin-Latour*
07·10·96–Jan 97	*Haviland Foundation* Photographs
07·10·96–Jan 97	*New Acquisitions*
07·10·96–Jan 97	*Charles Le Coeur*
Feb 97–Jun 97	*Théophile Gautier*
Feb 97–Jun 97	*Orsay Museum's Collection of Medals*

Paris

GALERIE NATIONALE DU JEU DE PAUME
Place de la Concorde 75001 Paris Director: Daniel Abadie
☎ +33 1 47031250 📠 +33 1 47031251
Open: Tuesday 12.00-21.30 Wednesday-Friday 12.00-19.00
Saturday, Sunday 10.00-19.00
Closed: Monday

COLLECTION | No permanent collection.

EXHIBITIONS
21·05·96–15·09·96 | *A Century of English Sculpture* Rock Drill (1913-1914) by Jacob Epstein brought England into the age of modern art. English sculptors since then have embraced all modern styles, producing unique and exceptionally powerful works. This is the first large exhibition to trace the continuous development of modern sculpture since the beginning of the century. Works are presented by Henry Moore, Barbara Hepworth, Anthony Caro, Philip King and contemporary artists such as Barry Flanagan, Tony Cragg and Richard Deacon.

08·10·96–01·12·96 | *Sean Scully and Jean-Marc Bustamante*

16·12·96–15·02·97 | *Jesus-Raphael Soto*

Paris

MUSÉE DU PETIT PALAIS
Avenue Winston Churchill 75008 Paris Director: Thérèse Burollet
☎ +33 1 42651273 📠 +33 1 42652460
Open: Tuesday-Sunday 10.00-17.00
Closed: Monday

COLLECTION | The Petit Palais exhibits a general survey of Western art from antiquity to 1925. The art of the Renaissance and the Northern schools (including stained glass, ceramics, and the work of French and German clockmakers from the 16th and 17th century) occupies a prominent place.
The Italian Renaissance is represented by an important collection of majolica, furniture, and paintings by Mantegna and Botticelli. Works by 17th-century Flemish and Dutch masters include paintings by Jordaens, Rubens, Rembrandt, Téniers, Metsu, Van Goyen, Ruysdael and Hobbema. A collection of 18th-century paintings, sculpture and other works of art is also on display.
Romantic painting is represented by the work of Chassériau and Delacroix, while artists of the Realist school include Millet, H.Daumier and Gustave Courbet. Landscape painting from the

second half of the 19th century highlights the development of French art from the Romantic period (Huet and Isabey) through Impressionism (Monet, Pissarro, Sisley and Guillaumin), the modified Realism of Corot, and the more vivid Realism of Rousseau, Harpignies and Breton.
The collection contains impressionist portraits by Cézanne, Monet, Pissarro, Renoir, Cassatt, Morisot and Toulouse-Lautrec, as well as sculptures by Carpeaux, Dalou, Carriès and other artists.

EXHIBITIONS

04·04·96–21·07·96 *Albrecht Dürer* *Engravings* The museum possesses 122 wood and 102 burin engravings, almost all of Dürer's work in this medium. The exhibition includes the series 'The Apocalypse and the Passion', as well as three masterpieces from the Dutuit Collection, 'The Horseman', 'Death' and 'The Devil'. Dürer was a master of wood as well as leather engraving. His themes include the Bible, mythology, genre subjects and portraits.

14·11·96–02·03·97 *The Forbidden City* The public and private life of the emperors of China in the period 1644-1911.

Paris

CENTRE NATIONAL DE LA PHOTOGRAPHIE
Hôtel Salomon de Rothschild
11, Rue Berryer 75008 Paris Director: Robert Delpire
☎ +33 1 53761232 📠 +33 1 53761233
Open: Wednesday-Monday 12.00-19.00
Closed: Tuesday and August

COLLECTION No permanent collection.

Hôtel Salomon de Rothschild, Paris; exhibition area of Centre National de la Photographie

EXHIBITIONS

06·05·96–29·07·96 *Marc Riboud* *China 56-96* This exhibition, shown simultaneously in Paris and Beijing, presents the work of one of the very few reporters who has been permitted to photograph Chinese society from the 1950s up to the present. Over one hundred photographs have been gathered for this exhibition. Together, they testify to the enormous changes that have occurred in China over the past forty years.

18·09·96–21·10·96 *Umbo* Born in Germany in 1902, Umbo was deeply influenced by the Bauhaus. He studied photography, soon became a famous portraitist, and pursued his career taking pictures for news reports and publicity. His pictures were published in several European magazines between the two world wars. Umbo has developed a specific vision of the world, embracing surrealistic tendencies, mixing light with shadow, residing halfway between the real and the unreal.

18·09·96–21·10·96   ***Moins Trente 96***   This biennial competition is open to photographers under the age of thirty, of French nationality or resident in France for at least one year. The exhibition presents the work of the winners of the competition and is intended to show the diversity of the art among young photographers.

18·09·96–21·10·96   ***Prix Niépce 96***   Awarded by the Association Gens d'Images, with the participation of Hewlett Packard France. The previous three winners were Marie-Paule Nègre (1995), Xavier Lambours (1994) and Jean-Claude Coutausse (1993).

06·11·96–20·01·97   ***Peter Beard*** *Africa*   Born in New York in 1938, Peter Beard has spent most of his life in Kenya. He knows Africa intimately and his illustrated notebooks show portraits of modern painters (Lindner, Bacon), as well as images of the slaughtering of crocodiles and the emblems of the Masai. One of his main inspirations has been wild animals, portrayed without exoticism. His work combines strength and sincerity.

Paris

MUSÉE PICASSO
5, Rue de Thorigny   75003 Paris   Director: Gérard Regnier
☎ +33 1 42712521 📠 +33 1 48047546
Open: Wednesday-Monday 1 Apr-30 Sep 09.30-18.00 1 Oct-31 Mar 09.30-17.30
Closed: Tuesday

COLLECTION   The museum's collection consists primarily of works by Picasso, including 203 paintings, 158 sculptures, 16 papiers collés, 29tableaux-reliefs, 88 ceramic pieces, over 3 000 drawings and prints, sketchbooks, illustrated books and manuscripts.
A chronological visit to the museum begins with the Blue Period 'Self-Portrait' which marks the arrival of the artist in Paris in 1901. It is followed by 'Celestina' (1904), 'Three Figures Under a Tree' (1907) and the 'Demoiselles d'Avignon'. The Cubist Period is expressed by the bronze 'Head of Fernande' (1909) and the 'Still Life with Chair Caning' from 1912, along with a series of constructions and collages. Works from Picasso's so-called Classical Period, such as 'Portrait of Olga' (1917), 'Pipes of Pan' (1923) and numerous drawings, are followed by those of the Surrealist Period: 'The Kiss' (1925) and 'The Crucifixion' (1930). The sculpture collections are dominated by the complete series of monumental 'Heads' made at Boisgeloup in 1931. Austere still-lifes from the war years and ceramics and sculptures from the Vallauris Period at the beginning of the 50s are also displayed. Finally, works can be viewed from the last decade of Picasso's life, such as 'Seated Old Man' (1970-1971). Because of their fragility, drawings and prints are exhibited on a rotating basis as a complement to the permanent collection.
The museum also displays Picasso's personal collection of some fifty works by artists he admired (Renoir, Cézanne, Rousseau) and his friends (Braque, Matisse, Miró).
The mansion in which the museum is housed was built between 1656 and 1659 by Pierre Aubert, Lord of Fontenay. The classic courtyard and garden arrangement were designed by Jean Boullier. Acquired by the City of Paris in 1964 after an eventful history with various occupants and functions, the mansion was given the status of Historical Monument in 1968 and restored.

EXHIBITIONS
Autumn 96   ***Engravings by Picasso***

Spring 97   ***Picasso and Photography III***

Paris

CENTRE NATIONAL D'ART ET CULTURE GEORGES POMPIDOU
19, Rue Beaubourg 75004 Paris Director: François Barré
☎ +33 1 44781233 📠 +33 1 444781216
Open: Monday, Wednesday-Friday 12.00-22.00 Saturday, Sunday 10.00-22.00
Closed: Tuesday

COLLECTION

The brightly painted 'inside-out' architecture of the Centre National d'Art et Culture Georges Pompidou was designed by the English architect Richard Rogers and the Italian architect Renzo Piano in 1977. The centre is comprised of a number of galleries and exhibition spaces including the Musée National d'Art Moderne, the Galerie d'Art graphique, the Galerie du Musée, the Galerie Photo, the Grande Galerie, the Galerie Nord, the Galerie Sud, and the Forum. The museum's collection covers the period from 1904 to the present day. The collection contains works by the Fauves with the emphasis on Matisse. The schools of Cubism, Dadaism and Surrealism are well represented with works by such artists as Picasso, Braque, Duchamp, Picabia, Man Ray, Ernst, Magritte and Dali. Other works of interest featured in the collection are mobiles by Calder, sculptures by Giacometti and works by Kandinsky, Klee, Mondrian, Pollock, Miró, Bacon and Rothko among others.

EXHIBITIONS

[Plastic Art]

08·05·96–30·06·96

Picabia 1922
This exhibition contains 30 paintings hung as they were by Picabia himself at the Dalmau Gallery in Barcelona in 1922. His 'mechanical' works combine academic tradition and the modernistic ideas of Dadaism, displaying Picabia's iconoclastic, subversive and humoristic attitude.

22·05·96–26·08·96

L'Informe (Anti-Formal Art)   The idea that Modernism is a succession of changes in form is challenged by avant-garde artists who are resolutely anti-formalistic. Based on the ideas of Georges Bataille, the term 'informe' (formless) signifies removal of the distinction between figure and background, form and material, form and content, etc. Four rooms representing four concepts contain works by Jackson Pollock (horizontality), Marcel Duchamp (temporality in the visual field), Lucio Fontana (materialism) and Robert Smithson (entropy), as well as contrasting works by other artists.

04·07·96–21·10·96

Francis Bacon   This is the first Bacon retrospective in Paris since 1971. It contains works from public and private collections in France and elsewhere. The exhibition, organised by David Sylvester, shows different periods ranging from the 30s up to the artist's death.

10·07·96–30·09·96

Contemporary designs from the Basle Museum   In addition to its collection of designs and etchings by Old Masters such as Hans Holbein the Younger and Urs Graf, the Basle Museum also has more than 150 sketches by Paul Cézanne, 11 Cubist designs by Georges Braque and 200 etchings by the American artist Jasper Johns. Also on display are works by the German and Swiss artists Joseph Beuys, Georg Baselitz, A.R. Penck, Martin Disler and Rosemarie Trockel, the Italian artist Francesco Clemente and the American artists Claes Oldenburg, Jonathan Borofsky, Bruce Nauman, Brice Marden and Roni Horn.

[Photography]

21·03·96–27·05·96

American Photography 1890-1965   *From the Collection of the Museum of Modern Art, New York*   The exhibition presents 183 works covering a century of photography.

[Design]

26·06·96–07·10·96   **Gaetano Pesce**   This retrospective exhibition of the work of Gaetano Pesce, internationally renowned architect and designer, was compiled by the artist himself. It shows the original manner in which he used and synthesised materials, and presents such recent architectural and interior design projects as the vertical garden in Osaka (1991), the Mourmans Gallery in Knokke-le-Zoute (1992) and the Chiat Day offices in New York (1993).

[Architecture]

20·03·96–27·05·96   **Christian de Portzamparc** *Scenes from a Studio*
The French architect Christian de Portzamparc received the Pritzker Prize for architecture in 1994. In a studio atmosphere, the exhibition presents original designs and sketches, paintings, models and photographs which trace the development of his main projects from 1974 to today in France, Japan and the United States, moving from idea to realisation. It shows urban and other projects in France, including l'Opéra Bastille and Eurodisney, as well as skyscrapers in Tokyo and New York.

22·05·96–26·08·96   **Free Form** *The 1950s*   This movement seeks to bring 'poetry and lyricism' back into the functionalist tradition. The multi-disciplinary exhibition brings together architecture and design, plastic art, photography and film. It shows architecture by André Bruyère, Emile Aillaud and Le Corbusier, furniture by Sori Yanagi and Isamu Noguchi, dwellings and sculptures by André Bloc, works by Ray and Charles Eames, sculptures by Hans Arp, Max Bill and Alexander Calder, and paintings by Bram van Velde, Vasarély and César Doméla.

22·05·96–23·09·96   **Antoine Grumbach**   This exhibition presents the work of the French architect and city planner Antoine Grumbach. It is divided into four sections: the first shows personal design and architectural themes; the second analyses several Paris districts; the third shows major projects constructed in Poitiers, including the Collège universitaire Vauban in Saint-Quentin and Yvelines (1991-92); the fourth presents architectural studies and urban plans which were made in 1982 for the World Fair of 1989.

03·07·96–21·10·96   **Frederick Kiesler (1890-1965)**   This multidisciplinary Kiesler retrospective is the first French exhibition dedicated to the Austrian architect-artist, who emigrated to the United States in 1926. He was an intellectual nomad, more involved with artists like Theo van Doesburg, Hans Arp and Marcel Duchamp than with his fellow architects. He embraced movements such as De Stijl, the biomorphism of the 30s and Surrealism.

Paris

MUSÉE RODIN
77, Rue de Varenne 75007 Paris   Director: Jacques Vilain
☎ +33 1 44186110 📠 +33 1 45511752
Open: Daily Oct-Mar 09.30-16.45   Apr-Sep 09.30-17.45

COLLECTION   The museum contains many original works, including bronze and marble sculptures and drawings, by the Late Romantic sculptor Auguste Rodin (1840-1917). It is housed in the Hôtel Biron, a mansion built c. 1730 for the Duke of Biron, later used as a convent and purchased by the State in 1901. The building was used from 1907 as a studio by Rodin, whose secretary Rainer Maria Rilke also lived there from 1908 to 1909. It was agreed that Rodin would bequeath his collection to the State.

Rodin made many sculptures of prominent literary and musical figures. He sculpted busts of Mahler, Carrier-Belleuse, Lady Sackville-West, Victor Hugo and Balzac. 'The Age of Bronze' was done after studying Michelangelo's work in Italy. Other works on display include 'The Kiss', 'The Hand of God', 'Orpheus', 'Eve' 'Young mother and her dying daughter', 'The Good Genius', 'Eternal Spring' and a sculpture of the artist's father. There are models for the 'Gates of Hell', a bronze museum door commissioned but never completed which served as inspiration for several independent sculptures, including the 'Three Shadows'. Among the bronzes and marbles displayed in the gardens are 'The Thinker', 'The Burghers of Calais' and 'Balzac'. Many studies and models are displayed, as well as paintings from Rodin's collection by Renoir, Monet and Van Gogh.

EXHIBITIONS

06·05·96-28·07·96   *Drawings by Bourdelle*

Sep 96-Dec 96   *Marbles by Thyssen*

Paris

LA CITÉ DES SCIENCES ET DE L'INDUSTRIE
30, Avenue Corentin-Cariou 75930 Paris Cédex 19 Director: Gérard Théry
☎ +33 1 40057000 📠 +33 1 40058237
Open: Tuesday-Sunday 10.00-18.00
Closed: Monday

COLLECTION

Twenty minutes from the heart of Paris, La Cité des Sciences et de l'Industrie is one of the world's largest cultural centres aimed at popularising science and promoting understanding of the world in which we live.

Cité des Sciences et de l'Industrie, Paris

Opened in 1986, La Cité is situated within the 55 hectare Parc de la Villette, in northeast Paris in a striking building converted from the city's old slaughterhouse. It is now one of the most popular attractions in Paris, along with the Eiffel Tower, the Louvre and Centre Pompidou. La Cité receives over 5 million visitors annually. Unlike more traditional museums or places of learning, La Cité is very much a 'hands on' experience with fully interactive exhibitions and participatory attractions providing fun and knowledge for all groups.
'Explora' is the core permanent exhibition area in the Cité, and new temporary exhibitions are opened throughout the year, many of which are now translated into English. As well as exhibitions, attractions ranging from a full-scale hunting submarine and planetarium to the 'Géode' omnimax theatre, and the 'Cinaxe' simulator theatre can be seen. There is also the highly popular 'Cité

des Enfants', a children's science village devoted to entertaining and educating children aged from 3 to 12 years.

EXHIBITIONS
until 31·08·96

Renaissance Engineers   From Brunelleschi to Leonardo da Vinci
About 50 scale models and images show how these Renaissance machines would have worked. 350 drawings and an audio-visual presentation illustrate the achievements of the artist-engineers who made possible the great creations of the Italian Renaissance. The exhibition opens with Leonardo's flying machine.

until 31·08·96.

Measuring and the Unmeasurable   This large exhibition (2000 square metres spread over three levels) has been mounted by Jean Nouvel. It has three themes: how we measure, in a objective sense, including working out measures, setting up standards and rules; how we measure and are measured in a more subjective sense, including the relationship of the body to the act of measuring, as well as the role of behaviour and opinions in taking measurements; and finally, a section on extreme measures, including measuring what's furthest away, biggest, smallest, and most inaccessible.

Pau

MUSÉE NATIONAL DU CHÂTEAU DE PAU
64000 Pau Director: Paul Nironneau
☎ +33 59823800 ▯ +33 59823818
Open: Daily 9.30-11.45 / 14.00-17.15

COLLECTION

The town of Pau grew up around a medieval fortress, later transformed into a Renaissance chateau by the kings of Navarre. In the 19th century Louis Philippe and Napoleon III commissioned architects to do considerable work on the chateau and the result is an example of the furnishings of the years 1830 to 1860. The furnishings were supplied by purveyors to the crown. The interior is a good example of the style of decoration common under the July monarchy. The tapestry collection is one of the most valuable in France: the tapestries were selected from the royal furniture repository to complement the interior decorations of the Chateau. Most of the hangings represent mythological scenes or portray aristocratic life and help to recreate the special atmosphere of the chateau.

EXHIBITIONS
15·04·96–15·05·96

Eye-Catching Objects   This is an exhibition in which the contemporary photographer Yvan Terestchenko takes an original look at the castle and its collections as they existed in the 19th century.

Oct 96–Jan 97

Ramiro Arrue   The Pyrenées from the Perspective of a Great Artist
About 100 works of Ramiro Arrue, who is generally only known for landscapes and regional themes, are included in an exhibition that asserts this Basque artist's position as a major national figure and examines the aesthetic and plastic qualities of his art.

Périgueux

MUSÉE DU PÉRIGORD
22, Cours Tourny 24000 Périgueux Curator: Véronique Merlin-Anglade
☎ +33 53531642
Open: Wednesday-Monday Apr-Sep 10.00-12.00 / 14.00-18.00
Oct-Mar 10.00-12.00 / 14.00-17.00
Closed: Tuesday

COLLECTION	Built on the site of an Augustinian monastery, the Musée de Périgord has an exceptional collection of prehistoric relics, as well as sculptures and Gallo-Roman mosaics. Many of the artefacts were recovered from excavations in the Périgord region, an area rich in prehistoric remains.

EXHIBITIONS

15·06·96–15·07·96	**Maurice Albe**
20·10·96–09·01·97	**Jean Marc Rubio** Contemporary art.
05·12·96–09·01·97	**'Salon du Livre Gourmand'** Puyforcat-St. Louis (Vaisselle)

Perpignan

MUSÉE H. RIGAUD
16, Rue de l'Ange 66000 Perpignan Director: Marie Claude Valairon
☎ +33 68354340
Open: Wednesday-Monday 09.00-12.00 / 14.00-18.00
Closed: Tuesday

COLLECTION	The museum has been moved to the Hotel de Lazerme, a 17th century mansion which can be considered one of the most beautiful dwellings in Perpignan. The collection, ranging from 13th-century masters to contemporary art, includes Hispano-Moresque ceramics, Catalan Primitives and portraits by Hyacinthe Rigaud. Amongst the well-known artists represented are Maillol, Dufy, Alechinsky, Brueghel, Bram van Velde, Calder, Clavé, Greuze, Géricault, Ingres, Krasno, Marie Laurencin, Appel, Saint Aubin and Picasso. The museum also exhibits a collection of 211 paintings by 211 contemporary artists.
EXHIBITIONS	No exhibitions plannned.

Reims

MUSÉE DES BEAUX-ARTS
8, Rue Chanzy 51100 Reims Director: Véronique Alemany-Dessaint
☎ +33 26472844 📠 +33 26777533
Open: Wednesday-Monday 10.00-12.00 / 14.00-18.00
Closed: Tuesday and 1 May, 14 Jul, 1 and 11 Nov, 25 Dec

COLLECTION	Founded in 1794, the museum is currently one of the ten largest provincial museums in France. On the ground floor, a remarkable collection of ceramics from 19th and 20th-century French and European potteries is on display, as well as a number late-19th and early-20th-century sculptures. The first floor has a unique series of religious paintings executed between 1460 and the mid-1500s. Thirteen 16th-century portraits by Lucas Cranach the Elder and his son, Lucas Cranach the Younger, as well as two by Barthel Bruyn, have been given a special place in the museum. The 17th century is represented by a collection of Flemish, Dutch and French paintings, while an assortment of 18th-century art objects and furniture recreates the intimate ambience of that epoch. The following section traces developments from the dawn of the 19th century (Neo-Classicism with David's 'Marat') to the 20th century (Dufy, Matisse, Puy, Vuillard, Bonnard). Landscapes have a privileged place, beginning with a comprehensive collection of Corots and continuing with the Barbizon School (T. Rousseau, Diaz, Millet, Dupré, Chintreuil, Daubigny). Works by Boudin, Jongking, Monet, Mauffra, Moret, Sisley and Pissarro are also on display.

A remarkable series of visionary paintings by the Czech artist Sima completes the collection.

EXHIBITION
21·06·96–15·11·96

Clovis and his Artistic Commemoration   An exhibition on the occasion of the 1500th anniversary of the baptism of Clovis. An iconography of people and events marking the foundation of the Kingdom of France.

Rennes

MUSÉE DES BEAUX-ARTS
20, Quai Emile Zola 35000 Rennes Director: Jean Aubert
☎ +33 99285585 📠 +33 99285599
Open: Wednesday-Monday 10.00-12.00 / 14.00-18.00
Closed: Tuesday

COLLECTION

Established with works seized from religious institutions and aristocrats during the French Revolution, the Musée des Beaux-Arts de Rennes considerably enlarged its collection in the course of the 19th century with donations, bequests and acquisitions from numerous sources. Today, with 1 045 paintings, 3 000 drawings, 2 400 engravings and 300 sculptures, the museum provides a comprehensive overview of the visual arts from the 14th to the 20th century. In addition, there is an extensive collection of Ancient Egyptian and Graeco-Roman art. The museum is housed in the former University complex designed by Vincent Boullée on the banks of the Vilaine River.

EXHIBITIONS
May 96

A new presentation of the permanent collection

May 96

Publication of the guide to the collection, published in collaboration with the Association of National Museums

Oct 96

An exhibition centred around Gauguin's painting 'La ronde des petites Bretonnes', on loan from the National Gallery in Washington

Rouen

MUSÉE DES BEAUX-ARTS
Square Verdrel 76000 Rouen Director: Claude Petry
☎ +33 35712840 📠 +33 35154323
Open: Thursday-Monday 10.00-12.00 / 14.00-18.00 Wednesday 14.00-18.00
Closed: Tuesday, Wednesdaymorning and public holidays

COLLECTION

The museum has a collection of paintings and sculpture from the 16th to the 20th century. The sculpture garden has works by Etex, ('Le Tombeau de Géricault'), Leroux, ('Le Fruit'), Bourdelle and Grun. The early paintings include a polyptych by Perugino from c.1500, 'Christ ending the Plague' by Veronese, an anonymous Spanish 'Adoration of the Magi', Caravaggio's 'Flagellation of Christ', 'The Good Samaritan' by Luca Giordano and works by Guerchin, David and Metsys. The collection contains a Brussels tapestry from 1525 and a series of 30 Russian icons from the 16th to the 19th century. Among the Spanish works are 'Democritus' by Velásquez and 'Zachariah' by Ribera. French paintings include 'The Storm' by Poussin and 'God Creating the Universe' by Philippe de Champaigne. There are also works by Rubens, Jan Steen and Ter Borch. French paintings include portraits by Watteau,

'Blanchisseuses' by Fragonard, 'Portrait of Delacroix' by the Rouen painter Géricault, 'Portrait of Gachot' by Millet, 'Chrysanthemums' by Renoir and nine paintings by Monet. There are also collections of Rouen faience, silver, jewellery and oriental works of art.

EXHIBITION
17·04·96–01·07·96 | **'L'école de Roi'** *From Impressionism to Marcel Duchamp*

Saint-Etienne

MUSÉE D'ART MODERNE
La Terrasse 42000 Saint-Etienne Director: Bernard Ceysson
☎ +33 77795252 📠 +33 77795250
Open: Daily 10.00-18.00
Closed: 1 Jan, 1 May, 1 Nov, 25 Dec

COLLECTION
The museum's collection of modern art includes works by such artists as Chabaud, Delaunay, Exter, Gleizes, Hélion, Kandinsky, Koudriachov, Kupka, Magnelli, Matisse, Monet, Rodin and Severini. It features four paintings by Picasso and two major works by Léger, as well as a large selection of paintings and Dada objects from Surrealists such as Arp, Victor Brauner, Duchamp, Ernst, Masson, Miro, Picabia, Schwitters and Tanguy.
Other artistic movements are also represented here, including works by Bissière, Dubuffet, Fautrier, Hartung, Manessier, Soulages and Bram van Velde and sculptures by Germaine Richier, Jacobsen, etc. The trends and movements marking the 60s and 70s, such as Pop Art and New Realism, are particularly well-represented and include works by Arman, César, Dine, Hains, Klein, Lichtenstein, Oldenburg, Spoerri, Villeglé, Warhol and Wesselmann. Minimal Art objects can also be admired, among which works by Andre, Cane, Fabro, Flavin, Grand, Judd, LeWitt, Merz, Morris, Noland, Pagès, Saytour, Stella, Viallat and Zorio. Finally, the museum also has a collection of works by German artists, including Baselitz, Lüpertz, Penck, Richter, etc.

EXHIBITIONS
28·03·96–03·06·96 | *Dmitrij Prigow*

29·03·96–02·06·96 | *Christian Jaccard*

21·06·96–08·09·96 | *Mono-ha*

27·09·96–01·12·96 | *Philippe Favier*

18·12·96–16·03·97 | *A View on History 1940-1968*

Saint-Germain-en-Laye

MUSÉE DES ANTIQUITÉS NATIONALES
Château de Saint-Germain-en-Laye 78103 Saint-Germain-en-Laye
☎ +33 1 34515365 📠 +33 1 34517393
Open: Wednesday-Monday 09.00-17.15
Closed: Tuesday

COLLECTION
The Museum of National Antiquities is housed in a castle built by Louis VI in the 12th century. Rebuilt three times, and enlarged by Louis XIV, it owes its present aspect to Millet, who restored it in the 19th century. Today the museum shows archaeological collections from the first man-made tools up to the 9th century. They have since grown with the discovery of many rare objects and masterpieces during archaeological excavations in the 19th and

20th centuries. The museum includes sections devoted to the Palaeolithic, Neolithic and Bronze Ages, the Celts, the Gallo-Romans, the Merovingians, and comparative archaeology.

Horse,
mammoth ivory
Late Palaeolithic,
from Magdalénien

Musées des
Antiquités
Nationales, Saint-
Germain-en-Laye

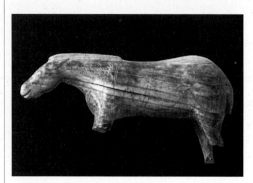

EXHIBITION
03·04·96–08·07·96

The Prehistoric Art of the Pyrenees   The exhibition presents about 400 rare pieces of work of Palaeolithic art, many of them master-pieces. These objects are so fragile that many of them are never exhibited, and thus the exhibition is an exceptional event. The artefacts are carved and sculpted out of bone, ivory, stone and antler. The Pyrenees are one of the most important areas for the study of prehistoric art. The exhibition provides the unique opportunity to discover the richness and homogeneity of the Magdalenian civilisation in the Pyrenees from 17 000 B.C. until 10 000 B.C.

Saint-Paul

FONDATION MAEGHT
06570 Saint-Paul Director: Jean Louis Prat
☎ +33 93328163 📠 +33 93325322
Open: Daily Oct-Jun 10.00-12.30 / 14.30-18.00 Jul-Sep 10.00-19.00

COLLECTION

Located in a lush, verdant setting, the Marguerite and Aimé Maeght Foundation is an outstanding example of a private foundation functioning as a museum in Europe. Its architectural design was specially conceived to exhibit contemporary and modern art in all its aspects. Painters and sculptors worked in direct collaboration with Catalan architect Josep-Lluis Sert to create works of art, often monumental in scale, that were incorporated into the building's design and blended into the surrounding nature. The Giacometti Court, the Miró Labyrinth enlivened with sculptures and ceramics, mosaic murals by Chagall and Tal-Coat, stained glass by Miró, Braque and Ubac, and a fountain by Pol Bury are some examples. The Maeght Foundation owns one of Europe's most important collections of 20th-century painting, sculpture, drawing and graphic work. Works by such prominent artists as Arp, Bonnard, Braque, Calder, Chagall, Dubuffet, Giacometti, Gonzalez, Hartung, Kandinsky, Lam, Léger, Miró, Tal-Coat, Ubac, Bram and Geer van Velde are displayed alongside works of Bazaine, Bury, Chillida, Sam Francis, Hantai, Kelly, Matta, Mitchell, Palazuelo, Riopelle, Soulages, Steinberg Tapies and other notable artists representing the young generation, including Adami, Alechinsky, Arroyo, Cane, Erró, Klapheck, Madden, Moninot, Monory, Oppenheim, Récalcati, Rouan, Stampfli, Szafran, Gasiorowsky and Viallat.

EXHIBITION
05·04·96–05·06·96

Germaine Richier   Retrospective

Sceaux

MUSÉE DE L'ILE DE FRANCE
Chateau de Sceaux 92330 Sceaux Director: Jean-Georges Lavit
☎ +33 46610671 📠 +33 46610088
Open: Wednesday-Monday 1 Apr-30 Sep 10.00-18.00 1 Oct-31 Mar 10.00-17.00
Closed: Tuesday

COLLECTION

The Ile-de-France Museum is housed in a chateau built by the second Duke and Duchess of Trévise and restored by the current owner of the building, the Department of Hauts-de-Seine. It has served as a museum since 1937. In addition to exhibits dealing with the history of the property surrounding the chateau, and a documentation center on the ground floor focusing on the history of Ile-de-France, the museum includes a variety of artistic exhibits. Paintings and furniture provide insight into life in the royal and princely residences of Ile-de-France. Landscapes by artists including Michel, Dunouy, Lépine, Huet, Lepère, Utrillo, le Sidaner, Foujita, and others depict Ile-de-France from the 17th to the 20th century. Ceramics on display include a unique collection of objects manufactured in Sceaux. The museum collection also includes contemporary artworks. Graphic works, engravings and old photographs are on display throughout the chateaux.

EXHIBITIONS

No exhibitions planned.

Sèvres

MUSÉE NATIONAL DE CÉRAMIQUE
Place de la manufacture 92310 Sèvres Conservator: Antoinette Hallé
☎ +33 1 41140420 📠 +33 1 45346788
Open: Wednesday-Monday 10.00-17.00
Closed: Tuesday

COLLECTION

The museum's collection is devoted exclusively to ceramics. Although founded by Alexandre Brongniart, the director of the Sèvres Porcelain Manufacturing Company from 1800 to 1847, the collection is by no means limited to ceramics from this company. The collections present a panoramic view of all that has been accomplished in the field of ceramics and include Oriental ceramics, European glazed ceramics, pottery, Islamic ceramics, Spanish Muslim ceramics, Italian and European ceramics and 16th to 18th-century tin-glazed wares and porcelains. A selection of contemporary ceramics is displayed in the entrance hall and is changed at frequent intervals.

EXHIBITIONS
Jun 96–end Aug 96

Pierre Bayle, Ceramist

Oct 96–Dec 96

Gard Pottery 18th-20th Century

Strasbourg

MUSÉE ARCHÉOLOGIQUE
Palais Rohan 2, Place du Château 67000 Strasbourg Curator: B. Schnitzler
☎ +33 88525000 📠 +33 88525009
Open: Wednesday-Monday 10.00-12.00 / 13.30-18.00 Sunday 10.00-17.00
Closed: Tuesday

COLLECTION

Located on the lower floor of the Rohan palace, the Archaeological Museum - one of the most important in France because of the size of its collections - invites you to discover several thousand of years

Funeral stela:
*A soldier driving a
chariot drawn by
two mules,*
1st centuy A.D.

*Musée
Archéologique,
Strasbourg*

of history of the Alsace from 600 000 B.C. to 800 A.C. The paleolithic mammouth hunters, the first agriculturers of the neolithic era, the necropolis of the Bronze and Iron ages, the everyday life of the gallo-romans and the richness of the merovingian civilisation in Alsace.

EXHIBITION
19·04·96–31·08·96

De la Roche à la Hache

Strasbourg

MUSÉE DES ARTS DÉCORATIFS
Palais Rohan 2, Place du Château 67000 Strasbourg Curator: Etienne Martin
☎ +33 88525000 📠 +33 88525009
Open: Wednesday-Monday 10.00-12.00 / 13.30-18.00 Sunday 10.00-17.00
Closed: Tuesday

COLLECTION

Located on the main floor of the Rohan palace, the former residence of the bishop princes built between 1731 and 1742, this museum is composed of two sections: the sumptuous apartments of the cardinals on the one hand, and the collections of Strasbourg decorative arts covering the period from 1681 to the middle of the nineteenth century on the other hand (world renown Hannong ceramics, furniture, sculpture and paintings, clockmaking, wrought iron, pewter ware, gold and silver ware). The museum also houses the famous toy collection from the Tomi Ungerer Donation.

Palais Rohan, Salon
des Evêques
Constructed between
1732 and 1742 by
Robert de Cotte,
Principal architect to
the King, for Cardinal
Armand Gaston de
Rohan-Soubise

*Musée des Arts
Décoratifs,
Strasbourg*

EXHIBITIONS

No exhibitions planned.

Strasbourg

MUSEE D'ART MODERNE ET CONTEMPORAIN
5, Place du Château 67000 Strasbourg Curator: Nadine Lehni
☎ +33 88525000 📠 +33 88525009
Open: Wednesday-Monday 10.00-12.00 / 13.30-18.00 Sunday 10.00-17.00
Closed: Tuesday

COLLECTION

Created in 1973, the most recent museum of Strasbourg, the Museum of Modern Art, displays collections from Impressionism to today. The historical part of the collection (1870-1960) provides a fine survey of major movements, good representing the modern art revolution. The collection constantly grows by new acquisitions of contemporary art, both french and foreign. These works illustrate the major contemporary movements in European art. There are, among other famous works by: Monet, Renoir, Gauguin, Rodin, Klimt, Braque, Klee, Arp, Ernst, Brauner, Filliou, Sarkis, Boltanski, Penone, Paladino, Immendorf, Baselitz, etc. In the temporary site now occupied by the museum, the collection is only partially exhibited and the presentation continually renewed.

With the construction commissioned to the Architect Adrien Fainsilber, of a new Museum for Modern and Contemporary Art, Strasbourg more than ever wants to play its role as the cultural capital of Europe. The originality of its collections (a small part of which is actually accessible at the Museum of Modern Art, 5 Place du Château) will reside in the intensity of the dialogue engaged between the works of some of the greatest innovators in the twentieth century. Thus this museum will be an authentic staging of modernity. Besides the collections of modern and contemporary art, the new building will also have a gallery of graphic arts, a gallery dedicated to Gustave Doré, a gallery for temporary exhibitions, an art library, an auditorium, an eductional service, and a bookshop. It will be constructed on the bank of the Ill, on the site of the 'Ancienne Commanderie des Chevaliers de St. Jean'.

The opening is scheduled for the end of 1998.

Gustave Klimt
(1862- 1918)
The Achievement,
c. 1909

Musée d'Art
Moderne et
Contemporain,
Strasbourg

EXHIBITIONS

01·03·96–05·05·96

Le Rhin, Der Rhein, De Waal   The River Rhine in the Art and Culture of the 20th Century [Ancienne Douane Exhibition Hall].

18·10·96–15·12·96

Joseph Beuys/Herbert Zangs   [Palais Rohan – Robert Heitz Gallery]

18·10·96–09·02·97

Eugene Carriere   Reality with the Magic of the Dream [Ancienne Douane Exhibition Hall].

Strasbourg

MUSÉE DES BEAUX-ARTS
Palais Rohan 2, Place du Château 67000 Strasbourg Curator: Jean-Louis Faure
☎ +33 88525000 📠 +33 88525009
Open: Wednesday-Monday 10.00-12.00 / 13.30-18.00 Sunday 10.00-17.00
Closed: Tuesday

COLLECTION

At the Museum of Fine Art located on the first floor of the Rohan
Palace, the european painting collections from the Middle Ages to
1870: the Italian and Flemish Primitives (with amongst others, works
of Giotto and Memling); Renaissance and Mannerism, (Botticelli
Raphael, Veronese, Lucas de Leyde, el Greco); Baroque, Realism and

Raffaello Sanzio dit
Raphaël (1483- 1520)
*Portrait of La
Fornarine, c. 1520*

*Musée des Beaux-
Arts, Strasbourg*

Classicism in the seventeenth and eighteenth centuries (Rubens,
Van Dyck, Dutch landscape and still-life paintings, Vouet,
Philippe de Champaigne, Largillière, Boucher, Canaletto, Tiepolo,
Ribera, Goya); works of the nineteenth century (Corot, Courbet).

EXHIBITION
26·04·96–27·10·96

Italian paintings of the Musée des Beaux-Arts

Strasbourg

MUSÉE DE L'OEUVRE NOTRE-DAME
3, Place du Château 67000 Strasbourg Curator: Cécile Dupeux
☎ +33 88525000 📠 +33 88525009
Open: Wednesday-Monday 10.00-12.00 / 13.30-18.00 Sunday 10.00-17.00
Closed: Tuesday

COLLECTION

Located since 1939 in buildings that were initially used by the
administration of the cathedral masons, this museum shows the
evolution of the arts in Strasbourg and in the regions of the upper
Rhine between the eleventh and the seventeenth centuries:
masterpieces of medieval sculpture from the Strasbourg cathedral,
major works from the Rhenish fifteenth century (for instance works
of Conrad Witz and Nicolas Gerhaert van Leyden), collections of
stained-glass windows, tapestry, gold or silver ware and furniture, a
still-life collection of Sebastien Stoskopff.
(See illustration on next page)

EXHIBITIONS

No exhibitions planned.

Nicolas de Leyde
Bust of pensive man,
c. 1467

*Musée de l'Oeuvre
Notre-Dame,
Strasbourg*

Toulouse

MUSÉE DES AUGUSTINS
21, Rue de Metz 31000 Toulouse Director: Alain Daguerre de Hureaux
☎ +33 61222182 📠 +33 61113469
Open: Wednesday-Monday Summer: 10.00-18.00 Winter: 10.00-17.00
Closed: Tuesday

COLLECTION

The museum, situated in a 14th-century Augustinian monastery, is
one of the oldest museums in France. The Gothic sculptures include
a marble effigies, a 14th-century Virgin and Child and monumental
figures of apostles and saints.
Religious paintings from the 14th to 18th century from several
European schools are displayed in the nave of the church, including
works by Murillo, Van Dyck, Jan Jansen, Charles de La Fosse, Rubens
and anonymous 14th-century French artists. The church also
contains 16th-century terracotta statues from the Saint-Sernin
cloister and a German Baroque organ.
The Neo-Gothic ship contains Romanesque sculpture, with a capital
from Saint-Sernin illustrating the 'War of Angels', and capitals from
the cloisters of the Daurade and St. Etienne. There are also early
Christian sarcophagi.

The first floor houses a collection of Italian, Flemish and Dutch
paintings mainly from the 17th to 19th century. These include works
by Matteo Rosselli, Valentin, Fontebasso, Guido Reni and works by
Francken, De Momper, Rombouts, Van Goyen, Van de Velde and
others. There are Medieval portraits of 'Capitouis', those allowed
the privilege of having their portraits painted, and portraits of
other prominent persons of Toulouse. The Romantic period is
represented by 'Muley Abd-ar-Rahman, sultan du Maroc, sortant de
son palais de Meknès' (1845) by Delacroix, 'L'Etoile du matin' by
Corot, 'Le Ruisseau au puits noir' by Courbet. There are also works
by Toulouse-Lautrec, Berthe Morisot, Vuillard, Utrillo, Rodin and
Maillol.

EXHIBITIONS

Jul 96-Aug 96   *Le Comte de l'An Mil*

18·09·96-16·12·96   *The Gold of the Andes*

14·10·96-20·01·97   *18th-Century Sculpture from Toulouse*

in 1997   *Henri Rousseau* *An Orientalist Painter*

Toulouse

MUSÉE PAUL DUPUY
13, Rue de la Pleau 31000 Toulouse Director: Jean Penent
☎+33 61222175
Open: Wednesday-Monday Oct-May 10.00-17.00 Jun-Sep 10.00-18.00
Closed: Tuesday and public holidays

COLLECTION

Paul Dupuy (1867-1944) bought and restored the former 'Hôtel de Besson' in order to house his collections and, during his lifetime, to establish a museum there bearing his name. The Musée Paul Dupuy was considerably enlarged after 1949 as a result of the efforts of its first curator, Robert Mesuret, and is now in the care of the city. It was expanded following a redistribution of the city collections and after renovations taking place from 1980 until 1985, and now houses extensive collections ranging from the Middle Ages to 1939. The department of prints and drawings contains a rich collection of works by artists from Toulouse and the Languedoc. The department of applied arts is divided into several sections: ivories (including the famous 'cor de Roland'), enamels, silver, ceramics (mainly from Toulouse, Bordeaux, Montpellier, Marseille, Moustiers, Nevers and Strasbourg), glass, wrought iron, textiles (ranging from the 14th-century antependium from the Cordeliers church to 18th and 19th-century costumes), furniture (dressers from the Toulouse area and 17th-century medicine cabinets from a Jesuit pharmacy), and wood carving. Besides the world-famous Gélis collection of timepieces, the museum also contains an interesting collection of weaponry, musical instruments, and a large collection of magic lanterns and vintage cameras. There are also sections on weights and measures, numismatics, and seals.

EXHIBITIONS
Until 28·05·96

Egypt   *The Egyptian Collection of the Musée Georges Labit*

24·06·96–15·09·96

De la Mer Chine au Tonkin   *A Journey along the Yang-tze and the Red River*

Tours

MUSÉE DES BEAUX-ARTS
18, Place François Sicard 37000 Tours Director: Jacques Nicourt
☎+33 47056873 📠 +33 47216936
Open: Wednesday-Monday 09.00-12.45 / 14.00-18.00
Closed: Tuesday and 1 Jan, 1 May, 14 Jul, 1 and 11 Nov, 25 Dec

COLLECTION

The Tours Museum of Fine Arts is housed in a former archiepiscopal palace set in a delightful French garden. Its renowned collections are displayed throughout sumptuously furnished rooms which reflect the atmosphere of 18th-century palace life.
Diana Gallery   This former synod room, painted in false marble after the original colours, owes its name to the statue of Diana by Jean-Antoine Houdon (1740-1828). Other works on exhibit were submitted by aspiring artists to the Royal Academy of Painting and Sculpture during the 18th century.
Louis XV Reception Hall   The paintings of François Boucher and a magnificent commode signed by Jean Demoulin (1715-1798) form a good illustration of the combination of sensitivity, refinement and libertinage which characterised the age of Louis XV.
Mantegna Gallery   The two panels painted between 1456 and 1460 for the San Zeno church in Verona by Andrea Mantegna (1431-1506), one of the major artists of the Northern Italian Renaissance, are considered to be the most significant works of art in the museum.

Delacroix and Orientalism   Delacroix' 'The Arab Comedians or Buffoons' reflects the impact made on the artist by the intense light, bright colours and picturesque scenes of the East.

Around Impressionism: Degas, Monet, Henri Martin. This diverse assortment of Impressionist works includes Degas' masterly study of Mantegna's Crucifixion.

20th Century: Alexander Calder   Several works by Alexander Calder (1898-1976) are on display, including a watercolour and a tapestry as well as mobiles.

Rembrandt Gallery   The small 'Flight to Egypt' which is on display, a youthful work monogrammed and dated 1627, marks the beginning of a more introspective phase in the artist's career.

Rubens Gallery   The fresh colours and fluid transparency of 'Ex Voto of the Virgin presenting the Child to the Donor', painted in 1615, reflect the stimulating influence which Peter Paul Rubens (1577-1640) had on his times.

EXHIBITIONS

23·11·96-03·03·97   ***International Gothic and the Renaissance***

16·05·97-31·08·97   ***150 Years of Freemasonry in Tours***   This international exhibition celebrates the 150th anniversary of the Démophile Lodge in Tours.

Valenciennes

MUSÉE DES BEAUX-ARTS
Boulevard Watteau   59300 Valenciennes   Director: Patrick Ramade
☎ **+33 27225720**   📠 **+33 27225722**
Open: Wednesday-Monday 10.00-12.00 / 14.00-18.00
Closed: Tuesday

COLLECTION   With renovation and expansion now completed, the museum's collection can be viewed in its new galleries and spaces for the first time.

Jean Baptiste
Carpeaux (1827-1875)
Rotunda

Musée des Beaux-Arts, Valenciennes

The Fine Arts Collection, initially based on works of art seized from religious communities and aristocratic families during the French Revolution, was gradually enlarged during the 19th and 20th centuries through purchases, gifts and legacies.

The Flemish School is particularly well represented, with well-known religious paintings and altar pieces from Valenciennes churches by artists such as Rubens (whose triptych, 'The Martyrdom of St. Stephen', is a famous example of the Baroque style), Abraham Janssens (including his masterpiece, 'Christ on the Cross'), Jordaens, Van Dyck and Pourbus.

French painting is represented primarily by the works of Antoine Watteau, a native of Valenciennes, including his 'Portrait of Antoine Pater' and 'La Vraie Gaieté'.

The collection of 19th-century sculpture is highlighted by an extensive exhibition of the work of Jean-Baptiste Carpeaux (150 sculptures, 50 paintings and more than 2 000 drawings).

The Archaeological Collection has been assembled on the basis of finds made during the course of construction and excavation in the area. This eclectic collection features miniature masks from the Celtic period, Gallo-Roman wall paintings and Merovingian ornaments, as well as recumbent figures and funeral paintings from the Middle Ages.

EXHIBITIONS

14·05·96–30·09·96

Museum under Construction   Six contemporary photographers show their work during the renovation of the museum (1992-1995).

Nov 96–Jan 97

François Dilasser   A retrospective of 10 years of painting by the contemporary artist.

Versailles

CHÂTEAU DE VERSAILLES ET DE TRIANON
78000 Versailles Director: Jean-Pierre Babelon
☎ +33 1 30847400 📠 +33 1 30847648
Open: Tuesday-Sunday 09.00-17.30
Closed: Monday, public holidays and for official ceremonies

COLLECTION

The Château and Gardens of Versailles are some of the finest examples of French 17th-century art in existence. King Louis XIII's former hunting lodge was transformed and enlarged by his son Louis XIV and new apartments were added during the reigns of Louis XV and Louis XVI. Versailles was abandoned by the royal family and court within days of the outbreak of the French Revolution. In 1837, King Louis-Philippe opened the Château museum which was to be devoted to glorious events in the history of France.

The Château's interior features numerous works of art; highlights include the Hercules Drawing Room which serves as an anteroom to the Kings State Apartment and houses Veronese's 'The Meal at the House of Simon'. The other drawing rooms are decorated with 17th-century mythological scenes, marble panelling, antiques and works of art such as Bernini's bust of Louis XIV. In Mansart's Hall of Mirrors, the ceiling by Le Brun evokes the wars of Louis XIV. The Queen's Bedchamber looks just as it did during Marie-Antoinette's reign and features brocade and Tours silk furniture. The private apartments include the Kings Bedchamber, the Clock Cabinet with its astronomical clock by Passement and Caffieri, the Private Cabinet featuring a medal cabinet by Gaudreaux, secretaires by Oeben and Riesener and candelabra of the American War of Independence by Thomire. The Royal Opera and the Royal Chapel by Gabriel and Mansart respectively are elaborately decorated, the former with trompe l'oeil paintings and the latter with carved scenes from the Old and New Testaments. On the ground floor, the Princes' Apartments have been restored and redecorated with 18th-century furniture. The Château's wings house a collection of 17th to 19th-century paintings of French historical subjects. The Grand Trianon (by Mansart) is decorated with mythological paintings commissioned by Louis XIV, as well as Napoleonic furniture.

The Small Trianon (by Gabriel) is surrounded by an English garden. The gardens surrounding the Château were designed by Le Nôtre and feature perspective avenues, marble statues, the Orangery and fountains.

EXHIBITIONS

15·02·96–12·05·96 | *The Exotic Hunting Parties of Louis XV*

17·10·96–02·02·97 | *Morceaux de Réception*

Villeneuve d'Ascq

MUSÉE D'ART MODERNE
1, Allée du Musée 59650 Villeneuve d'Ascq Curator: Joëlle Pijaudier
☎ +33 20054246 📠 +33 20919892
Open: Wednesday-Monday 10.00-18.00
Closed: Tuesday

COLLECTION

The Musée d'Art Moderne is housed in a building designed by French architect Roland Simounet. The core of its collection is a donation from Mr. and Mrs. Masurel, which includes representative works by most of the major Pre-Avant-Garde artists who lived in France during the first half of the 20th century. The permanent collection includes a group of Cubist reference works by Georges Braque, Henri Laurens and Pablo Picasso. It also includes the third largest collection of Fernand Léger; the finest collection of Amedeo Modigliani in France; and important pieces by André Derain, Paul Klee, André Masson, Joan Miro, and Georges Rouault.

EXHIBITIONS

until Sep 96 | *Contemporary Art Collections*   The exhibition contains over 300 works from the museum's contemporary art collection. 'Courtyard', an installation by Laurent Joubert and fourteen female artists from South Africa, will be shown for the first time.

May 96–Dec 96 | *Discovering and Rediscovering the Masurel Donation*   The exhibition contains works donated by Geneviève and Jean Masurel as well as works from the National Museum of Modern Art (Braque, Laurens, Léger, Modigliani, Picasso, Torrès-Garcia) and a painting by Claude Rutault commissioned by the museum.

28·09·96–19·01·97 | *Alighiero Boetti (1940-1994)*   *Retrospective*   This exhibition, organised in collaboration with the Turin Museum of Modern and Contemporary Art, contains about 60 works created between 1966 and 1994 and is the first retrospective of the Italian artist.

Kiel

Bremen

Hannover

Münster   Bielefeld

Haltern

Essen   Dortmund   Paderborn

Duisburg   Kassel

Düsseldorf

Mönchengladbach   Leverkusen

Köln (Cologne)   Göttingen

Aachen   Bonn

Frankfurt
Mainz

Darmstadt

Trier

Mannheim
Ludwigshafen

Saarbrücken

Karlsruhe

Stuttgart
Baden-Baden   Esslingen

Freiburg

Weil am Rhein

Lübeck

Schwerin

Hamburg

Berlin

Braunschweig

Goslar

Leipzig

Dresden

Weimar

Chemnitz

Nürnberg
(Nuremberg)

Regensburg

Ulm

München (Munich)

Aachen

LUDWIG FORUM FÜR INTERNATIONALE KUNST
Jülicher Straße 97-109 52070 Aachen Director: Wolfgang Becker
☎ +49 241 18070 📠 +49 241 1807101
Open: Tuesday and Thursday 10.00-17.00 Wednesday and Friday
10.00-20.00 Saturday and Sunday 11.00-17.00
Closed: Monday

COLLECTION

The Ludwig Forum for International Art is a showcase for the presentation and confrontation of various forms of contemporary art. The sunken 'quadrum' in the middle of the main hall is the heart of the forum, from which the 'lighthouse', the galleries, the upper floors, the performance space, workshops, ateliers, garden, library and bookshop are all accessible. Rotating exhibitions are complemented with a range of performing arts including music, dance, performance art and film.

EXHIBITIONS

May 96–Sep 96

Meetings with China   Newly acquired works from China will be shown along with additional items from the permanent collection in this exhibition which attempt to answer questions about what defines Chinese art and what distinguishes it from 'Western' art. Chinese theatre, folklore, decorations and ornaments will be presented as well.

10·05·96–Sep 96

Chinese Art from Taiwan   In cooperation with the Taipei Fine Arts Museum, this exhibition will attempt to give the visitor insight into the work of contemporary Chinese artists from Taiwan. About 150 works by 12 artists will be presented, including paintings, drawings, installations and photographs.

04·06·96–18·08·96

'Massivfragil'   Exhibition of selected sculptures of international artists on the occasion of an international forging congress in Aachen, in collaboration with the 'Handwerkskammer' of Aachen.

06·09·96–27·10·96

Transfer Italy   The museum's exchange programme has the goal of bringing local artists into contact with foreign colleagues; in 1995, an Italian artist worked in the Ludwig Forum. This year, the museum makes a presentation of works by Italian and North Rhine-Westphalian artists.

Dec 96–Jan 97

Kunstpreis Aachen 1996 *Katharina Fritsch*   The German artist Katharina Fritsch, who was the German representative at the Biennial of Venice in 1995, was selected as winner of the sixth 'Kunstpreis Aachen' by an international jury. The presentation of the award to the artist is scheduled to take place in October or November 1996 in the Ludwig Forum.

Dec 96–Feb 97

Kala Chakra   Using coloured sand, 4 Tibetan monks will paint a Mandala - a complex Buddhist symbol of the universe - on the floor of the exhibition hall.

Aachen

SUERMONDT LUDWIG MUSEUM
Wilhelmstraße 18 52070 Aachen Director: Ulrich Schneider
☎ +49 241 479800 📠 +49 241 37075
Open: Tuesday-Friday 11.00-19.00 Wednesday 11.00-21.00
Saturday, Sunday 11.00-17.00
Closed: Monday

COLLECTION

Sculpture and Paintings   The museum is especially renowned for its Medieval wooden sculptures. Masterpieces in painting from

Germany, the Netherlands and Flanders dating from the 15th to the 17th century give an insight into the different iconographical approaches of these periods, especially the 17th century. Included are works from the Northern Netherlands, with its profane iconography, and the Southern Netherlands, with its ideas of the counter-reformation. Furthermore, the collection provides an interesting selection of Spanish and Italian painters. Important works illustrate the different historical developments and cover the period up to the 19th and 20th century.

Glass paintings Another highlight of the collection is the assemblage of glass windows from the 14th to the 20th century.

Prints and drawings The Print Room, with its 15 000 European prints and drawings, provides an excellent opportunity to study these works. Included are works such as the four series by Goya, the Carceri by Piranesi, and works by Dürer and Rembrandt.

Applied Arts and Textiles Precious courtly and sacred objects from the Renaissance to the Baroque periods, and over 200 examples of textiles, are housed in the museum.

Willem Claesz Heda
(1594-1678)
Still-life, 1640

Suermondt-Ludwig
Museum, Aachen

EXHIBITIONS

[Exhibition Hall]

10·05·96–24·07·96   *Raoul Ubac*   Paintings, sculptures, photographs and graphics.

Aug 96   *Ritzi Jacobi*   Sculptures and textiles.

Sep 96–Oct 96   *Frank Weidenbach*   Sculpture and architecture.

Oct 96–Nov 96   *Alf Schuler*   Sculpture and installation.

11·12·96–03·03·97   *Against the Current*   *Masterworks of Lower-Rhine Sculpture in the Period of the Reformation*   During the transition from the Middle Ages to the Renaissance and far into the 16th century, large sculpture workshops flourished in Xanten, Kalkar and Kleve on the Lower Rhine. This exhibition features works by representative artists such as Arnt von Kalkar, Henrick Douwerman, Dries Holthuis and Henrick van Holt.

[Graphic Department]

14·03·96–19·05·96   *Erich Müller-Kraus (1911-1967)*   Watercolours, woodcuts and linoleum cuts, donated by K.O. Götz.

29·05·96–04·08·96   *Expressionist Watercolours*   Paintings from a private collection including artists such as Schlemmer, Kirchner and Nolde.

15·08·96–27·10·96   *Mila Wirtz-Getz*   Watercolours from a journey through Greece.

07·11·96–Jan 97   *Walter Dohmen*   *Transition*

Feb 97–Mar 97	**Dürer and the German Renaissance in Prints** Works by Aldegrever, Burgkmair, Altdorfer and Beham.
	[Studio]
13·04·96–09·06·96	**Ilse Bing** *Photographs 1929-1954*
Jun 96–Jul 96	**Anke Erlenhoff**
21·08·96–20·10·96	**Stoelben** *Camera Obscura* **Gerda Schlembach** 'Projector'
Nov 96–Dec 96	**Ernst Wille ,** Colour phenomena: spiritual-pictorial-functional-technical facts.

Baden-Baden

STAATLICHE KUNSTHALLE BADEN-BADEN
Lichtentaler Allee 8a 76530 Baden-Baden Director: Jochen Poetter
☎ +49 7221 23250 ⅢⒼ +49 7221 38590
Open: Tuesday-Sunday 11.00-18.00 Wednesday 11.00-20.00
Closed: Monday

COLLECTION | No permanent collection.

EXHIBITIONS
11·05·96–09·06·96	*Annual Exhibition of the Society of Friends of Young Art*
22·06·96–01·09·96	*African Art from the Han Coray Collection, 1916-1928*
19·01·97–23·03·97	*Cindy Sherman*

Berlin

ALTE NATIONALGALERIE
Bodestraße 1-3 10178 Berlin Director: Peter-Klaus Schuster
☎ +49 30 20355257 ⅢⒼ +49 30 2004950
Open: Tuesday-Sunday 09.00-17.00
Closed: Monday and 24, 25 and 31 Dec, 1 Jan,
Tuesday after Easter and Whitsun

COLLECTION | The museum building, designed by Friedrich A. Stüler of the Schinkel School (1867-1876), houses examples of paintings and plastic arts from the 19th century.

Eduard Gaertner
*View of the back of
the houses on the
Schlossfreiheit, 1855*

*Alte Nationalgalerie,
Berlin*

The large canvasses by Adolph von Menzel provide interesting insights into court life and industrial activity under Frederick II, while the world of the Prussian Army is depicted in the works of court painter Franz Krüger.
The life of the poor is the province of portrait painter and social observer Max Lieberman.

French painting from the same period is represented by the predecessors of Impressionism (Barbizon School), Rousseau, Corot and Gustave Courbet as well as a splendid collection of Impressionist paintings, including works by Eduard Manet, Claude Monet, August Renoir, Camille Pissarro and Paul Cézanne. Examples of German Idealism include impressive paintings by German expatriates in Rome: Hans von Marées, Anselm Feuerbach and Arnold Böcklin.

The plastic arts are represented by notable works by Johann Gottfried Schadows and Christian Daniel Rauchs, as well as important sculptures by Hildebrand, Kolbe, Rodin, Maillol and Degas.

EXHIBITION   [Alten Museum, Am Lustgarten]

02·08·96–20·10·96   *Lovis Corinth*   Retrospective

Berlin

ANTIKENSAMMLUNG
Kupfergraben 10178 Berlin Director: Wolf-Dieter Heilmeyer
☎ +49 30 20355500 📠 +49 30 2082987
Open: Tuesday-Sunday 09.00-17.00
Closed: Monday and 24, 25 and 31 Dec, 1 Jan,
Tuesday after Easter and Whitsun

COLLECTION   The collection of ancient art is a part of the Pergamonmuseum. The museum was built between 1910 and 1930 according to the plans of Alfred Messel and finished by Ludwig Hoffmann. The display of ancient architectural remains, like the Pergamonaltar, made the museum world famous. The big central Hall houses the reconstruction of the west side of the Pergamonaltar in its original dimensions and the 2,30 m high frieze with the battle between olympic gods and giants. The big marble altar was erected during the reign of King Eumenes II (165-156 BC) and excavated by Carl Humann and Alexander Conze (1878-1886).

The other halls and rooms houses remains of excavations in many sites in Asia minor, like Milet, Priene, Magnesia.

Athena in combat wit the Giant Alkyoneus, from the east frieze of the Pergamon Altar, c. 180-159 B.C.

Antikensammlung, Berlin

The collection of Greek and Roman sculpture includes in the main floor masterworks of the archaic, classical, hellenistic and Roman period, like the 'Berliner Göttin', the Hera of Cheramyes, the seatted goddess of Tarantum, a good selection of gravestones and Roman copies of Greek sculptures.

The first floor includes masterpieces of Roman portrait art. The Green Head of Julius Caesar and the marble portrait of Cleopatra represent the high level of the collection. The collection contains also an important quantity of Greek and Roman mosaics.

EXHIBITIONS   No exhibitions planned.

Berlin

BAUHAUS-ARCHIV / MUSEUM FÜR GESTALTUNG
Klingelhöferstraße 14 10785 Berlin Director: Peter Hahn
☎ +49 30 2540020 📠 +49 30 25400210
Open: Wednesday-Monday 10.00-17.00
Closed: Tuesday

COLLECTION

The Bauhaus, now more than three quarters of a century old, was founded in 1919 in Weimar by Walter Gropius. Although it was a rather small school for architecture and applied arts and was soon suppressed by the Nazis, it became well-known throughout the world, mainly as a result of the design it pioneered. Many teachers of the Bauhaus achieved fame: Wassily Kandinsky, Paul Klee, Oscar Schlemmer and Lyonel Feininger for instance. The teaching strategies developed at the Bauhaus - especially by Johannes Itten, Josef Albers and Laszlo Moholy-Nagy - were adopted internationally. The Bauhaus Architecture is viewed as part of the International Style.

Bauhaus-Archiv/
Museum für
Gestaltung, Berlin

The attention which the Bauhaus has continued to attract is due to the achievements during the brief fourteen years of its existence between 1919 and 1933, the year in which the Bauhaus was closed down by the Nazis. The Bauhaus Archive focuses on that period. The museum devotes its energies to collecting, examining and presenting all kinds of information that is related to the Bauhaus. The museum contains architectural models, designs, paintings, drawings, works of applied art and industrial products as well as materials related to the teaching. In addition, works from the Bauhaus workshops such as furniture, ceramics, woven materials, metal objects, prints, typographical studies, sculptures, photographs and theatre designs are exhibited. Examples of architecture by Walter Gropius, Hannes Meyer and Ludwig Mies van der Rohe as well as works of art by the Bauhaus Masters are also on display.

EXHIBITIONS

Summer 96

Max Peiffer-Watenphul *Photographs from Italy.*

Winter 96

The Bauhochschule Weimar *The successor institution to the Bauhaus in Weimar.*

Berlin

BERLINISCHE GALERIE
MUSEUM FÜR MODERNE KUNST PHOTOGRAPHIE UND ARCHITEKTUR
Martin-Gropius-Bau Stresemannstraße 110 10963 Berlin Director: J. Merkert
☎ +49 30 254860 📠 +49 30 25486345
Open: Tuesday-Sunday 10.00-20.00
Closed: Monday

COLLECTION

The museum features paintings, drawings, sculpture, photography, architecture, and artistic archives of Berlin artists from the late 19th and 20th centuries. The collection of visual arts focuses on the painters of the Berlin Secession, Expressionist painters and the Dada collection. Important artists of the 20s included in the collection are Otto Dix, George Grosz, Rudolf Schlichter, Christian Schad, and the Russian artists Naum Gabo and Iwan Puni. Featured post-war artists include Werner Heldt, Alexander Camaro and Hans Uhlmann. Georg Baselitz, Eugen Schönebeck and K.H. Hödicke are representative of the 60s. There is also a substantial collection of contemporary Berlin artists. The photography collection focuses primarily on art photography and features works by Heinrich Zille, Erich Salomon, El Lissitzky, Laszlo Moholy-Nagy, and numerous contemporary photographers, including many from the ex-GDR. The architectural collection consists of material concerning the history of architecture and urban development, particularly after the Second World War. There is a very large collection of 'art and construction', including the estate of the 'Puhl und Wagner' factory for mosaics and glass. The museum's archives include the estates of the gallery Ferdinand Möller, and those from artists such as Hannah Höch, Raoul Hausmann, Naum Gabo, George Rickey, and others.

EXHIBITIONS

May 96

100 Drawings from the Collection of the Berlinische Galerie

Sep 96–Oct 96

Works by Young Berlin Artists Purchased with funds provided by the Deutsche Bank for the Berlinische Galerie graphics collection.

Berlin

BRÜCKE-MUSEUM
Bussardsteig 9 14195 Berlin Director: Magdalena Moeller
☎ **+49 30 8312029 ▥ +49 30 8315961**
Open: Wednesday-Monday 11.00-17.00
Closed: Tuesday

COLLECTION

The museum is devoted exclusively to the 'Brücke' group of artists. The building, designed by Werner Düttmann, and situated in the leafy suburb of Grünewald, consists of four rooms grouped around a small central courtyard and a graphic cabinet in the basement. It was opened in 1967.
The 'Brücke' group was active between 1905 and 1913. Central members of the group included Karl Schmidt-Rottluff and Erich Heckel (the two initiators of the museum), Ernst Ludwig Kirchner and Fritz Bleyl. Among other artists who belonged to the group for shorter or longer periods were Emil Nolde, Max Pechstein, Otto Meuller and Kees van Dongen. Their subjective-expressive approach to painting, with its strong colours and terse forms, laid the foundations of Expressionism.
The work of Heckel and Schmidt-Rottluff is strongly represented, along with Nolde and Pechstein (with several important works), Herbig, Kerschbaumer, Gramatté, Kaus and Roeder. In addition to paintings, the collection includes prints, watercolours, drawings, sculptures and glass windows by various artists. Other documents and publications of the group are also on display.

EXHIBITIONS

20·04·96–08·09·96

Die Brücke Paintings

20·04·96–08·09·96

Otto Mueller Paintings, drawings, print graphics from the collection of the museum.

22·09·96–01·01·97

Max Pechstein A retrospective of his paintings.

11·01·97–14·04·97	*Max Pechstein* Works on paper.
11·01·97–14·04·97	*Ernst Ludwig Kirchner* Photographs.
23·04·97–09·06·97	*Ernst Ludwig Kirchner* Drawings and watercolours from a private collection.

Berlin

DEUTSCHES HISTORISCHES MUSEUM GMBH
Zeughaus Unter den Linden 2 10117 Berlin Director: Christoph Stölzl
☎ +49 30 215020 📠 +49 30 21502402 Internet: http://www.dhm.def
Open: Thursday-Tuesday 10.00-18.00
Closed: Wednesday

COLLECTION

Founded in 1987, the Deutsches Historisches Museum was originally to have been given a new building; in 1990, however, the holdings of the dissolved Museum für Deutsche Geschichte were transferred to the Deutsches Historisches Museum, and the combined collection was ultimately accommodated in the Zeughaus.

The Zeughaus is one of the most beautiful Baroque buildings in Northern Germany. However, extensive remodelling is needed to turn it into a modern museum. Renovation, including an estimated 10 000 square meters of exhibition space divided over three storeys, will be completed in 2000.

A committee of noted German historians and museum specialists have developed the concept of the museum, which centres on enlightenment and communication. The permanent display will contain artefacts and documents from the 9th century to the present, depicting political, social and economic aspects of Germany's history within a European context.

The museum's varied holdings include the well-known Zeughaus collection of military paraphernalia relating to Brandenburg-Prussian history, as well as many posters and documents associated with the history of the labour movement.

The museum also boasts more than two million illustrations relating to German history from 1933 to the present.

EXHIBITIONS

11·06·96–20·08·96	*Art and Power* Art and Architecture in Europe 1930-1945
27·09·96–01·12·96	*Vice Versa* German Artists in America; American Artists in Germany 1813-1913
13·12·96–11·03·97	*On Commission* The State and the Iconography of the GDR
09·01·97–25·03·97	*Victoria and Albert* Vicky and Kaiser Bill - A Chapter from Anglo-German Family Relations

Berlin

GEMÄLDEGALERIE
Stauffenbergstraße 40 10785 Berlin Director: Henning Bock
☎ +49 30 2666 📠 +49 30 2662103
Open: Tuesday-Sunday 09.00-17.00
Closed: Monday and 24, 25 and 31 Dec, 1 Jan,
Tuesday after Easter and Whitsun

COLLECTION

The Gemäldegalerie in Dahlem, which occupies two floors in the right wing and one in the left wing of the old part of the museum, houses a major collection of European paintings from the 13th to the 18th centuries.

A second collection can be viewed in the Pinacotheca in the Bodemuseum on the Museum Island.
Both collections will be moved to the Kulturforum in the Berlin Zoo by the end of 1997.

Jan Gossaert,
gen. Mabuse
Maria with Child,
15/16 century

Gemäldegalerie,
Berlin

On the ground floor: Works from all schools of painting up to the end of the 16th century, including paintings by Glatz (Bohemian School), Hieronymus Holzschuhers and Jakob Muffels (German Renaissance), Albrecht Dürer, Hans Holbein, Albrecht Altdorfer (the Master of the Danube School) and Lucas Cranach the Elder.
One section of the gallery is dedicated to Dutch painting, with renowned works by artists such as Van Eyck, the Master of Flemalle and his pupil Rogier van der Weyden, Pieter Brueghel and Hieronymus Bosch.
The section feauturing French painting includes works by J. Fouquet (15th century) and 18th-century artists such as A. Pesne and Chardin.
Italian Painting (13th-16th century) is represented by Giotto and Botticelli (Florentine School), Mantegna (Early Renaissance), Raphael and Titian.
The upper floor: Flemish and Dutch painting (17th century), including works by Van Dyck, Rubens, Vermeer, Pieter de Hoogh, Van Goyen, Ruysdael, Jan Steen, Frans Hals and Rembrandt and his school.
Examples of French and Italian painting from the 17th and 18th century include works by George de la Tour and the masters of Italian Baroque, Caravaggio and Annibale Carracci. The Venetian Schools are represented by Tiepolo, Canaletto and Guardi. Works by the classic French landscape painters, Poussin and Claude Lorrain, are also on display.

EXHIBITIONS   No exhibitions planned.

Berlin

KUNSTGEWERBEMUSEUM
Matthäikirchplatz 10785 Berlin Director: Barbara Mundt
☎ **+49 30 2662902 🖷 +49 30 2662947**
Open: Tuesday-Friday 09.00-17.00 Saturday-Sunday 10.00-17.00
Closed: Monday and 24, 25 and 31 Dec, 1 Jan,
Tuesday after Easter and Whitsun

COLLECTION   Housed on three exhibition floors in a new building designed by Rolf Gutbrod, the museum offers an excellent survey of arts and crafts from the Middle Ages to the Modern Industrial Era.
Works from the Middle Ages are displayed on the ground floor.

The treasure from the Dionysius Cloister at Enger/Herford (Westphalia), with its valuable Purse Relic (Börsenreliquie) set with precious stones (second half of the 18th century), is on view right next to the entrance. In the centre of the hall, the Cupola Relic (Cologne, ca. 1175) is exhibited. Designed in the form of a Byzantine church, the Relic was intended to preserve the head of St. Gregory, which was brought from Constantinople in 1173. The portable Altar of St. Eilbertus dates from the same era, while the golden Cross-vault (11th century) is said to originate in Northern Italy.

The other rooms on the ground floor contain important collections of Italian majolica (14th-15th century) and Venetian glass (16th-17th century) as well as the Lüneburger Council Silver (Late Gothic and Renaissance) and work by the goldsmiths of Nuremberg. In addition, the ground floor houses the largest permanent exhibition of 20th-century international design (furniture, tableware, etc.) in Germany.

On the upper floor, the contents of a Pomeranian cupboard are displayed: shelves (Brett), card games, measuring instruments, body care utensils (15th-17th century), Chinese and German (Meissen, Berlin) porcelain from the 17th and 18th century and a Chinese cabinet.

Other exhibits on this floor include a timbered mirror cabinet from Castle Wiesentheid/Franken (1724-25), as well as Jugendstil and Art Deco porcelain, faience and glass objects.

Winter, porcelain group
Frankenthal, c. 1755-1759

Kunstgewerbe-museum, Berlin

EXHIBITIONS

until 31·07·96   ***The Domed Reliquary in the Guelph Treasure***

05·04·96–end Jun 96   ***Beautiful Flowers***

10·05·96–28·07·96   ***From the Workshops***   *Restored and conserved Furniture, Textiles and Porcelain*

Berlin

NEUE GESELLSCHAFT FÜR BILDENDE KUNST
Oranienstraße 25 10999 Berlin Director: Leonie Baumann
☎ +49 30 6153031 📠 +49 30 6152290
Open: Daily 12.00-18.30

COLLECTION | No permanent collection.

Berlin

NEUE NATIONALGALERIE
Potsdamer Straße 50 10785 Berlin Director: Dietrich Honisch
☎ +49 30 2662651 📠 +49 30 2624715
Open: Tuesday-Friday 09.00-17.00 Saturday-Sunday 10.00-17.00
Closed: Monday and 24, 25 and 31 Dec, 1 Jan, Tuesday after
Easter and Whitsun

COLLECTION

The museum, housed in a glass and steel building designed by Mies van der Rohe (1968), exhibits a varied collection of 20th-century painting and plastic arts, including important works by European exponents of Classic Modern art and a selection of American art from the 60s and 70s.

Auguste Renoir
(1841-1919)
Chestnut tree in blossom, 1881

Neue National-
galerie, Berlin

Beginning with the pioneers of Expressionism (Gaugin, Munch, Hodler), the collection continues with an impressive array of works by the Brücke artists (Kirchner, Schmidt-Rottluff, Heckel,

Otto Müller). Works by L. Corinth, O. Kokoschka, W. Lehmbruck and Ernst Barlach are also on display.

French Cubism is represented by Picasso and Juan Gris, Classic Modern art by the Bauhaus painters (Schlemmer and Kandinsky), George Grosz, Paul Klee and the Surrealist Max Ernst.

Highlights of the contemporary art collection include works by the Zero Group and Nouveau Réalisme artists as well as American Colour Painting.

Important sculptures on display in the central part of the gallery and on the terrace include 'Die Wäscherin' by Renoir, 'Köpfe und Schwänze' by Calder and Gerhard Marcks' graceful 'Maja'.

EXHIBITION
24.05.96–30.09.96 | *Georg Baselitz*

Berlin

MUSEUM FÜR OSTASIATISCHE KUNST
Lansstraße 8 14195 Berlin Director: Willibald Veit
☎ +49 30 8301382 📠 +49 30 8315972
Open: Tuesday-Friday 09.00-17.00 Saturday, Sunday 10.00-17.00
Closed: Monday and 24, 25 and 31 Dec, 1 Jan, Tuesday after
Easter and Whitsun

COLLECTION
The museum houses a comprehensive collection of archaeological artefacts and arts and crafts from China, Japan and Korea, including works in bronze, stone, wood, ivory, lacquer and ceramics from 3000 BC to the present.

Areas of special emphasis are Chinese and Japanese painting and calligraphy and East Asian wood carving.

Chôbunsai Eishi
Courtesan Hanaôgi,
Japan, c. 1790-1800

Museum für
Ostasiatische Kunst,
Berlin

EXHIBITIONS
No exhibitions planned.

Berlin

SKULPTURENSAMMLUNG
Arnimallee 23-27 14195 Berlin Director: Arne Effenberger
☎ +49 30 8301252 📠 +49 30 8316384
Open: Tuesday-Friday 09.00-17.00 Saturday, Sunday 10.00-17.00
Closed: Monday and 24, 25 and 31 Dec, 1 Jan,
Tuesday after Easter and Whitsun

COLLECTION

The collection includes masterworks of Byzantine and European sculpture from the 3rd to the 19th century. Excellent examples from the early Christian and Byzantine periods include the great ivory Berlin Pyxis (a 4th-century ciborium for consecrated wafers) and the stone and glass mosaic of Christ the Merciful from the 12th century. *The section of German statues* from the Middle Ages mainly features statues from Swabia and High Rhineland: outstanding wood carvings, such as the 'Schutzmantelmaria' from Ravensburg, the Christ and St. John's group and the Madonna of Dangolsheim. The four Evangelists and the Singing Angels represent two highlights of the work by Tilman Riemenschneider.
A life-size Maria as the queen of heaven (14th century) represents the French Gothic style.

Albert-Erneste
Carrier Belleuse
*Confidence, 1865-
1870*

Skulpturen-
sammlung, Berlin

The Italian Renaissance section features important sculptures of the Quattrocento: the graceful Madonna Pazzi by Donatello, the terra cotta Marias by Luca and Andrea della Robbia, small bronzes by Giovanni da Bologna.
The Baroque and Rococo section contains statues by the 18th-century German master Martin Zürns as well as work by Feuchtmayr.
Another part of the collection is exhibited at the Bodemuseum on the Museum Island in the centre of Berlin.

EXHIBITIONS

No exhibitions planned.

Berlin

MUSEUM FÜR VERKEHR UND TECHNIK
MUSEUM OF TRANSPORT AND TECHNOLOGY
Trebbiner Straße 9 10963 Berlin Director: Günther Gottmann
☎ +49 30 254840 📠 +49 30 25484175
Open: Tuesday-Friday 09.00-17.30 Saturday, Sunday 10.00-18.00
Closed: Monday

COLLECTION

The Museum of Transport and Technology is housed on the site of the former Anhalter railway station in Berlin-Kreuzberg. It continues a tradition of large technical museums in Berlin, the exhibits of many of which were destroyed during the Second World War. The museum's aim is to interpret the world as a complex interactive system as opposed to exhibiting isolated technical objects. Showing the interrelationship of technology, science, history, art, nature and its influence on people's everyday life is the museum's main objective. The 14 departments provide a unique insight into man's technical accomplishments. On view are exhibitions on aviation, road transport, railways, manufacturing techniques and household appliances, telecommunications, computer and automation technology, textiles, paper and printing technology, navigation and hydraulic engineering, scientific instruments, film and photo technology and power engineering. The museum is surrounded by a park including such exhibits as windmills, solar technology, a forge and a historical brewery. Numerous historical machines and models are explained and shown in operation. Visitors can take part in printing, weaving, dipping their own paper, grinding corn and much more.

The science centre SPECTRUM (separate entrance: Möckernstraße 26) is the interactive department of the museum where the visitor can experience science for himself - by getting his hands on one of the 220 exhibits.

EXHIBITIONS
08·03·96–30·09·96

Resurfaced *The Museum for Oceanography and its Inventory*
The Museum of Transport and Technology presents this exhibition on the history of the famous Museum for Oceanography, exactly 90 years after its inauguration and 50 years after its closing. The Museum for Oceanography was formerly the largest German maritime museum.

Dutch windmill (1911)

Museum für Verkehr und Technik, Berlin

24·05·96–20·10·96

Mill Models This exhibition consists of ten models which have been reconstructed in accordance with actual mills (scale 1:10). As the constructions have been left open on one side, the mill machinery, which is operational and can be demonstrated, can be observed in detail. These models provide insight into the variety of mills, including windmills, watermills and animal-operated machines, as one of the most important sources of locomotion for craft and industry right up to, and into, this century.

14·12·96–20·04·97

The History of the Berlin Gas Service The first gaslights were installed 170 years ago. Some 20 years later, the City Gas Services was founded. This exhibition presents the history and development of the gas service up to 1996, the year in which a switch will be made to natural gas. The main topics are the production, storage, transport, pressure regulation and use of gas. The exhibition also includes a survey on the equipment involved in the past, as well as in modern processes of pipe renewal.

Berlin

MUSEUM FÜR VÖLKERKUNDE
Lansstraße 8 14195 Berlin Director: Klaus Helfrich
☎ +49 30 8301226 📠 +49 30 8315972
Open: Tuesday-Friday 09.00-17.00 Saturday, Sunday 10.00-17.00
Closed: Monday and 24, 25 and 31 Dec, 1 Jan,
Tuesday after Easter and Whitsun

COLLECTION

The museum features an important collection from countries all over the world.
Central and South America: Tomb (steles) and stone sculptures from Cozumalhuapa (Guatemala) and objects from the Maya culture. Important objects of sacred and profane plastic art from the Aztecs (sacrificial blood dish).
Pre-Inca period: Colourfully patterned textiles and anthropomorphic ceramics from Peru. The golden room features splendid ornamental and cult objects from the 7th century B.C. up to the 11th century A.D.
The Pacific: Objects from collections which have been assembled since the end of the 18th century (partially from the expeditions of James Cook) include wooden sculptures and painted masks from New Guinea. Also on display are the Southern Pacific Boat and the wonderful garment of red and ochre coloured feathers of the King of Hawaii.
Africa, South and East Asia: Terra cotta statues from Ife (Nigeria), bronze works and painted wooden sculptures from the former kingdom of Benin belong to the more interesting part of the collection.

Painted ivory figure,
'Musician on camel'
Rajastan, India, late
18th century

Museum für
Völkerkunde, Berlin

EXHIBITIONS
until 02·06·96

Huichun *Chinese Medicine in Historical Objects and Images*

until Oct '96

Pre-Columbian Stone Sculpture from America

Bielefeld

KUNSTHALLE BIELEFELD (RICHARD-KASELOWSKY-HAUS)
Artur-Ladebeck-Straße 5 33602 Bielefeld Director: Jutta Hülsewig-Johnen
☎ +49 521 512479 📠 +49 521 513429
Open: Tuesday-Sunday 11.00-18.00; Wednesday 11.00-21.00;
Saturday 10.00-18.00
Closed: Monday

COLLECTION

Art of the 20th Century The Kunsthalle Bielefeld, which opened to the public in 1968, is the only building in Germany designed by the American architect Philip Johnson. The museum houses a rich collection of 20th-century art, especially strong in Expressionism. The collection includes works by painters associated with 'Die Brücke' and 'the Bauhaus', and Cubist sculptures. The museum's collection also includes paintings by Max Beckmann, and contemporary German and American works.

EXHIBITIONS

08·05·96-23·06·96
Truong Tan The first museum exhibition of this young artist from Hanoi, Vietnam.

09·06·96-17·07·96
Langlands & Bell Art about Architecture The London artists Nikki Bell and Ben Langlands produce sculptures, models and photographs which deal with the meaning of architecture in our life. Acting as 'archaeologists of the present', they reduce ground plans and models of major buildings to their essential aspects, revealing underlying typologies and structures.

10·07·96-25·08·96
Annual BBK Exhibition Exhibition of the Federal Association of Visual Artists (BBK), Ostwestfalen-Lippe region.

28·07·96-08·09·96
'New Abstraction' An international exhibition surveying contemporary abstract painting.

11·09·96-27·10·96
Gina Lee Felber This Cologne-based photographer and installation artist presents new work. Felber's poetic and encoded world of images resists rational analysis and refers to the chaos of our reality with its abundance of entangled sensory impressions.

19·09·96-17·11·96
Idea and Idyll *Mankind and Nature in the 19th Century* The 19th century was a time of exciting contrasts, with bourgeois ideology shaken by revolutions and scientific/industrial progress transforming social structures. The advent of the Modern at the end of the century was rooted in deep insecurity. The exhibition features masterpieces of Romanticism ranging from the late 18th to the early 20th century, demonstrating how rural idyll became a flight from reality.

13·11·96-Jan 97
Text - Pictures This exhibition documents pictures and texts from children's painting courses in the Kunsthalle Bielefeld.

08·12·96-mid Feb 97
Irma Stern and Expressionism: Africa and Europe *Paintings and Drawings up to 1945.*

Bonn

BONNER KUNSTVEREIN
August-Macke-Platz/Hochstadenring 22 53119 Bonn Director: Annelie Pohlen
☎ +49 228 693936 📠 +49 228 695589
Open: Tuesday-Sunday 11.00-17.00 Thursday 11.00-19.00
Closed: Monday

COLLECTION

Artothek im Bonner Kunstverein Founded in 1987, the main objective of the 'Artothek im Bonner Kunstverein' is to provide art for loan. Totalling c. 1000 works of art, the collection consists of comtemporary art stemming from the 60s until the present day. It includes the artists Joseph Beuys, Sigmar Polke, Felix Droese and Rosemarie Trockel, but consists largely of works from various younger artists. Because of frequent transport to private users, the collection focuses on works on paper which can be protected by frames.

EXHIBITIONS

13·05·96-21·07·96   ***The Calculability of the World***   The exhibition includes works by Alighiero e Boetti, B. Ecker, C. Höller, F. Hybert, On Kawara, M. McCaslin, T. Miyajima, R. Mields and J. Wisniewski.

30·07·96-15·09·96   ***Bon Direct II***   Female artists from Bonn.

24·09·96-29·09·96   ***Videonale VII***   International festival for art videos.

Bonn

**KUNST- UND AUSSTELLUNGSHALLE
DER BUNDESREPUBLIK DEUTSCHLAND**
Friedrich-Ebert-Allee 4 53113 Bonn Director: Wenzel Jacob
☎ +49 228 9171200 📠 +49 228 234154
Open: Tuesday-Sunday 10.00-19.00
Closed: Monday

COLLECTION   No permanent collection.

EXHIBITIONS

23·02·96–12·05·96   ***Claes Oldenburg*** *An Anthology*   In the years of the Pop Art movement, Claes Oldenberg became one of the most important American artists. His works include everyday objects that have been extended into gigantic proportions and created in unusual materials. In particular, this exhibition will present works from his various themes such as "The Street" and "The Store", soft objects from the 1970s as well as models of his monumental sculptures. With approximately 200 objects, this exhibition will be one of the most comprehensive that has ever been dedicated to this American artist.

*Kunst- und
Ausstellungshalle der
Bundesrepublik
Deutschland, Bonn*

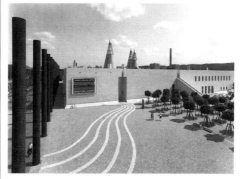

10·05·96-25·08·96   ***Wisdom and Compassion*** *The Sacred Art of Tibet*   With approximately 190 outstanding works of art, this exhibition shows the development of sacred art in Tibet from the 9th to the 19th century.

05·06·96–Spring 98   ***Future Garden***   In the roof garden of the Kunst- und Ausstellungs-halle, the American environment artists Helen Mayer Harrison and Newton Harrison will stage an ecological vision of the future. It will be possible to witness the endangered meadows of Europe and other installations.

05·07·96-12·01·97   ***The Great Collections IV: Moderna Museet, Stockholm***
The Moderna Museet in Stockholm will continue the Great Collections series in the Kunst- und Ausstellungshalle. The comprehensive collection of the Moderna Museet will be represented here by approximately 250 works of art ranging from early modern art to contemporary art. The Moderna Museet has the most important collection of modern art in Scandinavia.

27·09·96–10·11·96   ***Art from Austria 1896-1996***   This exhibition is devoted to Austria's painting, sculpture and architecture of the 20th century. On display will be 400 paintings, drawings and sculptures as well as architectural designs and photos by outstanding artists and architects who exemplify a period or an artistic movement.

16·12·96–02·03·97   ***The Great Collections V: Museo Nazionale di Capodimonte, Naples*** The Museo Nazionale di Capodimonte in Naples has one of Europe's most significant collections of paintings. For the first time the museum will be showing a selection of over 130 masterpieces outside Naples. These include major works by Andrea Mantegna, Raphael, Titian, El Greco, Pontormo, Lorenzo Lotto, Correggio, Annibale Carracci, Juseppe de Ribera, Guido Reni, Artemisia Gentileschi and others. There will also be paintings from the Neapolitan Baroque.

28·02·97–19·05·97   ***The Great Collections VI: Two Faces of the Hermitage (St. Petersburg)***   The first part of this exhibition is devoted to the gold of the Greeks and the Scythians and shows a selection of significant archaeological discoveries from the Altai region. With about 65 paintings and 50 drawings, the second part of the exhibition will present a representative selection of Baroque masterpieces from the Roman schools.

Bonn

KUNSTMUSEUM BONN
Friedrich-Ebert-Allee 2 53113 Bonn Director: Dieter Ronte
☎ **+49 228 776212** ⎙ **+49 228 776220**
Open: Tuesday-Sunday 10.00-18.00
Closed: Monday

COLLECTION   ***20th-Century Art***   The core of the museum's collection consists of a representative survey of German art since 1945, with an emphasis on works by August Macke and the Rhenish Expressionists. The museum began its systematic collecting activities after the Second World War with the work of August Macke, who lived in Bonn from 1900 onwards. The collection was extended with works by the Rhenish Expressionists, H. Campendonk, H. Thuar and the young Max Ernst, whose pictures were shown at an exhibition in Bonn (1913) organised by Macke.

As a result of the museum's acquisition policy, its holding of German art since 1945 is significant and thus receives pride of place in the museum. Works on view include those by young German artists which the Kunstmuseum collected and exhibited in its early days. When some of these artists gained a world-wide reputation, such as Beuys and his pupils at the Academy of Düsseldorf, the museum changed its collecting strategy and began to concentrate on the work of individual artists, such as Richter, Polke, Knoebel, Palermo, Ruthenbeck, Rückriem and Droese.

One of the museum's greatest acquisitions is the extensive collection of Beuys' 'Multiples' of 1965-1986. Neo-Expressionist figurative painting is represented by the work of Kiefer, Baselitz and Penck. Thanks to Ingrid Oppenheim, the museum owns an important stock of international art videos on view to the public at the Video Centre Ingrid Oppenheim. Finally the Kunstmuseum's holdings include a collection of international graphic art of the 20th century.

EXHIBITIONS	[Temporary Exhibition Area]
29·02·96–16·06·96	***China!*** The Kunstmuseum in Bonn shows it like it is.
end Jun 96	***The Art Award of the Volks- und Raiffeisenbanken*** In the Informal and Sixties Room.
26·06·96–18·08·96	***Willem de Kooning*** *The later work/The Eighties*
06·09·96–17·11·96	***The Dorothea von Stetten Art Award***
06·12·96–mid Feb 97	***Anselm Kiefer*** *New Works* (alternatively: Emilio Vedova retrospective, Rosemarie Trockel).
Mar–mid May 97	***Guiseppe Penone*** In collaboration with Galerie Kenewig.
	[Graphic Exhibition Rooms]
29·03·96–16·06·96	***Albert Renger-Patzsch*** *The Late Works* Trees, landscapes, rocks.
28·06·96–22·09·96	***Picasso*** *Illustrated Books*
mid Oct 96–Jan 97	***Wols*** *From the Graphic Collection*
Jan 97–Mar 97	***On the Existence of Objects*** Photography by Christopher Muller and Richard Caldicott
Mar 97–Jun 97	***Young Graphic Artists I*** This exhibition will provisionally feature Silvia Bächli, Camill Leberer, Nanne Meyer.

Bonn

RHEINISHES LANDESMUSEUM BONN
Colmanstraße 14-16 53115 Bonn Director: Hartwig Lüdtke
☎ **+49 228 72941 ▯▯ +49 228 7294299**
Open: Tuesday-Friday 09.00-17.00 Wednesday 09.00-20.00
Saturday and Sunday 10.00-17.00
Closed: Monday

COLLECTION	The Rheinisches Landesmuseum Bonn, founded in 1820, is one of the oldest museums in Germany. It houses a fine collection of art, applied art and cultural assets from the Rhineland. The region's historical and cultural development is presented from the Stone Age up to the present. One of its most famous objects is the only skull of a Neanderthal man ever discovered. Neanderthal people lived near Düsseldorf about 50 000 years ago. There are additional exhibits on the culture of the Celts, the Roman period, the Franconian period, art and applied art of the Middle Ages, Renaissance, Baroque, Rococo, and Classicism. Objects by noted artists, including paintings, sculpture, glass, furniture, earthenware, gold and photography, are presented within the period rooms.
EXHIBITIONS 13·03·96–27·05·96	***West Choir - East Portal***
24·04·96–16·06·96	***The Foundation-Stone Chest***
11·06·96–01·09·96	***The Franks and the Orient***
30·10·96–12·01·97	***Floris Neusüss***

Braunschweig

HERZOG ANTON ULRICH MUSEUM
Museumstraße 1 38100 Braunschweig Director: Jochen Luckhardt
☎ +49 531 4842400 📠 +49 531 4842408
Open: Tuesday-Sunday 10.00-17.00 Wednesday 10.00-20.00
Closed: Monday

COLLECTION

The collections are largely based on a ducal Baroque collection.
Old Masters 300 paintings are exhibited from the 1 200 Flemish,
Dutch, Italian, German and French paintings from between 1500
and 1800 in the collection. Highlights include a self-portrait by
Giorgione, 'Judith with the Head of Holofernes' by Rubens, a late
family portrait by Rembrandt, and 'Young Lady with a Glass of
Wine and Two Gentlemen' by J. Vermeer van Delft.

Jan Vermeer van
Delft (1632-1675)
*The girl with the
wineglass*

Herzog Anton Ulrich
Museum,
Braunschweig

Arts and Crafts The collection includes bronze statuettes and ivory
carvings mainly from the 16th and 17th century, early clocks, fine
furniture, an important collection of Venetian and Flemish lace and
16th and 17th-century Limoges enamels.
Oriental Arts Some exquisite examples of oriental art, mainly
lacquer work, are on display.
Antiquities The collection includes exhibits from Ancient Egypt,
Greek vases and Roman portrait busts and sculptures.
Drawings and Prints The comprehensive collection, dating from
the late Middle Ages to the Modern movement, includes almost
10 000 drawings, 100 000 prints and over 1000 sumptuously
illustrated books from the Baroque period.
Middle Ages The Medieval collection is displayed in Burg
Dankwarderode, the restored palace of Duke Henry the Lion.
Among the objects exhibited are some valuable liturgical works
including altars, altar fragments, altar utensils, liturgical books and
chasubles.

EXHIBITIONS
01·05·96–30·06·96

*Dutch Masters of the 17th Century, from the Fitzwilliam Museum in
Cambridge* Exhibits will include more than 100 drawings by
famous and less well-known Dutch masters, including Bloemaert,
Averkamp, Van Goyen, Berchem, Ruisdael and Rembrandt. Various
genres are represented, including Dutch and foreign landscapes,
seascapes, architectural views, figure and animal studies, flowers
and biblical scenes. These studies allow us a rare glimpse into the
working method of these artists.

Sep 96–Oct 96	***Prague Cabinet Painting around 1700, from the collections of the National Gallery in Prague*** As part of a long-term collaboration between the National Gallery in Prague and the Herzog Anton Ulrich-Museum in Braunschweig, this exhibition will present examples of cabinet paintings by Prague artists from around 1700. These painters followed the tradition of artists working a century earlier at the court of Emperor Rudolf II in Prague.
Nov 96–Jan 97	***From Gainsborough to Turner*** *British watercolours from the Whitworth Art Gallery, Manchester* No other artistic medium is as 'British' as the watercolour, and few other collections are as representative of the development of this genre between 1750 and 1850 as this Manchester collection. The exhibition offers a selection of the finest British watercolours of landscapes and architecture. The visionary, airy masterpieces by William Turner form a fitting centrepiece.
Mar 97–Apr 97	***Artists Look at Themselves*** *Graphic self-portraits from the 20th century* This exhibition draws on a recently acquired private collection containing more than 800 self-portraits by about 250 artists, executed as drawings or prints. Prominent German Expressionists are featured, as well as many other well-known modern artists.

Bremen

**FOCKE-MUSEUM BREMER LANDESMUSEUM
FÜR KUNST UND KULTURGESCHICHTE**
Schwachhauser Heerstraße 240 28213 Bremen Director: Jörn Christiansen
☎ +49 421 3613575 📠 +49 421 3613903
Open: Tuesday-Sunday 10.00-18.00
Closed: Monday

COLLECTION

The Focke-Museum came into existence following a merger between the Historical Museum of Bremen, which was founded by Johann Focke at the turn of the century, and the Bremen Museum of Arts and Crafts. Today, the Bremen State Museum displays collections which cover the economical, political and cultural aspects of the history of both the city and the state of Bremen.

From the glass
collection of the
Focke Museum:
Vase, 1911

*Focke Museum,
Bremen*

The collections, which range from the prehistoric to the most recent times, emphasise the history of this Hanseactic city, the history of shipping and overseas trade, and middle-class culture. The latter is represented by important collections of silver plate, china and glass. Objects of traditional applied art are supplemented with contemporary products and specimens of modern design.

Relics of peasant life and labour can be viewed in the various rural buildings which can be found on the museum grounds. One of these in particular, a farmhouse, illustrates the changes in village life that occurred as a result of industrialisation in the Bremen area.

EXHIBITION
24·05·96–31·08·96

The Key and the Eagle   *The History of Bremen's Statehood*
On June 1, 1646, Emperor Ferdinand III signed a charter in which Bremen was proclaimed an Imperial City. This event marks the foundation of the city-state which nowadays calls itself the Free Hanseactic City of Bremen. This exhibition is in honour of the 350th anniversary of Ferdinand's decision and covers the history of Bremen's statehood within the larger consecutive commonwealths of the Holy Roman Empire, the Germanic Confederation of 1815-1866, the Bismarckian German Empire and the republics of Weimar and Bonn; the key is the heraldic figure of Bremen, the eagle that of Germany. Two short periods in which Bremen temporarily lost its status of a state, from 1811-1813 when it was a provincial town in Napoleon's France, and from 1933-1945 when the German states were mere administrative districts of Hitler's Reich, are of particular interest.

Bremen

ÜBERSEE-MUSEUM BREMEN
Bahnhofsplatz 13 28195 Bremen Director: Viola König
☎ +49 421 3619176 📠 +49 421 3619291
Open: Tuesday-Sunday 10.00-18.00
Closed: Monday and 24, 25 and 31 Dec

COLLECTION

The South Seas Collection includes boats, houses and masks, and dioramas featuring this region's unique flora and fauna.
The Asian Collection includes a Rajasthani village illustrating the Indian agricultural economy, caste system, and art. A rubber plantation shows the problems and opportunities associated with aid to developing countries. Other displays include a Japanese garden, an exhibit on Shamanism, a traditional Chinese house and Indonesian musical instruments.
The American Collection includes exhibits of pipes, clothing, masks and basketry. Visitors can learn about the various Indian tribes. An exhibition of Pre-Columbian gold and Andean objects is opened in the summer of 1995.
Topics covered in **the African Collection** include Ancient Egypt, nomadism, the ecology of the Sahara Desert and the Sahel Crisis. Visitors can view a model of a farmstead, and dioramas of savanna animals. Since June 1995 a collection of African art and musical instruments is on display.
The origins and development of **the universe, the earth and life on earth** are explained using interactive models, photographs, and fossil and mineral displays. Included are a model of a cell, a weather satellite station, a dinosaur skeleton, and an electron microscope.

EXHIBITIONS
08·03·96–02·06·96

Design Time Bremen 1996: Alessandro Mendini *Design Changing, Products, Fetishes and Rituals*   This exhibition is based on the selection of Alessandro Mendini for the 'Internationales Design Jahrbuch 1996'.

end Apr 96 onwards

The Treasure Room of Columbian Gold and the Cultures of the Andes   The pre-Columbian gold treasure of the Übersee Museum is presented here for the first time in the newly erected treasure chamber.

02·06·96–25·08·96	**Jubilee Exhibition: Ghosts, Mummies and Exotics** *A Chamber of Curios from the Übersee Museum*
Aug 96	**The New Totem Pole is Produced** During this four-week period, the Red Indian carver and artist Nathan P. Jackson (originally from Alaska) will produce a totem pole measuring 13 m in height.
08·09·96–20·10·96	**Tales of Coffee, Cotton, Rundown Boots and New Approaches** A selection of tales and history relating to North-South connections in Bremen.
01·11·96–01·12·96	**Special Exhibition of the Society for Arts and Crafts** An exhibition celebrating the Museum Jubilee with the theme of 'collections'.
15·12·96–30·03·97	**Special Exhibition: Bremen** *City of Wine in the North* The exhibition presents the history of wine in Bremen, paying particular attention to the renowned Ratskeller under the City Hall and the cultural history of wine.
Apr 97–Jun 97	**Special Exhibition: Huichun** *Chinese Medicine*

Chemnitz

STÄDTISCHE KUNSTSAMMLUNGEN
Theaterplatz 1 09111 Chemnitz Director: Katharina Metz
☎ +49 371 4884424 📠 +49 371 4884499
Open: Tuesday-Sunday 11.00-17.00
Closed: Monday

COLLECTION

The Städtische Kunstsammlungen Chemnitz, founded in 1920, presently contains the following sections, which together hold about 80 000 exhibits: painting and sculpture, prints and textiles and applied art.
There are a large number of paintings and drawings by Karl Schmidt-Rottluff (one of the founders of the 'Brücke' group), who was born in Rottluff, a suburb of Chemnitz. Dresden Romanticism is represented by the painters C.D. Friedrich, C.G. Carus, J. Chr. Clausen-Dahl, G.F. Kersting and L. Richter. Among the German Impressionist paintings are works by R. Sterl, M. Liebermann, M. Slevogt and L. Corinth. There are also Expressionist paintings, Western European works from the Lühl Collection, art from the GDR and sculptures by Rodin, Lehmbruck, Barlach, Maillol and many others.
The large collection of textiles and applied art (Coptic fabrics, industrial design, furniture by H. v.d. Velde, historical posters, fine crafts and more) is one of the most important in Germany. The print collection contains over 20 000 works on paper by A. Dürer, M. Wohlgemut, Rembrandt, various Romanticists, K. Kollwitz, E. Munch, various Expressionists and many others. Parts of these collections are displayed in changing exhibitions.

EXHIBITIONS

24·03·96–26·05·96	**Sonia Delaunay** *Textile Design 1930-1960 (in collaboration with the Stedelijk Museum Amsterdam)*
16·06·96–08·09·96	**Lyonel Feininger (1871-1956)** An exhibition of privately owned wood engravings.
Sep 96–Oct 96	**Painting and Sculpture from the Lühl Collection** *Western European Art Since 1945*
Nov 96–Jan 97	**Concrete Art from the Jung Collection** An exhibition of privately owned paintings and objects.

Darmstadt

HESSISCHES LANDESMUSEUM DARMSTADT
Friedensplatz 1 64283 Darmstadt Director: Sybille Ebert-Schifferer
☎ +49 6151 165703 📠 +49 6151 28942
Open: Tuesday-Saturday 10.00-17.00 Wednesday 10.00-17.00 /19.00-21.00
Sunday 11.00-17.00
Closed: Monday

COLLECTION

The Hessian Regional Museum possesses a comprehensive section of Medieval mural paintings. Among the paintings from 1550 to 1800 are works by Pieter Brueghel, Domenichino and Rubens. The 19th–century collection includes works by Arnold Böcklin, Liebermann, Slevogt, Corinth and Darmstadt painters such as Schilbach and Lucas. The 20th century is represented by Feininger, Dix, Kirchner, Duchamp and others. The contemporary art section, with some 300 works includes 'Informal' and Pop Art, as well as works by Gerhard Richter, Arnulf Rainer and Sigmar Polke and German paintings from the 80s. The graphics collection illustrates the development of lithography and the art of drawing from the Late Middle Ages to the present day. It contains works by Italian, French and Dutch artists from the 16th to the 18th century and a collection of posters from about 1900 onwards. There is a collection of glass paintings from the 9th century to the present.

Works from the Carolingian era, a crucifixion group by Tilman Riemenschneider and Baroque sculptures by Zürn and Zamels are among the museum's sculptures. The Hübsch collection contains Medieval goldwork, carved ivory and enamel work. There are also goblets, hollow glassware and armour from the royal cabinet, archaeological finds from the Early Stone Age to Merovingian-Frankish times and provincial Roman objects.
The natural science sections contain a survey of the animal kingdom, rare specimens and a paleontology and mineralogy display.

EXHIBITIONS

21·03·96–27·05·96

The End of the World *Three Apocalyptic Sequences of the 15th and 16th Centuries* Taken from the Graphic Collection, pages are exhibited from three woodcut sequences of the 15th and 16th centuries on the theme of the Apocalypse of St. John. These include Albrecht Dürer's 'Apocalypsis cum figuris' (1498).

08·05·96–07·07·96

Joseph Beuys *MANRESA: A Photo Documentation* Some 60 photographs by Eva Beuys, Reiner Ruthenbeck and Walter Vogel document the MANRESA happening (1966), which took place in Galerie Schmela, Düsseldorf.

20·06·96–01·09·96

Colour Prints of the 18th Century

15·09·96–17·11·96

Christian Boltanski *An Installation*

12·12·96–Mar 97

Ernst Riegel (1871-1939) *A Jugendstil Goldsmith*

Darmstadt

SCHLOßMUSEUM DARMSTADT E.V.
Residenzschloß Marktplatz 15 64283 Darmstadt Director: Volker Illgen
☎ +49 6151 24035
Open: Monday-Thursday 10.00-13.00/14.00-17.00
Saturday, Sunday 10.00-13.00
Closed: Friday

COLLECTION

Founded in 1924 by Grand Duke Ernst Ludwig of Hesse, the museum covers the history of the former state, later Grand Duchy, of Hesse. Destruction by bombing in 1944 and dispersal to former East Germany has reduced the collection somewhat, though it remains representative.

There are over 20 rooms displaying pictures, artefacts, etc. relating to the social history of Darmstadt and surroundings. Parts of Landgrave Ernst Ludwig's carpentry workshop, the hunting diary of Ludwig VIII and militaria of Landgrave Ludwig XI are also on display.

The paintings include a large collection of local 18th and 19th-century artists and other masters such as Ziesenis, Winterhalter and Wilhelm Schadow. There are also 18th and 19th-century decorations, clothing and pre-1914 uniforms, including those of famous figures such as Bismarck and Moltke. Historic carriages, sedan chairs and riding gear, etc. from the House of Hesse are also exhibited. Central exhibit is the Madonna of the Bürgermeister of Basle, Jacob Meyer, painted by Hans Holbein the Younger in 1625 - one of the greatest German paintings, on the threshold between Gothic art and the Renaissance.

EXHIBITIONS

No exhibitions planned.

Dortmund

MUSEUM AM OSTWALL
Ostwall 7 44122 Dortmund Director: Ingo Bartsch
☎ +49 231 5023247 Ⅲ +49 231 5025244
Open: Tuesday-Sunday 10.00-17.00
Closed: Monday

COLLECTION

The pivot of the collection is formed by German Expressionism. In addition to works of the renowned 'Brücke' and 'Blauer Reiter' artists' groups, many associated German artists are also featured, including a considerable collection of works by August Macke and Alexej Jawlensky. Post-war European art is also strongly represented, with Geometric, Kinetic and Concrete art from such artists as Brüning, Mack, Götz, Uecker, Graeser and Spagnulo.

Max Beckmann
Self-portrait with cigarette, 1947

Museum am Ostwall, Dortmund

There is a wide-ranging collection of sculpture, both from the pre-war period (including works by Lehmbruck, Archipenko, H. Blumenthal, Maillol) and from the post-war era (including works by Moore, Calder, Arp, Chadwick, Melotti, Wotruba and Pistoletto).

Also on view is a representative selection from the major Cremer Collection consisting of diverse European works from the 50s to the 70s.

The museum also reserves a special space for important artists of the Fluxus and Happening movements (Beuys, Brecht, Filliou and Païk, among others), having exhibited these works permanently since 1972 and finally acquiring them from the Feelisch Collection in 1988. Since 1995, art regularly purchased by the Dörken Foundation for the Museum am Ostwall can be seen as well (Bury, Emde, Linnenbrink). The Bernhard Hoetger estate with its Expressionist architectonic maquettes and sculptures also belongs to the museum. The Graphics Collection focuses on Expressionism and international post-war drawings and prints.

EXHIBITIONS

12·05·96–21·07·96

Gerrit Thomas Rietveld   This Dutch artist (1888-1964), one of the most important architects of the 20th century, was revolutionary in his aesthetics as well as in the use of new forms and materials. His concern for the living and dwelling needs of modern society is reflected in his designs. The exhibition contains over 300 original objects, among them a fully furnished bedroom, offering for the first time a complete survey of Rietveld's creative work.

31·07·96–25·08·96

Bernhard Hoetger (1874-1949) Sculpture from the Dortmund Estate   The exhibition presents a selection from the estate of this sculptor and architect illustrating his diverse creative activity and changing style. The estate includes work influenced by Rodin and shaped by Impressionism as well as important works of Expressionist sculpture.

15·09·96–15·12·96

From 'Die Brücke' to 'Der Blauer Reiter' *Colour, Form and Expression in German Art 1905-1914*   Some 140 works (mainly paintings) are shown, contrasting and comparing the artists of the two movements: Heckel, Kirchner, Schmidt-Rottluff, Nolde, Pechstein, Mueller, Kandinsky, Marc, Jawlensky, Macke and Münter.

Dresden

GEMÄLDEGALERIE ALTE MEISTER
Semperbau am Zwinger 01067 Dresden Director: Harald Marx
☎ +49 351 4914620 📠 +49 351 4914694
Open: Tuesday-Sunday 10.00-18.00
Closed: Monday

COLLECTION

The Dresden Old Masters Picture Gallery has a collection of works by Italian Renaissance masters, including Raphael's 'Sistine Madonna', Giorgione's 'Sleeping Venus', Titian's 'The Tribute Money' and Correggio's 'Holy Night', as well as paintings from the Italian Baroque.

There are 17th-century Flemish and Dutch paintings by Rubens, Van Dyck and Jordaens, Rembrandt and his school, Jan Vermeer van Delft and the so-called Dutch 'minor masters'. This Gallery, created as the result of the passion for collecting of two Saxon Electors and Kings of Poland in the first half of the 18th century, also contains works by Spanish, French and German artists.

Some paintings were part of the 'Kunstkammer' (Art Chamber), founded as early as 1560 and considerably enlarged from the middle of the 17th century onwards. In 1707 the best paintings were removed from the 'Kunstkammer' and displayed separately in a room in the palace. They were eventually moved into the Great Hall and adjacent rooms, thus creating the first Dresden Picture Gallery within the Palace.

EXHIBITIONS

No exhibitions planned.

Dresden

GEMÄLDEGALERIE NEUE MEISTER
Albertinum, Brühlse Terrasse 01067 Dresden Director: Ulrich Bischoff
☎ +49 351 4914731 📠 +49 351 4914732
Open: Friday-Wednesday 10.00-18.00
Closed: Thursday

COLLECTION

Dresden's collection of 'Neue Meister' (artworks from the start of the bourgeois epoch in the 19th century through to the present day) has been accommodated in the rebuilt Albertinum since 1965, but its origins extend back to an annual financial donation instituted in 1843. A large number of works were either destroyed in the Second World War or expropriated shortly after and taken to Russia. New acquisitions have, however, partly made up for these losses.

The collection begins with German Romanticism and bourgeois Realism, including works from Böcklin, Thoma, Menzel, Uhde, Spitzweg, Friedrich, and the largest collection of the works of F. von Rayski. German and French Impressionism are also featured. German Expressionism forms a further focus, along with some remaining examples of the collection of 'Contemporary Socialist Art' from GDR days. One of the major works of the collection is Grundig's triptych 'The Thousand Year Reich', a prophetic anti-war work painted before the Second World War, now fittingly exhibited together with Otto Dix's 'War Triptych'.

EXHIBITIONS

[Modern Masters Picture Gallery]

18·03·96-Jun 96	***Theodor Rosenhauer*** *95th Birthday Commemoration*
08·07·96-15·09·96	***El Greco to Mondrian*** Pictures from a private Swiss collection.
30·09·96-08·12·96	***Oskar Kokoschka and Dresden***
Apr 97-Jun 97	***Ernst Ferdinand Oehme***

[Cabinet of Prints and Drawings]

16·12·96-Feb 97	***The Age of Tiepolos*** Venetian Masters from Ricci to Guardi.

Dresden

GRÜNES GEWÖLBE
Albertinum, Brühlse Terrasse 01067 Dresden Director: Dirk Syndram
☎ +49 351 4914590 📠 +49 351 4914599
Open: Friday-Wednesday 10.00-18.00
Closed: Thursday

COLLECTION

Between 1723 and 1729, King August the Strong converted the strong-rooms of the Dresden Schloß into a public treasure-chamber museum. Here he exhibited his outstanding collection of jewellery, goldsmiths' work, ivory and stone carvings, and bronze statuettes. Following the destruction of the Schloß in the Second World War, about half the original collection has been on view in four large halls of the Albertinum since 1974 and still forms the largest and more important treasure-chamber collection in Europe. It includes works of the Middle Ages, Renaissance, early Baroque and the reign of August the Strong himself. Particularly worthy of mention in the collection, which is one of the oldest museums for applied arts, are the ivory and ebony carvings of Balthasar Permoser and the goblets and jewelled works of Johann Melchior Dinglinger.

EXHIBITIONS

No exhibitions planned.

Dresden

PORZELLANSAMMLUNG
Zwinger Entrance 'Glockenspielpavillon' 01067 Dresden Director: U. Pietsch
☎ +49 351 4914627   📠 +49 351 4914629
Open: Friday-Wednesday 10.00-18.00
Closed: Thursday

COLLECTION

The Dresden Porcelain Collection was established by Augustus the Strong, King of Poland and Elector of Saxony, during a period of about fifteen years from 1715 and 1730. The nucleus of the collection still consists of Chinese and Japanese porcelain acquired during this period, and of Meissen porcelain manufactured for the king's porcelain palace known as the Japanese Palace. During the 19th century, following a long period of stagnation, the collection was expanded to include European porcelain (especially from Germany and Austria) of the 18th and 19th century. Since 1900, the Far Eastern collection has been enlarged with the addition of Chinese tomb figures from the Tang period, Chinese stoneware in the style of the Song period and Ming porcelain. The Meissen collection has been similarly enlarged with the addition of figures and tableware from the mid-18th century.

EXHIBITION
04·08·96-30·10·96

Johann Gregorius Höroldt In 1696 the first painter in the history of Meissen porcelain, Johann Gregorius Höroldt, was born. This exhibition, with works by the artist is in honour of the 300th anniversary of this event.

Dresden

SKULPTURENSAMMLUNG - STAATLICHE KUNSTSAMMLUNGEN DRESDEN
Georg-Treu-Platz 2 01067 Dresden Director: Heiner Protzmann
☎ +49 351 4914741   📠 +49 351 4956019
Open: Friday-Wednesday 10.00-18.00
Closed: Thursday

COLLECTION

The Sculpture Collection, that includes about 15 000 originals from over five millenniums, is divided into two main sections: the collection of art from the ancient world and the collection of European post-ancient sculptures dating from the Late Middle Ages to the present day.

The main works in the collection of art of the ancient world are marble sculptures, mainly valuable Roman replicas of Greek masterpieces from the Classical period to Hellenism. The pieces include 'Athena Lemnia' after Phidias, an ancient copy of Myron's 'Head of Athena', the three female statues from Herculaneum, the 'Head of Diadumenos', a statue of a Victor after Polyklet, 'Reclining Hercules' after Lysipp, 'Wine-pouring Satyr' after Praxiteles and the unique preserved copy of a Maenad by Skopas which is only otherwise mentioned in literature. There are also Greek originals such as funeral and votive reliefs and many precious examples of Greek, Etruscan and Roman ceramics, terracottas and bronzes.

The second part of the collection includes pieces from German, Italian, French and Dutch masters from the Middle Ages to the present day, notably the four smaller bronzes by Giambologna and sculptures by Adrian de Vries and Permoser. Sculptures from famous 19th and 20th-century artists, such as Schadow, Rauch, Degas, Rodin, Maillol, Meunier, Rosso, Lehmbruck, Kirchner, Kolbe and Glöckner are exhibited together with paintings from the Modern Masters Picture Gallery.

Duisburg

**WILHELM LEHMBRUCK MUSEUM DUISBURG -
EUROPEAN CENTER OF MODERN SCULPTURE**
Friedrich-Wilhelm-Straße 40   47049 Duisburg   Director: C. Brockhaus
☎ +49 203 2832630   🖷 +49 203 2833892
Open: Tuesday-Saturday 11.00-17.00   Sunday 10.00-18.00
Closed: Monday

COLLECTION

20th-century art   The collection features Wilhelm Lehmbruck's oeuvre, together with sculpture, painting, graphic art by other artists. Set in a wooded park in the heart of the city, the museum displays over 300 sculptures, 80 paintings and 100 works of graphic art by over 200 artists from 20 countries. Noteworthy are the sculpture garden and park.

A view of the collection with works by Wilhelm Lehmbruck

Wilhelm Lehmbruck Museum-European Center of Modern Sculpture, Duisburg

The core of the collection consists of Wilhelm Lehmbruck's oeuvre beginning with his early works created at the Düsseldorf Art Academy (1901-1908) and masterpieces from his Paris time (1910-1914), such as the 'Standing Female Figure' (1910), which was inspired by Maillol and established Lehmbruck's worldwide fame. Lehmbruck's drawings and graphic works reveal his ideas at their purest, while his paintings also show his expressionistic nature. Building on Lehmbruck's oeuvre is the collection of 20th-century international sculpture and object art, from Expressionist works by Barlach and Kollwitz to masterpieces of Cubism and Constructivism by Archipenko, Duchamp-Villon, Laurens, and others. Surrealism informs Picasso's and Arp's biomorphic shapes and the objets trouvés in Dali's and Ernst's works exemplify a whimsical and poetic approach to materials.
Following classical modern art is the steel sculpturing executed in many styles and techniques since 1945. Object art, Photo-Realism and Serial Art of the Zero evolved during the 1950s and 1960s. Finally there are works by Bill, Heerich, Le Witt, Judd, and Beuys, who, inspired by Lehmbruck, carried on his life work into the present.The collection of German paintings from the first half of the 20th century reviews artistic development from Expressionism to Bauhaus-oriented art, Surrealism and Informel.
The varied graphic collection concentrates on drawings, prints, and photographs by 20th-century sculptors represented in the permanent collection.

Düsseldorf

KUNSTMUSEUM DÜSSELDORF IM EHRENHOF
Ehrenhof 5   40479 Düsseldorf   Director: Hans Albert Peters
☎ +49 211 8992460 📠 +49 211 8929046
Open: Tuesday-Sunday 11.00-18.00   Library Graphic Dept. 11.00-17.00
Closed: Monday and 24 Dec, 25 Dec, 31 Dec, 1 Jan

COLLECTION

Old Masters   The Gallery of Old Masters shows magnificent examples of Dutch and Flemish painting of the 16th and 17th century and French and Italian painting of the 18th century. The highlights among the old masters are 'Venus and Adonis' and the 'Assumption of the Virgin' by Peter Paul Rubens. The 19th century is represented by paintings of the famous 'Düsseldorf School'.
Sculpture   The sculpture collection focuses on the Medieval and Baroque eras, including numerous Southern German Late Gothic sculptures.

August Macke
(1887-1914)
Four girls, 1912-1913

Kunstmuseum
Düsseldorf im
Ehrenhof, Düsseldorf

20th Century   The 20th century is represented by works of Expressionism, Neue Sachlichkeit and Constructivism. A particularly important ensemble consists of the Academy artists of Düsseldorf, including Otto Pankok and Joseph Beuys.
Glass   The Kunstmuseum features one of the leading glass collections of Europe. It shows a complete documentation of the development of glass-making from luxury glass of Pre-Roman times to the main trends of Art Nouveau and contemporary studio glass.
Prints and Drawings   With some 80 000 paper works from the 15th century up to the present, the collection of prints and drawings is one of the largest of its kind in the Federal Republic.
Arts and Crafts   The collection of arts and crafts features tapestry, furniture, old household implements and a large collection of ancient Iranian and Islamic crafts. The textile collection represents almost all textile techniques from the majority of European and Eastern countries. The 20th century is represented by an extensive collection of industrial design and applied arts.

EXHIBITIONS

24·09·95–Summer 96 | ***Paper Sculptures***   A new workshop in the Museum for young visitors.

03·04·96–05·05·96 | ***The Paik Class***

19·04·96–27·10·96 | ***Glass Design of the 20th Century***   Works from the museums's own collection. In the Grüner Saal, Tonhalle, Ehrenhof 1.

25·05·96–11·08·96 | ***Otto Piene Retrospective***   In the Kunstmuseum and Kunstpalast.

Autumn 96-mid 97 | ***The Seventh Year*** *Children's Pictures*   An exhibition in the Museum for young visitors.

begin Sep 96–
begin Nov 96 | ***Bertram Jesdinsky***

06·10·96–30·03·97 | ***In View of the Everyday*** *Genre motifs in Painting and Drawing 1830-1890*

10·11·96–Jan 97 | ***Glass from Murano 1930-1970*** *The Steinberg Foundation Collection* In the Kunstmuseum and the Grüner Saal, Tonhalle, Ehrenhof 1.

Düsseldorf

KUNSTHALLE DÜSSELDORF
Grabbeplatz 4 40200 Düsseldorf Director: Jürgen Harten
☎ **+49 211 8996241** 📠 **+49 211 8929168**
Open: Tuesday-Sunday 11.00-18.00
Closed: Monday

COLLECTION | No permanent collection.

EXHIBITIONS
16·05·96–07·07·96 | ***Happy End***   An exhibition featuring future and apocalyptic visions of the 90s.

Jan 97–Apr 97 | ***Michail Wrubel (1856-1910)***   An exhibition of paintings, watercolours, drawings and ceramics from Russia and the Ukraine.

Düsseldorf

KUNSTSAMMLUNG NORDRHEIN-WESTFALEN
Grabbeplatz 5 40102 Düsseldorf Director: Armin Zweite
☎ **+49 211 83810** 📠 **+49 211 8381202**
Open: Tuesday-Sunday 10.00-18.00
Closed: Monday

COLLECTION | The Kunstsammlung Nordrhein-Westfalen was established in 1960 when the regional government of North Rhine-Westphalia acquired a collection of 88 paintings and drawings by Paul Klee from the American private collector David Thompson, of Pittsburgh, and exhibited them in Schloss Jägerhof in Düsseldorf. The Klee collection was the basis for the establishment of the Stiftung Kunstsammlung Nordrhein-Westfalen in 1967.
Virtually all the significant artists, movements and streams of 20th–century painting are represented in the museum. The collection is comprised mainly of works of art produced before 1945, commencing with those many movements and streams at the beginning of the century which represented a drastic break with the traditional notion of art. Included in those movements are Fauvism, Expressionism and 'Der Blaue Reiter', Cubism and its many

ramifications, and 'Pittura Metafisica'. By the 20s and 30s, Dadaism and Surrealism were pre-eminent at one extreme, while Constructivism, Bauhaus and De Stijl dominated at the other. The museum's collection of works produced after 1945 ranges from Abstract Expressionism in the USA and Europe through Pop Art and Colour Field Painting.

Amadeo Modigliani
Caryatid 1911/1912

Kunstsammlung
Nordrhein Westfalen,
Düsseldorf

EXHIBITIONS

30·03·96–02·06·96   *Markus Lüpertz*   This exhibition comprises c. 70 paintings and several sculptures produced by Lüpertz during the past 30 years, with special focus on those more recent works in the series 'Men without Women: Parsival'. The principal motif in these works is the human face, head or mask hovering in space, a theme Lüpertz has used since the early 60s in every conceivable form and variation. While the exhibition thus has a retrospective character, it is not arranged chronologically, but instead opposes early works with later ones.

29·06·96–06·10·96   *Daniel Buren*   Since the end of the 60s, French artist Daniel Buren has been producing site-specific works whose structural elements consist of white and coloured stripes, in effect questioning the complexities of contemporary art and its environment framework. For this exhibition, Buren will create an installation which will relate to the unusual proportions of the exhibition hall on the ground floor of the museum.

23·11·96–02·03·97   *René Magritte*

Essen

MUSEUM FOLKWANG ESSEN
Goethestraße 41   45128 Essen   Director: Georg-W. Költzsch
☎ +49 201 888484   📠 +49 201 888450
Open: Tuesday-Sunday 10.00-18.00   Thursday 10.00-21.00
Closed: Monday

COLLECTION   The Folkwang Museum has an excellent collection of paintings, plastic arts, drawings, graphics (c. 25 000 pieces) and photography (c. 20 000 pieces) of the 19th and 20th century.
The collection features German Romanticists (Carus, Clausen Dahl, C.D. Friedrich, Hackert, Koch, Morgenstern) and Realists of the 19th century (Böcklin, Feuerbach, Leibl, Marées, Trübner, Thoma), in addition to French Realists (Corot, Courbet, Daumier, Delacroix) and

Impressionists (Cézanne, Gauguin, Van Gogh, Manet, Monet, Pissarro, Renoir, Signac, Sisley). Also strongly represented are the French Cubists (Braque, Delaunay, Gris, Léger, Picasso) and Surrealists (Dalí, Ernst, Miró, Magritte, Tanguy). The painters of the 'Brücke' (Heckel, Kirchner, Mueller, Nolde, Pechstein, Schmidt–Rottluff) and of the 'Blaue Reiter' (Kandinsky, Macke, Marc) and artists connected with ideas of those groups (Modersohn-Becker, Rohlfs), Bauhaus artists (Feininger, Klee, Maholy-Nagy, Molzahn, Schlemmer), all represent the variety of German Expressionism and of 20th-century art.

EXHIBITIONS

23·05·96–28·07·96	***Olivo Barbieri*** *Photographs Since 1978*
30·06·96–11·08·96	***Pedro Cabrita Reis*** *Installations*
08·08·96–06·10·96	***Biedermeier and Realism*** *Graphics from the Museum Collection*
25·08·96–06·10·96	***Contemporary Photography in North Rhine-Westphalia*** *Group Exhibition*
01·09·96–06·10·96	***Positions*** *Journeys to the Boundaries of Painting*
17·10·96–24·11·96	***Peter Keetman*** *Black and White Photographs*
03·11·96–17·11·96	***Prize-Winner of 'Villa Romana' 1996***
08·12·96–02·03·97	***Sean Scully*** *Work on Paper*
15·12·96–26·01·97	***Ansgar Nierhoff*** *Sculptures and Drawings*

Esslingen

GALERIE DER STADT ESSLINGEN
Villa Merkel Pulverwiesen 7300 Esslingen Director: R. Damsch-Wiehager
☎ +49 711 35122461 📠 +49 711 35122903
Open: Wednesday-Sunday 11.00-18.00 Tuesday 11.00-20.00
Closed: Monday

COLLECTION

Villa Merkel was built in the year 1873 for the Esslingen industrialist Oskar Merkel. The building was designed by the Stuttgart architect Otto Tafel.
The graphic collection of the city of Esslingen am Neckar was founded in the year 1957 by the Mayor of that time. Ever since, the collection has been enlarged continuously. In the year 1979, 1,300 works were registered in the first catalogue. In 1991 the second catalogue was published, featuring 1,940 items. By now the collection consists of about 2,800 works. The collection is entirely devoted to art of the 20th century. The emphasis lies on German Expressionism, French art of the 'École de Paris', contemporary European art and artists whose biographies are linked with Esslingen. The latter include high-quality works by Volker Böhringer, Adolf Fleischmann and Rolf Nesch. The foundation of the International Triennial of Photography at Esslingen in 1989 provided an occasion to enlarge the collection of selected examples of contemporary photography.
Villa Merkel is a municipal gallery with changing exhibitions of contemporary art. Besides the Triennial of Photography a small series of the international Zero-movement was initiated.

EXHIBITIONS

[Villa Merkel]

10·05·96–02·06·96	***Annual Exhibition of the Artists' Guild***

07·06·96–07·07·96	*Esslingen Art Society*
21·07·96–15·09·96	*Christian Marclay, Pipilotti Rist, Roman Signer, Jean Tinguely*
22·09·96–13·10·96	*New Acquisitions to the Graphic Collection of the Town of Esslingen*
27·10·96–08·12·96	*Martin Kippenberger*
15·12·96–25·01·97	*Esslingen Art Society*
	[Bahnwärterhaus]
26·04·96–27·05·96	*Cor Dera/Gerhard Friebe*
31·05·96–09·06·96	*Inga Svala Thorsdottir/Vanessa Beecroft*
21·07·96–29·09·96	*Eran Schaerf*
06·12·96–25·01·97	*Recipient of the Bahnwärter Grant*

Frankfurt am Main

DEUTSCHES ARCHITEKTUR-MUSEUM
Schaumainkai 43 60596 Frankfurt am Main Director: Wilfried Wang
☎ +49 69 21238844 📠 +49 69 21237721
Open: Tuesday, Thursday, Saturday, Sunday 11.00-18.00
Wednesday and Friday 12.00-20.00
Closed: Monday

COLLECTION The Architecture Museum, which opened in 1984, serves not only as an exhibition space and a discussion forum for German and international architecture and urban planning, but also as a repository for historically important architectural sketches, plans and models. Since the opening of the museum, some 80 exhibitions have taken place. The building, designed by Ungers, is meant to be more than a museum building — it is intended to illustrate the very essence of architecture. The collection currently includes 110 000 plans and drawings and 400 models, primarily of 20th-century buildings. In addition, the museum houses a libarary of more than 10 000 volumes on architectural history and theory since 1800, and numerous architectural monographs and periodicals of the 20th century. The museum's first permanent exhibition utilises scale models to depict the history of architecture and housing from the oldest known Stone Age hut to the urban dwellings of New York. A second, more comprehensive exhibition is currently in development.

EXHIBITIONS

22·03·96–09·06·96	*Weltbild Wörlitz* Design for a Cultural Landscape
29·06·96–01·09·96	*Erich Buchholz* An exhibition from the archives.
29·06·96–01·09·96	*Film Architecture* From Metropolis to Bladerunner
29·06·96–01·01·96	*Berlin Housing Architecture*
21·09·96–24·11·96	*Architecture for All the Senses* The Work of Eileen Gray
21·09·96–24·11·96	*Architecture in the 20th Century: Ireland*
14·12·96–23·02·97	*Ecological Architecture and Urban Planning*

Frankfurt am Main

MUSEUM FÜR KUNSTHANDWERK
Schaumainkai 17 60594 Frankfurt am Main Director: Arnulf Herbst
☎ +49 69 21234037 📠 +49 69 21230703
Open: Tuesday-Sunday 10.00-17.00 Wednesday 10.00-20.00
Closed: Monday

Museum für
Kunsthandwerk,
Frankfurt a. Main

COLLECTION

The municipal Museum of Decorative Art of the City of Frankfurt
has been in existence since 1877. Its collection of over 30 000 objects
from all areas of the applied arts is assembled in five departments.
The European Department covers the Middle Ages to the present,
as does the collection of book-art and graphics. The Near Eastern
Department presents Islamic arts and crafts of the 9th to the 19th
century. Art and applied art from China and Japan are to be found
in the Department for Eastern Asia. In 1988 the Icon Museum of the
City of Frankfurt, founded on Dr Schmidt-Voigt's generous gift and
housed in the nearby Deutschordenshaus, was incorporated as a
fifth department. One of the main aims of the museum lies in the
demonstration of relationships and influences between western and
eastern cultures.
All of the collections have found an appropriate setting in the
museum's new building designed by the New York architect Richard
Meier and constructed between 1982 and 1985.

EXHIBITIONS
18·04·96–27·05·96

Fokus 7   Passage Of Time   Ceramic sculptures by Ewen Henderson,
Great Britain.

28·03·96–02·06·96

Drawings

23·05·96–20·10·96

The Treasure House of Kuwait

20·06·96–18·08·96

Contemporary German Fashion Photography

Frankfurt am Main

MUSEUM FÜR MODERNE KUNST
Domstraße 10 60311 Frankfurt am Main Director: J.-C. Ammann
☎ +49 69 21230447 📠 +49 69 21237882
Open: Tuesday-Sunday 10.00-17.00 Wednesday 10.00-20.00
Closed: Monday

COLLECTION

The MMK is entirely devoted to contemporary art. The heart of its
collection is formed by a group of 84 works dating from the 60s.
The collection includes works by Chamberlain, de Maria, Johns,
Judd, Lichtenstein, Oldenburg, Rauschenberg, Rosenquist, Segal and

Warhol, as well as Bacon, Klein, Palermo, Rainer, Richter, Ruthenbeck and Walter.
From the mid-80s onwards this stock has been supplemented with contemporary art works.
Approximately every six months there is a 'Change of Scene' at the museum, which involves six to eight rooms being refitted.

EXHIBITIONS

14·06·96–12·01·97   *Change of Scene X*   As part of Change of Scene X, new work is being shown in new rooms. Exhibited artists include: Nobuyoshi Araki (photography), Larry Clark (photography), Jock Sturges (photography) and Anke Doberauer (painting).

31·01·97–04·05·97   *Change of Scene XI*   *Whitney Museum: Views from Abroad*

Frankfurt am Main

PORTIKUS FRANKFURT AM MAIN
Schöne Aussicht 2 60311 Frankfurt Director: Kasper König
☎ +49 69 60500830 ▥ +49 69 60500831
Open: Tuesday-Sunday 11.00-18.00 Wednesday 11.00-20.00
Closed: Monday

COLLECTION   No permanent collection.

EXHIBITIONS

30·03·96–19·05·96   *Esko Männikkö*

25·05·96–21·07·96   *Ulrike Grossarth*

27·07·96–22·09·96   *N.N.*

28·09·96–24·11·96   *Franz Ackermann*

30·11·96–end Jan 97   *Tobias Rehberger*

Frankfurt am Main

SCHIRN KUNSTHALLE
Römerberg 60311 Frankfurt am Main Director: Hellmut Seemann
☎ +49 69 2998820 ▥ +49 69 29989240
Open: Tuesday-Sunday 10.00-19.00 Wednesday, Thursday 10.00-22.00
Closed: Monday

COLLECTION   No permanent collection.

EXHIBITIONS

09·03·96–12·05·96   *Photo Prospect '96*   Contemporary photographic art, in cooperation with the Frankfurt Kunstverein.

08·06·96–01·09·96   *Lucio Fontana*   Retrospective.

20·09·96–08·12·96   *Sean Scully* *Twenty Years, 1976 - 1995*   In cooperation with the High Museum of Art, Atlanta, Georgia, USA (in conjunction with the presentation of 'Eire' at the Frankfurt Book Fair).

02·10·96–05·01·97   *Ferdinand Hodler*   In cooperation with the Kunstmuseum Solothurn, Switzerland.

14·12·96–30·03·97   *Collection of the Aargauer Kunsthaus*   In cooperation with the Aargauer Kunsthaus, Aarau, Switzerland.

25·01·97–06·04·97   *Gaston Chaissac*   Retrospective.

Frankfurt am Main

STÄDELSCHES KUNSTINSTITUT UND STÄDTISCHE GALERIE
Schaumainkai 63 60596 Frankfurt am Main Director: Herbert Beck
☎ +49 69 6050980 📠 +49 69 610163
Open: Tuesday-Sunday 10.00-17.00 Wednesday 10.00-20.00
Closed: Monday

COLLECTION

Founded in 1815 by the Frankfurt merchant Johann Friedrich Städel, the museum was originally conceived as both collection and art college, and is now the city's major art gallery. The museum building itself was seriously damaged during the war and was first restored in 1966, with an extension added in 1990. The museum's collections span almost all European schools from the 14th to 20th century and it continues to acquire contemporary works.
There are a number of particularly strong collections. German Renaissance painting is represented by fine works from Cranach, Dürer, Altdörfer, both Holbeins, Baldung and anonymous masters. There is an outstanding collection of early and later Flemish and Dutch Renaissance works, including Jan van Eyck's 'Lucca Madonna' and paintings by Campin, Van der Weyden, Van der Goes, Bosch and Memling; this is augmented by works from the Dutch Golden Age from Rembrandt, Vermeer, Rubens, Van Ruysdael, Hobbema, Brouwer, Steen, Hals and Kalff. Italian schools are also strongly represented, both of the Renaissance (Fra Angelico, Botticelli, Pontormo, Tintoretto, among others) and of the 18th century (Tiepolo). French painting of the 18th and 19th century is exemplified by such artists as Watteau, Chardin, Corot, Delacroix, Courbet, Monet, Renoir, Manet, Degas and Cézanne. German painting comes to the fore again in the 19th and 20th-century departments, with Böcklin and Feuerbach followed by a large collection of German Expressionists, including Beckmann, Nolde and Kirchner. The museum also has a major graphic collection.

EXHIBITIONS

08·05·96–30·10·96   **Hans Steinbrenner**   Sculptures (in the Städelgarten)

Jun 96–Sep 96   **Henri Matisse**   Jazz Series of graphic works

25·09·96–18·12·96   **The Second Russian Avant-Garde 1955-1985**

Autumn 96   **'Frankfurter Zugänge'**   A didactic cabinet exhibition in collaboration with study seminars.

Autumn 96–Winter 96   **The Woodcut**   60 Examples covering six centuries

Freiburg im Breisgau

AUGUSTINERMUSEUM
Augustinerplatz 79098 Freiburg i. Br. Director: Saskia Durian-Ress
☎ +49 761 2012531 📠 +49 761 2012597
Open: Tuesday-Friday 9.30-17.00 Saturday, Sunday 10.30-17.00
Closed: Monday

COLLECTION

The Augustiner Museum is located in the centre of Freiburg's Old Town in a former monastery for Augustinian monks. The setting is ideal for the display of the municipal art collection, which includes art and craft from many eras, with a focus on the art of the Upper Rhine region. The highlight of the museum is an extensive collection of Medieval stone and wooden sculptures, glass and panel paintings, tapestries, and gold and silver utensils. Many original ornamental sculptures from Freiburg Cathedral are also on display.

There are exhibits of goldsmiths' work dating back more than a thousand years, embroidered and knitted textiles from the High and Late Middle Ages, paintings by late Medieval masters, and unique specimens of book illumination. The Augustiner Museum also has a collection of Baroque sculptures, an extensive collection of historic furniture and interiors, a collection of glassware and a picture gallery of Baden paintings of the 19th century.

EXHIBITIONS

20·03·96–09·06·96

Late Baroque Esquisses of Oil Painting *The Reuschel Collection*
The Reuschel Collection contains several outstanding works of art by famous artists of Southern Germany, the Tyrol and the Academy of Art in Vienna, including works by Franz Anton Maulbertsch, Johann Wolfgang Baumgartner and Januarius Zick, as well as works of Italian origin.

20·03·95–09·06·96

New Acquistions During the last two years the Augustiner Museum has acquired, by purchase and donation, numerous works of art related to its special fields of collection. The most interesting of these are shown in this exhibition, including, for example, a rare piece of embroidery from about 1500, selected paintings of the 18th, 19th and 20th centuries, antique porcelain by various German producers, and a selection of drawings and etchings.

28·06·96–01·09·96

Saved for Baden *From the Margrave of Baden Auction*
During the sensational Sotheby's auction in 1995, the government of the German state of Baden endeavoured to secure important objects of art and history from the former collection of the Margrave of Baden for the public. The most interesting pieces among them are shown in this exhibition.

Oct 96–Nov 96

Henri de Toulouse-Lautrec *Works on Paper* The famous French painter Toulouse-Lautrec depicts, in his inimitable way, the way of life in Paris during the fin-de-siècle era. His drawings, lithographs and posters, created mainly in the cafés, cabarets and dance halls of Paris, show the special atmosphere of these places and reveal much about the mood of the people.

05·12·96–23·01·97

Christoph Daniel Schenck *The Constance Baroque Sculptor*
Christoph Daniel Schenck (1635-1691), who worked in the second half of the 17th century, usually in the Lake Constance region, was one of the eminent woodcarving artists of his day. This exhibition of his sculpture includes works from the Augustiner Museum's own collection.

Goslar

MÖNCHEHAUS-MUSEUM FÜR MODERNE KUNST
Mönchestraße 3 3380 Goslar Director: Th.K.Peter Schenning
☎ +49 5321 29570 ▥ +49 5321 42199
Open: Tuesday-Saturday 10.00-13.00 / 15.00-17.00 Sunday 10.00-13.00
Closed: Monday

COLLECTION

The 'Mönchehaus' was built in 1528 and is one of the oldest buildings in the centre of Goslar. The first floor contains the 'Apostelzimmer', an historical best room with one of the last existing plaster floors.
The permanent display in the museum and the sculpture garden consists of paintings, environment works and sculptures, in particular by recipients of the Kaiserring: Henry Moore, Max Ernst, Alexander Calder, Victor Vasarely, Joseph Beuys, Richard Serra, Max Bill, Günther Uecker, Willem de Kooning, Eduardo Chillida, Georg Baselitz, Christo, Gerhard Richter, Mario Merz, Anselm Kiefer,

Nam June Paik, Rebecca Horn, Roman Opalka and Bernd & Hilla Becher. Work by young artists is also on display, especially those who have won the Kaiserring Grant.

27·04·96–04·08·96   *Bernhard Heisig*   This exhibition presents an extensive cross-section of his paintings, including the critical historic pictures, portraits and landscapes, as well as various graphic works.

10·08·96–20·10·96   *Georges Braque*   This exhibition focused on Georges Braque continues the series of 'book of painter' exhibits. 'Books of painter', usually loose leaf, are special graphic editions in which the word/line tension is particularly effective, evidencing the graphic artist's critical examination of poetry and other literary forms.

20·10·96–Jan 97   *Kaiserring Grant 1996*   Support of young artists is a special interest of the Society for Furtherance of Modern Art in Goslar, which is underscored by the yearly awarding of a grant to a young artist and a one-man show of the recipient's works with a sales guarantee.

26·10·96–Jan 97   *Dani Karavan*   *Kaiserring Recipient 1996*   Dani Karavan (born 1930) belongs to those international artists who do not conceptualise their works directly for museums or private collections, but rather for social, urban spaces. In many cities Karavan has, through his art, been able to establish sense connections which previous additive planning had hindered.

Göttingen

STÄDTISCHE MUSEUM GÖTTINGEN
Ritterplan 7/8 37073 Göttingen Director: Jens-Uwe Brinkmann
☎ +49 551 4002843 📠 +49 551 4002059
Open: Tuesday-Friday 10.00-17.00 Saturday, Sunday 10.00-13.00
Closed: Monday

COLLECTION   The museum's collection of religious art presents a survey of the development of sculpture from the 12th century to the late Middle Ages, the Renaissance Age and the Baroque Age, up to the late 18th century.

Städtisches Museum
Göttingen

The oldest objects date from the Paleolithic period. There are also objects on display from the Neolithic period up to the Bronze Age. These give an impression of the development of human culture in

the Göttingen region. The history of the city of Göttingen is represented from the Merowingian period up to the end of the Second World War: beginning with a document from 953 first mentioning a village called 'Gutingi', up to models, pictures, photographs and everyday items from the 19th century.
Finally, objects from the departments of the 'Georgia Augusta', along with photographs, give a brief view of the development of Göttingen University, starting from its foundation in 1737. The culture and history of the city can also be viewed through some special collections of art and craft objects from Jewish culture and history, and collections on the history of literature and publishing.

EXHIBITIONS

05·05·96–30·06·96   **Ausglass**   An exhibition of glass art by 16 Australian artists.

14·07·96–01·09·96   **The Ball is Spherical**   Curious and funny things about football.

15·09·96–27·10·96   **55,000 Years Ago**   An early human settlement near Lichtenberg in the Lüchow-Dannenberg region.

10·11·96–08·12·96   **Göttingen**   Historical prospects of the city.

15·12·96–26·01·97   **Alfred Pohl** *Woodcuts, Etchings, Watercolours*

Feb 96–Apr 97   **Fighting Against Conflagration**   Firemen in Göttingen then and now.

Haltern

WESTFÄLISCHES RÖMERMUSEUM
Weseler Straße 100   45721 Haltern   Director: Rudolf Asskamp
☎ +49 2364 93760   📠 +49 2364 937630
Open: Tuesday-Friday 09.00-17.00   Saturday, Sunday 10.00-18.00
Closed: Monday

COLLECTION   This new museum, opened in 1993, displays old and new finds from the Haltern camps and other military installations established by the Romans along the Lippe River during the initial stages of their war against Free Germany from 12 B.C. to 16 A.D. The front of the building runs parallel to the partly reconstructed defences of the camp. Upon entering the museum across the Roman V-shaped ditch and rampart, the visitor is thus placed in the centre of Rome's easternmost outpost in the conquered German lands.

The exterior of the building is topped with fourteen skylights in the form of legionnaires' tents. The interior is one large exhibition hall flooded with light. More than 800 objects of daily life and soldiers' equipment, such as weapons, articles of clothing, tools of carpenters and metal workers, pottery, glass, coins and medical instruments are on display.

EXHIBITIONS   No exhibitions planned.

Hamburg

HAMBURGER KUNSTHALLE
Glockengießerwall 20095 Hamburg   Director: Uwe M. Schneede
☎ +49 40 24862612   📠 +49 40 24862482
Open: Tuesday-Sunday 10.00-18.00   Thursday 10.00-21.00
Closed: Monday and 3 Oct, 24 Dec, 31 Dec

COLLECTION   The Hamburger Kunsthalle is currently undergoing a stimulating period of renewal. The galleries housing the permanent collection have been renovated, paintings from the Old Masters up to the Classical Modernists have been rearranged and an extensive new building due to be opened in 1997 will house the Modern Art collection.

Medieval Art   The collection begins with art from the Middle Ages and includes one of the greatest and most moving paintings in North German Gothic art, the Grabow Altar ('Petri-Altar') of 1379 by Master Bertram. The twenty-four plates contain naive and lively scenes from the Old and New Testament. An interesting comparison can be made between this polyptych and the 'Thomas-Altar' by Master Franke, also in the collection.

Dutch 17th-Century Painting   Dutch 17th-century painting is represented by an early Rembrandt work ('Simeon in the Temple'), land and seascapes by Averkamp, Van Goyen, S. and J. Ruisdael, Van de Velde and genre paintings by Jan Steen and P. de Hoogh.

German Painting of the 19th Century   A particularly strong feature of the Kunsthalle, this part of the collection is centred around the works of the Romantic painters Caspar David Friedrich ('Das Eismeer', 'Wanderer über dem Nebelmeer') and Philipp Otto Runge ('Die Hülsenbeckschen Kinder', 'Der Morgen'), which together highlight the movement toward subjectivity in painting. The Kunsthalle also has works by Feuerbach, Von Marées and Böcklin. Additional highlights include the Menzel Room and the famous 'Drei Frauen in der Kirche' by the Realist Wilhelm Leibl. The Kunsthalle collection contains groups of works by Max Liebermann ('Die Netzflickerinnen'), Lovis Corinth and Edvard Munch ('Madonna'). The Classical Modernists are dominated by Max Beckmann and Oskar Kokoschka, together with artists from the 'Brücke' and 'Blauer Reiter' groups (Ernst Ludwig Kirchner, Emil Nolde, Franz Marc). 'Der Goldfisch' by Paul Klee also belongs in this context.

Contemporary art is featured in temporary room exhibitions of individual artists' work. One such room is devoted over a longer term to works by Joseph Beuys.

EXHIBITIONS	
22·03·96–16·06·96	**Egon Schiele** *The Leopold Collection, Vienna*
05·07·96–08·09·96	**The Great Draughtsmen** *From Ingres to Bonnard* French drawings from the Museum of Visual Arts in Budapest and from Swiss collections.
20·09·96–01·12·96	**Georg Hinz** *The Art Chamber Shelf*
27·10·96–29·12·96	**Hamburg Painting in the Biedermeier Period**
Jan 97–Mar 97	**Italian Renaissance Drawings**
Feb 97	**Opening of the Ungersbau**

Hamburg

MUSEUM FÜR KUNST UND GEWERBE HAMBURG
Steintorplatz 1 20099 Hamburg Director: Wilhelm Hornbostel
☎ +49 40 24862732 📠 +49 40 24862834
Open: Tuesday-Sunday 10.00-18.00 Thursday 10.00-21.00
Closed: Monday

COLLECTION   **Applied Arts from the Middle Ages to Historism**   The collection provides a fine survey of European arts and crafts. It includes sculptures, bronzes, articles of gold, ivory, glass, ceramics, tapestries, scientific instruments, majolica, faience, porcelain, period rooms, and musical instruments.

Art Nouveau The museum possesses one of the most important collections of Art Nouveau, acquired at the 1900 World Fair in Paris and representing a broad cross-section of the Art Nouveau trends.
Modern Applied Art and Industrial Design This section includes works in the French Art Deco style, German Expressionist graphics and sculpture, Bauhaus and De Stijl furniture, ceramics and studio pottery of the 20 and 30s, Kinetic objects and modern industrial design.
East Asia and the Islamic World Covering the period from antiquity to the Ming and Quing dynasties, the Chinese collection contains ceramics, jade, bronzes and paintings. The collection of Japanese art shows swordguards, woodcut prints and books. The Islamic collection consists of textiles, wall tiles, ceramics, glass, bronzes and the art of books.
Ancient Art The Ancient Art section includes Egyptian reliefs, bronzes, faience and painted mummy portraits, as well as Etruscan bronzes, vases and sculpture. Ancient Greece is represented by ceramics, bronzes, terracottas, sculpture, glass and jewellery. Ancient Rome is represented by a marble portrait collection, glass, and bronzes.
Graphic Design and Photography The graphic design collection includes ornamental engravings and a famous poster collection.The development of photography from its beginnings to the present is documented in a collection which includes daguerreotypes, other early techniques, and photos exemplifying the pictorialism characteristic of the turn of the century.

Museum für Kunst und Gewerbe, Hamburg Westfaçade, built 1877

EXHIBITIONS

29·03·96–23·06·96	**The Patient Planet** *A History of the World in 225 Photographs* An exhibition on the journal "du" in the period 1941-1995.
03·04·96–07·07·96	**Real Feelings** *Graphic Design of the 90s*
May 96–Jun 96	**Lamp Design**
Jun 96	**Uwe Loesch** *Communication Design*
Sep 96–Oct 96	**A.T. Schaefer** *Places of Colour* Photographs.
06·09·96–17·11·96	**Hamburg Faience**
06·09·96–17·11·96	**Japanese Laquer Pictures**
13·09·96–17·11·96	**Yves Saint Laurent**
Autumn	**Signs of Friendship** *Japanese Albums, Fans and Scroll Pictures* An exhibition selected from the Rose Hempel Collection.
Nov 96–Jan 97	**Thomas Schleede and Students**

08·11·96–27·01·97	***The Hats of Adele List***
29·11·96–18·12·96	***Annual Northern German Craftwork Fair***
Winter	***Michael Ruetz*** *The Perennial Eye*
	[Forum K]
14·04·96–19·05·96	***"e.g. Oak"*** *Furniture by the Hamburg Group Stückgut e.V.*
May 96–Jun 96	***Bag Art***
13·09·96–27·11·96	***The Stranger in Art***
	[Photography Forum]
10·05·96–23·06·96	***Alfred Steffen*** *Portraits* Photographs of well-known contemporary faces.
Aug 96–Sep 96	***Edgar Lissel*** *Houses of God* A journey through Germany with the camera obscura.
Oct 96–Nov 96	***Klaus Elle***

Hamburg

HAMBURGISCHES MUSEUM FÜR VÖLKERKUNDE
Rothenbaumchaussee 64 20148 Hamburg Director: Wulf Köpke
☎ +49 40 44195524 📠 +49 40 44195242
Open: Tuesday-Sunday 10.00-18.00 Thursday 10.00-21.00
Closed: Monday

COLLECTION

The museum's seven main departments house around 350 000 objects and 300 000 historical-ethnographical photographs. The museum's highlights include the famous 'Chamber of Gold' which houses Central and South American gold treasures, the bronze and ivory works of the kingdom of Benin, and the largest collection of Siberian artefacts outside Russia.
The museum also houses artefacts from the Near East, Middle East and Southern and Eastern Asia. The peoples and cultures of Oceania have always occupied a prominent position within the collection, and the Maori meeting house and the display of Oceanic religious objects are sure to leave a lasting impression. The building's Art Nouveau lobby and the lecture hall with its original fixtures are equally impressive.

EXHIBITIONS

No details available.

Hannover

HISTORISCHES MUSEUM
Pferdestraße 6 30159 Hannover Director: Waldemar R. Röhrbein
☎ +49 511 1682352 📠 +49 511 1685003
Open: Tuesday 10.00-20.00 Wednesday-Friday 10.00-16.00
Saturday-Sunday 10.00-18.00
Closed: Monday

COLLECTION

The Museum of History, which was founded in 1903, lost its building and a quarter of its collection during the war. It subsequently moved into its new accommodation in the old part of the town, in which the remnants of the Medieval town wall are integrated. The collection consists of three departments.

The central and largest department offers the visitor a chronological tour through the civic history of the City of Hannover from the Middle Ages up to the present. Medieval archaeological finds, town plans, models, paintings, graphics, photos, posters, porcelain, Hannover silver, household effects, furnished rooms and garments between 1760 and 1960 illustrate the development, the changes, the political and everyday life of the town. Handicraft tools, industrial products, vehicles and children's toys complete the picture.

The presentation of the union between Great Britain and Hannover from 1714 until 1837 is the largest section of the department of State History. Here, among other items, are displayed portraits of Guelph dukes, electors and kings, garments, banners, the rare garment of a mint apprentice, coins, relics of the mining industry in the Harz and Deister regions and military equipment. Also featured are the coaches from the Hannoverian royal stables, including the Gilded State Coach, built in London around 1783, and the Perchhigh Phaeton.

The development of country life and labour between the 17th century and the beginning of the 19th century are presented in the third department. There are a number of farmhouse models, a reconstructed fireplace, a farmhouse parlour from the middle of the 17th century, Fritz Mackensen's painting 'Church Service on the Moorland', country garments, a combine harvester and a threshing machine.

EXHIBITIONS

14·02·96–05·05·96

Bees-Plants-Man *Honey-Bees and Bee-Keepers Past and Present*
This exhibition attempts to visualise the centuries-old mutual relationship between bees, plants and mankind, with reference to the Northern German region.

24·08·96–17·11·96

Lower Saxony *State of the Federal Republic for the last 50 years*
Following a short glance back to the Second World War and the concentration camps, the exhibition covers the period of the British occupation of Northern Germany, as well as the changes in mentality, the political developments and the economic situation leading to the so-called 'Wirtschaftswunder' (economic miracle). Finally, attention is also focused on the main interests of the new generations, their concern for nature and social justice, and how they experience no longer being near the eastern frontier, but rather in the centre of the Republic of Germany.

Hannover

NIEDERSÄCHSISCHES LANDESMUSEUM HANNOVER
Am Maschpark 5 30169 Hannover Director: Heide Grape-Albers
☎ +49 511 98075 📠 +49 511 9807640
Open: Tuesday-Sunday 10.00-17.00 Thursday 10.00-19.00
Closed: Monday. Due to renovation parts of the museum are closed.

COLLECTION

Art Gallery The Niedersächsisches Landesgalerie exhibits paintings and sculptures dating from the Middle Ages to the 20th century, including works by Cranach, Riemenschneider, Botticelli, Rubens, Rembrandt, Poussin, Tiepolo, Caspar David Friedrich, Carl Spitzweg, Monet, Max Liebermann, Max Slevogt and Lovis Corinth and an important collection of drawings and prints.
Natural History The collections of the Natural History Department represent the biology and geology of Northern Europe, with special reference to Lower Saxony. Exhibitions on ecology aim to promote a better understanding of the natural environment.
Aquarium The Aquarium displays fish, amphibians, reptiles and insects in realistic reconstructions of their natural habitats.

Prehistory In the Department of Archaeology the most important archaeological finds from Lower Saxony are on display, illustrating the history of this county from Palaeolithic up to the Middle Ages. In the newly created 'Kindermuseum' children can explore prehistoric time with the help of realistic models made by children and activities like grinding corn or working stone tools.

Ethnology The permanent exhibition of the Department of Ethnology includes collections from Oceania, Asia, Africa and the Americas, and a special reflection on themes covering Ethnomedicine, Ethnobotany and Natural Philosophie.

Niedersächsisches Landesmuseum Hannover, Hannover (The Lower Saxony State Museum) Main façade, built 1897-1902

EXHIBITIONS

05·11·95-14·07·96

[Forum des Landesmuseums]
Given to be Shown   *Donations and Loans to the Lower Saxony State Art Gallery*   113 paintings and sculptures owned by the Lower Saxony State Art Gallery from the 17th to early 20th century, ranging from Rembrandt and Rubens to Monet and Corinth.

Apr 96-end Jun 96

Colour in Colorado   *The Art of Indian Children from Mexico* Wallpaintings by Indian children representing their daily life in Mexico.

Jun 96-Dec 96

Exhibition by the Department of Natural History

12·12·96-Feb 97

Age of Bronze   *Life, Faith and Death, 3000 Years ago* Cultural and historical aspects of the Bronze Age.

Hannover

SPRENGEL MUSEUM HANNOVER
Kurt-Schwitters-Platz 30169 Hannover Director: Ulrich Krempel
☎ +49 511 1683875 📠 +49 511 1685093
Open: Tuesday 10.00-22.00 Wednesday-Sunday 10.00-18.00
Closed: Monday

COLLECTION

Situated by the Maschsee, the large lake near the centre of Hannover, the Sprengel Museum houses major collections of classic modern and contemporary art. The museum was created in response to a donation to the city of more than 300 modern works by the industrialist Bernhard Sprengel in 1969. The museum building itself is notable: completed in two phases, in 1979 and 1992, it provides an optimal setting and protection for the collections while opening up to its surroundings. The architecture itself easily vies for attention with many of the exhibited works. The classic modern section has outstanding exhibits of German Expressionism (works from the 'Brücke' and 'Blaue Reiter' groups, Nolde, Beckmann and Kokoschka), French Cubism (Picasso, Léger, Laurens), 'Neue Sachlichkeit', Surrealism, Constructivism and excellent Kurt Schwitters and Paul Klee collections, together with sculpture by Arp, Barlach, Lehmbruck and Moore, among others. The contemporary collection is similarly constructed around particular artists, rather than taking an encyclopaedic approach. In addition to large quantities of excellent German art, other collections focus on the 'Ecole de Paris', work complexes by Baumeister, Nay and Schumacher, décollages by Rotella and Hains, Minimal Art by Judd, LeWitt, Rückriem and Sandback, and Conceptual Art by Barry, Kosuth, Sonnier, Tuttle, Walther and Weiner. A major graphic collection completes the overview of 20th–century art.

EXHIBITIONS No details available.

Karlsruhe

BADISCHES LANDESMUSEUM KARLSRUHE
Schloss 76131 Karlsruhe Director: Harald Siebenmorgen
☎ +49 721 9266542 📠 +49 721 9266549
Open: Tuesday-Sunday 10.00-17.00 Wednesday 10.00-20.00
Closed: Monday

COLLECTION The 'Grossherzoglich Badische Altertümersammlung', the 'Museum of Industry', founded in 1860, and part of the Grand Duke's personal collections are now the nucleus of the Badisches Landesmuseum Karlsruhe, founded in 1919. It is owned by the State of Baden-Württemburg.

Set with views of Karlsruhe
Fayence manufactury of Durlach, c. 1765

Badisches Landesmuseum, Karlsruhe

Prehistory, Egyptian art, Greek, Roman and Oriental antiquities, sculptures and decorative art of the Middle Ages, the Renaissance and the Baroque period are on display in the former residence of the margraves, later the Grand Dukes of Baden. In addition to these collections there are state and hunting weapons, coins, medals and the 'Turkish Booty' of the margrave Ludwig Wilhelm von Baden. European decorative art from Art Nouveau to Art Deco, arts, crafts and 20th-century design have been put on show in the 'Museum beim Markt', situated between the castle and Karlsruhe's marketplace.

An overall picture of the production of the Majolika-Factory Karlsruhe, founded in 1900 and still producing, can be seen in the 'Museum in der Majolika-Manufactur'.
There are branch museums in Hirsau, Staufen, Osterburken and Bruchsal with an interesting collection of mechanical musical instruments in the Bruchsal castle.

EXHIBITIONS
24·02·96–02·06·96

Delphi *The Oracle at the Navel of the World*   This exhibition, organised in collaboration with the museum in Delphi and the French School in Athens, presents the history of the Delphi oracle. It utilises original objects as well as models and computer programs.

13·03·96–09·06·96

Saved for Baden *The Acquisitions of the Badisches Landesmuseum Karlsruhe 1995 from the Collections of the Markgrafen and Großherzöge von Baden*   The Badisches Landesmuseum was able to purchase about 250 objects during 1995 at the famous auction in Baden-Baden. Including 'Kunstkammer' objects from the Middle Ages up to the 18th century, the famous paintings from the Salem altarpiece, and 18th and 19th-century decorative arts and furniture. These newly acquired objects are not only significant as objects of art, but also of considerable historic interest.

Karlsruhe

STAATLICHE KUNSTHALLE KARLSRUHE
Hans Thoma-Straße 2-6 76133 Karlsruhe Director: Horst Vey
☎ **+49 721 9263355** 📠 **+49 721 9266788**
Open: Tuesday-Friday 10.00-17.00 Saturday, Sunday 10.00-18.00
Closed: Monday and 24, 31 Dec and Carnival (Tuesday)

COLLECTION

The origins of the Staatliche Kunsthalle collection in Karlsruhe can be traced back to the art collection of the margraves, later to become Grand Dukes of Baden. Margrave Christopher I (1474-1515) commissioned Hans Baldung Grien in 1511 to paint a devotional image of him and his family praying to St. Ann, Mary and Christ. He was also responsible for the acquisition of important works of Old German Masters including Baldung's 'The Adoration of the Christ Child', Lucas Cranach the Elder's 'Madonna with Child' and 'The Judgement of Paris' and a collection of Flemish masters of the 17th century.

Margrave Karoline Luise (1723-1783) was largely responsible for the acquisition of the Dutch masters of the 17th century and French contemporary painters, together with the notable acquisitions of Rembrandt's sombre self-portrait and the four still lifes by Chardin. Acquisitions during the 19th century include the Hans Thoma collection which he donated himself while he was Director of the Kunsthalle and the panels 'Christ Carrying the Cross' and 'Christ on the Cross between Mary and John' by Grünewald.

The collection is further complemented by works from French and German masters, European sculpture from the 19th and 20th century, outstanding Italian painting from the 15th to 18th centuries, and German and French drawings and graphic art.

EXHIBITIONS
until 08·09·96

Children of Today Play Karlsruhe People   *The Weinbrenner Period 1800-1830*

03·04·96–30·06·96

The Karlsruhe Passion   *A Major Work of the Late Gothic Strasbourg School*   This exhibition, to celebrate the 150th anniversary of the Kunsthalle Karlsruhe, centres on the 'Karlsruhe Passion', five altar panels painted around 1450 by an unknown master of the Strasbourg school. The exhibition is supplemented by a wide range of other paintings, woodcuts, copperplate engravings and drawings produced in the same general period and region, together with documents, arms and armour.

May 96–Jun 96	*Jerry Zenink*
14·06·96–28·07·96	*Watercolour Masterpieces 1800-1850* Selected works from the Karlsruhe Kupferstichkabinett.
11·10·96–mid Feb 97	*Moritz von Schwind* Paintings, Drawings, Graphics
11·10·96–mid 1997	*Fairy Tale Games*

Kassel

MUSEUM FRIDERICIANUM KASSEL
Friedrichsplatz 18 34117 Kassel Director: Veit Loers
☎ +49 561 7072720 📠 +49 561 774578
Open: Tuesday-Sunday 10.00-17.00 Thursday 10.00-20.00
Closed: Monday

COLLECTION No permanent collection.

*P.P. Rubens
(1577-1640)
The triumph of the
Victor, c. 1614*

*Collection Staatliche
Museen Kassel,
Schloss
Wilhelmshöhe*

EXHIBITIONS

Until Nov 96 *120 Masterworks Highlights of a Princely Collection of Renaissance and Baroque paintings* The exhibition includes works by such artists as Dürer, Jordaens, Poussin, Rubens, Rembrandt, Cranach, Titian, etc.

04·02·96–05·05·96 *Collaborations Warhol/Basquiat/Clemente* An exhibition of the collaborative efforts of Andy Warhol, Jean-Michel Basquiat and Francesco Clemente, dating from the early 80s. On public display for the first time, the exhibition consists of 45 collaborations between Warhol and Basquiat, and 10 collaborations between Warhol, Basquiat and Clemente.

Kassel

GEMÄLDEGALERIE ALTE MEISTER
Schloß Wilhelmshöhe 34131 Kassel Director: Hans Ottomeyer
☎ +49 561 93777 📠 +49 561 315873
Closed: Closed for renovation

Kiel

KUNSTHALLE ZU KIEL
Düsternbrooker Weg 1 24105 Kiel Director: Hans-Werner Schmidt
☎ +49 431 5973751 📠 +49 431 5973754
Open: Tuesday-Sunday 10.30-18.00 Wednesday 10.30-20.00
Closed: Monday

COLLECTION

A collection of Schleswig-Holstein art from the 17th to the 20th century is represented by artists such as Ovens, Blunck, Jessen, Wrage, Feddersen and Olde. The 19th and early 20th- century gallery features works by Kersting, Dahl, Schwind, Feuerbach, Rodin, Rohlfs, Krøyer, Trübner, Liebermann, Corinth and Slevogt, and especially by the Russian painters (Aiwasoffski, Kramskoi, Lewitan, Repin, Schischkin and others).

The collection possesses fine examples of German Expressionism including paintings by Emil Nolde, sculptures by Ernst Barlach and works of the 'Brücke' artists Kirchner, Heckel, Schmidt-Rottluff and Pechstein, as well as works representative of New Objectivity and Magical Realism. Current acquisitions focus on art produced since 1945, such as works of the Informel, COBRA and SPUR groups, Constructive Art, and works exhibiting realistic tendencies. The gallery contains important paintings, sculptures and objects by contemporary artists such as Richter, Paik, Kubota, Ruthenbeck, Kirkeby, Baselitz and Knoebel.

The graphic collection includes more than 30 000 drawings, watercolours and prints from the 16th century to the 20th century, primarily by Dutch, German, Italian and French artists, and international contemporary graphic artworks

EXHIBITIONS

25·04·96-16·06·96   ***Karl Schmidt-Rottluff***   Brush drawings in black ink from the Brücke-Museum Berlin

05·05·96-16·06·96   ***Ekkekard Thieme***   Prints

02·06·96-18·08·96   ***'Ente Gut - Alles Gut'***   The inventors of the Disney cosmos: Carl Barks - Al Taliaferro - Floyd Gottfredson

23·06·96-18·08·96   ***'Doppelt Haut - Double Skin'***

23·06·96-18·08·96   ***Tattoo***   *Pictures which get under the Skin*

25·08·96-13·10·96   ***Gustav Kluge***   Watercolours and sculptures.

24·10·96-01·12·96   ***Jan Voss***   Retrospective

08·12·96-26·01·97   ***43rd Exhibition of the Schleswig-Holstein Artists Association***

Feb 97-Mar 97   ***Martin Assig***

Köln - Cologne

MUSEUM FÜR ANGEWANDTE KUNST / MUSEUM OF APPLIED ARTS
An der Rechtschule 50667 Köln Director: Brigitte Tietzel
☎ **+49 221 2213860 📠 +49 221 2213885**
Open: Tuesday-Friday 11.00-17.00 Saturday, Sunday 12.00-17.00
Closed: Monday

COLLECTION

The Museum of Applied Arts is one of the four major museums for arts and crafts in Germany. The items on display include fashions and jewellery, as well as objects of everyday use.

The full range of applied arts from the last 1000 years is on display on three floors, starting with contemporary design, moving back through the 60s and 50s to the Art Deco of the 30s and 40s and on to the Bauhaus and Werkbund styles. Specific aspects are shown in separate departments, e.g. the fashion collection, modern ceramics, textiles, furniture, sculpture, weapons, metals, as well as ceramic and glass art. There is also a graphic collection.

EXHIBITIONS
until 14·07·96

Art on Billboards *Posters from the Collection of the Cologne Museum of Applied Arts* This exhibition will present 200 of the best post-war German posters from the museum's collection. The exhibition includes posters by Pablo Picasso, Max Bill, Joseph Beuys, Robert Rauschenberg and Sigmar Polke. The interface between contemporary art and poster design manifests itself especially in the numerous drafts by poster designers such as Almir Mavignier, Robert Indiana or Willem Sandberg.

Breast ornament with the portraits of Czar Alexander II and Czar Alexander III
Russia, 2nd half of 19th century

From the collection Historical Museum, Moscow

23·08·96–08·12·96

Magnificent Empire of the Czars 1613-1917 *A Dynasty Looks to the West* The robes of Peter the Great and Catherine the Great, the diary of the last Czarina, the treasures of the court jeweller Fabergé, as well as the pearl-embroidered bonnets and robes of the rich merchants' wives are just some of the objects to be presented in this exhibition. The exhibition will illustrate the development of Russia from its political and cultural opening to the West, especially to Germany, up to the development of a Slavic, nationalist counter-movement. More than 500 applied art objects from the State Historical Museum in Moscow, including paintings, works on paper and documents, are included in this show.

Köln · Cologne

JOSEF-HAUBRICH-KUNSTHALLE
Josef-Haubrich-Hof 50676 Köln Director: Mia M. Storch
☎ +49 221 2212335 📠 +49 221 2214552
Open: Tuesday-Sunday 10.00-17.00 during exhibitions
Closed: Monday

COLLECTION   No permanent collection.

EXHIBITIONS
24·04·96–16·06·96

Ernst Wille *Paintings* Ernst Wille, born 1916 in Herne/Westphalia, has become one of the most prominent artists living and working in Cologne. During his years on the faculty at the 'Werkkunstschule' in Aachen, Wille developed a personal theory of colour, based on the materiality of colours used by artists. The exhibition in the Josef-Haubrich-Kunsthalle will present a retrospective of Ernst Wille's paintings from the later 1940s through to the early 90s, from his early figurative paintings to the abstract canvasses of his present work.

Oct 96–Dec 96

Star Trek *The Exhibition* 'Star Trek, The Exhibition' presents the entire history of the 'Starship Enterprise' and its crew, from the first episode of the famous television series right up to the most recent film 'Generations'. The exhibition includes a reconstructed deck of the Starship, original costumes, photographic documentation, video clips and models - all on loan from Paramount Studios.

early 1997

The Power of Women and the Supremacy of Man   *A Cross-Cultural Comparison of Gender Relationships*   This new exhibition presents the various forms of gender relationships found in ethnography, history and archaeology, as well as those found in European and non-European art. The exhibition examines the way in which gender roles are determined by history and culture, and how roles may change in the present and future.

Köln - Cologne

MUSEUM LUDWIG
Bischofsgartenstraße 1 50667 Köln Director: Marc Scheps
☎ **+49 221 2213491 ▥ +49 221 2214114**
Open: Tuesday-Friday 10.00-18.00 Saturday, Sunday 11.00-18.00
Closed: Monday

COLLECTION

Cologne's most recent museum contains works of art of the 20th century. It includes paintings and sculptures, found objects and 'environments', a collection of graphic art, as well as one of the largest sections of photography of Germany.

The collection, which initially consisted of key works of German Expressionism, was considerably enlarged in the 50s and 60s, thus forming the basis of the Modern Section of the 'Wallraf-Richartz' Museum.

More than 300 objects d'art of the Ludwig Collection were handed over to the municipality in 1976 under the name Ludwig Donation. As a result of the opening of the new museum, Cologne now has a complete survey of modern art at its disposal, a great part of which has been devoted to contemporary artists. Cubism, the works of the 'Brücke' and of Expressionism, Italian Futurism and Russian Avant-Garde illustrate the beginning of the 20th century with excellent examples.

Ernst Ludwig
Kirchner
*Female semi-nude
with hat*

*Museum Ludwig,
Köln*

European art of the 20s is present in works of Pittura Metafisica, Bauhaus, Constructivism, New Objectivity and Surrealism. The evolution of the works of Picasso over six decades can be followed. New Realism and British and American Pop-Art form the strong features of the museum. The flowering of German art from the end of the 60s up to the present day is amply documented. Other important expressions of art, situated between Minimal Art, Colour Field Painting and Individual Mythology complete the portrait of the last two decades.

EXHIBITIONS
01·06·96–25·08·96

The Expressionists   This ambitious exhibition presents work of artists from 'Die Brücke' and 'Der Blaue Reiter' movements, as well as many individual artists. In addition, lesser known aspects of the Expressionist movement will be investigated, and attention will be devoted to Nazi actions taken against German Expressionists. Important loans from European and American museums and private collections will be complemented by Expressionist masterpieces from the collection of the Museum Ludwig.

06·09·96–17·11·96

Benjamin Katz   *Living with Artists*   Photographer Benjamin Katz has been a keen and respected observer of the Cologne art scene for the last 20 years. The artistic quality of his simultaneously intense and sensitive photographs has found increasing recognition. He has visited artists in their studios and also documented numerous exhibitions and events throughout Germany.

18·09·96–17·11·96

The Speck Collection   *Seeing - Reading - Writing*   Dr Reiner Speck is one of the world's most renowned art collectors. His collection includes works by some of the most important artists of the second half of the 20th century. Reiner Speck's collection revolves around a number of themes and concepts ranging from those found in Arte Povera, Minimal and Conceptual Art, to the most recent trends of contemporary art, including such artists as Dan Asher, Walter Daho, Günther Förg, Georg Herold, Raymond Pettibon, Thomas Schütte and Rosemarie Trockel.

Köln - Cologne

MUSEUM FÜR OSTASIATISCHE KUNST MUSEUM OF EAST ASIAN ART
Universitätsstraße 100 50674 Köln Director: Adele Schlombs
☎ +49 221 9405180 📠 +49 221 407290
Open: Tuesday-Friday 10.00-16.00 Saturday, Sunday 11.00-16.00
Closed: Monday

COLLECTION

Germany's oldest museum of Far Eastern Art was moved to a modern building in 1977 by Kunio Mayekawa (1905-86), a student of Le Corbusier. The Japanese garden within the premises was designed by the contemporary artist Masayuki Nagare (born 1923).

The museum displays works of Chinese, Japanese and Korean art, from the Neolithic period to modern times. The Chinese ritual bronzes of the Shang dynasty (13th-11th century B.C.) are as renowned as the museum's vast collection of Buddhist art consisting of exquisitely sculpted stone, wood and lacquer images, delicately painted cult images and powerful Zen-related impressions of human beings and nature.

The collection of Chinese ceramics is especially well represented in the celadon range. The three-coloured tomb figurines together with other vessels are fine examples porcelain from the Tang dynasty (610-907) and later. The collection of Korean ceramics is one of the best in continental Europe. Chinese literati paintings, decorative hanging scrolls and folding screens from Japan as well as the profane, colourful Ukiyo-e prints introduce the visitor to the everyday life of times long past. New on display are early Chinese Buddhist and Daoist sculptures (8th-12th century) and the collection of Chinese furniture.

20·03·96-30·06·96	*Cultivation of Rice and Production of Silk in Chinese Painting and Graphic Arts*
23·04·96-21·07·96	*The World of the Samurais*
25·04·96-30·06·96	*Depiction of a Literary Scholar in Chinese and Japanese Art*
25·04·96-30·06·96	*Korean Ceramic Art by Young-Jae-Lee 1975-1995*
19·10·96-15·01·97	*20th-Century Chinese Painting Tradition and Innovation*

Köln - Cologne

RAUTENSTRAUCH-JOEST-MUSEUM MUSEUM OF ETHNOLOGY
Ubierring 45 50678 Köln Director: Gisela Völger
☎ +49 221 33694130 📠 +49 221 3369410
Open: Tuesday-Friday 10.00-16.00 Saturday, Sunday 11.00-16.00
Closed: Monday

COLLECTION

The museum collection includes approximately 65 000 objects from Melanesia, Polynesia, Micronesia and Australia, Africa south of the Sahara, Ancient Egypt, Southeast Asia, and North and South America. Additional highlights of the collection include textiles and documents from the Ottoman Empire. The collections are complemented by an important historical photographic archive and an excellent reference library. A primary focus of the museum's work is the scientific research of its collection. With its exhibitions, special programmes and publications, all stressing cross-cultural comparisons, the museum also fosters understanding and respect for 'foreign', non-European cultures and lifestyles. The concept for the new building now in the planning stage envisions the museum even more as a meeting place between members of the various cultures that are a vital presence in and around the city of Cologne.

*Idol from the
South Seas*
Nukuoro, before
1830

*Rautenstrauch-Joest-
Museum, Köln*

EXHIBITION
26·04·96–28·01·97

The Coconut Palm   A Tree with a thousand possibilities   The coconut palm is considered by many to be the best example of perfect ecological use. From the roots to the very top of the tree, it provides people living in the tropics with a great variety of products. Frequently, it forms the basis of nourishment. Coconut products have also been an object of trade with Europe for over 100 years. At present, the coconut palm is of special interest because, in discussions regarding environmentally responsible development, it represents a paradigm for the development and exploitation of a renewable resource. With several hundred objects, the many uses of the coconut palm, both traditional and newly developed, will be presented.

Köln - Cologne

RÖMISCH-GERMANISCHES MUSEUM
Roncalliplatz 4 50667 Köln Director: Hansgerd Hellenkemper
☎ +49 221 2214090 📠 +49 221 2214030
Open: Tuesday-Friday 10.00-16.00 Saturday, Sunday 11.00-16.00
Closed: Monday

COLLECTION

The Romano-Germanic Museum in Cologne is built upon the remains of a Roman civic villa and the medieval Imperial Palace, and includes a world famous floor mosaic, preserved on its original site, that has been incorporated into the museum's exhibition rooms. The archaelogical heritage of the city is on display, ranging from the prehistoric to the medieval, with documentation of ancient Roman Cologne of particular note. There are also displays from the Stone Age, the Bronze Age and the Iron Age, tracing history from 100 000 B.C. up to the 1st century B.C., and including clay vessels of superb quality, finds from the graves of free Germanic tribes from the time of the Roman Empire, and artefacts revealing traces of Frankish settlement in Cologne. Exhibits focusing on Roman times include mosaics and wall decorations, jewellery and ceramics. There are also exhibits of everyday life in Roman times.

EXHIBITIONS

04·06·96–27·10·96

Tu Felix Agrippina   To celebrate its 50th anniversary, the museum presents portraits of the founder of the Roman city of Cologne, the Empress Agrippina the Younger, and her imperial relatives of the iulo-claudian dynasty in outstanding examples originating primarily from Italian museums.

Jul 96–Oct 96

Roman Silver   Recent donations and purchases representing five centuries of antique silversmiths' craft.

Köln - Cologne

WALLRAF-RICHARTZ-MUSEUM
Bischofsgartenstraße 1 50667 Köln Director: Rainer Budde
☎ +49 221 2212372 📠 +49 221 2212629
Open: Tuesday-Friday 10.00-18.00 Saturday, Sunday 11.00-18.00
Closed: Monday

COLLECTION

The Wallraf-Richartz Museum is one of Germany's oldest museum foundations. The picture gallery is renowned for its three major collections.
Medieval Art   The Medieval department houses a unique range of panel paintings from the Cologne School and works from other regions. Together they provide an almost unbroken survey of panel painting from 1300 to 1550. The collection is augmented by a group of free-standing altar pieces. Later Gothic traditions and the new approaches of the early 16th century are seen emerging in numerous Dutch panel paintings and works by Old German Masters such as Dürer.

16th to 18th century   The museum's extensive collection of 16th to 18th-century Dutch and Flemish paintings include some of the best works of the Golden Age of the 17th century. The Rubens collection is especially fine and the Rembrandt self-portrait represents a high point in his late work. Great examples of Mediterranean art are also on display, including works by the Italian Paris Bordone, the French artist Claude Gellée and the great Spanish artists of the early Golden Age.

19th century The comprehensive 19th-century collection opens with Romantic and Realist paintings and one of Germanies finest Leibel collections. German Impressionism is represented by Liebermann and Slevogt. The French paintings include works by the Realist Courbet, Renoir (the early portrait of the Sisleys), Monet, Sisley, Degas, Manet and Cézanne. The collection is completed by Symbolist paintings by Ensor and Munch, together with works by Van Gogh, Gauguin and Bonnard that take us beyond Impressionism towards the art of our own century.

EXHIBITIONS

23·02·96–05·05·96 | *The Play of Colour* Armand Guillaumin (1841-1927)
A forgotten Impressionist.

10·12·96–end Feb 97 | *Capriccio as Artistic Principle* An exhibition reaching from Leonardo through Turner, illuminating the roots of the Modern in the 18th century.

Jan 97–end Mar 97 | *Tiepolo* Drawings

end Mar 97–
end Jun 97 | *Barthel Bruyn the Elder*

Leipzig

MUSEUM DER BILDENDEN KÜNSTE LEIPZIG MUSEUM OF FINE ARTS
Dimitroffplatz 1 04107 Leipzig Director: Herwig Guratzsch
☎ **+49 341 2169920** 🖷 **+49 341 286529**
Open: Tuesday and Thursday-Sunday 09.00-17.00 Wednesday 13.00-21.30
Closed: Monday

COLLECTION | The museum's total holdings number 2 700 paintings from the late Middle- Ages to the present, 750 sculptures and more than 55 000 drawings and prints.
The permanent display includes Old German and Early Dutch and Flemish masterpieces, such as the renowned 'Liebeszauber' (Love Spell) by a Lower Rhine master from the late 15th century, paintings by Rogier van der Weyden, Lucas Cranach the Elder and Hans Baldung Grien, and outstanding Dutch 17th-century paintings by Frans Hals, Jan van Goyen and many others.

The museum's representative collection of German painting from the 20th century includes works by Anton Graff, Caspar David Friedrich, Wilhelm Leibl, Arnold Böcklin, Max Liebermann, Lovis Corinth, Max Klinger, Oskar Kokoschka and Max Beckmann.
The graphic collection bears witness to the development of the graphic arts in Europe from the early days to the present. Highlights of the collection include works by Martin Schongauer and Lucas Cranach the Elder, as well as Italian Baroque drawings by Gianlorenzo Bernini and Salvator Rosa. There is also an unusually wide representation of Dutch 19th-century drawings.

EXHIBITIONS

29·03·96–27·05·96 | *Hartwig Ebersbach* Paintings, Sculptures, Installations
Approximately 130 works of art from this abstract artist (born in Zwickau in 1940), one of the most renowned of those working artists originating from the former East Germany.

31·07·96-15·09·96	**Karl Schmidt-Rotluff** Marking the 20th anniversary of Schmidt-Rotluff's death (1884-1976), this exhibition displays 130 drawings with wash, most of them from the estate of the artist (now in the Brücke-Museum, Berlin, from which this exhibition is on loan) which have not been previously shown to the public. The works date from 1906 to 1968.
14·08·96-29·09·96	**Picasso** *Lithographs* This exhibition shows 150 lithographs from a private German collection dating from 1945 to 1960.
18·12·96-16·02·97	**Otto Mueller** This exhibition groups some 10 paintings, 10 drawings and 40 prints (woodcuts and lithographs) around the 'Liebespaar' painting by Mueller.

Leverkusen

STÄDTISCHES MUSEUM LEVERKUSEN SCHLOß MORSBROICH
Gustav-Heinemann-Straße 80 51377 Leverkusen Director: Rolf Wedewer
☎ +49 214 56007 📠 +49 214 56000
Open: Tuesday 11.00-21.00 Wednesday-Sunday 11.00-17.00
Closed: Monday

COLLECTION

This Late Baroque castle has been home to a museum for contemporary art since 1941. The sculpture park with its old trees is an extra point of interest to visitors from home and abroad.
The international collection of the museum consists of approximately 300 paintings, sculptures and objects, as well as about 3 000 works on paper. All main post-war styles are represented.
Besides regular display of all collections, between eight and twelve temporary exhibitions are held every year. These present internationally renowned artists or illuminate cultural-historical connections on the basis of various themes.

Städt. Museum Leverkusen, Schloss Morsbroich

EXHIBITIONS

17·03·96-02·06·96	**Rudolf Schoofs** *Work from the Walter Collection.*
24·03·96-02·06·96	**Maria Lassnig** *Drawings and Watercolours 1946-1995*
15·06·96-06·10·96	**Works from the Graphics Collection**
23·06·96-01·09·96	**Mic Enneper** *The Arsenal 1987-1996*
27·10·96-05·01·97	**Gregor-Torsten Kozik** *Drawings and Woodcuts*

Workshop for copperplate engraving and intaglio, copperplate print
Augsburg, 1621

Gutenberg-Museum Mainz

In the mezzanine, an exhibition explains how books were made before Gutenberg invented his printing process, what his process entails and what the impact of his invention was. The final exhibit in the mezzanine traces the development of bookbinding.

The second floor exhibition traces the history of writing and early alphabets. The East Asian collection of polychrome woodcuts and examples of printing reveals that printing with separate blocks for separate characters was used in Asia before Gutenberg. The works of William Morris displayed in the Art Nouveau section had an enormous influence on the development of book printing in the late 19th and early 20th century. The rest of this section is devoted to Art Nouveau book art from England and Germany, book plates (ex-libris) and early 20th-century posters.

The mezzanine above this section contains the book art of the 20th century, a history of paper, artist's books, children's books, paper theatres, and a selection of the most beautiful German books of the year.

EXHIBITIONS

16·04·96–30·06·96   *The Ideal Book*   *William Morris and the Kelmscott-Chaucer of 1896*

19·04·96–30·06·96   *The Poet Arrabal and his Illustrators*

Jul 96–Sep 96   *Mechtild Lobisch*   *Contemporary Bookbinding*

Oct 96–Dec 96   *Bülent Erkmen*   *Graphic Design by a Turkish Artist*   The exhibition includes posters, book designs and logotypes.

Mainz

LANDESMUSEUM MAINZ
Große Bleiche 49-51   55116 Mainz   Director: Gisela Fiedler-Bender
☎ +49 6131 28570   📠 +49 6131 285757
Open: Tuesday 10.00-20.00   Wednesday-Sunday 10.00-17.00
Closed: Monday

COLLECTION   The diverse collection of the Landesmuseum Mainz ranges from objects showing the existence of human habitation in the Mainz area as far back as 300 000 B.C., to artworks from the 1990s. Objects demonstrating Roman influence along the Rhine are on display, as are objects in the Prince Johann Georg Collection from Rome, Greece and Egypt. There are works from the early Middle Ages (450-900 A.D.) and both religious and secular works from the 14th and 15th centuries. The museum possesses a variety of Renaissance and Baroque works by German, French and Italian painters and sculptors, and 17th-century Dutch masterpieces by P. Brueghel the Elder, J. Jordaens, J. van Goyen and S. van Ruysdael. Porcelain and pottery from factories in Mainz and elsewhere in Germany are also on display. The 19th and 20th-century collection includes significant Art Nouveau (Jugendstil) objects produced in France, Germany, Austria and Bohemia. There is also a vast collection of watercolours, drawings and prints, and a notable collection of Judaica. The history of the city of Mainz is chronicled in exhibits which include models, pictures, coins, medals, documents and tools, as well as photographs from both before and after the Second World War.

EXHIBITIONS

28·04·96–09·06·96 | ***History of Gravel***   A large number of Roman objects, discovered in a former bed of the Rhine River near Xanten.

02·05·96–09·06·96 | ***Heike Kern***   *Luck in the Angle*   Plastic works from mixed media.

30·06·96–01·09·96 | ***Media-Museum/Cultural Summer 1996***   Fabrizio Plessi, video installation; Experiment Landesmuseum, with a variety of works by young artists.

10·07·96–01·09·96 | ***Erwin Wortelkamp***   Works on paper (1963-1996) and sculptures.

22·09·96–27·10·96 | ***Sinje Dillenkofer***   *Photo Objects*   Winner of the Paul-Strecker Prize for 1995.

24·09·96–27·10·96 | ***Käthe Kollwitz***   Graphic works from the collection of the Landesmuseum Mainz.

Mannheim

REIß-MUSEUM
Zeughaus C5 68159 Mannheim Director: Karin von Welck
☎ **+49 621 2933150/51** 📠 **+49 621 2933099**
Open: Tuesday-Sunday 10.00-17.00 Thursday 12.00-17.00
Closed: Monday

COLLECTION | ***Museum for Archaeology and Ethnology***   The archaeological collections comprise objects from the Stone Age up to modern times, the highlights being Roman tombstones and finds dating from the Ancient Greek and Roman epochs.
The ethnological collections are particularly known for their African and Asian exhibits. Among the most attractive sights are the reconstruction of a Tuareg tent, the famous Begin collection and a Japanese tea house, where tea ceremonies are performed occasionally.
Museum for Art, City and Theatre History   Well-known are the porcelain, faience and furniture collections. The local history section shows the development of the city of Mannheim through four centuries. Numerous exhibits like prints, maps, town models or early bicycles such as the Draisine give a good impression of how people lived in Mannheim. The permanent exhibition 'Religion, the Court and the Bourgeoisie - Mannheim in the 18th century' gives a good insight into life at the court of the Elector Palatine.
Based on the important archives of the Mannheim National Theatre, the theatre collection documents the history of the theatre in Mannheim. Among its greatest treasures are a set model dating

from the time of the theatrical manager Dalberg and its library with the promptbook for the original performance of Schiller's 'Robbers'.
Museum for Natural History The beginnings of the Natural History collections go back to the time of the Elector Palatine Karl Theodor and his famous 'Naturalienkabinett'.
The permanent exhibition 'Life in the Ice Age' gives a good idea of life in that important period of the history of life on our planet.

EXHIBITIONS

15·02·96-02·07·96

Zemann Portraits In the 1960s Hilde Zemann worked at the National Theater in Mannheim as a photographer, creating many fine scenographic photos. This exhibition, however, shows her black-and-white portaits of actors. With her subtle and sympathetic approach in the studio she is able to get behind the mask of the often camera-shy performers, revealing the underlying personality in a respectful way.

20·07·96-06·10·96

The Children of Bombay *Photos by Dario Mitidiere* In 1992 the photographer spent a year working with the street childen of Bombay. His images are a tribute to the courage of the children and a testimony to the paradoxes of their existence.

08·09·96-06·01·97

The Franks *The Pioneers of Europe* During the final phase of the Roman Empire the Franks became familiar with the Roman state structure and later inherited much of it after Roman power crumbled. As a Germanic people in a Christian-Roman environment, the Franks form a major link between the classical and medieval periods, preparing the ground for Europe. The exhibition documents the growth of Frankish culture under the Merowingian dynasty and portrays the lives of the Franks, ranging from royalty to serfs.

Mönchengladbach

SCHLOß RHEYDT
Schloßstraße 508 41238 Mönchengladbach Director: Carsten Sternberg
☎ **+49 2166 928900** 📠 **+49 2166 9289049**
Open: Tuesday-Saturday 14.00-20.00 Sunday 11.00-20.00
Closed: Monday

COLLECTION

Schloss Rheydt is a castle originally dating back to the 12th century, which houses the municipal museum of the town of Mönchengladbach in North Rhine-Westphalia. Parts of the current structure date back to the 15th century. Extensive restorations have been undertaken in recent years and today the manor house, with some of the original furnishings, as well as the grounds, the gatehouse, the keep, the ramparts and bastions are integral parts of the museum. The museum has an extensive collection pertaining to local history, with some objects dating back to Roman and prehistoric times. It has also built a collection devoted to the arts and decorative crafts of the Renaissance and installed displays depicting the technological history of the area, which has been a major centre for the manufacture of textiles.
The municipal history department has organised the displays at the Schloss Rheydt according to several basic themes: history of settlement, tracing the history of the community; personalities, focusing on the men and women of the community who have distinguished themselves; visual artists of Mönchengladbach; and industrial and social development, focusing especially on 19th and 20th-century developments and including 5 looms in working order. In the cellar vaults of the manor house there is a display devoted to the architectural history of Schloss Rheydt. The bastion, which is currently being renovated, will house archaeological displays when the work is completed.

EXHIBITIONS

17·03·96-26·05·96	**'Spitzenkräfte'** Pillow-lace work from Upper Franconia.
21·03·96-28·07·96	**The Four Seasons**
28·04·96-28·07·96	**Werner Labbé** A Rheydt artist in southern light.
18·07·96-22·09·96	**The Neuenhofer Collection** An exhibition of glasswork.
11·08·96-29·12·96	**Hans Rilke** An exhibition on the 50th anniversary of the death of the Rheydt painter.

Mönchengladbach

STÄDTISCHES MUSEUM ABTEIBERG
Abteistraße 27 41061 Mönchengladbach
☎ +49 2161 252631 📠 +49 2161 252659
Open: Tuesday-Sunday 10.00-18.00
Closed: Monday

COLLECTION

The museum was founded in 1904; in 1922 a donation from Walter Kaesbach transformed it into a collection of contemporary art based on German Expressionism. In 1982 the new building by the architect Hans Hollein was opened. Nowadays it is chiefly a collection of international contemporary art from 1960 up to the present. The specialisations include Pop Art, Minimal Art, Concrete Art and Radical Painting. Works by Joseph Beuys, Marcel Broodthaers, Ulrich Rückriem, Richard Serra, Gerhard Richter, Sigmar Polke, Lawrence Weiner, Palermo, Dorothee von Windheim, Günter Umberg, Joseph Marioni, Roni Horn etc. are on display. The collection includes a large number of site-specific works and installations.
The museum also owns a 20th-century collection of prints and drawings.

EXHIBITIONS

12·05·96-15·09·96	**Paul Bradley** The British artist Paul Bradley exhibits a site-specific installation which is partly an autonomous sculpture and partly a functional object as it might be used in a game. Radical reduction of means, subtle humour and social criticism are combined in a very strong and ambivalent work of art.
06·10·96-07·01·97	**Gundi Berghold** Austrian-born Gundi Berghold has her first solo exhibition in a museum. Iron video sculptures will be arranged to form a site-specific ensemble.
Nov 96-Dec 96	**Liligant (Restauraxion)** *Cosima von Bonin, Kai Althoff, Tobias Rehberger* This exhibition of three young German artists will first be shown in the Museum of Contemporary Art, Sao Paulo. Personal memories, individual associations, fiction and utopia are combined in different kinds of works.

München - Munich

ALTE PINAKOTHEK
Barer Straße 27 80799 München Director: J.G. Prinz Von Hohenzollern
☎ +49 89 23805215 📠 +49 89 23805221
Closed for renovations between 1994 and 1997

COLLECTION

Old Masters   The Alte Pinakothek is one of the largest and most beautiful painting galleries in the world. It was commissioned by King Ludwig I, designed by the architect Leo von Klenze and built between 1826 and 1836. The collection unites previous galleries of various branches of the Wittelsbach family. King Ludwig added a considerable collection of Old German, Old Dutch and Italian paintings, which form the most important sections of the gallery, together with the Flemish, Dutch and French Baroque paintings. The 'Four Evangelists' by Dürer, the Columba Altar by Rogier van der Weyden, Raphael's 'Holy Family Canigiani', 60 paintings by Rubens and numerous pictures by Rembrandt, as well as excellent work from Poussin and Lorrain are part of the 800 paintings on permanent display.

Dürer, Albrecht
The four Apostles

Alte Pinakothek,
München

The Alte Pinakothek and Neue Pinakothek, the State Gallery of Modern Art, the Schack Gallery and its 15 branches throughout Bavaria are all part of the Bavarian National Painting Collection. Between 1994 and 1997 the Alte Pinakothek will be closed due to renovations. During that period 300 of the masterpieces will be exhibited at the Neue Pinakothek.

EXHIBITIONS

No exhibitions planned.

München - Munich

STAATLICHE ANTIKENSAMMLUNGEN UND GLYPTOTHEK
Königsplatz München Director: Raimund Wünsche
☎ +49 89 598359 (Antikensammlungen) +49 89 286100 (Glyptothek)
📠 +49 89 5503851
Open: Antikensammlungen: Tuesday-Sunday 10.00-16.30
Wednesday 12.00-20.30
Glyptothek: Tuesday-Sunday 10.00-16.30 Thursday 12.00-20.30
Closed: Monday

At the start of the 19th century, King Ludwig I of Bavaria had the Königsplatz built in imitation of ancient Athens. The 'Propyläen', which form the entrance to the 'King's Place', also serve as a huge town gate. Two monumental buildings, the Antikensammlungen (Collections of Antiquities) and the Glyptothek, each resembling a Classical temple, stand on either side of the lawn-covered public square.

[Antikensammlungen]

COLLECTION

In building the Antikensammlungen, the architect Georg Friedrich Ziebland was inspired by Roman podium temples. The museum's monumental façade forms the south front of the classical Königsplatz. The museum posses a collection of antiquities ranging from the 14th century B.C. to the 4th century A.D.

In the collection are painted Attic black and red-figured vases by some of the best practioners of this art, including Exekias, Andokides and Euphronios. Among these works is the famous cup depicting Dionysos, the god of wine and ecstasy, making a voyage across the sea. Another vase depicts the poetess Sappho, celebrated for her love poems.
There is also an outstanding collection of terracotta statuettes from Tanagra and Myrina. The colourfully painted figurines, showing the beauty and elegance of Greek women, offer a glimpse of everyday life in ancient times.

The basement houses the collection of goldsmiths' work, including a Hellenistic burial wreath from Armento and a superb diadem of a Greek lady from the Black Sea. These pieces and others reveal another aspect of the artistry of ancient times. The collection of Roman silverware provides evidence of the high standard of metalworking as well as the luxurious lifestyle of the time.

On the upper floor of the museum, the world of the Etruscans, known best through their graves, is presented. A carriage found at Castel San Mariano, used by an Etruscan lady for her wedding and then for her last journey, is on display in the staircase. The function of many other object remains a mystery, however.

EXHIBITIONS   No details available.

[Glyptothek]

COLLECTION   The Glyptothek was built as a museum between 1816 and 1830 by the renowned architect Leo von Klenze. The museum houses a collection of antique sculpture, covering all periods of ancient Greece and Rome.
The 'Munich Kouros' and the 'Apollo of Tenea' are fine examples of the Archaic period. Other highlights of the collection are the two groups of figures originating from the pediments of the Temple of Aphaia on the Greek island of Aegina. They were discovered by British and German scholars in 1811. The sculptures date from around 500 B.C. and were made of marble from the island of Paros. Each group represents a battle between Greek and Trojan heroes. Also on display are works by Classical Greek artists such as Polycletes' 'Diadumenos' and the 'Eirene' of Kephisodot. There are busts of Plato, Euripides and Homer, and a collection of portraits representing famous Roman emperors and citizens.

EXHIBITIONS   No details available.

München - Munich

HAUS DER KUNST
Prinzregentenstraße 1 80538 München Director: Christoph Vitali
☎ +49 89 211270 📠 +49 89 21127157
Open: Tuesday-Friday 10.00-22.00 Saturday-Monday 10.00-18.00

COLLECTION   No permanent collection.

EXHIBITIONS
03·05·96-21·07·96   ***Lovis Corinth***   *Retrospective*

10·05·96-04·08·96   ***The Russian Avant-Garde***   *The Costakis Collection, Athens and the Tretyakov Gallery, Moscow*

24·05·96-28·07·96   ***Umbo***   *From Bauhaus to Photo-Journalism*   *An overview of the work of the Bauhaus photographer.*

23·08·96-20·10·96	*Imi Knoebel* Work Overview
03·11·96-26·01·97	*Francis Bacon* Retrospective
15·11·96-26·01·97	*BLAST* Ezra Pound and the Artists of the English Avant-Garde

München · Munich

KUNSTHALLE DER HYPO-KULTURSTIFTUNG
Theatinerstraße 15 80333 München Director: Peter A. Ade
☎ +49 89 224412 📠 +49 89 29160981
Open: Daily 10.00-18.00 Thursday 10.00-21.00

COLLECTION No permanent collection.

EXHIBITIONS

22·03·96–16·06·96	*Christian Rohlfs* A Retrospective This retrospective of Christian Rohlfs (1849-1938) displays about 120 paintings and 30 drawings.
05·07·96–15·09·96	*American Art after 1960* The collection of Ileana and Michael Sonnabend The Sonnabend collection encompasses the most important artistic directions after 1960. The exhibition includes work by Cy Twombly, Jasper Johns, Robert Rauschenberg, Andy Warhol, Richard Serra, Bruce Nauman and Roy Lichtenstein, among others.
04·10·96–06·01·97	*Kingdoms along the River Nile* Treasures of Ancient Sudan 200 works on loan from museums in Boston, Khartoum, Berlin, Leipzig, Munich, London and several collections.

München · Munich

STÄDTISCHE GALERIE IM LENBACHHAUS · KUNSTBAU LENBACHHAUS
Luisenstraße 33 80333 München Director: Helmut Friedel
☎ +49 89 2332000 📠 +49 89 23332003
Open: Tuesday-Sunday 10.00-18.00 Kunstbau: Tuesday-Sunday 10.00-20.00
Closed: Monday

COLLECTION At the peak of his career, the highly successful portrait painter Franz von Lenbach (1836-1904) commissioned the architect Gabriel von Seidl to construct his residence in Munich. This architectural 'Gesamtkunstwerk' was later purchased by the City of Munich, which opened the Städtische Galerie im Lenbachhaus to the public in 1929. The original collection featured works by artists of the 19th and early 20th-century Munich school.

Lenbachhaus
München

This collection has since been expanded and presently includes works by Jawlensky, Kandinsky, Klee, Macke, Marc, Münter and others who worked in Munich before the First World War. The Alfred Kubin archive was purchased from the Hamburg collector Kurt Otte.

In recent years the museum has acquired contemporary works of art, including works by Arakawa, Joseph Beuys, Oyvind Fahlström, Michael Heizer, Asger Jorn, Anselm Kiefer, Hermann Nitsch, A.R. Penck, Sigmar Polke, Arnulf Rainer, Sean Scully and the artists' group Spur.

The Lenbachhaus restructured its exhibition activities with the opening of the Kunstbau in 1994. This new gallery, located 100 metres from the Lenbachhaus, has already proven its value as a flexible space for widely differing concepts of art.

EXHIBITIONS

[Lenbachhaus]

27·03·96–09·06·96 **Serial Structures** A selection from the museum's permanent collection including works by Arnulf Rainer, Hanne Darboven, Anna and Bernhard Johannes Blume and Jürgen Klauke.

26·06·96–08·09·96 **Mel Bochner** *Thought made Visible* A retrospective of drawings, photographs and installations from the period 1966-1973.

25·09·96–17·11·96 **Heimrad Prem (1934-1978)** *Retrospective* Working at the interface between 'Art informel' and the New Figuration, Heimrad Prem, a co-founder of the artists' group Spur (1956-65), was one of the foremost German painters of the 60s.

04·12·96–Jun 97 **American Art** This exhibition, displaying all of the museum's acquisitions of American Art, includes works by Andy Warhol, Michael Heizer, Ellsworth Kelly, Dan Flavin, William Copley, James Turrell, Jenny Holzer and Lawrence Weiner.

[Kunstbau Lenbachhaus]

03·04·96–26·06·96 **Michelangelo Pistoletto** *Memoria - Intelligenzia - Providenzia* The exhibition is a major retrospective, displaying an extensive selection of works from every phase of the artist's oeuvre and documenting its principal themes and techniques.

17·07·96–06·10·96 **Olaf Metzel** Metzel's sculptures and installations are based on a critical analysis and aesthetic appropriation of themes encountered through a direct perception of reality, in this case specific aspects of consumer culture, such as sport and tourism.

23·10·96–05·01·97 **Jeff Wall** Jeff Wall is the first artist to be awarded the newly established Munich Art Prize which, in addition to the prize money, includes this opportunity to realise an exhibition in Kunstbau.

München - Munich

NEUE PINAKOTHEK
Barer Straße 29 80799 München Director: J.G. Prinz Von Hohenzollern
☎ +49 89 23805195 🖷 +49 89 23805221
Open: Wednesday-Sunday 10.00-17.00 Tuesday and Thursday 10.00-20.00
Closed: Monday

COLLECTION

19th Century Paintings The Neue Pinakothek, a gallery for contemporary art, was commissioned by King Ludwig I and built between 1846 and 1853 opposite the Alte Pinakothek. The museum was destroyed during the Second World War; since its renovation in 1981 is has featured German painting of the

Manet, Edouard
*Breakfast in the
studio*

Neue Pinakothek,
München

19th century, as well as internationally important works of art from between 1800 and 1900, from Classicism up to Jugendstil. It includes major works by David, Goya, Turner, Courbet, Manet, Monet and Van Gogh. Paintings by the Nazarenes, C.D. Friedrich, Menzel, Spitzweg, Waldmüller, Marées, Feuerbach and Leibl are also on display.

EXHIBITIONS | No exhibitions plannned.

München - Munich

PRÄHISTORISCHE STAATSSAMMLUNG
Lerchenfeldstraße 2 80538 München Director: Hermann Dannheimer
☎ +49 89 293911 📠 +49 89 225238
Open: Tuesday-Sunday 09.00-16.00 Thursday 09.00-20.00
Closed: Monday

COLLECTION | The Prehistoric collection of the Bavarian State dates back to 1885, but it first received its own modern museum premises in 1977.
The contents of the collection tell the story of Bavarian settlement, from the earliest finds of the Palaeolithic era (120 000 B.C.) on through prehistory into the Middle Ages (16th century).
The main topics of the museum are the Stone Age and the Bronze Age, the Urnfield culture and the Iron Age with the Hallstatt era, the La Tène era and the Oppidum Manching. The Roman era and the Middle Ages are also represented with many objects. Opposite the entrance, the museum has a hall devoted to special exhibitions for which a separate admission is charged. The permanent exhibition is arranged in chronological order; the large historical timescale in each of the rooms lists the particular era shown in the room and links it with contemporary events in other parts of the world.

EXHIBITIONS | No details available.

München - Munich

DIE NEUE SAMMLUNG
Prinzregentenstraße 3 80538 München Director: Florian Hufnagl
☎ +49 89 227844 📠 +49 89 220282
Open: (only during special exhibitions) Tuesday-Sunday 10.00-17.00
Closed: Monday

COLLECTION | With a unique collection of almost 40 000 products and artefacts documenting the history of industrial design, graphic design and crafts, 'Die Neue Sammlung' is one of the leading international museums of 20th-century applied art - and the largest museum of industrial design in the world. The inspiration for the establishment of this institution came from the German 'Werkbund' movement in Munich in 1907. From 1912 onwards a collection of 'modern-day model artefacts' was gradually built up.

The traditional areas of the arts and crafts are represented by a comprehensive collection of everyday objects. In addition, the museum devotes much of the available space to mass-produced products of modern industrial design. The graphic design section covers the range from posters, packaging and book design to photography. Over the last decade the museum has also built up a number of specialised collections. These cover areas such as the automobile, sports equipment, secondary architecture and the field of system development.

EXHIBITIONS

Apr 96–Sep 96

For a Museum of Tomorrow This exhibition presents selected masterpieces of the Neue Sammlung, acquired during the last five years in anticipation of the two new museum buildings planned for 20th-century art in Munich and Nuremberg. The exhibition provides a representative cross-section of the museum's permanent collections from the end of the last century until the present.

Oct 96–Jan 97

Applied Art of Today Danner Award 96

München - Munich

SCHACK-GALERIE
Prinzregentenstraße 9 80538 München Director: J.G. Prinz Von Hohenzollern
☎ +49 89 23805224 🖷 +49 89 23805221
Open: Wednesday-Monday 10.00-17.00
Closed: Tuesday

COLLECTION

19th Century Paintings This is the former private collection of Count Adolf Friedrich von Schack. The collection consists of 274 paintings, 181 of which are constantly on display in a wing of the former Prussian Consulate on the Prinsregentenstraße.
Several paintings by Anselm von Feuerbach, Arnold Böcklin and Moritz von Schwind are the main features of the collection.

EXHIBITIONS

No exhibitions planned.

München - Munich

STAATSGALERIE MODERNER KUNST
Prinzregentenstraße 1 80538 München Director: J.G. Prinz Von Hohenzollern
☎ +49 89 21127137 🖷 +49 89 23805227
Open: Tuesday-Sunday 10.00-17.00 Thursday 10.00-20.00
Closed: Monday

COLLECTION

Classical Modern Contemporary Art The Staatsgalerie Moderner Kunst has been built up since the Second World War. Its collection consists of works from the Classical Modern period ranging up to contemporary art. Thanks to gifts and works given in loan it became possible to focus on new trends, such as Surrealism. The best-known works include 'Struggling Forms' by Franz Marc, 'Dreamlike Improvisation' by Kandinsky, 'Full Moon' by Paul Klee, the paintings by Kirchner, a large collection of paintings by Max Beckmann, works of American Abstract Expressionism and Joseph Beuys' monumental work 'The End of the 20th Century'.

EXHIBITIONS

No exhibitions planned.

München - Munich

VILLA STUCK
Prinzregentenstraße 60 81675 München Director: Jo-Anne Birnie Danzker
☎ +49 89 4555510 📠 +49 89 4555124
Open: Tuesday-Sunday 10.00-17.00 Thursday 10.00-21.00
Closed: Monday

COLLECTION

Not only is the Villa Stuck an important historical monument and a work of art itself, but its dramatic history reflects that of the city of Munich: the heady days of turn-of-the-century Munich as the City of Art, the dark days of the Second World War, the first post-war exhibitions of formerly banned artists such as Max Beckmann in the Villa Stuck, the gallery's emergence as a centre for major private galleries, and the gallery's conversion to a private and then to a public museum. Eyewitness accounts of these events have been recorded by a television team in an oral history project entitled 'Memory Bank - Villa Stuck'. Excerpts from these interviews will be on view daily.

EXHIBITIONS
09·05·93-07·07·96

Franz von Stuck and Photography *The Staged and Documentary Image* Franz von Stuck used photography as a technical aid and visual compositional source for genre constume scenes and portraits and also for mythological and symbolistic paintings. This exhibition documents Stuck's intensive use of photography and places it in the context of the lively relationship of photography and painting in the 19th century. The exhibition presents almost 300 original photographs by the Munich painter from the period 1889 to 1928.

25·07·96-29·09·96

Collaborations *Warhol, Basquiat, Clemente* The Collaborations bring together three different characters, cultures and generations: New York Pop-Art, Afro-American graffiti culture and the influence of Indian philosophy and culture, respectively. The meeting took place in New York 1984/85, with each artist involved in a lively exchange while staying true to his own position. The museum will be showing 44 large-format works.

24·10·96-12·01·97

Max Klinger *Drawings, 'Zustandsdrücke', Cycles* The growing interest in turn-of-the-century art is reflected in the fresh debate on artists such as Von Stuck or Klinger, their self-portraits and their portrayals of women. In collaboration with the Munich Graphische Sammlung and the Museum der Bildende Künste in Leipzig, more than 425 works on paper by Klinger will be shown. New selections culled throughout Germany will be exhibited in addition to the previously shown graphic cycles.

Münster

WESTFÄLISCHES LANDESMUSEUM FÜR KUNST UND KULTURGESCHICHTE
Domplatz 10 48143 Münster Director: Klaus Bußmann
☎ +49 251 590701 📠 +49 251 5907210
Open: Tuesday-Sunday 10.00-18.00
Closed: Monday and 1 May, 24 and 31 Dec, 1 Jan

COLLECTION

The collection of the Westphalian State Museum of Art and Cultural History consists of artworks and objects ranging from the Middle Ages up to the contemporary era.
Old Masters In this section the focus is on sacred Westphalian art from the Romanic up to the Late Gothic period. Highlights are the 'Soester Antependium' (c. 1170), the 'Unnaer Marienklage' (c. 1380) and the 'Halderner Altar' by the Master of Schöppingen (c. 1440).

The main pieces from the Renaissance period are the works by the Brabender family of artists (sculptures) and by tom Ring (paintings). The Baroque period is represented by Dutch paintings from the 17th century and decorative art from the 18th century (silver, porcelain, furniture). The 19th century gallery contains examples of German paintings, including work by Rincklake, Carus, Blechen, Hasenclever and Makart.

Modern Art   The Modern Art department, mainly consisting of paintings and sculptures, starts with works from the Jugendstil period and German Impressionism (Pankok, Corinth, Slevogt). Other highlights are German Expressionism, New Objectivity, Art Informel and Constructivism (Kirchner, Heckel, Schmidt-Rottluff, Macke, Nolde, Rohlfs, Albers, Schumacher, Serra). In this field the museum is internationally oriented.

Johann Brabender
The temptation of Adam and Eve, c. 1545

Westfälisches Landesmuseum, Münster

Special Collections   These include a large graphic collection: graphic art from the 16th to the 20th century, documentary graphics as part of the history of Germany and Westpalia in particular and portraits. In addition, the museum has a coin cabinet and a section with architectural designs focusing on the Baroque period in Westphalia (J.C. Schlaun).

EXHIBITIONS
19·05·96–28·07·96

Morris Louis   A retrospective of the American painter Morris Louis (1912-1962). His major work was created in the last five years of his life and is mostly enormous in scale: the 'Veils' (curtain-like, intermeshing, transparent flows of colour), the 'Unfurleds' (irregular broad, separated colour strips, flowing diagonally downward) and the 'Stripes' (parallel bundles of straight colour stripes, mostly vertical and sometimes horizontal). Some 25 works will be on display.

01·09·96–10·11·96

The tom Ring Family of Painters   The painter Ludger tom Ring and his two sons (Münster, 16th century) combined elements of German, Dutch and Flemish styles in their work. The exhibition brings all their work together for the first time in 70 years, with still-lifes (animal and flower pictures), religious tableaus and portraits.

01·12·96–16·02·97

Paul Signac and the Liberation of Colour in Europe   The French painter Paul Signac (1863-1935) was a seminal figure in 20th-century art. Exhibited in 1912 alongside Van Gogh, Munch and Cézanne, he exerted a great influence on Matisse and the 'Fauves', Mondrian, Kirchner, Kandinsky and many other major early 20th-century European figures.

Nürnberg · Nuremberg

GERMANISCHES NATIONALMUSEUM
Kartäusergasse 1 90402 Nürnberg Director: Ulrich Großmann
☎ +49 911 13310 🖷 +49 911 1331200
Open: Tuesday-Sunday 10.00-17.00 Wednesday 10.00-21.00
Closed: Monday and 1 Jan, Shrove Tuesday, Good Friday, 24, 25 and 31 Dec

COLLECTION

Founded in 1852, the Germanisches Nationalmuseum today houses about 1.2 million objects relating to the artistic and cultural history of German-speaking Central Europe between prehistoric times and the present day. The permanent exhibitions display some 20 000 objects including prehistoric and early historic artefacts, paintings and stained glass, sculpture, decorative arts, furniture, textiles, toys and doll houses, historical musical and scientific instruments, historical weapons and hunting gear, collections devoted to the healing arts, the crafts and guilds, and folk arts.

The museum's study collections and research facilities include a department of prints and drawings and a cabinet of coins and medals, historical archives, and a fine art archive of papers left by artists and art historians. There is also a vast research library.

The core of the museum complex is a 14th-century Carthusian monastery with its church, cloisters, monks' houses and refectory. A recently opened wing provides modern facilities for special exhibitions, conferences, concerts and conservation workshops. Of particular note is the environmental installation, 'Way of Human Rights', by Israeli artist Dani Karavan, displayed in front of the new entrance.

The permanent exhibitions include prehistoric artefacts, medieval and Renaissance painting and sculpture, 15th and 16th-century German armour, German Baroque and Rococo sculpture, painting and porcelain, gold and silverware, and the world's largest collection of pianos.

View of the new main entrance with pillars of the Street of Human Rights

Germanisches Nationalmuseum, Nürnberg

EXHIBITIONS

14·12·95-28·07·96

Faces of Bourgeois Art and Culture *From Neoclassicism to the Era of the International Expositions* This exhibition presents, for the first time, the museum's entire holdings of fine and applied art from the 19th century and illustrates the spectrum of artistic and cultural development in Germany between 1780 and 1880.

14·03·96-07·07·96

Ways of Abstraction *Rudolf Jahns (1896-1983)* Jahns, who was and is rightly regarded as the poet among abstractionists, is the subject of a centennial retrospective.

21·03·96-28·04·96

Michael Mathias Prechtl *The Illustrated Books* On the occasion of the noted Nuremburg artist's 70th birthday, the exhibition presents an overview of his works of book illustration since 1960.

28·03·96-30·06·96   ***Leopold Widhalm and the Production of Lutes and Violins in Nuremburg***   This exhibition features instruments from the museum's own collection which document Nuremburg's preeminence in the field of lute-making and violin-making in the 17th and 18th centuries.

Jun 96-06·10·96   ***Past, Present, Future - From all Draw Pleasure***   *The Art of the Medallion in Europe from the Renaissance to the Present* 500 masterpieces from the world's largest collection of coins and medallions, the Münzkabinett of the Staatliche Museum Berlin.

25·07·96-22·09·96   ***With Level and Compass***   *Four Centuries of Architectural and Technical Drawings*   Holdings in the museum's collection of prints and drawings provide the basis for this exhibition.

29·08·96-03·11·96   ***Eberhard Fiebig***   *Works and Documents*   An exhibition of the work of the contemporary sculptor known for his use of steel beams.

03·10·96-24·11·96   ***Johann Christoph Erhard***   *A Graphic Artist of the Romantic Period* This exhibition of the work of a short-lived and underrated graphic artist of the early 19th century will feature drawings and watercolours created in Rome, where Erhard was influenced by Joseph Anton Koch.

31·10·96-12·01·97   ***Expressionistic Paintings***   *The Ahlers Group Collection* This exhibition will present in its entirety an important and previously little-known private corporate collection which contains masterpieces of Expressionist painting by Nolde, Kandinsky, Marc, Kirchner, Beckmann and others. Of particular interest is a group of works by Alex von Jawlensky.

05·12·96-02·02·97   ***Jochen Gerz***   *'The French Wall'*   The first complete presentation of the 88 component parts of a work (1971-1975) by an artist preoccupied with the problems of perception and the complex reality of images and media.

Nürnberg · Nuremberg

KUNSTHALLE NÜRNBERG
Lorenzer Straße 32   90402 Nürnberg   Director: Lucius Grisebach
☎ +49 911 2312853   📠 +49 911 2313721
Open: Tuesday-Sunday 10.00-17.00 Wednesday 10.00-20.00
Closed: Monday and 1 May, 24, 25 and 31 Dec

COLLECTION   The collection is comprised of c. 1500 works of international art dating from the late 50s up to the present and including works by Richard Lindner, Jiri Kolar, Richard Long and Ulrich Rückriem, as well as by younger artists such as Stephan Balkenhol, Guillaume Bijl, Ange Leccia and Thomas Ruff.

EXHIBITIONS

11·04·96-12·05·96   ***Raimund Girke***   *Paintings*   A retrospective of the well-known German 'fundamental' painter Raimund Girke (born in 1930), revealing the artist's development from the late 50s up until the present. The exhibition is organised by the Sprengel Museum in Hannover.

23·05·96-30·06·96   ***Hans Peter Reuter***   *Seven Rooms - Seven Paintings*   Site-specific installation of seven new paintings by German artist Hans Peter Reuter (born in 1942) showing abstract, architectural interiors comprised of spatial visions of blue tiles.

11·07·96–25·08·96 | ***Tracking the Thoughts*** A selection of drawings from the collection of the Kaiser Wilhelm Museum in Krefeld, Germany, which focuses on the changing role of the drawing as an autonomous category of art since the late 50s. The exhibition includes works by Beuys, Caramelle, Chamberlain, Clemente, Darboven, Deacon, Domer, Eva Hesse, Hockney, Kiecol, Yves Klein.

19·09·96–01·12·96 | ***Tadeusz Kantor*** A comprehensive exhibition of works by the Polish artist Tadeusz Kantor (1915-1990), who is well-known for his avant-garde theatre work. This selection includes assemblages, drawings, paintings and theatre props and was compiled by Jaromir Jedlinski, director of the Museum Sztuki, Lodz, Poland.

Paderborn

**WESTFÄLISCHES MUSEUM FÜR ARCHÄOLOGIE -
MUSEUM IN DER KAISERPFALZ**
Am Ikenberg 33098 Paderborn Director: Matthias Wemhoff
☎ +49 5251 10510 📠 +49 5251 281892
Open: Tuesday-Sunday 10.00-18.00
Closed: Monday

COLLECTION | The Archaeological Museum is housed in the rooms of the rebuilt Ottonian Palace which was discovered during excavation in the years 1964-1970. Since parts of the excavated foundations and remaining walls stood several metres high, it was decided to reconstruct the dimensions and character of the 11th-century edifice.
In front of the rebuilt palace are the walls of Charlemagne's first palace in Saxony, 'Karlsburg', built in 776. In 799 Charlemagne received Pope Leo III in Paderborn; in the course of these talks the emperor's coronation in Rome was planned. The exhibition gives a full inventory of what the palace contained: coins, ornaments, fragments of precious glassware, remains of Carolingian murals, roof and ornamental tiles, floor materials, fragments of pillars, metal objects and especially pottery.

St. Bartholomee
Chapel
Chapel of the
Ottonian Palace,
consecrated in 1017

*Museum in der
Kaiserpfalz,
Paderborn*

EXHIBITIONS
07·10·95-30·08·96 | ***Excavation Campaign*** *New Medieval Excavations in Paderborn*
The exhibition presents objects from the 12th to the 17th century from a new excavation in Paderborn.

Regensburg

MUSEUM OSTDEUTSCHE GALERIE
Dr.-Johann-Maier-Straße 5 93049 Regensburg Director: Lutz Tittel
☎ +49 941 22031 📠 +49 941 29129
Open: Tuesday-Sunday 10.00-16.00
Closed: Monday

COLLECTION

The museum is dedicated to the collection and exhibition of paintings, graphics and sculptures by 19th and 20th-century artists from the former East German provinces, as well artists from Eastern and Southeastern Europe. But the museum also presents a representative sample of other German art. Work of artists from East Prussia, Pomerania, Silesia, Bohemia, Moravia, the Baltic Provinces and Transylvania, rooted in the development of European art, are featured.

19th-century art is represented by Menzel, Gaertner, Von Max, Grützner, Von Werner, members of the Düsseldorf School, the Berlin Secessionism, Impressionism and Expressionism. The 20th century is represented by works of the Abstract and Constructive art movements, Realist tendencies appearing after the First World War, and art of the 30s, including works by Kokoschka, Feininger, Schlemmer, Molzahn, Sintenis, and sculptures by Käthe Kollwitz. There are also important contemporary works, and a sizeable collection of prints, drawings, portfolios and illustrated books.

EXHIBITIONS

19·05·96–23·06·96

Reiner Zitta   Born 1944 in Buchelsdorf (Bohemia), the artist lives in Altdorf near Nuremburg. Preferring wood and 'objets trouvés' as working materials, he produces painted stelae ('forefathers' boards'), figurines and charms in African and primitive styles to represent private or collective myths.

07·07·96–18·08·96

Helmut Rieger *Retrospective*   Born 1931 in Neisse, Silesia, the artist lives in Steinebach near Munich. A founding member of the 'Wir' group, he sought a personal style in opposition to Abstract Expressionism and Informel, which he found in a transformation of a dynamic baroque. In the 60s he produced dynamic 'Anti-Objects'. Later he returned to the early figurative matter, developing a personal style showing extreme life situations in a mysterious darkness.

01·09·96–27·10·96

Art as Concept *Concrete and Geometrical Tendencies since 1960 in the Work of German Artists from Eastern and South-Eastern Europe*
This exhibition will show the role that the artists of the former East German provinces have played in the development of German concrete art between 1960 and 1995. In an exhibition of 200 paintings, sculptures and graphics, 25 artists demonstrate a variety of approaches in concrete art, including constructionist, geometrical, serial, Op-Art, structural in meditative-monochrome works, etc.

13·10·96–17·11·96

Borderline Photographs 1986-1996 *Germany-Austria-Czechia*
An exhibition of the Adalbert Stifter Society, Munich. Alterations of the topographical, economic, social and cultural situation in close proximity to the border before and after the political change between East and West will be on display.

Spring 97

Gudrun Wasserman   A follow-up to the 1995 exhibition in Kiel and Tallinn entitled 'Not Light, Nor Yet Darkness', this exhibition will show works developed since that time, in particular those executed for the museum. They are characterised by the use of natural light supplemented by various photographic techniques and projections.

Saarbrücken

SAARLAND MUSEUM
Bismarckstraße 11-19 66111 Saarbrücken Director: Ernst-Gerhard Güse
☎ +49 681 99640 📠 +49 681 66393
Open: Tuesday-Sunday 10.00-18.00 Wednesday 12.00-20.00
Closed: Monday

COLLECTION

Modern Collection The Saarland Museum, in its present-day conception, was established in 1950 by Rudolf Bornschein. The museum is known for a collection of 19th and especially 20th-century paintings and sculptures, as well as a sculpture park. The styles represented range from Impressionism to Contemporary art, including works by Max Beckmann and Alexander Archipenko. Focal points of the collection are its examples of Expressionism and Art Informel.

Graphic Collection The 'Graphisches Kabinett' includes drawings and prints by Manet, Ensor, Kubin, and Beuys, among others, and forms a complement to the collection of paintings.

Antique Collection The 'Alte Sammlung' presents fine art from Saarland, Lorraine and Luxembourg dating from the 12th to the 19th century. Included are a large number of paintings, sculptures, china, silversmith and goldsmith works, coins and furniture. The High Medieval sculptures from Lorraine are especially noteworthy, as are the 17th and 18th-century landscape paintings which include representative works of the Frankenthal School by Huysmans, Savery and Lorrain.

State Gallery The 'Landesgalerie' presents works by 20th-century artists from the region.

EXHIBITIONS

21·04·96-27·05·96 ***Boris Savelev***

19·05·96-14·07·96 ***The Early Renaissance in Italy***   14th and 15th-century drawings from the Berliner Kupferstichkabinett.

09·06·96-01·09·96 ***Martin Assig***   Pictures and drawings.

Michelangelo
Buonarroti
Group of three
standing men facing
left
in the exhibition
'Drawings from
Tuscany, The Age of
Michelangelo;
Saarland Museum,
Saarbrücken

Collection Graphische
Sammlung Albertina,
Wien

22·09·96-03·11·96 ***Drawings from Tuscany***   *The Age of Michelangelo*   This exhibition covers the time from the death of Lorenzo the Magnificent in 1492 until the death of his one-time protegé Michelangelo in 1564, a period which witnessed the birth of nearly all the works of the most significant artists of the Cinquecento as well as the works of Leonardo da Vinci in the preceding generation. This corresponds roughly with the period which Vasari and his successors saw as the actual culminating phase in the 'rebirth' of the arts.

24·11·96-19·01·97	**Gerhard Hoehme** *Aetna Cycle* These paintings are the result of intensive reserach which Hoehme undertook between 1980 and 1982 on Mt. Aetna. The creation of the cycle accompanied a study of the geology, history, and mythology of the volcano. [Graphisches Kabinett]
17·06·96-09·08·96	**Max Liebermann** Paintings, drawings and prints.
14·10·96-15·11·96	**Erich Heckel**
09·12·96-31·01·97	**Café du Dôme** Matisse Weisgerber, Pascin, Levy.

Schwerin

**STAATLICHES MUSEUM SCHWERIN-KUNSTSAMMLUNGEN.
SCHLÖSSER UND GÄRTEN**
Alter Garten 3 19055 Schwerin Director: Kornelia von Berswordt-Wallrabe
☎ +49 385 592400 📠 +49 385 563090
Open: Art Collection: Tuesday 10.00-20.00 Wednesday-Sunday 10.00-17.00
Castles (Schwerin, Ludwigslust, Güstrow) 15 Apr-14 Oct Tuesday-Sunday
and Easter 10.00-18.00; 15 Oct-14 Apr Tuesday-Sunday 10.00-17.00
Closed: Monday

COLLECTION

The State Museum Schwerin, the national art museum of Mecklenburg-Vorpommern, exhibits extensive collections from the Middle Ages to contemporary art in the Gallery in Schwerin and in three former residences of the Mecklenburg dynasty, the castles Schwerin, Ludwigslust and Güstrow. The collection, started in the 18th century, contains 550 paintings and 4 000 graphics from the 'Golden Age' of Dutch and Flemish painting. Nearly all the painters, including Brueghel, Rubens, Rembrandt, Hals and Mieris, are represented by more than one work. There are 34 paintings and 56 sketches by the 18th-century French Court artist Jean Baptiste Oudry.
Schwerin has a large collection of porcelain by Meissen and other European manufacturers. The residence-castles are highlights of historic North German architecture.

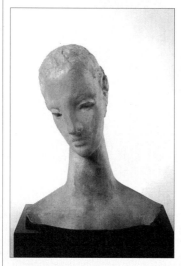

Wilhelm Lehmbruck
(1881-1919)
*Head of pensive
man, 1913/1914*

*Staatliches Museum
Schwerin, Schwerin*

EXHIBITIONS
12·05·96-07·07·96

Quicksand   Contemporary Art from Mecklenburg.

21·07·96-15·09·96 | ***Mail Art in Eastern Europe*** Mail Art, which first appeared in the U.S. during the 1950s, is an exchange of ideas by sending art through the mail. The demand for this type of communication was increased because of imposed isolation, and thus was of particular importance among dissidents from Poland, Hungary, Czechoslovakia, Yugoslavia, Rumania, Bulgaria, the USSR and East Germany.

Oct 96 onwards | ***Sigmar Polke***

Stuttgart

GALERIE DER STADT STUTTGART
Schloßplatz 2 70173 Stuttgart Director: Johann-Karl Schmidt
☎ +49 711 2162188 📠 +49 711 2167820
Open: Tuesday-Sunday 11.00-18.00 Wednesday 11.00-20.00
Closed: Monday

COLLECTION | ***19th Century*** The collection of 19th-century paintings was founded in 1924 and now includes works by Philipp Friedrich Hetsch, Johan Baptist, Seele and other artists of Swabian Classicism. Together with the works of the School of Open-Air Painting from the turn of the century by Hermann Pleuer, Otto Reiniger and Christian Landenberger, they form the historical section of the museum's collection.
Modern Art The Galerie der Stadt Stuttgart houses the largest and most famous public collection of works by the Realist, Expressionist and Dadaist Otto Dix. His work paralleled the German Old Masters in holding up a mirror to the troubled times of Germany and the German people during the First and Second World Wars and the intervening period. One of his major works, the 'Großstadt', is central to the Stuttgart collection.
Abstract art is represented by works from Adolf Hoelzel and his students Oskar Schlemmer and Willi Baumeister. Hoelzel was the first to step beyond representational images at the beginning of the century. A collection of more than 300 paintings and drawings from Fritz Winter, a protagonist of non-figurative art after 1945, was given to the museum and is now on display.
Contemporary Art The permanently displayed collection of paintings, sculptures and installations from the 60s up to the present day includes work by Diter Roth, Walter Stöhrer, Horst Antes, Dieter Krieg, Joseph Kosuth, Markus Lüpertz, Michael Buthe and Felix Droese.

EXHIBITIONS
23·03·96-30·06·96 | ***Dieter Krieg***

Oct 96-Nov 96 | ***Camill Leberer***

Dec 96-Feb 97 | ***Alessandro Mendini***

Stuttgart

STAATSGALERIE STUTTGART
Konrad-Adenauer-Straße 30-32 70173 Stuttgart Director: Christian von Holst
☎ +49 711 2124050 📠 +49 711 2124068
Open: Tuesday-Sunday 10.00-17.00 Tuesday and Thursday 10.00-20.00
Closed: Monday

COLLECTION | Built in the neoclassical style of the early 19th century, the original building, the 'Alte Staatsgalerie', accommodates works from the 14th to the 19th century, as well as the museum's

Graphics Collection, with its copious stock of drawings, water-colours, collages, original prints, illustrated books, posters and photographs. Originating from the collection of the Duchy of Württemberg, the museum's outstanding paintings by Old Masters - Jerg Ratgeb, Canaletto, Memling and Rembrandt are just four examples - set the themes of the individual departments. The 19th-century department contains, besides its special collection of works of 'Swabian Classicism', exemplary works of the most important art movements of the time, from the Pre-Raphaelites to the Symbolists, from the Romantics to the Impressionists.

Adjoining the old museum on the gallery level is the 'Neue Staatsgalerie', the extension designed by James Stirling. This new museum building is dedicated to art of the 20th century. Since the end of the Second World War, the main points of emphasis of the collection have been Classic Modernism and contemporary painting and sculpture. The museum's concentration on significant groups of works from various movements ('Les Fauves', 'Die Brücke', 'Der Blaue Reiter' and Cubism), and on outstanding groups by individual artist including Picasso, Beckmann, Schlemmer, Beuys and Kiefer, accounts for the high international prestige which the Staatsgalerie Stuttgart enjoys today.

Staatsgalerie
Stuttgart, 1977-1984

Architects: James
Stirling, Michael
Wilford and
Associates

Trier

RHEINISCHES LANDESMUSEUM TRIER
Weimarer Allee 1 54290 Trier Director: Hans-Peter Kuhnen
☎ +49 651 97740 📠 +49 651 9774222
Open: Tuesday-Friday 09.30-17.00 Saturday, Sunday and public holidays
10.30-17.00
Closed: Monday except Easter Monday and Whit Monday

COLLECTION

This museum, the largest in Trier, spans the period from prehistory to early modern times, extensively displaying the civilisation, settlement, religion and art of the first four centuries A.D. Burial monuments illustrate life and commerce along the Moselle. The 'Landesmuseum' houses about 200 colourful floor mosaics.

The collection contains early imperial glassware, terra cotta and bronze figurines, and an abundance of household pottery and terra sigillata vessels from over 70 local pottery makers. Roman glassmaking is represented by cups, flasks, bowls and the 'diatret' vessel from Niederemmel.

There are also about 40 000 coins of Trier mintage, the largest collection in Western Germany, and weapons, jewellery, glassware, necklaces, fibulae, gold discs and harnesses from the Frankisch period. The Middle Ages and early modern times are represented by Romanesque and Gothic sculpture and architecture and ceramics from the Rhine-Moselle area.

Marble relief of the Roman Imperial deities Jupiter, Juno and Minerva in the exhibition 'Religio Romana'

Rheinisches Landesmuseum Trier, Trier

EXHIBITION

17·04·96–17·11·96

Religio Romana *Religious Monuments in the Trier Region*
Roman Gaul is characterised by a great variety of gods and cults. Trier, the capital of the province of Gallia Belgica, illustrates particularly clearly the fusion of the old Celtic deities with the Classical Roman pantheon following the conquest by Caesar. From the 2nd century onwards mystical and redemptive oriental cults with new cult practices and places of worship found increasing favour with the Gallo-Roman population. By the end of the late 3rd century such cults were laying the foundations for Christianity in Trier, the oldest bishopric in Germany. This historical development provides the background for the special exhibition at the Landesmuseum Trier, with its wealth of archaeological monuments, models, reconstructions and documentation.

Ulm

ULMER MUSEUM
Marktplatz 9 89073 Ulm Director: Brigitte Reinhardt
☎ +49 731 1614300 📠 +49 731 1611626
Open: Tuesday-Sunday 11.00-17.00 Thursday 11.00-20.00
Closed: Monday

COLLECTION

Since its establishment in 1924 the concept of the Ulm Museum has been to give equal attention to the cultivation and collection of both ancient and modern art. The core of the Ancient Art section is a unique collection of Late Gothic painting and sculpture from Ulm and Upper Swabia. Excellent examples of regional arts and crafts can be seen, in particular goldsmith's work and Ulm cupboards and cabinets.

The 'Weickmannianum' is unique. It is a collection of exotic rarities collected in the 17th century by Christoph Weickmann and is one of the oldest collections in Germany.

The museum also has a Prehistoric section devoted to the history of archaeology and modern archaeological methods, together with natural science. The 32 000 year-old animal/man sculpture is the oldest in Central Europe.

The Kurt Fried Collection   This collection of contemporary art was donated by Kurt Fried in 1978. The collection includes paintings, graphic art, sculptures and other objects. It boasts excellent examples of all the important post-war trends.

EXHIBITIONS

17·03·96–19·05·96

Verre Églomisé   *Pictures from the Danube Countries*

21·04·96–23·06·96

Ernst Ludwig Kirchner   *Unknown Drawings*   Some 90 drawings spanning the entire creative period of the artist, from 1904 to 1937, are on view for the first time.

23·06·96–06·10·96

The Romans on the Danube and Illner   *New Research and Finds*
This exhibition, with loans from various other museums, gives a comprehensive survey of Roman history from the 1st to 5th century A.D. on the Upper Danube and Lower Illner. Finds from old and new excavations, including weapons, jewellery, coins, pottery, tools and gravestones, illuminate the infrastructure of forts, villages and estates.

30·06·96–25·08·96

Maria Lassnig   *Drawings and Watercolours 1945-1995*   The exhibition, with c. 100 drawings and watercolours, surveys the work of this important Austrian artist. After early experiments with Surrealism, Maria Lassnig moved on to Abstract Informalism with a visual investigation of 'body awareness' which continues to the present day. Based on her own sensibility, she gives shape to the invisible and formless.

01·09·96–13·10·96

Andy Warhol   *Screen Print Retrospective*   The pictures of Andy Warhol deal with themes of the consumer society, advertising and the media. The serious and the banal, fashion, beauty and ugliness coexist to mirror the urban experience. The exhibition shows works from a period of 30 years, some hardly known, which were all produced with the screen print technique that he helped to develop.

20·10·96–01·12·96

Annual Exhibition of the Baden-Württemberg Artists' Society

15·12·96–09·02·97

The Visible World   *Dutch Painting of the 16th and 17th Century*
17th-century Dutch painting perceived the world in a completely new way: as an immediate environment, without a heavenly sky and Italian Renaissance ideals. Realism seemed to triumph -

but new studies show hidden depths. Some 60 oil paintings and works on paper include examples by Backhuysen, Cuyp, Dusart, Porcellis and Van Vliet, taken from the Christoph Müller Collection.

Weil am Rhein

VITRA DESIGN MUSEUM
Charles-Eames-Straße 1 79576 Weil am Rhein Director: A. von Vegesack
☎ +49 7621 702200 📠 +49 7621 77493
Open: Tuesday-Friday 14.00-18.00 Saturday, Sunday and public holidays 11.00-17.00
Closed: Monday

COLLECTION

The Vitra Design Museum has one of the foremost collections of modern furniture design in the world. Over 1800 objects document major periods and styles, from early industrial production and the bent-wood furniture of the 19th century to Pop Art designs and the post-industrial furniture sculpture of the 80s and 90s. The highlight of the collection is the estate of Charles and Ray Eames, which was acquired in 1988. Other points of interest are Functionalist steel-tube furniture from the 20s and 30s, Gerrit Rietveld, key Scandinavian designs (1930-1960), Alvar Aalto, American furniture designers from the Shakers to Robert Venturi, Italian design from the 50s to the present day, George Nelson, Verner Panton and Jean Prouvé. The museum also houses an extensive archive which includes the estates of Anton Lorenz and George Nelson.
A collection of modern lamps is currently being set up.

Vitra Design Museum
Weil am Rhein

EXHIBITIONS
27·01·96–19·05·96

Rooms in Time Design from the 50s to the 80s   The exhibition attempts to recapture the feeling of these four decades, taking the example of furniture design to show how diverse the interrelations were between private lives and the designed human environment. There is a sample room for each decade, with an atmosphere created by light and music. Additional select items include avant-garde designs which were pioneering for their day as well as examples of mass-production. An illustrated chronology points out the most important political, economic and social events of the time.

25·05·96–Nov 96

Scandinavian Design   This exhibition consists of a complete original room from the Paimio Sanatorium (by Alvar Aalto) and a home environment (by Verner Panton). Together they represent the evolution of Scandinavian design.

Weimar

KUNSTSAMMLUNGEN ZU WEIMAR
Burgplatz 4 99423 Weimar Director: Rolf Bothe
☎ +49 3643 5460 📠 +49 3643 546101
Open: Tuesday-Sunday 10.00-18.00
Closed: Monday

COLLECTION

The Weimar Collection is one of the most important collections of the former GDR, with work ranging from classical to contemporary times. It is housed in the impressive Schloß Weimar complex which includes buildings dating from between the early 18th century and the mid-19th century. One of the outstanding features of the museum is the Cranach Gallery which features more than 20 works by both Cranachs, including the portraits of Luther and of Sibylle of Cleves, and the 'Battle of Naked Men and Lamenting Women'. Dürer's double portrait of Hans and Felicitas Tucher is also noteworthy. Another major focus is formed by Dutch and Flemish painting of the 16th to 18th century, which includes portraits, landscapes and still-lifes by such artists as Honthorst, Van der Helst, Ruysdael, Van Ostade, Heda and Kalff. Other important collections feature Russian icons, mainly from the Moscow and Novgorod Schools; a small selection of Italian Renaissance painting with works by Ribera, Tiepolo, Tintoretto and Veronese, among others; and a large collection of Classical, Romantic and Realist German painting from the period 1750-1850, including works by Dahl, Hackert, Tischbein and Runge. The Weimar School is represented by artists such as Brendel, Hagen, Buchholz, Von Hoffmann and Beckmann, together with single works by Böcklin, Liebermann, Monet and Rodin. Contemporary art is chiefly represented by artists of the former GDR, with proponents of the Dresden, Leipzig and Berlin Schools. Many Schloß interiors are also on display, including the 'Dichterzimmer' which commemorates the famous poets of Weimar.

EXHIBITIONS

No exhibitions planned.

Aberdeen

ABERDEEN ART GALLERY
Schoolhill Aberdeen AB9 1FQ Head: A. Hidalgo
☎ +44 1224 646333 📠 +44 1224 632133
Open: Monday-Saturday 10.00-17.00 Thursday 10.00-20.00
Sunday 14.00-17.00

COLLECTION

Aberdeen Art Gallery houses an important art collection ranging from 18th-century portraits by Raeburn, Hogarth, Ramsay and Reynolds to powerful 20th-century works by Paul Nash, Ben Nicholson and Francis Bacon. The collection also includes paintings by Impressionists such as Monet, Pissaro, Sisley and Bonnard. Other permanent displays feature a significant collection of Scottish silver and other decorative arts. The Gallery seeks where possible to provide a platform for new and emerging artists and hosts an active programme of special exhibitions throughout the year.

EXHIBITIONS

13·04·96–27·05·96 **El Greco:** 'Christ Driving the Traders from the Temple' (on loan from the National Gallery)

04·05·96–25·05·96 **Aberdeen Artists' Society Annual Exhibition**

01·06·96–27·07·96 **Artists' Portraits** From Aberdeen Art Gallery's extensive collection, featuring works from Victorian painters to the present day. Artists represented include Toulouse-Lautrec, Francis Bacon, Alma-Tadema, Millais, Melville, John Singer-Sargent, Stanley Spencer, John Bellany, Ken Currie, Gilbert and George.

03·08·96–07·09·96 **Lil Nelson** An exhibition of contemporary Scottish landscape paintings and prints.

21·09·96–19·10·96 **Ceramics (title to be confirmed)** A series of exhibitions featuring the work of Britain's leading potters including David Cohen, Ken Eastman and Ewan Henderson.

26·10·96–30·11·96 **Ian Fleming Retrospective** One of Scotland's most innovative and imaginative artists whose work was initially in the school of strict and meticulous Realism; later his use of line became freer and his tonal range greater. Fleming also played a fundamental part in the local art world of North-East Scotland.

26·10·96–30·11·96 **William MacGillivray Bicentenary** A celebration of the life and work of Scotland's forgotten genius in the field of natural history. The exhibition will feature a selection of his watercolours of birds, fish and mammals, on loan from the Natural History Museum.

25·01·97–22·02·97 **Woven Image** An exhibition of contemporary British tapestry.

01·03·97–05·04·97 **Scottish Silver** Historic and contemporary silver presented in association with the Scottish Gallery, Edinburgh.

08·03·97–05·04·97 **First Exhibition Award** Open to all post-graduate students at Scottish Art Schools, this award offers the best graduate his/her first exhibition in a major Scottish Gallery. The winner will be announced in July 1996.

Bath

HOLBURNE MUSEUM AND CRAFTS STUDY CENTRE
Great Pulteney Street Bath Avon BA2 4DB Curator: Barly Roscoe
☎ +44 1225 466669 📠 +44 1225 333121
Open: Monday-Saturday 11.00-17.00 Sunday 14.30-17.30
Closed: Mid Dec to Mid Feb and Mondays November to Easter

COLLECTION

The collection of decorative and fine art was made by Sir William
Holburne (1793-1874) and includes English and continental silver,
porcelain, Italian majolica and bronzes, together with glass,
furniture, miniatures and Old Master paintings. Since his time the
collection has been increased by gifts and bequests, with the
emphasis still on the 17th and 18th centuries.

Examples of work by 20th-century British artist-craftspeople are also
on view. This collection and archive was formed by the Study Arts
Centre and includes printed and woven textiles, pottery, furniture
and calligraphy as well as reference books, documents, photographs
and craftsmen's working notes. There is also a selection of work by
contemporary artist-craftspeople on long term loan from the Crafts
Council collection. Study facilities are available for those who wish
to examine work more closely or to study the reference material.

Thomas
Gainsborough
(1727-1788)
Louisa, Lady Clarges,
1778

Holburne Museum
and Crafts Study
Centre, Bath

EXHIBITIONS
12·09·96-27·10·96

Quilt Art   A touring exhibition of contemporary quilts.

12·11·96-15·12·96

William Morris and the Crafts Today   A touring exhibition
organised by the William Morris Society of Designer-Craftsmen.

Belfast

ULSTER MUSEUM
Botanic Gardens Belfast BT9 5AB N. Ireland Director: John C. Nolan
☎ +44 232 667769 📠 +44 232 681885
Open: Monday-Friday 10.00-17.00 Saturday 13.00-17.00 Sunday 14.00-17.00

COLLECTION

The Ulster Museum possesses diverse collections of scientific,
cultural, and artistic materials.

Its Irish archaeological collections date from around 7000 B.C. until
the late 17th century. The non-Irish collections feature notable
holdings of Pacific Island and Australasian materials, specimens
from North American Indian, African, and Egyptian cultures, and
some 95 percent of the world's authenticated material from Spanish
Armada ships which foundered off the coast of Ireland.

The Fine Art holdings cover a wide spectrum of works, encompassing a representative collection of Irish painting and sculpture from the late 17th century to the present day, as well as 20th-century British art. There are also small collections of contemporary international art and British and continental 'Old Master' paintings.

In its collection of applied art are important examples of Irish ceramics, silver and glass, as well as modern European ceramics and glass, costumes and textiles, and jewellery.

Scientific displays include exhibits on botany and zoology, displays of minerals and gemstones, and a popular dinosaur gallery featuring a skeleton of 'Anatosaurus annectens'. The museum also possesses large collections of preserved plants and animals of great scientific importance. The Local History collections reflect the political and industrial history of Ulster from about 1600. The main galleries are devoted to the political and social history of Ulster and the origins of the city of Belfast.

EXHIBITIONS

05·05·96-02·06·96

Nature's Bounty   Through the centuries man has made use of the natural resources provided by the environment. Nearly all animals, vegetables and minerals have been used at some time for the benefit of the human race in pre-industrial societies. Using objects from the museum's collections, from ancient Ireland and Egypt to the 20th century, this exhibition explains what natural materials were used, how they were used and why.

29·03·96-08·09·96

A Celebration of Riches   From the wealth of the museum's collections of fine and decorative arts comes a dramatic exhibition providing a showcase of the museum's finest pieces, among them Turner's 'The Dawn of Christianity', the silver-gilt 'Kildare Toilet Service', on public display for the first time, the 'Lennox Quilt' and Morris Louis' 'Golden Age'. From paintings and drawings, silver and glass, to ceramics and wood, textiles and costumes, a series of tableaux leads the visitor from the 16th century to the present day.

19·04·96-01·09·96

·***Images Sacred and Secular***   Sacred and secular imagery of Christ from the 16th century to the present day.

10·05·96-01·09·96

Dressed for Battle   Weapons and equipment used in warfare by many societies through the ages.

26·07·96-29·09·96

Treasures of the Royal Horticultural Society   From the Royal Horticultural Society's rich collections of botanical illustrations numbering around 18 000 drawings, some 70 of the best have been brought together to provide an impressive selection of the work of artists from the 16th century onwards.

26·07·96-29·09·96

Raymond Piper's Orchids   People may be surprised to hear that there are wild orchids - about 50 varieties - growing in Ireland. Piper has spent 30 years studying and drawing them and this exhibition is a rare opportunity to view some of these delicate watercolours by Northern Ireland's most famous living botanical artist·

Aug 96-Sep 96

Royal Ulster Academy   Annual exhibition of works by members of the Royal Ulster Academy.

25·10·96-23·02·97

Irish Fashion since 1950   To celebrate the achievements of Irish fashion in the second half of the 20th century, the Ulster Museum has put together a new, major exhibition providing a stunning visual impression of the development of Irish fashion, its individual character and its place in mainstream European fashion.

Opening Oct 96

Early Ireland   The first phase of an exciting re-development of the museum's permanent galleries, 'Early Ireland' provides a narrative history from 10 000 B.C. to 1500 B.C., telling the story of the first settlers in Ireland, the spread of farming and the earliest metalworkers. Visitors can discover how the prehistoric peoples of Ireland lived, who they were and what we know of their food, houses, weapons and tools.

24·11·96-02·02·97   ***Wildlife Photographer of the Year***   Prize-winning photographs illustrating the best of natural history photography.

Birmingham

THE BARBER INSTITUTE OF FINE ARTS
The University of Birmingham   Edgbaston   Birmingham B15 2TS
Director: R. Verdi
☎ **+44 121 4147333**   📠 **+44 121 4143370**
Open: Monday-Saturday 10.00-17.00   Sunday 14.00-17.00

Vigee-Le Brun,
Elisabeth
Countess Golovine

The Barber Institute
of Fine Arts,
Birmingham

COLLECTION

The Barber Institute of Fine Arts was founded in 1932 'for the study and encouragement of art and music' and has since grown to become one of the finest small picture galleries in the world. Located at the East Gate of the University of Birmingham, it houses an outstanding collection of Old Master and Modern paintings, drawings and sculpture, and a magnificent Art Deco concert hall. The collections include major works by Bellini, Poussin, Rubens, Gainsborough and Turner, and also Rossetti, Whistler, Monet, Degas, Renoir and Magritte. Other important exhibits include Roman and Byzantine coins, illuminated manuscripts, rare books and objets d'art.

EXHIBITIONS

No details available.

Birmingham

BIRMINGHAM MUSEUM AND ART GALLERY AND THE GAS HALL
Chamberlain Square   Birmingham B3 3DH   Director: Evelyn A. Silber
☎ **+44 121 2352834**   📠 **+44 121 2356227**
Open: Monday-Saturday 10.00-17.00   Sunday 12.30-17.00
Closed: Phone to check Christmas and New Year closures

COLLECTION

Covers fine and applied art, from middle ages to present, archaeology, ethnography, local history and natural sciences.

Highlights of the collection are 18th and 19th century English watercolours, paintings, sculpture, stained glass and drawings by the Pre-Raphaelites. A select Old Master selection includes works by S. Martini, G. Bellini, P. Giovanni, O. Gentileschi, C. Dolci, Canaletto, Reynolds, Gainsborough, Turner, Degas, Pissarro, Sisley, Renoir.

The applied art collection is especially strong in silver and metalwork, jewellery, stained glass and ceramics. The work of W. de Morgan, William Morris & Co. and the Arts and Crafts Movement are well represented.
There are innovative displays of ethnographic material in Gallery 33.

EXHIBITIONS | [Museum and Art Gallery]

24·02·96–12·05·96 | **The Land is Bright**   *The Colour Woodcuts of Elizabeth Field*
Scenes of Birmingham and the Cotswolds are shown alongside the original woodblocks and tools which the artist has recently presented to the museum. She was a founding member in 1927 of the Central Club of Colour Woodblock Engravers.

26·05·96–29·09·96 | **Visions of Love and Life**   *Pre-Raphaelite Art from the Birmingham Collection*   Renowned as one of the world's finest collections of Pre-Raphaelite art, this exhibition has recently completed a highly successful tour of America which attracted more then 200 000 paying visitors, and is now back home in all its glory. Among the 118 works are Millais's 'The Blind Girl', 'The Long Engagement' by Arthur Hughes and many of Birmingham's Pre-Raphaelite drawings.

26·10·96–29·12·96 | **Tony Phillips**   **The City**   Born in Liverpool and living in Shropshire, Tony Phillips' work reflects his interest in urban life. His new paintings, drawings and prints of Paris, New York and Liverpool merge with a more general look at the way cities work today. Specially commissioned etchings of Birmingham and related work by students from Josiah Mason Sixth Form College are also on view.

[Gas Hall]

17·05·96–29·09·96 | **Monster Creepy Crawlies**   Visitors will enter a world of larger-than-life insects, come face to face with a giant ant, a scorpion as big as a car, a huge wasp and a monster mosquito. Models of a garden shed and a kitchen, with lift-up lids, show the invertebrates that lurk there; children can join the 'Insect Orchestra' and learn about the sounds insects make, or dig in a sandpit and discover what's living there.

26·10·96–02·02·97 | **William Morris Revisited**   *Questioning the Legacy*   The designs of William Morris have been so influential over the last century that many are still in production today, particularly wallpapers and textiles. To mark the centenary of his death this major exhibition will show his work and later examples by designers who have acknowledged Morris' influence on them, dating from the early 20th century to the present day.

Bournemouth

RUSSELL-COTES ART GALLERY AND MUSEUM
East Cliff Bournemouth BH1 3AA Head: Simon Olding
☎ **+44 1202 451800 📠 +44 1202 451851**
Open: Tuesday-Sunday 10.00-17.00
Closed: Monday

COLLECTION | Built in 1894, East Cliff Hall was originally the home of Sir Merton and Lady Annie Russell-Cotes. Richly decorated with stained glass, stencilwork and elaborate woodwork, the house formed the perfect setting for the many works of art which they brought home from extensive world travels. Bournemouth Council opened Russell-Cotes to the public in 1922, following the donation of the house, its collections and the later Art Galleries. The museum's collection consists of an impressive assortment of Victorian and Edwardian paintings, complemented by sculpture, decorative art and furniture, as well as a modern art collection. Furthermore, important commissions of contemporary craft and sculpture are sited in the Display Space, Art Galleries and Garden.

Evelyn de Morgan
Aurora Triumphans
(c. 1886)

Russell-Cotes Art
Gallery and Museum,
Bournemouth

EXHIBITIONS

11·05·96-01·09·96   ***Paul Eachus and Helen Coxall***   A site-specific installation addressing interpretation and cultural identity.

21·09·96-20·04·97   ***Evelyn de Morgan***   First retrospective of an important Victorian woman artist.

Brighton

BRIGHTON MUSEUM & ART GALLERY
Church Street   Brighton BN1 1UE   Director: Jessica Rutherford
☎ **+44 1273 603005**   ▥ **+44 1273 608202**
Open: Monday, Tuesday Thursday-Saturday 10.00-17.00   Sunday 14.00-17.00
Closed: Wednesday and Good Friday, 25, 26 Dec, 1 Jan

COLLECTION   The Brighton Museum & Art Gallery possesses rich collections of both local and national importance, included Art Nouveau and Art Deco works ranging from Gallé to Clarice Cliff, non-Western items from textiles to masks, and archaeological artefacts from flint axes to silver coins. There is also a fashion gallery and a toy cabinet, and the museum has exhibits of fine art. From time to time, the museum presents temporary exhibitions and conducts special events.

EXHIBITIONS

20·04·96-27·05·96   ***Land of Tempests***   *New Art from Guatemala, El Salvador and Nicaragua*   This is the first show of its kind to focus specifically on Central America and includes paintings, prints, sculptures and installations by nine contemporary artists, eight of whom are exhibiting in Britain for the first time.

07·06·96–21·07·96   ***'The Green Room' and other Paintings (1985-1995) by Graham Dean*** An exhibition consisting of large-scale vibrant watercolour paintings and other works by the Brighton-based artist, Graham Dean. The 'Green Room' paintings refer specifically to incidents in the artist's life.

08·08·96–15·09·96   ***The Impossible Science of Being***   *Dialogues between Anthropology and Photography*   An exploration of the parallel histories of anthropology and photography from a contemporary critical standpoint. This exhibition will show archival photographs and images from the museum's collections with commissioned work by three British artists of Afro-Caribbean and Asian origin - Faisal Abdu'Allah, Zarina Bhimji and Dave Lewis.

28·09·96–10·11·96   **Teatro Gioco Vita**   *Italian Shadow Puppets*   An exhibition of Italian puppets with video, animated puppets and startling theatrical backdrops. The show reveals the innovative work of the 'Teatro Gioco Vita' working in collaboration with Lele Luzzatti, well-known Italian theatre designer and children's illustrator since 1978.

30·11·96–06·01·97   **The Inner Eye**   A show which explores how artists and others make tangible the spiritual and the invisible, translating inner emotions into visible material objects. A wide variety of work will be included, ranging from medieval woodcuts, 'spontaneous' miraculous photographs of the Virgin Mary, ex-votos, icons and crystal balls to works by Old Masters, William Blake, Paul Klee and contemporary artists.

Bristol

CITY MUSEUM AND ART GALLERY
Queen's Road   Bristol BS8 1RL   Director: H. McGowan
☎ +44 117 9223571   🖷 +44 117 9222047
Open: Daily 10.00-17.00

COLLECTION   The City Museum and Art Gallery houses an outstanding collection that can be divided into 6 main categories: decorative art, fine art, Eastern art and culture, archaeology and history, geology and natural history. The collection of decorative art encompasses European ceramics, glass, textiles, metalwork and furniture dating from the 17th century to the present. The fine art collection includes French 16th to 20th-century paintings, a number of charming Victorian paintings and works by the Bristol School.

Victorian Picture Gallery

City Museum and Art Gallery, Bristol

The collection of Eastern art is internationally significant and displays Chinese art, Japanese ceramics, carved ivories, metal sword fittings, Far Eastern lacquerware and the arts of the Indian sub-continent, Asia and the Islamic countries. Archaeological material from the Bristol area and from many parts of the world is displayed in the museum. The Egyptian Gallery contains exhibits illustrating ancient Egyptian beliefs about death and the afterlife and includes a display detailing the scientific unwrapping of a 21st-Dynasty mummy. The Bristol area is of special geological interest and the museum has a major collection of fossils and a mineral gallery. These are displayed in such a way that they help explain how the earth was formed and how species evolved through geological time.

EXHIBITIONS
until 27·10·96 *The Life, Death and Times of Horemkenesi*   An exhibition presenting the results of the Bristol Mummy Project.

04·05·96–23·06·96   *Imagining Rome*   The portrayal of Ancient Rome in 19th-century British paintings.

11·07·96–01·09·96   *The Natural History Museum's Discovery Centre* Hands-on activities for children exploring the natural world.

Apr 97–Oct 97   *Cabot 500*   A series of exhibitions celebrating John Cabot's voyage in 1497 from Bristol to what later became Canada.

Cambridge

CAMBRIDGE UNIVERSITY MUSEUM OF ARCHAEOLOGY AND ANTHROPOLOGY
Downing Street Cambridge CB2 3DZ Director: D.W. Phillipson
☎ +44 1223 333511 📠 +44 1223 333503
Open: Monday-Friday 14.00-16.00 Saturday 10.00-12.30
Closed: Sunday

COLLECTION | Although primarily a University institution devoted to teaching and research, the museum's galleries contain much to interest the non-specialist visitor. The Archaeology Gallery surveys world history from the origins of mankind to the rise of literate civilisation. The Anthropology Gallery surveys cultures from all continents. Some subject areas, among which Oceanian anthropology and American and European archaeology, are particularly comprehensive.

EXHIBITIONS
until Summer 96 | *Living Traditions* *Continuity and Change, Past and Present*   One of the themes of this exhibition is the creation and maintenance of cultural boundaries, particularly during periods of rapid change. By placing recent acquisitions alongside historical and archaeological material, the adaptive and creative forces of individual artists can be expressed. The exhibition focuses on seven distinct cultural areas and historical periods: Aboriginal Australia, The Swahili in Eastern Africa, Concheros dancers in Mexico, Powwows in North America, the Northwest Coast of Canada, Roman Britain and the University of Cambridge.

Autumn 96-onwards | *African Metalwork*

Cambridge

FITZWILLIAM MUSEUM
Trumpington Street Cambridge CB2 1RB Director: S.S. Jervis
☎ +44 1223 332900 📠 +44 1223 332923
Open: Tuesday-Saturday 10.00-17.00 Sunday 14.15-17.00
Closed: Monday (except Easter Monday, Spring and Summer Bank Holidays)
Good Friday, May Day Bank Holiday, 24 Dec-1 Jan

COLLECTION | The museum possesses rich collections of Egyptian objects, Greek and Roman art, antiquities from Mesopotamia and the kingdoms of Ur, Babylon, Assyria, Persia, and Arabia, as well as sculpture, bronzes, glass, jewellery, gems, grave furnishings and applied art covering the period from the Paleolithic to early Christian eras. The applied arts include international ceramics, notably early European pottery; majolica; Korean, Chinese and Japanese porcelain and pottery; glass; armour; choice silver; furniture; notable English clocks; sculpture; textiles and fans.

There are important collections of Greek, Roman, and Medieval coins, additional collections of engraved gems and cameos, and fine Italian and foreign medals.

The museum's varied collection of paintings includes Italian paintings from the 15th century onwards, examples of the Dutch and Flemish schools, representative works of the French school, Impressionist and Post-Impressionist paintings and works by English artists including Hogarth, Reynolds, Gainsborough, Turner, Stubbs and Constable. There are also numerous English watercolours, miniatures, drawings and prints.

The museum also possesses a library containing fine illuminated, literary and music manuscripts, and fine printed books.

Fitzwilliam Museum, Cambridge

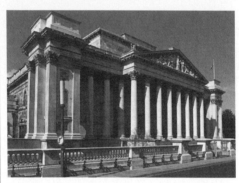

EXHIBITIONS

23·01·96-02·06·96   ***Primavera*** *Pioneering Craft and Design* [Adeane Gallery]
The Primavera craft shop was opened by Henry Rothschild in London in 1946 and provided a unique forum for many talented craftspeople and designers. This exhibition includes fine ceramics and textiles, specially commissioned interior furnishings from the 1950s and 60s, British rural crafts, and traditional arts and crafts from Poland, Sardinia, India, Africa and Peru.

13·02·96-12·05·96   ***Colour Prints from the Beddington Collection*** [Charrington Print Room]   18th-century coloured mezzotints and stipple engravings, as well as the painting by Angelica Kauffmann for a print by Francesco Bartolozzi.

20·02·96-24·05·96   ***Coinage in Ireland*** [Cripps Gallery]

09·04·96-07·07·96   **'Colledge Goods'** *400 Years of Sidney Sussex College* [Octagon]
In the course of four centuries Sidney Sussex College has acquired an impressive range of treasures. To commemorate its founding in 1596, important items in the collection are on display, including a masterpiece of Jacobean goldsmith's work, the ewer and basin given John 2nd Lord Harrington, works by 18th and 20th-century goldsmiths, 40 manuscripts and early printed books, and other curiosities.

23·04·96-30·06·96   ***Surimono*** *Hokusai and his Pupils* [Shiba Room]

14·05·96-01·09·96   ***Burne-Jones and William Morris*** *Illustrations for the Kelmscott Chaucer and the Aeneid* [Graham Roberts Room]

21·05·96-22·09·96   ***Tennyson and Trollope*** *Book Illustrations by John Everett Millais* [Charrington Print Room]

25·06·96-25·10·96   ***The Development of Portraiture on Greek Coinage*** [Cripps Gallery; Tue-Fri 14.00-16.00]

09·07·96-13·10·96	***Japanese Drawings from the Museum's Collection*** [Shiba Room]
23·07·96-22·12·96	***Variations on Ceramic Themes*** *Big is Beautiful* [Octagon] This exhibition includes a selection of large European and Oriental pieces which are extraordinary feats of potting and decorating.
24·09·96-Jan 97	***John Downman (1750-1824)*** *Landscape, Genre and Portraits of 'Rank and Fashion'* [Graham Robertson Room]
08·10·96-Feb 97	***Rembrandt and the Nude*** [Charrington Print Room] This second exhibition devoted to the Fitzwilliam's outstanding collection of Rembrandt etchings reveals new information about the paper Rembrandt used for printing, and investigates ideas of nakedness and nudity as revealed in some of Rembrandt's most intimate studies of the female and male figure.
08·10·96-22·12·96	***The Golden Century*** *Dutch Master Drawings from the Fitzwilliam Museum* [Adeane Gallery] This exhibition features landscapes, seascapes, animal and flower drawings, figure drawings and drawings with religious themes. Artists represented include Rembrandt, Cuyp, Van Huysum, Goltzius, Bloemaert, Saftleven and the Van de Veldes. A fully illustrated catalogue will be available.
22·10·96-22·12·96	***The Utagawa School*** [Shiba Room]

Cardiff

NATIONAL MUSEUM OF WALES
Cathays Park Cardiff CF1 3NP Director: Colin Ford
☎ +44 1222 397951 📠 +44 1222 373219
Open: Tuesday-Saturday 10.00-17.00 Sunday 14.30-17.00
Closed: Monday, except public holidays

COLLECTION

The National Museum of Wales includes exhibitions on Natural History as well as Fine Art.
'The Evolution of Wales' gallery is a major interdisciplinary exhibition tracing the development of Wales from its earliest geological origins up to the end of the last great Ice Age, when the present landscape was moulded. The exhibition actually 'begins' with the origins of the universe, the solar system, the Earth and life on Earth, and introduces the concepts of plate tectonics and continental drift, up to the point in time when that piece of the Earth's crust which is now called Wales was located at latitude 50 south of the equator. It continues up through the age of dinosaurs to the emergence of man.

'The Natural History of Wales' is a new exhibition which illustrates the marine and woodland environments of modern Wales.
Six new art galleries display the museum's internationally acclaimed collection of fine art. The Davies Collection of French Impressionist art is especially noteworthy. Other galleries show Welsh, British and European paintings, as well as an impressive collection of sculpture and ceramics.

EXHIBITIONS
16·03·96-16·06·96

Inscribed in Stone The focus of this exhibition is the full-size marble replica of the Trajanic inscription from Caerleon (Roman Isca), set in a recreated workshop of a stone engraver. The exhibition recreates the excitement of producing the replica stone in its most precise detail. In the study of its context, content, composition, letter-forms and cutting technique, the project reveals the way in which the Roman designer and artist craftsmen operated.

01·04·96–31·05·96   *Pollination of Plants on Stamps*   Exploring the various methods of pollination, not only by wind and water but also the wide variety of insects and birds that play a major role in the process.

Cheltenham

CHELTENHAM ART GALLERY & MUSEUM
Clarence Street Cheltenham GL50 3JT Director: George Breeze
☎ +44 1242 237431 📠 +44 1242 262334
Open: Monday-Saturday 10.00-17.20
Closed: Sunday and public holidays

COLLECTION

Cheltenham Art Gallery & Museum possesses an internationally significant collection related to the Arts and Crafts Movement: that period at the turn of the century inspired by William Morris. Particularly strong in furniture, the collection also includes silver, textiles and paintings, much of which has a Cotswold connection. Cheltenham is the most complete Regency town in Britain and the museum houses a wide range of objects associated with its history. There is also a gallery devoted to one of the town's famous sons, Edward Wilson, who died with Captain Scott on their way back from the South Pole in 1912.

Many other fascinating collections are on view, with the notable collection of Dutch and Flemish paintings, donated by the Baron de Ferrieres in 1898, of particular interest. A fine collection of oriental ceramics has been assembled from the many pieces brought back to Cheltenham by retiring civil servants who had served in the Far East. There are additional displays of archaeological treasures from the Cotswolds and a series of historical galleries depicting life from the Middle Ages to the 20th century.

Arts and Crafts
interior, showing
furniture and
metalwork designed
by Ernest Gimson and
Ernest Barnsley,
dating from
1905-1930

Cheltenham Art
Gallery & Museum,
Cheltenham

EXHIBITIONS

15·06·96–28·08·96   *Simply Stunning*   *The Pre-Raphaelite Art of Dressing*
Paintings, photographs and dresses from the period 1860-1910, drawn from collections all over the UK, showing how the Pre-Raphaelite artists and their models broke with convention by setting a trend for clothes which were loose-fitting, simple and elegant, reflecting their admiration for medieval costume.
Art influenced dress and vice versa, as is revealed in work by Rossetti, Burne-Jones, Kate Greenaway, May Morris and others.

23·11·96–04·01·97   *Rodmarton Manor*   *'Not a Drawing Room Sort of House'*
One of the last great country houses, Rodmarton Manor, near Cirencester, was designed by Ernest Barnsley between 1909 and 1926. Both the architect and the client, the Hon. Claude Biddulph, saw it as an opportunity to put Arts and Crafts ideals into practice, to revive local craft traditions and provide a focal point for the

community. The exhibition will document the building of the house and illustrate some of its treasures; it is Cheltenham's contribution to the William Morris Centenary.

Chichester

PALLANT HOUSE GALLERY
9 North Pallant Chichester West Sussex PO19 ITJ Director: David Coke
☎ **+44 1243 774557 🖷 +44 1243 536038**
Open: Tuesday-Saturday 10.00-17.15
Closed: Sunday, Monday and public holidays

COLLECTION

The museum displays a collection of works by 20th-century artists, displayed in an 18th-century setting. There are works by Henry Moore, Graham Sutherland, Paul Nash, John Piper, Ivor Hitchens, Barbara Hepworth, Ben Nicholson and many other British Masters as well as Europeans including Klee, Cézanne, Picasso, Severini, Léger and others.

EXHIBITIONS

07·05·96-15·06·96 **L.S. Lowry** *Seascapes and Barren Landscapes* Unexpected work by this well-known modern Primitive.

07·05·96-15·06·96 **Recent Paintings by Jane Andrews** Fantastic images with a strong theatrical feeling and a refreshing humour.

29·06·96-20·07·96 **Chichester Festivities** Sculptors working at Pallant House as well as maquettes for sculpture.

06·08·96-14·09·96 **Alan Davie (1920)** *Recent Work* Richly symbolic and magical paintings.

05·11·96-04·01·97 **Brendan Neilan R.A. (1941)** Recent screenprints and a chance to see the complex techniques involved in their production.

[Garden Gallery Exhibitions]
11·05·96-22·06·96 **Bernard Charles** *Spirit of the Downs* Ceramics and watercolours.

29·06·96-10·08·96 **Eric James Mellon** New ceramic work and graphic work.

17·08·96-28·09·96 **Keith Clements** New vistas: Sussex from the Bypass.

Coventry

HERBERT ART GALLERY & MUSEUM
Jordan Well Coventry CV1 5QP Director: Peter Pinnell
☎ **+44 1203 832385 🖷 +44 1203 832410**
Open: Monday-Saturday 10.00-17.30 Sunday 14.00-17.00

COLLECTION

20th-Century Art The collection features the work of numerous British artists.
Graham Sutherland The gallery is one minute from Coventry Cathedral and contains the Iliffe Collection of over 150 of Sutherland's studies for the 75-foot high tapestry which forms the centrepiece of this showpiece of Modernism.
Topographical Art The collection covering the period from 1650 to 1980 includes many paintings, watercolours, prints and drawings, mostly of Coventry, as well as of Warwick and Kenilworth Castles.
Other Art Collections Additional collections include British Figure Drawings, 1875-1975; British Watercolours, 1775-1980; Local Artist David Gee (1793-1872); Paintings of Lady Godiva; and Luca Giordano's immense 'Bacchus and Ariadne'.

Natural History The museum possesses approximately 250 000 specimens, including large and extensive insect collections spanning most insect orders, as well as a moderately-sized collection of stuffed birds and animals, bird's eggs and fossils.

Social History These collections are comprised principally of Stevengraphs, silk ribbons and Coventry-made clocks and watches. There are also examples of objects manufactured in the city over the past 1000 years.

Archaeology There is an excellent collection of Medieval artifacts, particularly rich in ceramics, metals and leather objects.

EXHIBITIONS

01·05·96–09·06·96 | **The Motor Show** [Galleries 4&5] A collection of paintings, drawings and graphic works by contemporary British artists who feature representations of road vehicles in their work. Also a small section of historical works, by artists including Burra, Bratby and Carel Weight.

15·06·96–28·07·96 | **The Mirror in the Sea** Photographic work by Michael Hockney of Nova Scotia. Hockney presents a challenging personal portrait of this enchanting region of the world through his powerful panoramic colour photography and distinctive black and white studies.

19·06·96–28·07·96 | **Barry Bermange** Found and Lost Documents [Gallery 5] Photographs deeply rooted in themes of fear, poverty, loneliness and uncertainty, influenced by the suffering of his family who were refugees from Eastern Europe. His images have visual references to the collage paintings and constructions of Robert Rauschenberg and are drawn largely from time-worn deposits of torn printed imagery found on city billboards. Specially curated by the artist for this venue.

08·08·96–15·09·96 | **Synaptica** [Galleries 4&5] Installations by John Herbert, Bill Jackson, Lisa Durk, Ray Spence and Laura Malacart.

28·09·96–10·11·96 | **Made in the Middle** [Galleries 4&5] Innovative craft by some of the Midland's top makers. Articles include jewellery, textiles and ceramics.

20·11·96–05·01·97 | **Year of the Car** [Gallery 4] A culmination of the many activities which have taken place as part of the Year of the Car.

20·11·96–05·01·97 | **Cash's and Stevengraphs** [Gallery 5] To celebrate the 150th anniversary of Cash's, complemented by a display of stevengraphs. Curated by Hew Jones.

11·01·97–16·02·97 | **Ology Gallery Pilot** [Gallery 5] A pilot for a major 'ology' gallery due to open in the year 2000. To include archaeological, ecological and geological objects from the permanent collection.

19·02·97–30·03·97 | **Coventry Women's Show** [Gallery 5] A celebration of art produced by women working and living in Coventry, alongside paintings by women working in some of Coventry's twin cities. To celebrate International Women's Week. The artists will be working in the gallery to produce an exhibition for International Women's Week, which will then be displayed until the end of March.

26·02·97–06·04·97 | **Derek Southall** [Gallery 4] A major retrospective by Coventry-born artist Derek Southall.

14·04·97–25·05·97 | **Heart of England Biennial 2** [Galleries 4&5] The second Biennial exhibition open to people living and working in Coventry, Warwick and Solihull. It includes paintings, prints, drawings and sculptures.

Derby

DERBY MUSEUM & ART GALLERY
The Strand Derby DE1 1BS Director: David Fraser
☎ +44 1332 255587 📠 +44 1332 255804
Open: Monday 11.00-17.00 Tuesday-Saturday 10.00-17.00
Sunday and public holidays 14.00-17.00

COLLECTION

The Derby Museum & Art Gallery possesses a diverse collection of art, art objects, and historical displays. Featured in the collection are paintings by the 18th- century Derby artist Joseph Wright (1734-1797), including portraits, landscapes, and scenes depicting scientific and industrial activity. Also featured are examples of fine Derby porcelain ranging from the middle of the 18th century to the present. There are also local military regimental collections on display. Natural history exhibits depict the geology and wildlife of Derbyshire. Additional exhibits present local archaeology and history.

EXHIBITIONS

No exhibitions planned.

Derby

PICKFORD'S HOUSE MUSEUM
41 Friar Gate Derby DE1 1DA Directors: Diane Moss & Elizabeth Spencer
☎ +44 1332 255363 📠 +44 1332 255804
Open: Monday 11.00-17.00 Tuesday-Saturday 10.00-17.00 Sunday and
public holidays 14.00-17.00

COLLECTION

Built in 1770 by the architect Joseph Pickford as his family home and work premises, the museum contains displays concerning domestic life in the 18th and early 19th century. Period room settings include a dining room, morning room, drawing room, kitchen, Georgian bedroom and a servant's bedroom. There are additional displays of costumes and textiles from the museum's permanent collection, and the Frank Bradley collection of toy theatres.

EXHIBITIONS

20·01·96–05·01·97

Fashion and Freedom *Women's Fashions from the 1920s* After the end of the Edwardian period, a revolution in women's clothing took place. For a variety of social and economic reasons clothing became less restrictive as lifestyles changed. This exhibition explores some of the reasons why these changes occurred, as well as displaying the dresses typical of the 1920s. Included in the exhibition will be several dresses by well-known designers like Chanel, as well as ready-made clothes that could be purchased on the high street.

27·04·96–07·07·96

Cutlery from Sheffield An exhibition of cutlery on loan from Sheffield Museum. In the exhibition, over 300 items will be on display, dating from the 18th century to the present day. Included in the exhibition are table cutlery, penknives, razors and scissors, all made in Sheffield.

Dorchester

DORSET COUNTY MUSEUM
High West Street Dorchester Dorset DT1 1XA Director: Richard de Peyer
☎ +44 1305 262735 📠 +44 1305 257499
Open: Monday-Friday 10.00-17.00 Jul and Aug Sunday 10.00-17.00
Closed: Saturday and Sunday

COLLECTION

The Dorset County Museum displays the principal county collections of archaeology, natural history and fossil geology, substantial local and rural history galleries and the world's major collection of manuscripts by Thomas Hardy. There is also a reconstruction of Thomas Hardy's study from Max Gate, Dorchester.

Maggie Richardson
Bronze bust of
Thomas Hardy
(1840-1928)

Dorset County
Museum, Dorchester

EXHIBITIONS

26·04·96-01·06·96 — ***Dinosaur Roadshow***   This exhibition of dinosaurs is designed to be understood by grown-ups as well as children, and includes the cast skeleton of a 20-foot megalosaurus, dinosaur droppings, and rare and precious fossils.

28·04·96-02·06·96 — ***British Gas Wildlife Photographer of the Year 1994***   A chance to see the results of this famous competition acclaimed for its evocative and sympathetic insight into the natural world.

08·06·96-20·07·96 — ***The Flowers of the Countryside***
This exhibition of paintings by Mary Tarraway combines her deep botanical knowledge acquired over many years with a keen eye for colour and form.

15·06·96-14·09·96 — ***Man and the Land***   *150 Years of Dorset Farming*   The museum celebrates its 150th anniversary with a big exhibition on Dorset's most important industry - farming.

27·07·96-14·09·96 — ***Goal!***   An exhibition for collectors and sportsmen celebrating 100 years of football in Dorset and beyond.

14·09·96-26·10·96 — ***John Bratby***   The largest selling show of Bratby's late works since his death in 1992.

02·11·96-14·12·96 — ***Poole Printmakers***   Dorset's premier printmaking cooperative includes over 60 amateur and well-known print producers in a wide variety of techniques.

Durham

THE BOWES MUSEUM
Barnard Castle Durham DL12 8NP Director: Elizabeth Conran
☎ +44 1833 690606 ▦ +44 1833 367163
Open: Monday-Saturday 10.00-17.30 Sunday 14.00-17.00
variant closing times: Mar/Apr/Oct 17.00 Nov-Feb 16.00

COLLECTION

The Bowes Museum was founded by John Bowes and his wife Josephine in the second half of the 19th century.
The chateau-like building was designed in Second Empire style by a Parisian architect and stands in 20 acres of gardens and parkland surrounded by countryside.
The founders were assiduous collecters of Fine and Decorative Arts of Western Europe, mainly in the time between 1850 and 1874.
The collection of about 1 400 paintings covers most European schools and includes works by Sassetta, Primaticcio, Tiepolo, Canaletto, El Greco, Goya, Borgoña, Carreño de Miranda, Champaigne, Boucher, Vernet, Robert, Courbet, Van Heemskerck, Vinckeboons, De Vlieger and Snyders.

The many European and English ceramics are broad in range, taking in majolica, faience, delftware, stoneware etc. and porcelain from numerous well-known factories, such as Sèvres and Meissen. There is also a small collection of Oriental porcelain.
Sculptures, wood-carvings, silverware, glass and ivories form part of the collection as well. In addition, there are examples of tapestry, textiles, needlework and costumes together with dolls, doll's houses and toys. The vaults of the museum contain Prehistoric, Roman, Medieval and Modern archaeological finds of the region and items pertaining to the social history of Teesdale.

EXHIBITIONS

30·03·96-02·06·96

Flesh and Spirit *Velázquez and Painters in 17th-Century Madrid*
The development of a national school of Spanish painting.

03·05·96-28·07·96

Private View An exhibition showing works by modern British and European artists, integrated into the collection to suggest how John and Josephine Bowes might have collected today.

25·05·96-01·09·96

Walking the Landscape *With Cotman and Turner in Teesdale*
This is an exhibition showing views of Teesdale past and present, timed to coincide with 'The Marking of the Ways' project on the River Tees.

21·09·96-10·12·96

Dutch, Venetian, Cumber and Print *Barnard Castle Carpets* This exhibition presents a detailed survey of the carpet-making industry in Barnard Castle in the 18th and 19th centuries.

Edinburgh

NATIONAL GALLERY OF SCOTLAND
The Mound Edinburgh EH2 2EL Director: Timothy Clifford
☎ +44 131 5568921 📠 +44 131 2200917
Open: Monday-Saturday 10.00-17.00 Sunday 14.00-17.00

Titian
The three Ages of Man

National Gallery of Scotland, Edinburgh

COLLECTION

The National Gallery of Scotland houses an outstanding collection of paintings, drawings and prints by renowned masters from the Renaissance to Post-Impressionism, and includes works by Velasquez, El Greco, Rembrandt, Vermeer, Turner, Constable, Monet and Van Gogh.

EXHIBITIONS

07·03·96–06·05·96

David Le Marchand (1674-1726) *An Ingenious Man for Carving In Ivory*   David Le Marchand, formerly of Dieppe but who settled in Edinburgh in 1696, produced exquisite cameo portraits which are among the most impressive ever carved in ivory. Among the distinguished patrons who flocked to him for portrait busts and cameos were royalty - Queen Anne and George I - aristocrats such as the Duke of Marlborough, politicians and intellectuals including Sir Isaac Newton.

25·04·96–14·07·96

Awash with Colour *American Watercolours from Boston*
This exhibition presents a collection of over 50 watercolours, selected from the magnificent holdings of the Museum of Fine Arts in Boston, which will be seen in Europe for the first time. Works by Winslow Homer, Edward Hopper and Georgia O'Keeffe and the English artist John Singer Sargent will be shown together in this exhibition.

08·08·96–20·10·96

Velázquez in Seville

Nov 96–Jan 97

German Renaissance Prints

Edinburgh

ROYAL MUSEUM OF SCOTLAND (NATIONAL MUSEUMS OF SCOTLAND)
Chambers Street Edinburgh EH1 1JF Director: Mark Jones
☎ +44 131 2257534 📠 +44 131 2204819
Open: Monday-Saturday 10.00-17.00 Sunday 12.00-17.00

COLLECTION

The National Museums of Scotland present the art, culture, and technology of Scotland to the world, as well as presenting the world to Scotland. In particular, the Royal Museum of Scotland houses a wide variety of international collections covering the decorative arts; science, technology and working life; geology; and natural history. These collections are displayed in the elegant surroundings of one of the finest examples of Victorian architecture, designed by Captain Francis Fowke. Permanent galleries include 'European Art: 1200-1800', 'Western Decorative Art: 1850-2000', 'Twentieth Century Jewellery', 'World in Our Hands' and 'Bird Biology'.

EXHIBITIONS

08·06·96–15·09·96

Pride and Passion *The National Burns Exhibition*   This exhibition explores the life and times of the Scottish poet Robert Burns. Exhibits include poems, letters and songs written in Burns' own hand, paintings illustrating his poetry and portraits of the man himself, as well as objects which help to create a picture of what life was like 200 years ago.

01·10·96–14·10·96

Behind the Screens   An exhibition which looks at the past 100 years of cinema from the pioneering days of the travelling showman to the multiplexes of the 1990s, as seen through the eyes of the manager, projectionist, usherette, chocolate boy, pianist and doorman.

12·10·96–03·11·96

Passing Out   This jewellery exhibition is the annual showcase for the best student degree work from all the colleges in Britain which have jewellery and silversmithing courses.

The main hall in the Royal Museum of Scotland, Edinburgh

02·11·96–12·01·97 | ***The Art of Protection*** This exhibition illustrates a number of key developments in European arms and armour between the 14th and 17th centuries. The military uses of the objects are described but the emphasis is on broader historical concepts. For instance, changes in the design of armour over the years are explored not only in terms of changes in weapons and military tactics but of technological, industrial, social and economic developments.

01·12·96–26·05·97 | ***The Scottish Home*** This exhibition communicates ideas about the nature of the home and its changing role in people's lives.

Feb 97–Mar 97 | ***Shell Valentine Card Collection*** An exhibition of 200 Valentine cards dating from the early 19th century, collected by Jane Samuels, owner of 'The Valentine Shop in the Strand'.

Apr 97–Jun 97 | ***Beauty and the Banknote*** This unusual exhibition from the British Museum explores the scope and significance of images of women on paper money. The extraordinary range includes imperious allegories, crowned monarchs, women working in factories and paddy fields, and a computer operator from Macedonia.

Edinburgh

SCOTTISH NATIONAL PORTRAIT GALLERY
1 Queen Street Edinburgh EH2 1JD Curator: Duncan Thomson
☎ +44 131 5568921 📠 +44 131 2267649
Open: Monday-Saturday 10.00-17.00 Sunday 14.00-17.00

COLLECTION | The Scottish National Portrait Gallery was founded in 1882 to illustrate Scottish history by means of authentic portraits. The collection policy has been broadened over the years to include topographical views of Scotland, contemporary depictions of historical events and portraits that are notable landmarks in the history of Scottish portrait painting. The Gallery also now contains a constantly updated Reference Archive and Social History Index, as well as the Scottish National Photography collection.
Most of the best known figures of Scottish history are represented, including Mary, Queen of Scots, Bonnie Prince Charlie and Robert Burns. Contemporaries include the dress designer Jean Muir, the novelist Muriel Spark and the footballer Danny McGrain.
The distinctive Neo-Gothic building, specifically designed for its current function by Sir Rowand Anderson, is remarkable in its own

right. The entrance hall contains a painted frieze showing a progression of the most celebrated Scottish men and women from ancient times to the end of the 19th century. Above are murals illustrating Scottish battles for independence.

Allan Ramsey
Hume, David

Scottish National Portrait Gallery, Edinburgh

EXHIBITIONS

Apr 96–Sep 96 — **Speaking Likeness**

20·09·96–24·11·96 — **David Roberts Bicentenary**

26·09·96–01·12·96 — **Look, Love and Follow** *Jacobite Prints*

12·12·96–23·02·97 — **Buccleauch Portrait Miniatures**

Edinburgh

SCOTTISH NATIONAL GALLERY OF MODERN ART
Belford Road Edinburgh EH4 3DR Curator: Richard Calvocoressi
☎ +44 131 5568921 ▯ +44 131 3324939
Open: Monday-Saturday 10.00-17.00 Sunday 14.00-17.00

F.C.B. Cadelli
Lady in Black

Scottish National Gallery of Modern Art, Edinburgh

COLLECTION — The Scottish National Gallery of Modern Art possesses Scotland's finest collection of 20th-century painting, sculpture and graphic art.

The collection includes works by Picasso, Matisse, Magritte, Moore, Baselitz, Davie, Freud, Bellany, Campbell and Wiszniewski.

EXHIBITIONS

06·06·96–22·09·96   *Alberto Giacometti 1901-1966*   This will be the first major exhibition of Giacometti's work to be staged in Britain since the restrospective held at the Tate Gallery in 1965. The exhibition will be comprised of 80 sculptures, 30 paintings and a selection of drawings. These will include sketches and paintings that were made by Giacometti in his youth, Surrealist sculptures produced during the early 1930s, and the celebrated series of tall standing figures which was begun immediately after the Second World War. Many of Giacometti's greatest works will be featured in the exhibition.

Nov 96–Jan 97   *Anne Redpath*

Glasgow

ART GALLERY AND MUSEUM
Kelvingrove Glasgow G3 8AG Director: Julian Spalding
☎ +44 141 3573929 📠 +44 141 3574537
Open: Monday-Saturday 10.00-17.00 Sunday 11.00-17.00
Closed: 1 Jan, 25 Dec

COLLECTION   The Art Gallery and Museum is housed in a red sandstone building completed in 1902. The collection includes paintings by Botticelli, Giorgione, Rembrandt, Millet, Monet, Van Gogh, Derain, Picasso and Dufy, as well as works by contemporary artists. There are also displays of historic and modern silver, jewellery, glass and ceramics; European armour, swords and firearms; and clothing, weapons and tools from prehistoric times. The museum conducts an extensive programme of temporary exhibitions.

Art Gallery and
Museum, Glasgow

EXHIBITIONS

until 25·08·96   *St. Kilda Explored*   This exhibition looks at the St. Kilda archipelago, off the west coast of Scotland, and the work which has gone on there since it was evacuated in 1930. The work of historians, vernacular architects, archaeologists and natural scientists is examined by means of interactive displays, a reconstruction of a typical house and a simulated excavation.

13·06·96–mid Aug 96   *Jessie M. King*   Jessie M. King was best known for her illustrations, with their distinctive rhythmic linear style. She also designed jewellery, textiles, wallpaper and decoration for ceramics.

Sep 96–Oct 96   ***Prize Winners Art Competition***   This competition attracts approximately 3000 entries, generally of remarkably high standard, from local schoolchildren. Most of the students are presented with a subject and complete a work within three hours.

20·09·96–23·03·97   ***Claws***   This exhibition looks at the world of domestic and feral cats, with an emphasis on natural history and human-feline interaction beginning in the days of Ancient Egypt.

07·10·96–16·12·96   ***Information Superhighway***   From the Science Box series of the London Museum of Science, this exhibition looks at the facts behind the hype of the Information Superhighway. Eight terminals give visitors the chance to explore the Internet themselves.

24·11·96–02·02·97   ***The British Gas World Wildlife Photographer of the Year Awards*** The winning entries in the Wildlife Photographer of the Year Competition are on display, featuring images from around the globe.

Glasgow

THE BURRELL COLLECTION
2060 Pollokshaws Road Glasgow G41 1AT Director: Julian Spalding
☎ +44 141 6497151   🖷 +44 141 6360086
Open: Monday-Saturday 10.00-17.00 Sunday 11.00-17.00
Closed: 1 Jan, 25 Dec

COLLECTION   The Burrell Collection, housed in a building of red sandstone, Portland limestone and timber, three miles south of Glasgow's centre, was assembled by a wealthy shipowner from Glasgow, Sir William Burrell, and contains more than 8000 items. In the Hutton Castle rooms, a reconstruction of rooms in Burrell's home, works from ancient civilisations and decorative arts of Northern Europe are displayed. The Oriental Collection includes Chinese ceramics, jades, bronzes, Japanese prints and a collection of Middle Eastern carpets and rugs. There is also a collection of European paintings, including many fine works by Degas.

EXHIBITIONS
06·06·96–06·10·96   ***Lynne Curran***   This exhibition presents Lynne Curran's tapestries, samplers and drawings. The artist will be in situ at the exhibition, completing a tapestry commissioned by Glasgow City Museums.

29·11·96–31·03·97   ***Russian Gold***   More than 150 objects from the museums of Rostov and Azov will be on display, documenting cultures of the Ukraine and Black Sea Regions dating from the 5th century B.C. to the 5th century A.D. The show will include exquisite jewellery, stoneware, plate and ornaments.

Glasgow

MCLELLAN GALLERIES
270 Sauchiehall Street Glasgow G2 3EH Director: Julian Spalding
☎ +44 141 3311854   🖷 +44 141 3329957
Open: Monday-Saturday 10.00-17.00 Sunday 11.00-17.00
Closed: 1 Jan, 25 Dec and between exhibitions

COLLECTION   No permanent collection.

25·05·96–30·09·96

Charles Rennie Mackintosh This is the largest-ever exhibition of Scotland's most celebrated architect and designer. It brings together material drawn from international collections, including some never previously exhibited. The various aspects of his work are explored through original works of art, room settings, reconstructions, models and video presentations. A highlight of the exhibition is the reconstruction of the Ladies' Luncheon Room from Miss Cranston's Ingram Street Tearooms, designed in 1900.

Nov 96–Dec 96

The Royal Glasgow Institute 135th Annual Anniversary The RGI annual exhibition is open to professional artists and others and aims to display the best of contemporary painting and sculpture in Scotland. Selection is by a committee of RGI council members and the exhibition forms the third-largest collection of its kind in Britain.

Glasgow

GALLERY OF MODERN ART
Queen Street Glasgow G1 3AZ Director: Julian Spalding
☎ +44 141 3311854 📠 +44 141 3329957
Open: Monday-Saturday 10.00-17.00 Sunday 11.00-17.00
Closed: 1 Jan, 25 Dec

COLLECTION

Glasgow's Gallery of Modern Art, which opened in March 1996, is housed in a refurbished neo-classical Georgian building in the heart of the city. The museum collection consists of post-war art and design, including a great many works acquired since 1990 through a specially created modern art fund.

The Gallery is spread over four floors of exhibition space, with each floor linked thematically to one of the four natural elements of fire, earth, water or air. The world-class works on display include pieces by innovators with international reputations, such as Niki de Saint Phalle, David Hockney, Sebastiao Salgado and Eduard Bersudsky, and a diverse cross-section of other international artists from countries as far afield as Papua New Guinea, Ethiopia, Australia and Mexico.
Some of Scotland's best-known artists are also represented in the museum's collection, including Peter Howson, John Bellany, Alan Davie, Adrian Wiszniewski, Steven Campbell and Alison Watt. Both in exhibitions and in the building itself, contemporary craft and design play an important role, with commissions awarded for the design of public seating, tiling and window recesses as part of the renovation of the building.

Apr 96–May 96

The Lord Provost's Prize The £12 000 City of Glasgow Lord Provost's Prize is awarded annually to an artist chosen by three expert judges and by votes of the public. Six shortlisted artists each submit one recent work and these works are then displayed at the Gallery of Modern Art so that visitors can vote for their favourite.

14·06·96–08·09·96

Craigie Aitchison This exhibition is intended as a 70th birthday tribute to the much respected and popular Scottish painter, Craigie Aitchison. The works on display include models, portraits, landscapes, still-lifes and his famous Bedlington terrier and Crucifixion paintings.

Grasmere

THE WORDSWORTH MUSEUM
Dove Cottage Grasmere Cumbria LA22 9SH Director: Robert Woof
☎ +44 15394 35544 📠 +44 15394 35748
Open: Daily 09.30-17.30
Closed: 24-26 Dec and 4 weeks in Jan-Feb

COLLECTION

Dove Cottage was the home of the poet William Wordsworth (1770-1850) from December 1799 until May 1808. It was here that he wrote 'Michael', 'Resolution and Independence', 'Ode: Intimations of Immortality', and 'The Prelude (1805)' in its entirety. The award-winning museum opened to the public in 1935. The Wordsworth Collection contains primary verse and letter manuscripts of Wordsworth, his family and circle of friends. There is a collection of portraits and printed early editions of these figures including Wordsworth himself, Samuel Taylor Coleridge, Lord Byron, Robert Southey and Thomas De Quincey. The Trust has a fine art collection centring on landscape drawings, paintings and prints emerging from the developing culture surrounding the Lake District, 1750-1850.

EXHIBITIONS

01·07·96–03·11·96 | *Benjamin Robert Haydon*   Painter and Writer

Feb 97 onwards | **The Ancient Mariner**

Hull

FERENS ART GALLERY
Queen Victoria Square Hull HU1 3RA Director: Michael Stanley
☎ +44 1482 593902 📠 +44 1482 593710
Open: Monday-Saturday 10.00-17.00 Sunday 13.30-16.30

COLLECTION

The Ferens Art Gallery possesses a collection of European and British works of art dating from the 15th century to the present. Chronological displays in the museum begin with Dutch and European Old Masters. Refined 18th-century portraiture, moralising and narrative Victorian images and the radical artistic developments of the early 1900s carry the story into the 20th century, with Post-War art and a varied selection of contemporary works.
In addition to these chronological displays, there are marine paintings and local scenes offering insights into Hull's thriving maritime past.
The museum also possesses a Live Art Space and auditorium, where traditional art forms can mix freely with film, video, computers and installations to produce new works, the latest in 'crossover' performance and time-based art.

EXHIBITIONS

24·02·96–12·05·96 | *A Collection for the Future*   Acquisitions made by the Ferens Art Gallery in a three-year funding partnership with the Contemporary Art Society and the Arts Council of England.

27·04·96–16·06·96 | *Art Unlimited* Multiples of the 1960s and 1990s from the Arts Council Collection   A national touring exhibition from the South Bank Centre, including works by Joseph Beuys, Christo and Richard Hamilton.

06·07·96–25·08·96 | *Sound and Fury*   The art and imagery of Heavy Metal; exhibition toured by Cartwright Hall, Bradford.

24·08·96–22·09·96 | *The Parents*   Photographs by Colin Gray.

07·10·96–20·10·96	*Root 96* International Festival of Live Art - performance and installation.
16·11·96–21·12·96	*Terry Street* Photographs by Robert Whittaker.
Nov 96–Dec 96	*Jacqueline Morreau* Work from the last ten years.
Feb 97–Mar 97	*Ferens Annual Winter Exhibition* Annual open submission show.

Kirkcaldy

KIRKCALDY MUSEUM AND ART GALLERY
War Memorial Gardens Kirkcaldy Fife KY1 1YG Curator: Dallas M. Mechan
☎ +44 1592 260732 ⬛ +44 1592 646260
Open: Monday-Saturday 10.30-17.00 Sunday 14.00-17.00

COLLECTION

The Kirkcaldy Museum and Art Gallery, set in the attractive garden grounds of the town's War Memorial Gardens, houses a collection of fine and decorative arts of local and national importance. The museum owns what is probably the largest public collection of the works of William McTaggart and Scottish colourist S.J. Peploe existing outside the National Galleries of Scotland. The collection also includes works by Sickert, Lowry and Cadell, and features an award-winning permanent local history exhibition. A lively changing exhibition programme of art, craft, history and photography runs throughout the year. Tbe museum café features a fine display of Wemyss Ware pottery, the colourful local ceramic ware which was produced in the town between the 1890s and 1930.

EXHIBITIONS

29·06·96–31·07·96	*Inuit Art* An exhibition of printmaking and soapstone and bone sculpture by Inuit artists from Cape Dorset, Northwest Territories, Canada.
17·08·96–20·10·96	*Claiming the Kingdom* An exhibition of artwork by outstanding contemporary artists of Fife.
31·08·96–22·09·96	*Behind the Screens* In celebration of the Centenary of Cinema, this small-scale social history exhibition explores the cinema as experienced by projectionists, managers and usherettes from the early days of the travelling cinematograph booth right up to today's modern multiplexes.
02·11·96–29·11·96	*Fife Art Exhibition* This annual event provides an unrivalled opportunity for amateur artists in Fife to display their creations. Over 600 works will be on display, ranging from paintings and photographs to sculpture and craft work.
14·12·96–09·02·97	*The Chair in Fife, 1660-1960* A pioneering exhibition featuring a selection of 'common' chairs made from local materials and with local features which illustrate how, before the age of mass production, the furniture of Fife had a distinct personality.
14·12·96–09·02·97	*Sitting Pretty* An exhibition of contemporary chairs made in Scotland both by industry and by artisan-makers, highlighting the internationalist context in which furniture design flourishes today.
22·02·97–20·04·97	*Raw Materials* *Contemporary Scottish Textiles* A selection of 62 pieces by 23 artisans who demonstrate the rich diversity of approaches to the textile arts in Scotland today.

Leeds

LEEDS CITY ART GALLERY
The Headrow Leeds LSl 3AA Director: Evelyn Silber
☎ +44 113 2478248 📠 +44 113 2449689
Open: Monday-Friday 10.00-17.30 Wednesday 10.00-21.00
Saturday 10.00-16.00
Closed: Sunday and Bank Holiday Mondays and following Tuesdays

COLLECTION

The collection includes Old Masters, a representative collection of 19th-century art, including Victorian academic paintings, landscapes by Constable, Turner and Crome, Barbizon paintings and paintings by Sisley, Renoir, Signac and Fantin-Latour. There are works by Derain, Bonnard and others from the early 20th century.

20th-century art is the main focus of the Gallery's collection and covers all the main movements this century from Camden Town through Vorticism to the present day. There are works from the inter-war years by Wadsworth, Spencer and others and the post-war artists include, among others, Francis Bacon, John Walker and Leon Kossoff.

Among the prints and drawings are a collection of Dürer prints and Rembrandt etchings. The English watercolours are strongly represented.

The sculpture collection contains work by Jacob Epstein, Henry Moore, Barbara Hepworth and Eduardo Paolozzi, with some earlier pieces by Canova and Rodin. More recent trends are represented by Richard Long, Bill Woodrow and others.

Henry Moore
(1898-1986)
Shelter scene- Two seated figures 1941

Leeds City Art Galleries, Leeds

EXHIBITIONS

Mar 96-Jun 96

Conversations with Pictures A series of interludes through the Gallery's permanent collection, designed to make the visitor linger longer and ponder; contemporary artists select a painting and engage it in a 'dialogue'. Participants include Bridget Riley, Paula Rego and Canadian artist Eric Cameron.

14·03·96-02·06·96

Real Art: 'A New Modernism' *British Reflexive Painters in the 1990s* A show about painting as much as a show of paintings, this two-part exhibition brings together some forty abstract works by six painters from a new generation of British artists.

18·04·96-02·06·96

Jake Attree *Visions of the City*

27·04·96-02·06·96

Jack B. Yeats *A Celtic Visionary* Jack B. Yeats (1871-1957), brother of the poet W.B. Yeats, is recognised as the foremost Irish painter of the 20th century. This exhibition brings together a selection of his remarkable late pictures, painted with a bold, expressionistic and almost mystical vision.

13·06·96-27·07·96	***The Impossible Science of Being*** *Dialogues between Anthropology and Photography* Exploring the history and influence of anthropological photography from a contemporary critical standpoint, this exhibition presents archival material from the Royal Anthropological Institute juxtaposed with new commissioned work by Faisal Addu'Allah, Dave Lewis and Zarina Bhimji, three contemporary artists of African and Asian origin.
mid Jun 96-Oct 96	***Wunderkammer*** *The Secret Life of Objects* This large-scale project sets out to create a number of critical and creative explorations by living artists into the nature of contemporary museum culture.
Aug 96-Sep 96	***Open Exhibition*** The Gallery's annual exhibition, held in the Lyons Galleries and open to all artists resident in the Yorkshire and Humberside regions, presents work in painting, drawing, sculpture, printmaking and photography.
04·09·96-23·11·96	***David Nash*** *Drawings and Sculpture* David Nash (born 1945) is widely regarded as one of Britain's leading sculptors, regularly exhibiting internationally. His sculpture, invariably in wood, responds to the natural environment, and in particular to its inner forces, often translating natural forms into new constructs.
02·10·96-05·01·97	***David Le Marchand (1674-1726)*** *An Ingenious Man for Carving in Ivory* Looking at the career of this ivory carver who found the principal market for his work in Britain.
02·10·96-05·01·97	***Peter Scheemakers (1691-1781)*** *The Famous Statuary* Studies in a sculptor's career, his monumental commissions and his market in Britain, traced largely through his drawings.

Leicester

LEICESTERSHIRE MUSEUM AND ART GALLERY
New Walk Leicester LE1 7EA Director: Tim Schadla-Hall
☎ **+44 116 2554100 📠 +44 116 2473011**
Open: Monday-Saturday 10.00-17.30 Sunday 14.00-17.30
Closed: Good Friday, 25, 26 Dec

COLLECTION	A major regional venue with local and national collections. New galleries include Variety of Life (natural history), Leicestershire's Rocks (geology), Ancient Egyptians and Discovering Art. The displays range from beautiful decorative arts, including ceramics, silver and glass and the internationally famous German Expressionist collection; to the Rutland Dinosaur, stunning minerals, and hundreds of butterflies.
EXHIBITIONS 23·03·96–12·05·96	***An Intelligent Rebellion*** *Women Artists of Pakistan* This exhibition of photography, collage, printing and painting is the first to feature contemporary art from Pakistan.
23·03·96–19·05·96	***Easter Eggstravaganza*** This exhibition explores the natural and social history of the egg and brings together the collections of the museum's biology section with its famous Dryad crafts collection.
01·06·96–26·06·96	***Artworks*** A new selection of paintings and recent acquisitions from the Leicestershire Museums, Arts and Records Service Artworks Collection is featured in this exhibition.
02·06·96–21·07·96	***Messel Fossils*** A window on the past: 50 million year-old complete skeletons of bats, crocodiles, snakes and birds from a unique discovery made at the Messel Pit in Germany.

06·07·96–22·09·96	*Indian Miniatures* Festivals of India
14·07·96–15·09·96	*'Now Showing'* Posters and Ephemera from Popular Indian Cinema, 1950s-1970s
03·08·96–22·12·96	*Immensely Industrious* The Watercolours of George Moore Henton (1861-1924)

Liverpool

LIVERPOOL MUSEUM
William Brown Street Liverpool L3 8EN Curator: Eric Greenwood
☎ **+44 151 4784747** **+44 151 4784390**
Open: Monday-Saturday 10.00-17.00 Sunday 12.00-17.00
Closed: 1 Jan, Good Friday, 24-26 Dec

| COLLECTION | The Liverpool Museum houses a collection with subjects ranging from the wonders of the rain forest to the mysteries of outer space. Permanent displays include a vivarium and an aquarium, historic transport, archaeology, ethnology, the award-winning Natural History Centre, the Time and Space Gallery and a planetarium. |
| EXHIBITION 11·01·96–28·08·96 | *The Arts of the Samurai* 14th-19th Century This exhibition is drawn from the museum's Japanese collections, which have never been previously displayed. The exhibits consist of Japanese armour, swords, sword-fittings and lacquer work collected by Liverpool businessman Randal Hibbert from the late 19th century until around 1925. The exhibition illustrates the European perception of the Japanese, following the opening of Japan to Western trade in 1868. |

Liverpool

MERSEYSIDE MARITIME MUSEUM
Albert Dock Liverpool L3 4AA Curator: Mike Stammers
☎ **+44 151 2070001** **+44 151 4784590**
Open: Daily 10.30-17.30

| COLLECTION | Set in the heart of Liverpool's magnificent waterfront, the museum is dedicated to the history of the great port of Liverpool, its ships and its people. With its unique blend of floating exhibits, craft demonstrations and five floors of permanent displays including a new permanent Transatlantic Slavery gallery, the museum covers all aspects of Merseyside maritime activity. |
| EXHIBITIONS | No exhibitions planned. |

Liverpool

TATE GALLERY LIVERPOOL
Albert Dock Liverpool L3 4BB Curator: Lewis Biggs
☎ **+44 151 7093223** **+44 151 7093122**
Open: Tuesday-Sunday 10.00-18.00
Closed: Monday, except for public holidays

| COLLECTION | No permanent collection. |
| EXHIBITIONS Until Apr 97 | *Home and Away* Internationalism and British Art 1900-1990 This collection display looks at how artistic developments in Britain |

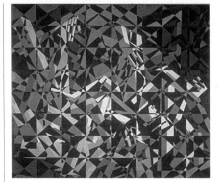

David Bomberg
(1890- 1957)
*In the Hold, 1913 -
1914*
Exhibition
'Home and Away-
Internationalism and
British Art 1900-1990'

*Tate Gallery,
Liverpool*

have been influenced both by the travels of artists abroad and by
the presence of foreign artists working in Britain. Ranging across
the whole of the century, it includes celebrated works by Walter
Sickert, Jacob Epstein, Henri Gaudier-Brzeska, Henry Moore, David
Hockney, Rachel Whiteread and Damien Hirst.

16·03·96–Apr 97 | ***Characters and Conversations*** *A Portrait of Modern British Art
1900-1930* This display explores the characterisation of the British
artist in the early years of the 20th century. Focusing on the image
projected by self-proclaimed 'modern' artists, it includes self-
portraits, portraits of friends and associates, group portraits and
studio interiors produced by a diverse selection of artists working in
the early part of the 20th century. Many of the artists knew each
other, and the display looks at various communities of artists,
including those associated with the Royal Academy, the Slade
School, the Bloomsbury and Vorticist groups.

30·03·96–Aug 96 | ***Wandering About in the Future*** *New Tate Acquisitions*
Taking its title from one of the exhibited works, Cathy de
Monchaux's 'Wandering About in the Future, Looking Forward In
the Past', this is a display of art recently acquired for the national
collection. Sculpture by Louise Bourgeois, Juan Muñoz, Miroslaw
Balka, Robert Gober and Georg Baselitz; paintings, photography
and wall-based work by Ian McKeever, Gerhard Richter, Cindy
Sherman and Cathy de Monchaux, and a video work by Bruce
Nauman offer an insight into the Tate's collecting policy for
'cutting-edge' contemporary art.

13·04·94–27·05·96 | ***New Contemporaries 96*** New Contemporaries is relaunched at
Tate Gallery Liverpool this Spring. Selected by Mark Wallinger,
Maria de Corral and Richard Shone, this exhibition continues to be a
unique platform for young artists to show their work in a
professional atmosphere.

14·09·96–03·11·96 | ***Rachel Whiteread*** Sculptor Rachel Whiteread is known for her
much acclaimed work 'House' and as winner of the 1993 Turner
Prize. This exhibition will include works which have not previously
been seen in Britain and will be the first solo show of her work
outside London.

Liverpool

WALKER ART GALLERY
William Brown Street Liverpool L3 8EL Curator: Julian Treuherz
☎ +44 151 2070001 📠 +44 151 4784190
Open: Monday-Saturday 10.00-17.00 Sunday 12.00-17.00
Closed: 1 Jan, Good Friday, 24-26 Dec

COLLECTION

The Walker Art Gallery houses an outstanding collection of European art from 1300 to the present day. It is especially rich in European Old Masters, Victorian and Pre-Raphaelite paintings and modern British art. It also houses an award-winning sculpture gallery.

EXHIBITIONS

Nov 96–Feb 97

Sir Charles Reilly and the Liverpool School of Architecture
Sir Charles Reilly (1874-1948) was one of the most influential figures of 20th-century British architecture. He designed some distinguished buildings, but was more important as a teacher, polemicist and source of inspiration. This exhibition examines his own buildings as well as the work of his students and associates, who designed many of Liverpool's most prominent landmarks.

Mar 97–Jun 97

Sir Lawrence Alma Tadema   One of the most famous and successful of Victorian artists, Alma Tadema specialised in paintings of life in classical times, showing elegantly dressed Romans in their sumptuous villas, visiting the baths or idling on marble benches overlooking the deep blue sea. Tadema was especially noted for his exquisite rendering of fine detail, exotic flowers, rich fabrics, precious objects and the sheen of marble.

London

ROYAL ACADEMY OF ARTS
Burlington House Piccadilly London W1V 0DS Director: Pears Rodgers
☎ +44 171 4945615 📠 +44 171 4394998
Open: Daily 10.00-18.00

COLLECTION

No permanent collection.

EXHIBITIONS

28.03.96-23.06.96

Gustave Caillebotte 1848-1894 *The Unknown Impressionist*   This will be the first comprehensive exhibition in Britain to celebrate the work of Gustave Caillebotte, the least known of the Impressionist painters.

09.06.96-18.08.96

(Closed 17 June)
228th Summer Exhibition   The Royal Academy's annual Summer Exhibition, now in its 228th year, brings together over 1100 paintings, sculptures, drawings and models by many of Britain's most distinguished artists and architects.

11.07.96-08.09.96

Roger de Grey Painter   An exhibition of the work of Sir Roger de Grey, President of the Royal Academy, who died in February 1995.

Jul 1996

Royal Academy Schools Final Year Show   Work by some of this country's most promising young artists who have completed their three-year postgraduate course at the RA Schools. Many of the works will be for sale.

12.09.96-17.11.96

Bridging the City   This exhibition focuses on the current debate surrounding the revitalisation of the Thames through London. Addressing issues about the ways in which rivers were variously bridged - from the simple path bridge to the multifunctional 'inhabited' bridge - it draws upon examples from the past as well as future projects designed specifically for the River Thames.

07.11.96-19.01-97

From Mantegna to Picasso *100 Drawings from the Thaw Collection at the Pierpont Morgan Library, New York*   This will be the first showing in Europe of one hundred Master Drawings from the private collection of Eugene and Clare Thaw, which has been put together over the past few decades. The exhibition includes important examples by Mantegna, Altdorfer and Fra Bartolommeo, but focuses on the collection's eighteenth- and nineteenth-century drawings, including significant holdings of Cézanne, Delacroix, Degas en Redon.

16.01.97-06.04.97   ***Late Braque***   Together with Pablo Picasso, Georges Braques was the founder of Cubism. This exhibition will be devoted to the last twenty-five years of Braque's career, when he returned to the ideas and techniques that had first preoccupied him during his Cubist period.

London

ACCADEMIA ITALIANA
8-9 Grosvenor Place London SW1X 7SH   Director: Rosa Maria Letts
☎ **+44 171 2350303** 📠 **+44 171 2350404**
Open: Tuesday-Saturday 10.00-17.20 Sunday 12.00-17.30

COLLECTION   No permanent collection.

EXHIBITIONS
Spring 96–Summer 96   ***Leonardo*** *Artist, Inventor, Scientist*   This comprehensive exhibition, including paintings, drawings, models and interactive computer-generated images, examines the full scope of Da Vinci's genius.

Accademia Italiana
London

Sep 96   ***Randy Klein*** *Transformations*   Presented as a magical journey through a gigantic book: a presentation of the work of this remarkable young sculptor, inspired by classical mythology and Dante's Divine Comedy.

Sep 96   ***Sconfinamenti*** *Italian/British Visual Art Exchange*
A contemporary art exhibition of various works by young British and Italian artists.

Oct 96   ***Pushkin Exhibition***   From the Pushkin Museum in Moscow, in celebration of its centenary, a fascinating collection of portraits, artefacts, letters and manuscripts of this major literary figure.

Nov 96   ***La Dolce Vita from Grosz to Guttuso*** *The Art Collection of Marta Marzotto, the Celebrated Italian Personality and Liberated Muse*
A range of work including intimate portraits by Renato Guttuso and a number of major works by European and Italian 20th-century artists.

Dec 96   ***Orneore Metelli***   A captivating exhibition of this Italian artist,
              giving an evocative retrospective of Terni, capital of Umbria, from
              1900 to 1940. Humour and daring perspectives distinguish the
              paintings of this newly discovered master of the 'naive'.

Spring 97   ***Russian Imperial Tables***   Taken from the collections of the State
              Museum of Ceramics and the 18th-century Kuskova Estate, this
              exhibition presents an important survey of Russian history.

London

BARBICAN ART GALLERY
Level 8 Barbican Centre London EC2Y 8DS Director: Melvyn Barnes
☎ **+44 171 6384141 📠 +44 171 6280364**
Open: Monday, Wednesday-Saturday 10.00-18.45 Tuesday 10.00-17.45
Closed: Sunday

COLLECTION   No permanent collection.

EXHIBITIONS
09·05·96–18·08·96 ***Eve Arnold***   *A Retrospective*   This exhibition of over 200 black and
              white and colour photographs covers all aspects of the work of one
              of the century's most influential and humane photographers, Eve
              Arnold. For more than four decades she has witnessed through
              camera and words many of the major figures and events of the
              latter half of the 20th century. Figures featured in her photographs
              include political figures Malcolm X and Margaret Thatcher, heads of
              state Dwight Eisenhower and Indira Gandhi, and movie stars Clark
              Gable and Marilyn Monroe.

09·05·96–18·08·96 ***Derek Jarman***   The first ever retrospective of the life and work of
              Derek Jarman (1942-1994), this exibition considers his diverse career
              as artist, filmmaker and designer.

12·09·96–15·12·96 ***Erwin Blumenfeld*** *A Fetish of Fashion*   Erwin Blumenfeld
              (1897–1969), most famous for his innovative fashion photography in
              the 1930s for Paris 'Vogue', was also an active participant in the
              anarchist Dada movement. This major restrospective on Blumenfeld
              will cover all aspects of his oeuvre, tracing his development as a
              photographer, and also featuring his paintings, drawings, collages
              and written work.

12·09·96–15·12·96 ***Icons and Innovators***   This exhibition will be a window to the most
              fresh and exciting developments in the hitherto undervalued arena
              of British fashion design, fashion photography, video, advertising
              and youth culture. The exhibition will, by inviting the participation
              of those at the cutting edge of style in fashion, music and the
              media, celebrate the energy and creativity that arise outside
              mainstream art practice.

Jan 97–Apr 97 ***Modernism in Britain***   Taking a look at art in Britain during the
              period brief between 1910 and 1914, this exhibition will juxtapose
              works of British artists with works from Europe that were exhibited
              in Britain at this time. Barbican Art Gallery hopes to include works
              by Picasso, Cézanne and Matisse in the show, alongside celebrated
              artists such as Vanessa Bell and Duncan Grant.

London

THE BRITISH MUSEUM
Great Russell Street London WC1B 3DG Director: R.G.W. Anderson
☎ +44 171 6361555 📠 +44 171 3238118
Open: Monday-Saturday 10.00-17.00 Sunday 14.30-18.00
Closed: 1 Jan, 5 Apr, 6 May, 24-26 Dec

COLLECTION

Founded in 1753, the British Museum has a large collection of works of man stemming from Prehistoric times until the present day. There are permanent displays of antiquities from Egypt, Western Asia, Greece, Rome and the Orient, as well as collections of works from the Prehistoric, Romano-British, Medieval, Renaissance and Modern periods. The museum's collections of prints and drawings, coins and medals and Japanese antiquities are displayed in a series of temporary exhibitions, while the Ethnographic collections are housed at the Museum of Mankind.

Examples of the artefacts which can be viewed at the British Museum include the following: The Rosetta Stone and Egyptian mummies (Egyptian antiquities), sculptures from the Parthenon, the Mausoleum of Halicarnassus and the Temple of Artemis at Ephesus, and the Portland Vase (Greek and Roman antiquities), the Sutton Hoo Treasure, Lewis Chessmen, and the 'Nef' Ships Clock (Medieval and Later antiquities), Indian sculptures from Amaravati and Chinese porcelain (Oriental antiquities), the Lindow Man and the Mildenhall Treasure (Prehistoric and Romano-British antiquities), and Assyrian lionhunt reliefs and the Oxus Treasure (Western Asiatic antiquities).
Recently the museum opened a new gallery 'The Hellenistic World' and more galleries are planned for the next year.

William Crosbie
*Young Man learning
(No, No, No, No,),*
1935

*British Museum,
London*

EXHIBITIONS

05·03·96–18·08·96 ***Excavating Ancient Beirut***

07·03·96–08·09·96 ***Commemorating the 19th Century*** *Coins and Medals by the Wyon Family*

13·03·96–14·07·96 ***Vases and Volcanoes*** *Sir William Hamilton and his Collection*

15·05·96–14·07·96 ***The Art of Kayama Matazó*** *(closed June 17 for changeover)*

23·05·96–30·06·96 ***Oriental Antiquities*** *Recent Acquisitions*

23·05·96–15·09·96 ***The Grotesque*** *Ornamental Prints from the British Museum*

23·05·96–15·09·96 ***19th-Century French Drawings from the British Museum***

23·05·96–15·09·96	*David Le Marchand (1674-1726), Ivory Carver*
24·05·96–28·07·96	*South Indian Painting and Sculpture* An exhibition for the South India Festival.
26·07·96–29·09·96	*20th-Century Chinese Painting* *Tradition and Innovation* An exhibition on loan from the Hong Kong Museum of Art.
Aug 96–Oct 96	*Japanese Paintings and Prints*
10·09·96–02·03·97	*The Coins and Archaeology of the Abbasid Caliphate*
13·09·96–05·01·97	*Mysteries of Ancient China* An exhibition sponsored by The Times
27·09·96–05·01·97	*The Malcolm Collection of Drawings*
16·10·96–12·01·97	*Japanese Prints during the Allied Occupation (1945-1952)*
24·01·97–20·04·97	*Modern Scandinavian Printmaking*
24·01·97–20·04·97	*Jacques Bellange, Mannerist Printmaker*
Mar 97–Jul 97	*Ancient Faces* *Mummy Portraits from Roman Egypt*

London

COURTAULD GALLERY
Somerset House Strand London WC2 Director: John Murdoch
☎ +44 171 8732526 🖷 +44 171 8732589
Open: Monday-Saturday 10.00-18.00 Sunday 14.00-18.00

COLLECTION

A fine collection of Impressionist paintings in Britain, as well as masterpieces by Botticelli, Tiepolo, Rubens, and Goya, housed in Somerset House, one of the most beautiful 18th-century buildings in London.

EXHIBITIONS

22·02·96–26·05·96

Thomas Gainsborough *40 Drawings from the Collection* Landscapes, portraits and studies by the great 18th-century master.

14·06·96–27·08·96

The Four Elements   Prints and drawings from the collection on the theme of fire, water, earth and air. Artists include Turner, Manet, Dürer, Rowlandson, Guercino and Brueghel.

10·10·96–05·01·97

William Chambers and Somerset House   Somerset House has been called the most remarkable public building of the Enlightenment in London, and yet both it and its architect are little known. This exhibition will examine Chambers as an architect, as well as the actual construction of his masterpiece.

London

DESIGN MUSEUM
28 Shad Thames London SE1 2YD Director: Paul Thompson
☎ +44 171 4036933 🖷 +44 171 3786540
Open: Monday-Friday 11.30-18.00 Saturday, Sunday 12.00-18.00
Closed: 25, 26 Dec

COLLECTION

The Design Museum offers visitors a readily accessible insight into the role that design plays in our everyday lives, from the origins of mass production up to the present day. The Collection Gallery on the top floor of the museum provides examples of the development of design in mass production. It is organised into a series of thematic displays showing changes in use and meaning, and the origins of mass production. Many displayed items and methods are still in use today. The Review Gallery examines contemporary design in an international context. On display are concepts, prototypes and finished products from furniture to cameras and cars to computers, providing visitors with an unparalleled opportunity in this country to see some of the most innovative products produced by designers from all over the world. Both these galleries host exciting programmes of regularly changing displays which profile a single product, designer or company in greater depth. Graphic and photographic displays are held in the foyer of the museum.

EXHIBITIONS

24·04·96–06·10·96

100 Masterpieces   *Furniture that made the 20th Century*
100 classics of furniture design by the world's leading designers are on display in the UK for the first time during the summer of 1996.

24·10·96–Apr 97

Charlotte Perriand   *A Way of Life*   Charlotte Perriand, who worked with Le Corbusier for 10 years, is one of the most significant figures in the development of Modernism. This is the first retrospective exhibition in the UK devoted to her long and distinguished career.

London

DULWICH PICTURE GALLERY
College Road London SE21 7AD Director: Giles Waterfield
☎ +44 181 6935254 📠 +44 181 6930923
Open: Tuesday-Friday 10.00-17.00 Saturday 11.00-17.00 Sunday 14.00-17.00
Closed: Monday and public holidays

COLLECTION

Dulwich Picture Gallery has an outstanding collection of Old Master paintings, primarily from 17th-century artists, as well as many well-known 18th-century artists.

Rembrandt van Rijn
Girl at a window,
1645

Dulwich Picture
Gallery, London

The collection came into existence as a result of political events in 17th-century Europe. A London art dealer named Noel Desenfans was commissioned by the King of Poland to acquire paintings for a Polish national collection, but the king was forced to abdicate his throne and the pictures were left without a home. An heir of Desenfans, Sir Francis Bourgeois, established the gallery in Dulwich. The building was designed for the collection in 1811 by Sir John Soane and was Britain's first public art gallery. The founders of the Gallery lie in the mausoleum which Soane designed for them in the centre of the Gallery.

29·02·96-12·05·96   **Soane and Death**   Dulwich Picture Gallery, the first purpose-built art gallery in England, was designed by Sir John Soane. He was fascinated by the art of death and mausoleums which, with their lack of imposed conventions and disciplines, allowed him freedom for individual expression. This exhibition explores Soane's interest in this field and is centred on his most celebrated burial chamber: the mausoleum which he intended for the three founders of the museum.

19·06·96-18·08·96   **Martha Fleming** *Open Book*   Martha Fleming, the Canadian contemporary artist, will create a new, temporary artwork for Dulwich, combining Sir Joshua Reynolds' own portable camera obscura and his painting 'A Girl and a Baby', one of the most popular pictures in the Dulwich Picture Gallery's collection.

03·07·96-29·09·96   **Dutch Flower Painting 1600-1750**   In the age when a single tulip bulb cost more than a town house, Dutch flower paintings varied from delicate contemplative studies to exuberant confections. Many of the paintings in this exhibition, including works by Ambrosius Bosschaert, Van Huysum, Rachel Ruysch, Jan Davidsz de Heem and Balthasar van der Ast, are from private collections and have never been on display before.

London

HAYWARD GALLERY
Belvedere Road London SE1 8XZ Director: Henry Meyric Hughes
☎ +44 171 9283144 ◫ +44 171 4012664
Open: Daily 10.00-18.00 Tuesday, Wednesday 10.00-20.00

   No permanent collection.

06·06·96-18·08·96   **Claes Oldenburg** *An Anthology*   Claes Oldenburg is probably best known for his soft sculptures depicting ordinary objects such as toilets, typewriters and foodstuffs, but this exhibition traces his career from the installations of the early 60s, rendered in brightly painted canvas soaked in plaster, through his series of drawings, in the late 60s, for proposed colossal monuments of everday objects, to his efforts over the past 20 years to realise the proposed monuments.

19·09·96-01·12·96   **ACE!** *Arts Council Collection New Purchases*   This exhibition, highlighting purchases made since 1989, presents about 50 works by some of Britain's best known artists, plus examples from an emerging generation. Featured are paintings by Gillian Ayres, Michael Craig-Martin, Gary Hume and Zebedee Jones, photographic and time-based work by Jane and Louise Wilson, Catherine Yass, Lucy Gunning and Sarah Jones, sculpture by Rachel Whiteread, Damien Hirst, Grenville Davey, Eric Bainbridge and Hadrian Pigott, and Antony Gormley's epic installation, entitled 'Field for the British Isles'. Also a Mapplethorpe photographs exhibition will accompany this event.

London

ICA INSTITUTE OF CONTEMPORARY ARTS
The Mall London SW1Y 5AH Director: Mik Flood
☎ +44 171 9300493 ◫ +44 171 8730051
Open: Daily 12.00-19.30 Friday 12.00-21.00

   No permanent collection.

Vija Celmins
Stones and painted
bronzes

Institute of
Contemporary Arts,
London

EXHIBITIONS

10·05·96—07·07·96	*Jake and Dinos Chapman*
23·07·96—29·09·96	*Gothic*
01·11·96—22·12·96	*Vija Celmins*
15·01·97—16·03·97	*Gabriel Orozco*

London

LEIGHTON HOUSE MUSEUM & ART GALLERY
12 Holland Park Road London W14 8L2 Director: Julia Findlater
☎ +44 171 6023316 📠 +44 171 3712467
Open: Monday-Saturday 11.00-17.30
Closed: Sunday and public holidays

COLLECTION

Leighton House was the home of Frederic, Lord of Leighton (1830-1896), the great Classical painter and President of the Royal Academy. The house was built between 1864 and 1879 to designs by George Aitchison, and is the expression of Leighton's vision of a private palace devoted to art.
The Arab Hall is the centrepiece of Leighton House. The gilt mosaic frieze, depicting birds and scenes of mythology, the sound of the fountain in the centre of the Arab Hall, and the intricate designs of the Isnik tiles all create an extraordinary oriental ambiance. This atmosphere extends throughout the other rooms of the house, culminating in Leighton's Studio, which is the heart of the house and the reason for its existence. Leighton House contains a fine collection of Victorian art. Paintings by Leighton, Burne-Jones, Millais and their contemporaries are displayed throughout the House. There is also an extensive exhibition programme in the adjacent art galleries.

EXHIBITIONS

13·05·96—25·05·96	*A Middle Eastern Surprise*
03·06·96—22·06·96	*Society of Scribes*
01·07·96—05·07·96	*Tabitha Salmon*
22·07·96—10·08·96	*Kensington & Chelsea Artists' Exhibition*
27·08·96—28·09·96	*Randolph Caldecott*
14·10·96—02·11·96	*Paper as a Sculptural Medium*
11·11·96—23·11·96	*James Childs*
02·12·96—14·12·96	*Silversmiths*

London

MUSEUM OF MANKIND -
THE ETHNOGRAPHY DEPT. OF THE BRITISH MUSEUM
6 Burlington Gardens London W1X 2EX Director: J. Mack
☎ +44 171 6361555   +44 171 3238013
Open: Monday-Saturday 10.00-17.00 Sunday 14.30-18.00
Closed: 1 Jan, 5 Apr, 6 May, 24-26 Dec

COLLECTION

Ethnography The Museum of Mankind is the British Museum's Department of Ethnography. Its main concern is studying and collecting items from recent and contemporary Indigenous societies in Africa, the Americas, Asia, Oceania and parts of Europe. The archaeology of sub-Saharan Africa is also a subject of one of the museum's collections.
Examples of items on display include Benin bronzes and ivories from West Africa, textiles and wood sculpture from West and Central Africa, stone and mosaic work from pre-Columbian times and Meso-America, collections made in the Pacific and on the north-west coast of America during the voyage of Captain Cook and Vancouver, and the Raffles collection from the early 19th century.

EXHIBITIONS

Until 03·06·96   *Display and Modesty* North African Textiles

Until 16·06·96   *Secular and Sacred* Ethiopian Textiles

Until 16·06·96   *Great Benin, a West African Kingdom*

Until 16·06·96   *The Power of the Hand* African Arms and Armour

Until Sep 96   *Play and Display* Masquerades of Southern Nigeria
An exhibition for the Africa '95 season.

25·04·96 onwards   *Pagay, Rice and Life in the Northern Philippines*

16·05·96 onwards   *The Gilded Image* Pre-Columbian Gold from Central and South America

Nov 96 onwards   *Maori*

London

THE NATIONAL GALLERY
Trafalgar Square London WC2N 5DN Director: Neil MacGregor
☎ +44 171 7472885   +44 171 9304764
Open: Monday-Saturday 10.00-18.00 Sunday 14.00-18.00
Closed: 1 Jan, Good Friday, 24 -26 Dec

COLLECTION

The National Gallery houses the national collection of Western European painting, comprising more than 2 000 pictures dating from the late 13th to the early 20th century: in other words, from Giotto to Picasso. The pictures belong to the public and access to them is free, as it has been since the Gallery was founded in 1824. All pictures are normally on show.
The Gallery's unique strength lies in the balance of the collection across all European schools. Virtually all the great artists are represented by masterpieces and the collection is hung to emphasise the international nature of European painting at all periods since the Renaissance.
The Sainsbury Wing (Painting from 1260 to 1510) exhibits works by Van Eyck, Piero della Francesca, Botticelli, Leonardo da Vinci, Bellini, Raphael and others. Paintings by artists such as Cranach,

Michelangelo, Holbein, Titian, Veronese and El Greco are on display in the West Wing (Painting from 1510 to 1600), while in the North Wing (Painting from 1600 to 1700) works by Rubens, Poussin, Velázquez, Van Dyck, Claude, Rembrandt and Vermeer can be viewed. Canvasses by Gainsborough, Turner, Constable, Cézanne, Monet, Van Gogh, Seurat and Picasso are exhibited in the East Wing (Painting from 1700 to 1920).

Bronzino
An Allegory with Venus and Cupid

The National Gallery, London

EXHIBITIONS

[Sainsbury Wing]

22·05·96–26·08·96

Degas *Beyond Impressionism*   This exhibition is the first major exhibition devoted to the late work of Edgar Degas. This late work has never been properly studied and the exhibition will bring together paintings, pastels, drawings and sculptures from public and private collections around the world to present a fuller and more coherent picture of the highly innovative Degas in his last decades.

17·10·96–19·01·97

Making & Meaning *Rubens' Landscapes*   The fourth exhibition in this series will concentrate on Rubens' landscapes. The Gallery holds the most outstanding group of his landscape paintings to be found anywhere in the world: the five paintings including the large and celebrated 'Chateau de Steen', the picture Rubens made of his own country estate.

[Sunley Room]

22·05·96–26·08·96

Degas as a Collector   To coincide with the Degas exhibition in the Sainsbury Wing, this exhibition looks at Degas' own collection of paintings, drawings and prints. The Gallery acquired eleven works, including examples by Ingres, Delacroix and Manet, at the Degas sale in 1918, and these are joined by loans from collections in Britain and abroad featuring works by Van Gogh, Gauguin and Cézanne, among others.

25·09·96–05·01·97

Peter Blake *Associate Artist at The National Gallery*   In 1994, Peter Blake was invited to become the Gallery's third Associate Artist. This exhibition will show work produced during his two years with the Gallery.

[Room 30]

22·02·96–19·05·96

Masterpieces from the Doria Pamphilj Gallery, Rome   The Doria Pamphilj Gallery is one of the most celebrated princely collections in

Rome and contains many masterpieces of 16th and 17th-century painting. For the first time, a group of its finest works is being shown outside Italy, including Velázquez's famous portrait of 'Pope Innocent X', Caravaggio's 'Rest on the Flight into Egypt' and paintings by Titian and Raphael.

[Room 1]

06·03·96–27·05·96 | ***Pesellino's Trinity Altarpiece*** This display examines the great 'Trinity' altarpiece by the 15th-century artist Pesellino, one of the Gallery's most complex and puzzling works. Completed after the artist's death, it was later broken up and acquired by the Gallery in pieces. These were reassembled together with a fragment that belongs to the Royal Collection. Only recently was a missing predella panel identified in the collection of the Hermitage Museum and is here reunited with the rest of the altarpiece for the first time.

05·06·96–07·07·96 | ***El Greco's 'Christ Driving the Traders from the Temple'*** This work is on return from its UK tour and is the third of the present series of touring exhibitions.

17·07·96–29·09·96 | ***National Gallery Collectors*** John Julius Angerstein

London

NATURAL HISTORY MUSEUM
Cromwell Road London SW7 5BD Director: Neil Chalmers
☎ **+44 171 9389123** 📠 **+44 171 9389267**
Open: Monday-Saturday 10.00-17.50 Sunday 11.00-17.50
Closed: 23-26 Dec

COLLECTION | The museum is home of national collections of living and fossil animals and plants, rocks and meteorites and the finest dinosaur exhibition for 65 million years. In addition, there are various interactive exhibitions, including Ecology, Creepy Crawlies, Human Biology, Discovering Mammals and the Origin of Species.

EXHIBITION
25·10·96–23·02·97 | ***The British Gas Wildlife Photographer of the Year 1996*** Winning and highly commended photographs from the world's finest wildlife photography competition will be on display in an exhibition at the Natural History Museum.

London

NATIONAL MARITIME MUSEUM
Romney Road, Greenwich London SE10 9NF Director: Richard Ormond
☎ **+44 181 8584422** 📠 **+44 181 3126632**
Open: Monday-Saturday 10.00-17.00 Sunday 12.00-17.00
Closed: 24 - 26 Dec

COLLECTION | Accomodated in historical buildings, the museum displays its collections which include extensive international holdings of marine art, ship models, globes, plans, navigational and astronomical instruments and historical manuscripts. Permanent galleries display many paintings and artefacts illustrating Britain's role in exploration, colonisation and naval actions. The 20th-century Seapower Gallery uses videos and reconstructions to illustrate advances in both military and merchant shipping.
The Old Royal Observatory delineates the Greenwich Meridian, Longitude 0, and contains Harrison's marine chronometers and

many of the other clocks that helped to make Greenwich famous as the reference for international time zones. The Queen's House, designed by Inigo Jones, was built for the wives of Stuart monarchs and is decorated in the vivid colours favoured by the flamboyant Henrietta Maria. The marine art collection is also noteworthy. Library, book publishing, education, and photo library and research facilities are available.

EXHIBITION

summer '95-onwards

Nelson   Using Nelson's possessions, this exhibition sets the scene of conflict between Britain and France in which Nelson achieved fame. Illustrated with impressive tableaux, oil paintings and artefacts, the displays depict major naval actions and the popular acclaim for a man who died at the moment of his greatest victory.

London

NATIONAL PORTRAIT GALLERY
Saint Martin's Place London WC2H OHE Director: Charles Saumarez Smith
☎ +44 171 3060055 📠 +44 171 3060058
Open: Monday-Saturday 10.00-18.00 Sunday 12.00-18.00

COLLECTION:

The National Portrait Gallery was founded in 1856 to collect the likenesses of famous British men and women. Today the collection is the most comprehensive of its kind in the world and constitutes a unique record of the men and women who created (and are still creating) the history and culture of the nation. The Gallery houses a primary collection of over nine thousand works, as well as an immense archive. There is no restriction on medium - there are oil paintings, watercolours, drawings, miniatures, sculptures, caricatures, silhouettes and photographs.

Clark, Michael 1954-
Derek Jarman 1993

Picture Library,
National Portrait
Gallery, London

The collection, arranged chronologically, begins on the top floor (level 5) with the Tudors and their predecessors. Each room has a particular historical theme. The collection includes: Holbein's Cartoon of Henry VIII, the 'Ditchley' portrait of Queen Elizabeth I and the 'Chandos' portrait of Shakespeare. Among the Victorians (level 3) are the portraits of Queen Victoria, Prince Albert, politicians, scientists, artists, writers and explorers of the era. The early 20th-century Galleries (level 2) cover the period from 1914 to 1945. The display includes First World War portraits and a fine collection of the War Poets. Politicians, scientists, sportsmen and major figures from all sections of the arts are displayed alongside a superb collection of Bloomsbury portraits. The late 20th-century Galleries (level 1) feature contemporary portraits from 1945 to the present day. The collection includes works by Andy Warhol, David Hockney, Allen Jones and Lucian Freud.

EXHIBITIONS

23·02·96–02·06·96 **The Room in View** Organised by the Education Department, this exhibition explores the importance of background in portraiture. Paintings, drawings and photographs spanning three centuries are organised in four sections: artists at work, scientists at work, other people at work, and people at rest.

22·03·96–07·07·96 **David Livingstone and the Victorian Encounter with Africa** This exhibition will look at the life and work of the explorer and missionary David Livingstone, at the myth which developed around his name, and at the Africa which he encountered during the middle decades of the 19th century. Exhibits will include contemporary photographs and press reports, notebooks, and artefacts collected during his travels.

12·04·96–07·07·96 **John Deakin** This exhibition comprises 100 to 120 black and white vintage prints with an emphasis on Deakin's portraits, which remain distinctive for their very lack of 'style', their honesty, vigour and integrity. His fashion and urban landscapes (Paris, Rome and London) are included, as well as a selection of the portrait photographs taken for Francis Bacon to paint from, found in the painter's studio after his death.

21·06·96–06·10·96 **Family Albums** The intention of this exhibition is to trace the link between the documentation of the family and successive developments in the technology of representation, such as photography, film, video and, more recently, computer-centred multimedia.

26·07·96–20·10·96 **BP Portrait Award 1996 and BP Travel Award** The 17th annual exhibition of portraits entered for the BP Portrait Award, a competition for young artists between the ages of 18 and 40.

04·10·96–05·01·97 **Private Eye Times** For 35 years, this most successful of all satirical magazines has continued to amuse the British public and to enrage the Establishment in almost equal measure. 'Private Eye Times' is a celebration of the magazine's years of success.

08·11·96–09·02·97 **John Kobal Photographic Portrait Award 1996** The fourth John Kobal Photographic Portrait Award exhibition will include the winners and a selection of entries from the 1996 Award Competition.

08·11·96–09·02·97 **The Art of the Picture Frame** *Artists' Patrons and the Framing of Portraits in Britain* Nearly 200 framed pictures will be displayed in this exhibition examining function, technique, style, the influence of the frame on the viewer's perception, and particularly, the question of choice: how frames are chosen by artist, sitter, patron, architect and framemaker.

London

THE SERPENTINE GALLERY
Kensington Gardens London WC2 3XA Director: Julia Peyton-Jones
☎ +44 171 4026075 📠 +44 171 4024103
Open: Daily 10.00-18.00

COLLECTION No permanent collection.

EXHIBITIONS
30·04·96-26·05·96

Langlands and Bell   This exhibition is a major survey of the collaborative works by the British artists Ben Langlands and Nikki Bell. The 40 or so sculptures on display express the nature of architecture, its symbolic significance and the ways in which it reflects and determines human behaviour. The plans and views, depicted in floor and wall-based works, are derived from actual buildings and fall into various architectural categories, such as ecclesiastical, prison and corporate. The geometrical, abstract and formal quality of the works paradoxically belie a wealth of meaning which pervades our built environments.

12·06·96-21·07·96

Fischli and Weiss   This will be the first major exhibition in Britain of the collaborative works by the Swiss artists Peter Fischli and David Weiss. Developed from their recent installation at this year's Venice Biennale, it will consist of sculptures and numerous video films, the latter being screened on monitors or projected onto gallery walls. Characteristically, it will assert the eloquence of banal objects and events, referring indirectly to the binds and inevitabilities of the human condition through everyday phenomena.

London

SIR JOHN SOANE'S MUSEUM
13 Lincoln's Inn Fields London WC2A 3BP Director: P.K. Thornton
☎ **+44 171 4052107** 📠 **+44 171 8313957**
Open: Tuesday-Saturday 10.00-17.00 and on first Tuesday of each month
18.00-21.00
Closed: Sunday, Monday and public holidays

COLLECTION

Architecture   Sir John Soane (1753-1837), one of the leading British architects of his time, designed and built No. 13 Lincoln's Inn Fields both as his private residence and to house his collection of paintings, drawings, sculpture and antiquities.
The architecture reflects his own personal style with shallow vaulted ceilings, mirrors to reflect and suggest extensions of space, planes opening to reveal more pictures hung behind, openings between rooms and in floors to give unusual views, and many overhead skylights often incorporating coloured glass which provide dramatic and picturesque lighting. The collection contains architectural models of classical buildings and Soane's own architectural works.
Old Masters   The painting include two series by Hogarth, 'The Rake's Progress' and 'An Election', and works by Canaletto, Watteau, Reynolds, Lawrence, Turner and Piranesi.
Sculpture   Original marbles and plasters by Bandini, Quellin, Flaxman, Westmacott, Chantry, Banks, and others are on display.
Antiquities   Works on display include the alabaster sarcophagus of Seti I of Egypt (c. 1300 B.C.), fragments from the Erectheum, the Pantheon, originals and casts of architectural and sculptural fragments, and Greek fragments.
Drawings   The Research Library houses an important collection of 30 000 architectural drawings by Thorpe, Wren, Kent, Chambers, Adam, both Dances, and Soane, as well as others Italian drawings from the 16th to 18th century.

EXHIBITIONS
29·03·96–31·08·96

Soane Revisited   *A Journey of Rediscovery of the Buildings of Sir John Soane*   This exhibition presents a journey across Britain made between August 1994 and December 1995 by a young architect, Ptolemy Dean, in which he visited Soane's buildings - ranging from cow sheds to country houses to church monuments to the Bank of England - and documented them in a series of vivid pen and wash sketches.

Oct 96–May 97   ***Robert Adam***   *The Creative Mind from Sketch to Finished Drawing*
The exhibition draws on the museum's collection of 8000 drawings by Adam.

London

TATE GALLERY
Millbank London SW1P 4RG Director: Nicholas Serota
☎ **+44 171 8878000** 📠 **+44 171 8878007**
Open: Monday-Saturday 10.00-17.50 Sunday 14.00-17.50

COLLECTION

The Tate Gallery houses the national collection of British painting from the 16th century to the present day. It is also the national gallery for Modern art, encompassing painting and sculpture made in Britain, Europe, America, and other countries associated with the European tradition in this century. The collection also includes substantial holdings of drawings and watercolours after 1945. The Clore Gallery, added in 1987, houses the paintings, watercolours, drawings and sketchbooks of J.M.W. Turner, left to the nation on his death.

Tate Gallery, London

EXHIBITIONS
06·06·96-01·09·96

Leon Kossoff   The first ever retrospective exhibition of work by the artist. Born in 1926, Kossoff is one of the most important post-war British artists. The exhibition features about 80 paintings, including loans from abroad, and will survey the development of his work from the 1950s to the present day.

10·10·96-05·01·97

The Grand Tour   *The Lure of Italy in the 18th Century*
For many centuries Italy has enjoyed a reputation as the home of the greatest art and architecture. In the 18th century especially, artists and writers, royalty and nobility travelled there to absorb the atmosphere of antique ruins and to seek inspiration from Renaissance paintings. This exhibition will investigate their journey and show painting and sculpture, drawings and prints from distinguished collections across the world. The survey includes work by Batoni, Canaletto, Piranesi, Reynolds and Zoffany.

Feb 97-May 97

Lovis Corinth (1858-1925)   In the closing years of the 19th century, Lovis Corinth played a central role in the German exhibiting societies, which broke with academic tradition and laid the foundations for Expressionist art. Although an innovator, Corinth drew much inspiration from Rembrandt and Rubens, and aimed to renew European tradition. He painted historical and biblical subjects, nudes, flower still-lifes, portraits and landscapes, often in a raw, uncompromising and melancholy manner. This is the first major retrospective of his work in the UK.

London

VICTORIA AND ALBERT MUSEUM
Cromwell Road South Kensington London SW7 2RL Director: Alan Borg
☎ +44 171 9388500 🖷 +44 171 9388341
Open: Tuesday-Sunday 10.00-17.50 Monday 12.00-17.50
Closed: Good Friday, May Day Bank Holiday, 24-26 Dec

The Dome
Victoria and Albert
Museum, London

COLLECTION

The museum's collections comprise sculpture, furniture, fashion and textiles, paintings, silver, glass, ceramics, jewellery, books, prints and photographs from Britain and all over the world. Highlights include the world's greatest collection of Constables and the national collection of watercolours; the famous 15th-century Devonshire Hunting Tapestries; the Dress Court showing fashion from 1500 to the present day; a superb Asian collection, including the much-loved Tippoo's Tiger; Medieval treasures; magnificent collections of Renaissance and Victorian sculpture; the Jewellery Gallery including the Russian Crown Jewels; and the 20th-Century Gallery, devoted to contemporary art and design. There are also magnificent new galleries devoted to European art and design, glass and ceramics, ironwork, Chinese, European and Indian art, 20th-century design and the architect Frank Lloyd Wright.
Galleries opening in 1996 are the Leighton Frescoes (15 February), the Raphael Gallery (October) and the Silver Gallery (27 November).

EXHIBITIONS
04·04·96–29·09·96

Arts and Crafts Architecture   This display explores the development, from the 1850s onward, of a style of domestic architecture sympathetic to the ideals of William Morris. It includes works by Philip Webb, Norman Shaw, W.E. Nesfield, C.R. Ashbee and C.F.A. Voysey.

09·05·96–01·09·96

William Morris   The most comprehensive exhibition ever mounted on the life and work of the influential British designer, poet, philosopher, socialist, and founder of the Arts and Crafts Movement. Over 500 objects explore the range, versatility, skill and innovation of this remarkable man.

12·06·96–22·09·96   ***Graphic and Artistic Responses to AIDS***   For over a decade, artists, graphic designers and photographers have been creating work which reflects not only the impact of AIDS, but also the spread of the epidemic. This exhibition looks at goverment posters, and the literature of action groups, local authorities and charities, as well as the work of artists and photographers who have been affected in some way by AIDS.

14·11·96–26·01·97   ***American Photography 1890-1965***   75 years of American photography, drawn from the collection of the Museum of Modern Art, New York. The exhibition features works by the most important and celebrated photographers of the century, including Alfred Stieglitz, Walker Evans, Dorothea Lang, Paul Strand, Ansel Adams and Irving Penn.

London

THE WALLACE COLLECTION
Hertford House Manchester Square   London W1M 6BN   Director: R. Savill
☎ +44 171 9350687   📠 +44 171 2242155
Open: Monday-Saturday 10.00-17.00   Sunday 14.00-17.00
Closed: 1 Jan, Good Friday, 1 May, 24-26 Dec

COLLECTION | The Wallace Collection displays superb works of art against the sumptuous backdrop of Hertford House.

Frans Hals,
1580 ? - 1666
*The Laughing
Cavalier*

The Wallace
Collection, London

In the richly decorated rooms are fine Old Master paintings by Titian, Canaletto, Rembrandt, Hals, Rubens, Velasquez and Gainsborough, among others, and excellent collections of French 18th-century painting, furniture and Sevre porcelain. There are also four impressive galleries for the display of an outstanding collection of arms and armour, miniatures, gold boxes, French and Italian sculpture, and Renaissance works of art, including Limoges enamels, majolica, glass, silver, cuttings from illuminated manuscripts and carvings in ivory, rock crystal and boxwood.
Under the terms of Lady Wallace's bequest, the collection may not be enlarged, nor may items be loaned from it. It thus remains a testament to the tastes and interests of a single wealthy family over a period of four generations.

EXHIBITIONS | No exhibitions planned.

London

WHITECHAPEL ART GALLERY
Whitechapel High Street London E1 7QX Director: Catherine Lampert
☎ +44 171 5227888 🖷 +44 171 3771685
Open: Tuesday-Sunday 11.00-17.00 Wednesday 11.00-20.00
Closed: Monday

COLLECTION

No permanent collection.

EXHIBITIONS

13·03·96-05·05·96

Jeff Wall   This exhibition features fifteen recent photographic works by leading Canadian artist Jeff Wall (born 1946), each comprised of a lightbox and a single still image - often of monumental size. Wall's works depict carefully staged tableaux: they can evoke street scenes, landscapes, history paintings or Hollywood movies, but are always notable for their uncanny rendering of photographic 'reality'. In recent years, the artist has experimented with digital technology to combine different shots into a single seamless image.

17·05·96-07·07·96

Renato Guttuso   Renato Guttuso (1912-1987) was one of modern Italy's greatest figurative painters. Born in Sicily, Guttuso settled in Rome in 1937 and made his name there as a Social Realist, before fleeing the capital in 1943 to join the Resistance. Guttuso is best known for the sweeping narratives of Italian street life and contemporary events which he began to paint in the 1930s. However, he was also a brilliant painter of still life and of the Bohemian world of the café and studio. This is Guttuso's first British retrospective.

19·07·96-15·09·96

The Open and The Open Studios   The 'Open' is a regular exhibition which features new work by East London artists. The exhibition (held every two years) extends to film, video and installation, as well as to painting and sculpture, and includes works by established artists as well as unknowns.

Manchester

MANCHESTER CITY ART GALLERIES
Mosley Street Manchester M2 3JL Director: Richard Gray
☎ +44 161 2365244 🖷 +44 61 2367369
Open: Monday-Saturday 10.00-17.45 Sunday 14.00-17.45
Closed: 25, 26 Dec, 1 Jan, Good Friday

COLLECTION

Manchester City Art Galleries' collection of fine art is particularly rich in the field of 19th-century British paintings, including work by Turner and the Pre-Raphaelites as well as important 18th-century works by Gainsborough and Stubbs. The galleries' collection of 20th-century art is also very strong, with works by Henry Moore, Ben Nicholson, Augustus John, Francis Bacon and Lucian Freud.

The decorative arts collection includes Greek vases from the 4th century and more contemporary pieces by the best artists in Britain and abroad. The decorative arts in the upper galleries are shown in the context of the paintings with which they are displayed. Downstairs, in the collection 'A New Look at Decorative Arts', ceramics, glass and silver are displayed thematically. Visitors are encouraged, for example, to compare a rare 17th-century slipware dish with a plate designed and decorated by Picasso.

EXHIBITIONS

until 30·06·96

Whitefriars Glass   The Art of James Powell and Sons

06·04·96-27·05·96	*Willy Ronis* Photographs 1926-1995
08·06·96-01·09·96	*Offside!* Football and Contemporary Art
14·09·96-03·11·96	*The Inner Eye* An exhibition selected by Marina Warner.
21·09·96-19·01·97	*Finnish Glass*
16·11·96-02·02·97	*David Hockney* Putting you in the Picture

Middlesbrough

MIDDLESBROUGH ART GALLERY
320 Linthorpe Road Middlesbrough TS1 4AW Assistant Curator: Alison Lloyd
☎ +44 1642 247445 📠 +44 1642 813781
Open: Tuesday-Saturday 10.00-17.30
Closed: Sunday and Monday

COLLECTION

The Middlesbrough Art Gallery's collection of 20th-century art includes work by Frank Auerbach, David Bomberg, Gaudier Brzeska, Gwen John, Stanley Spencer and Paula Rego. The museum's most recent acquisition is a crayon and pencil work on paper by Claes Oldenburg, entitled 'Bottle of Notes'.
The Middlesbrough Art Gallery presents an exciting and varied programme of contemporary art and related events.

EXHIBITIONS

11·05·96-15·06·96 *Soccerscape* Stephen Gill and Tim Hetherington   A photographic exhibition documenting Middlesbrough Football Club's move to its new Riverside Stadium and their promotion to the English Premier League.

22·06·96-03·08·96 *Claes Oldenburg* Multiples   The exhibition consists of around 150 objects, plus notebook pages, drawings and prints, and is based upon an earlier European Tour, which included Frankfurt, Vienna and Tel Aviv.

10·08·96-21·09·96 *Lynn Silverman* Corporation House   This exhibition will bring together a new series of photographs made during an extensive period of work at Corporation House in Central Middlesbrough.

28·09·96-23·11·96 *Marina Abramovic* The House - 5 Rooms and Storage   For the last 20 years, Maria Abramovic has been a key figure in contemporary art, incorporating sound, video, photographs and sculpture into her work. The House, as a metaphor for the body, has continued to fascinate Marina Abramovic. At Middlesbrough Art Gallery she will transform the exhibition spaces into Bedroom, Bathroom, Kitchen, Television Room, Living Room and Storage.

08·02·97-05·04·97 *Speculative Proposals*   Artists will be invited to explore issues concerning the transformation of urban landscapes and related social issues.

New Bridge

SCOTTISH AGRICULTURAL MUSEUM (NATIONAL MUSEUMS OF SCOTLAND)
Rhas Showground New Bridge Midlothian EH28 8NB Director: Mark Jones
☎ +44 131 3332674 📠 +44 131 333 2674
Open: 1 Apr-30 Sep Daily 1 Oct-31 Mar Monday-Friday
Closed: 1 Oct-31 Mar Saturday, Sunday and Christmas-New Year

COLLECTION

Historical items The collections trace the history of rural life in Scotland and the progress from hand skills to mechanisation in farming and crofting communities. The main themes of the permanent displays are: The Agricultural Revolution to the coming of the tractor and combine harvester; the social and economic life of the countryside; the traditional use of materials in the countryside; and the changing relationship between people and animals. Objects include tools, implements, photographs and folk art.

EXHIBITIONS

20·06·96–23·06·96

Fergusson Tractors This exhibition is presented to mark the 50th anniversary of Fergusson, and will take place during the Royal Highland Show.

May 96–Sep 96

Bees A display of honey bees, bumble bees and wasps, comprising living bees in a working hive with an observation hive to enable visitors to observe their behavior.

Newcastle upon Tyne

THE HATTON GALLERY
Newcastle University Newcastle upon Tyne Director: Gavin Robson
☎ +44 191 2226057 Ⅲ +44 191 2611182
Open: Monday-Friday 10.00-17.30
Saturday (University term time only) 10.00-16.30
Closed: Sunday and public holidays

COLLECTION

The Hatton Gallery collection was founded in the 1920s when Professor Hatton of the King Edward VII School of Art in Newcastle donated a small collection of Indian miniatures and an edition of Burgkmair's 'Triumphal Procession'. Paintings ranging through the Renaissance to Modern periods were acquired in the 1940s and 1950s, and these now form the core of the collection. Further expansion followed from the 1950s to the 1980s. A large body of contemporary British art was donated by the Contemporary Art Society, including works by Patrick Herron, Francis Bacon and

The Hatton Gallery

Newcastle University,
Newcastle upon Tyne

Prunella Clough. Among important bequests made to the Gallery are the Bosanquet collection of textiles, the Hall Bequest of Baxter and Victorian prints, and the Charlton Bequest, comprising watercolours, drawings, prints and oils by the Charlton brothers and other artists from their circle, such as Crawhall. Recent bequests include Kurt Schwitter's 'Merzbarn' donated by Harry Pierce in 1965, and the Uhlman Collection of African Sculpture donated in 1985.

EXHIBITIONS

29·04·96–24·05·96

Artlanta Artlanta is the first stage of an exchange exhibition with artists in Atlanta. Works by painters, sculptors and printmakers currently active in the North of England will be displayed at the Hatton Gallery, before touring to the King Plow Arts Centre in Atlanta, Georgia.

17·06·96-13·07·96   **BA Degree Show**   This highly successful exhibition consists of works by graduate students of the Fine Art Department at Newcastle University, and includes paintings, sculptures and prints. These can be viewed both in the Hatton Gallery and in the Fine Art Department.

02·09·96-08·10·96   **Derek Jarman** *A Retrospective*   Few people realise that the distinguished film maker Derek Jarman was originally a painter who studied at the Slade School of Art in the 60s. This exhibition presents his paintings, drawings and sculpture prints, as well as his innovative stage and garden designs.

19·10·96-28·11·96   **From Folk Art to Fine Art** *The Russian Revolution in Art & Design 1900-1925*   The exhibition reflects the innate creativity and visual inventiveness of Russian art during this period, as well as the continuity existing between Russian folk tradition and the work of the avant-garde. Using two private collections, one a collection of paintings, watercolours and drawings by the Russian avant-garde, the other a unique collection of Russian folk art, the exhibition demonstrates how folk art tradition was carried over into the Rayist, Suprematist and Constructivist movements.

06·12·96-25·01·97   **Artists in Atlanta**   The exhibition aims to present a moment of great cultural tension and creativity in Atlanta and the South at a time of cultural pluralism. It is a vivid examination of the social and cultural dislocation of African-Americans, American Indians, Asian-born artists and Spanish communities.

Newcastle upon Tyne

LAING ART GALLERY
Higham Place Newcastle upon Tyne NEI 8AG Director: John Millard
☎ **+44 191 2327734 ▯▣ +44 191 2220952**
Open: Monday-Saturday 10.00-17.00 Sunday 14.00-17.00
Closed: Good Friday

COLLECTION   The Laing Art Gallery is the North East's principal gallery with a collection of paintings, watercolours, costumes, silver, glass, pottery and sculpture as well as a permanent programme of temporary exhibitions, talks and activities. Among the highlights of the permanent collection are works by Gauguin, William Holman Hunt, Burne-Jones and the Northumberland-born Victorian painter John Martin. Modern art is also represented with works by Stanley Spencer and Henry Moore. The Laing Art Gallery has the award-winning 'Art On Tyneside' exhibition on permanent display. This explores the region's art from the Middle Ages to the present. Games, videos and reconstructions make this journey through history particularly enjoyable.

EXHIBITIONS
01·06·96-26·08·96   **Treasures from the Lost Kingdom of Northumbria**   This exhibition explores Northumbria's Anglo-Saxon heritage with displays of illuminated manuscripts, ornate sculpture and precious gold and silver jewellery. The focus is the region's Golden Age between A.D. 600 and 800, when the Kingdom of Northumbria became the centre of a remarkable flowering of Latin learning and artistic brilliance.

13·09·96-03·11·96   **A Palace of Victorian Art**   This exhibition, devoted to London's Grosvenor Gallery, presents over 100 works by Victorian artists including Burne-Jones, Whistler, G.F. Watts and Alma-Tadema. The exhibition also explores the many personalities associated with the Grosvenor Gallery including John Riskin, Oscar Wilde, Lilly Langtry and Henry Jones.

16·11·96–07·02·97   *Serious Games*   *Art for the 21st Century*   This exhibition explores serious issues through the participatory 'game' nature of various media including CD-ROM, virtual reality and the Internet. It brings together high-tech and low-tech interactive works of art in a stunning and intriguing exhibition which looks forward to the new millenium.

Northampton

CENTRAL MUSEUM AND ART GALLERY
Guildhall Road   Northampton NN1 1DP   Director: Sheila Stone
☎ +44 1604 233500   📠 +44 1604 238720
Open: Monday–Saturday 10.00–17.00   Sunday 14.00–17.00

COLLECTION

Northampton possesses the largest collection of footwear in Britain and one of the most important collections of this kind in the world. *Footwear on display* ranges from Roman and Medieval examples to present-day boots and shoes. There are even unusual specimens such as the boots worn by 'Jumbo' the elephant in a re-creation of Hannibal's trek across the Alps.

A number of specially commissioned works, such as a depiction of Saint Crispin, the patron saint of shoemakers, illustrate subjects associated with the footwear industry. There is also a number of paintings and other illustrations of shoemakers and shoemaking as well as two indexes, one of shoemakers and shoemaking companies and another of 'concealed shoes' (shoes hidden in buildings for good luck).

The Fine Arts Gallery possesses a small but important collection of Italian works. Although focusing on late Venetian artists, all the most important artistic centres of Italy are represented. Other pieces in the collection are displayed on a rotating basis.

The Decorative Arts Gallery displays a selection from its fine collection of British ceramics and its comprehensive collection of Oriental ceramics. British and Irish glass dating from the mid-17th century to the late 20th century is displayed along with one of the earliest complete dated bottles in existence (1657).

The archaeological and social history displays focus on the development of Northampton and range from prehistoric worked flint to furniture designed by the Scottish architect Charles Rennie Mackintosh for the home of local model-maker W.J. Bassett Lowke.

EXHIBITIONS

30·03·96–18·08·96   *Newcomers*   *The Story of Northampton People*   Over 2000 years of settlement in Northampton.

24·08·96–22·09·96   *Young Images*   Young artists' observations, attitudes and issues in the 1990s.

28·09·96–20·10·96   *Simple Science*   A hands-on exhibition for 5-7 year-olds.

28·09·96–17·11·96   *Personal Perspectives*   Photography by Richard Oldfield.

26·10·96–24·11·96   *Boxes and Bowls?*   Cuir bouilli: experimental forming of leather.

30·11·96–05·01·97   *The Town and County Art Society*   83rd Annual Exhibition.

Norwich

CASTLE MUSEUM
Norwich NR1 3JU Curator: Andrew Moore
☎ +44 1603 223624 📠 +44 1603 765651
Open: Monday-Saturday 10.00-17.00 Sunday 14.00-17.00
Closed: 5 Apr, 24 - 26 Dec

COLLECTION

This regional museum houses a collection of watercolours and oils
by John Sell Cotman and the Norwich School of Artists, together
with displays of Norwich silver, Lowestoft porcelain, English
ceramics and the Twining Teapot Gallery. Dutch oils by Hobbema
and Jan van Goyen are also featured, as well as etchings by
Rembrandt. The Castle Museum also cares for a public collection of
contemporary craft and the museum shop sells selected work. The
Modern Art collection is diverse and includes work by Ernst, Nolde
and Warhol in the Adeane Bequest.

The Castle Keep, designed as a royal palace before 1100, was built
partly from Caen stone and houses some of the large archaeological
collections which tell the story of the people of Norfolk. Egyptian
mummies are also displayed along with material from other ancient
civilisations. Gold and silver found at Snettisham includes the largest
collection of Iron Age gold neck rings anywhere in Europe, and
many examples of Roman craftsmanship found in the region are
also shown in the Archaeology Gallery.

The Natural History galleries house specimens of unique animals
and plants from the wildlife areas in Norfolk. There are also Ice Age
fossils found in Norfolk and the 600 000 year-old elephant remains
discovered on the Cromer coast.

EXHIBITIONS

03·02·96–22·09·96

Paper Dreams *Twentieth Century Works on Paper*   An exhibition
from the museum's art collection including examples by Klee,
Chagall, Nolde, Spencer, Howard Hodgkin, Gilbert and George, and
Maggi Hambling.

30·03·96–Mar 97

Norwich *A Cathedral City*   An exhibition of watercolours to
celebrate Cathedral 900.

04·05·96–29·09·96

The Great Treasure Hunt   An interactive Experience for all Ages.

12·10·96–05·01·97

The Prime Minister, the Empress and the Heritage   The story of Sir
Robert Walpole's country home at Houghton Hall, Norfolk, his
collection and the sale of his paintings to Catherine the Great of
Russia.

Stephen Slaughter
Sir Robert Walpole,
1742
in the exhibition
'The Prime Minister,
the Empress and the
Heritage'

Castle Museum,
Norwich

Norwich

SAINSBURY CENTRE FOR VISUAL ARTS
University of East Anglia Norwich NR4 7TJ Director: Nicola Johnson
☎ +44 1603 456060 📠 +44 1603 259401
Open: Tuesday-Sunday 11.00-17.00
Closed: Monday and throughout University Christmas vacation

COLLECTION

The museum and gallery of the University of East Anglia was designed by the world-famous architect Sir Norman Foster to house the Robert and Lisa Sainsbury Collection, which was given to the University in the 1970s. Modern European sculpture and painting, including works by Bacon, Degas, Epstein, Giacometti, Moore and Picasso are displayed alongside one of the finest British collections of non-Western art outside London.

EXHIBITIONS

06·02·96–09·06·96   *Swords of the Samurai* *Japanese Masterpieces from the British Museum*

04·06·96–07·07·96   *Museology MA Exhibition 'Carnival'*

25·06·96 onwards   *Francis Bacon* *Paintings in the Sainsbury Collection*

14·07·96–07·09·96   *EAST*

Oct 96–Dec 96   *Patrick Bailly Maitre Grand Anderson Collection of Art Nouveau*

Jan 97–Apr 97   *Derek Jarman* *Paintings Retrospective*

Oxford

ASHMOLEAN MUSEUM AND UNIVERSITY GALLERIES
Beaumont Street Oxford OX1 2PH Director: Christopher White
☎ +44 1865 278000 📠 +44 1865 278018
Open: Tuesday-Saturday 10.00-16.00 Sunday 14.00-16.00
Closed: Monday and during St. Giles' Fair, Christmas, 5-7 April

COLLECTION

The Ashmolean Museum, established in 1683, is the oldest museum to be open to the public in Great Britain. The present building, designed by C.R. Cockerell and completed in 1845, is one of the best examples of Neo-Grecian architecture in Britain and provides a highly sympathetic interior for displays of works of art.
The collections are diverse, ranging in time from an 8 000 year-old human skull excavated at Jericho to 20th-century works of art. On permanent display are the University's collections of antiquities from Egypt, Greece, Rome and the Near East; British and European paintings including Italian, Dutch and Flemish, French Impressionist and Pre-Raphaelite works; Asian art, including Chinese bronzes, Islamic and Japanese ceramics, and Indian sculpture; sculpture and applied art (ceramics, silver, glass, etc.) and European stringed instruments. Temporary exhibitions highlight some of the prints and drawings, and coins and medals in the museum's collections.

EXHIBITIONS

13·02·96–12·05·96   *16th-Century French Ornament Drawings* *Designs for Medals and Jewels by Etienne Delaune (1518-1578)*   The Ashmolean's collection of 16th-century French ornament drawings is one of the most extensive of its kind in existence. The designs for jewels are of particular interest; several can be identified as designs for Catherine de Medici and Henry II, Diane de Poitiers and Mary Queen of Scots.

12·03·96–12·05·96   *Designs for the Ashmolean* Architectural plans and drawings for

Detail from Attic red-figure cup from Orvieto, by the Anthipon Painter, c. 480 BC

Ashmolean Museum, Oxford

the building of the Ashmolean Museum in the 1840s, by the architect C.R. Cockerell (1788-1863). The series of contract drawings are handsome drawings in their own right and allow one to follow the evolution of the building through successive modifications. The exhibition marks the 150th anniversary of the completion of the building in 1846.

14·05·96–Aug 96 **Life Drawing**   A selection of drawings from the Ashmolean's permanent collection, ranging from the 16th to the 20th century. The drawings fall in the main into two categories - studies of the posed model as an academic exercise and studies made in preparation for figures in painting or sculpture. Artists represented will include Michelangelo, Raphael, Rembrandt, Rubens and Cézanne.

21·05·96–15·10·96 **Ruskin and Oxford**   Ruskin always had close links with Oxford. After his appointment as the first Slade Professor he decided to found an Art School in the University, at which his principles could be put into practice. This exhibition, drawn largely from the Ashmolean's collections, will illustrate this surprisingly little-documented aspect of Ruskin's aims.

24·09·96–01·12·96 **Modern Chinese Paintings** *From the Jose Mauricio and Angelita Trinidad Reyes Collection*   As a result of the acquisition of the Reyes Collection, presented to the Ashmolean in 1995, the museum has become the major European repository of modern Chinese painting. More than 100 hanging scrolls and albums by leading Chinese artists of the late 19th and 20th centuries are included in the collection. The exhibition focuses on landscapes in the 'literati' tradition.

Oxford

MUSEUM OF MODERN ART
30 Pembroke Street Oxford OX1 1BP Director: David Elliott
☎ +44 1865 722733 📠 +44 1865 722573
Open: Tuesday-Saturday 10.00-18.00 Thursday 10.00-21.00
Sunday 14.00-18.00
Closed: Monday

COLLECTION | No permanent collection.

EXHIBITIONS
28·04·96–30·06·96 **Carl Andre**   Carl Andre is widely considered to be one of America's

most important sculptors. In the 1960s Andre's work was primarily horizontal in format - ribbons of pipes and nails; and sequences of large, flat, metal squares. Along with Donald Judd and Robert Morris, he became a crucial figure in the minimalist movement, and broke with the age-old European tradition of the vertical format in sculpture. The exhibition will include the series 'Equivalent' of which the famous 'Tate bricks' ('Equivalent VIII') is a part, as well as many of Andre's lesser-known works.

14·07·96–22·09·96   ***Scream and Scream Again***   This exhibition will bring together a number of recent film and video installationss produced by two generations of European and American artists. Some use the imagery and format of early cinema; others take the video monitor as an element in a larger sculptural assemblage, treating the moving video image as a physical sculptural material.

06·10·96–29·12·96   ***Taxonomy***   *Photography Art and the Order of Things*   In the 19th century, the theories of Linnaeus and Darwin stimulated the belief that the contents of the universe were subject to scientific classification. Photography was perceived as providing objective documentation of the physical world in this process of classification. In the 20th century, a number of artists have undermined this approach by adhering to its conventions but producing work with aesthetic rather than scientific intentions. The exhibition will place 19th-century photographs alongside those of contemporary artists, and consider how these artists have subverted the 19th-century approach.

Southampton

SOUTHAMPTON CITY ART GALLERY
Civic Centre Southampton SO14 7LP Keeper: Margot Heller
☎ +44 1703 832743   📠 +44 1703 832153
Open: Tuesday-Friday 10.00-17.00 Thursday 10.00-20.00
Saturday 10.00-16.00 Sunday 14.00-17.00
Closed: Monday

COLLECTION   The Southampton City Art Gallery's permanent collection spans 6 centuries of European art, including 17th-century Dutch landscapes, 18th-century portraiture and a small number of French Impressionist works, Edward Burne-Jones's 'Perseus Series' and a new installation 'with the Arcades, work in Situ 1994' by Daniel Buren. 20th-century British art is particularly well represented: the collection includes many fine works of art by artists such as Stanley Spencer, Anthony Gormley, Gilbert and George, Barry Flanagan, Rachel Whiteread and Helen Chadwick.

Sir Matthew Smith
Dulcie, 1915

Southampton City
Art Gallery,
Southampton

05·04·96-02·06·96   **Freedom**   Organised by Amnesty International, this exhibition brings together contemporary works in a range of media (including video, painting, sculpture and photography) on the theme of 'freedom'. It includes works by Willie Doherty, Mona Hatoum and Keith Piper.

04·06·96-04·08·96   **Sir John Everett Millais**   This display of works from the family's collection will be exhibited to mark the centenary of Millais' death.

04·06·96-Aug 96   **Boudin to Dufy** *Impressionist and other Masters from the Musée des Beaux Arts, Le Havre*   This exhibition brings together key works from Le Havre's fine collection of Impressionist painting and will include works by Sisley, Pissarro and Monet.

16·08·96-06·10·96   **A Celebration of Southampton's Art Collection**   An exhibition to display the rich diversity of Southampton's permanent collection of both new and historic art.

18·10·96-05·01·97   **Triplicate**   Katherine Clarke, Susan Collins, Anne Eggebert, John Kippin, Edward Stewart and Jo Stockham, six young and mid-career British artists, were commissioned to create new works through which a comparison could be made of three art galleries (Southampton City Art Gallery, The Towner Art Gallery, and Eastbourne and the Tate, St. Ives) in terms of the galleries' architecture, collections, visitors and atmospheres.

17·01·97-16·02·97   **Southampton Open**   An exhibition selected from works submitted by artists in the region. It will include the Moore & Blatch prize for outstanding works by art students in the region.

28·02·97-11·05·97   **Drawing Breath**   An exhibition of works in a broad range of media, including early 20th-century self-portraits and works by such artists as Alison Watt, Helen Chadwick and Mona Hatoum.

St. Ives

TATE GALLERY ST. IVES
Porthmeor Beach St Ives TR26 1TG Director: Michael Tooby
☎ +44 1736 796226 📠 +44 736 794480
Open: 1 Apr-31 Oct Sunday and public holidays 11.00-17.00
Monday-Saturday 11.00-19.00 Tuesday and Thursday 11.00-21.00;
1 Nov-31 Mar Tuesday-Sunday 11.00-17.00
Closed: 1 Nov-31 Mar Monday, 24, 25 Dec

   The Tate Gallery St. Ives opened in 1993 in a stunning new building overlooking the spectacular Cornish coastline. The building is designed to show works of art in an environment which has inspired artistic development in the area for over a hundred years. The Tate Gallery St. Ives presents changing displays of 20th-century art in the context of Cornwall, focusing on the modern tradition with which St. Ives is associated. Exhibitions are composed of artworks drawn from the Tate Gallery's collection and are supplemented by loans. Key artists represented in the collection include Alfred Wallis, Ben Nicholson, Barbara Hepworth, Naum Gabo, Patrick Heron, Terry Frost and Wilhelmina Barns-Graham. In addition to the annual rotation of the main exhibits, the study display gallery houses exhibitions devoted to a particular artist or theme which change three times a year.

Through its programme of artist's projects and residencies, the Tate Gallery St. Ives is dedicated to providing working opportunities in Cornwall for artists from both Great Britain and abroad, resulting in a continuous programme of displays by invited contemporary artists. The Barbara Hepworth Museum and Sculpture Garden have been run by the Tate Gallery since 1980 and are now an integral part of the Tate Gallery St. Ives. The Museum offers a remarkable insight into the work and outlook of one of Britain's most important 20th-century sculptors.

EXHIBITIONS
04·05·96-03·11·96

Mark Rothko   Mark Rothko (1903-1970) was one of the leading figures of American Abstract Expressionism. His work has rarely been seen outside London, and this exhibition will offer an opportunity to compare this major artist with his contemporaries in Britain.

16·11·96-02·11·97

Displays 1996-97

16·11·96-20·04·97

Christopher Wood   *In conjunction with the Musée des Beaux Arts, Quimper*   Christopher Wood (1901-1930) found the connection between Cornwall and Brittany particularly significant in his paintings. While he is a celebrated artist in Britain, this will be the first time that his work will be shown in France since his death.

Truro

ROYAL CORNWALL MUSEUM
River Street Truro Cornwall TR1 2SJ Director: Caroline Dudley
☎ +44 1872 72205 📠 +44 1872 40514
Open: Monday-Saturday 10.00-17.00
Closed: Sunday and Bank Holidays

COLLECTION

The Royal Cornwall Museum is one of the largest and most diverse regional museums in the UK with collections of minerals, human history, art, applied art, natural history, toys, numismatics and a large archive of photographs dating from the 1840s to the present day.
Minerals   The Rashleigh collection of minerals is particularly rich in copper ores, collected when copper mining in Cornwall was at its height. A highlight in the collection is the world's largest specimen of liroconite. A new gallery is devoted to the history of Cornish mining and minerals.

R. Borlase Smart
(1881-1947)
*Morning Light,
St. Ives, 1922*

*Royal Cornwall
Museum, Truro*

Human History   The museum is the primary repository for all officially excavated archaeological material from Cornwall and includes three of the only four known Bronze Age gold collars found in England.
Art   The Fine Art collection centres on a collection of more than 300 Old Master drawings from the 14th to the 20th century and includes important drawings by Turner, Constable, Rossetti, Blake, Rubens, Claude and Gericault. There are also collections of European prints and 19th and 20th-century oil paintings.
Applied Art   The museum has collections of ceramics ranging from

the Medieval period to the 20th-century studio potters such as Bernard Leach and Michael Cardew. Smaller but high-quality collections include Japanese and Chinese applied art, West Country silver, British pewter, textiles and European ceramics.

EXHIBITIONS

04·05·96–01·06·96	***Cornwall Photographic Alliance 25th Anniversary Exhibition***
01·06·96–30·06·96	***Cornwall Buildings Group Annual Awards Exhibition***
08·06·96–07·07·96	***Arts in Trust*** Work by local schools in collaboration with artists and the National Trust.
10·08·96–31·08·96	***Truro Art Society Annual Exhibition***
07·09·96–27·09·96	***Mermaid Appeal*** An art exhibition and auction.
05·10·96–07·11·96	***Branch Out*** *Art and Special Needs*
Nov 96–Dec 96	***City of Light*** Lantern Project in collaboration with Kneehigh Theatre.

Wakefield

WAKEFIELD ART GALLERY
Wentworth Terrace Wakefield WF1 3QW Director: Gordon Watson
☎ +44 1924 305796 📠 +44 1924 305769
Open: Monday-Saturday 10.30-17.30 Sunday 14.30-17.00
Closed: 1 Jan, 25, 26 Dec

COLLECTION

Two of the most outstanding British sculptors of the 20th century, Henry Moore and Barbara Hepworth, were born within a few miles of Wakefield Art Gallery and, not surprisingly, the Gallery has acquired some significant early sculpture and drawings by these now internationally celebrated artists. These and important work from other major British modern artists form the core of the collection. Works from other periods and European schools are also on display.

Displays at nearby Wakefield Museum include the Waterton Collection - exotic birds and animals collected in South America and elsewhere by Charles Waterton, the remarkable 19th-century traveller and naturalist.

EXHIBITIONS

04·05·96–16·06·96	***'From Yorkshire with Love'*** Yorkshire as seen through the eyes of the celebrated artist Ashley Jackson.
29·06·96–01·09·96	***Decorative Arts*** A historical survey of Wakefield's own collection.
07·09·96–27·10·96	***Suzanne McIvor*** Recent large abstract paintings by this Ilkley-based artist.
09·11·96–12·01·97	***Introduction to Weaving*** An exhibition of woven textiles from the Crafts Council Collection.
Mar 97–Apr 97	***Margaret Harrison*** New work by one of the most influential British feminist artists.

York

YORK CITY ART GALLERY
Exhibition Square York Y01 2EW Curator: Richard Green
☎ +44 1904 551861 📠 +44 1904 551866
Open: Monday-Saturday 10.00-17.00 Sunday 14.30-17.00
Closed: 1 Jan, Good Friday, 25, 26 Dec

COLLECTION

The collection of the York City Art Gallery comprises 600 years of European painting, from early Italian gold-ground panels to the art of the 20th century. Exceptional in its range and interest, the collection includes pictures by Parmigianino and Bellotto, Lely and Reynolds, Frith and Boudin, Lowry and Nash, and nudes by York-born William Etty. There is also an outstanding collection of modern stoneware pottery.

EXHIBITIONS

06·04·96–26·05·96

Carel Weight *A War Retrospective* Carel Weight (born 1908) is one of Britain's most respected living artists. This exhibition brings together the paintings he made during the Second World War as a soldier, an army art advisor and an official war artist. The exhibition includes works produced in England, Italy, Austria and Greece.

11·05·96–14·07·96

Unseen Etty William Etty (1787-1849), York's most successful painter, was famous in his day for his history pictures, and has always been admired for his studies of the nude. This stairwell display presents a selection of Etty's drawings and sketchbooks alongside portraits of the artist from the Gallery's collection.

01·06·96–30·06·96

Georg Baselitz *Prints* Georg Baselitz is best known for turning the figures in his pictures upside down in order to question the meaning of art. This exhibition of prints by the leading contemporary German artist combines the humour of inversion with a serious concern for materials and colour.

14·07·96–08·09·96

Folk Art in Britain Art made by and for ordinary people in the 18th and 19th centuries is the subject of this exhibition. It includes naive paintings by Alfred Wallis and anonymous sign writers, colourful shop signs and weather-vanes.

21·09·96–20·10·96

Yorkshire Sculptors' Group A selected exhibition of work by members of this local sculptors' group.

02·11·96–08·12·96

York Open A select selling exhibition of work by York artists.

14·12·97–26·01·97

London Knees *Claes Oldenburg Multiples 1964-1990*
A life-size cast of a pair of knees is the starting point for an exhibition of multiples by one of America's wittiest and most popular artists.

York

YORKSHIRE MUSEUM
Museum Gardens York YO1 2DR Director: Brian Hayton
☎ +44 1904 629745 📠 +44 1904 651221
Open: Apr-Oct Daily 10.00-17.00 Nov-Mar Monday-Saturday 10.00-17.00
Sunday 13.00-17.00

COLLECTION

Archaeology The Yorkshire Museum houses one of the finest archaeological collections in Europe, ranging from prehistoric times through the Roman, Anglo-Saxon, Viking and Medieval periods. There is a large and outstanding collection of Roman sculptures, mosaics, jewellery and other objects. Anglo-Saxon artefacts include the fine 8th-century silver gilt bowl from Ormside and the Gilling sword as well as sculptures and personal ornaments. The renowned Viking collection comprises decorated metalwork, stone carvings and a variety of organic objects. The Medieval section is particularly known for its sculpture, including the life-size Romanesque figures of the Apostles from St. Mary's Abbey.

Yorkshire Museum, York

Numismatics The Yorkshire Museum has one of the country's most important collections of coins, comprising about 35 000 specimens. Particular areas of strength include the coinages of Roman Britain and of Anglo-Saxon and Medieval England.

Decorative Art The museum's collection of ceramics is of national importance, including comprehensive assortments of tin-glazed Delftware, Leeds creamware and Rockingham porcelain as well as pieces from most Yorkshire potteries, examples of county pottery and late-Victorian art pottery production and work by York silversmiths. Selected items from the collection are on view in the pottery gallery on the first floor of the museum.

Geology The museum has an extensive geological collection comprising more than 100 000 specimens, as well as the Tempest Anderson Collection of some 5000 negatives of vulcanological topics from around the world (1880-1913).

EXHIBITION
01·01·96 onwards

Venom This exhibition presents the biology and behaviour of an astonishing variety of deadly animals. The exhibition combines museum models, live specimens and interactive displays.

Dublin ■

Dublin

IRISH MUSEUM OF MODERN ART
Royal Hospital Kilmainham Dublin 8 Director: Declan McGonagle
☎ +353 1 6718666 📠 +353 1 6718695
Open: Tuesday-Saturday 10.00-17.30 Sunday and public holidays 12.00-17.30
Closed: Monday and Good Friday, 24-26 Dec

COLLECTION

Founded in 1991, the Irish Museum of Modern Art presents a wide cross-section of Irish and international art of the 20th century, including pivotal figures such as Picasso, Giacometti and Joseph Beuys, and leading contemporary artists.

EXHIBITIONS

11·01·96–04·06·96

Literary Themes Modern artists have largely revolted against the dominance of literature in their field but a select number continue to make images in response to the written word. This exhibition examines the relationships between word and image and influences evident in both directions.

14·03·96–17·05·96

Glen Dimplex Artists Award 1996 An exhibition of the work of the five artists shortlisted for the 1996 IMMA Glen Dimplex Artists Award. They are performance artist Marina Abramovic, sculptor and installation artist Janine Antoni, painter Mark Francis, multimedia artist Jaki Irvine and sculptor and painter Alice Maher. The award of £15000 is open to Irish artists and to non-Irish artists who have exhibited in Ireland.

30·03·96–16·06·96

Works on Paper from the Weltkunst Collection This exhibition of sculptors' drawings and prints provides valuable insight into the development of their works.

24·04·96–30·06·96

Distant Relations 'Distant Relations' is a large-scale exhibition exploring the shared cultural experience of Irish, Mexican and Chicano artists. It comprises the work of 12 artists who have achieved recognition not only in their own context, but also in a wider environment.

11·05·96–15·09·96

Sculpture This exhibition from the museum collection will include selected works which use the immediate architectural space, but also make reference to the urban and rural environments beyond the gallery. Artists included Damien Hirst, Michael Landry, Juan Munoz, Barrie Cooke, Richard Long and Chung Eun Mo.

30·05·96–25·08·96	**Sean Scully** *Twenty Years (1976-1995)* Sean Scully's large-scale abstract paintings carry on the rich legacy of post-war abstract art. His paintings are notable for their highly disciplined vocabulary, with vertical, horizontal and diagonal stripes of varying length and thickness forming the basis of his work.
31·05·96	**Maytime Festival Exhibition** The annual Maytime Festival for older people is run in conjunction with the national organisation Age & Opportunity. The focus this year is a painting exhibition on the theme of a 'sense of place'.
Jun 96–Dec 96	**Figuration** Continuing the collection presence in the west ground floor galleries, there will be an exhibition of painting, sculpture and mixed-media works looking at a variety of themes ranging from the body in action to gender issues.
12·09·96–Jan 97	**The Event Horizon** *A Season of Exhibitions, Films and Projects on European Identity* This series explores issues of national identity, immigration and cultural phenomena. A central theme is the belief that the 'new' Europe must be built on an amalgam of old and new, and in order to retain vitality, it must incorporate a sense of flexibility.
27·09·96–Jan 97	**Beverly Semmes** *Sculpture/Installation* American artist Beverly Semmes is one of a number of younger artists working with issues involving the body and feminism. Recent work to be included in this exhibition introduces a kinetic element to her art.
17·10·96–Feb 97	**Louis le Brocquy** *Retrospective* Louis le Brocquy (born Dublin, 1916) has always been preoccupied with capturing an aspect of the body as an image of the human being. This retrospective exhibition comprises more than 90 paintings spanning his entire career.

Dublin

NATIONAL GALLERY OF IRELAND
Merrion Square (West) Dublin 2 Director: Raymond Keaveney
☎ +353 1 6615133 ▥ +353 1 6615372
Open: Monday-Saturday 10.00-17.30 Thursday 10.00-20.30
Sunday 14.00-17.00
Closed: 24, 25 Dec, Good Friday

COLLECTION	**Italian School** The collection of Italian art includes a number of acknowledged masterpieces, most notably Fra Angelico's 'Attempted Martyrdom of Saints Cosmas and Damian'. Works from the sixteenth century North Italian school include Titian's 'Ecco Uomo' and Tiepolo's 'Allegory of Immaculate Conception'. The Gallery has an impressive collection of Florentine seventeenth-century art. Caravaggio's highly dramatic painting, 'The Taking of Christ' is one of the highlights. **German and Early Netherlandish Schools** The German collection represents works dating from the fifteenth and sixteenth centuries. Highlights include: Portraits by Conrad Faber, Wolf Huber, George Pencz and Bernard Strigel. Also in this collection is 'The Peasant Wedding' by Pieter Brueghel the Younger. **Dutch school** The Dutch School is one of the strongest in the Gallery's collection. Among them, Rembrandt's 'Landscape with the Rest on the Flight into Egypt', Jan Steen's 'Village School', Ferdinand Bol's 'David's Dying Charge to Solomon', Hobbema's Wooded Landscape-'The Path on the Dyke' and Jacob van Ruisdael's 'The Castle of Bentheim'.

Other important paintings include 'Marriage Feast at Cana' by Jan Steen, 'Lute-Playe'r by Frans Hals and 'Lady writing a Letter' by Johannes Vermeer.

Later Flemish School   Flemish paintings date from the seventeenth to the nineteenth century. Highlights of this collection include works by Jordaens, Rubens and Van Dyck.

Spanish School   The Gallery's holding of Spanish paintings comprises works by Nicolás Francés and a number of works by Murillo including the complete set of six paintings on the theme of the prodigal son.Other important works include 'The Immaculate Conception' by Zurbarán, 'St. Francis receiving the Stigmata' by El Greco, Goya's 'Lady in a Black Mantilla', 'The Kitchen Maid with the Supper at Emmaus' by Velázquez and 'Still-live with Mandolin' by Picasso.

French School   The French collection includes masterpieces from the seventeenth to the nineteenth century. Worth noting are works by Nicolas Poussin, Jaques-Louis David and Eugène Delacroix. The collection of French Impressionist and early twentieth century paintings include 'A River Scene' by Claude Monet, 'Bords du Canal du Loing à St-Mammes' by Alfred Sisley and 'Ballet Dancers' by Edgar Degas.

Caravaggio
(1571- 1618)
The taking of Christ

National Gallery of
Ireland, Dublin

British School   The British collection is strong in eighteenth century portraiture with works by William Hogarth, Thomas Gainsborough, Joshua Reynolds and George Romney. The nineteenth century is highlighted by a collection of 35 Turner Watercolours. Among the modern works are four Augustus John portraits.

Irish School   The Irish School spans works from the seventeenth century to the present day. Among the most notable Irish landscape artists are Thomas Roberts, Robert Carver, George Barret and William Ashford. Portraiture include works by John Michael Wright, James Latham, Thomas Frye and Nathaniel Hone the Elder. A major exponent of the nineteenth century history painting was Daniel Maclise.

One of the greatest Irish artists of the twentieth century is Jack B. Yeats, whose work reveals his fascination with the people, places and legends encountered in his youth in Sligo.

EXHIBITIONS

07·05·96–16·06·96

Mrs Delaney's Flower Collages   A selection of fragile collages from the British Museum will represent the first visiting exhibition to be mounted in the Gallery's newly refurbished space dedicated to works on paper.

11·06·96–28·07·96

Miró (1893-1983)   This exhibition comprises 100 prints and 17 illustrated books by Joan Miró, from the Muséo Nacional Centro de Arte Reina Sofía, Madrid, and is the most important collection of Miró's works ever to be presented in Ireland.

02·07·96–11·08·96 ***Acquisitions*** An exhibit showing the Gallery's recent acquisitions.

08·10·96–15·12·96 ***William Leech (1881-1968)*** A favourite 'Irish Impressionist', Leech studied at the Metropolitan School of Art and then at the Royal Hibernian School with Walter Osborne. In 1901 he continued his studies in Paris, moving to Brittany in 1903 where the sunshine and plein air effects gradually replaced his darker, academic works. 'The Goose Girl' and 'Convent Garden' are among the most popular works in the Gallery's collection. This is the first monograph exhibition dedicated to the artist.

29·10·96–15·12·96 ***Treasures from the Royal Horticultural Society*** This exhibition has been selected from approximately 18 000 paintings and drawings in the Society's possession. It consists of about 70 images ranging from 17th-century Dutch flower studies to plant portraits by leading botanical artists of the present day.

01·01·97–31·01·97 ***Turner Watercolours*** Of the Gallery's 35 watercolours and drawings by J.M.W. Turner (1775-1851), 31 were bequeathed to the Gallery by Henry Vaughan in 1900, who stipulated that they should only be exhibited in January when the sunlight is weakest. This request has been strictly adhered to and as a result, they remain in pristine condition.

Dublin

NATIONAL MUSEUM OF IRELAND
Kildare Street Dublin 2 Director: Patrick F. Wallace
☎ +353 1 6777444 Fax +353 1 6766116
Open: Tuesday-Saturday 10.00-17.00 Sunday 14.00-17.00
Closed: Monday and 25 Dec

COLLECTION

The National Museum houses collections consisting of antiquities, historical objects and works of decorative art tracing the development of Irish civilisation from the Mesolithic period, ca. 7000 B.C., to the 20th century.

Permanent exhibitions include 'Prehistoric Ireland', which covers the period from the Mesolithic to the Iron Age and complements the metalwork on display in the other exhibitions, as well as 'Ireland's Gold' which focuses on the museum's collection of Bronze Age gold; one of the most comprehensive of its kind in Western Europe.
'The Treasury' traces the history of Irish art from the Celtic Iron Age, ca. 300 B.C., to the late Middle Ages. An audio-visual presentation lasting ten minutes and available with English, French or German commentary provides an introduction to this exhibition.

The exhibition 'Ireland - the Viking Age' deals with the Viking invasions during the late Middle Ages and the impact of these on Irish society.
The historical display includes such exhibits as 'The Road to Independence', tracing the events which led to the foundation of the modern Irish State.

EXHIBITIONS

No exhibitions planned.

■ Luxembourg

Luxembourg

CASINO LUXEMBOURG
41, Rue Notre Dame 2240 Luxembourg Director: J. Kox
☎ +352 225045 📠 +352 222000
Open: Tuesday-Sunday 10.00-18.00 Thursday 10.00-20.00
Closed: Monday

COLLECTION | No permanent collection.

EXHIBITIONS

22·05·96-14·07·96 | **Sean Scully** *The Catherine Paintings* Despite the great simplicity of Scully's motifs - alternating bands or squares in two colours - the abstract paintings of this Dublin-born artist (born 1945) express a powerful personality and suggest places and moments in the painter's life.

24·07·96-15·09·96 | **Sculptural Suggestions** *Jürgen Albrecht (or Franz West), Richard Deacon, Reinhard Mucha, Peer Veneman, Didier Vermeiren and Erwin Wurm* An exhibition exploring form and material as well as the relations between space, the history of sculpture and its presentation. 'Sculptural Suggestions' presents a sample of the plastic and poetic power of contemporary sculpture.

25·09·96-17·11·96 | **'Actions Directs'** *Filippo Falaguasta, Robert Milin, Antoine Prum* Artistic actions such as installations or performances undertaken by these artists, interacting with the artistic or social community and part of the population of the City of Luxembourg, will be documented through photographs, videos, texts, etc.

25·09·96-17·11·96 | **Giovanni Anselmo** *Invited by Michel Assenmaker* Anselmo works with weight, torsion, gravity, direction, the divisibility of material, induction, and similar physical forces and properties.

27·11·96-09·02·97 | **'Stanze' for Painting** Juxtaposition of works by Kelly, Toroni, Viallat, Federle, Frize, Jean-Pierre Bertrand, Baselitz, Penck, Richter, Polke, Büthe, Rutault, etc. with works of earlier painters (Le Brun, Heda, Patel, Natoire, Monet, etc.) from the famous collection of the Museum of Modern Art of St. Etienne.

| Feb 97-Apr 97 | **Didier Bay** *Retrospective* Using photographs, videos, texts and art history, and the use of themes such as landscapes, nudes, or sexuality, Didier Bay has been expressing ideas about our conception of images and stereotypes since the beginning of the 1970s. This exhibition is the first large retrospective of the work of Didier Bay. |

Luxembourg

MUSÉE D'HISTOIRE DE LA VILLE DE LUXEMBOURG
14, Rue du Saint-Esprit 1475 Luxembourg Conservator: Danièle Wagener
☎ +352 47962766 📠 +352 471707
Open: Tuesday-Sunday 10.00-18.00 Thursday 10.00-20.00
Closed: Monday

COLLECTION

Luxembourg City's new historical museum offers an opportunity to discover the city's more than 1000 years of history from different perspectives. One of the main tasks of the city has been the preservation and enhancement of its architectural heritage. For this reason, the new museum has been installed in a group of four restored houses in the heart of the old part of Luxembourg. One of the main features is the panoramic elevator which virtually travels through time by passing though the museum's six exhibition levels. Both the building and the museum's collections reflect Luxembourg's history within an architectural, military, social and cultural context. Ancient views of the city, portraits of some of the great figures of local history, items of the citizens' daily life, weapons, furniture, costumes and dresses, as well as liturgical objects are on display.

EXHIBITIONS

No exhibitions planned.

Luxembourg

MUSÉE NATIONAL D'HISTOIRE ET D'ART
Marché-aux-Poissons 2345 Luxembourg Director: Paul Reiles
☎ +352 4793301 📠 +352 223760
Open: Tuesday-Friday 10.00-16.45 Saturday 14.00-17.45 Sunday 10.00-11.45 / 14.00-17.45
Closed: Monday

COLLECTION

The museum is housed in a former governor's mansion which has been completely restored. Its collection, ranging from prehistoric to modern times, includes Celtic numismatics and Celto-Roman finds from excavations in the area. The Romans had settlements, mansions and farms in Luxembourg; models of the 18th and 19th century archaeological sites are on display. There are medieval sculptures, a medieval retable, folk art and folklore, ceramics, a collection of arms and armour and a 16th-century travellers' currency guidebook. The Natural History section covers the fields of palaeontology, geography, geology, mineralogy, ornithology and botany, and the museum also has a small planetarium. The Fine Art section has works by Pieter Brueghel the Younger ('Calvary'), Pieter Brueghel III ('Village Wedding'), Lucas Cranach, Van Dyck, Jacob Jordaens, David Teniers, Adriaan Brouwer ('The Foot Operation'), David Rijckaert ('Smokers in the Tavern') and others. There is also an exhibit of contemporary Luxembourg art.

EXHIBITIONS

No details available.

WILLEM LENSSINCK

SCULPTOR

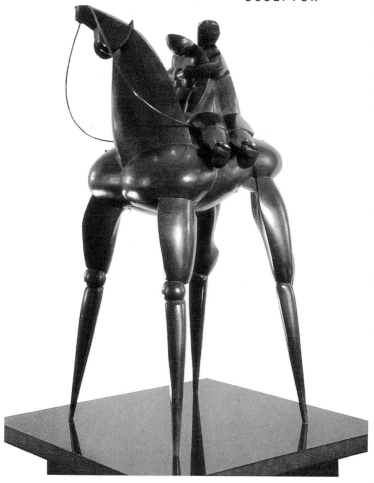

"Horse called desire "- bronze   hardstone -
123 x 70 cm hxb.

GALLERY   LAIMBöCK

other artists :
**Fons Bemelmans - Pieter d'Hont
Federico Carasso -   Paul Grégoire
Guus Hellegers - Gerhard Lentink
Francisca Zijlstra -   Juan Ripollès
Lia Laimböck - Jos van Vreeswijk**

Daily open by appointment: Doornseweg 10
Langbroek   3947 ME   The Netherlands.
tel/fax +31 343 561699

Amsterdam

ALLARD PIERSON MUSEUM
Archaeological Collection of the University of Amsterdam
Oude Turfmarkt 127 1012 GC Amsterdam Director: H.A.G. Brijder
☎ +31 20 5252556 📠 +31 20 5252561
Open: Tuesday-Friday 10.00-17.00 Saturday-Sunday 13.00-17.00
Closed: Monday

COLLECTION

The collection contains three sections: Egypt; the Near East, Cyprus and Prehistoric Greece; and the Greek World, Etruria, and the Roman Empire.

The Egyptian civilisation is displayed by means of mummies and sarcophagi, images of gods and Egyptians, and objects relating to everyday life. Scale models of the pyramids of Giza and the temple of Edfu help to unlock the secrets of the Egyptian pharaohs, Greek kings and Roman emperors who ruled here from 5000 B.C. to 700 A.D.
Jewellery, weapons, statuettes, vases and cuneiform tablets offer a glimpse into religious and daily life of Iran, Mesopotamia, Syria, Palestine and Anatolia between 5000 B.C. and 800 A.D. Pottery and marble idols display early civilisations on the Cycladic Islands, Crete and the Greek mainland.

Greek colonists took their culture to Italy where elements of it were adopted by the Etruscans and then by the Romans. This Graeco-Roman civilisation then spread throughout the Roman Empire,

greatly influencing Western ideas. Stone statues and portraits, bronzes and glass, pottery, jewellery and household items give an impression of how these people lived.

EXHIBITION
Jun 96–Sep 96 | ***The Olympic Games in Ancient Times***

Amsterdam

VAN GOGH MUSEUM
Paulus Potterstraat 7 1007 CX Amsterdam Director: R. de Leeuw
☎ **+31 20 5705200** 🖷 **+31 20 6735053**
Open: Daily 10.00-17.00
Closed: 1 Jan

COLLECTION | With more than 200 paintings and some 500 drawings, the museum maintains the largest and most varied Van Gogh collection in the world. Many of the paintings are on permanent exhibition in chronological order, from the sombre canvasses of Brabant to the brightly coloured works of his late period, providing a fine survey of Van Gogh's development as an artist. Highlights include 'The Potato Eaters', 'Self-Portrait with Felt Hat', 'Still Life with Sunflowers', 'Wheat Field with Crows', etc.
The collection of contemporary works, also largely on permanent exhibition, comprises paintings by Toulouse-Lautrec, Gauguin, Fantin-Latour, Monet, Isaac Israëls and many other artists known to Van Gogh. The museum is striving to expand the collection with paintings, drawings, pastels and sculpture from the 1840-1920 period.

Vincent van Gogh
(1853-1890)
Self-portrait with
straw hat, 1887

Van Gogh Museum,
Amsterdam

EXHIBITIONS
29·03·96-23·06·96 | ***The Passage of Time*** Paintings and Drawings by Caspar David Friedrich and Philipp Otto Runge

10·05·96-15·09·96 | ***Vincent van Gogh*** The Drawings of the Van Gogh Museum. Part 1: The Early Work (1880-1883)

26·07·96-17·11·96 | ***The Colour of Sculpture 1840-1910*** a.o. Klinger, Rodin, Gauguin, Picasso

29·11·96-02·03·97 | ***Sir Lawrence Alma-Tadema (1836-1912)*** Retrospective

Amsterdam

AMSTERDAM HISTORICAL MUSEUM
Kalverstraat 92 1012 RM Amsterdam Director: P.W. Kruseman
☎ +31 20 5231822 📠 +31 20 6207789
Open: Monday-Friday 10.00-17.00 Saturday-Sunday 11.00-17.00
Closed: 30 Apr, 25 Dec, 1 Jan

COLLECTION

The Amsterdam Historical Museum is the custodian of the older Fine and Applied art collection of the city of Amsterdam. This collection has been augmented by bequests, legacies, loans and acquisitions. The paintings, furniture, art objects and everyday artefacts in the museum relate the story of the city of Amsterdam and its inhabitants.

One of the highlights of the collection is formed by the group portraits of civic guards and regents from the 16th, 17th and 18th century. Many of these are on permanent display in the museum's 'Civic Guard Gallery'. The anatomical lessons form a separate category within this collection, an important piece among the museum's holdings being Rembrandt's 'Dr. Deijman's Anatomy Lesson'. The silver showpieces of the 16th and 17th-century civic guard guilds are an interesting feature of the museum's decorative art collection. In addition, the museum possesses some good examples of carved wooden furniture as well as a large collection of everyday artefacts. There are also collections of silver, china, pewter and decorated glassware.

The Print Room houses a large number of drawings and prints. These include drawings by Rembrandt, Rubens, Ruysdael and Van Ostade. The museum is renowned for its large collection of prints and drawings by Jan and Caspar Luiken.

EXHIBITIONS

07·03·96–18·08·96 **Boys and Girls**   An exhibition on life in Amsterdam's City Orphanage.

04·04·96–23·06·96 **Anatolia in Amsterdam**   An exhibition for and about people from Turkey and their neighbours in Amsterdam.

22·08·96–27·10·96 **Open House**   An exhibition dealing with life in an Amsterdam neighbourhood at the end of the 19th century.

03·10·96–07·01·97 **Fans and Lace**   *An Amsterdam Collection*

15·12·96–15·04·97 **Czar Peter The Great and Holland**

Amsterdam

JOODS HISTORISCH MUSEUM - JEWISH HISTORICAL MUSEUM
Jonas Daniël Meijerplein 2-4 1011 RH Amsterdam Director: J. Belinfante
☎ +31 20 6269945 📠 +31 20 6241721
Open: Daily 11.00 - 17.00
Closed: Day of Atonement (23 Sep 96)

COLLECTION

The permanent collection illustrates the many aspects, both of the past and present, of Judaism in the Netherlands; the religion, culture and history of Jews in this country form the central theme. At the start of this tour, in the New Synagogue, five elements are presented which play a part in the Dutch-Jewish identity today: religion, the bond with Israel, the experiences of the Shoah, personal history (including the story of Charlotte Salomon), and the influence of Dutch culture on Jewish culture. The presentation in the Great Synagogue explains the Jewish life cycle, festivals and the differences between the various Jewish religious communities in the

Netherlands. The story of the Jewish socio-economic history in this country is told in the presentations which can be viewed in the galleries of the synagogue.

Introductory panel in
the gallery of the
Great Synagogue
during the exhibition
'Dat is de kleine man'
1995

*Joods Historisch
Museum, Amsterdam*

EXHIBITIONS

15·12·95-19·05·96   ***Jerusalem in Judaism, Christianity and Islam***   The tradition of Abraham originated in Jerusalem, giving rise to three monotheistic religions (Jews, Christians and Muslims). All three consider Jerusalem as the Holy City, though each from a different perspective. Using illustrations, maps, photographs, models and ceremonial objects, the museum presents several themes conveying the cultural and religious ties of these three faiths with Jerusalem and with each other.

22·03·96-08·09·96   ***Peter Hunter/Otto Salomon, Emigrant in London***   *Photographs 1935-1945*   Peter Hunter was born Otto Salomon in Berlin in 1913. After fleeing Nazi Germany in 1935, he made impressive photographic essays of political and cultural events in London before the Second World War. During the war, Hunter photographed the liberation of Italy. This exhibition will coincide with an exhibition at the Historical Museum of The Hague featuring photographs by Hunter's father (the acclaimed founding father of parliamentary photography) and entitled 'Erich Salomon in Holland, Photographs from 1933-1945'.

07·06·96-24·11·96   ***Civil Equality***   2 September, 1996, marks the 200th anniversary of the 'Decree Awarding Jews Equal Status With All Other Citizens', which was adopted by the National Assembly of The Hague. This is celebrated in this exhibition of the Jewish emancipation in the Netherlands, which also includes an anthology of articles on various aspects of the Jewish emancipation.

13·09·96-Dec 96   ***Jules Chapon***   The artist Jules Chapon was born in Haarlem in 1914 and has resided in France since 1973· This exhibition presents a retrospective of his artistic achievements from the start of his work during the Second World War up to the present.

Amsterdam

DE NIEUWE KERK
Gravenstraat 17 1012 NL Amsterdam Director : E.W. Veen
☎ +31 20 6268168 📠 +31 20 6226649
Open: Opening times vary

COLLECTION | No permanent collection.

EXHIBITIONS
14·07·96–01·09·96   *Russian Summer* *Palech Exhibition and Photography Wubbo de Jong*

17·12·96–13·04·97   *Russian Winter* *Catherine the Great Exhibition*

22·04·97–Jun 97 | *World Press Photo*

Amsterdam

MUSEUM HET REMBRANDTHUIS
Jodenbreestraat 4-6 1011 NK Amsterdam Director: A.R.E. de Heer
☎ +31 20 6249486 📠 +31 20 6232246
Open: Monday-Saturday 10.00-17.00 Sunday and public holidays 13.00-17.00

COLLECTION

Once Rembrandt van Rijn's residence, the museum houses a virtually complete collection of the master's etchings. Of the 280 prints Rembrandt made, 250 are on display, together with paintings by his teachers and pupils.

When Rembrandt moved into this three-story house in 1639, he was already a well-established and wealthy artist. However, the cost of buying and furnishing the house eventually led to his financial downfall in 1656. When Rembrandt was declared insolvent, an inventory of the contents of the house was drawn up, which listed more than 300 paintings by Rembrandt himself and some by his teacher, Pieter Lastman, and his friends, Peter Paul Rubens and Jan Lievens. To meet his debts, Rembrandt was forced to sell most of his possessions. He ultimately moved out in 1660.

The museum is now home to his graphic art. Rembrandt's prints reveal his eye for detail and his skill in creating dramatic effects of light and dark. He depicted a varied range of subjects, including landscapes, patriarchs, emaciated beggars, children at play, and himself in numerous self-portraits.

EXHIBITIONS
05·10·96–05·01·97

The Old Testament in Dutch 16th and 17th-Century Printmaking
Rembrandt, his predecessors and pupils
Religious scenes constitute an important part of Dutch 16th and 17th-century imagery. In particular, dramatic events from the Old Testament, such as The Fall, Abraham's Sacrifice and Susanna and the Elders, were popular subjects for artists. The exhibition shows the drama of the Old Testament through the eyes of artists such as Rembrandt, Goltzius, Lucas van Leyden and Maarten van Heemskerk.

Amsterdam

RIJKSMUSEUM
Stadhouderskade 42 1071 ZD Amsterdam Director: H.W. van Os
☎ +31 20 6732121 📠 +31 20 6798146
Open: Monday-Sunday 10.00-17.00
Closed: 1 Jan

COLLECTION

The Rijksmuseum is Holland's principal museum and houses a large and wide-ranging collection of objects.
Paintings   The core of the collection is made up of Dutch paintings from the 17th century. Rembrandt is well represented with 19 works, of which 'The Nightwatch' has a central place in the museum. This period is also represented with paintings by such artists as Hals, Vermeer, Steen and Ter Borch. Artists from the 15th and 16th centuries are also on display, including Jan Scorel, Maerten van Heemskerck, Lucas van Leyden and Hendrick Goltzius. A small

collection of paintings of Foreign Schools, among which Rubens, Murillo and Tintoretto, is also on display.

Sculpture and Decorative Arts Sculpture and decorative arts stemming from the Middle Ages to Jugendstil and Art Nouveau can be viewed. The museum focuses on its collections of Medieval sculpture, 16th and 17th-century silver and its Delftware and Meissen collections.

Dutch History The display consists of all kinds of memorabilia (ship models, flags, objects of gold and silver, documents, etc.) relating mainly to the political and military history of the Netherlands.

Asiatic Art A large part of this collection of art objects from South and South-East Asia and the Far East is on loan from the Society of Friends of Asiatic Art.

Print Room The collection covers Dutch Drawing from the 15th to the 20th century, including drawings by Rembrandt and his pupils and Dutch graphic artists of the 16th and 17th century. International schools, among which Japanese Art, are also well represented.

EXHIBITIONS

11·05·96-04·08·96

Disegni *Three Centuries of Italian Drawing from the Rijksmuseum* Not many people know about the Rijkmuseum's collection of Italian drawings. Although not large, this part of the collection includes many intriguing items. The exhibition consists of some 80 drawings dating from the 15th to the 18th century. Masterpieces by Pierio di Cosimo, Sebastiano del Piombo, Frederico Barocci, Carlo Marata and Giambattista Tiepolo are among the works on display.

't GEELHUYS
OOSTERHOUT
Gallery

FINE ARTS 1820-1920

Romanticism, The Hague School, Impressionism.

Prominent painters such as Bauer, Corot, Dupré, Israels, Jongkind, Koekkoek, Leickert, Lépine, Maris, Monticelli, Roelofs, Schelfhout, Weissenbruch.

Address: Leijsenstraat 51, 4901 PC Oosterhout
☎ +31 162 434 357.
Director: B. Paulus van Pauwvliet.

By appointment.

08·06·96-29·09·96

Dutch Weapons from Russia   An exhibition of 75 weapons from the Kremlin and Hermitage collections. The weapons, including numerous rifles and pistols, have been recently restored in the Netherlands.

10·08·96-27·10·96

The Great American Watercolour   *American Watercolours 1860–1940*   This will be the first European exhibition to focus on American watercolours. Having originally painted in European styles, American artists began to establish a tradition of their own towards the end of the 19th century. Major among these artists were Winslow Homer, a master of watercolour technique, John Singer Sargent, with his brilliant portraits and landscapes, produced with originality and flair, and most American of all, Edward Hopper, who depicted America with a clear and simple style. The exhibits are from the Museum of Fine Arts in Boston.

Jan Steen
The Hennery

In the exhibition
'Jan Steen – Painter
and Storyteller',
Rijksmuseum,
Amsterdam

Collection
Mauritshuis, Den
Haag

21·09·96-12·01·97

Jan Steen   *Painter and Storyteller*   Jan Steen was more than just a comic; he was a unique artist. His use of colour was masterly and he could portray a group of figures in such a way that they seemed involved in some intriguing activity. Moreover, he was able to present wonderfully atmospheric scenes in which humour was far from dominant. His comedy could vary from refined to coarse, from basic to sophisticated. The Rijksmuseum's major winter exhibition features 50 paintings from around the world and focuses on his talent as a storyteller and his qualities as a painter.

02·11·96-02·02·97

Reflections on the Everyday   *Dutch Genre Prints from the 16th and 17th century*   In the late 15th century, woodcut artists and engravers began portraying scenes of everyday life in prints: amourous couples, farmers on their way to the market, groups of musicians. Scenes such as these were especially popular in the 17th century. This exhibition provides a delightful survey of the genre prints. Lucas van Leyden, Rembrandt and Adriaen van Ostade are amply represented. There are also some surprising, for the most part unknown, prints on display here. The exhibition attempts to explain the deeper significance of the themes and motifs.

Amsterdam

NEDERLANDS SCHEEPVAARTMUSEUM AMSTERDAM
Kattenburgerplein 1 1018 KK Amsterdam
Director a.i.: E.S. van Eyck van Heslinga
☎ **+31 20 5232222** 📠 **+31 20 5232213**
Open: Tuesday-Saturday 10.00-17.00 Sunday and public holidays 12.00-17.00;
15 Jun-15 Sep Monday 10.00-17.00
Closed: Monday (15 Sep-15 Jun) and 1 Jan, 30 Apr

COLLECTION

The large storehouse, now home to the Netherlands Maritime Museum, once contained munitions, ropes and sails for the Dutch Navy. Today, the building houses a permanent exhibition displayed on two floors and covering the entire Dutch seafaring history. There are ship's models, modern and historical paintings, nautical instruments, sea charts, weapons and an attic full of yachts. There is also a radar hut with an interactive computer programme, a periscope with a view of the entire city and the Royal Barge.

The towering masts of the VOC ship 'Amsterdam' can be seen from the Central Station. It is a replica of the ill-fated East Indiaman 'Amsterdam' that went down on its maiden voyage to Asia in 1749. It has a complete crew who perform all the appropriate action on board the ship. The helmsman sets course, the cook prepares an authentic seaman's meal, the sailors swab the deck, the guns are fired and the cargo is loaded.

You can experience the long and dangerous voyage to the East Indies in our Philips HD Multi Media Theatre. Using the latest techniques, the film realistically shows the visitor what it is like to be on board and bound for Batavia.

EXHIBITIONS

until Summer 96

Fighting for Freedom, 1940-1945   This exhibition focuses on the adventures and struggles of the war at sea during the Second World War. It also provides an idea of the actual size of the maritime contribution to the war effort.

02·03·96–30·06·96

Bontekoe, the Captain, the Journal, the Boys   An exhibition about the famous adventures of Bontekoe and his sailors during their trip with the Dutch East Indian Company.

29·03·96–12·01·97

Vinke & Co.   An exhibition about the company Vinke & Co. of Amsterdam, which contributed to the Amsterdam shipping and trading business.

12·10·96–Apr 97

Trapped in Ice   *Life in the 'Behouden Huys' 1596-1597*
An exhibition about the journey of Willem Barentsz and his stay on Nova Zembla, where he and his crew spent the winter of 1596-1597.

Amsterdam

STEDELIJK MUSEUM MUSEUM OF MODERN ART
Paulus Potterstraat 13 1071 CX Amsterdam Director: Rudi Fuchs
☎ +31 20 5732737 🖷 +31 20 5732789
Open: Dailiy 1 Oct-31 Mar 11.00-17.00 1 Apr-30 Sep 11.00-19.00
Closed: 1 Jan

COLLECTION

The Stedelijk Museum is an important museum of modern and contemporary art in The Netherlands. It is a dynamic museum that presents developments in the visual arts. A number of works is permanently on view from the Stedelijk Museum's renowned collection of paintings and sculpture, drawings, prints, photographs, graphic design, applied art and design.

Highlights of the collection are some fifty paintings, watercolours and drawings by the Russian artist Malevitch and works by Kandinsky, Chagall, Picasso, Monet, Cézanne, Matisse and Dubuffet. German Expressionism is represented by Kirchner and Campendonck, and Dutch art by Van Gogh, Breitner, 'De Stijl' painters Mondrian and Doesburg, the 'Cobra' painters Appel, Constant and Corneille, as well as others such as Willink, Jan Toorop and Charley Toorop.

Other styles include Pop Art by Rauschenberg, Liechtenstein and Warhol, Hard Edge paintings, Minimal Art and Nouveau Réalisme.

The collection also contains furniture by Gerrit Rietveld, industrial design, audio-visual art, kinetic art and installations.

EXHIBITIONS

06·04·96–26·05·96 | **Peiling** *Recent Dutch Art*

16·04·96–09·06·96 | **Edvard Munch** Beginning in April, the Stedelijk Museum presents, for the first time, a major exhibition of paintings by Edvard Munch (1863-1944). Along with Van Gogh, Munch was one of the foremost 19th-century Expressionist pioneers. The emphasis in the selection for this exhibition is on works created between 1920 and 1942, including landscapes, still-lifes, portraits and figure compositions. Munch's paintings are displayed alongside works of several contemporary artists who have expressed great admiration for him or whose work reflects his influence. Among others, they include Jannis Kounellis, Joseph Beuys, Günther Förg, Georg Baselitz and Karel Appel.

11·05·96–30·06·96 | **Doors Project** 30 doors by Piet Hein Eek.

11·05·96–30·06·96 | **Barbara Broekman** *Tapestries*

08·06·96–25·08·96 | **Gerrit Komrij's Selections** Writer Gerrit Komrij serves as guest curator for this exhibition of works from the collection of the Stedelijk Museum.

22·06·96–18·08·96 | **Photographs from the Museum Collection** Highlights from the photography collection.

29·06·96–25·08·96   **Under Capricorn**   The aim of this exhibition is to show how contemporary art reflects the experience of living on a shrinking planet. Space exploration, developments in satellite and computer technology, global environmental problems and the collapse of communism have all intensified awareness of the world as a whole.

12·07·96–15·09·96   **Cobra and the Stedelijk**   The 'CoBrA' movement (from Copenhagen, Brussels and Amsterdam) was founded in 1948 by Amsterdam-based artists Karel Appel, Constant and Corneille, along with the Danish painter Asger Jorn and the Belgian writers Christian Dotremont and Joseph Noiret. Their use of primitive and naive art and children's drawings as sources of inspiration, and their surrender to what spontaneously welled up from the subconscious, provoked considerable indignation. In this exhibition, the Stedelijk presents about 150 works of the Cobra movement from the period between 1948 and 1962.

K. Malevich
Girls in the fields,
1928-1932

Permanent
collection,
Stedelijk Museum,
Amsterdam

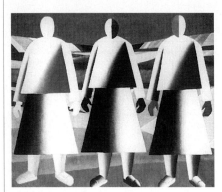

13·07·96–08·09·96   **August Sander**

07·09·96–27·10·96   **Marcus Lupertz**

14·09·96–10·11·96   **Art from Surinam 1975-1995**

23·11·96–Jan 97   **20th-Century Italian Art**   This important exhibition presents Italian art of the 20th century. The retrospective covers the period from the Futurist movement through the most recent developments, and includes works by Gino Severini, Giorgio Morandi, Giorgio De Chirico, Alberto Burri, Lucio Fontana, Mario Merz, Jannis Kounellis and others. It will be the first time that such a broad overview of Italian art can be seen in the Netherlands. Seldom, either in Italy or elsewhere in Europe, has such a broad-scale retrospective exhibition been presented. In total, about 300 works will be included.

Amsterdam

TROPENMUSEUM
Linnaeusstraat 2   1092 CK Amsterdam   Director: H.J. Gortzak
☎ +31 20 5688200   ⅢG +31 20 5688331
Open: Monday-Friday 10.00-17.00   Saturday-Sunday and
public holidays 12.00-17.00
Closed: 1 Jan, 30 Apr, 5 May, 25 Dec

COLLECTION   The Tropenmuseum houses about ten permanent collections which offer a many-sided picture of human life in the tropics and subtropics. There are a number of lifelike exhibits in which one can imagine oneself in a different world. A few examples include: walking through an Arab street to the sound of buyers, sellers and donkey-drivers, hearing the monotonous singing of the monks at a Buddhist temple, and finding one's way through shelters similar to those found in the cities of Bombay and Calcutta. Furthermore, objects reflecting the history and culture of the peoples in the tropics are on display in showcases. A special exhibition for children aged 6-12 can be visited in the Children's Museum (different opening hours).

Lighthall
Tropenmuseum,
Amsterdam

EXHIBITIONS

until 01·09·96

Puppetry in Africa and Asia   This exhibition puts many different and often beautiful puppets on display, and also features a special question-and-answer trail for children. Puppetry is still a lively tradition in many African and Asian countries, serving both educational and entertainment functions, and often relating the ancient stories about good and evil. Puppet shows are also used for health education and to safely express criticism of social conditions in the societies. For this reason, puppetry remains popular among the young and the old.

Nov 96–Aug 97

Amazonia   'Amazonia' focuses on one of the most impressive natural areas of the world. Pre-Columbian settlements and the colonial period are featured, but the main stress is on the 20th century. 'Amazonia' presents the beauty of the material cultures, but also the shocking reality of dislocated societies and abused natural scenery.

until Apr 97

[Children's Museum - hours differ from Tropenmuseum; call 020.56.88.300 for information]
Stories to Know where to Go   An exhibition about a group of Aborigines in the north of Australia: the people of the Wild Honey. The exhibition deals with their land and with the way in which they pass on their knowledge about the land to their children in their songs, dances and paintings.

Apeldoorn

PALEIS HET LOO - NATIONAAL MUSEUM
Koninklijk Park 1 7315 JA Apeldoorn Director: A.W. Vliegenthart
☎ +31 55 5772400 ⅢⒻ +31 55 5219983
Open: Tuesday-Sunday 10.00-17.00
Closed: Monday (except public holidays) and 25 Dec

COLLECTION

Het Loo Palace, in the woodland setting of Apeldoorn in the heart of the Netherlands, was the favourite summer residence of the Viceregents and the Royal Family of the Netherlands from 1686 to 1975. Since 1984 the palace has served as a museum following a significant restoration of the buildings and the gardens which returned them to their original 17th-century state. The palace, with its interiors dating from William and Mary up to the reign of Queen Wilhelmina, reflects the lifestyles of the members of the family of the Dutch House of Orange-Nassau over three centuries.

The wings, with their permanent and visiting exhibitions of historical objects, documents, paintings, china, silver, royal garments and court costumes, present a picture of the historical ties of the House of Orange-Nassau with the Netherlands.

A large collection of national and international orders and decorations is housed in the Museum of the Chancery of the Netherlands Orders of Knighthood.

The spring and summer planting of the Baroque garden parterres, surrounded by terraces, pergolas, statues and vases, is in exactly the same fashion as in the 17th century.

The Royal Stables house royal carriages, hunting carriages, sleighs and vintage court cars, including the 'wagon' in which Queen Wilhelmina went out on painting excursions.

The entire complex is surrounded by extensive woodland, dotted with lakes, and is fully open to the public.

EXHIBITIONS

27·04·96-27·05·96	**Future through Tradition** This exhibition is organised by 'Tesselschade-Arbeid Adelt' and includes such themes as For Women, By Women, The professional training of Dutch Women, Good Needlework and The Royal Patronage.
23·05·96-27·05·96	**Kitchen Art Fair**
Jul 96-Aug 96	**A Royal View over the Garden** Every Wednesday in July and August, access to the Palace roof.
05·07·96-14·07·96	**National Lathyrus Show (Sweet Peas)**
31·08·96	**Royal Fireworks** Royal fireworks in the Gardens.
25·10·96-02·04·97	**Between Two Thrones** Treasures from Peterhof, from Peter The Great to Nicolas II Exquisite furniture, art objects, costumes and paintings stemming from the residential period of Czar Peter The Great up to Czar Nicolas II.

Apeldoorn

VAN REEKUM MUSEUM
Churchillplein 2 7314 BZ Apeldoorn Director: Frits Bless
☎ +31 55 5219155 ▥⒡ +31 55 5225456
Open: Tuesday-Saturday 10.00-17.00 Sunday 13.00-17.00
Closed: Monday and 1 Jan, 16 Apr, 25 May, 4 Jun, 25 Dec

COLLECTION

The emphasis of the museum is on Dutch art since 1960. There are works by Cesar Domela, Carel Visser, Jan Schoonhoven, Johan Claassen, Cees Andriessen, Waldo Bien, Frank van Hemert, Berend Hoekstra, Sjoerd Buisman, Mark Brusse and many others. Artists from other countries are also featured, and include Joseph Beuys, François Morellet, Franz Eggenschwiler, Leon Tarasewicz, KCHO, Belkis Ayon, Marcos Lora Read, etc.

The Van Reekum Museum also houses a photography collection with work by, among others, Bernard Faucon, Teun Hocks, Anja de Jong, Paul de Nooyer, Duane Michals, Lydia Schouten and David Ward.

There is also an interesting collection of modern art jewellery by designers such as Emmy van Leersum, Marion Herbst, Coen Mulder, Birgit Laken, Susanna Heron and Caroline Broadhead.

Since 1989 the museum has collaborated closely with the Museum Sztuki in Lódz (Poland). This partnership is reflected in the reconstruction of the Neoplastic Room by Wladislaw Strzeminski (1893-1952), on permanent display in the Van Reekum Museum. Strzeminski designed this room in 1948 for one of the Sztuki Museum's galleries. The Van Reekum Museum acquired the replica in 1989.

Arnhem

MUSEUM VOOR MODERNE KUNST ARNHEM - MUSEUM OF MODERN ART ARNHEM
Utrechtseweg 87 6812 AA Arnhem Director: L. Brandt Corstius
☎ +31 26 3512431 📠 +31 26 4435148
Open: Tuesday-Saturday 10.00-17.00 Sunday and public holidays 11.00-17.00
Closed: Monday

COLLECTION

The permanent collection of Contemporary Fine Art includes paintings by the Magical Realists and their contemporaries, such as Carel Willink, Pyke Koch, Dick Ket and Charley Toorop. The museum's acquisitions place the accent on contemporary art, in particular figurative works by Dutch artists. The museum also possesses an important collection of modern Dutch jewellery.

[A Series of Contemporary Applied Art in 'De Koepel']

02·06·96-11·08·96   **Lam de Wolf**   *Textile Installation 'Empty'*   Following the first series of monumental 'wall works' in 1991, it is clear that de Wolf has now entered a new phase in her development: using the borders of handkerchiefs. Although this series is less three-dimensional than earlier works, the mutual relationship between the various elements as a result of careful positioning remains an important aspect of this artist's work.

25·08·96-20·10·96   **Piet Stockmans**   In the case of Piet Stockmans (born 1940), the combination of activities as industrial designer and free-style ceramist has led to a unique kind of work. He creates series of works (vases, bowls, masks and other forms) by transforming the plaster moulds in such a way that they remain recognisable as a series, but the exact similarities disappear. In addition to variations in form, the artist also applies blue glazing, decorating white porcelain with subtle streaks of blue.

09·11·96-12·01·97   **Ri-Jeanne Cuppens**   Using coloured earthenware and concrete, ceramist Ri-Jeanne Cuppens (born 1963, Limburg) makes geometrical castings which resemble architectural constructions. The repetition of castings and the alternation of open and closed parts create an impression of a row of houses.

Feb 97-Mar 97   **Barbara Broekman**   Tapestries are out. They belong in the 15th century or in the 70s. Barbara Broekman (born 1955) is self-willed. This artist creates tapestries using various materials and techniques. Her work is characterised by stratification, resulting in almost abstract compositities.

Assen

DRENTS MUSEUM
Brink 1 - 5   9401 HS Assen   Director: G.G. Horstmann
☎ +31 592 312741 📠 +31 592 317119
Open: Tuesday-Sunday 11.00-17.00
Closed: Monday and 25 Dec, 1 Jan

Egbert van Drielst
(1745-1818)
Winter in Annen

*Drents Museum,
Assen*

COLLECTION   The archaeological department of the museum presents treasures from Drenthe's distant past, including flint axes and a 10 000 year-old dugout canoe, made from the trunk of a fir tree, which is the oldest known vessel in the world. In addition, the famous bog body known as the 'Girl from Yde' is on display.
The Art Nouveau and Art Deco department includes a collection of art and products of applied and industrial design from the first decades of the 20th century.

There is also a tax collector's house with period rooms displaying furniture, wall coverings and decoration, lighting, china and a fully equipped kitchen typical of a prosperous family in Drenthe in the 17th or 18th century. The exhibition 'Drenthe 1920-1940' shows how dramatically Drenthe changed between the two world wars. The textile and costume departments concentrate on 'urban' and traditional costumes from 1750 up to the present. The applied art department focusses on furniture, glass and ceramics, base metals, gold and silver, folklore, and coins and pennies from Drenthe. The museum's collection of paintings from Drenthe extending from the 18th to the 20th century is displayed in the halls and stairways. Highlights are paintings from the Hague School.

EXHIBITION
05·10·96-12·01·97   *Iron Spoons*

Den Haag - The Hague

HAAGS GEMEENTEMUSEUM
Stadhouderslaan 41 2517 HV Den Haag Director: J.L. Locher
☎ +31 70 3381111 +31 70 3557360
Open: Tuesday-Sunday 11.00-17.00
Closed: Monday

COLLECTION

The Haags Gemeentemuseum collection encompasses the three very different fields of modern art, applied art and music.
The modern art collection of 19th and 20th-century art includes work by Weissenbruch, Monet, Van Gogh, Kandinsky, Constant, Sol LeWitt and the largest collection of Mondrians in the world. The extensive collection of prints and drawings includes works by Redon, Bresdin, Mondrian, Escher, Beckmann and Westerik.

The permanent collection of applied arts on display include western and colonial furniture, Hague silver, ceramics and glass from Europe, the Islamic world, Japan and China. There are also period rooms dating from the 17th, 18th and late 19th centuries. Displays include pieces from the 'Art Nouveau' Dutch Jugendstil movement. A new collection currently being created is devoted to contemporary glass and ceramics with work by Sipek, Sotsass and Frijns. The large costume collection is also housed in this section.

Kirchner, E.L.
Czardas dancers,
1907

Haags
Gemeentemuseum,
Den Haag

The music collection has examples of western musical instruments including oboes by the Richter family, recorders by A. van Aardenberg and keyboard instruments from the Ruckers family and the Erard brothers. There is a unique collection of electronic musical instruments, notably the set-up for the Stockhausen composition 'Microphonie' and Kagel's 'Zwei-Mann-Orchester'.

17·02·96–27·05·96   **Fabric in Form**   This exhibition includes original painted and textured fabrics by Ella Koopman as well as designs made from Koopman's fabrics.

02·03·96–16·06·96   **Frank van Hemert**   Frank van Hemert (1956) is a leading contemporary Dutch artist. This first-ever retrospective shows works from 1981 to the present.

09·03·96–02·06·96   **Delft in the Time of Vermeer**   A number of Vermeer's paintings include representations of Delftware. This exhibition, timed to concide with the exhibition of 17th-century painting masterpieces in the Mauritshuis, displays examples of Delft pottery.

09·03·96–02·06·96   **Hague Porcelain**

16·03·96–26·05·96   **Gary Lang**   Gary Lang will develop an installation consisting of a 'mirror' made of coloured tape placed on the wall.

27·04·96–02·06·96   **World Wide Video Festival**   Over 150 videotapes, CD-ROM, CD-i and Internet productions plus 18 installations will be on view in the course of the forthcoming 14th World Wide Video Festival.

08·06·96–08·09·96   **Ruud Kuijer**   Ruud Kuijer's sculptures are built up of elements cast together. Of special importance is the interrelationship of these elements to each other in space.

08·06·96–08·09·96	**Ossip** This exhibition presents a broad overview of mostly recent work by this original artist who utilises manipulated photographs and objects.
14·06·96–15·09·96	**Traditional Gems - Modern Jewellery**
13·07·96–06·10·96	**French Masters from Moscow** *From Monet to Matisse* A selection of 60 top works from the collection of turn-of-the-century French paintings held by the Pushkin Museum in Moscow. The exhibition comprises major works from the earliest days of modern art, by artists such as Monet, Cézanne, Gauguin, Bonnard, Picasso, Braque, Matisse, and others.
01·03·97–11·05·97	**The Golden Age in Denmark**
01·03·97–01·06·97	**German Expressionism** This exhibition is constructed around a painting by Ernst Ludwig Kirchner in the Haags Gemeentemuseum's modern art collection.

Den Haag · The Hague

HAAGS HISTORISCH MUSEUM
Korte Vijverberg 7 2513 AB Den Haag Director: M.C. van der Sman
☎ +31 70 3646940 📠 +31 70 3646942
Open: Tuesday-Friday 11.00-17.00 Saturday-Sunday 12.00-17.00
Closed: Monday and 25 Dec, 1 Jan

COLLECTION	The museum shows the development of the Hague from village to city and the life of its inhabitants. History is displayed by means of guild silver, Rozenburg porcelain, antique furniture, a doll's house, photographs (also in stereo), models and numerous paintings. There is also a nearly five-metre wide 'View of the Hague' by the famous painter Jan van Goyen as well as other cityscapes by Jan Steen, the La Fargue family, Jan ten Compe and Floris Arntzenius.
EXHIBITIONS 01·03·96–02·06·96	**Dutch Life in the Days of Vermeer**
16·03·96–23·06·96	**Erich Salomon in Holland** *Photographs 1933-1940*
mid Jun 96–Sep 96	**Count Floris V of Holland (1254-1296)**
mid Sep 96–mid Nov 96	**Art and History** *Floor Rubbings by Ton Martens*
mid sep 96–mid Nov 96	**The Dollhouse of Lita de Ranitz**
Dec 96–mid Feb 97	**The House of Orange and the Romanovs**
Mar 97–end Apr 97	**Designs by the Court Architect Pieter de Swart (1709-1773)**

Den Haag · The Hague

MAURITSHUIS
Korte Vijverberg 8 2513 AB Den Haag Director: F.J. Duparc
☎ +31 70 3469244 📠 +31 70 3653819
Open: Tuesday-Saturday 10.00-17.00 Sunday 11.00-17.00
Closed: Monday

COLLECTION	The Mauritshuis, a 17th-century palace, is uniquely situated in the centre of The Hague, at a corner of the Hofvijver, directly adjacent to the seat of the Dutch government. It was built between 1634 and

1644 for Johan Maurits van Nassau Siegen, who was a nephew of Viceregent Frederik Hendrik. The Mauritshuis was designed by Jacob van Campen and, in collaboration with Pieter Post, constructed in the Dutch Classicist style. In 1822 the Mauritshuis became a museum. The museum houses a collection of world-famous paintings from the Dutch Golden Age, with works such as 'The Anatomy Lesson' by Rembrandt, Vermeer's 'View of Delft' and paintings by Jan Steen, Frans Hals, Paulus Potter and others. In 1994 the collection was enriched with a magnificent landscape by Meindert Hobbema. The collection of works by Flemish and Dutch masters of the 15th and 16th century includes works by Rogier van der Weyden, Rubens and Van Dyck.

EXHIBITION
01·03·96-02·06·96

Johannes Vermeer   Johannes Vermeer (1632-1675) left behind a modest oeuvre of approximately 35 paintings, a large number of which will be on view in this exhibition. Vermeer is admired for his painting technique, his superb depiction of light and shade and his illusionism. This exhibition, organised by the National Gallery of Art in Washington and the Mauritshuis, includes works on loan from museums in London, Paris, Berlin, Dublin, Edinburgh and New York, among others, and offers the first representative survey of the work of this master of the Dutch Golden Age.

Den Haag - The Hague

HET PALEIS
Lange Voorhout 74 2514 EH Den Haag Director: J.L. Locher
☎ **+31 70 3381111** ▥ **+31 70 3557360**
Open: Tuesday-Sunday 11.00-17.00
Closed: Monday

COLLECTION   No permanent collection.

Front façade
Museum Paleis Lange
Voorhout, Den Haag

EXHIBITIONS
13·04·96–16·06·96

Frantisek Kupka (1871-1957) *Prague - Paris*   Before becoming a pioneer of abstract art, Kupka had already achieved fame as a Symbolist and Expressionist painter and an Art Nouveau book illustrator. Important paintings illustrating various aspects of his oeuvre will be shown, drawing on examples from the collections of the Centre Beaubourg (Paris) and the Narodni Galeri (Prague). A series of drawings on the theme 'Prometheus' (Private Collection, Paris) will be exhibited for the first time.

29·06·96–01·09·96

Leon Spilliaert (1881-1946) and M.C. Escher   Born in the Belgian seaside resort of Ostende, like Ensor, Spilliaert developed a fantasy world of his own, on the dark side of Belgian symbolism. His early self-portraits speak of morbid dreams and total isolation. His work connects Symbolism and Expressionism. Parallel to this exhibition, a selection of highlights from the graphic work of M.C. Escher will be on display.

21·09·96–01·12·96   **Princely Possessions**   The Archives of the Dutch Royal Family are undergoing restoration. As a result, it is now possible to show a selection from the family's rich collections. Jewellery, clothing, rare photographs and portraits will be included. This exhibition emphasises the history of Het Paleis with particular attention directed to Queen Emma and her son-in-law Prince Hendrik.

14·12·96–16·02·97   **Suze Robertson**

Dordrecht

DORDRECHTS MUSEUM
Museumstraat 40   3311 XP Dordrecht   Director: J.M. de Groot
☎ +31 78 6134100 ▉ +31 78 6141766
Open: Tuesday-Saturday 10.00-17.00   Sunday and public holidays 13.00-17.00
Closed: Monday and 25 Dec, 1 Jan

COLLECTION

The museum has an interesting collection of paintings, prints and drawings, with the emphasis on Dutch painting from the 17th century up to the present day.
The Golden Age   The collection includes works from famous Dutch Masters of the Golden Age with prize pieces from the Cuyp family and Rembrandt's local students. Dordrecht's past prominence is reflected in the museum's masterpieces by Albert Cuyp, Nicolaes Maes and Samuel van Hoogstraten. Work by Jan van Goyen and less famous masters such as Cornelis Bisschop and Jacob van Geel are also well represented.
From Romanticism to Impressionism   Paintings from the 18th, 19th and early 20th century occupy a special place in the museum. Highlights include the landscapes by Jacob van Strij and Romantic masterpieces from B.C. Koekkoek and A. Schelfhout. Work by Ary Scheffer, the 19th-century Franco-Dutch painter, is permanently displayed. The collection of works from the Hague and the Amsterdam schools is impressive with paintings by Mauve, Breitner and the Maris brothers.
Old and New Developments   The collection of 20th-century paintings, prints and drawings includes work by important pre-war masters such as Jan Toorop and Jan Sluyters. More recent developments are well represented with work from the Cobra group including Appel, Constant and Wolvecamp and important contemporary masters such as J.C.J. van der Heyden, Lataster and Armando.

EXHIBITIONS
07·04·96–16·06·96   **After Scheffer**   Ten contemporary painters, sculptors and engravers who received scholarships from the Ary Schefferfoundation.

17·05·96–25·08·96   **Dordrecht in Print 1650-1800**   People approaching Dordrecht are struck by the beauty of the waterfront with its centuries-old houses, warehouses and churches, and by the contrast between the activity of outgoing and incoming ships and the apparent peace of the riverbank. These scenes are depicted in this selection of prints and drawings from the collections of the Dordrechts Museum and the Municipal Archive of Dordrecht.

08·09·96–17·11·96   **Robert Zandvliet**   This contemporary artist is often inspired by paintings in museum collections, such as by

Hendrik Johannes Weissenbruch's (1824-1903) 'North of the Village Nieuwkoop', in the collection of the Dordrechts Museum.

15·09·96–17·11·96   **Masters of Dordrecht of the 19th Century**   Paintings, drawings and prints by 19th-century artists, including landscapes by Jacob van Strij (1756-1815), river views by J.C. Schotel (1787-1838) and birdpieces and wallpapers by Aart Schouman (1710-1792).

30·11·96–03·02·97   **Bea de Visser**   A contemporary artist.

Eindhoven

STEDELIJK VAN ABBEMUSEUM
Vonderweg 1 5611 BK Eindhoven Director: J. Debbaut
☎ +31 40 2755275 ⑈ +31 40 2460680
Open: Tuesday-Sunday 11.00-17.00
Closed: Monday, except public holidays

COLLECTION

The Van Abbemuseum has always geared its acquisition policy to its exhibition policy and vice versa. As a result, its permanent collection charts, to a large extent, the history of its exhibitions. Major works such as Richard Serra's 'T-junction', Joseph Beuy's installation 'Voglio vedere i miei montagne' occupying an entire room, and Mario Merz's 'Igloo Nero' were made especially for exhibitions at the museum. Through its adventurous exhibition policy, relatively early works by such artists as Christo, Frank Stella, Anselm Kiefer and Donald Judd have come into the museum's collection. To provide a context for these contemporary, post-war works, the museum also possesses examples of the historic avant-garde including important works by Picasso, Chagall, Braque, Léger, Mondrian, Delaunay, Kandinsky, Kokoschka, Van Doesburgh and Moholy-Nagy, among others. In addition, the Van Abbemuseum has a large collection of major works by the Russian Constructivist El Lissitzky. In recent years the museum has built up significant ensembles of the work of a new generation of sculptors including Thomas Schütte, Jan Vercruysse, Jean-Marc Bustamante, Juan Muñoz, Miroslaw Balka and Rachel Whiteread.
As of 1 January 1995 the Van Abbemuseum on the Bilderdijklaan is closed for expansion and renovation. All museum departments have been temporarily relocated to Vonderweg 1 in Eindhoven (opposite the PSV football grounds).

EXHIBITIONS
20·04·96-02·06·96   **Jubilee Exhibition 1**   60 Years of the Van Abbemuseum

15·06·96-01·09·96   **Jubilee Exhibition 2**

14·09·96-24·11·96   **Brabant**   200 Years of History

Enschede

RIJKSMUSEUM TWENTHE
Lasondersingel 129 7514 BP Enschede Director: D.A.S. Cannegieter
☎ +31 53 4358675 ⑈ +31 53 4359002
Open: Tuesday-Sunday 10.00-17.00
Closed: Monday and 1 Jan

COLLECTION

The collection presently comprises three departments: Pre-modern Art, Modern Art, and Crafts.
The Pre-modern Department   focuses on an extensive collection of 15th to 19th-century paintings. The Art of the Middle Ages,

religious art, 16th and 17th-century landscapes, 18th-century still lifes and portraits, and 19th-century paintings from the Romantic Period, the Barbizon School and the Hague School are well represented. The museum is also fortunate enough to possess some Late Medieval woodcarvings (sculptures), manuscripts, and some early examples of the art of printing.

The Department of Modern Art is made up almost exclusively of works produced by Dutch artists and is represented mainly by pre-war and post-war Expressionist and Abstract-geometric trends. Pieces produced by working artists continue to be added to this collection.

The Department of Crafts contains an extensive collection of 17th and 18th-century delftware. Included in this department is the Gobelin Hall which was built to house some large Gobelins (tapestries) from Brussels.

Monet, Claude
Cliffs near Pourville,
1882

Rijksmuseum
Twenthe, Enschede

EXHIBITIONS
01·05·96–23·06·96 | *Ben Akkerman*

Jul 96–Aug 96 | *Henry William Bunbury (1750-1811)*

Sep 96 | *Pjotr Müller*

Gouda

CATHARINA GASTHUIS
Oosthaven 9/Achter de kerk 14 2801 PB Gouda Director: N.C. Sluijter-Seijffert
☎ +31 182 588440 ⌨ +31 182 588671
Open: Monday-Saturday 10.00-17.00 Sunday and public holidays 12.00-17.00
Closed: 25 Dec, 1 Jan

W.B. Tholen
The Arntzenius
sisters

Museum het
Catharina Gasthuis,
Gouda

COLLECTION

The Catharina Gasthuis was originally established as a hospital at the beginning of the 14th century and remained a hospital until 1910. The adjoining chapel dates from 1474. The collection's highlights include 16th-century altarpieces which survived that century's iconoclasm, antique toys, an old city dispensary, a surgeon's guild room, an 18th-century kitchen, an isolation cell, instruments of torture and 19th-century paintings from the 'Barbizon' and 'Hague' Schools.

EXHIBITIONS

No exhibitions planned.

Groningen

GRONINGER MUSEUM
Museumeiland 1 Groningen Director: Reyn van der Lugt
☎ **+31 50 3666555** ⅢⒻ **+31 50 3120815**
Open: Tuesday-Sunday 10.00-17.00
Closed: Monday and 1 Jan, 28 Aug, 25 Dec

COLLECTION

Archaeology The Archaeology display contains objects from the Bronze Age, urns found in urnfields in Westerwolde, Iron Age objects, and Roman urns and artefacts discovered during archaeological excavations of the city up to 1993. Wherever possible, the objects are displayed against a background which reflects the site in which they were found: sand, bog or terp.

Groninger Museum,
1994
Groningen

Architects: A. en F.
Mendini

History Maces, guild silver, city seals and a coin and medal collection form the core of this department's collection. Topographical material, including city portraits by Cornelis Pronk, Johannes Bulthuis and A.J. van Prooijen, 16th and 17th-century church treasures and textiles, and portraits by Herman Collenius, Philips van Dijk and Janszoon de Stomme can also be viewed here.
Decorative Art The core of the collection is formed by Chinese and Japanese export porcelain shipped to the Netherlands by the VOC (Dutch East India Company) in the 17th and 18th century. The collection also features porcelain, stoneware and earthenware from Korea, Vietnam and Thailand.
Art after 1950 This department aims to acknowledge, collect and preserve new trends in art, starting at the earliest stages of their development. Examples on display here include Figuration Libre, German Neo-Expressionism, Mülheimer Freiheit, graffiti artists, Pattern & Decoration, staged photography, work which can be described as 'between art, architecture and design' and Art Business, in which visual artists include business elements in their artistic concepts.
Old Art (1500-1950) The collection gives a picture of the history of art in the Netherlands from 1600-1950. It includes works by

members of the De Ploeg group, the society of Expressionist artists in Groningen, the R.J. Veendorp collection, works by the Hague School and the collection of Dr. C. Hofstede de Groot, among which Fabritius, Heda and Rubens and drawings by Rembrandt.

EXHIBITIONS

until 19·05·96	***St. Walfridus Legacy***
until 09·06·96	***Virtualistic Vibes*** *Recent Work by Micha Klein*
21·04·96–16·06·96	***Utopia In Plastic***
04·06·96–22·09·96	***Highlights of the V.O.C. Collection in the Groninger Museum***
11·06·96–18·08·96	***30 Years of Acquisitions***
30·06·96–01·09·96	***Dick Bruna & Paul Huf***
Dec 96–Jan 97	***Johan Dijkstra,*** *member of the group of artists 'De Ploeg' in Groningen*
Spring 97	***Andres Serrano*** *- American photographer*

Haarlem

FRANS HALSMUSEUM-DE HALLEN
Groot Heiligland 62 2011 ES Haarlem Director: D.P. Snoep
Vleeshal Verweyhal Grote Markt 16 2011 RD Haarlem
☎ +31 23 5164200 📠 +31 23 5311200
Open: Monday-Saturday 11.00-17.00 Sunday and public holidays 13.00-17.00
Closed: 25 Dec, 1 Jan

COLLECTION

Apart from the Frans Halsmuseum itself, there are two branch museums in Haarlem: the Vleeshal and the Verweyhal, both located on the old marketplace (Grote Markt).

View of the inner garden of the Frans Hals Museum, Haarlem

The museum's permanent collection of 17th-century portraits, landscapes, genre paintings and still-lifes includes works by the likes of Hendrick Goltzius, Judith Leyster, Johannes Verspronck, Pieter Claesz, Willem Heda, Adriaen van Ostade and Jacob van Ruisdael. Frans Hals' eight group portraits of militia companies and regents form the high point of the collection. The museum also houses a large collection of period furniture, Haarlem silver and ceramics.

The collection of Modern and Contemporary art includes paintings, sculptures, the graphic arts, objects and ceramics. It features work by the Dutch Impressionists and Expressionists, the Cobra group, contemporary art and work by artists from the Haarlem area. Artists such as Isaac Israëls, Herman Kruyder, Jan Sluyters, Corneille, Constant, Karel Appel, Reinier Lucassen, Armando, Mari Boeyen and Ger Dekkers are included in the permanent collection. The museum's two other buildings on the Grote Markt are devoted to temporary exhibitions and Classic Modern art respectively.

EXHIBITIONS

[Museum]

23·03·96–12·05·96   **A Firmament of Flowers**   An exhibition of flowers in a remodelled Frans Halsmuseum. A unique, recently acquired set of 17th-century bed curtains with embroidered flower motifs, shown together with vases, flowers in the museum garden and works of art on the theme of 'the flower'.

31·03·96–26·05·96   **Sewing Kits 17th-19th Century**   Sewing kits as paintings with lids - a selection from private collections and the collection of the Frans Halsmuseum.

01·04·96–19·05·96   **Anne van Waerden**   *Crystal Objects*

20·05·96–07·07·96   **Milan Kunc**

13·07·96–25·08·96   **Jun Kaneko**   *Ceramic Objects*

[Verweyhal]

06·04·96–16·06·96   **Verwey's House**   The legacy of a highly individualistic Haarlem painter - Kees Verwey (1900-1995). Paintings, watercolours and studio items. Photographs of the interior by Piet van Leeuwen.

29·06·96–11·08·96   **Classic Moderns**   A selection from the museum collection.

24·11·96–23·02·97   **Herman Kruyder**   A special exhibition of the work of the painter Herman Kruyder (1881-1935).

[Vleeshal]

31·08·96–03·11·96   **Pop-Up**   An exhibition showing the 'moveable book' in all of its varied forms, from the 17th century up to and including today's interactive media.

15·09·96–24·11·96   **Earthly Paradises**   An exhibition dealing with the garden in the imagination of Dutch artists, 1470-1770, as depicted in paintings, prints, ceramics, etc.

14·12·96–09·02·97   **Kunst zij ons doel**   A presentation of the work of the Haarlem artists' society 'Kunst zij ons doel' (May art be our aim).

Haarlem

TEYLERS MUSEUM
Spaarne 16 2011 CH Haarlem Director: E. Ebbinge
☎ +31 23 5319010 📠 +31 23 5342004
Open: Tuesday-Saturday 10.00-17.00 Sunday and public holidays 12.00-17.00
Closed: Monday, 25 Dec and 1 Jan

COLLECTION

The Teylers Museum was established by Pieter Teyler van der Hulst, a prosperous merchant born in Haarlem in 1702. In his last will and testament, he provided for its establishment by endowing the Teyler Foundation, part of whose task would be to further progress in the arts and sciences.

Ever since his death in 1778, his ideals have been given concrete expression through the museum. For example, the Neo-Classical Oval Hall was built in 1784 for the display of the collection and demonstrations of physics. The museum's first curator, Wybrand Hendriks, acquired a portion of the Queen of Sweden's collection of 16th and 17th-century drawings by Italian masters. Subsequent curators have continued to add to the collection, which now includes five centuries of Dutch draughtsmanship, works produced by the Romantic and The Hague Schools, and Impressionist prints. The museum's first director, Martinus van Marum, encouraged scientific research and laid the foundations for the scientific collections belonging to the Teyler Museum, including fossils and mineral specimens. There is also an important collection of coins and medals.

Michelangelo
Buonarroti
(1475- 1564)
*Study for the Sixtine
Chapel, c. 1511*

*Teylers Museum,
Haarlem*

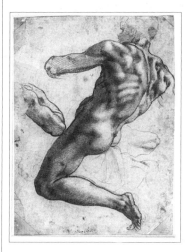

A new wing provides space for a gallery for temporary exhibitions, a smaller space to exhibit books from the Library and a pavilion for didactic programmes.
Selections from the international renowned collection of drawings, will be on display in the new Printroom.

EXHIBITIONS [The New Wing]

02·03·96-12·05·96 ***Giorgio Morandi (1890-1964)*** To mark the opening of its new wing, the museum is organising an exhibition of works by the famous Italian painter and draughtsman Giorgio Morandi.

25·05·96-28·07·96 ***Heer Bommel & Tom Poes*** A well-known Dutch cartoon character is the subject of this exhibition, which coincides with the 'Haarlemse Stripdagen', i.e. Haarlem's Comic Strip Days.

10·08·96-10·11·96 ***Time and Life*** Biophysical research in the Netherlands.

Dec 96-Feb 97 ***Dutch Drawings of the 17th Century*** Selections from the museum's own collection, to mark the publication of a new catalogue.

Feb 97-Apr 97 ***Leonard Springer (1855-1940),*** *Landscape and Garden Architect*

[Printroom]

02·03·96-02·06·96 ***Italian Drawings 1400-1700***

14·06·96-15·08·96 ***Master Drawings from the Permanent Collection***

| 31-08-96-27-10-96 | ***The History of a Haarlem Drawing Academy*** *'Art Be Our Goal'* *turns 175* |
| Nov 96-Dec 96 | ***Johan Sybo Sjollema (1900-1990)*** *Drawings* |

's-Hertogenbosch

NOORDBRABANTS MUSEUM
Verwersstraat 41 5211 HT 's-Hertogenbosch Director: Margriet van Boven
☎ +31 73 6877800 📠 +31 73 6877899
Open: Tuesday-Friday 10.00-17.00 Saturday-Sunday and public holidays
12.00-17.00
Closed: Monday

COLLECTION

The North Brabant Museum is located in the former residence of the Governors of Noord-Brabant. Two modern wings haven been added. The museum's permanent collection is based on the rich past of the Duchy of Brabant during the late Middle Ages, Renaissance and Baroque.
Keeping up-to-date with recent developments, the museum frequently organizes extensive exhibitions on an international art level.

EXHIBITIONS

16-05-96–25-08-96	***Gardens in Dutch Art*** *16th and 17th Century* This exhibition includes over 100 paintings, prints, manuscripts and objects featuring the formal garden in Dutch art from the 15th until the 18th century. It provides a splendid overview for garden and art lovers.
14-09-96–24-11-96	***The Muse as Driving Force*** *Visual Arts and the Development of Modern Brabant, 1796-1996* To mark the bicentennial of the independence of the province of Brabant, located in the South of the Netherlands, this exhibition covers the development of art and culture during a 200 year period, one which ran parallel to the emancipation of the province as such.
12-12-96–10-03-97	***Jewish Culture in North Brabant during the 19th and 20th Centuries***
28-03-97–08-06-97	***Children's Culture*** *From the Middle Ages up to the 20th Century*

Laren

SINGER MUSEUM
Oude Drift 1 1251 BS Laren Director: E.J.C. Raassen-Kruimel
☎ +31 35 531565 📠 +31 35 5317751
Open: Tuesday-Saturday 11.00-17.00 Sunday and public holidays 12.00-17.00
Closed: Monday and 1 Jan, 30 Apr, 25 Dec

COLLECTION

The museum started with the private collection of the American painter W.H. Singer and his wife. Singer lived and worked in Laren at the beginning of the 20th century. It was here that he built a house that nowadays forms part of the museum. The museum was built in 1956 and renovated in 1994. In 1996 the 40th anniversary will be celebrated.
The collection mainly consists of paintings, watercolours and drawings of Laren painters, French artists from the School of Barbizon, works of a few American painters and of French and Dutch sculptors from the 19th and 20th century. The French painter Henri Le Sidaner, who was a friend of William Singer, is represented

with twelve paintings. A great number of works by William Singer has been added to this collection. The Foundation of Friends of the private Singer Museum has enabled the acquisition of more important works from the School of The Hague and of Amsterdam Impressionists. Through the years, numerous gifts and legacies have completed the collection, such as the Hart Nibbrig endowment and in 1995 the gift of the Groeneveld Collection.

EXHIBITIONS

12·05·96-23·06·96 | ***Paul Huf***   *Portraits of a Photographer*

09·06·96-14·07·96 | ***Henk Wolvers***   *Ceramics*

23·06·96-18·08·96 | ***Sjoerd de Vries***   *Paintings*

30·06·96-18·08·96 | ***Margot Zandstra***   *Objects*

F. Hart Nibbrig
(1866-1915)
*On the dunes at
Zandvoort, 1892*

*Singer museum,
Laren*

25·08·96-03·11·96 | ***F. Hart Nibbrig (1866-1915)***   A special exhibition to celebrate the 40th anniversary of the Singer Museum.

07·10·96-10·11·96 | ***Johnny Rolf***   *Graphic Work*

17·11·96-05·01·97 | ***Graphics Now 7***   Bi-annual exhibition of graphic works of art from the Netherlands.

19·01·97-16·03·97 | ***Reimond Kimpe (1885-1970)***   *Paintings And Drawings*

01·04·97-20·06·97 | ***Henri le Sidaner***   *Drawings*

Leeuwarden

FRIES MUSEUM
Turfmarkt 11 8911 KS Leeuwarden Director: R.H.C. Vos
☎ +31 58 2123001 📠 +31 58 2132271
Open: Monday-Saturday 11.00-18.00 Sunday and public holidays 13.00-17.00
Closed: 25 Dec, 1 Jan

COLLECTION | The first part of an entirely renovated Fries Museum opened on 15 April, 1995. The museum has been expanded with the addition of the facing 16th-century 'kanselarij' (Chancellery). The collections of the Fries Museum include paintings from the 16th century through to the 20th century, a large collection of drawings and graphics, a significant costume collection, a famous collection of Frisian silver and many archaeological objects. There is also a section devoted to the Second World War, and various period rooms open to the public.

EXHIBITIONS

08·03·96 onwards   This exhibition focuses on the research and conservation of the portrait of Fookel van Walta and her daughter Tiedt van Botnia, which was painted by Adriaan van Cronenburg.

13·04·96–02·06·96   *The War on the Table*   As the earnestness of the war seems so remote from the playful innocence of games and jigsaw puzzles, the subject of this exhibition may appear to be of only minor importance. It becomes clear however that, early on, such innocent games were deployed as an aide to pursuing politics and war propaganda.

15·04·96–07·07·96   *Playing with the War*   The toy collection.

May 96–Jun 96   *Posters on the Subject of Magic and Variety Show/Theatre*

01·06·96–01·09·96   *From Royal Ownership*   The Collections of the Family of Orange In honour of the 100th anniversary of the Private Archives of the House of Orange, a selection of portraits, sculptures, historical photographic material, crockery, costumes and precious gold and silver will be on display to the public in this exhibition.

13·07·96–06·10·96   *Written in the Book*   The collection of books containing hand-written comments, stamps and signatures.

14·09·96–27·10·96   *Special Exhibition of the Works of Harmen Abma*

13·10·96–07·01·97   *It Fires*   The collection of small arms.

Leeuwarden

KERAMIEKMUSEUM HET PRINCESSEHOF
Grote Kerkstraat 11 8911 DZ Leeuwarden Director: J.A. Mulder
☎ +31 58 2127438 ▯▤ +31 58 2122281
Open: Monday-Saturday 10.00-17.00 Sunday and public holidays 14.00-17.00
Closed: 25 Dec, 1 Jan

COLLECTION   Once the official residence of Princess Maria-Louise of Hessen-Kassel, widow of the Frisian Viceregent John William Friso, Prince of Orange, the palace now houses the National Museum of Ceramics (since 1917). The dining-room on the ground floor is decorated with stucco ceiling, gold curtains, various portraits and Chinese porcelain. There are a total of thirty rooms containing collections of porcelain, pottery and stoneware pieces. The museum's extensive collections can be divided into four main categories: Oriental ceramics, European ceramics, the Tile department and Modern and contemporary ceramics.
The Princessehof's main collection consists of Asian ceramics, including works from Japan, China, Vietnam and Thailand. In its entirety, the collection of Chinese ceramics illustrates the development of this industry: starting with terracotta pieces made in the 3rd millenium B.C. and leading up to objects manufactured during the Ching dynasty (1644-1912). There are also objects belonging to the famous Famille Verte, Noire and Rose. The European ceramics include Italian Renaissance earthenware (majolica), delftware, Wedgwood, porcelain and Art-Nouveau and Art-Deco ceramics. The museum also houses an extensive collection of tiles from the Middle-East, Spain, Portugal, France and the Netherlands. Finally, contemporary ceramics from several European countries, particularly the Netherlands, are also on display.

EXHIBITIONS

EXHIBITIONS

15·03·96-03·06·96   *Frisian Ceramics*

21·06·96-02·09·96   *Johan van Loon, the Netherlands*   *Modern Ceramics*

20·09·96-25·11·96   *Ceramics from Morocco*

mid Dec 96-end Feb 97   *Modern Ceramics - two exhibitions*   The exhibition includes a collection of American modern ceramics from the Everson collection of New York, and a collection of English contemporary salt-glazed ceramics.

Leiden

RIJKSMUSEUM VAN OUDHEDEN NATIONAL MUSEUM OF ANTIQUITIES
Rapenburg 28 2301 EC Leiden Director: P.J.Th. Schoots
☎ +31 71 5163163 📠 +31 71 5149941
Open: Tuesday-Saturday 10.00-17.00 Sunday and public holidays 12.00-17.00
Closed: Monday and 1 Jan, 3 Oct, 25 Dec

COLLECTION   The National Museum of Antiquities, set up at the behest of King William I in 1818, exhibits artefacts that were long considered miracles due to their age and unique histories. The display of works from Classical Greek antiquity includes distinctive square-bearded sculptured heads, intimate sculptured funeral scenes and tragic theatre masks. The Near East comes alive through ritual statuettes, figurines of priests and inscriptions. The collection includes an inscription relating the story of King Nebuchadnezzar II's hanging gardens of Babylon. The Egyptian collection of mummies, funeral requisites, temple statues and utensils evoke this wondrous civilisation. Highlight of this section is the Isis Sanctuary, the temple of Taffeh.

The Netherlands has often been 'flooded'; not just by water but also by foreign peoples and their cultures. These events have left telltale clues in the Dutch soil, ranging from fishing tackle and snares (c. 1000 years B.C.), the flint implements of reindeer hunters and Roman altars from the coast of Zeeland, to Frankish and Saxon treasures. The display 'Archaeology in the Netherlands' offers a survey of national history from Prehistory to Medieval times. Most of the exhibits were recovered by archaeologists from the National Museum.

EXHIBITIONS

until 10·06·96   *Wine! Wine! Wine!*   *Wine in Greek and Roman Antiquity*
An exhibition which focuses on different aspects of viniculture in the Greek and Roman world, including reconstructions of a symposium, an ancient shipwreck with amphorae, a Roman 'pub', and a splendid dining hall.

19·03·96-05·08·96   *The Olympic Games in Ancient Greece*   The exhibition focuses on similarities and differences between the modern and ancient Olympic Games.

Sep 96-Jan 97   *Hands On*   An exhibition where visitors (both children and adults) can touch, view, smell and listen to archaeology and archaeological objects.

Oct 96-Mar 97   *Double-Crossing*   *Forgeries in Dutch Archaeology*   Forgeries offer an exciting and fascinating view of Dutch archaeology; the forger, his work and the reaction of the deceived archaeologists. The exhibition consists of 20 different cases of forgery. On the one hand these forgeries tell their own story. On the other hand they show the development of Dutch archaeology as a science over the last 150 years.

Leiden

STEDELIJK MUSEUM DE LAKENHAL
Oude Singel 28-32 2312 RA Leiden Director: H. Bolten-Rempt
☎ +31 71 5165360 📠 +31 71 5134489
Open: Tuesday-Friday 10.00-17.00 Saturday, Sunday and public holidays
12.00-17.00
Closed: 3 June-1 Sep due to internal restaurations Monday and 25 Dec, 1 Jan

COLLECTION

The Municipal Museum of Leiden is a museum of typical Dutch urban culture from the 16th century to the present. Since 1874 it has been housed in the Lakenhal, the former clothmakers' hall built in 1640 by Arent van 's Gravensande. A series of 16th-century paintings by Isaac van Swanenburgh depicting the various stages of the wool production process is supplemented by a loom, sample books, scissors, stamps, etc. Events from Leiden's history are also depicted, such as the siege of the city and its relief on 3 October 1574. The collection contains Leiden silver, engraved glass, pewter, tiles and paintings by 16th-century Leiden artists. The 17th century is represented by the young Rembrandt, Lievens, David Bailly, Jan Steen, Gerard Dou and the Leiden 'Precise School'. The 18th century is presented in rooms furnished in the style of the period. The 19th-and 20th-century collection contains work by Bakker, Korff, Jan Toorop, H.P. Bremmer, Floris Vester, Kamerlingh Onnes, Hendrik Valk, Theo van Doesburg and early examples of 'De Stijl'. Works from the contemporary collection are exhibited every summer.

EXHIBITIONS

24·02·96–28·05·96 *Orientation* Contemporary art by 5 Dutch and 5 Indonesian artists.

12·10·96–13·01·97 *Jan van Goyen* This exhibition is to celebrate the fact that Jan van Goyen (1596-1656), leading landscape artist, was born in Leiden 400 years ago. A striking survey consisting of 60 paintings and drawings from Dutch and foreign collections will focus on his role as the renewer of the art of landscaping in the Golden Age. Biographic documents and letters will reveal parts of his life, especially his role as a trader in tulip bulbs.

Leiden

RIJKSMUSEUM VOOR VOLKENKUNDE
Steenstraat 1 2312 BS Leiden Director: S.B. Engelsman
☎ +31 71 5168800 📠 +31 71 5128437
Open: Tuesday-Friday 10.00-17.00 Saturday, Sunday and public holidays
12.00-17.00
Closed: Monday and 1 Jan, 3 Oct

COLLECTION

The National Museum of Ethnology in Leiden is one of the oldest scientific ethnological museums in the world. It has grown out of an ethnological museum established in 1837 by Dr. Ph. F. von Siebold, who had served as a physician to a Dutch trading post near Nagasaki, Japan, and who opened his well-documented Japanese collection to the public a few years after his return to the Netherlands.
The museum's collections have been greatly expanded over the years, and now include items from many non-Western cultures, including Sub-Saharan Africa, the Arctic, China, the islands of Southeast Asia, Japan and Korea, Southwest and Central Asia, Latin America, North America, Oceania, and the mainland of Southeast Asia.
The museum is currently undergoing extensive renovations, and the exhibitions are restricted to special temporary exhibitions, guided tours, films, lectures and demonstrations.

Girl with bead
neckband
Inuit, Groenland

Rijksmuseum voor
Volkenkunde, Leiden

EXHIBITIONS
continuing for
several years

Japan Around 1850 Impressive lacquerware, headrests, bowls and chopsticks, as well as many more examples combining beauty and functionality, serve to illustrate the everyday life of the merchant class in 19th-century Japan.

11.10.96-May 97

Veils (working title) The subject of veils and veiling is currently one of the most emotive subjects within costume history, both for the participants and observers. This exhibition is intended to show that the development and use of veiling has ancient antecedents, which are spread throughout Europe, the Mediterranean and the Middle East.

Maastricht

BONNEFANTENMUSEUM
Avenue Ceramique 250 6221 KX Maastricht Director: A. van Grevenstein
☎ +31 43 3290190 📠 +31 43 3290199
Open: Tuesday-Sunday 11.00-17.00
Closed: Monday (except public holidays) and Carnival week
(Saturday-Tuesday), 25 Dec, 1 Jan

COLLECTION

The Bonnefantenmuseum is the Province of Limburg's museum for fine arts and archaeology.
Archaeology The archaeology collection consists of finds from Limburg dating from approximately 250 000 B.C. to the Modern Era. At the heart of the collection are important archaeological assemblages from the Stone Age, the Roman period, and the early Middle Ages.

Bonnefanten-
museum,
Maastricht

Medieval to 18th Century The collection of Medieval to 18th century art is divided into three main categories: Medieval sculpture, early Italian painting (1325-1525) and painting of the Southern Netherlands from the 16th and 17th centuries. Pieter Brueghel the Younger highlights this collection.

Contemporary The collection of contemporary art covers a select number of artists. At its core is the Seminal Collection, which includes Beuys, Broodthaers, Dibbets, Fabro, Kounellis, LeWitt, Mangold, Merz, Ryman, and Serra. The museum also houses a number of smaller collections, including Maastricht earthenware and silver.

EXHIBITIONS	
until 02·06·96	*Willem de Kooning* *Sculptures*
11·02·96-01·09·96	*Sol LeWitt* *Mural*
09·03·96-09·06·96	*The Neutelings Collection* *Sculpture from the Middle Ages*
06·04·96-01·09·96	*Fons Haagmans*
27·04·96-29·09·96	*Pierre Kemp* A collection of approximately 80 paintings by the Dutch poet Pierre Kemp (1886-1967); these works have never been on display before.
03·05·96-08·09·96	*The Océ-Van der Grinten Collection* Works by young (mostly Dutch) artists.
20·09·96-end Nov 96	*Gary Hume*

Middelburg

ZEEUWS MUSEUM
Abdij 4331 BK Middelburg Director: J.V.T. van Spaander
☎ +31 118 626655 📠 +31 118 638998
Open: Monday-Saturday 10.00-17.00 Sunday and public holidays 12.00-17.00
Closed: 24 and 30 Dec after 15.00 and 25 Dec, 1 Jan

COLLECTION

The Zealand Museum is housed in a centuries-old Norbertine Abbey in Middelburg. The collections recount thousands of years of Zealand's history and include archaeological finds such as the votive stones dedicated to the goddess Nehalennia, 18th-century rarity cabinets, 17th and 18th-century porcelain and silver from the society collections, and an overview of Zealand's regional costumes.
Classic and Modern Art The collection includes works by the 17th–century painters François Rijckhals and Adriaen van de Venne. Among the 20th-century artists inspired by Zealand's landscape are Jan Toorop, Jacoba van Heemskerck, the Hungarian painter Maurice Goth and his daughter Sarika Goth, Charley Toorop and Reimond Kimpe, Jan van Munster, Paul de Nooijer, Marinus Boezem and Piet Dieleman.
16th-Century Tapestries The series of 16th-century tapestries illustrating the battle between Zealand's 'geuzen' (Protestant fighters) and the Spanish on the Schelde rivers during the Eighty Years' War (1568-1648) was commissioned by the Provincial Council of Zealand and woven in Delft and Middelburg.

EXHIBITIONS

until 18·08·96

Hushed in Beauty *Jan Heyse (1882-1954)* Jan Heyse was part of the artist group from Domburg which centred around the Dutch artists Jan Toorop and Piet Mondrian. This double exhibition (in cooperation with the Marie Tak van Poortvliet Museum in Domburg) includes 100 paintings, woodcuts and drawings. This artist's work bears comparison with that of the Flemish Hans Memling and the Italian Andrea Mantegna.

14·06·96-onwards

Middelburg and the VOC (East India Company) Presentations on the subject of the Dutch East India Company are being organised by various museums in the Netherlands in 1996. Vlissingen and

Middelburg are among those in Zealand. This particular presentation focuses on the construction of the city, the administrators who lived in Middelburg and the equipage (dockyard, rope walks and sawmills) in the 17th century.

06·07·96-01·09·96 | *Stills* *Photographic Works by Wim Riemens* Wim Riemens (1933–1995) was a many-sided and self-willed artist-photographer from Middelburg. Among other works, portrayals of the Zeeland landscape is one particular theme on display here: a countless number of representations each with a different colour intensity.

20·09·96-14·01·97 | *Contemporary Art* *A Selection from the Collection by Lex ter Braak*

Spring 97 | *Reimond Kimpe (1885-1970)* An exhibition of paintings by this artist from Middelburg, in cooperation with the Singer Museum in Laren.

Nijmegen

NIJMEEGS MUSEUM COMMANDERIE VAN SINT-JAN
Franse Plaats 3 6511 VS Nijmegen Director: G.Th.M. Lemmens
☎ +31 24 3229193 📠 +31 24 3605073
Open: Monday-Saturday 10.00-17.00 Sunday and public holidays 13.00-17.00
Closed: 25 Dec

COLLECTION | The municipal museum of the city of Nijmegen derives its name from the cloister/hospital Commanderie van St. Jan, dating from 1296 and originally belonging to the order of the Knights of St. John. The museum houses a cultural-historical collection, comprising the town's collection in the field of history, art and applied art from the 11th until the 19th century, as well as a collection of modern art.
The 'Kanis Family Triptych', the monumental view of the Valkhof citadel by Jan van Goyen, and the painting of the Peace of Nijmegen by Henry Gascard are highlights of the collection. The museum also has a unique collection of Nijmegen silver. The modern art collection consists of more than 500 paintings and over 2000 works on paper, mainly focusing on a number of movements in Dutch art since the 60s, including Pop Art, Fundamental Art, Reliefs/Assemblies, and especially Contemporary Expressionism.

EXHIBITIONS
20·04·96–26·06·96 | *Contemporary Ceramics* In this retrospective exhibition, the works of 18 prominent Dutch ceramists are on display. The diversity in use of materials and glazing techniques is especially remarkable. There are works of ceramists who aspire to aethetic perfection as well as baroque forms and vases built up in geometric patterns.

13·04·96–19·05·96 | *Collette Deblé* This artist from Paris exhibits her drawings of female figures. This exhibition is held in conjunction with the cycle of lectures organised by the Studium Generale of the Catholic University Nijmegen.

22·06·96–01·09·96 | *Omdat dair in die kleijne arme verlaten Weeskens in toe stellen* This is one of a number of thematic historical exhibitions focusing on parts of the town's collections. It examines orphan care in Nijmegen in the 16th century. The ups and downs of the two Nijmegen orphanages with their buildings and inventories are the theme of this exhibition.

07·09·96–13·10·96 | *Servie Janssen (1949)* Servie Janssen uses a variety of mediums, such as drawing and painting, performance, and installations. This exhibition in the Commanderie, which includes the artist's existing paintings and assemblies, has the character of a large installation.

19·10·96–01·12·96   *Biennale Gelderland*   For the third time in succession, this biennial salon is presented in four museums in Gelderland, in cooperation with the artists' association G.B.K. The works of about 40 artists are simultaneously shown in Nijmegen, Arnhem, Apeldoorn and Zutphen.

Nijmegen

PROVINCIAAL MUSEUM G.M. KAM
Museum Kamstraat 45 6522 GB Nijmegen Director: A.M. Gerhartl-Witteveen
☎ +31 24 3220619 ▯▤ +31 24 3604799
Open: Tuesday-Friday 10.00-17.00 Saturday, Sunday and public holidays
13.00-17.00
Closed: Monday and 25 Dec

COLLECTION   In the G.M. Kam Provincial Museum, the archaeology of the province of Gelderland comes to life. Exhibitions from the permanent collection as well as temporary exhibitions present a picture of the earliest history of the province, and in particular of Roman Nijmegen.
In recent decades, extensive excavations have taken place, adding many revealing finds to the museum collection. New and unexpected discoveries are still being brought to light. Since the museum serves as the archaeological repository for the province, the greater part of those discoveries in Gelderland are stored there.

EXHIBITION
14·02·96-23·06·96   *Death on the Ridge*   A small exhibition about 30 centuries of burials on a ridge formed by pressure from ice.

Otterlo

KRÖLLER-MÜLLER MUSEUM
Houtkampweg 6 6731 AW Otterlo Director: Evert J. van Straaten
☎ +31 318 591241 ▯▤ +31 318 591515
Open: Tuesday-Sunday and public holidays 10.00-17.00
Closed: Monday except public holidays and 1 Jan

COLLECTION   The Kröller-Müller Museum houses a world-famous collection of fine art, mainly from the 19th and 20th century, incorporating paintings, sculptures, drawings, graphic and applied arts. A focal point of the museum's collection is the wide collection of works by Vincent van Gogh, representing one of the most comprehensive collections of this artist's work to be found anywhere in the world. The museum also boasts important paintings by many other great artists including Georges Seurat, Pablo Picasso, Fernand Léger and Piet Mondrian, to name but a few.

Vincent van Gogh
(1853-1890)
Café terrace at night,
'Place du Forum',
Arles 1888

Kröller-Müller
Museum, Otterlo

Sculpture of the late 19th and 20th century also occupies an important place in the Kröller-Müller Museum. The sculpture garden, covering 21 hectares, is one of the largest in Europe. Accomodating a unique collection of works in the setting of a varied landscape, the sculpture garden offers the visitor a fascinating survey of the manner in which sculptural art has developed from the end of the 19th century up to the present. Among the sculptors represented are August Rodin, Henry Moore, Barbara Hepworth, Richard Serra, Mario Merz, Jean Dubuffet and Claes Oldenburg.

EXHIBITION

Autumn 96

Franz West *Retrospective*

NRC 🛡 HANDELSBLAD

Rotterdam

MUSEUM BOYMANS-VAN BEUNINGEN
Museumpark 18-20 3015 CX Rotterdam Director: Chris Dercon
☎ +31 10 44194700 📠 +31 10 4360500
Open: Tuesday-Saturday 10.00-17.00 Sunday and public holidays 11.00-17.00
Closed: Monday and 1 Jan, 30 Apr, 25 Dec

COLLECTION

The collection of *Old Masters* provides a fine survey of Western European art dating from the 14th to the mid-19th century. Particularly well represented is Northern and Southern Netherlandish art from the 15th and 16th century and Dutch painting from the 17th century. Highlights of the collection include 'The Vagabond' by Hieronymus Bosch, Brueghel's 'Tower of Babel', Rembrandt's 'Portrait of Titus' and works by Van Eyck, Rubens, Titian and Saenredam.

Covering *the period from 1850 to the present,* the collection contains famous works by the Surrealists Magritte and Dali. The Modern Classics Department boasts superb paintings by Monet, Van Gogh, Kandinsky and Van Dongen. There are also important examples of recent German and American art and contemporary sculpture.

The *Department of Applied Art and Design* houses precious objects and everyday utensils dating from the Middle Ages to the present. There are important collections of majolica, pewter, silver, glass, pre-industrial utensils and modern decorative art. In recent years work from the field of industrial design has come to occupy a prominent place in the museum.

As well as having a large number of prints, the *Print Room* has custody of one of the world's biggest and most important collections of drawings. Numerous schools from the Middle Ages to the present are represented, as well as masters such as Dürer, Rembrandt, Goya, Giorgione, Watteau, Manet, Cézanne and Picasso.

Pieter Brueghel the
Elder (1525- 1569)
The Tower of Babel

*Museum Boymans
van Beuningen,
Rotterdam*

EXHIBITIONS

24·01·96–18·08·96 **Bruce Nauman**   A small presentation of 'Rotating Glass Walls',
4 film loops Super 8, 10, 1970.

10·03·96–19·05·96 **Cindy Sherman**   This major retrospective includes approximately
80 photo-works, which are concentrated in four groups: Film Stills
(of a melancholy nature), Disgust Series (abstract), Sex Pictures
(dolls) and Horror Series.

28·04·96–04·08·96 **Mannerist Prints from the Collection of the German Artist Baselitz**
Georg Baselitz owns a superb collection of Mannerist prints, the
majority of which date from the 16th century.

09·06·96–25·08·96 **Manifesta**   For the Manifesta of 1996, five international exhibition-
makers (Katalyn Néray, Rosa Martínez, Victor Misiano, Hans-Ulrich
Obrist and Andrew Renton) will present works by young European
artists.

09·06·96–25·08·96 **The Multiples of Lawrence Weiner**

09·06·96–18·08·96 **Guest Curator, Hans Haacke**   Every two years, the Boymans-van
Beuningen Museum invites a prominent figure in the international
art world to guest-curate an exhibition selected from the museum's
large and varied holdings. Preceded by Harald Szeeman, Peter
Greenaway and Robert Wilson, Hans Haacke, an artist with a strong
political engagement, has consented to stage this exhibition.

08·09·96–01·12·96 **Willem de Kooning**   A retrospective covering the period from 1981
to 1987, supplemented by works from the 70s from the collection of
the Stedelijk Museum.

10·11·96–05·01·97 **Kees van Dongen 1897-1914**   Early drawings and watercolours,
supplemented by 16 major paintings and works by contemporaries,
including Picasso.

22·12·96–16·02·97 **Praise of the High Seas**   *17th-Century Dutch Marine Painting*
Like architectural painting, marine painting addressed a theme that
emerged towards the end of the 16th century. The Haarlem painter
Hendrik Cornelisz. Vroom (c. 1566-1640), regarded as the inventor
of the genre, often received government commissions for
spectacular works recording historic events at sea. The two leading
exponents in the field were Willem van de Velde I and II. Other
important marine painters were Adam Willaerts, Jan Porcellis,
Simon de Vlieger and Jan van de Cappelle. The exhibition consists of
some 110 paintings.

Rotterdam

KUNSTHAL ROTTERDAM
Westzeedijk 341 3015 AA Rotterdam Director: W. van Krimpen
☎ +31 10 4400300 📠 +31 10 4367152
Open: Tuesday-Saturday 10.00-17.00 Sunday and public holidays 11.00-17.00

COLLECTION	No permanent collection.
EXHIBITIONS	
10·02·96-02·06·96	*Han van Meegeren (1889-1947)* *From Artist (manqué) to Master Forger*
23·03·96-12·05·96	*Studio Dumbar* *Behind the Screen*
23·03·96-25·05·96	*Breukel & Kooiker* *Contemporary photography*
23·03·96-27·05·96	*The Reel World* *Film Poster Art 1895-1995*
30·03·96-23·06·96	*Feast for the Eye* *Four Centuries of Erotic art*
18·05·96-01·09·96	*Gerard van den Berg*
08·06·96-18·08·96	*Manifesta I,* *European Art Manifestation*
08·06·96-15·09·96	*Surrealism from Dutch Collections*

24·08·96-27·10·96	*Mary Ellen Mark* Retrospective
24·08·96-10·11·96	*African Sculpture* from the Museum of Ethnography
07·09·96-17·11·96	*The Erasmus Bridge*
02·11·96-05·01·97	*The Motorway* A Photoproject of Theo Baart and Tracy Metz
18·11·96-20·11·96	*The Art of Cooking*
06·12·96-23·02·97	*Sea in Sight* Dutch Marine Painting in the 18th and 19th century

Rotterdam

MARITIEM MUSEUM 'PRINS HENDRIK'
Leuvehaven 1 3011 EA Rotterdam Director: ad interim
☎ **+31 10 4132680 📠 +31 10 4137342**
Open: Tuesday-Saturday 10.00-17.00 Sunday and public holidays 11.00-17.00
Closed: Monday and 1 Jan, 30 Apr, 25 Dec

COLLECTION

Vademecum A shipping manual in the form of an exhibition offers an introduction to shipping.
'Professor Splash' An interactive exhibition is recently completely renewed and bigger now. 'Professor Splash' allows children aged 4-12 to experiment, experience and discover for themselves, making it fun to find out about ships, shipping and basic maritime principles.
Men Aboard, Life at Sea in the 17th-18th Century The collection focuses on the sailors who worked and lived on the Dutch sailing ships during the time of the Republic. It includes handwritten ship's logs, rare nautical charts and atlases, engravings of disasters at sea, pictures of sea battles and navigational instruments.
Open Storeroom A look behind the scenes: showcases, shelves and cupboards containing clothing, coins, crockery and various other items.
Museumship 'Buffel' Built in 1868 and largely restored to its original state, this former armourclad turret-ram of the Royal Dutch Navy features a fully-equipped upper deck and furnished officers' quarters. Within the ship are a number of displays on such subjects as life on board, navigation, and artillery.

EXHIBITIONS
05·10·96-09·03·97

The Dockworker in Rotterdam 1890-1960 A Go-Getter This exhibition gives an impression of the housing conditions, working environment and living conditions of dock labourers in Rotterdam. The diary of Hein Mol, an important dock labourer at the beginning of this century, forms the thread connecting the various themes of this display.

28·03·97-14·09·97

Ships for the Environment As the title suggests, this exhibition focusses on various activities within the field of shipping which are directed towards maintaining and improving the quality of the environment. The ships themselves play an important role. Research vessels, ships equipped with special incinerators and salvage vessels are just a few of the ships presented in this display.

Rotterdam

NATUURMUSEUM ROTTERDAM
Westzeedijk 345 3015 AA Rotterdam Director: J.W.F. Reumer
☎ **+31 10 4364222 📠 +31 10 4364399**
Open: Tuesday-Saturday 10.00-17.00 Sunday and public holidays 11.00-17.00
Closed: Monday and 30 Apr, 25 Dec, 1 Jan

COLLECTION	The Natuurmuseum Rotterdam was established in 1927. It is the only museum in the region with exhibitions, activities, information and collections concerning natural history and environmental issues.
	The museum possesses an important collection of stuffed birds, fossilised remains of mammals, skulls and skeletons, insects, shells, minerals, and a collection of preserved organisms. The Natuurmuseum, along with the four other museums which surround it, is an antique mansion flanked by a modern pavilion and is situated in the new cultural heart of Rotterdam called the Museumpark.

EXHIBITIONS		
until 09·06·96	*Precious Possession*	20 curators, 20 selections from the collection.
09·06·96–19·08·96	*Manifesta I*	A unique contemporary European Art Event.
09·06·96–until further notice	*Biological Diversity*	The multiformity of life in water, on land and in the air.
09·06·96–until further notice	*Dr. A.B. Van Deinse's Collection*	Whales and zoological curiosities.

Rotterdam

NAI NEDERLANDS ARCHITECTUURINSTITUUT
NETHERLANDS ARCHITECTURE INSTITUTE
Museumpark 25 3015 CB Rotterdam Director: H. van Haaren
☎ **+31 10 4401200 📠 +31 10 4366975**
Open: Tuesday-Saturday 10.00-17.00 Sunday and public holidays 11.00-17.00
Closed: Monday (except Easter Monday and Whit Monday)
and 25 Dec, 1 Jan and 30 Apr

COLLECTION	The Institute's Collection Department manages some 300 archives, 100 collections of the most prominent Dutch architects and urbanists of the 19th and 20th century, and various partial collections containing models, furniture, posters and a large number of glass negatives and slides.

Nederlands Architectuur Instituut (NAI) Rotterdam

EXHIBITIONS	
09·03·96-16·06·96	*The Architect's Discipline* [Balcony Room] This exhibition offers a behind-the-scenes look into the architect's career as it recounts the history of architecture education and provides the public with an understanding of the specific know-how and skills which the architect requires.
04·04·96-07·07·96	*The Modern Years The 50s and 60s - The Spreading of Contemporary Architecture* [Main Room] The far-reaching

modernisation of Dutch society and, with it, of architecture and urban development, is the theme of this exhibition. The 50s and 60s were a period of large-scale changes: buildings were built against the background of reconstruction, housing shortage, theoretical debates between functionalism and traditionalism and the transformation of an agricultural society into an industrial one.

29·06·96-20·10·96   *Dutch Interior* [Balcony Room]   This exhibition, which also features material from the NIA collection, coincides with the publication of the book 'Dutch Interiors from the Neo-Renaissance to Post-Modernism'. Both reveal how interior architecture has been subject to constant change in the past century: the emphasis moving from entire interiors to a focus on furniture and household appliances. Today, the boundaries between architecture, interior architecture and design are becoming increasingly blurred.

10·08·96-17·11·96   *Real Space in Quick Times, Triennale of Milan* [Main Room] Revolutionary developments in communication, a leap to unprecedented production processes and virtual reality will have a profound impact on society. The influence of advanced computer applications on the design of cities and buildings is already manifesting itself. This is the theme of the NIA-organised entry for the 19th Milan Triennale. Content and composition by Ole Bouman, design by architect Ben van Berkel.

10·11·96-1997   *The Collection Gispen* [Gallery]   W.H. Gispen is known for his designs of steel tube furniture and Giso lamps. The NIA is curator of a major collection of furniture, lamps and product catalogues from the Gispen firm, a selection of which is presented here. Gispen often collaborated with other artists, including photographers Paul Schuitema and Jan Kamman.

07·12·96-Feb 97   *The Netherlands goes to School* [Main Room]   In 1996, the Ministry of Education, Culture and Science will transfer its financial responsibility for school construction to lower authorities and school boards. The history of school construction is associated with the names of virtually all leading architects: Berlage, Dudok and Duiker to Van den Broek & Bakema, Hertzberger, Mecanoo and Koolhaas, as well as a number of less famous designers. The exhibition covers the history of architectural and educational ideas as a source of inspiration for the construction of future school buildings.

Spring 97   *Michel de Klerk* [Main Room]   This large-scale exhibition not only presents the work of Michel de Klerk as a master of the Amsterdam school, but also focusses on his position and that of his contemporaries in the international field. The rational aspects of De Klerk's oeuvre, which has always been categorised as expressionistic, are paid special attention.

Rotterdam

WITTE DE WITH CENTER FOR CONTEMPORARY ART
Witte de Withstraat 50 3012 BR Rotterdam Director: Bartomeu Marí
☎ +31 10 4110144 📠 +31 10 4117924
Open: Tuesday-Sunday 11.00-18.00
Closed: Monday

COLLECTION   No permanent collection.

EXHIBITIONS

23·03·96-19·05·96   *Voorwerk 5*   Bartomeu Marí's first exhibition as director of Witte de With contains works by Yvonne Dröge-Wendell, Christoph Fink,

Sigalit Landau and Ana Prada. The contrasting individual approaches of these four young artists reflect the lack of connection among contemporary art movements. During the exhibition, the Dutch artist Zeger Reyers will present a project involving living organisms in the stairwell of Witte de With.

08·06·96–18·08·96　　*Manifesta 1*　In the context of the European Manifesta project, five young international curators have organised exhibitions for Witte de With and other museums and institutes in Rotterdam.

07·09·96–27·10·96　　*Tony Brown*　*Kinetic Sculptures/Installations*　The Canadian artist Tony Brown employs light, movement and sound, exploring new technologies and bringing several disciplines together in a 'Gesamt-kunstwerk'.

09·11·96–15·01·97　　*Frederick Kiesler*　The Austrian architect and philosopher Frederick Kiesler (1890-1965), builder of the shrine that houses the Dead Sea Scrolls, was involved in the European avant-garde of the 20s. He has influenced American artists such as Jasper Johns, Willem de Kooning and others. The exhibition presents a collection of Kiesler's drawings for several utopian architectural projects.

Jan 97–Mar 97　　*Tacita Dean and Gerco de Ruyter*　This exhibition is in connection with the 26th Rotterdam Film Festival. The British artist Tacita Dean combines fact and fiction in the film 'Girl Stowaway' and the video 'How to Put a Boat in a Bottle'.
The highly experimental photographs and films of Gerco de Ruyter include shots made with a camera mounted on a kite.

Schiedam

STEDELIJK MUSEUM SCHIEDAM
Hoogstraat 112 3111 HL Schiedam Director: P.Th. Tjabbes
☎ **+31 10 4269066 ▥ +31 10 4732780**
Open: Tuesday-Saturday 11.00-17.00 Sunday 12.30-17.00
Closed: Monday

COLLECTION　　The collection consists of works from modern Dutch artists, mainly from the post-war period: Cobra collection, Abstract-Geometric art, Pop-Art, New Figurative art, Elementarism and art of the past years in which figuration once again plays a role. The collection is not on permanent display, but a selection can be seen at the so-called Open Depot on request.

EXHIBITIONS
18·05·96–30·06·96　　*Célia Cymbalista, Ester Grinspum, Carmela Gross and Geórgia Kyriakakis*　*Ceramic Statues and Installations*　The exhibition presents ceramic works by six young Brazilian female artists who attended the European Ceramic Work Centre in 's-Hertogenbosch. Their work is experimental rather than traditional, ranging from fragile installations to massive sculptures.

11·05·96–30·06·96　　*From the Museum's Collection*　In conjunction with the above exhibition, the museum will present several sculptors whose work is in some way similar to that of the Brazilian artists.

07·07·96–15·09·96　　*Summer Exhibition from the Museum's Collection*　A large number of works of art and historical objects will be displayed, including 'Portrait of the Artist as a Young Man' (1966-1991), an installation by Marinus Boezem.

Sep 96　　*Art Relay*　The theme of the annual provincial Art Relay is 'connection'. Schiedam may choose the theme 'marriage', portrayed in multimedia art forms.

15·09·96–24·11·96	*Autumn Exhibition of Contemporary Art*
29·11·96–01·12·96	*Kunstwerkt Foundation Art Fair* The annual art fair of the Kunstwerkt Foundation will be organised as in previous years.
Dec 96–Jan 97	*Historical Christmas Exhibition* *The Station and its Surroundings and/or Municipal Archives 100 Years Old*
Dec 96 onwards	*Historical Exhibition from the Museum's Collection* The museum plans to hold long-term exhibitions relating to the history of Schiedam and based on the museum's collection of historical objects.

Utrecht

MUSEUM CATHARIJNECONVENT
Nieuwegracht 63 3512 LG Utrecht Director: H.L.M. Defoer
☎ +31 30 2313835 🖷 +31 30 2317896
Open: Tuesday-Friday 10.00-17.00 Saturday, Sunday and public holidays 11.00-17.00
Closed: Monday and 1 Jan

COLLECTION

Museum Catherijneconvent, the cloisters of Utrecht, is housed in a 15th-century convent in the centre of Utrecht. It contains a collection of paintings, sculpture, textiles, manuscripts and gold and silver illustrating the evolution of Christianity in the Netherlands from its beginnings to the present. The medieval art section is the most important in the Netherlands.
The evolution of Catholic and Protestant churches is shown in its historical context. Various themes are addressed: construction, style and decorative elements of churches, the religious world and the works of art it inspired, the different ceremonies, the role of faith in daily life and the relationship between Church and State.
The museum also contains works by 17th-century Dutch masters such as Rembrandt, Frans Hals and Pieter Saenredam.

EXHIBITIONS

31·08·96–17·11·96	*The Utrecht Psalter* The Utrecht Psalter (c. 820-840) is one of the most fascinating manuscripts to emerge from the early Middle Ages and one of the most important surviving manuscripts from France. The Psalter is named after Utrecht, the town where the book has been preserved in the University Library since 1716 and where a major exhibition is devoted to the manuscript and the art objects it inspired.
Dec 96 onwards	*Russian Popular Prints and Drawings from the State Historical Museum, Moscow* The exhibition comprises approximately 100 to 120 popular prints from the State Historical Museum in Moscow. These biblical, religious and historical representations, many of them vividly coloured, date from the 18th and 19th centuries.
22·03·97–01·06·97	*Preachers* A survey of the preacher's vocation from the 16th century to the present, from the simple, uneducated minister to the dignified 19th-century parson, ending with the modern 'pastor'. The aspects treated in this presentation include education, the performance of duties, the politically and socially active parson, the preacher-poet and pastoral work.

Utrecht

CENTRAAL MUSEUM UTRECHT
Agnietenstraat 1 3512 XA Utrecht Director: Sjarel Ex
Rietveld Schröderhuis
Prins Hendriklaan 50a 3583 EP Utrecht
☎ +31 30 2362362 🖷 +31 30 2332006
Open: Tuesday-Saturday 10.00-17.00 Sunday and public holidays 12.00-17.00
Closed: Monday

COLLECTION

The **Centraal Museum,** the oldest municipal museum in the
Netherlands, has developed from modest beginnings to become
one of the most important museums in the Netherlands. The large
and varied collection of works of art is spread over a complex of
buildings around a beautiful enclosed garden.

The main building houses the collection of art from before 1900,
including fashion and dress, period rooms, arts and crafts, and
paintings by Utrecht masters. The entire top floor is devoted to the
history of the city of Utrecht. The building also houses a coin and
medal collection, a print collection, and in the basement, an
extremely rare Utrecht ship dating from the 12th century. Other
highlights of the museum include a 17th-century doll's house, the
paintings of Jan van Scorel and the so-called Utrecht Caravaggists
(Bloemaert, Ter Brugghen, Van Honthorst, etc.) and the silver
produced by the Van Vianen family of silversmiths. A very unusual
double chapel, built around 1514 as part of the former Agnieten-
klooster (Convent of St. Agnes) is also located in this section of the
museum.

The former artillery stables, converted into an exhibition room in
1986, now generally house a collection of modern art providing a
comprehensive survey of 20th century Dutch art. The stables are
sometimes used for temporary exhibitions. The Nicolaikerk (Nicholas
Church), a Gothic church dating from the middle of the 15th
century, serves as an unusual exhibition room, and is accessible via
the museum during the summer months.

The Rietveld Schröder House The Rietveld Schröder house, an
outstanding example of the 'De Stijl' architectural style, is an
integral and important part of the Centraal Museum. The house
was designed in 1924 by architect Gerrit Rietveld in close
cooperation with Truus Schröder-Schräder, and was restored in
1987. The primary colours, the styling and use of space make the
house entirely unique. It also possesses some of the functionalist
characteristics which Rietveld was to elaborate on further during
the 1930s. It is a 15-minute walk from the Centraal Museum.

EXHIBITIONS

16·05·96–11·08·96

Touche's Nine   Each year, the Touche Art Foundation of the
Netherlands presents awards to young sculptors. There are nine
artists who were awarded a prize in the past three years:
Frederico D'Orazio, Mark Manders, Karin Arink, Krijn de Koning,
Fransje Killaars, Marijke van Warmerdam, Marieke van Diemen,
Moritz Ebinger and Sylvie Zijlmans. Their work will be displayed in
this special exhibition.

31·08·96–27·10·96

Collection of Contemporary Drawings, Province of Utrecht This
exhibition presents contemporary drawings collected by the
Province of Utrecht.

31·08·96–27·10·96

Take 2 *Contemporary Art*

Zwolle

STEDELIJK MUSEUM ZWOLLE
Melkmarkt 41 8011 ML Zwolle Director: H.J. Aarts
☎ +31 38 4214650 📠 +31 38 4219248
Open: Tuesday-Saturday 10.00-17.00 Sunday and public holidays 13.00-17.00
Closed: Monday, 1 Jan, 7 Apr, 26 May, 9-18 Aug and 25 Dec

COLLECTION | The collection contains paintings, prints and drawings, silver, furniture and textiles concerning the province of Overijssel and in particular the city of Zwolle. Several of these objects are presented in a historical context. Highlights of the collection are the paintings by Gerard Ter Borch and the Zwolle city council's silver.

EXHIBITIONS

04·05·96-16·06·96 | *The Baptists*

29·06·96-25·08·96 | *Cats in the Visual Arts*

16·11·96-05·01·97 | *Late Medieval Manuscripts from Salland*

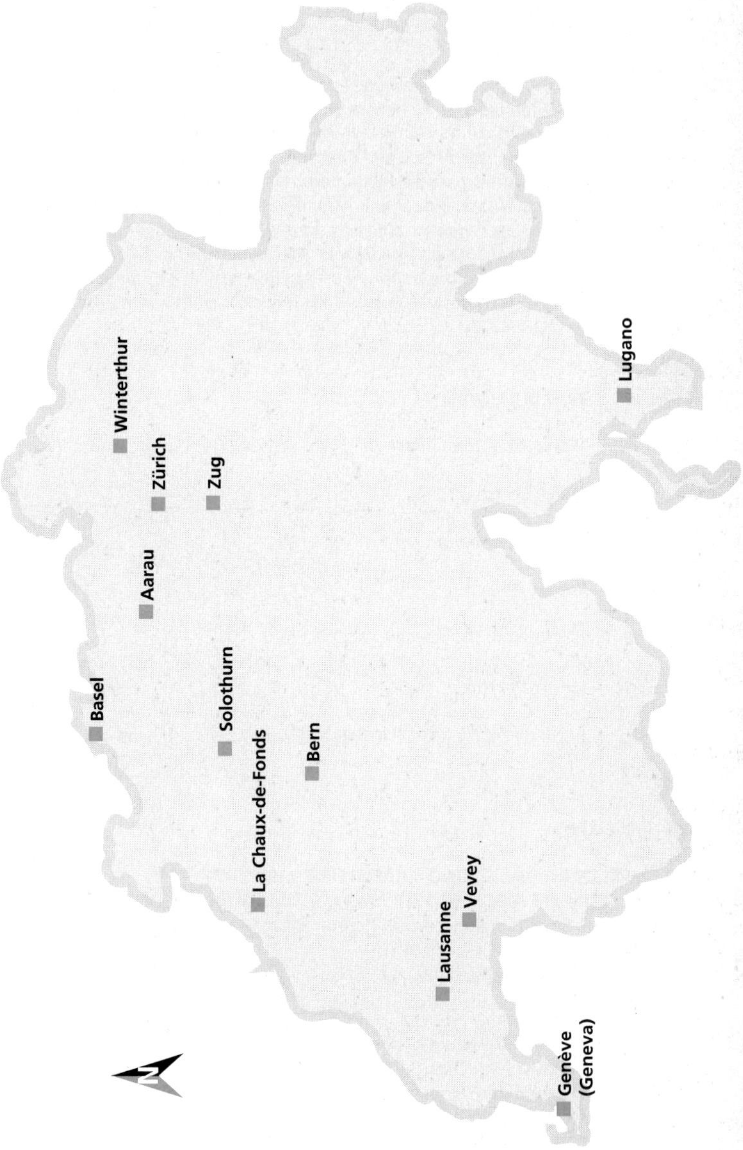

Winterthur

Zürich

Zug

Aarau

Lugano

Basel

Solothurn

La Chaux-de-Fonds

Bern

Vevey

Lausanne

Genève
(Geneva)

Aarau

AARGAUER KUNSTHAUS AARAU
Aargauerplatz 5001 Aarau Director: Beat Wismer
☎ +41 62 8352330 📠 +41 62 8352329
Open: Tuesday-Sunday 10.00-17.00 Thursday 10.00-20.00
Closed: Monday

COLLECTION

The museum's collection gives a picture of the development of art in Switzerland from the late 18th century until the present day. Some 18th-century artists whose works are displayed here include Johann Heinrich Füssli and Caspar Wolf. Swiss art in the 19th century is represented by numerous landscape paintings, as well as works by Albert Anker and Arnold Böcklin. Finally, the Modern age of Swiss art is illustrated by works of such artists as Ferdinand Hodler, Cuno Amiet and Giovanni Giacometti. The collection also includes Swiss contemporary artists. Due to a lack of adequate space, it is often only possible to view parts of the permanent collection.

EXHIBITIONS

30·03·96-19·05·96	*Ingeborg Lüscher*
30·03·96-09·06·96	*Works from the Collection* *Sculptures and Works on Paper*
14·04·96-09·06·96	*Jan Hubertus*
02·06·96-11·08·96	*Jan Schoonhoven*
23·06·96-08·09·96	*Robert Müller*
24·08·96-17·11·96	*Works from the Aargau Art Collection*
28·09·96-17·11·96	*Carmen Perrin*
07·12·96-12·01·97	*Annual Exhibition of Aargau Artists*

Basel - Basle

ANTIKENMUSEUM BASEL UND SAMMLUNG LUDWIG
BASLE MUSEUM OF ANCIENT ART AND LUDWIG COLLECTION
St. Albangraben 5 4010 Basel Director: Peter Blome
☎ +41 61 2712202 📠 +41 61 2711861
Open: Tuesday-Friday 10.00-17.00
Closed: Monday

COLLECTION

The Basle Museum of Ancient Art is the only Swiss museum devoted exclusively to Classical Antiquity. The exhibits housed by the museum date from the 3rd millennium B.C. to 300 A.D. and are mostly Greek, but there are also objects of Ancient Italian, Etruscan and Roman origin. Sculptures and ceramics form the core of the permanent exhibition, but bronze statuettes, clay figurines, gold jewellery and coins are represented as well. The majority of the pieces are gifts from private collectors of our time, such as Robert Käppeli and Giovanni Züst. In 1980 Peter and Irene Ludwig donated their collection to the museum, an event that led to the enlargement of the premises.

An interesting feature of the museum is the diversity of its architecture. Two connected classical townhouses contain the vases and smaller objects, while the sculptures can be found in the skylight gallery of the modern annex and in the vaulted cellar

(Roman sarcophagi and portraits). A courtyard with trees and flowers forms the heart of this block of buildings.

The Educational department of the museum runs instructive exhibitions and workshops in an adjacent building (Luftgässlein 5). The collection of plaster casts is located on the Mittlere Strasse 17 and provides the first comprehensive survey of the Parthenon.

Head of Athena. Roman copy after a bronze statue c. 430 B.C. from the circle of Phidias.

The Basle museum of Ancien Art and Ludwig Collection, Basle

EXHIBITIONS

28·04·96-23·06·96   *Pandora*   Women in Classical Greece.

20·03·97-13·07·97   *Egypt - Moments of Eternity*   Hidden treasures in Swiss private collections.

Basel · Basle

MUSEUM FÜR GEGENWARTSKUNST
St. Alban-Rheinweg 60   4010 Basel   Curator: Theodora Vischer
☎ +41 61 2728183   📠 +41 61 2710536
Open: Tuesday-Sunday 10.00-17.00 and Easter Monday, Whit Monday
Closed: Monday and 26, 28 Feb, Good Friday, 1 May, 1 Aug,
24, 25, 31 Dec

COLLECTION   The Museum of Contemporary Art is a joint project of the Emanuel Hoffmann Foundation, the Christoph Merian Foundation and the canton of Basle-Stadt. The architects Wilfried and Katharina Steib linked a 19th-century factory to a new structure to create an appealing complex that blends harmoniously into the surrounding old part of the city. The works on display date from the 1960s to the present, starting with Minimal Art, Conceptual Art and 'Wild Painting' and continuing up to the latest in installation art. Focal points are works by Frank Stella, Bruce Nauman, A.R. Penck. Joseph Beuys and Rosemarie Trockel.

EXHIBITIONS

01·06·96–29·09·96   *FremdKörper - Corps Etrangers - Foreign Bodies*   The focal point of this exhibition is a concept of the human being in which the borders between strange and familiar, real and unreal, inner perspective and external view have become open and transparent and are up for discussion. The confrontation of artists with their own bodies as foreign bodies has never had such great importance as it now does. This exhibition will testify to that fact with selected video installations.

Jonathan Borofsky
(1942-)
Flying man, 1983

Museum
für Gegenwartskunst,
Basel

26·10·96–Mar 97

Dan Graham/Andrea Zittel   Dan Graham (born 1942 in Urbana, Illinois) has been documenting mass-produced suburban developments in the United States with photographs and commentaries since the mid-60s. The 'living spaces' of Andrea Zittel (born 1965 in Escondido, California) are living units satisfying a number of needs in very small spaces, attempting to offer a simple and liberating alternative to the complexity of modern life. The point of departure in both artists' work is the actual living space of individual man in post-modernist mass society.

Basel · Basle

KUNSTHALLE BASEL
Steinenberg 7 4051 Basel Director: Thomas Kellein
☎ +41 61 2724833 📠 +41 61 2724826
Open: Tuesday-Sunday 11.00-17.00 Wednesday 11.00-20.30
Guided tours on Sunday 11.00
Closed: Monday

COLLECTION

No permanent collection.

EXHIBITIONS
10·03·96–12·05·96

Beat Klein   The artist Beat Klein studies objects and their history, as well as the way we deal with them. Size, proportions and materials all play a role.

10·03·96–12·05·96

Nobuyoshi Araki, Larry Clark, Thomas Struth, Christopher Williams
Four contrasting but complementary photographers. The viewer is confronted with a polyvalent system composed of constructions and images, the public and the private, obsessions and order.

10·03·96–12·05·96

Michel Majerus   The young Berlin painter Majerus creates startling work in a specific German tradition between conceptual art and painterly technique. He makes room-size installations which transform every surface into painting.

09·06·96–25·08·96

Franz West, Edward Krasinski, Jason Rhoades

15·09·96–03·11·96

Liz Larner, Zoe Leonard

24·11·96–11·01·97

Annual Exhibition of Basle Artists

Basel - Basle

KUNSTMUSEUM
St. Alban-Graben 16 4010 Basel Director: Katharina Schmidt
☎ +41 61 2710828 ▥ +41 61 2710845
Open: Tuesday-Sunday 10.00-17.00 and Easter Monday, Whit Monday During
the exhibition Canto d'amore 27 Apr-11 Aug also Wednesday 10.00-21.00
Closed: Monday and 26-28 Feb, Good Friday, 24, 25 Dec, 31 Dec

COLLECTION

The Museum of Fine Arts houses the collections of the Departments
of Painting and of Prints and Drawings. The emphasis is on Upper
Rhenish paintings and drawings from 1400 to 1600 and on 19th and
20th-century art. The Öffentliche Kunstsammlung Basle has the
world's largest collection of works by the Holbein family. The
Renaissance is also represented by numerous major works. These old
masterpieces largely originate from the collection, purchased in
1661, of Basilius Amerbach. Paintings by the Basle artist Arnold
Böcklin form one highlight of the 19th-century exhibits.
20th-century art focuses on Cubism, German Expressionism, Abstract
Expressionism and Pop Art.

Picasso, Pablo
Seated harlequin,
1923

Kunstmuseum, Basel

EXHIBITIONS

27·04·96–11·08·96

Canto d'Amore Classicist Modernism in Music and the Visual Arts
1914-1935   The emergence of modernism at the beginning of the
20th century revolutionised the arts. In music and painting, an
avant-garde developed, while connections with the classicist
traditions also remained. Many artists and musicians knew each
other, and sometimes collaborated. This selection of masterworks
discloses one of the most intense artistic epochs of the 20th century
in terms of European music and painting, and includes paintings,
sculptures and drawings by Picasso such as 'Three Women at the
Spring' and 'Harlequin Holding a Half Mask', autographs of
Stravinsky's major works, music by Milhaud, Satie and Casella to
accompany artworks by Matisse, De Chirico, and other works by
Bonnard, Maillol, Arthur Honegger and Manuel de Falla.

18·05·96–25·08·96

Engraving - Etching - Aquatint Works from Schongauer to Baselitz
from the Kupferstichkabinett Basel   This exhibition deals with the
techniques of intaglio from its beginning to the present time.

07·09·96–10·11·96

Watercolours Works from the 15th to the 20th Century from the
Kupferstichkabinett Basel   This exhibition grasps the particular
nature of watercolours, in which the paper itself shines through the
transluscent layers of colour, with the ground lending them a
brilliance which is not manifest in the reflecting pigment alone.

28·09·96–19·01·97   ***Put into Light II*** *Paintings from the 15th-18th Century Collection seen from a different angle*   The first exhibition in a series, entitled 'With Turban and Flag – Aelbert Cuyp's Basel Family Portrait Rediscovered', which brings together information on a specific work of art.

23·11·96–26·01·97   ***Russian Avant-Garde 1910-1924*** *Prints by Malevich, El Lissitzky, Rodchenko, Ljubov'Popova, Rozanova et al., from the Cabinet des Estampes, Geneva*   This exhibition focuses on the development of an avant-garde in Russia with connections to modern art in France, Italy, the Netherlands, Italy and Germany. This Russian avant-garde was in turn significant for the development of Constructivism.

14·12·96–09·03·97   ***The Collection Anne-Marie and Ernst Vischer-Wadler*** *A Legacy* This exhibition features 116 items by 40 artists out of bequest to the Öffentliche Kunstsammlung Basel and the Ethnological Museum. The selection includes works by Picasso, Léger, Arp, Tanguy, Meret Oppenheim, Wols, Tobey, Giacometti, Chillida, Al Held, Robert Mangold, Donald Judd, Richard Tuttle and Jackson Pollock.

Bern

BERNISCHES HISTORISCHES MUSEUM
Helvetiaplatz 5   3000 Bern 6   Director: Georg Germann
☎ +41 31 3511811 ▥ +41 31 3510663
Open: Tuesday-Sunday 10.00-17.00
Closed: Monday

COLLECTION   ***History***   A wide variety of exhibits focus on different aspects of Berne's history from the Middle Ages to the present.
Large Flemish tapestries once belonging to the dukes of Burgundy and the bishops of Lausanne exemplify the sumptuous courtly style of the Late Middle Ages in Burgundy and the Republic of Berne.

Traian and Herkinbald carpet, Tournai c. 1450 Detail with the entourage of Emperor Traian

Bernisches Historisches Museum, Bern

The 'Pourtalès Salon' offers a faithful representation of upper class life during the 18th century, 'the Golden Age of Berne'. A portrait gallery, together with displays of luxurious silver, glass and porcelain objects, and furniture pieces help to illustrate the way of life during this period. Additional exhibits, including a scale-model of Berne constructed in the 1850s, document the town's subsequent development.
Guild silver pieces, a portrait gallery of various Lord Mayors of the City of Berne, and their chairs of state illustrate the life of the ranking classes of old Berne. Other contrasting exhibits depict the new political order that began with the French invasion in 1798. A cycle of portraits by the painter Josef Reinhart provides a realistic and undistorted picture of 18th-century Swiss peasantry.
Prehistory and early history   A wealth of artefacts document several thousand years of human occupation, beginning with life among Stone Age hunter groups, and extending through early

agrarian life, metal crafting, the development of Celtic culture, the
subsequent Roman conquest, and the arrival of the Alemanni.
Ethnography The department consists of the Oriental-Islamic
Henry Moser Charlottenfels collection and a collection which was
built up by the Bernese painter Johan Wäber, who accompanied
Captain Cook to the South Seas, Alaska and Siberia.
Numismatics The core of the museum's coin collection includes
coins from the Roman Empire, Bernese and Swiss coins and medals,
and an assortment of coins from Central Asia.

EXHIBITIONS
Jun 96–Sep 96 　　　***Pharaonic and Coptic Burial Treasures***

Dec 96–Mar 97 　　　***Stained Glass Designs and Armorial Glass of 16th and 17th Century
Switzerland***

Bern

KUNSTMUSEUM BERN
Hodlerstrasse 8-12　3000 Bern 7　Director: Toni Stooss
☎ +41 31 3110944　📠 +41 31 3117263
Open: Wednesday-Sunday 10.00-17.00　Tuesday 10.00-21.00
Closed: Monday

COLLECTION

The Museum of Fine Arts Bern has an outstanding collection of
national and international art ranging from the 14th to 20th
centuries.
In the lower rooms of the Old Building, the visitor is presented with
Italian paintings from the 14th to 16th centuries as well as works by
Swiss artists from Niklaus Manuel Deutsch to Albert Anker. On the
upper stories, works by later Swiss artists are presented, from
Arnold Böcklin and Ferdinand Hodler and continuing up to the 20th
century.
Important collections of works by Paul Klee are shown on the
ground floor in the New Building.
Artists represented on the top floor include Pierre Bonnard,
Georges Braque, Paul Cézanne, Gustave Courbet, Salvador Dali,
Edgar Degas, Robert Delaunay, Vincent van Gogh, Juan Gris, Vassily
Kandinsky, Ludwig Kirchner, Eduard Manet, Franz Marc, Henri
Matisse, Joan Miró, Amedeo Modigliani, Pablo Picasso, Camille
Pissarro, Auguste Renoir, Chaim Soutine and many more.

EXHIBITIONS
27·03·96–02·06·96

John Webber (1751-1793) *South Sea Voyager and Landscape
Painter* John Webber, who was born in Bern, originally came to
the public's attention for the magnificent illustrations he created
during Captain Cook's third and last voyage around the world
(1776-1780) on behalf of the British Admiralty. In Bern, however,
the focus will be mainly on his gouaches and drawings which he
completed during his extensive tours throughout Europe and
England between 1787 and 1793.

29·03·96–02·06·96

Drawing Is Seeing *Masterpieces from Ingres to Bonnard taken
from the Budapest Museum of Fine Arts and from Swiss Collections*
Approximately 75 works from the splendid collection kept at the
Budapest Museum of Fine Arts - famous drawings by Delacroix,
Daumier, Courbet, Victor Hugo, Manet, Millet, Cézanne and Rodin -
will be complemented by outstanding works from various Swiss
collections. This major exhibition will present a total of 150 works
by leading French artists of the 19th century.

19·06·96–18·08·96

Life, a Dream *Ernst Kreidolf (1863-1956)* This exhibition has been
staged with the twin aims of confirming Ernst Kreidolf's reputation

as a superb illustrator of picture books, and of showing work by him rarely seen in public before. The exhibition will include pencil drawings and sketch books, landscape drawings and watercolours completed in Partenkirchen and on the island of Sylt, oil paintings, and highly original greeting cards and costumes.

La Chaux-de-Fonds

MUSÉE DES BEAUX-ARTS
33, Rue des Musées 2300 La Chaux-de-Fonds Director: Edmond Charrière
☎ +41 39 230444 🖷 +41 39 236193
Open: Tuesday-Sunday 10.00-12.00 / 14.00-17.00 Wednesday 10.00-12.00 / 14.00-20.00
Closed: Monday

COLLECTION

The museum houses a permanent collection of paintings, sculptures, engravings, drawings, photographs and tapestries from the 19th and 20th century.
Art from La Chaux-de-Fonds, Neuchâtel and other parts of Switzerland is represented with works by Kaiser, L'Eplattenier, Le Corbusier, Anker, Vallotton and Baily.
A special exhibition is devoted to the Romantic painter and native of La Chaux-de-Fonds, Leopold Robert (1794-1835), celebrated for his portrayals of Italian brigands.
Works by Lieland, Constable, Delacroix, Van Gogh, Matisse, Deran, Rouault and Soutine form part of a prestigious legacy, the René and Madeleine Junod Collection.
The contemporary abstract tradition is represented with works by Buchet, Bissière, Manessier, Winter, Jacobsen, Poraodoro, Morellet and others.

Le Corbusier
(1887-1965)
Seated woman, 1933

Musée des Beaux-Arts, La Chaux-de-Fonds

EXHIBITIONS

30·03·96–19·05·96   **Christian Lindow** *1945-1990*   Paintings, drawings and prints.

22·06·96–25·08·96   **Three Painters' Collections** *Collections of Martin Disler, Günther Foerg, Olivier Mosset*

28·09·96–10·11·96   **François Morellet**   Grids.

30·11·96–05·01·97   **Young Painters from Madrid and La Chaux-de-Fonds**
A confrontation.

Genève - Geneva

MUSÉE ARIANA
10, Avenue de la Paix 1202 Genève Director: Cäsar Menz
☎ +41 22 4185450 📠 +41 22 4185451
Open: Wednesday-Monday 10.00-17.00
Closed: Tuesday

COLLECTION

The Musée Ariana is the Swiss glass and ceramics museum. Built by Gustave Revilliod (1817-1890) for his private collections of glass and ceramics and completed in 1884, this Italianate palace is situated in the quarter of the international organisations. At his death Revilliod left his museum, its collections and the surrounding park to the city of Geneva. In 1934 it became part of the Musée d'art et d'histoire. The collections reflect seven centuries of creation - from the Middle Ages to the present - in Europe, the Middle East and Asia. All the main techniques of glass and ceramic-making are represented, and the contemporary scene is given special attention.
In addition to the permanent collection and research/teaching facilities, space has been allotted for temporary exhibitions.

Façade Musée
Ariana,
Genève

EXHIBITIONS

31·05·96-31·08·96

Dutch Majolica   The exhibition, from a private collection, will present the first Dutch majolica pieces (1550-1650), conceived in the style of Italian Renaissance majolica.

21·11·96-26·01·97

Setsuko Nagasawa   Setsuko Nagasawa (born Kyoto 1941), a contemporary ceramicist, whose approach is specifically contemporary in its constant investigation of technique and material. Formed in the Japanese tradition where ancient philosophical and religious ideals provide the foundation for artistic production, her work explores the creative potential in the everyday object.

Genève - Geneva

MUSÉE D'ART ET D'HISTOIRE
2, Rue Charles-Galland 1206 Genève 3 Director: Cäsar Menz
☎ +41 22 4182600 📠 +41 22 4182601
Open: Tuesday-Sunday 10.00-17.00
Closed: Monday

COLLECTION

The Musée d'art et d'histoire is one of the largest museums in Switzerland. It brings together archaeological, applied art and fine art collections.
Ancient Egyptian and Greco-Roman art is represented by an important group of sculptures, decorated vases, coins, engraved

stones and metalwork (the Missorium, a Roman silver plate). The Orient has long fascinated Geneva, and is present in both the archaeological and applied art collections (Byzantine metalwork, Coptic textiles, Ottoman embroidery) and a fine collection of icons.

Façade Musée d'art et d'histoire, Genève

Medieval sculpture and stained glass are exhibited in the Historic Rooms, as well as Geneva interiors of the 16th to the 18th centuries. The altarpiece of Konrad Witz (1444), a precursor of realistic landscape painting in the Western world, portrays a biblical scene against the backdrop of Lake Geneva and its mountains. French and Italian painting from the 16th to the 18th centuries and a charming Avercamp attest to the high quality of Geneva collections of this period. The Genevese artist Jean-Etienne Liotard is represented by one of the largest collections of his pastels and oils, featuring scenes from oriental life.

Geneva Romantic and Impressionist landscape painting (Töpffer, Agasse, Calame) is displayed alongside oils by Corot, Renoir, Monet and Cézanne. Works by the prominent artists Vallotton and Hodier mark the beginnings of modern art. The 20th-century collection, which includes works by Giacometti and Bram van Velde among other contemporary artists, is constantly growing, and is the source of frequent exhibitions.

EXHIBITIONS

18·04·96–06·10·96

The Alps as Seen by Geneva Romantics Through his writings, Rodolphe Töpffer inspired Geneva artists to conquer the heights of Swiss mountains, to capture the poetry of their peaks and the wild grandeur of the Alps. Under his influence François Diday (1802–1877), Alexandre Calame (1810-1864) and their followers produced original graphic works and powerful oils which were enthusiastically received by the public of their time.

19·04·96–14·07·96

Bronze and Gold *Two Faces of Marcus Aurelius, Emperor, Soldier, Moralist* This exhibition constitutes the first exhibition outside of Hungary of an oversized head in bronze found in Pécs at the site of a Roman military camp. It is a realistic portrait of the Emperor Marcus Aurelius (120-180 A.D,) who fought in Pannonia on the Danube. The work will be shown in tandem with the famous gold bust of Avenches, which has rarely been exhibited. The history and personality of Marcus Aurelius - emperor, soldier and moralist - will be illustrated through iconographic and scientific material.

20·09·96–early 1997

The Episcopate of Geneva: The First Financial Centre? Certain facets of the rich coin collection acquired in 1995 by the Musée d'art et d'histoire shed new light on the history of the Episcopate of Geneva in the period between the Kingdom of Burgundy and the Empire (1019-1032).

12·12·96–28·04·97	***Greek, Melchite and Russian Icons*** This exhibition will contain over 100 Greek, Melchite and Russian pieces, belonging to a Lebanese collector, owner of one of the most important private collections of icons in existence today. The works date from the 14th to the 18th century, and come from Greece (principally Crete and the North), from the Arabian East (Aleppo, Damas, Antioch, Homs, Tripoli), and Russia (Moscow and in particular Novgorod). They attest to the central place the icon holds in Eastern Christian worship, and to the cultural and spiritual diversity of Lebanon.
Jan 97–Apr 97	***Fragments of Italiote Vases*** *The Cahn Collection*

Genève · Geneva

CENTRE D'ART CONTEMPORAIN DE GENÈVE
10, Rue des Vieux-Grenadiers 1205 Genève Director: Paolo Colombo
☎ +41 22 3291842 📠 +41 22 3291886
Open: Tuesday-Sunday 11.00-18.00
Closed: Monday

COLLECTION	No permanent collection.

EXHIBITIONS	
28·03·96–15·06·96	*Katia Bassanini*
08·05·96–01·09·96	*Ingeborg Luescher*
15·05·96–01·09·96	*Pipilotti Rist*
Nov 96–Jan 97	*Winners of the Swiss Federal Grants in the Visual Arts*
Feb 97–May 97	*Italian Art Today*

Genève · Geneva

CENTRE GENEVOIS DE GRAVURE CONTEMPORAINE
17, Malagnou 1208 Genève Director: Véronique Bacchetta
☎ +41 22 7351260 📠 +41 22 7352897
Open: Monday-Friday 14.00-18.00 Saturday 14.00-17.00
Closed: Sunday

COLLECTION	The stated goal of the Centre Genevois de Gravure Contemporaine is to promote an appreciation of engraving in the context of contemporary art. Established in 1966, the Centre Genevois de Gravure Contemporaine is open to international artists as well as artists from Geneva and the rest of Switzerland. Since 1986 it has been actively involved in the publication of engravings, artists' books and photographic prints, and the production of videos. It endeavours to focus attention on the problems intrinsic to reproducible pictures and objects. Artists are provided with an environment conducive to experimentation and to reflection on the possible links between contemporary art and the techniques of reproduction. Their work is presented in editions which the Centre produces and shows. Among the works which have been exhibited are large monotypes by John Armleder, metal points by Philippe Favier, monochrome engravings by Olivier Mosset, lithographs by Jean-Michel Othoniel, artists' books by Emmett Williams and Claude Closky, engravings by Ian Anüll and Alex Hanimann, and a video by Roman Signer. The Centre has also held a retrospective of the graphic work of

Marcel Broodthaers. The works on exhibit are illustrative of the diversity of attitudes and approaches to the printing process and, more generally, to the reproduction of objects.

EXHIBITIONS

May 96–mid Jun 96   **_Kristin Oppenheim (USA)_**   _Book and Exhibition_   The artist lives and works in New York.

28·06·96–28·09·96   **_Alexandre Bianchini, Nicolás Fernández, Jérôme Hentsch and Alain Julliard_**   _Books and Exhibitions_   The artists live and work in Geneva.

mid Oct 96–Dec 96   **_Heimo Zobernig_**   _Book and Exhibition_   The artist lives and works in Vienna, Austria.

Genève · Geneva

CABINET DES ESTAMPES DU MUSÉE D'ART ET D'HISTOIRE
5, Promenade du Pin   1204 Genève   Director: Cäsar Menz
☎ +41 22 4182770   📠 +41 22 4182771
Open: Tuesday-Sunday 10.00-12.00 / 14.00-18.00
Closed: Monday

COLLECTION

The Cabinet des estampes owns an estimated 300 000 examples of engraving dating back over 500 years, and offers an overview of the evolution of the art of engraving from its origins. Highlights of the collection include works by Piranesi, Callot, Hogarth, Carrière, Redon and Meryon. Particularly distinctive is a rare ensemble of glass plate prints by Camille Corot.

In its acquisitions policy regarding modern works, the Cabinet des estampes has chosen to focus on specific currents and artists. Avant-garde Russian and Hungarian prints from the period between 1913 and 1925 are represented in one of the best collections in Europe. Also notable is the collection of works by Giorgio de Chirico, Jean Fautrier, Antonio Saura, Bram van Velde, Markus Raetz, Georg Baselitz, Urs Lüthi and John M. Armleder.

The engravings of the Lausanne artist Felix Valloton provide a complement to the collection of his paintings in the Musée d'art et d'histoire.

Ljubov Popova (1889-1924)
Untitled, 1921

Cabinet des Estampes, Genève

Prominent in the collection is a group of artists' books, ranging from sumptuous collectors' editions from the beginning of the

century to booklets produced during the 1960s.
While the collections are not on permanent display, specific works can be viewed by appointment.

EXHIBITIONS

06·06·96–08·09·96   *Only in Geneva*   'Only in Geneva' presents a selection of works from the permanent collection which, by their rarity or their exceptional quality, make Geneva a pole of attraction for the world of prints. The exhibition will include innovative creations of the Russian and Hungarian avant-garde (Lissitzky, Popova, Rozanova and Peri), the complete collection of Urs Graf's standard bearers, an original iron printing plate by Daniel Hopfer, original/multiples of Jean Fautrier, as well as unique works by De Chirico, Schwitters, Man Ray and many others.

26·09·96–03·11·96   *Hors Scène II*   Following 1995's 'Hors scène I: Notes on Print', which focused on works by eight European and American contemporary artists around an exceptional suite of 1962 lithographs by Robert Morris, 'Hors scène II' will again assemble a selection of contemporary creators around a central theme, this time in relation to the photographic image.

28·11·96–19·01·97   *Robert Müller*   *Prints 1983-1995*   On the occasion of the publication of Volume II of the Cataloque Raisonné of the Swiss artist Robert Müller, the Cabinet des Estampes exhibits his engravings, covering the last ten years of his work. The work combines elements of pre-Renaissance art with references to Art Brut.

Genève · Geneva

MUSÉE DE L'HORLOGERIE
15, Route de Malagnou 1208 Genève Director: Cäsar Menz
☎ +41 22 4186470 📠 +41 22 4186471
Open: Wednesday-Monday 10.00-12.00 / 14.00-18.00
Closed: Tuesday

COLLECTION   The history of watchmaking is related in a collection of clocks, watches and clockmaking tools covering four centuries, from 1550 to 1950. Miniatures, jewellery, snuffboxes, mainly from Geneva, complete this attractive ensemble. Present-day work in the field of enamel, jewellery and watchmaking is exhibited in changing displays.

EXHIBITIONS   No exhibitions planned.

Genève · Geneva

PETIT PALAIS, MUSÉE D'ART MODERNE
2, Terrasse Saint Victor 1206 Genève President: Oscar Ghez
☎ +41 22 3461433 📠 +41 22 3465315
Open: Monday-Friday 10.00-12.00 / 14.00-18.00 Saturday-Sunday 10.30-13.00 / 14.00-17.00

COLLECTION   The Petit Palais contains modern art from the period 1880-1930 by both famous and lesser-known artists. The collection illustrates the transitions and interconnections of the various movements. Beginning with Courbet, it includes works by Impressionists such as Manet, Monet, Sisley, Pissarro, Renoir, Degas, Cézanne, Berthe Morisot, Marie Bracquemond, Guillaumin, Whistler, Lebourg,

Fantin-Latour, Caillebotte and Thaulow; the Post-Impressionists Albert André, Georges d'Espagnat, Moret, Montezin, Louis Carrand and Charreton; painters of the Nabi movement such as Gauguin, Sérusier, Maurice Denis, Bonnard, Vuillard, Meyer de Haan and others; Pointillists such as Seurat and his followers Luce, Cross, Angrand and Théo van Rysselberghe; the Fauvists Louis Valtat, Dufy, Friesz, Van Dongen, Matisse, Manguin, Puy, Camoin and August Chabaud, Larionov and Gontcharova; Montmartre artists such as Steinlen, Bottini, the engraver Galanis, Picasso, Edmond Heuzé, Suzanne Valadon and her son Maurice Utrillo, and Quizet. The Paris School is represented by the Cubists Braque, Fernand Léger, Juan Gris, La Fesnaye, Le Fauconnier, Henry Hayden, Kisling, Maria Blanchard and Marie Laurencin. 20th-century Primitives, or Naïfs, are exhibited ex-voto style in the crypt.

EXHIBITION
until 30·05·96

'Montmartre Vivant' *From Toulouse-Lautrec to Utrillo*

Genève · Geneva

MUSÉE RATH
Place Neuve 1204 Genève Director: Cäsar Menz
☎ +41 22 3105270 📠 +41 22 3121858
Open: Tuesday and Thursday-Sunday 10.00-17.00 Wednesday 12.00-21.00
Closed: Monday

COLLECTION

At the time of its opening in 1828, the Musée Rath was the first Swiss museum devoted to the fine arts. The museum's objective was to exhibit and house original works of art and plaster casts used for the study of art. Since the Musée d'Art et d'Histoire came into existence, the Musée Rath, under its auspices, has been used exclusively for major temporary exhibitions.

EXHIBITIONS
26·04·96–28·07·96

Rodolphe Töpffer (1799-1846) *Graphic Adventures* This exhibition is an exploration of the rich universe of this inexhaustibly imaginative and creative individual, today recognised as the inventor of the comic strip. An incisive cartoonist, Töpffer was also the sensitive illustrator of his own writings, an ironic observer of Switzerland's burgeoning tourist trade, a poet of the Alps and an active commentator on the artistic output of his epoch.

13·09·96–05·01·97

Dieter Roth Specifically for this exhibition, this internationally-known Swiss artist, who works outside the limits of classic artistic standards, will create a large-scale installation composed of everyday objects and materials. Through his extravagant machines and his organised disorder, where each element has its place and function according to the artist's unique logic, Dieter Roth is a pitiless observer of today's world.

Genève · Geneva

MUSÉE D'HISTOIRE DES SCIENCES VILLA BARTHOLONI
128, Rue de Lausanne 1202 Genève Director: Cäsar Menz
☎ +41 22 7316985 📠 +41 22 7411308
Open: Wednesday-Monday 13.00-17.00
Closed: Tuesday

COLLECTION

Geneva boasts a collection of scientific instruments sufficiently important to merit its own museum. Historically, 18th-century Geneva was home to scholars, many from families of substantial means, whose keen interest in science led them to acquire scientific instruments from the finest manufacturers of the time in Europe. Over the years the collection has been steadily increased through acquisitions, and provides a broad picture of the evolution of science.

EXHIBITION
14·06·96–Spring 97 | ***Anatomical Models***   A group of anatomical models illustrating dermatological diseases.

Genève · Geneva

MAISON TAVEL
6, Rue du Puits-Saint-Pierre 1204 Genève Director: Cäsar Menz
☎ **+41 22 3102900**
Open: Tuesday-Sunday 10.00-17.00
Closed: Monday

COLLECTION | The oldest private residence in Geneva (13th-14th century), built by the patrician Tavel family and occupied over the centuries by a number of prominent Genevans, the Maison Tavel was acquired by the city in 1963 and, following extensive restoration, opened to the public in 1986.
This historic monument of national importance houses a museum devoted to the history of Geneva as a city, and to its domestic traditions. Objects, drawings, engravings and photographs, coins, furniture and silver illustrate Geneva's past from the Middle Ages to the beginning of the 20th century. An impressive historic model of the city shows it as it was in the times of Calvin and Rousseau.

EXHIBITIONS
07·06·96–31·12·96 | ***Rodolphe Töpffer***   *Chronicler of Daily Life*   A choice of Töpffer's drawings available on computer will be shown on the second floor, along with everyday objects from the artist's period.

07·06·96–31·12·96 | ***The Alps in Detail***   Landscape drawings and prints from the 18th and 19th century attest to the epoch's fascination with the exploration of the Alpine scene, and in particular Mont Blanc, first by road, then a path, and then nothing but stone and ice. Tiny figures against the landscape depicted by artists of the time provide the measure of the immensity of this new world.

Lausanne

MUSÉE CANTONAL DES BEAUX-ARTS
Place de la Riponne 6 1014 Lausanne Director: Jörg Zutter
☎ **+41 21 3128332** ▣ **+41 21 3209946**
Open: Tuesday, Wednesday 11.00-18.00 Thursday 11.00-20.00
Friday-Sunday 11.00-17.00
Closed: Monday

COLLECTION | The Museum of Fine Arts houses the collections of the cantonal departments of painting, prints, drawings and sculpture. The emphasis is on Swiss paintings from 1750 through to 20th-century art. These works are permanently exhibited in the first three galleries. The Museum of Fine Arts has the world's largest collections of works by the famous watercolourist Louis Ducros (1748-1810), the academic painter Charles Gleyre (1806-1874), the highly respected wood engraver and painter Félix Valloton (1865-1925) and the 'art brut' artist Louis Sourter (1871-1942).

15·05·96–22·09·96

Aristide Maillol   Aristide Maillol (1861-1944) is one of the main representatives of the important current of European sculpture of the 1920s and 1930s that sought to revive and renew the classical ideal. This exhibition aims to present the much wider range of his artistic work. In addition to sculpture in various formats and materials, the more than 100 works on display include paintings, tapestries, book illustrations, hand drawings and lithographs.

06·10·96–08·12·96

Thomas Huber   *Paintings 1990-1995*   The work of Thomas Huber aims to explain the meaning and to legitimise the process of artistic creation. Huber is primarily interested in the didactic message of paintings or objects and his creation develops around specific themes such as marriage, family, the studio, the library and the bank, among others.

Lugano

MUSEO CANTONALE D'ARTE
Via Canova 10 6900 Lugano Director: Manuela Kahn-Rossi
☎ +41 91 9104760 📠 +41 91 9104789
Open: Tuesday 14.00-17.00 Wednesday-Sunday 10.00-17.00
Closed: Monday

In addition to several Renaissance works, the permanent collection of the museum consists of paintings, sculptures and graphic works of the 19th and 20th century and photographs of the 20th century. It aims to give an overview of the various art movements of the last two centuries, especially in relation to the Ticino Canton, which is situated strategically on one of the main routes between Northern and Southern Europe. The Ticinese artists of the 19th century include C.A. Meletta, V. Vela, A. Ciseri, F. Feragutti-Visconti, L. Rossi, E. Berta, F. Franzoni, L. Chialiva and F. Agnelli. The earlier part of the 20th century is represented by F. Boldini, C. Cotti, G. Gonzato, F. Filippini, S. Brignoni, R. Rossi and E. Dobrzansky, while contemporary artists include M. Cavalli, L. Bernasconi, R. Ferrari, F. Paolucci, N. Toroni and N. Snozzi.
There are also works from the internationally known 19th-century artists E. Degas, A. Renoir C. Pissarro and M. Rosso and turn-of-the-century works by the Swiss artists F. Hodler, C. Amiet and S. Righini. The present century is mainly represented by Avant-Garde artists who lived in Ticino for varying lengths of time. Besides O. Schlemmer, J. Arp, S. Taeuber-Arp, A. von Jawlenski, P. Klee, M. von Werefkin, H. Richter, W. Varlin and J. Bissier, there are works by artists of the Swiss Expressionist group from the 1920s which was known as Rot-Blau.
The collection is completed by a number of works by artists belonging to two Italian movements: Novecento Italiano (C. Carrà, A. Funi and F. Casorati) and Corrente (R. Birolli and I. Valenti).

May 96

The Collection of the Museo Cantonale d'Arte   Fine arts of the 19th and 20th centuries.

Jun 96

Video Art   *From Experimentation to Specific Language*

08·09·96–17·11·96

Odilon Redon   *The Nature of the Invisible* Paintings and drawings.

Lugano

MUSEUM OF EXTRA-EUROPEAN CULTURES _
The Serge and Graziella Brignoni Collection
Via Cortivo 24 6976 Lugano/Castagnola Curator: Carla Burani Ruef
☎ +41 91 9717353 📠 +41 91 9719575
Open: Mar-Oct Tuesday-Sunday 10.00-17.00
Closed: Monday and Nov-Feb

COLLECTION | The permanent collection of art form tribal cultures of Oceania, Asia and Africa, consists of approximately 600 objects, mostly wooden figures from Melanesia, Polynesia and Indonesia. There are ceremonial objects, amulets, masks, skull-racks, fragments of cult houses, musical instruments and shields from New Guinea (Sepik, Maprik, Asmat and the Gulf of Papua) and New Ireland (malanggans and ulis from the northern and central parts of the islands). The collection also includes items from the other Melanesian islands, Polynesia, and the Asian tribal cultures of Nias, Sumatra and Kalimantan. The collection also includes wooden masks, primarily from western Sub-Saharan regions.

The character of this collection is intimately tied to the painter Serge Brignoni, who collected these objects with the eye of an artist, and continues to collect today. Beyond the ethno-anthropological significance of the collection, the collection also addresses the historical aspects of collecting, exoticism, primitivism and surrealism.

EXHIBITIONS | No details available.

Lugano

FONDAZIONE THYSSEN-BORNEMISZA
Villa Favorita 6976 Lugano-Castagnola Director: Maria De Peverelli
☎ +41 91 9721741 📠 +41 91 9716151
Open: 5 Apr-3 Nov Friday-Sunday 10.00-17.00
Closed: Monday-Thursday and 4 Nov 1996 - 28 Mar 1997

COLLECTION | The Gallery of the Villa Favorita has been presenting an exhibit of about 150 European and American 19th and 20th-century paintings and watercolours from the Thyssen-Bornemisza Collection since 1992. A third of these works are 19th-century American paintings. They include works from 1835 to 1900 by the major exponents of Luminism and the Hudson River School of painting, as well as leading American Impressionists and Western painters such as Cole, Hassam, Hade, Kensett, Robinson, Twatchman and Wittredge. The remaining one hundred paintings illustrate the development of the art of the 20th century on both sides of the Atlantic through representative examples of every major style, including Cubism, German Expressionism, Russian Avant Garde, Dada, Surrealism, American Scene painting and Precessionism, Abstract Expressionism, Pop Art and Photorealism. The works include oil paintings, works on paper and some sculpture. Artists with works in the collection include Chashnik, de Chirico, Ernst, Freud, Itten, Larionov, Macke, Malevich, Marc, Masson, Munch, Nolde, Schiele, Benton, Davis, Demuth, Estes, Henri, Homer, Hopper, Marin, Parrish, Pollock, Shahn, Wesselmann and Wyeth.

EXHIBITIONS | No details available.

Solothurn

KUNSTMUSEUM SOLOTHURN
Werkhofstrasse 30 4500 Solothurn Director: Andre Kamber
☎ +41 65 222307 ▮▯ +41 65 225001
Open: Thursday-Saturday 10.00-12.00 / 14.00-17.00 Tuesday 10.00-12.00 /
14.00-21.00 Sunday 10.00-17.00
Closed: Monday

COLLECTION

The Solothurn Museum of Art unites the collections of the city, the art association and the Dübi-Müller, Josef Müller and Max Gubler foundations. Although the museum's collection is defined as Swiss, its first works were two small Medieval German paintings. A range of 19th-century Swiss art by Buchser, Fröhlicher, Hodler, Amiet, Trachsel, Berger and Gubler characterises the collection, though it also contains more European works of art by the likes of Degas, Van Gogh, Matisse, Braque, Gris and Léger.

Contemporary art is represented by the work of artists such as Roth, Thomkins, Eggenschwiler, Oppenheim, Luginbühl, Tinguely, R. Müller and Wiggli. The Kunstmuseum also houses a section devoted to Primitive art (in cooperation with the Musée Barbier-Müller in Geneva) and a section dedicated to the graphic arts - mainly new Swiss drawing.

EXHIBITIONS

24·02·96–19·05·96

Ben Vautier   The first Swiss general overview of the work of this artist (born Geneva, 1935), including 'Le Magasin, 1958-1973, 1984, 1994' from the Pompidou Centre in Paris. His work combines images and text in a critical and often humorous mode.

15·06·96–22·09·96

Friendships and Artistic Sense   *The Former Solothurn Ferdinand Hodler Collection*   This exhibition of the work of Hodler is based on the private collections of the Müller family at the beginning of the century. It features more than 80 pictures, mostly painted after 1900, including major works such as 'The Beechwood', 'Love', 'The Holy Hour' and more than 30 landscapes.

15·06·96–22·09·96

Art from Africa, Asia and Pre-Columbian America   *From the Former Collections of our Donors*   The Müller family, and in particular Josef Müller, were also enthusiastic collectors of older and non-European art. This exhibition features figures, masks and objects from Africa, pre-Columbian America and Asia. Of special interest are the 'barbus Müller': volcanic stone sculptures of mysterious origin.

15·06·96–22·09·96

The Müller Family's Photographs of Ferdinand Hodler
An exhibition of varied photos of Hodler, mostly taken by Gertrud Dübi-Müller but also by her sister Margrit Kottmann-Müller and possibly Josef Müller.

Vevey

SWISS CAMERA MUSEUM
6, Ruelle des Anciens-Fosses 1800 Vevey Director: P. & J-M. Bonnard Yersin
☎ +41 21 9219460 ▮▯ +41 21 9216458
Open: Daily Mar-Oct 10.30-12.00 / 14.00-17.30 Nov-Feb 14.00-17.30

COLLECTION

The museum is housed in a refurbished 18th-century building, combining old and modern architecture. Each floor, with its own theme, has a different colour. The basement, or level 1, is yellow and contains studio cameras, laboratory equipment and other photographic items.

The blue level 0 displays cameras arranged according to country of origin. The red level 1 has a chronological display of stereoscopic cameras. Level 2, grey, houses regularly changing exhibitions, and the attic, level 3, features the exhibition on projection, ranging from magic lanterns to state-of-the-art projectors.

One notable exhibit is the Leica showcase that displays the work of Oscar Barnack: almost inadvertently, he invented the Leica 35mm still camera while trying to develop a prototype for 35mm motion film without wasting too much film. Other notable exhibits include Le Compass, a technical marvel manufactured by the watchmakers Le Coultre, and an amazing panoramic camera with a 360 degree image produced by Alpa.

EXHIBITIONS

24·02·96-27·05·96   ***Dominique Derisbourg, a Fashion Photographer***   This French photographer, who studied photography in Vevey, has brought an appealing blend of freshness and audacity to the photographs published by FEMINA, the Swiss-French magazine for which he frequently works in Paris.

08·06·96-13·10·96   ***The World in Three Dimensions***   The fascination of stereo photography, or everything that has been invented for the reproduction of 3D images.

19·10·96-end Jan 97   ***Carlo Ponti, Image Wizard***   In the 19th century, Carlo Ponti, a Swiss-Italian who had settled in Venice, invented an extraordinary machine for viewing photographs which enabled modification of the image. The Swiss Camera Museum possesses such a 'Megaletoscope', as well as a series of images. The restoration of such photographs, also presented here, is both complicated and fascinating.

Winterthur

THE OSKAR REINHART FOUNDATION
Stadthausstraße 6 8400 Winterthur Director: Peter Wegmann
☎ +41 52 2675172 📠 +41 52 2676228
Open: Tuesday-Sunday 10.00-17.00
Closed: Monday

COLLECTION   The collection is housed in the Old Gymnasium, built by Leonhard Zeugheer between 1838 and 1842, and includes around 600 works by German, Swiss and Austrian artists from the 18th to the 20th century. Swiss painting is especially well represented with work from Liotard to Füssli, Graff, Wolf, Agasse, Töpffer, Calame, Menn, Böcklin and Anker up to Hodler, Segantini and Amiet. The art of German Romanticism (Friedrich, Runge, Kersting, Blechen, Schwind, Spitzweg), Realism and Idealism (Waldmüller, Menzel, Thoma, Leibl, Trübner, Feuerbach, Marées) as well as Impressionism (Uhde, Liebermann, Slevogt) also form focal points.

EXHIBITIONS   No exhibitions planned.

Zug

KUNSTHAUS ZUG
Dorfstrasse 27 6301 Zug Director: Matthias Haldemann
☎ +41 42 211150 📠 +41 42 224465
Open: Tuesday-Friday 12.00-18.00 Saturday-Sunday 10.00-17.00
Closed: Monday

COLLECTION   The focus of the collection is on objects belonging to the realms of

Surrealism and Fantastic art, and includes the works of such artists as Moeschlin, Seligmann, Von Moos, Ballmer, Jacob, Kuhn, Weber, Wipf and Wölffli. In addition, the collection contains various works from the Viennese sculptor Fritz Wotruba (1907-1975), figurative Swiss sculptures, concrete art and art from central Switzerland. The various parts of the collection are alternatingly on display and can be viewed at regular intervals.

EXHIBITIONS

02·06·96-01·09·96

Tadashi Kawamata   Work in Progress in Zug   The Japanese artist Tadashi Kawamata (born 1953) has earned an international reputation with large, architectural installations in wood. His pieces are the result of an intensive interaction with spatial, social, cultural and historical conditions in the places where he works. Often, he counters the sleek containers of urban civilisation with evocations of simple, basic building activity.

02·06·96-01·09·96

Richard Tuttle   Replace the Abstract Picture Plane   Ever since the 1960s, Richard Tuttle (born 1941) has been one of the great individualists of American art. With uncanny sure-footedness, Tuttle defies every artistic convention to conjure a constant succession of surprising and poetic configurations out of the most varied materials. At first, the pieces often seem random, faulty, incomplete, weak and chaotic, but then they develop a presence of their own. Tuttle plans a large installation extending through several rooms for this exhibition.

15·09·96-03·11·96

Heinz Gappmayr   Text Images   Heinz Gappmayr (born 1925) lives in Innsbruck and has long been one of the major proponents of visual poetry. His works have their place on the frontier between image and language. Place, time, space, colour, number and measure - the elementary conditions of existence and thought - are the central concerns of his work.

Zürich

FOUNDATION E.G. BÜHRLE COLLECTION
Zollikerstrasse 172 8008 Zürich Director: Christian Bührle
☎ +41 1 4220086 📠 +41 1 4220347
Open: Tuesday and Friday 14.00-17.00 Wednesday 17.00-20.00
Closed: Monday, Thursday, Saturday, Sunday

Pierre Auguste
Renoir (1841-1919)
Little Irene, 1880

Foundation E. G.
Bührle Collection,
Zürich

COLLECTION | The Emil G. Bührle Collection is a private art collection exhibited in a 19th-century villa. It comprises Medieval wood carvings and paintings by the old masters, but above all works by French artists of the 19th and 20th century.

The French Impressionists form a nucleus embracing eight works by Manet, seven each by Cézanne and Van Gogh and five by Gauguin. The collection includes the trio of portraits by Cézanne consisting of 'The Artist's Wife in an Armchair', the 'Self-Portrait with Palette' and 'The Boy in the Red Waistcoat'. In addition, there are works of Monet, Renoir, Pissarro, Sisely, Degas and Toulouse-Lautrec as well as works by the Nabis, the Fauves and the Cubists.
The 18th-century Venetian school is represented by Canaletto, Guardi and Tiepolo. The Dutch Baroque paintings include the 'Portrait of a Man' by Frans Hals.
Thirty sculptures from the 12th to the 16th century are also on display.

EXHIBITIONS | No exhibitions planned.

Zürich

HAUS FÜR KONSTRUKTIVE UND KONKRETE KUNST
Seefeldstrasse 317 8008 Zürich Director: Elisabeth Grossmann
☎ +41 1 3813808 📠 +41 1 3820592
Open: Tuesday-Friday 10.00-12.00 / 14.00-17.00 Saturday, Sunday 10.00-17.00
Closed: Monday

COLLECTION | The heart of the display is the long-term presentation of an 'imaginary collection' of the Zürich Concrete artists, in particular Bill, Glarner, Graeser, Hinterreiter, Loewensberg and Lohse. All of them participated to a large extent in the development of Constructivist art in Zürich; their influence can still be felt in contemporary art.

The exhibition is changed once a year; it is created through the collaboration with collectors and museums and the relevant curators.
Besides works by Graeser and Lohse, young Swiss and foreign artists are also represented.

EXHIBITIONS

12·04·96–09·06·96 | **Dadamaine** 'I fatti della vita'

12·04·96–27·10·96 | **Work Groups in Long-Term Presentations** Work by Bill, Glarner, Grasser, Hinterreiter, Loewensberg and Lohse.

21·06·96–18·08·96 | **Hartmut Böhm**

30·08·96–27·10·96 | **Florin Granwehr** 'Stand der Lage'

08·11·96–19·01·97 | **The Colour WHITE** From Zero to Today

Zürich

KUNSTHAUS ZÜRICH
Heimplatz 1 8024 Zürich Director: Felix Baumann
☎ +41 1 2516755 📠 +41 1 2512464
Open: Tuesday-Thursday 10.00-21.00 Friday-Sunday 10.00-17.00
Closed: Monday and public holidays

COLLECTION

Old Masters   A selection of sculptures and paintings, mainly by the Masters of Carnation, represents Medieval art. Pictures from the Ruzicka and Koetser Foundations highlight the Baroque period. A comprehensive department is devoted to Zürich painting after the Reformation, culminating in the work of Saloman Gessner and Henry Fuseli.

Swiss Artists   This representative collection includes works by Koller, Zünd, Böcklin, Welti, Segantini, Hodler, Augusto Giacometti, Vallotton, Amiet and Giovanni Giacometti. It also covers the realistic and surrealistic figuration of the inter-war period, Zürich 'concrete art' and post-1945 sculpture.

Classical Moderns   Works by Edvard Munch, Kokoschka, Beckmann, Corinth, Matisse (mainly sculpture), Picasso, Max Ernst and Miró are on display in this collection.

New Tendencies   Examples on display include works by Baselitz, Penck and Kiefer, Bacon, Disler and Cucchi.

Graphic Art Collection   A collection of approx. 80 000 prints and drawings, including Old Master drawings, Swiss landscape drawing, 20th-century art, works of Zero movements and Minimal and Conceptual art.

Swiss Foundation of Photography   The works of Swiss and foreign photographers, both past and present, can be admired in this display, as well as a collection of original photographic prints and publications.

Wassily Kandinsky
(1866-1944)
The black patch, 1921

*Kunsthaus Zürich,
Zürich*

EXHIBITIONS
15·03·96–19·05·96

Erotika   The enormous range of the theme 'erotica', from trivial to banal to grotesque to sublime, is displayed here through works by Gessner, W.S. Burroughs, Rodin, Rist, Hogarth, Wiedeman, Picasso and others.

04·04·96–14·07·96

Ancient China Images of Men and Gods   *New Archeological Finds from The People's Republic of China*   The exhibition, 'Ancient China', covers 5000 years of Chinese history and focusses on images of men and gods in the art of prehistoric and early imperial China. Approximately 200 objects, mainly from spectacular new finds and most of which have never left China before, provide a fascinating insight into the development of Chinese civilization from c. 5000 B.C. to 220 A.D. The extraordinary artistry and historical significance of these great works of art open up new avenues to our knowledge of China's civilization and religions. These exhibits made of bronze, jade, ceramics and other materials illustrate such themes as the first known images of man, early mythology, ancestral cults, and the origins of writing.

12·04·96–23·06·96	*Hans Danuser* Photographic Works
07·06·96–18·08·96	*Inez van Lamsweerde* Photographic Works
05·07·96–03·11·96	*Peter Fischli/David Weiss* Video Installation
23·08·96–10·11·96	***In Artificial Light*** Photographs from the collections of the Swiss Foundation of Photography, the Young Art Group of the Association of Zürich Friends of the Arts, and the Zürich Art Association, give insight into the international history of photography in the 20s and 30s, and the renaissance of this medium in the 'artificial light' of the 70s.
30·08·96–27·10·96	***Pierrick Sorin*** Video Installation This artist is one of the most notable of the French Art scene of the 90s. Though the scenes in his videos sometimes express slapstick comedy and irony, his pessimistic view on life is ever obvious.
08·11·96–05·01·97	*Marianne Olsen/Walter Siegfried*
08·11·96–12·01·97	***Hans Baumgartner*** A presentation of Baumgartner's life work, in which the main themes include: 'man at work' and landscapes.
06·12·96–23·02·97	***Austria in a Net of Roses*** Following earlier exhibitions of works by Austrian artists from the creative Vienna of 1990, the moment has come to follow this spirit to the present: 'Austria im Rosennetz', an exhibition as a spiritual portrait.

Zürich

THE SWISS NATIONAL MUSEUM
Museumstrasse 2 8023 Zürich Director: Mr. Furger
☎ **+41 1 2186511 📠 +41 1 2112949**
Open: Tuesday-Sunday 10.00-17.00
Closed: Monday

COLLECTION

The Swiss National Museum, which was opened in 1898 and housed in a building designed by Gustav Gull, displays the cultural diversity of Switzerland with exhibits dating from the Stone Age to the 19th century. The museum's collections cover prehistoric and early history, weapons, gold, silver, copper and brass work, pewter and

Jost Bürgi
Celestial globe, bras, gilded; 1594

Schweizerisches
Landesmuseum,
Zürich

ceramic artefacts, textiles and costumes, jewellery, coins, medallions and seals.

The museum also features glass painting, painting and sculpture, furniture and interiors, watches and musical instruments. The National Museum houses Ferdinand Hodler's famous 'Retreat of the Swiss Confederates at Marignano' (1899-1900). A number of special collections such as catalogues and photographs can be viewed by appointment only. The museum's library has restricted lending facilities.

<table>
<tr><td>EXHIBITIONS</td><td></td></tr>
<tr><td>15·03·96–02·06·96</td><td>Those who can get a job Work! The Swiss National Museum examines the theme of unemployment in this exhibition. An important aspect of the show is the contributions of unemployed German and French-speaking Swiss citizens who collaborated on the project. A great number of everyday objects and art objects are on display, inviting a comparison between unemployment as it existed in the 19th century and unemployment today.</td></tr>
<tr><td>19·07·96–27·10·96</td><td>Art of Sound Two Centuries of Mechanical Musical Instruments 200 years ago, Antoine Favre-Salomon, a Swiss watchmaker from Geneva, invented the mechanical principle of music boxes consisting of thin steel reeds made to vibrate and thus produce sound. The production of music boxes in Geneva and in Sainte-Croix was an important branch of Swiss industry between 1830 and 1900, and secured for Switzerland an international reputation for fine precision work.</td></tr>
</table>

Zürich

MUSEUM RIETBERG ZÜRICH - VILLA WESENDONCK - PARK-VILLA RIETER
Gablerstraße 15 8002 Zürich Director: Eberhard Fischer
☎ +41 1 2024528 📠 +41 1 2025201
Branch: Haus zum Kiel Hirschengraben 20 8001 Zürich
☎ +41 1 2619652 📠 +41 1 2025201
Open: Tuesday-Sunday 10.00-17.00;
Park-Villa Rieter: Tuesday-Saturday 13.00-17.00 Sunday 10.00-17.00
Closed: Monday

<table>
<tr><td>COLLECTION</td><td>The Museum Rietberg, located in Rieter Park, is a small museum with important works of art from Asia, Africa, the Americas and Oceania. Built in 1857, the Villa Wesendonck was the social and cultural centre of Zürich for many years. The internationally recognised sculptures bequeathed to the City of Zürich by Baron Eduard von der Heydt constitute the core of the permanent collection. Two to three special exhibitions of international significance are presented each year.
The Museum Rietberg presents its collection of Asian painting in the Park-Villa Rieter, which is also located in Rieter Park. The associated 'Haus zum Kiel', a small gallery located in the heart of Zürich, is used by the museum for temporary exhibitions.</td></tr>
<tr><td>EXHIBITIONS</td><td>[Haus zum Kiel Hirschengraben 20]</td></tr>
<tr><td>24·05·96–27·10·96</td><td>Keris Handles from the Malayan Archipelago The Malayan keris is considered to be a mediator between the supernatural and the human world, between the ancestors and the living. It is also considered a status symbol and a sign of the bearer's clan. The exhibition presents the most outstanding keris from the Von der Heydt collection, as well as some masterpieces from Swiss museums and private collections.</td></tr>
</table>

29·11·96–02·03·97 | **Côte d'Ivoire** *Ethnographic Research by Hans Himmelheber on Craftsmen and Artists of the Baule and Guro* Hans Himmelheber's dissertation 'Negerkünstler' (1939) is an in-depth study of the role of the individual carvers of the Guro and Baule from the Ivory Coast. It describes how carving skills were taught in a traditional African society, which tools were employed and which ideals of beauty were represented by the carvers.
This exhibition presents photographs, never published before, from two of Himmelheber's expeditions. Photographs by Martin Lippmann, who accompanied Himmelheber on his second expedition to the Ivory Coast in 1936, are also on display.
Besides these field photographs, the exhibition also includes objects collected during the expeditions.

[Museum Rietberg: Villa Wesendonck]

04·04·96–04·07·96 | **Mandate of Heaven** *Emperors and Artists in China* Mandate of Heaven is an exhibition consisting of a representative number of magnificent ink paintings from the collection of the Metropolitan Museum of Art in New York. It presents paintings and calligraphies from the 11th to the 18th centuries and lays emphasis on the diverse relations between the Chinese emperors and the artists. An exhibition of early Chinese works of art, titled Ancient China, is simultaneously on display at Kunsthaus Zürich.

03·11·96–30·03·97 | **Sican** *A Princely Tomb from Ancient Peru in Collaboration with the Peruvian Ministry of Culture* Not far from the northern coast of Peru lies the region of Batan Grande. Between 900 and 1000 A.D. this site was the ceremonial centre of the pre-Columbian Sican culture. Archaeological research by Professor Iszumi Shimada enables profound insight into this vanished culture. The tomb of a high-ranking man, in which human sacrifices were included in his honour as well as objects of gold, was found in this region and is on display here.

ADVERTISING IN THE

European MUSEUM Guide

brings your company or product to the attention of a very large public.

	Maximum size	Price
	100 mm wide and 40 mm high	NLG 790.–
	100 mm wide and 50 mm high	NLG 880.–
	100 mm wide and 60 mm high	NLG 970.–
	100 mm wide and 70 mm high	NLG 1060.–
	100 mm wide and 80 mm high	NLG 1150.–
1/2 page	100 mm wide and 105 mm high	NLG 1300.–
1/1 page	100 mm wide and 210 mm high	NLG 2400.–

- The prices are exclusive of 17,5% VAT.
- The prices above are for b/w advertisements;
- Surcharge for full-colour NLG 1800.–
- Prices are based on delivery of film material ready for use.
- Reservations for the '97I'98 edition should be made before December 20, 1996.

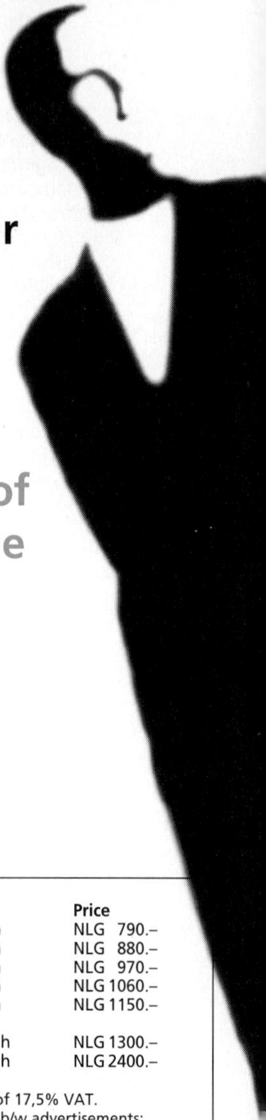

INDEX
Cities

MUSEUM MEDIA PUBLISHERS

Cities in alphabetical order by country.

AUSTRIA

CITY	MUSEUM	PAGE
Graz	Joanneum, Bild- und Tonarchiv (Landesmuseum)	6
Graz	Joanneum (Alte Galerie des Steiermärkischen Landesm.)	6
Innsbruck	Tiroler Volkskunstmuseum	7
Linz	Neue Galerie der Stadt Linz (Wolfgang-Gurlitt-Museum)	7
Salzburg	Residenzgalerie Salzburg	8
Salzburg	Rupertinum	9
Wien - Vienna	Akademie der bildenden Künste (Gemäldegalerie der)	10
Wien - Vienna	Belvedere (Österreichische Galerie)	11
Wien - Vienna	Graphische Sammlung Albertina	11
Wien - Vienna	Kunsthalle Wien	13
Wien - Vienna	Kunstforum Bank Austria	12
Wien - Vienna	KunstHausWien	13
Wien - Vienna	Kunsthistorisches Museum	14
Wien - Vienna	Ludwig Wien (Museum moderner Kunst Stiftung)	15
Wien - Vienna	Völkerkunde (Museum für)	16
Wien - Vienna	Volkskunde (Österreichisches Museum für)	17
Wien - Vienna	Wiener Secession	17

BELGIUM

CITY	MUSEUM	PAGE
Antwerpen - Antwerp	Beeldhouwkunst Middelheim (Openluchtmuseum voor)	22
Antwerpen - Antwerp	Hedendaagse Kunst Antwerpen (Museum van)	20
Antwerpen - Antwerp	Mayer van den Bergh (Museum)	21
Antwerpen - Antwerp	Plantin-Moretus (Museum)	23
Antwerpen - Antwerp	Rubenshuis	24
Antwerpen - Antwerp	Scheepvaartmuseum (Nationaal)	22
Antwerpen - Antwerp	Schone Kunsten (Koninklijk Museum voor)	20
Antwerpen - Antwerp	Stedelijk Prentenkabinet	24
Brugge - Bruges	Arentshuis (The Brangwyn Museum)	25
Brugge - Bruges	Groeninge Museum	26
Brugge - Bruges	Gruuthuse Museum	27
Brugge - Bruges	Memling Museum	27
Bruxelles - Brussels	Architecture (Fondation pour l')	28
Bruxelles - Brussels	Art Ancien –Royaux des Beaux-Arts de B. (Musée d')	29
Bruxelles - Brussels	Art Moderne –Royaux des Beaux-Arts de B. (Musée d')	30
Bruxelles - Brussels	Beaux-Arts (Palais des)	30
Bruxelles - Brussels	Musical Instruments (Brussels Museum of)	28
Bruxelles - Brussels	Natuurwetenschappen (Museum Kon. Belg. Inst. voor)	31
Charleroi	Beaux-Arts (Musée des)	32
Charleroi	Photographie (Musée de la)	32
Deurle	Dhondt-Dhaenens (Museum)	33
Gent - Ghent	Bijlokemuseum	33
Gent - Ghent	Hedendaagse Kunst (Museum van)	34
Gent - Ghent	MIAT (Museum for Industrial Archaeology and Textiles)	35
Gent - Ghent	Schone Kunsten (Museum voor)	36
Gent - Ghent	Sierkunst en Vormgeving (Museum voor)	37
Liège - Luik	Ansembourg (Musée d')	37
Morlanwelz	Mariemont (Musée Royal de)	38
Namur	Arts Anciens du Namurois (Musée des)	39
Oostende - Ostend	PMMK - Museum voor Moderne Kunst	39
Tervuren	Midden-Afrika (Koninklijk Museum voor)	40

FRANCE

CITY	MUSEUM	PAGE
Agen	Beaux-Arts (Musée des)	44
Aix-en-Provence	Granet (Musée)	44
Aix-les-Bains	Faure (Musée)	45
Albi	Toulouse-Lautrec (Musée)	45
Alençon	Beaux-Arts et de la Dentelle (Musée des)	46
Amiens	Picardie (Musée de)	47
Angers	Beaux-Arts (Musée des)	48
Angoulême	Beaux-Arts (Musée des)	49

Cities in alphabetical order by country.

Cities in alphabetical order by country.

Cities in alphabetical order by country.

Cities in alphabetical order by country.

GERMANY

CITY	MUSEUM	PAGE
Stuttgart	Galerie der Stadt Stuttgart	193
Stuttgart	Staatsgalerie Stuttgart	193
Trier	Rheinisches Landesmuseum	195
Ulm	Ulmer Museum	196
Weil am Rhein	Vitra Design Museum	197
Weimar	Kunstsammlungen zu Weimar	198

GREAT BRITAIN

CITY	MUSEUM	PAGE
Aberdeen	Aberdeen Art Gallery	200
Bath	Holburne Museum and Crafts Study Centre	201
Belfast	Ulster Museum	201
Birmingham	Art Gallery & The Gas Hall (Birmingham Museum and)	203
Birmingham	Barber Institute of Fine Arts	203
Bournemouth	Russell-Cotes Art Gallery and Museum	204
Brighton	Brighton Museum & Art Gallery	205
Bristol	City Museum and Art Gallery	206
Cambridge	Archaeology and Anthropology (University M. of)	207
Cambridge	Fitzwilliam Museum	207
Cardiff	National Museum of Wales	209
Cheltenham	Cheltenham Art Gallery & Museum	210
Chichester	Pallant House Gallery	211
Coventry	Herbert Art Gallery & Museum	211
Derby	Derby Museum & Art Gallery	213
Derby	Pickford's House Museum	213
Dorchester	Dorset County Museum	213
Durham	Bowes Museum (The)	214
Edinburgh	National Gallery of Scotland	215
Edinburgh	Royal Museum of Scotland (National M. of Scotland)	216
Edinburgh	Scottish National Gallery of Modern Art	218
Edinburgh	Scottish National Portrait Gallery	217
Glasgow	Art Gallery and Museum	219
Glasgow	Burrell Collection (The)	220
Glasgow	McLellan Galleries	220
Glasgow	Modern Art (Gallery of)	221
Grasmere	Wordsworth Museum (The)	222
Hull	Ferens Art Gallery	222
Kirkcaldy	Kirkcaldy Museum and Art Gallery	223
Leeds	Leeds City Art Gallery	224
Leicester	Leicestershire Museum and Art Gallery	225
Liverpool	Liverpool Museum	226
Liverpool	Merseyside Maritime Museum	226
Liverpool	Tate Gallery Liverpool	226
Liverpool	Walker Art Gallery	227
London	Accademia Italiana	229
London	Barbican Art Gallery	230
London	British Museum (The)	231
London	Courtauld Gallery	232
London	Design Museum	232
London	Dulwich Picture Gallery	233
London	Hayward Gallery	234
London	ICA Institute of Contemporary Arts	234
London	Leighton House Museum & Art Gallery	235
London	Maritime Museum (National)	238
London	Museum of Mankind Ethnography Dept. of British M.	236
London	National Gallery	236
London	Natural History Museum	238
London	Portrait Gallery (National)	239
London	Academy of Arts (Royal)	228
London	Serpentine Gallery (The)	240
London	Sir John Soane's Museum	241
London	Tate Gallery	242
London	Victoria and Albert Museum	243

Cities in alphabetical order by country.

Cities in alphabetical order by country.

INDEX
Museums

MUSEUM MEDIA PUBLISHERS

Museums in alphabetical order by country.

Museums in alphabetical order by country.

FRANCE

MUSEUM	CITY	PAGE
Louvre (Musée du)	Paris	88
Maeght (Fondation)	Saint-Paul	106
Magnin (Musée)	Dijon	67
Marine (Musée de la)	Paris	91
Marmottan (Musée)	Paris	92
Matisse (Musée)	Le Cateau-Cambrésis	60
Matisse (Musée)	Nice	80
Modern and Contemporary Art (Museum of)	Nice	81
Moyen Age Musée/Thermes de Cluny	Paris	92
Nicéphore Niépce (Musée)	Chalon-sur-Saône	61
Normandie (Musée de)	Caen	57
Oeuvre Notre-Dame (Musée de l')	Strasbourg	110
Orangerie (Musée National de l')	Paris	94
Orsay (Musée d')	Paris	95
Périgord (Musée du)	Périgueux	102
Petit Palais (Musée du)	Avignon	52
Petit Palais (Musée du)	Paris	96
Photographie (Centre National de la)	Paris	97
Picardie (Musée de)	Amiens	47
Picasso (Musée)	Antibes	49
Picasso (Musée)	Paris	98
Pompidou (Centre National d'Art et Culture Georges)	Paris	99
Réattu (Musée)	Arles	50
Renaissance (Musée National de la)	Écouen	69
Rigaud (Musée H.)	Perpignan	103
Rodin (Musée)	Paris	100
Sciences et de l'Industrie (La Cité des)	Paris	101
Thomas Henry (Musée)	Cherbourg	64
Tissus (Musée des)	Lyon	74
Toulouse-Lautrec (Musée)	Albi	45
Unterlinden (Musée d')	Colmar	64
Versailles et de Trianon (Château de)	Versailles	114

GERMANY

MUSEUM	CITY	PAGE
Abteiberg (Städtisches Museum)	Mönchengladbach	178
Alte Meister (Gemäldegalerie)	Dresden	142
Alte Meister (Gemäldegalerie)	Kassel	164
Alte Nationalgalerie	Berlin	120
Angewandte Kunst (Museum für)	Köln - Cologne	165
Antikensammlung	Berlin	121
Antikensammlungen und Glyptothek (Staatliche)	München - Munich	179
Archäologie/M. Kaiserpfalz (Westfälisches Museum für)	Paderborn	189
Architektur-Museum (Deutsches)	Frankfurt am Main	150
Augustinermuseum	Freiburg im Breisgau	153
Badisches Landesmuseum	Karlsruhe	162
Bauhaus-Archiv / M. für Gestaltung	Berlin	122
Berlinische Galerie/Mod. Kunst Photographie und Arch.	Berlin	122
Brücke-Museum	Berlin	123
Die Neue Sammlung	München - Munich	183
Ehrenhof (Kunstmuseum Düsseldorf im)	Düsseldorf	146
Focke-Museum M. für Kunst und Kulturgeschichte	Bremen	137
Folkwang Essen (Museum)	Essen	148
Fridericianum Kassel (Museum)	Kassel	164
Galerie der Stadt Stuttgart	Stuttgart	193
Galerie der Stadt Esslingen	Esslingen	149
Gemäldegalerie	Berlin	124
Germanisches Nationalmuseum	Nürnberg - Nuremberg	187
Grünes Gewölbe	Dresden	143
Gutenberg-Museum Mainz	Mainz	174
Hamburger Kunsthalle	Hamburg	156

Museums in alphabetical order by country.

GERMANY

MUSEUM	CITY	PAGE
Haus der Kunst	München - Munich	180
Herzog Anton Ulrich Museum	Braunschweig	136
Hessisches Landesmuseum	Darmstadt	140
Historisches Museum	Hannover	159
Historisches Museum (Deutsches)	Berlin	124
Hypo-Kulturstiftung (Kunsthalle der)	München - Munich	181
Josef-Haubrich-Kunsthalle	Köln - Cologne	166
Kunst- und Ausstellungshalle Bundesr. Deutschland	Bonn	133
Kunst und Gewerbe (Museum für)	Hamburg	157
Kunst und Kulturgeschichte (Westfälisches M. für)	Münster	185
Kunstgewerbemuseum	Berlin	125
Kunsthalle Baden-Baden (Staatliche)	Baden-Baden	120
Kunsthalle Bielefeld (Richard-Kaselowsky-Haus)	Bielefeld	131
Kunsthalle Düsseldorf	Düsseldorf	147
Kunsthalle Nürnberg	Nürnberg - Nuremberg	188
Kunsthalle zu Kiel	Kiel	164
Kunsthandwerk (Museum für)	Frankfurt am Main	151
Kunstmuseum Bonn	Bonn	134
Kunstsammlung Nordrhein-Westfalen	Düsseldorf	147
Kunstsammlungen zu Weimar	Weimar	198
Kunstverein (Bonner)	Bonn	132
Landesmuseum Mainz	Mainz	175
Lenbachhaus (Städtische Galerie im)	München - Munich	181
Ludwig Forum für Internationale Kunst	Aachen	118
Ludwig (Museum)	Köln - Cologne	167
Moderne Kunst (Museum für)	Frankfurt am Main	151
Moderner Kunst (Staatsgalerie)	München - Munich	184
Mönchehaus- Museum für Moderne Kunst	Goslar	154
Museum am Ostwall	Dortmund	141
Museum der Bildenden Künste	Leipzig	171
Neue Gesellschaft für Bildende Kunst	Berlin	126
Neue Meister (Gemäldegalerie)	Dresden	143
Neue Nationalgalerie	Berlin	127
Niedersächsisches Landesmuseum Hannover	Hannover	160
Ostasiatische Kunst (Museum für)	Berlin	128
Ostasiatische Kunst (Museum für)	Köln - Cologne	168
Ostdeutsche Galerie (Museum)	Regensburg	190
Overbeck-Gesellschaft (Contemporary Art)	Lübeck	173
Pinakothek (Alte)	München - Munich	178
Pinakothek (Neue)	München - Munich	182
Portikus Frankfurt am Main	Frankfurt am Main	152
Porzellansammlung	Dresden	144
Prähistorische Staatssammlung	München - Munich	183
Rautenstrauch-Joest-Museum (Ethnology)	Köln - Cologne	169
Reiß-Museum	Mannheim	176
Rheinisches Landesmuseum	Trier	195
Rheinisches Landesmuseum Bonn	Bonn	135
Römermuseum (Westfälisches)	Haltern	156
Römisch-Germanisches Museum	Köln - Cologne	170
Saarland Museum	Saarbrücken	191
Schack-Galerie	München - Munich	184
Schirn Kunsthalle	Frankfurt am Main	152
Schloß Morsbroich (Städtisches Museum Leverkusen)	Leverkusen	172
Schloß Rheydt	Mönchengladbach	177
Schloßmuseum	Darmstadt	140
Schwerin-Kunstsammlungen, Schlösser und Gärten	Schwerin	192
Skulpturensammlung	Berlin	128
Skulpturensammlung - Staatliche Kunstsammlungen	Dresden	144
Sprengel Museum	Hannover	161
Staatliche Kunsthalle Karlsruhe	Karlsruhe	163
Staatsgalerie Stuttgart	Stuttgart	193
Städelsches Kunstinstitut und Städtische Galerie	Frankfurt am Main	153
Städtische Kunstsammlungen	Chemnitz	139
Städtische Museum Göttingen	Göttingen	155

Museums in alphabetical order by country.

Museums in alphabetical order by country.

Museums in alphabetical order by country.

Museums in alphabetical order by country.

INDEX
Exhibitions

MUSEUM MEDIA PUBLISHERS

Exhibitions in chronological order.

AUSTRIA

DATE	CITY	MUSEUM	ARTIST/THEME
Jan 96 - Dec 96	Wien - Vienna	Graphische Sammlung Albertina	Master Drawings of the Albertina
01·03·96 - 27·05·96	Wien - Vienna	Kunstforum Bank Austria	Early Van Gogh
14·03·96 - 09·06·96	Linz	Neue Galerie der Stadt Linz	Gaston Chaissac (1910-1964)
14·03·96 - 16·06·96	Wien - Vienna	Belvedere (Österreichische Galerie)	Claude Monet
16·03·96 - 19·05·96	Wien - Vienna	Ludwig (Moderner Kunst Stiftung)	Franz West
21·03·96 - 01·09·96	Wien - Vienna	Museum für Völkerkunde	Foreign Vienna Xenographic P.
30·03·96 - 27·05·96	Wien - Vienna	Ludwig (Moderner Kunst Stiftung)	Susana Solano
Apr 96-Jul 96	Salzburg	Residenzgalerie Salzburg	Grünspan & Schildlaus
Apr 96-Jun 96	Wien - Vienna	Museum für Volkskunde	Iron Handicraft
05·04·96 - 09·06·96	Salzburg	Rupertinum	Paul Strand World on My Doorstep
May 96-Sep 96	Wien - Vienna	Museum für Volkskunde	Lace from Pag (Croatia)
09·05·96 - 14·07·96	Salzburg	Rupertinum	Lun Tuchnowski Sculptures
09·05·96 - 07·07·96	Salzburg	Rupertinum	Karl Schleinkofer Drawings
15·05·96 - 16·06·96	Wien - Vienna	Kunsthalle Wien /Museumquartier	Mail Art
15·05·96 - 23·06·96	Wien - Vienna	Kunsthalle Wien /Museumquartier	Magnum Cinema
15·05·96 - 30·06·96	Wien - Vienna	Wiener Secession / Hauptraum	Carsten Höller Installation
15·05·96 - 30·06·96	Wien - Vienna	Wiener Secession / Galerie	Manfred Erjautz
15·05·96 - 01·09·96	Wien - Vienna	KunstHausWien	Raoul Dufy
18·05·96 - 07·07·96	Salzburg	Rupertinum	Alberto di Fabio Works on Paper
18·05·96 - 07·07·96	Salzburg	Rupertinum	Cy Twombly Drawings
20·05·96 - 26·08·96	Wien - Vienna	Kunsthistorisches Museum	Auguste Rodin 1840-1917
24·05·96 - 22·09·96	Wien - Vienna	Kunsthistorisches Museum	Treasures from the Land of the Bible
01·06·96 - 30·09·96	Graz	Landesmuseum Joanneum	Treasures and Visions
Jul 96 - Sep 96	Salzburg	Residenzgalerie Salzburg	My Life, Let Me Shake Your Hand
04·06·96 - 04·08·96	Wien - Vienna	Graphische Sammlung Albertina	Between the Times
05·06·96 - 04·08·96	Wien - Vienna	Kunstforum Bank Austria	Drawing In Austria 1908-1938
05·06·96 - 15·10·96	Wien - Vienna	Ludwig (Moderner Kunst Stiftung)	Coming Up Young Art in Austria
13·06·96 - 14·07·96	Salzburg	Rupertinum	Erich Lessing
14·06·96 - 08·09·96	Wien - Vienna	Ludwig (Moderner Kunst Stiftung)	Errò
20·06·96 - end Sep 96	Innsbruck	Tiroler Volkskunstmuseum	Human Images in Folk Art
20·06·96 - 24·08·96	Linz	Neue Galerie der Stadt Linz	Masterpieces of Graphic Art
21·06·96 - 06·01·97	Wien - Vienna	Museum für Völkerkunde	Shining South Seas
Jul 96-Aug 96	Salzburg	Rupertinum	Georg Eisler
11·07·96 - 20·10·96	Salzburg	Rupertinum	Richard Gerst / The Landscapes
12·07·96 - 01·09·96	Wien - Vienna	Wiener Secession / Hauptraum	Young Scene
12·07·96 - 01·09·96	Wien - Vienna	Wiener Secession / Galerie	Marijke van Warmerdam
12·07·96 - 01·09·96	Wien - Vienna	Wiener Secession / Graf. Kabinett	Alexander Braun Writing Pictures
20·07·96 - 13·10·96	Salzburg	Rupertinum	Oskar Kokoschka
24·07·96 - 27·10·96	Salzburg	Rupertinum	Louise Bourgeois Objects
Aug 96-Dec 96	Salzburg	Residenzgalerie Salzburg	Jacopo Borges in the Residenzgalerie
29·08·96 - 24·11·96	Wien - Vienna	Kunstforum Bank Austria	Art of the Mentally Ill
30·08·96 - 03·11·96	Wien - Vienna	Kunsthalle Wien / Karlsplatz	Illusion - Emotion - Reality
Sep 96-Nov 96	Wien - Vienna	Kunsthalle Wien /Museumquartier	Gottfried Bechthold
05·09·96 - 13·10·96	Linz	Neue Galerie der Stadt Linz	Jack Ox
11·09·96 - 18·10·96	Wien - Vienna	Wiener Secession / Hauptraum	Martin Walder
11·09·96 - 27·10·96	Wien - Vienna	Wiener Secession / Galerie	Nobuyoshi Araki/Larry Clark
11·09·96 - 27·10·96	Wien - Vienna	Wiener Secession / Graf. Kabinett	Zoe Leonhard
Autumn 1996	Wien - Vienna	Kunsthistorisches Museum	The Restored Pictures. Hall VIII
Oct 96-Feb 97	Wien - Vienna	Museum für Volkskunde	Filigree Jewellery
17·10·96 - 15·01·97	Linz	Neue Galerie der Stadt Linz	Ernst Haas Photographs
17·10·96 - 01·12·96	Salzburg	Rupertinum	Karl Schmidt-Rotluff
24·10·96 - 15·12·96	Salzburg	Rupertinum	Ulrich Waibel New Drawings
24·10·96 - 15·12·96	Salzburg	Rupertinum	Franz Ringel Pictures 1970-1990
26·10·96 - 10·11·96	Wien - Vienna	Ludwig (Moderner Kunst Stiftung)	Abstract/Real
27·10·96 - Feb 97	Wien - Vienna	Kunsthistorisches Museum	The Message of Music
31·10·96 - 01·12·96	Wien - Vienna	Wiener Secession / Hauptraum	Philip Taaffe Paintings
31·10·96 - 08·12·96	Wien - Vienna	Wiener Secession / Galerie	Dorothee Golz Objects

Exhibitions in chronological order.

AUSTRIA

DATE	CITY	MUSEUM	ARTIST/THEME
Nov 96-Jan 97	Wien - Vienna	Museum für Völkerkunde	Erotic Art of ancient Peru
04·11·96 - 01·12·96	Salzburg	Rupertinum	Creative Children's Exhibition
21·11·96 - 12·01·97	Wien - Vienna	M. mod. K. Stiftung Ludwig Wien	Ákos Birkás
04·12·96 - Feb 97	Salzburg	Rupertinum	Annemarie Avramidis
05·12·96 - Feb 97	Salzburg	Rupertinum	Adolf Wolfli Works on Paper
13·12·96 - 19·01·97	Wien - Vienna	Wiener Secession / Hauptraum	James Coleman Multimedia
18·12·96 - 02·03·97	Wien - Vienna	Belvedere (Österreichische Galerie)	Oskar Kokoschka and Dresden
19·12·96 - Feb 97	Salzburg	Rupertinum	The Wolfgang Graninger Collection
Winter 96/97	Innsbruck	Tiroler Volkskunstmuseum	Sledges and Toboggans
Spring 97	Wien - Vienna	Belvedere (Österreichische Galerie)	Rudolf Hoflehner

BELGIUM

DATE	CITY	MUSEUM	ARTIST/THEME
24·02·96 - 02·06·96	Antwerpen-Antwerp	Stedelijk Prentenkabinet	Focus on Paul van Ostaijen
15·03·96 - 05·05·96	Gent - Ghent	Museum Sierkunst en Vormgeving	Danish ceramics
21·03·96 - 21·09·96	Tervuren	Koninklijk Museum Midden-Afrika	ÆTHIOPIA
22·03·96 - Spring 96	Antwerpen-Antwerp	Open Air M. Sculpture Middelheim	Henk Visch
22·03·96 - 16·06·96	Morlanwelz	Musée Royal de Mariemont	D'une Oeuvre l'Autre
26·03·96 - 26·05·96	Bruxelles - Brussels	Musée d'Art Ancien	In the Margins of the Book
30·03·96 - 12·05·96	Gent - Ghent	Museum van Hedendaagse Kunst	Carl de Keyzer
12·04·96 - 02·06·96	Antwerpen-Antwerp	Museum van Hedendaagse Kunst	Guillaume Bijl The Collection
20·04·96 - 26·05·96	Gent - Ghent	Museum van Hedendaagse Kunst	Dan Graham Pavilions
23·04·96 - 09·06·96	Bruxelles - Brussels	Fondation pour l'Architecture	In Praise of Simplicity
27·04·96 - 08·06·96	Charleroi	Musée des Beaux-Arts	The Liège School of Engraving
03·05·96 - 02·06·96	Gent - Ghent	Bijlokemuseum	Agnes van den Bossche
04·05·96 - 16·06·96	Oostende - Ostend	PMMK - Museum Moderne Kunst	Raoul de Keyzer
12·05·96 - 23·06·96	Deurle	Museum Dhondt-Dhaenens	Philippe Van Snick, Manfred Jade
12·05·96 - 01·09·96	Charleroi	Musée de la Photographie	The Three Grand Egyptians.
12·05·96 - 01·09·96	Charleroi	Musée de la Photographie	The Catastrophe of Bois du Cazier
Jun 96-Sep 96	Namur	Musée des Arts Anciens du Namurois	Enamels from Limousin
07·06·96 - 08·09·96	Bruxelles - Brussels	Palais des Beaux-Arts	Art in Resistance
07·06·96 - 08·09·96	Bruxelles - Brussels	Palais des Beaux-Arts	Ilya Kabakov On the Roof
07·06·96 - 31·10·96	Antwerpen-Antwerp	National Maritime Museum	The History of the Belgian Navy
15·06·96 - 29·09·96	Bruxelles - Brussels	Musée d'Art Ancien	The Dog, a Friend
15·06·96 - 29·09·96	Gent - Ghent	MIAT (Indust. Archaeology /Textiles)	Industrious and Picturesque Belgium
15·06·96 - 29·09·96	Gent - Ghent	MIAT (Indust. Archaeology /Textiles)	Man and Machine
21·06·96 - 15·09·96	Antwerpen-Antwerp	Museum van Hedendaagse Kunst	Power/Powerlessness
22·06·96 - 15·09·96	Gent - Ghent	Museum Sierkunst en Vormgeving	Ian Eisenloeffel (1876-1957)
25·06·96 - 31·12·96	Bruxelles - Brussels	Fondation pour l'Architecture	Art Deco Architecture in Brussels
29·06·96 - 15·09·96	Oostende - Ostend	PMMK - Museum Moderne Kunst	Pol Bury
29·06·96 - 15·09·96	Oostende - Ostend	PMMK - Museum Moderne Kunst	Emiel Claus Retrospective Exhibition
29·06·96 - 15·09·96	Oostende - Ostend	PMMK - Museum Moderne Kunst	Walter Leblanc
29·06·96 - 29·09·96	Antwerpen-Antwerp	Museum Plantin-Moretus	Music Books Printed in Antwerp
30·06·96 - 15·09·96	Deurle	Museum Dhondt-Dhaenens	Paul Robbrecht and Hilde Daem
06·09·96 - 05·10·96	Charleroi	Musée des Beaux-Arts	50th Anniversary of the Academy
06·09·96 - 03·11·96	Antwerpen-Antwerp	Museum van Hedendaagse Kunst	David Nash, Max Couper
07·09·96 - 08·12·96	Charleroi	Musée de la Photographie	A. Minkinnen, E. Boubat, F. Tuefferd
13·09·96 - 15·12·96	Bruxelles - Brussels	Musée d'Art Moderne	From Magritte to Magritte
20·09·96 - 08·12·96	Morlanwelz	Musée Royal de Mariemont	Colours for the Four Seasons
21·09·96 - 20·01·97	Antwerpen-Antwerp	Stedelijk Prentenkabinet	Jan Cox
22·09·96 - 27·10·96	Deurle	Museum Dhondt-Dhaenens	Rik Moens, Logos (Moniek Darge)
Autumn 96	Gent - Ghent	Museum Sierkunst en Vormgeving	Murano Glass 1900 to today
Autumn 96-Winter 96	Antwerpen-Antwerp	Museum Mayer van den Bergh	The Mayer van den Bergh Breviary
Autumn 96-Spring 97	Bruxelles - Brussels	Museum Natuurwetenschappen	Bats Masters of the Night
Oct 96-Jan 97	Namur	Musée des Arts Anciens du Namurois	Tins from the Meuse Area
04·10·96 - 08·12·96	Bruxelles - Brussels	Musée d'Art Ancien	S.O.S. Panel Paintings

Exhibitions in chronological order.

BELGIUM

DATE	CITY	MUSEUM	ARTIST/THEME
05·10·96 - 02·02·97	Oostende - Ostend	PMMK - Museum Moderne Kunst	From Ensor to Delvaux
05·10·96 - 02·02·97	Oostende - Ostend	PMMK - Museum Moderne Kunst	Etienne Elias
15·10·96 - 15·12·96	Bruxelles - Brussels	Musée d'Art Ancien	Léon Spilliaert (1881-1946)
18·10·96 - 17·01·97	Antwerpen-Antwerp	Museum Plantin-Moretus	The Moretuses
03·11·96 - 08·12·96	Deurle	Museum Dhondt-Dhaenens	Ria Pacquée, Jon Thompson
09·11·96 - 12·01·97	Charleroi	Musée des Beaux-Arts	Vasarély
22·11·96 - 12·01·97	Antwerpen-Antwerp	Museum van Hedendaagse Kunst	Marijke van Warmerdam
24·11·96 - 16·02·97	Antwerpen-Antwerp	Koninklijk Museum Schone Kunsten	Naturalism in Belgium and Europe
30·11·96 - 30·03·97	Gent - Ghent	Bijlokemuseum	Religious Art in Ghent
13·12·96 - 02·03·97	Charleroi	Musée de la Photographie	Stefan De Jaeger, Larry Fink
14·12·96 - 01·06·97	Gent - Ghent	MIAT (Indust. Archaeology /Textiles)	This is How Great-Grandmother Lived
15·12·96 - 02·03·97	Antwerpen-Antwerp	Koninklijk Museum Schone Kunsten	From a Different World

FRANCE

DATE	CITY	MUSEUM	ARTIST/THEME
until 19·05·96	Amiens	Musée de Picardie	Anne and Patrick Poirier
until 28·05·96	Toulouse	Musée Paul Dupuy	Egypt
until 31·08·96	Paris	La Cité des Sciences et de l'Industrie	Renaissance Engineers
until 31·08·96	Paris	La Cité des Sciences et de l'Industrie	Measuring and the Unmeasurable
until Sep 96	Villeneuve d'Ascq	Musée d'Art Moderne	Contemporary Art Collections
30·01·96 - 12·05·96	Paris	Cognacq-Jay Museum	The Animal, Mirror of Man
31·01·96 - 15·06·96	Paris	M. National d'Histoire Naturelle	Fantasy of Precious Stones
05·02·96 - 19·05·96	Paris	Musée d'Orsay	From Beirut to Damascus
07·02·96 - 30·06·96	Paris	Musée des Arts Décoratifs	Les Dubuffet de J. Dubuffet
15·02·96 - 12·05·96	Versailles	Château de Versailles et de Trianon	The Exotic Hunting Parties of Louis XV
16·02·96 - 12·05·96	Alençon	Musée des Beaux-Arts &Dentelle	Tribute to Michel Macréau
19·02·96 - 19·05·96	Paris	Musée d'Orsay	Offenbach
19·02·96 - 19·05·96	Paris	Musée d'Orsay	The Halévy Family (1760-1960)
23·02·96 - 27·05·96	Nîmes	Carré d'Art-Musée d'Art Contemp.	Jean-Pierre Bertrand
28·02·96 - 27·05·96	Paris	Galeries Nationales du Grand Palais	Corot (1796-1875)
01·03·96 - 05·05·96	Strasbourg	Musee d'Art Moderne et Cont.	Le Rhin, Der Rhein, De Waal
02·03·96 - 27·05·96	Nantes	Musée des Beaux Arts	Olav Christopher Jenssen
02·03·96 - 19·05·96	Agen	Musée des Beaux-Arts	F.R.A.M. Regional Project
03·03·96 - 05·06·96	Caen	Musée des Beaux-Arts	Normandy Paintings
09·03·96 - 13·05·96	Dijon	Musée des Beaux-Arts	Claudio Parmiggiani Drawings
12·03·96 - 16·06·96	Angers	Musée des Beaux-Arts	A Wallpaper Adventure
13·03·96 - 10·06·96	Paris	M. Moyen Age Thermes de Cluny	A Gothic Treasure
16·03·96 - 02·06·96	Colmar	Musée d'Unterlinden	Celtic and Gallic Treasures
20·03·96 - 27·05·96	Paris	Centre Georges Pompidou	Christian de Portzamparc
21·03·96 - 30·06·96	Orléans	Musée des Beaux-Arts	Mémoire du Nord
21·03·96 - 27·05·96	Paris	Centre Georges Pompidou	American Photography 1890-1965
Spring 96-Summer 96	Grenoble	Musée de Grenoble	Black and White Stories
22·03·96 - 02·06·96	Marseille	Cantini d'Art Moderne et Cont.	Pierre Girieud
23·03·96 - 19·05·96	Albi	Musée Toulouse-Lautrec	Bazaine and Poetry
23·03·96 - 26·05·96	Calais	M. des Beaux Arts et de la Dentelle	Diller & Scofidio Investments
23·03·96 - 28·05·96	Castres	Musée Goya	José Subira-Puig
23·03·96 - 16·06·96	Nice	M. Modern and Contemporary Art	Giovanni Anselmo
28·03·96 - 03·06·96	Saint-Etienne	Musée d'Art Moderne	Dmitrij Prigow
29·03·96 - 02·06·96	Saint-Etienne	Musée d'Art Moderne	Christian Jaccard
Apr 96-mid Jun 96	Montauban	Musée Ingres	A la Lisière du Trouble
mid Apr 96-12·06·96	Chartres	Musée des Beaux-Arts	Jacques Le Brusq
02·04·96 - 30·06·96	Paris	Musée Carnavalet	The Russians in Paris
03·04·96 - 08·07·96	Saint-Germain-en-Laye	Musée des Antiquités nationales	The Prehistoric Art of the Pyrenees
04·04·96 - 25·05·96	Limoges	FRAC Limousin	J. Grigley, FRAC Limousin
04·04·96 - 21·07·96	Paris	Musée du Petit Palais	Albrecht Dürer Engravings
05·04·96 - 23·06·96	Paris	ARC- M. Art Moderne Ville de Paris	Pierre Soulages Restrospective

Exhibitions in chronological order.

FRANCE

DATE	CITY	MUSEUM	ARTIST/THEME
05-04-96 - 05-06-96	Saint-Paul	Fondation Maeght	Germaine Richier Retrospective
05-04-96 - 08-07-96	Paris	Musée du Louvre	Recent Acquisitions
06-04-96 - 27-05-96	Dijon	Musée Archéologique de Dijon	A Story of Pot
11-04-96 - 24-06-96	Nantes	Musée des Beaux Arts	Ans, Guillard, Lemasson, Ruault
12-04-96 - 12-06-96	Bordeaux	capcMusée d'Art Contemporain	The Grande Lande Farm
12-04-96 - 12-06-96	Bordeaux	capcMusée d'Art Contemporain	Jean-Paul Thibeau
12-04-96 - 12-06-96	Bordeaux	capcMusée d'Art Contemporain	'Johannesburg: As in School'
12-04-96 - 12-06-96	Bordeaux	capcMusée d'Art Contemporain	For Hiroshima
12-04-96 - 17-06-96	Nice	Musée Matisse	La Ceramique Fauve
15-04-96 - 15-05-96	Pau	Musée National du Château de Pau	Eye-Catching Objects
15-04-96 - 28-07-96	Paris	Musée d'Orsay	Menzel (1815-1905)
16-04-96 - 15-07-96	Paris	Galeries Nationales du Grand Palais	The Romantic Years
17-04-96 - 01-07-96	Rouen	Musée des Beaux-Arts	'L'école de Roi'
18-04-96 - 16-06-96	Paris	ARC- M. Art Moderne Ville de Paris	Felix Gonzales-Torres
18-04-96 - 16-06-96	Paris	ARC- M. Art Moderne Ville de Paris	Willie Doherty
18-04-96 - 16-06-96	Paris	ARC- M. Art Moderne Ville de Paris	Nigel Rolfemid
19-04-96 - 31-08-96	Strasbourg	Musée Archéologique	De la Roche à la Hache
24-04-96 - 29-07-96	Besançon	M. des Beaux-arts et d'Archéologie	François-Marius Granet's Drawings
26-04-96 - 15-06-96	Dijon	Le Consortium	Rirkrit Tiravanija (USA)
26-04-96 - 30-06-96	Marseille	Musée des Beaux-Arts	Philippe de Champaigne
26-04-96 - 27-10-96	Strasbourg	Musée des Beaux-Arts	Italian paintings
May 96 - 31-12-96	Calais	M. des Beaux Arts et de la Dentelle	The Adventure of Lace in Calais
May 96 - Jul 96	Douai	Musée de la Chartreuse	Georges Demeny
May 96 - Jul 96	Fontainebleau	M. du château de Fontainebleau	Porcelains, earthenwares and enamels
May 96	Rennes	Musée des Beaux-Arts	Presentation permanent collection
May 96	Rennes	Musée des Beaux-Arts	Publication guide to the collection
May 96 - Dec 96	Villeneuve d'Ascq	Musée d'Art Moderne	The Masurel Donation
03-05-96 - 02-09-96	Nantes	Musée des Beaux Arts	Henry Moore
06-05-96 - 29-07-96	Paris	Centre National de la Photographie	Marc Riboud China
06-05-96 - 28-07-96	Paris	Musée Rodin	Drawings by Bourdelle
08-05-96 - 30-06-96	Paris	Centre Georges Pompidou	Picabia 1922
10-05-96 - 15-07-96	Arras	M. d'Arras Abbaye Saint-Vaast	Paysages Anglais
10-05-96 - 05-08-96	Paris	Musée du Louvre	Pisanello
11-05-96 - 30-06-96	Amiens	Musée de Picardie	Bizarre Objects
11-05-96 - 16-06-96	Bayonne	Musée Bonnat	By Invitation: Eric Decelle
11-05-96 - 01-09-96	Le Cateau-Cambrésis	Musée Matisse	Del Marle
11-05-96 - 25-05-96	Lyon	Musée des Tissus	The Art of Quilt, Treasury of Silk
13-05-96 - 30-07-96	Nancy	Musée des Beaux-Arts	Around Clodion
14-05-96 - 30-09-96	Valenciennes	Musée des Beaux-Arts	Museum under Construction
15-05-96 - 14-08-96	Avignon	Musée du Petit Palais	Architectural Drawings by Rodin
Mid May 96-18-08-96	Paris	Musée Carnavalet	Georges Aerni Parisian Façades
21-05-96 - 15-09-96	Paris	Galerie Nationale du Jeu de Paume	A Century Of English Sculpture
22-05-96 - 26-08-96	Paris	Centre Georges Pompidou	L'Informe (Anti-Formal Art)
22-05-96 - 26-08-96	Paris	Centre Georges Pompidou	Free Form The 1950s
22-05-96 - 23-09-96	Paris	Centre Georges Pompidou	Antoine Grumbach
22-05-96 - 08-01-97	Paris	M. National d'Histoire Naturelle	Exhibition of Meteorites
24-05-96 - 26-08-96	Chantilly	Musée Condé	Clouet in Chantilly
24-05-96 - 26-08-96	Paris	Musée du Louvre	Clouet at the Louvre
26-05-96 - 09-09-96	Auxerre	Abbaye Saint Germain	Jean-Pierre Risos
Jun 96-end Aug 96	Sèvres	Musée national de Céramique	Pierre Bayle, Ceramist
01-06-96 - 05-08-96	Caen	Musée des Beaux-Arts	Barry Flanagan Engravings
Jun 96-Oct 96	Caen	Musée de Normandie	Voyagers and Hermits
01-06-96 - 16-02-97	Lyon	Musée des Beaux-Arts	Treasure of Place des Terreaux
08-06-96 - 28-10-96	Agen	Musée des Beaux-Arts	Dreams of Light
14-06-96 - 15-09-96	Calais	M. des Beaux Arts et de la Dentelle	Alison Wilding Sculptures
14-06-96 - 09-09-96	Nantes	Musée des Beaux Arts	Philippe Cognée
15-06-96 - 15-09-96	Alençon	M. des Beaux-Arts et de la Dentelle	Lace

Exhibitions in chronological order.

FRANCE

DATE	CITY	MUSEUM	ARTIST/THEME
15·06·96 - 08·09·96	Bordeaux	Musée des Beaux-Arts	Greece in Revolt
15·06·96 - 22·09·96	Nîmes	Carré d'Art-Musée d'Art Cont.	Gerhard Richter
15·06·96 - 1998	Paris	M. National d'Histoire Naturelle	Natural History of Radioactivity
15·06·96 - 15·07·96	Périgueux	Musée du Périgord	Maurice Albe
17·06·96 - 15·09·96	Paris	Musée d'Orsay	Landscapes Photographs
17·06·96 - 15·09·96	Paris	Musée d'Orsay	Drawings by Fantin-Latour
20·06·96 - 03·11·96	Cherbourg	Musée Thomas Henry	Ceramics in Normandy
21·06·96 - 29·09·96	Amiens	Musée de Picardie	Russian Romanticism
21·06·96 - 28·09·96	Limoges	FRAC Limousin	M. François, FRAC Limousin
21·06·96 - 15·11·96	Reims	Musée des Beaux-Arts	Clovis and his Artistic Commemoration
21·06·96 - 08·09·96	Saint-Etienne	Musée d'Art Moderne	Mono-ha
Summer 96	Bayonne	Musée Bonnat	Works Regional Fund for Cont. Art
Summer 96	Montauban	Musée Ingres	Robert Lapoujade (1921-1993)
22·06·96 - 15·09·96	Biot	Musée National Fernand Léger	'Jean Fautrier, the hothead'
22·06·96 - 25·08·96	Caen	Musée de Normandie	Dragons and Drakkars
22·06·96 - 05·09·96	Dijon	Le Consortium	Dan van Golden (NL)
22·06·96 - 28·10·96	Dijon	Musée des Beaux-Arts	Ages and Faces of Asia
22·06·96 - 31·08·96	Lyon	Musée des Tissus	Kimonos of the Hata Family
24·06·96 - 15·09·96	Toulouse	Musée Paul Dupuy	De la Mer Chine au Tonkin
26·06·96 - 07·10·96	Paris	Centre Georges Pompidou	Gaetano Pesce
28·06·96 - 30·09·96	Antibes	Musée Picasso	1946
28·06·96 - 29·09·96	Bordeaux	capcMusée d'Art Contemporain	Annette Messager
28·06·96 - 29·09·96	Bordeaux	capcMusée d'Art Contemporain	Cindy Sherman Works 1985-1995
28·06·96 - 29·09·96	Bordeaux	capcMusée d'Art Contemporain	Tony Oursler Video Installations
28·06·96 - 28·10·96	Chartres	Musée des Beaux-Arts	Pinchus Kremegne
28·06·96 - 04·11·96	Dijon	Musée Archéologique de Dijon	Registered Designs
28·06·96 - 07·10·96	Nice	Musée Matisse	Matisse et Bonnard
29·06·96 - 18·09·96	Nice	M. Moderne et Contemporain	'Chimériques Polymères'
29·06·96 26·10·96	Angers	Musée des Beaux-Arts	Anthony Car
30·06·96 - 29·09·96	Albi	Musée Toulouse-Lautrec	From Picasso to Barcelo
Jul 96-Sep 96	Bayonne	Musée Bonnat	Treasures of English Painting
Jul 96-Oct 96	Nice	Musée Archeologique de Cimiez	Life and handicraft
Jul 96-mid Oct 96	Paris	ARC-Musée d'Art Moderne	Alexander Caldermid
Jul 96-Aug 96	Toulouse	Musée des Augustins	Le Comte de l'An Mil
03·07·96 - 21·10·96	Paris	Centre Georges Pompidou	Frederick Kiesler (1890-1965)
04·07·96 - 21·10·96	Paris	Centre Georges Pompidou	Francis Bacon
05·07·96 - 06·10·96	Castres	Musée Goya	Jumel de Noireterre
05·07·96 - end Sep 96	Marseille	Cantini d'Art Moderne et Cont.	Auguste Chabaud
06·07·96 - 28·10·96	Honfleur	Musée Eugène Boudin	Still-Life Evolution in the 19th Century
10·07·96 - 30·09·96	Paris	Centre Georges Pompidou	Contemporary Designs Basle Museum
mid Jul 96-end Oct 96	Montpellier	Musée Fabre	On Nature
29·07·96 - 02·12·96	Besançon	M. Beaux-Arts et d'Archéologie	Homage to Four Forgotten Sculptors
07·08·96 - 04·11·96	Besançon	M. Beaux-Arts et d'Archéologie	Drawings of the Barbizon School
Sep 96-Jan 97	Chantilly	Musée Condé	Watteau and his circle in the Collections
Sep 96-Nov 96	Chartres	Musée des Beaux-Arts	Marceau
Sep 96-Nov 96	Paris	Musée de la Marine	The Clippers
Sep 96-Dec 96	Paris	Musée Rodin	Marbles by Thyssen
07·09·96 - 01·12·96	Colmar	Musée d'Unterlinden	Otto Dix and the Old Masters
mid Sep 96-Jan 97	Montauban	Musée Ingres	Xavier Krebs & Jean Suzanne
15·09·96 - Oct 96	Dijon	Le Consortium	Liam Gillick (GB)
16·09·96 - 18·11·96	Nancy	Musée des Beaux-Arts	Henri-Leopold Lévy (1840-1904)
17·09·96 - 09·12·96	Paris	Galeries Nationales du Grand Palais	Nara
18·09·96 - 21·10·96	Paris	Centre National de la Photographie	Umbo
18·09·96 - 21·10·96	Paris	Centre National de la Photographie	Moins Trente 96
18·09·96 - 21·10·96	Paris	Centre National de la Photographie	Prix Niépce 96
18·09·96 - 16·12·96	Toulouse	Musée des Augustins	The Gold of the Andes
19·09·96 - 01·12·96	Lyon	Musée des Beaux-Arts	New acquisitions & restored works

Exhibitions in chronological order.

FRANCE

DATE	CITY	MUSEUM	ARTIST/THEME
20·09·96 - 25·11·96	Arras	Ancienne Abbaye Saint-Vaast	La Tenture de la 'Vie de la Vièrge'
20·09·96 - 30·11·96	Calais	M. Beaux Arts et de la Dentelle	Felix Del Marle
20·09·96 - 10·01·97	Nantes	Musée des Beaux Arts	Troels Wörsel
Autumn 96	Douai	Musée de la Chartreuse	Henri Edmond Cross
Autumn 96	Paris	Musée Picasso	Engravings by Picasso
24·09·96 - 01·01·97	Paris	Galeries Nationales du Grand Palais	Manet, Van Gogh, Gauguin, Matisse
27·09·96 - 01·12·96	Saint-Etienne	Musée d'Art Moderne	Philippe Favier
28·09·96 - 16·12·96	Grenoble	Musée de Grenoble	Morris Louis
28·09·96 - 09·12·96	Nice	M. Moderne et Contemporain	Tom Wesselmann
28·09·96 - 19·01·97	Villeneuve d'Ascq	Musée d'Art Moderne	Alighiero Boetti (1940-1994)
30·09·96 - 30·01·97	Marseille	Musée des Beaux-Arts	Rodin
Oct 96-Jan 97	Alençon	M. Beaux-Arts et de la Dentelle	Cambodia
Oct 96-Nov 96	Chartres	Musée des Beaux-Arts	Robert Nicoidsky
Oct 96-Mar 97	Orléans	Musée des Beaux-Arts	Un Automne Italien
Oct 96-08·01·97	Paris	ARC-Musée d'Art Moderne	Georg Baselitz
Oct 96-Jan 97	Pau	Musée National du Château de Pau	Ramiro Arrue
Oct 96	Rennes	Musée des Beaux-Arts	Gauguin's 'La ronde des petites ...'
Oct 96-Dec 96	Sèvres	Musée National de Céramique	Gard Pottery 18th-20th Century
03·10·96 - 03·11·96	Limoges	FRAC Limousin	Martine Aballéa, Chapelle saint Libéral
04·10·96 - 06·01·97	Paris	Musée du Louvre	Barye
05·10·96 - 05·01·97	Nice	Musée des Beaux-Arts	Wine, vineyards, ...
07·10·96 - Jan 97	Paris	Musée d'Orsay	Haviland Foundation Photographs
07·10·96 - Jan 97	Paris	Musée d'Orsay	New Acquisitions
07·10·96 - Jan 97	Paris	Musée d'Orsay	Charles Le Coeur
08·10·96 - 01·12·96	Paris	Galerie Nationale du Jeu de Paume	Sean Scully and Jean-Marc Bustamante
14·10·96 - 20·01·97	Toulouse	Musée des Augustins	18th-Century Sculpture from Toulouse
15·10·96 - 20·01·97	Paris	Musée Carnavalet	Madame de Sévigné
15·10·96 - 20·01·97	Paris	Galeries Nationales du Grand Palais	Portraits by Picasso
17·10·96 - 02·02·97	Versailles	Château de Versailles et de Trianon	Morceaux de Réception
18·10·96 - 15·12·96	Strasbourg	Art Moderne et Contemporain	Joseph Beuys Herbert Zangs
18·10·96 - 09·02·97	Strasbourg	Art Moderne et Contemporain	Eugene Carriere
20·10·96 - 09·01·97	Périgueux	Musée du Périgord	Jean Marc Rubio
21·10·96 - 20·01·97	Paris	Musée du Louvre	Recent Acquisitions
Autumn 96	Lyon	Musée des Tissus	Church Vestments of the 19th Century
23·10·96 - 23·02·97	Paris	Musée des Arts Décoratifs	A Vision of the City in Toys
25·10·96 - Jan 97	Bordeaux	capcMusée d'Art Contemporain	Jean-Charles Blais Retrospective
25·10·96 - 15·02·97	Nantes	Musée des Beaux Arts	Paul-Armand Gette
25·10·96 - 02·02·97	Nîmes	Carré d'Art-Art Contemporain	Nîmes in the Mirror of its Museums
28·10·96 - 06·01·97	Bordeaux	Musée des Arts Décoratifs	A Glance at the Basque Region
28·10·96 - 28·01·97	Paris	Musée Carnavalet	Mois de la Photo 96
Nov 96-Feb 97	Caen	Musée des Beaux-Arts	Italian Contemporary Painting
Nov 96-Jan 97	Chartres	Musée des Beaux-Arts	Ofer Lellouche
Nov 96-Dec 96	Dijon	Le Consortium	Pierre Huyghe (F)
Nov 96-Dec 96	Le Cateau-Cambrésis	Musée Matisse	Illuminated Drawings
Nov 96-Jan 97	Valenciennes	Musée des Beaux-Arts	François Dilasser
01·11·96 - Nov 96	Biot	Musée National Fernand Léger	Drawings from the Collection
06·11·96 - 08·01·97	Nice	Musée Matisse	Trois Oeuvres à l'Étude
06·11·96 - 20·01·97	Paris	Centre National de la Photographie	Peter Beard Africa
14·11·96 - 02·03·97	Paris	Musée du Petit Palais	The Forbidden City
15·11·96 - 31·01·97	Agen	Musée des Beaux-Arts	Julio Villani
15·11·96 - 15·02·97	Amiens	Musée de Picardie	The Marionettes of Picardy
23·11·96 - 03·03·97	Tours	Musée des Beaux-Arts	Gothic and the Renaissance
Dec 96-Feb 97	Chartres	Musée des Beaux-Arts	An Italian Autumn
Dec 96-Apr 97	Orléans	Musée des Beaux-Arts	Romanticism
Dec 96-Feb 97	Paris	Musée de la Marine	The Salon de la Marine
05·12·96 - 09·01·97	Périgueux	Musée du Périgord	'Salon du Livre Gourmand'
13·12·96 - 17·03·97	Dijon	Musée des Beaux-Arts	Bernard Plossu Photographer

Exhibitions in chronological order.

FRANCE

DATE	CITY	MUSEUM	ARTIST/THEME
14·12·96 - end Feb 97	Calais	M. Beaux Arts et de la Dentelle	The Hand-Made Lace Collection
16·12·96 - 15·02·97	Paris	Galerie Nationale du Jeu de Paume	Jesus-Raphael Soto
18·12·96 - 16·03·97	Saint-Etienne	Musée d'Art Moderne	A View on History 1940-1968
1997	Grenoble	Musée de Grenoble	Signac and the Liberation of Colour
1997	Nice	Musée Matisse	La Côte d'Azur et la Modernité
1997	Toulouse	Musée des Augustins	Henri Rousseau An Orientalist Painter
Jan 97-Apr 97	Paris	ARC-Musée d'Art Moderne	The 1930s in Europe
23·01·97 - 06·04·97	Lyon	Musée des Beaux-Arts	Kees van Dongen
Feb 97-Jun 97	Paris	Musée d'Orsay	Théophile Gautier
Feb 97-Jun 97	Paris	Musée d'Orsay	Orsay Museum's Collection of Medals
11·02·97 - 02·06·97	Paris	Galeries Nationales du Grand Palais	Khmer Art
05·03·97 - 08·07·97	Paris	Galeries Nationales du Grand Palais	'Masterpieces' of the MNATP? or Saura?
18·03·97 - 01·07·97	Paris	Galeries Nationales du Grand Palais	France-Belgium
Spring 97	Paris	Musée Picasso	Picasso and Photography III
21·04·97 - 21·07·97	Paris	Musée du Louvre	Centenary of the Friends of the Louvre
16·05·97 - 31·08·97	Tours	Musée des Beaux-Arts	150 Years of Freemasonry in Tours

GERMANY

DATE	CITY	MUSEUM	ARTIST/THEME
until 02·06·96	Berlin	Museum für Völkerkunde	Huichun Chinese Medicine
until 14·07·96	Köln - Cologne	Museum für Angewandte Kunst	Art on Billboards
until 31·07·96	Berlin	Kunstgewerbemuseum	The Domed Reliquary/Guelph Treasure
until 08·09·96	Karlsruhe	Staatliche Kunsthalle Karlsruhe	Children of Today Play Karlsruhe People
until Oct 96	Berlin	Museum für Völkerkunde	Pre-Columbian Stone Sculpture
09·05·93 - 07·07·96	München - Munich	Villa Stuck	Franz von Stuck and Photography
20·03·95 - 09·06·96	Freiburg im Breisgau	Augustinermuseum	New Acquistions
24·09·95 - Summer 96	Düsseldorf	M. Düsseldorf im Ehrenhof	Paper Sculptures
07·10·95 - 30·08·96	Paderborn	Archäologie - M.in der Kaiserpfalz	Excavation Campaign
05·11·95 - 14·07·96	Hannover	Niedersächsisches M. Hannover	Given to be Shown
14·12·95 - 28·07·96	Nürnberg-Nuremberg	Germanisches Nationalmuseum	Faces of Bourgeois Art and Culture
19·01·96 - end 96	Berlin	Neue Gesellschaft für Bildende Kunst	Art instead of Advertising
27·01·96 - 19·05·96	Weil am Rhein	Vitra Design Museum	Rooms in Time
Feb 96-Apr 97	Göttingen	Städtische Museum Göttingen	Fighting Against Conflagration
04·02·96 - 05·05·96	Kassel	Museum Fridericianum Kassel	Collaborations
14·02·96 - 05·05·96	Hannover	Historisches Museum	Bees-Plants-Man
15·02·96 - 02·07·96	Mannheim	Reiß-Museum	Zemann Portraits
23·02·96 - 12·05·96	Bonn	Kunst- und Ausstellungshalle Bund.	Claes Oldenburg An Anthology
23·02·96 - 05·05·96	Köln - Cologne	Wallraf-Richartz-Museum	The Play of Colour Armand
24·02·96 - 02·06·96	Karlsruhe	Badisches Landesmuseum Karlsruhe	Delphi the Oracle
29·02·96 - 16·06·96	Bonn	Kunstmuseum Bonn/Temp. Ex. Area	China!
08·03·96 - 30·09·96	Berlin	Museum für Verkehr und Technik	Resurfaced
08·03·96 - 02·06·96	Bremen	Übersee-Museum Bremen	Design Time Bremen 1996
08·03·96 - 23·06·96	Dresden	Skulpturensammlung - Staatliche K.	Renaissance and Baroque Bronzes
09·03·96 - 12·05·96	Frankfurt am Main	Schirn Kunsthalle	Photo Prospect '96
13·03·96 - 27·05·96	Bonn	Rheinisches Landesmuseum Bonn	West Choir - East Portal
13·03·96 - 09·06·96	Karlsruhe	Badisches Landesmuseum Karlsruhe	Saved for Baden
14·03·96 - 19·05·96	Aachen	Suermondt Ludwig Museum/Graphic	Erich Müller-Kraus (1911-1967)
14·03·96 - 07·07·96	Nürnberg-Nuremberg	Germanisches Nationalmuseum	Ways of Abstraction
16·03·96 - 19·05·96	Ludwigshafen	Wilhelm-Hack-Museum	Rembrandt Fecit The Etchings
17·03·96 - 02·06·96	Leverkusen	M. Leverkusen Schloß Morsbroich	Rudolf Schoofs
17·03·96 - 26·05·96	Mönchengladbach	Schloß Rheydt	'Spitzenkräfte'
17·03·96 - 19·05·96	Ulm	Ulmer Museum	Verre Églomisé Pictures
18·03·96 - Jun 96	Dresden	Gemäldegalerie Neue Meister	Theodor Rosenhauer
20·03·96 - 09·06·96	Freiburg im Breisgau	Augustinermuseum	Late Baroque Esquisses of Oil Painting
20·03·96 - 30·06·96	Köln - Cologne	Museum für Ostasiatische Kunst	Chinese Painting and Graphic Arts
21·03·96 - 27·05·96	Darmstadt	Hessisches Landesmuseum Darmstadt	The End of the World

Exhibitions in chronological order.

Exhibitions in chronological order.

GERMANY			
DATE	**CITY**	**MUSEUM**	**ARTIST/THEME**
04·05·96 - 01·09·96	Stuttgart	Staatsgalerie Stuttgart	500 Years of Art on Paper
04·05·96 - 13·10·96	Stuttgart	Staatsgalerie Stuttgart	Italian Gothic Painting
04·05·96 - 13·10·96	Stuttgart	Staatsgalerie Stuttgart	German Painting
04·05·96 - onwards	Stuttgart	Staatsgalerie Stuttgart	The Marcel Duchamp Cabinet
05·05·96 - 30·06·96	Göttingen	Städtische Museum Göttingen	Ausglass
05·05·96 - 16·06·96	Kiel	Kunsthalle zu Kiel	Ekkekard Thieme Prints
08·05·96 - 23·06·96	Bielefeld	K.Bielefeld (Richard-Kaselowsky - H.)	Truong Tan
08·05·96 - 07·07·96	Darmstadt	Hessisches Landesm. Darmstadt	Colour Prints of the 18th Century
08·05·96 - 30·10·96	Frankfurt am Main	Städelsches Kunstinstitut/Galerie	Hans Steinbrenner Sculptures
10·05·96 - 24·07·96	Aachen	Suermondt Ludwig Museum	Raoul Ubac
10·05·96 - Sep 96	Aachen	Ludwig Forum für Int. Kunst	Chinese Art from Taiwan
10·05·96 - 28·07·96	Berlin	Kunstgewerbemuseum	From the Workshops
10·05·96 - 25·08·96	Bonn	Kunst- und Ausstellungshalle Bund.	The Sacred Art of Tibet
10·05·96 - 02·06·96	Esslingen	G. der Stadt Esslingen / Villa Merkel	Annual Exhibition of the Artists' Guild
10·05·96 - 23·06·96	Hamburg	Museum für Kunst und Gewerbe	Alfred Steffen Portraits
10·05·96 - 04·08·96	München - Munich	Haus der Kunst	The Russian Avant-Garde
11·05·96 - 09·06·96	Baden-Baden	Staatliche Kunsthalle Baden-Baden	The Society of Friends of Young Art
12·05·96 - 21·07·96	Dortmund	Museum am Ostwall	Gerrit Thomas Rietveld
12·05·96 - 15·09·96	Mönchengladbach	Städtisches Museum Abteiberg	Paul Bradley
12·05·96 - 07·07·96	Schwerin	Schwerin-, Schlösser und Gärten	Quicksand
13·05·96 - 21·07·96	Bonn	Bonner Kunstverein	The Calculability of the World
15·05·96 - 01·09·96	Dresden	Skulpturensammlung - Dresden	Michael Schoenholtz
16·05·96 - 07·07·96	Düsseldorf	Kunsthalle Düsseldorf	Happy End
19·05·96 - 28·07·96	Münster	M. Kunst und Kulturgeschichte	Morris Louis
19·05·96 - 23·06·96	Regensburg	Museum Ostdeutsche Galerie	Reiner Zitta
19·05·96 - 14·07·96	Saarbrücken	Saarland Museum	The Early Renaissance in Italy
23·05·96 - 28·07·96	Essen	Museum Folkwang Essen	Olivo Barbieri
23·05·96 - 20·10·96	Frankfurt am Main	Museum für Kunsthandwerk	The Treasure House of Kuwait
23·05·96 - 30·06·96	Nürnberg-Nuremberg	Kunsthalle Nürnberg	Hans Peter Reuter
24·05·96 - 30·09·96	Berlin	Neue Nationalgalerie	Georg Baselitz
24·05·96 - 20·10·96	Berlin	Museum für Verkehr und Technik	Mill Models
24·05·96 - 31·08·96	Bremen	Focke-Museum	The Key and the Eagle
24·05·96 - 28·07·96	München - Munich	Haus der Kunst	Umbo From Bauhaus to Photo-j.
25·05·96 - 11·08·96	Düsseldorf	Kunstm. Düsseldorf im Ehrenhof	Otto Piene Retrospective
25·05·96 - 21·07·96	Frankfurt am Main	Portikus Frankfurt am Main	Ulrike Grossarth
25·05·96 - Nov 96	Weil am Rhein	Vitra Design Museum	Scandinavian Design
29·05·96 - 04·08·96	Aachen	Suermondt Ludwig Museum/Graphic	Expressionist Watercolours
30·05·96 - 14·07·96	Ludwigshafen	Wilhelm-Hack-Museum	Young Artists Promotion Award
31·05·96 - 09·06·96	Esslingen	G. Stadt Esslingen / Bahnwärterhaus	Inga Svala Thorsdottir/Vanessa Beecroft
Jun 96 - Jul 96	Aachen	Suermondt Ludwig Museum/Studio	Anke Erlenhoff
Jun 96	Berlin	Neue Gesellschaft für Bildende Kunst	Beth B. Under Lock and Key
Jun 96 - Sep 96	Frankfurt am Main	Städelsches Kunstinst. Städtische G.	Henri Matisse
Jun 96	Hamburg	M. Kunst und Gewerbe Hamburg	Uwe Loesch Communication Design
Jun 96 - Dec 96	Hannover	Niedersächsisches M. Hannover	The Department of Natural History
Jun 96 - 06·10·96	Nürnberg-Nuremberg	Germanisches Nationalmuseum	Past, Present, Future
01·06·96 - 25·08·96	Köln - Cologne	Museum Ludwig	The Expressionists
02·06·96 - 25·08·96	Bremen	Übersee-Museum Bremen	Ghosts, Mummies and Exotics
02·06·96 - 18·08·96	Kiel	Kunsthalle zu Kiel	'Ente Gut - Alles Gut'
02·06·96 - 14·07·96	Lübeck	Overbeck-Gesellschaft (Cont. Art)	Carla Accardi Paintings
04·06·96 - 18·08·96	Aachen	Ludwig Forum Int. Kunst	'Massivfragil'
04·06·96 - 27·10·96	Köln - Cologne	Römisch-Germanisches Museum	Tu Felix Agrippina
05·06·96 - Spring 98	Bonn	Kunst- und Ausstellungshalle Bundes.	Future Garden
07·06·96 - 03·09·96	Berlin	Deutsches Historisches Museum	Art and Power
07·06·96 - 07·07·96	Esslingen	G. der Stadt Esslingen / Villa Merkel	Esslingen Art Society
08·06·96 - 01·09·96	Frankfurt am Main	Schirn Kunsthalle	Lucio Fontana
09·06·96 - 17·07·96	Bielefeld	K. Bielefeld (Richard-Kaselowsky-H.)	Langlands + Bell
09·06·96 - 01·09·96	Saarbrücken	Saarland Museum	Martin Assig Pictures and Drawings

Exhibitions in chronological order.

GERMANY

DATE	CITY	MUSEUM	ARTIST/THEME
11·06·96 - 01·09·96	Bonn	Rheinisches Landesmuseum Bonn	The Franks and the Orient
13·06·96 - 11·08·96	Ludwigshafen	Wilhelm-Hack-Museum	Brancusi Photographs
14·06·96 - 12·01·97	Frankfurt am Main	Museum für Moderne Kunst	Change of Scene X
14·06·96 - 28·07·96	Karlsruhe	Staatliche Kunsthalle Karlsruhe	Watercolour Masterpieces 1800-1850
15·06·96 - 21·07·96	Berlin	Neue Gesellschaft für Bildende Kunst	A Monument to Bakunini
15·06·96 - 06·10·96	Leverkusen	M. Leverkusen Schloß Morsbroich	Works from the Graphics Collection
16·06·96 - 08·09·96	Chemnitz	Städtische Kunstsammlungen	Lyonel Feininger (1871-1956)
17·06·96 - 09·08·96	Saarbrücken	Saarland Museum	Max Liebermann
20·06·96 - 18·08·96	Frankfurt am Main	Museum für Kunsthandwerk	Cont. German Fashion Photography
Summer 96	Berlin	Bauhaus-Archiv / M. für Gestaltung	Max Peiffer-Watenphul
end Jun 96	Bonn	Kunstmuseum Bonn/Temp. Exh.	The Art Award of the Banks
22·06·96 - 01·09·96	Baden-Baden	Staatliche Kunsthalle Baden-Baden	African Art from Han Coray Collection
23·06·96 - 18·08·96	Kiel	Kunsthalle zu Kiel	'Doppelt Haut - Double Skin'
23·06·96 - 18·08·96	Kiel	Kunsthalle zu Kiel	Tattoo
23·06·96 - 01·09·96	Leverkusen	M. Leverkusen Schloß Morsbroich	Mic Enneper the Arsenal 1987-1996
23·06·96 - 06·10·96	Ulm	Ulmer Museum	The Romans on the Danube and Illner
26·06·96 - 18.08.96	Bonn	Kunstmuseum Bonn/Temp. Exh.	Willem de Kooning
26·06·96 - 08·09·96	München - Munich	Lenbachhaus	Mel Bochner Thought Made Visible
28·06·96 - 22·09·96	Bonn	Kunstmuseum Bonn/Graphic Exh.	Picasso Illustrated Books
28·06·96 - 01·09·96	Freiburg im Breisgau	Augustinermuseum	Saved for Baden
29·06·96 - 06·10·96	Düsseldorf	Kunstsamml. Nordrhein-Westfalen	Daniel Buren
29·06·96 - 01·09·96	Frankfurt am Main	Deutsches Architektur-Museum	Erich Buchholz
29·06·96 - 01·09·96	Frankfurt am Main	Deutsches Architektur-Museum	Film Architecture
29·06·96 - 01·09·96	Frankfurt am Main	Deutsches Architektur-Museum	Berlin Housing Architecture
29·06·96 - 08·09·96	Stuttgart	Staatsgalerie Stuttgart	The Graphic Art of Barnett Newman
30·06·96 - 11·08·96	Essen	Museum Folkwang Essen	Pedro Cabrita Reis
30·06·96 - 01·09·96	Mainz	Landesmuseum Mainz	Media-Museum/Cultural Summer 1996
30·06·96 - 25·08·96	Ulm	Ulmer Museum	Maria Lassnig Drawings/Watercolours
Jul 96-Oct 96	Köln - Cologne	Römisch-Germanisches Museum	Roman Silver
Jul 96-Sep 96	Mainz	Gutenberg-Museum Mainz	Mechtild Lobisch Cont. Bookbinding
05·07·96 - 12·01·97	Bonn	Kunst- und Ausstellungshalle Bundes.	The Great Collections IV
05·07·96 - 08·09·96	Hamburg	Hamburger Kunsthalle	The Great Draughtsmen
05·07·96 - 15·09·96	München - Munich	Kunsthalle der Hypo-Kulturstiftung	American Art After 1960
07·07·96 - 18·08·96	Regensburg	Museum Ostdeutsche Galerie	Helmut Rieger Retrospective
08·07·96 - 15·09·96	Dresden	Galerie Neue Meister	El Greco to Mondrian
10·07·96 - 01·09·96	Mainz	Landesmuseum Mainz	Erwin Wortelkamp
11·07·96 - 25·08·96	Nürnberg-Nuremberg	Kunsthalle Nürnberg	Tracking the Thoughts
13·07·96 - 18·08·96	Duisburg	Wilhelm Lehmbruck M. Duisburg	New Works Duisburg Artists' Group
14·07·96 - 01·09·96	Göttingen	Städtische Museum Göttingen	The Ball Is Spherical
17·07·96 - 06·10·96	München - Munich	Städtische Galerie im Lenbachhaus	Olaf Metzel
18·07·96 - 22·09·96	Mönchengladbach	Schloß Rheydt	The Neuenhofer Collection
20·07·96 - 06·10·96	Mannheim	Reiß-Museum	The Children of Bombay
21·07·96 - 15·09·96	Esslingen	Galerie der Stadt Esslingen / Villa	C. Marclay, P. Rist, R. Signer, J. Tinguely
21·07·96 - 29·09·96	Esslingen	G. Stadt Esslingen / Bahnwärterhaus	Eran Schaerf
21·07·96 - 15·09·96	Schwerin	Staatliches Museum Schwerin	Mail Art in Eastern Europe
25·07·96 - 29·09·96	München - Munich	Villa Stuck	Warhol, Basquiat, Clemente
25·07·96 - 22·09·96	Nürnberg-Nuremberg	Germanisches Nationalmuseum	With Level and Compass
27·07·96 - 01·09·96	Berlin	Neue Gesellschaft für Bildende Kunst	Félix González-Torres (1957-1996)
27·07·96 - 22·09·96	Frankfurt am Main	Portikus Frankfurt am Main	N.N.
27·07·96 - 01·09·96	Ludwigshafen	Wilhelm-Hack-Museum	Alan Reynolds Retrospective Show
28·07·96 - 08·09·96	Bielefeld	K. Bielefeld (Richard-Kaselowsky-H.)	'New Abstraction'
28·07·96 - 28·08·96	Lübeck	Overbeck-Gesellschaft Cont. Art	Sigurdur Gudmundsson Painting
30·07·96 - 15·09·96	Bonn	Bonner Kunstverein	Bon Direct II
31·07·96 - 25·08·96	Dortmund	Museum am Ostwall	Bernhard Hoetger (1874-1949)
31·07·96 - 15·09·96	Leipzig	M. der Bildenden Künste Leipzig	Karl Schmidt-Rotluff
Aug 96	Aachen	Suermondt Ludwig Museum	Ritzi Jacobi
Aug 96	Bremen	Übersee-Museum Bremen	The New Totem Pole is Produced

Exhibitions in chronological order.

GERMANY

DATE	CITY	MUSEUM	ARTIST/THEME
Aug 96-Sep 96	Hamburg	M. Kunst und Gewerbe Hamburg	Edgar Lissel Houses of God
03·08·96 - 03·11·96	Stuttgart	Staatsgalerie Stuttgart	Maria Nordman Sculpture/City
04·08·96 - 30·10·96	Dresden	Porzellansammlung	Johann Gregorius Höroldt
08·08·96 - 06·10·96	Essen	Museum Folkwang Essen	Biedermeier and Realism1
10·08·96 - 20·10·96	Goslar	Mönchehaus- M. moderne Kunst	Georges Braque
11·08·96 - 29·12·96	Mönchengladbach	Schloß Rheydt	Hans Rilke
14·08·96 - 29·09·96	Leipzig	M. der Bildenden Künste Leipzig	Picasso Lithographs
15·08·96 - 27·10·96	Aachen	Suermondt Ludwig M. / Graphic	Mila Wirtz-Getz
17·08·96 - 16·01·97	Berlin	Neue Gesellschaft für Bildende Kunst	The Best Years
21·08·96 - 20·10·96	Aachen	Suermondt Ludwig Museum/Studio	Stoelben Camera Obscura
22·08·96 - 27·10·96	Ludwigshafen	Wilhelm-Hack-Museum	Hannelore Landrock-Schumann
23·08·96 - 08·12·96	Köln - Cologne	M. Angewandte Kunst	Magnificent Empire of the Czars
23·08·96 - 20·10·96	München - Munich	Haus der Kunst	Imi Knoebel Work Overview
24·08·96 - 17·11·96	Hannover	Historisches Museum	Lower Saxony
25·08·96 - 06·10·96	Essen	Museum Folkwang Essen	Photography in North Rhine-Westphalia
25·08·96 - 13·10·96	Kiel	Kunsthalle zu Kiel	Gustav Kluge
29·08·96 03·11·96	Nürnberg-Nuremberg	Germanisches Nationalmuseum	Eberhard Fiebig Works and Documents
Sep 96 - Oct 96	Aachen	Suermondt Ludwig Museum	Frank Weidenbach
Sep 96 - Oct 96	Berlin	Berlinische Galerie M. Mod. Kunst	Works by Young Berlin Artists
Sep 96 - Oct 96	Braunschweig	Herzog Anton Ulrich Museum	Prague Cabinet Painting around 1700
Sep 96 - Oct 96	Chemnitz	Städtische Kunstsammlungen	Painting/Sculpture from the Lühl Coll.
Sep 96 - Oct 96	Hamburg	M. Kunst und Gewerbe Hamburg	A.T. Schaefer Places of Colour
begin Sep 96- Nov 96	Düsseldorf	M. Düsseldorf im Ehrenhof	Bertram Jesdinsky
01·09·96 - 03·11·96	Duisburg	Wilhelm Lehmbruck M. Mod. Sculp.	Mario Merz The Igloo
01·09·96 - 06·10·96	Essen	Museum Folkwang Essen	Positions
01·09·96 - 10·11·96	Münster	M. Kunst und Kulturgeschichte	The Tom Ring Family of Painters
01·09·96 - 13·10·96	Ulm	Ulmer Museum	Andy Warhol
05·09·96 - 20·10·96	Berlin	Neue Gesellschaft für Bildende Kunst	Family of Man
06·09·96 - 27·10·96	Aachen	Ludwig Forum Int. Kunst	Transfer Italy
06·09·96 - 17.11.96	Bonn	Kunstmuseum Bonn/Temp. Exh.	The Dorothea von Stetten Art Award
06·09·96 - 17·11·96	Hamburg	M. Kunst und Gewerbe Hamburg	Hamburg Faience
06·09·96 - 17·11·96	Hamburg	M. Kunst und Gewerbe Hamburg	Japanese Laquer Pictures
06·09·96 - 17·11·96	Köln - Cologne	Museum Ludwig	Benjamin Katz Living with Artists
07·09·96 - 13·10·96	Berlin	Neue Gesellschaft für Bildende Kunst	Walter Niedermeyer
08·09·96 - 20·10·96	Bremen	Übersee-Museum Bremen	Tales of Coffee, Cotton, Rundown Boots
08·09·96 - 06·01·97	Mannheim	Reiß-Museum	The Franks The Pioneers of Europe
11·09·96 - 27·10·96	Bielefeld	K. Bielefeld (Richard-Kaselowsky-H.)	Gina Lee Felber Photographs
13·09·96 - 17·11·96	Hamburg	M. Kunst und Gewerbe Hamburg	Yves Saint Laurent
13·09·96 - 27·11·96	Hamburg	M. Kunst und Gewerbe Hamburg	The Stranger in Art
14·09·96 - 01·12·96	Ludwigshafen	Wilhelm-Hack-Museum	Andy Warhol
15·09·96 - 17·11·96	Darmstadt	Hessisches Landesmuseum Darmstadt	Christian Boltanski An Installation
15·09·96 - 15·12·96	Dortmund	Museum am Ostwall	From 'Die Brücke' to 'Der Blauer Reiter'
15·09·96 - 27·10·96	Göttingen	Städtische Museum Göttingen	55 000 Years Ago
15·09·96 - 20·10·96	Lübeck	Overbeck-Gesellschaft Cont. Art	Young Art International 1996
18·09·96 - 17·11·96	Köln - Cologne	Museum Ludwig	The Speck Collection
19·09·96 - 17·11·96	Bielefeld	K.Bielefeld (Richard-Kaselowsky-H.)	Mankind and Nature in 19th Century
19·09·96 - 01·12·96	Nürnberg-Nuremberg	Kunsthalle Nürnberg	Tadeusz Kantor
20·09·96 - 08·12·96	Frankfurt am Main	Schirn Kunsthalle	Sean Scully Twenty Years, 1976 - 1995
20·09·96 - 01·12·96	Hamburg	Hamburger Kunsthalle	Georg Hinz The Art Chamber Shelf
21·09·96 - 24·11·96	Frankfurt am Main	Deutsches Architektur-Museum	Architecture in the 20th Century
21·09·96 - 24·11·96	Frankfurt am Main	Deutsches Architektur-Museum	Architecture for All the Senses
22·09·96 - 01·01·97	Berlin	Brücke-Museum	Max Pechstein
22·09·96 - 13·10·96	Esslingen	G. Stadt Esslingen / Villa Merkel	New Acq. to the Graphic Collection
Autumn 96-mid 97	Düsseldorf	M. Düsseldorf im Ehrenhof	The Seventh Year Children's Pictures
Autumn 96	Frankfurt am Main	Städelsches K. und Städtische Galerie	'Frankfurter Zugänge'
Autumn 96-Winter 96	Frankfurt am Main	Städelsches K. und Städtische Galerie	The Woodcut
Autumn 96	Hamburg	M. für Kunst und Gewerbe Hamburg	Signs of Friendship

Exhibitions in chronological order.

GERMANY

DATE	CITY	MUSEUM	ARTIST/THEME
22·09·96 - 27·10·96	Mainz	Landesmuseum Mainz	Sinje Dillenkofer Photo Objects
22·09·96 - 03·11·96	Saarbrücken	Saarland Museum	Drawings from Tuscany
24·09·96 - 29·09·96	Bonn	Bonner Kunstverein	Videonale VII
24·09·96 - 27·10·96	Mainz	Landesmuseum Mainz	Käthe Kollwitz
25·09·96 - 18·12·96	Frankfurt am Main	Städelsches K. und Städtische Galerie	The Second Russian Avant-Garde
25·09·96 - 17·11·96	München - Munich	Lenbachhaus	Heimrad Prem (1934-1978)
27·09·96 - 10·11·96	Bonn	Kunst- und Ausstellungshalle Bundes.	Art from Austria 1896-1996
28·09·96 - 24·11·96	Frankfurt am Main	Portikus Frankfurt am Main	Franz Ackermann
28·09·96 - 24·11·96	Stuttgart	Staatsgalerie Stuttgart	Froehlich Foundation
30·09·96 - 08·12·96	Dresden	Gemäldegalerie Neue Meister	Oskar Kokoschka and Dresden
Oct 96-Nov 96	Aachen	Suermondt Ludwig Museum/Exh.	Alf Schuler
Oct 96-Nov 96	Freiburg im Breisgau	Augustinermuseum	Henri de Toulouse-Lautrec
Oct 96-Nov 96	Hamburg	M. Kunst und Gewerbe Hamburg	Klaus Elle
Oct 96-Dec 96	Köln - Cologne	Josef-Haubrich-Kunsthalle	Star Trek The Exhibition
Oct 96-Dec 96	Mainz	Gutenberg-Museum Mainz	Bülent Erkmen
Oct 96-Jan 97	München - Munich	Die Neue Sammlung	Applied Art of Today Danner Award
Oct 96 onwards	Schwerin	M. Schwerin-K., Schlösser und Gärten	Sigmar Polke
Oct 96-Nov 96	Stuttgart	Galerie der Stadt Stuttgart	Camill Leberer
02·10·96 - 05·01·97	Frankfurt am Main	Schirn Kunsthalle	Ferdinand Hodler
03·10·96 - 24·11·96	Nürnberg-Nuremberg	Germanisches Nationalmuseum	Johann Christoph Erhard
04·10·96 - 06·01·97	München - Munich	Kunsthalle der Hypo-Kulturstiftung	Kingdoms along the River Nile
06·10·96 - 30·03·97	Düsseldorf	Museum Düsseldorf im Ehrenhof	In View of the Everyday
06·10·96 - 07·01·97	Mönchengladbach	Städtisches Museum Abteiberg	Gundi Berghold
10·10·96 - 10·12·96	Berlin	Deutsches Historisches Museum	Vice Versa
11·10·96 - mid Feb 97	Karlsruhe	Staatliche Kunsthalle Karlsruhe	Moritz von Schwind
11·10·96 - mid 1997	Karlsruhe	Staatliche Kunsthalle Karlsruhe	Fairy Tale Games
12·10·96 - 05·01·97	Stuttgart	Staatsgalerie Stuttgart	Félix Thiollier (1842-1914)
13·10·96 - 17·11·96	Regensburg	Museum Ostdeutsche Galerie	Borderline Photographs 1986-1996
14·10·96 - 15·11·96	Saarbrücken	Saarland Museum	Erich Heckel
mid Oct 96-Jan 97	Bonn	Kunstmuseum Bonn/Graphic Exh.	Wols From the Graphic Collection
17·10·96 - 24·11·96	Essen	Museum Folkwang Essen	Peter Keetman
19·10·96 - 24·11·96	Berlin	Neue Gesellschaft für Bildende Kunst	Limited Limitlessness
19·10·96 - 15·01·97	Köln - Cologne	Museum für Ostasiatische Kunst	20th-Century Chinese Painting
19·10·96 - 19·01·97	Stuttgart	Staatsgalerie Stuttgart	Johann Heinrich Füssli and John Milton
20·10·96 - Jan 97	Goslar	Mönchehaus-M. für mod. Kunst	Kaiserring Grant 1996
20·10·96 - 01·12·96	Ulm	Ulmer Museum	The Baden-Württemberg Artists' Society
23·10·96 - 05·01·97	München - Munich	G. im Lenbachhaus - K. Lenbachhaus	Jeff Wall
24·10·96 - 01·12·96	Kiel	Kunsthalle zu Kiel	Jan Voss Retrospective
24·10·96 - 12·01·97	München - Munich	Villa Stuck	Max Klinger
26·10·96 - Jan 97	Goslar	Mönchehaus-M. für moderne Kunst	Dani Karavan Kaiserring Recipient 1996
27·10·96 - 08·12·96	Esslingen	G. Stadt Esslingen / Villa Merkel	Martin Kippenberger
27·10·96 - 29·12·96	Hamburg	Hamburger Kunsthalle	Hamburg Painting in the Biedermeier
27·10·96 - 05·01·97	Leverkusen	M. Leverkusen Schloß Morsbroich	Gregor-Torsten Kozik
30·10·96 - 12·01·97	Bonn	Rheinisches Landesmuseum Bonn	Floris Neusüss
31·10·96 - 12·01·97	Nürnberg-Nuremberg	Germanisches Nationalmuseum	Expressionistic Paintings
Nov 96-Dec 96	Aachen	Suermondt Ludwig Museum/Studio	Ernst Wille
Nov 96-Jan 97	Braunschweig	Herzog Anton Ulrich Museum	From Gainsborough to Turner
01·11·96 - 01·12·96	Bremen	Übersee-Museum Bremen	The Society for Arts and Crafts
Nov 96-Jan 97	Chemnitz	Städtische Kunstsammlungen	Concrete Art from the Jung Collection
Nov 96-Jan 97	Hamburg	M. Kunst und Gewerbe Hamburg	Thomas Schleede and Students
Nov 96-Dec 96	Mönchengladbach	Städtisches Museum Abteiberg	Liligant [Restauraxion]
03·11·96 - 17·11·96	Essen	Museum Folkwang Essen	Prize-Winner of 'Villa Romana' 1996
03·11·96 - 12·12·96	Lübeck	Overbeck-Gesellschaft Cont. Art	Katharina Grosse Murals
03·11·96 - 26·01·97	München - Munich	Haus der Kunst	Francis Bacon Retrospective
07·11·96 - Jan 97	Aachen	Suermondt Ludwig Museum/Graphic	Walter Dohmen Transition
07·11·96 - 05·01·97	Ludwigshafen	Wilhelm-Hack-Museum	Horst Bartnig Woodcuts
08·11·96 - 27·01·97	Hamburg	M. Kunst und Gewerbe Hamburg	The Hats of Adele List

Exhibitions in chronological order.

GERMANY

DATE	CITY	MUSEUM	ARTIST/THEME
10·11·96 - Jan 97	Düsseldorf	M. Düsseldorf im Ehrenhof	Glass from Murano 1930-1970
10·11·96 - 08·12·96	Göttingen	Städtische Museum Göttingen	Göttingen
15·11·96 - 26·01·97	München - Munich	Haus der Kunst	BLAST
17·11·96 - 05·01·97	Duisburg	Wilhelm Lehmbruck M. Duisburg	André Volten Brass Sculptures
23·11·96 - 02·03·97	Düsseldorf	K. Nordrhein-Westfalen	René Magritte
24·11·96 - 19·01·97	Saarbrücken	Saarland Museum	Gerhard Hoehme Aetna Cycle
29·11·96 - 18·12·96	Hamburg	M. Kunst und Gewerbe Hamburg	Annual German Craftwork Fair
30·11·96 - end Jan 97	Frankfurt am Main	Portikus Frankfurt am Main	Tobias Rehberger
Dec 96-Jan 97	Aachen	Ludwig Forum für Int. Kunst	Kunstpreis Aachen 1996
Dec 96-Feb 97	Aachen	Ludwig Forum für Int. Kunst	Kala Chakra
Dec 96-Feb 97	Stuttgart	Galerie der Stadt Stuttgart	Alessandro Mendini
01·12·96 - 16·02·97	Münster	M. für Kunst und Kulturgeschichte	Paul Signac
04·12·96 - Jun 97	München - Munich	Lenbachhaus	American Art
05·12·96 - 23·01·97	Freiburg im Breisgau	Augustinermuseum	Christoph Daniel Schenck
05·12·96 - 02·02·97	Nürnberg-Nuremberg	Germanisches Nationalmuseum	Jochen Gerz 'The French Wall'
06·12·96 - mid Feb 97	Bonn	Kunstmuseum Bonn/Temp. Exh.	Anselm Kiefer New Works
06·12·96 - 25·01·97	Esslingen	G. Stadt Esslingen / Bahnwärterhaus	Recipient of the Bahnwärter Grant
07·12·96 - Jan 97	Berlin	Neue Gesellschaft für Bildende Kunst	The Telematic Space II
07·12·96 - 16·02·97	Stuttgart	Staatsgalerie Stuttgart	Tiepolo & Venetian Art of Drawing
08·12·96 - 25·02·97	Bielefeld	K. Bielefeld (Richard-Kaselowsky-H.)	Irma Stern and Expressionism
08·12·96 - 02·03·97	Essen	Museum Folkwang Essen	Sean Scully Work on Paper
08·12·96 - 26·01·97	Kiel	Kunsthalle zu Kiel	The Schleswig-Holstein Artists Ass.
09·12·96 - 31·01·97	Saarbrücken	Saarland Museum	Café du Dôme
10·12·96 - end Feb 97	Köln - Cologne	Wallraf-Richartz-Museum	Capriccio as Artistic Principle
11·12·96 - 03·03·97	Aachen	Suermondt Ludwig M./Graphic Dep.	Against the Current
12·12·96 - Mar 97	Darmstadt	Hessisches M. Darmstadt	Ernst Riegel (1871-1939)
12·12·96 - Feb 97	Hannover	Niedersächsisches M. Hannover	Age of Bronze
13·12·96 - 11·03·97	Berlin	Deutsches Historisches Museum	On Commission
14·12·96 - 20·04·97	Berlin	Museum für Verkehr und Technik	The History of the Berlin Gas Service
14·12·96 - 23·02·97	Frankfurt am Main	Deutsches Architektur-Museum	Ecological Arch. and Urban Planning
14·12·96 - 30·03·97	Frankfurt am Main	Schirn Kunsthalle	Collection of the Aargauer Kunsthaus
14·12·96 - Feb 97	Ludwigshafen	Wilhelm-Hack-Museum	Konkret International I
14·12·96 - 31·03·97	Stuttgart	Staatsgalerie Stuttgart	The Magic of Numbers
15·12·96 - 30·03·97	Bremen	Übersee-Museum Bremen	Bremen City of Wine in the North
15·12·96 - 26·01·97	Essen	Museum Folkwang Essen	Ansgar Nierhoff
15·12·96 - 25·01·97	Esslingen	G. Stadt Esslingen / Villa Merkel	Esslingen Art Society
15·12·96 - 26·01·97	Göttingen	Städtische Museum Göttingen	Alfred Pohl Woodcuts
15·12·96 - 09·02·97	Ulm	Ulmer Museum	The Visible World
16·12·96 - 02·03·97	Bonn	Kunst- und Ausstellungshalle Bund.	The Great Collections V
16·12·96 - Feb 97	Dresden	Gemäldegalerie Neue Meister	The Age of Tiepolos
16·12·96 - Apr 97	Dresden	Skulpturensammlung - Staatliche K.	Western European Plastic Art
18·12·96 - 16·02·97	Leipzig	Museum der Bildenden Künste	Otto Mueller
Winter 96/97	Berlin	Bauhaus-Archiv / M. für Gestaltung	The Bauhochschule Weimar
Winter 96/97	Hamburg	M. Kunst und Gewerbe Hamburg	Michael Ruetz The Perennial Eye
Jan 97-Mar 97	Bonn	Kunstmuseum Bonn/Graphic Exh.	On the Existence of Objects
Jan 97-Apr 97	Düsseldorf	Kunsthalle Düsseldorf	Michail Wrubel (1856-1910)
Jan 97-Mar 97	Hamburg	Hamburger Kunsthalle	Italian Renaissance Drawings
Jan 97-end Mar 97	Köln - Cologne	Wallraf-Richartz-Museum	Tieplol Drawings
early 1997	Köln - Cologne	Josef-Haubrich-Kunsthalle	Power of Women & Supremacy of Man
09·01·97 - 25·03·97	Berlin	Deutsches Historisches Museum	Victoria and Albert
11·01·97 - 14·04·97	Berlin	Brücke-Museum	Max Pechstein Works on Paper.
11·01·97 - 14·04·97	Berlin	Brücke-Museum	Ernst Ludwig Kirchner Photographs.
19·01·97 - 23·03·97	Baden-Baden	Staatliche Kunsthalle Baden-Baden	Cindy Sherman
25·01·97 - 06·04·97	Frankfurt am Main	Schirn Kunsthalle	Gaston Chaissac
31·01·97 - 04·05·97	Frankfurt am Main	Museum für Moderne Kunst	Change of Scene XI
Feb 97-Mar 97	Aachen	Suermondt Ludwig Museum/Studio	Dürer and the German Renaissance
Feb 97	Hamburg	Hamburger Kunsthalle	Opening of the Ungersbau

Exhibitions in chronological order.

GERMANY

DATE	CITY	MUSEUM	ARTIST/THEME
Feb 97-Mar 97	Kiel	Kunsthalle zu Kiel	Martin Assig
28·02·97 - 19·05·97	Bonn	Kunst- und Ausstellungshalle Bund.	The Great Collections VI
begin Mar-May 97	Bonn	Kunstmuseum Bonn/Temp. Exh.	Guiseppe Penone
Mar 97-Jun 97	Bonn	Kunstmuseum Bonn/Graphic Exh.	Young Graphic Artists I
Mar 97-Apr 97	Braunschweig	Herzog Anton Ulrich Museum	Artists Look at Themselves
Mar 97-May 97	Ludwigshafen	Wilhelm-Hack-Museum	Victor Vasarely Retrospective Show
end Mar 97-end Jun 97	Köln - Cologne	Wallraf-Richartz-Museum	Barthel Bruyn the Elder
Spring 97	Regensburg	Museum Ostdeutsche Galerie	Gudrun Wasserman
Apr 97-Jun 97	Bremen	Übersee-Museum Bremen	Huichun Chinese Medicine
Apr 97-Jun 97	Dresden	Gemäldegalerie Neue Meister	Ernst Ferdinand Oehme
23·04·97 - 09·06·97	Berlin	Brücke-Museum	Ernst Ludwig Kirchner Drawings

GREAT BRITAIN

DATE	CITY	MUSEUM	ARTIST/THEME
until 27·10·96	Bristol	City Museum and Art Gallery	Horemkenesi
until Summer 96	Cambridge	Univ.M. Archaeology&Anthropology	Living Traditions
until 25·08·96	Glasgow	Art Gallery and Museum	St. Kilda Explored
until Apr 97	Liverpool	Tate Gallery Liverpool	Home and Away
until 03·06·96	London	Museum of Mankind - Ethnography	Display and Modesty
until 16·06·96	London	Museum of Mankind - Ethnography	Secular and Sacred
until 16·06·96	London	Museum of Mankind - Ethnography	Great Benin, a West African Kingdom
until 16·06·96	London	Museum of Mankind - Ethnography	The Power of the Hand
until Sep 96	London	Museum of Mankind - Ethnography	Play and Display
until 30·06·96	Manchester	Manchester City Art Galleries	Whitefriars Glass
13·04·94 - 27·05·96	Liverpool	Tate Gallery Liverpool	New Contemporaries 96
Summer 95-onwards	London	National Maritime Museum	Nelson
01·01·96 - onwards	York	Yorkshire Museum	Venom
11·01·96 - 28·08·96	Liverpool	Liverpool Museum	The Arts of the Samurai
20·01·96 - 05·01·97	Derby	Pickford's House Museum	Fashion and Freeedom
23·01·96 - 02·06·96	Cambridge	Fitzwilliam Museum/Adeane Gallery	Primavera Pioneering Craft and Design
03·02·96 - 22·09·96	Norwich	Castle Museum	Paper Dreams
06·02·96 - 09·06·96	Norwich	Sainsbury Centre for Visual Arts	Swords of the Samurai
13·02·96 - 12·05·96	Cambridge	Fitzwilliam Museum/Adeane Gallery	Colour Prints from the Beddington Coll.
13·02·96 - 12·05·96	Oxford	Ashmolean M. and Univ. Galleries	16th-Century French Orn. Drawings
20·02·96 - 24·05·96	Cambridge	Fitzwilliam Museum/Cripps Gallery	Coinage in Ireland
22·02·96 - 26·05·96	London	Courtauld Gallery	Thomas Gainsborough
22·02·96 - 19·05·96	London	The National Gallery	Masterpieces from the Doria Pamphilj
23·02·96 - 02·06·96	London	National Portrait Gallery	The Room in View
24·02·96 - 12·05·96	Birmingham	M. Art Gallery and The Gas Hall	The Land is Bright
24·02·96 - 12·05·96	Hull	Ferens Art Gallery	A Collection for the Future
29·02·96 - 12·05·96	London	Dulwich Picture Gallery	Soane and Death
Mar 96-Jun 96	Leeds	Leeds City Art Gallery	Conversations with Pictures
05·03·96 - 18·08·96	London	The British Museum	Excavating Ancient Beirut
06·03·96 - 27·05·96	London	The National Gallery	Pesellino's Trinity Altarpiece
07·03·96 - 06·05·96	Edinburgh	National Gallery of Scotland	David Le Marchand (1674-1726)
07·03·96 - 08·09·96	London	The British Museum	Commemorating The 19th Century
12·03·96 - 12·05·96	Oxford	Ashmolean M. and Univ. Galleries	Designs for the Ashmolean
13·03·96 - 14·07·96	London	The British Museum	Vases and Volcanoes
13·03·96 - 05·05·96	London	Whitechapel Art Gallery	Jeff Wall
14·03·96 - 02·06·96	Leeds	Leeds City Art Gallery	Real Art: 'A New Modernism'
16·03·96 - 16·06·96	Cardiff	National Museum of Wales	Inscribed in Stone
16·03·96 - Apr 97	Liverpool	Tate Gallery Liverpool	Characters and Conversations
Spring 96-Summer 96	London	Accademia Italiana	Leonardo Artist, Inventor, Scientist
22·03·96 - 07·07·96	London	National Portrait Gallery	David Livingston
23·03·96 - 12·05·96	Leicester	Leicestershire M. and Art Gallery	An Intelligent Rebellion
28·03·96 - 23·06·96	London	Royal Academy of Arts	Gustave Caillebotte

Exhibitions in chronological order.

GREAT BRITAIN

DATE	CITY	MUSEUM	ARTIST/THEME
29·03·96 - 08·09·96	Belfast	Ulster Museum	A Celebration of Riches
29·03·96 - 31·08·96	London	Sir John Soane's Museum	Soane Revisited
30·03·96 - 02·06·96	Durham	The Bowes Museum	Flesh and Spirit
30·03·96 - Aug 96	Liverpool	Tate Gallery Liverpool	Wandering About in the Future
30·03·96 - 18·08·96	Northampton	Central Museum and Art Gallery	Newcomers
30·03·96 - Mar 97	Norwich	Castle Museum	Norwich A Cathedral City
01·04·96 - 31·05·96	Cardiff	National Museum of Wales	Pollination of Plants on Stamps
Apr 96-Sep 96	Edinburgh	Scottish National Portrait Gallery	Speaking Likeness
Apr 96-May 96	Glasgow	Gallery of Modern Art	The Lord Provost's Prize
04·04·96 - 29·09·96	London	Victoria and Albert Museum	Arts and Crafts Architecture
05·04·96 - 02·06·96	Southampton	Southampton City Art Gallery	Freedom
06·04·96 - 27·05·96	Manchester	Manchester City Art Galleries	Willy Ronis Photographs 1926-1995
06·04·96 - 26·05·96	York	York City Art Gallery	Carel Weight A War Retrospective
09·04·96 - 07·07·96	Cambridge	Fitzwilliam Museum	'Colledge Goods'
12·04·96 - 07·07·96	London	National Portrait Gallery	John Deakin
13·04·96 - 27·05·96	Aberdeen	Aberdeen Art Gallery	El Greco
18·04·96 - 02·06·96	Leeds	Leeds City Art Gallery	Jake Attree Visions of the City
19·04·96 - 01·09·96	Belfast	Ulster Museum	Images Sacred and Secular
20·04·96 - 27·05·96	Brighton	Brighton Museum & Art Gallery	Land of Tempests
23·04·96 - 30·06·96	Cambridge	Fitzwilliam Museum	Surimono Hokusai and his Pupils
24·04·96 - 06·10·96	London	Design Museum	100 Masterpieces
25·04·96 - 14·07·96	Edinburgh	National Gallery of Scotland	Awash with Colour
25·04·96 - onwards	London	Museum of Mankind - Ethnography	Pagay, Rice and Life
26·04·96 - 01·06·96	Dorchester	Dorset County Museum	Dinosaur Roadshow
27·04·96 - 07·07·96	Derby	Pickford's House Museum	Cutlery from Sheffield
27·04·96 - 16·06·96	Hull	Ferens Art Gallery	Art Unlimited
27·04·96 - 02·06·96	Leeds	Leeds City Art Gallery	Jack B. Yeats A Celtic Visionary
28·04·96 - 02·06·96	Dorchester	Dorset County Museum	British Gas Wildlife Photographer
28·04·96 - 30·06·96	Oxford	Museum of Modern Art	Carl Andre
29·04·96 - 24·05·96	Newcastle upon Tyne	The Hatton Gallery	Artlanta
30·04·96 - 26·05·96	London	The Serpentine Gallery	Langlands and Bell
01·05·96 - 09·06·96	Coventry	Herbert Art Gallery & Museum	The Motor Show
May 96-Sep 96	New Bridge	Scottish Agricultural Museum	Bees
03·05·96 - 28·07·96	Durham	The Bowes Museum	Private View
04·05·96 - 25·05·96	Aberdeen	Aberdeen Art Gallery	Aberdeen Artists
04·05·96 - 23·06·96	Bristol	City Museum and Art Gallery	Imagining Rome
04·05·96 - 29·09·96	Norwich	Castle Museum	The Great Treasure Hunt
04·05·96 - 03·11·96	St. Ives	Tate Gallery St. Ives	Mark Rothko
04·05·96 - 01·06·96	Truro	Royal Cornwall Museum	Cornwall Photographic Alliance
04·05·96 - 16·06·96	Wakefield	Wakefield Art Gallery	'From Yorkshire With Love'
05·05·96 - 02·06·96	Belfast	Ulster Museum	Nature's Bounty
07·05·96 - 15·06·96	Chichester	Pallant House Gallery	L.S. Lowry
07·05·96 - 15·06·96	Chichester	Pallant House Gallery	Recent Paintings by Jane Andrews
09·05·96 - 18·08·96	London	Barbican Art Gallery	Eve Arnold A Retrospective
09·05·96 - 18·08·96	London	Barbican Art Gallery	Derek Jarman
09·05·96 - 01·09·96	London	Victoria and Albert Museum	William Morris
10·05·96 - 01·09·96	Belfast	Ulster Museum	Dressed for Battle
10·05·96 - 07·07·96	London	ICA Institute of Contemporary Arts	Jake and Dinos Chapman
11·05·96 - 01·09·96	Bournemouth	Russell-Cotes Art Gallery and M.	Paul Eachus and Helen Coxall
11·05·96 - 22·06·96	Chichester	Pallant House Gallery	Bernard Charles Spirit of the Downs
11·05·96 - 15·06·96	Middlesbrough	Middlesbrough Art Gallery	Soccerscape
11·05·96 - 14·07·96	York	York City Art Gallery	Unseen Etty
13·05·96 - 25·05·96	London	Leighton House M. & Art Gallery	A Middle Eastern Surprise
14·05·96 - 01·09·96	Cambridge	Fitzwilliam Museum	Burne-Jones and William Morris
14·05·96 - Aug 96	Oxford	Ashmolean M. and Univ. Galleries	Life Drawing
15·05·96 - 14·07·96	London	The British Museum	The Art of Kayama Matazó
16·05·96 - onwards	London	Museum of Mankind - Ethnography	The Gilded Image

Exhibitions in chronological order.

GREAT BRITAIN

DATE	CITY	MUSEUM	ARTIST/THEME
17·05·96 - 29·09·96	Birmingham	M. Art Gallery and the Gas Hall	Monster Creepy Crawlies
17·05·96 - 07·07·96	London	Whitechapel Art Gallery	Renato Guttusomid
21·05·96 - 22·09·96	Cambridge	Fitzwilliam Museum	Tennyson and Trollope
21·05·96 - 15·10·96	Oxford	Ashmolean M. and Univ. Galleries	Ruskin and Oxford
22·05·96 - 26·08·96	London	The National Gallery	Degas Beyond Impressionism
22·05·96 - 26·08·96	London	The National Gallery	Degas as a Collector
23·05·96 - 30·06·96	London	The British Museum	Oriental Antiquities
23·05·96 - 15·09·96	London	The British Museum	The Grotesque
23·05·96 - 15·09·96	London	The British Museum	19th-Century French Drawings
23·05·96 - 15·09·96	London	The British Museum	David Le Marchand, Ivory Carver
24·05·96 - 28·07·96	London	The British Museum	South Indian Painting and Sculpture
25·05·96 - 01·09·96	Durham	The Bowes Museum	Walking the Landscape
25·05·96 - 30·09·96	Glasgow	McLellan Galleries	Charles Rennie Mackintosh
26·05·96 - 29·09·96	Birmingham	M. Art Gallery and The Gas Hall	Visions of Love and Life
01·06·96 - 27·07·96	Aberdeen	Aberdeen Art Gallery	Artists' Portraits
01·06·96 - 26·06·96	Leicester	Leicestershire M. and Art Gallery	Artworks
01·06·96 - 26·08·96	Newcastle upon Tyne	Laing Art Gallery	Treasures of Northumbria
01·06·96 - 30·06·96	Truro	Royal Cornwall Museum	Cornwall Buildings Group
01·06·96 - 30·06·96	York	York City Art Gallery	Georg Baselitz Prints
02·06·96 - 21·07·96	Leicester	Leicestershire M. and Art Gallery	Messel Fossils
03·06·96 - 22·06·96	London	Leighton House M. & Art Callery	Society of Scribes
04·06·96 - 07·07·96	Norwich	Sainsbury Centre for Visual Arts	Museology MA Exhibition 'Carnival'
04·06·96 - 04·08·96	Southampton	Southampton City Art Gallery	Sir John Everett Millais
04·06·96 - Aug 96	Southampton	Southampton City Art Gallery	Boudin to Dufy
05·06·96 - 07·07·96	London	The National Gallery	Christ Driving the Traders f. the Temple
06·06·96 - 22·09·96	Edinburgh	Scottish National G. of Modern Art	Alberto Giacometti 1901-1966
06·06·96 - 06·10·96	Glasgow	The Burrell Collection	Lynne Curran
06·06·96 - 18·08·96	London	Hayward Gallery	Claes Oldenburg An Anthology
06·06·96 - 01·09·96	London	Tate Gallery	Leon Kossoff
07·06·96 - 21·07·96	Brighton	Brighton Museum & Art Gallery	'The Green Room' and other Paintings
08·06·96 - 20·07·96	Dorchester	Dorset County Museum	The Flowers of the Countryside
08·06·96 - 15·09·96	Edinburgh	Royal Museum of Scotland	Pride and Passion
08·06·96 - 01·09·96	Manchester	Manchester City Art Galleries	Offside! Football and Contemporary Art
08·06·96 - 07·07·96	Truro	Royal Cornwall Museum	Arts in Trust
09·06·96 - 18·08·96	London	Royal Academy of Arts	228th Summer Exhibition
12·06·96 - 21·07·96	London	The Serpentine Gallery	Fischli and Weiss
12·06·96 - 22·09·96	London	Victoria and Albert Museum	Graphic and Artistic Responses to AIDS
13·06·96 - mid Aug 96	Glasgow	Art Gallery and Museum	Jessie M. King
13·06·96 - 27·07·96	Leeds	Leeds City Art Gallery	The Impossible Science of Being
14·06·96 - 08·09·96	Glasgow	Gallery of Modern Art	Craigie Aitchison
14·06·96 - 27·08·96	London	Courtauld Gallery	The Four Elements
15·06·96 - 28·08·96	Cheltenham	Cheltenham Art Gallery & Museum	Simply Stunning
15·06·96 - 28·07·96	Coventry	Herbert Art Gallery & Museum	The Mirror in the Sea
15·06·96 - 14·09·96	Dorchester	Dorset County Museum	Man and the Land
mid Jun 96-Oct 96	Leeds	Leeds City Art Gallery	Wunderkammer
17·06·96 - 13·07·96	Newcastle upon Tyne	The Hatton Gallery	BA Degree Show
19·06·96 - 28·07·96	Coventry	Herbert Art G. & Museum(Gallery 5)	Barry Bermange
19·06·96 - 18·08·96	London	Dulwich Picture Gallery	Martha Fleming Open Book
20·06·96 - 23·06·96	New Bridge	Scottish Agricultural Museum	Fergusson Tractors
21·06·96 - 06·10·96	London	National Portrait Gallery	Family Albums
22·06·96 - 03·08·96	Middlesbrough	Middlesbrough Art Gallery	Claes Oldenburg Multiples
25·06·96 - 25·10·96	Cambridge	Fitzwilliam Museum	The Development of Portraiture
25·06·96 - onwards	Norwich	Sainsbury Centre for Visual Arts	Francis Bacon
29·06·96 - 29·07·96	Chichester	Pallant House Gallery	Chichester Festivities
29·06·96 - 10·08·96	Chichester	Pallant House Gallery	Eric James Mellon
29·06·96 - 31·07·96	Kirkcaldy	Kirkcaldy Museum and Art Gallery	Inuit Art
29·06·96 - 01·09·96	Wakefield	Wakefield Art Gallery	Decorative Arts

Exhibitions in chronological order.

GREAT BRITAIN

DATE	CITY	MUSEUM	ARTIST/THEME
01·07·96 - 03·11·96	Grasmere	The Wordsworth Museum	Benjamin Robert Haydon
01·07·96 - 05·07·96	London	Leighton House M. & Art Gallery	Tabitha Salmon
Jul 96 - mid Sep 96	London	Whitechapel Art Gallery	Whitechapel Open and East London
03·07·96 - 29·09·96	London	Dulwich Picture Gallery	Dutch Flower Painting 1600-1750
06·07·96 - 25·08·96	Hull	Ferens Art Gallery	Sound and Fury
06·07·96 - 22·09·96	Leicester	Leicestershire M. and Art Gallery	Indian Miniatures Festivals of India
09·07·96 - 13·10·96	Cambridge	Fitzwilliam Museum	Japanese Drawings
11·07·96 - 01·09·96	Bristol	City Museum and Art Gallery	The Natural History Museum
11·07·96 - 08·09·96	London	Royal Academy of Arts	Roger de Grey, Painter
14·07·96 - 15·09·96	Leicester	Leicestershire M. and Art Gallery	'Now Showing'
14·07·96 - 07·09·96	Norwich	Sainsbury Centre for Visual Arts	EAST
14·07·96 - 22·09·96	Oxford	Museum of Modern Art	Scream and Scream Again
14·07·96 - 08·09·96	York	York City Art Gallery	Folk Art in Britain
17·07·96 - 29·09·96	London	The National Gallery	John Julius Angerstein
22·07·96 - 10·08·96	London	Leighton House M. & Art Gallery	Kensington & Chelsea Artists' Exhibition
23·07·96 - 22·12·96	Cambridge	Fitzwilliam Museum	Variations on Ceramic Themes
23·07·96 - 29·09·96	London	ICA Institute of Contemporary Arts	Gothic
26·07·96 - 29·09·96	Belfast	Ulster Museum	Treasures of the Royal Horticultural Soc
26·07·96 - 29·09·96	Belfast	Ulster Museum	Raymond Piper's Orchids
26·07·96 - 20·10·96	London	National Portrait Gallery	BP Award 1996
26·07·96 - 29·09·96	London	The British Museum	20th-Century Chinese Painting
27·07·96 - 14·09·96	Dorchester	Dorset County Museum	Goal!
Aug 96-Sep 96	Belfast	Ulster Museum	Royal Ulster Academy
Aug 96-Sep 96	Leeds	Leeds City Art Gallery	Open Exhibition
Aug 96-Oct 96	London	The British Museum	Japanese Paintings and Prints
03·08·96 - 07·09·96	Aberdeen	Aberdeen Art Gallery	Lil Nelson
03·08·96 - 22·12·96	Leicester	Leicestershire M. and Art Gallery	Immensely Industrious
06·08·96 - 14·09·96	Chichester	Pallant House Gallery	Alan Davie (1920) Recent Work
08·08·96 - 15·09·96	Brighton	Brighton Museum & Art Gallery	The Impossible Science of Being
08·08·96 - 15·09·96	Coventry	Herbert Art Gallery & Museum	Synaptica
08·08·96 - 20·10·96	Edinburgh	National Gallery of Scotland	Velázquez in Seville
10·08·96 - 21·09·96	Middlesbrough	Middlesbrough Art Gallery	Lynn Silverman Corporation House
10·08·96 - 31·08·96	Truro	Royal Cornwall Museum	Truro Art Society Annual Exhibition
16·08·96 - 06·10·96	Southampton	Southampton City Art Gallery	Southampton's Art Collection
17·08·96 - 28·09·96	Chichester	Pallant House Gallery	Keith Clements
17·08·96 - 20·10·96	Kirkcaldy	Kirkcaldy Museum and Art Gallery	Claiming the Kingdom
24·08·96 - 22·09·96	Hull	Ferens Art Gallery	The Parents
24·08·96 - 22·09·96	Northampton	Central Museum and Art Gallery	Young Images
27·08·96 - 28·09·96	London	Leighton House M. & Art Gallery	Randolph Caldecott
31·08·96 - 22·09·96	Kirkcaldy	Kirkcaldy Museum and Art Gallery	Behind the Screens
Sep 96 - Oct 96	Glasgow	Art Gallery and Museum	Prize Winners Art Competition
Sep 96	London	Accademia Italiana	Randy Klein Transformations
Sep 96	London	Accademia Italiana	Sconfinamenti
02·09·96 - 08·10·96	Newcastle upon Tyne	The Hatton Gallery	Derek Jarman A Retrospective
04·09·96 - 23·11·96	Leeds	Leeds City Art Gallery	David Nash
07·09·96 - 27·09·96	Truro	Royal Cornwall Museum	Mermaid Appeal
07·09·96 - 27·10·96	Wakefield	Wakefield Art Gallery	Suzanne McIvor
10·09·96 - 02·03·97	London	The British Museum	Coins & Archaeology of the Abbasid
12·09·96 - 27·10·96	Bath	Holburne M. and Crafts Study Centre	Quilt Art
12·09·96 - 15·12·96	London	Barbican Art Gallery	Erwin Blumenfeld A Fetish of Fashion
12·09·96 - 15·12·96	London	Barbican Art Gallery	Icons and Innovators
13·09·96 - 05·01·97	London	The British Museum	Mysteries of Ancient China
13·09·96 - 03·11·96	Newcastle upon Tyne	Laing Art Gallery	A Palace of Victorian Art
14·09·96 - 26·10·96	Dorchester	Dorset County Museum	John Bratby
14·09·96 - 03·11·96	Liverpool	Tate Gallery Liverpool	Rachel Whiteread
14·09·96 - 03·11·96	Manchester	Manchester City Art Galleries	The Inner Eye
19·09·96 - 01·12·96	London	Hayward Gallery	ACE!

Exhibitions in chronological order.

GREAT BRITAIN			
DATE	**CITY**	**MUSEUM**	**ARTIST/THEME**
20·09·96 - 24·11·96	Edinburgh	Scottish National Portrait Gallery	David Roberts Bicentenary
20·09·96 - 23·03·97	Glasgow	Art Gallery and Museum	Claws
21·09·96 - 19·10·96	Aberdeen	Aberdeen Art Gallery	Ceramics
21·09·96 - 20·01·97	Bournemouth	Russell-Cotes Art Gallery and M.	Evelyn de Morgan
21·09·96 - 10·12·96	Durham	The Bowes Museum	Dutch, Venetian, Cumber and Print
21·09·96 - 19·01·97	Manchester	Manchester City Art Galleries	Finnish Glass
21·09·96 - 20·10·96	York	York City Art Gallery	Yorkshire Sculptors' Group
Autumn 96-onwards	Cambridge	Archaeology and Anthropology Univ.	African Metalwork
23·09·96 - 10·11·96	Brighton	Brighton Museum & Art Gallery	Teatro Gioco Vita
24·09·96 - Jan 97	Cambridge	Fitzwilliam Museum	John Downman
24·09·96 - 01·12·96	Oxford	Ashmolean M. and Univ. Galleries	Modern Chinese Paintings
25·09·96 - 05·01·97	London	The National Gallery	Peter Blake
26·09·96 - 01·12·96	Edinburgh	Scottish National Portrait Gallery	Look, Love and Follow Jacobite Prints
27·09·96 - 05·01·97	London	The British Museum	The Malcolm Collection of Drawings
28·09·96 - 10·11·96	Coventry	Herbert Art Gallery & Museum	Made in the Middle
28·09·96 - 23·11·96	Middlesbrough	Middlesbrough Art Gallery	Marina Abramovic
28·09·96 - 20·10·96	Northampton	Central Museum and Art Gallery	Simple Science
28·09·96 - 17·11·96	Northampton	Central Museum and Art Gallery	Personal Perspectives
Oct 96	Belfast	Ulster Museum	Early Ireland
Oct 96	London	Accademia Italiana	Pushkin Exhibition
Oct 96-May 97	London	Sir John Soane's Museum	Robert Adam
Oct 96-Dec 96	Norwich	Sainsbury Centre for Visual Arts	Patrick Bailly
01·10·96 - 14·10·96	Edinburgh	Royal Museum of Scotland	Behind the Screens
02·10·96 - 05·01·97	Leeds	Leeds City Art Gallery	David Le Marchand (1674-1726)
02·10·96 - 05·01·97	Leeds	Leeds City Art Gallery	Peter Scheemakers (1691-1781
04·10·96 - 05·01·97	London	National Portrait Gallery	Private Eye Times
05·10·96 - 07·11·96	Truro	Royal Cornwall Museum	Branch Out Art and Special Needs
06·10·96 - 29·12·96	Oxford	Museum of Modern Art	Taxonomy
07·10·96 - 16·12·96	Glasgow	Art Gallery and Museum	Information Superhighway
07·10·96 - 20·10·96	Hull	Ferens Art Gallery	Root 96
08·10·96 - Feb 97	Cambridge	Fitzwilliam Museum	Rembrandt and the Nude
08·10·96 - 22·12·96	Cambridge	Fitzwilliam Museum	The Golden Century
10·10·96 - 05·01·97	London	Courtauld Gallery	William Chambers and Somerset House
10·10·96 - 05·01·97	London	Tate Gallery	The Grand Tour
12·10·96 - 03·11·96	Edinburgh	Royal Museum of Scotland	Passing Out
12·10·96 - 05·01·97	Norwich	Castle Museum	Prime Minister, Empress and Heritage
14·10·96 - 02·11·96	London	Leighton House M. & Art Gallery	Paper as a Sculptural Medium
16·10·96 - 12·01·97	London	The British Museum	Japanese Prints
17·10·96 - 19·01·97	London	The National Gallery	Rubens' Landscapes
18·10·96 - 05·01·97	Southampton	Southampton City Art Gallery	Triplicate
19·10·96 - 28·11·96	Newcastle upon Tyne	The Hatton Gallery	From Folk Art to Fine Art
22·10·96 - 22·12·96	Cambridge	Fitzwilliam Museum/Shiba Room	The Utagawa School
24·10·96 - Apr 97	London	Design Museum	Charlotte Perriand A Way of Life
25·10·96 - 03·02·97	Belfast	Ulster Museum	Irish Fashion since 1950
25·10·96 - 23·02·97	London	Natural History Museum	The British Gas Wildlife Photographer
26·10·96 - 30·11·96	Aberdeen	Aberdeen Art Gallery	Ian Fleming Retrospective
26·10·96 - 30·11·96	Aberdeen	Aberdeen Art Gallery	William MacGillivray Bicentenary
26·10·96 - 29·12·96	Birmingham	M. Art Gallery and The Gas Hall	Tony Phillips The City
26·10·96 - 02·02·97	Birmingham	M. Art Gallery and The Gas Hall	William Morris Revisited
26·10·96 - 24·11·96	Northampton	Central Museum and Art Gallery	Boxes and Bowls?
Nov 96-Jan 97	Edinburgh	National Gallery of Scotland	German Renaissance Prints
Nov 96-Jan 97	Edinburgh	Scottish National G. of Modern Art	Anne Redpath
Nov 96-Dec 96	Glasgow	McLellan Galleries	The Royal Glasgow Institute Anniversary
Nov 96-Dec 96	Hull	Ferens Art Gallery	Jacqueline Morreau
Nov 96-Feb 97	Liverpool	Walker Art Gallery	Sir Charles Reilly
Nov 96	London	Accademia Italiana	La Dolce Vita from Grosz to Guttuso
Nov 96 - onwards	London	Museum of Mankind - Ethnography	Maori

Exhibitions in chronological order.

GREAT BRITAIN

DATE	CITY	MUSEUM	ARTIST/THEME
Nov 96-Dec 96	Truro	Royal Cornwall Museum	City of Light
01·11·96 - 22·12·96	London	ICA Institute of Contemporary Arts	Vija Celmins
02·11·96 - 14·12·96	Dorchester	Dorset County Museum	Poole Printmakers
02·11·96 - 12·01·97	Edinburgh	Royal Museum of Scotland	The Art of Protection
02·11·96 - 29·11·96	Kirkcaldy	Kirkcaldy Museum and Art Gallery	Fife Art Exhibition
02·11·96 - 08·12·96	York	York City Art Gallery	York Open
05·11·96 - 04·01·97	Chichester	Pallant House Gallery	Brendan Neilan R.A. (1941)
08·11·96 - 09·02·97	London	National Portrait Gallery	Photographic Portrait Award 1996
08·11·96 - 09·02·97	London	National Portrait Gallery	The Art of the Picture Frame
09·11·96 - 12·01·97	Wakefield	Wakefield Art Gallery	Introduction to Weaving
11·11·96 - 23·11·96	London	Leighton House M. & Art Gallery	James Childs
12·11·96 - 15·12·96	Bath	Holburne M. and Crafts Study Centre	William Morris and the Crafts Today
14·11·96 - 26·01·97	London	Victoria and Albert Museum	American Photography 1890-1965
16·11·96 - 21·12·96	Hull	Ferens Art Gallery	Terry Street
16·11·96 - 02·02·97	Manchester	Manchester City Art Galleries	David Hockney
16·11·96 - 07·02·97	Newcastle upon Tyne	Laing Art Gallery	Serious Games
16·11·96 - 02·11·97	St. Ives	Tate Gallery St. Ives	Displays 1996-97
16·11·96 - 20·04·97	St. Ives	Tate Gallery St. Ives	Christopher Wood
20·11·96 - 05·01·97	Coventry	Herbert Art Gallery & Museum	Year of the Car
20·11·96 - 05·01·97	Coventry	Herbert Art Gallery & Museum	Cash's and Stevengraphs
23·11·96 - 04·01·97	Cheltenham	Cheltenham Art Gallery & Museum	Rodmarton Manor
24·11·96 - 02.02.97	Belfast	Ulster Museum	Wildlife Photographer of the Year
24·11·96 - 02.02.97	Glasgow	Art Gallery and Museum	Wildlife Photographer of the Year
29·11·96 - 31·03·97	Glasgow	The Burrell Collection	Russian Gold
30·11·96 - 06·01·97	Brighton	Brighton Museum & Art Gallery	The Inner Eye
30·11·96 - 05·01·97	Northampton	Central Museum and Art Gallery	The Town and County Art Society
Dec 96	London	Accademia Italiana	Orneore Metelli
01·12·96 - 26·05·97	Edinburgh	Royal Museum of Scotland	The Scottish Home
02·12·96 - 14·12·96	London	Leighton House M. & Art Gallery	Silversmiths
06·12·96 - 25·01·97	Newcastle upon Tyne	The Hatton Gallery	Artists in Atlanta
12·12·96 - 23·02·97	Edinburgh	Scottish National Portrait Gallery	Buccleuch Portrait Miniatures
14·12·96 - 09·02·97	Kirkcaldy	Kirkcaldy Museum and Art Gallery	The Chair in Fife, 1660-1960
14·12·96 - 09·02·97	Kirkcaldy	Kirkcaldy Museum and Art Gallery	Sitting Pretty
14·12·96 - 26·01·97	York	York City Art Gallery	London Knees Claes Oldenburg
Jan 97-Apr 97	London	Barbican Art Gallery	Modernism in Britain
Jan 97-Apr 97	Norwich	Sainsbury Centre for Visual Arts	Derek Jarman
11·01·97 - 16·02·97	Coventry	Herbert Art Gallery & Museum	Ology Gallery Pilot
15·01·97 - 16·03·97	London	ICA Institute of Contemporary Arts	Gabriel Orozco
17·01·97 - 16·02·97	Southampton	Southampton City Art Gallery	Southampton Open
24·01·97 - 20·04·97	London	The British Museum	Modern Scandinavian Printmaking
24·01·97 - 20·04·97	London	The British Museum	Jacques Bellange, Mannerist Printmaker
25·01·97 - 22·02·97	Aberdeen	Aberdeen Art Gallery	Woven Image
Feb 97-Mar 97	Edinburgh	Royal Museum of Scotland	Shell Valentine Card Collection
Feb 97 - onwards	Grasmere	The Wordsworth Museum	The Ancient Mariner
Feb 97-Mar 97	Hull	Ferens Art Gallery	Ferens Annual Winter Exhibition
Feb 97-May 97	London	Tate Gallery	Lovis Corinth (1858-1925)
08·02·97 - 05·04·97	Middlesbrough	Middlesbrough Art Gallery	Speculative Proposals
19·02·97 - 30·03·97	Coventry	Herbert Art Gallery & Museum	Coventry Women's Show
22·02·97 - 20·04·97	Kirkcaldy	Kirkcaldy Museum and Art Gallery	Raw Materials
26·02·97 - 06·04·97	Coventry	Herbert Art Gallery & Museum	Derek Southall
28·02·97 - 11·05·97	Southampton	Southampton City Art Gallery	Drawing Breath
Mar 97-Jun 97	Liverpool	Walker Art Gallery	Sir Lawrence Alma Tadema
Mar 97-Apr 97	Wakefield	Wakefield Art Gallery	Margaret Harrison
Mar 97-Jul 97	London	The British Museum	Ancient Faces
01·03·97 - 05·04·97	Aberdeen	Aberdeen Art Gallery	Scottish Silver
08·03·97 - 05·04·97	Aberdeen	Aberdeen Art Gallery	First Exhibition Award
Spring 97	London	Accademia Italiana	Russian Imperial Tables

Exhibitions in chronological order.

GREAT BRITAIN

DATE	CITY	MUSEUM	ARTIST/THEME
Apr 97-Oct 97	Bristol	City Museum and Art Gallery	Cabot 500
Apr 97-Jun 97	Edinburgh	Royal Museum of Scotland	Beauty and the Banknote
14·04·97 - 25·05·97	Coventry	Herbert Art Gallery & Museum	Heart of England Biennial 2

IRELAND

DATE	CITY	MUSEUM	ARTIST/THEME
11·01·96 - 04·06·96	Dublin	Irish Museum of Modern Art	Literary Themes
14·03·96 - 17·05·96	Dublin	Irish Museum of Modern Art	Glen Dimplex Artists Award 1996
30·03·96 - 16·06·96	Dublin	Irish Museum of Modern Art	Works on Paper
24·04·96 - 30·06·96	Dublin	Irish Museum of Modern Art	Distant Relations
07·05·96 - 16·06·96	Dublin	National Gallery of Ireland	Mrs Delaney's Flower Collages
11·05·96 - 15·09·96	Dublin	Irish Museum of Modern Art	Sculpture
30·05·96 - 25·08·96	Dublin	Irish Museum of Modern Art	Sean Scully Twenty Years
31·05·96 - 31·05·96	Dublin	Irish Museum of Modern Art	Maytime Festival Exhibition
Jun 96 - Dec 96	Dublin	Irish Museum of Modern Art	Figuration
11·06·96 - 28·07·96	Dublin	National Gallery of Ireland	Miró (1893-1983)
02·07·96 - 11·08·96	Dublin	National Gallery of Ireland	Acquisitions
12·09·96 - Jan 97	Dublin	Irish Museum of Modern Art	The Event Horizon
27·09·96 - Jan 97	Dublin	Irish Museum of Modern Art	Beverly Semmes
08·10·96 - 15·12·96	Dublin	National Gallery of Ireland	William Leech (1881-1968)
17·10·96 - Feb 97	Dublin	Irish Museum of Modern Art	Louis le Brocquy Retrospective
29·10·96 - 15·12·96	Dublin	National Gallery of Ireland	The Royal Horticultural Society
01·01·97 - 31·01·97	Dublin	National Gallery of Ireland	Turner Watercolours

LUXEMBOURG

DATE	CITY	MUSEUM	ARTIST/THEME
22·05·96 - 14·07·96	Luxembourg	Casino Luxembourg	Sean Scully The Catherine Paintings
24·07·96 - 15·09·96	Luxembourg	Casino Luxembourg	Sculptural Suggestions
25·09·96 - 17·11·96	Luxembourg	Casino Luxembourg	'Actions Directs'
25·09·96 - 17·11·96	Luxembourg	Casino Luxembourg	Giovanni Anselmo
27·11·96 - 09·02·97	Luxembourg	Casino Luxembourg	'Stanze' For Painting
Feb 97 - Apr 97	Luxembourg	Casino Luxembourg	Didier Bay Retrospective

THE NETHERLANDS

DATE	CITY	MUSEUM	ARTIST/THEME
continuing for years	Leiden	Rijksmuseum voor Volkenkunde	Japan Around 1850
until Summer 96	Amsterdam	Ned. Scheepvaartmuseum A'dam	Fighting for Freedom, 1940-1945
until 01·09·96	Amsterdam	Tropenmuseum	Puppetry in Africa and Asia
until Apr 97	Amsterdam	Tropenmuseum	Stories to Know Where to Go
until 19·05·96	Apeldoorn	Van Reekum Museum	Dick van Arkel After Brueghel
until 19·05·96	Groningen	Groninger Museum	St. Walfridus Legacy
until 09·06·96	Groningen	Groninger Museum	Virtualistic Vibes
until 02·06·96	Maastricht	Bonnefantenmuseum	Willem de Kooning Sculptures
until 18·08·96	Middelburg	Zeeuws Museum	Hushed in Beauty Jan Heyse
until 09·06·96	Rotterdam	Natuurmuseum Rotterdam	Precious Possession
until 10·06·96	Leiden	Rijksm. van Oudheden M. Antiquities	Wine! Wine! Wine!
15·12·95 - 19·05·96	Amsterdam	Joods Historisch M. - Jewish Hist. M.	Jerusalem
24·01·96 - 18·08·96	Rotterdam	M. Boymans-van Beuningen	Bruce Nauman
10·02·96 - 02·06·96	Rotterdam	Kunsthal Rotterdam	Han van Meegeren
11·02·96 - 01·09·96	Maastricht	Bonnefantenmuseum	Sol LeWitt Mural
14·02·96 - 23·06·96	Nijmegen	Provinciaal M. / G.M. Kam	Death on the Ridge
17·02·96 - 27·05·96	Den Haag-The Hague	Haags Gemeentemuseum	Fabric In Form
23·02·96 - 12·05·96	Rotterdam	NAI Ned. Arch. instituut-Architecture	Drawings by Daniel Castor
24·02·96 - 28·05·96	Leiden	Stedelijk M. De Lakenhal	Orientation

Exhibitions in chronological order.

THE NETHERLANDS

DATE	CITY	MUSEUM	ARTIST/THEME
01·03·96 - 02·06·96	Den Haag-The Hague	Haags Historisch Museum	Dutch Life in the Days of Vermeer
01·03·96 - 02·06·96	Den Haag-The Hague	Mauritshuis	Johannes Vermeer
02·03·96 - 16·06·96	Den Haag-The Hague	Haags Gemeentemuseum	Frank van Hemert
02·03·96 - 30·06·96	Amsterdam	Ned. Scheepvaartmuseum A'dam	Bontekoe
02·03·96 - 12·05·96	Haarlem	Teylers Museum	Giorgio Morandi (1890-1964)
02·03·96 - 02·06·96	Haarlem	Teylers Museum	Italian Drawings 1400-1700
07·03·96 - 18·08·96	Amsterdam	Amsterdam Historical Museum	Boys and Girls
08·03·96 - onwards	Leeuwarden	Fries Museum	Adriaan van Cronenburg
09·03·96 - 02·06·96	Den Haag-The Hague	Haags Gemeentemuseum	Delft in the Time of Vermeer
09·03·96 - 02·06·96	Den Haag-The Hague	Haags Gemeentemuseum	Hague Porcelain
09·03·96 - 09·06·96	Maastricht	Bonnefantenmuseum	The Neutelings Collection
09·03·96 - 16·06·96	Rotterdam	NAI Ned. Arch. instituut-Architecture	The Architect's Discipline
10·03·96 - 19·05·96	Rotterdam	M. Boymans-van Beuningen	Cindy Sherman
15·03·96 - 03·06·96	Leeuwarden	Keramiekmuseum Princessehof	Frisian Ceramics
16·03·96 - 26·05·96	Den Haag-The Hague	Haags Gemeentemuseum	Gary Lan
16·03·96 - 23·06·96	Den Haag-The Hague	Haags Historisch Museum	Erich Salomon in Holland
19·03·96 - 05·08·96	Leiden	Rijksm. van Oudheden M. Antiquities	The Olympic Games in Ancient Greece
22·03·96 - 08·09·96	Amsterdam	Joods Historisch M. - Jewish Hist. M.	Peter Hunter/Otto Salomon
23·03·96 - 12·05·96	Haarlem	Frans Halsmuseum/Museum	A Firmament of Flowers
23·03·96 - 25·05·96	Rotterdam	Kunsthal Rotterdam	Breukel & Kooiker
23·03·96 - 27·05·96	Rotterdam	Kunsthal Rotterdam	The Reel World
23·03·96 - 12·05·96	Rotterdam	Kunsthal Rotterdam	Studio Dumbar
23·03·96 - 19·05·96	Rotterdam	Witte de With/Cont. Art	Voorwerk 5
25·03·96 - 19·05·96	Arnhem	M. Moderne Kunst-M. Modern Art	Jury Game
29·03·96 - 12·01·97	Amsterdam	Ned. Scheepvaartmuseum A'dam	Vinke & Co.
29·03·96 - 23·06·96	Amsterdam	Van Gogh Museum	The Year and the Day
30·03·96 - 23·06·96	Rotterdam	Kunsthal Rotterdam	Feast for the Eye
31·03·96 - 26·05·96	Haarlem	Frans Halsmuseum/Museum	Sewing Kits 17th-19th Century
01·04·96 - 19·05·96	Haarlem	Frans Halsmuseum/Museum	Anne van Waerden Crystal Objects
04·04·96 - 23·06·96	Amsterdam	Amsterdam Historical Museum	Anatolia in Amsterdam
04·04·96 - 07·07·96	Rotterdam	NAI Ned. Arch. instituut-Architecture	The Modern Years
06·04·96 - 26·05·96	Amsterdam	Stedelijk Museum M. of Modern Art	Peiling Recent Dutch Art
06·04·96 - 16·06·96	Haarlem	Frans Halsmuseum/Verweyhal	Verwey's House
06·04·96 - 01·09·96	Maastricht	Bonnefantenmuseum	Fons Haagmans
07·04·96 - 16·06·96	Dordrecht	Dordrechts Museum	After Scheffer
13·04·96 - 16·06·96	Den Haag-The Hague	Het Paleis	Frantisek Kupka (1871-1957)
13·04·96 - 02·06·96	Leeuwarden	Fries Museum	The War on the Table
13·04·96 - 19·05·96	Nijmegen	M. Commanderie van Sint-Jan	Collette Deblé
15·04·96 - 07·07·96	Leeuwarden	Fries Museum	Playing with the War
16·04·96 - 09·06·96	Amsterdam	Stedelijk Museum M. of Modern Art	Edvard Munch
20·04·96 - 02·06·96	Eindhoven	Stedelijk Van Abbemuseum	Jubilee Exhibition 1
20·04·96 - 26·06·96	Nijmegen	M. Commanderie van Sint-Jan	Contemporary Ceramics
21·04·96 - 16·06·96	Groningen	Groninger Museum	Utopia In Plastic
27·04·96 - 27·05·96	Apeldoorn	Paleis Het Loo - Nationaal M.	Future Through Tradition
27·04·96 - 02·06·96	Den Haag-The Hague	Haags Gemeentemuseum	World Wide Video Festival
27·04·96 - 29·09·96	Maastricht	Bonnefantenmuseum	Pierre Kemp
28·04·96 - 07·07·96	Arnhem	M. Moderne Kunst-M. Modern Art	Ria Pacquée
28·04·96 - 04·08·96	Rotterdam	M. Boymans-van Beuningen	Mannerist Prints
May 96-Jun 96	Leeuwarden	Fries Museum	Posters
01·05·96 - 23·06·96	Enschede	Rijksmuseum Twenthe	Ben Akkerman
03·05·96 - 08·09·96	Maastricht	Bonnefantenmuseum	The Océ-Van der Grinten Collection
04·05·96 - 16·06·96	Zwolle	Stedelijk Museum Zwolle	The Baptists
10·05·96 - 15·09·96	Amsterdam	Van Gogh Museum	Vincent van Gogh
11·05·96 - 04·08·96	Amsterdam	Rijksmuseum	Disegni
11·05·96 - 30·06·96	Amsterdam	Stedelijk Museum M. of Modern Art	Doors Project
11·05·96 - 30·06·96	Amsterdam	Stedelijk Museum M. of Modern Art	Barbara Broekman Tapestries
11·05·96 - 30·06·96	Schiedam	Stedelijk Museum Schiedam	From the Museum's Collection

THE NETHERLANDS

DATE	CITY	MUSEUM	ARTIST/THEME
12-05-96 - 23-06-96	Laren	Singer Museum	Paul Huf Portraits of a Photographer
16-05-96 - 25-08-96	's-Hertogenbosch	Noordbrabants Museum	Gardens in Dutch Art
16-05-96 - 11-08-96	Utrecht	Centraal Museum Utrecht	Touche's Nine
17-05-96 - 25-08-96	Dordrecht	Dordrechts Museum	Dordrecht in Print 1650-1800
18-05-96 - 01-09-96	Rotterdam	Kunsthal Rotterdam	Gerard van den Berg
18-05-96 - 18-08-96	Rotterdam	NAI Ned. Arch. instituut-Architecture	Metro Benelux Section / Metro Stations
18-05-96 - 30-06-96	Schiedam	Stedelijk Museum Schiedam	Ceramic Statues and Installations
20-05-96 - 07-07-96	Haarlem	Frans Halsmuseum/Museum	Milan Kunc
23-05-96 - 27-05-96	Apeldoorn	Paleis Het Loo - Nationaal M.	Kitchen Art Fair
25-05-96 - 28-07-96	Haarlem	Teylers Museum	Heer Bommel & Tom Poes
Jun 96 - Sep 96	Amsterdam	Allard Pierson Museum	The Olympic Games in Ancient Times
01-06-96 - 01-09-96	Leeuwarden	Fries Museum	From Royal Ownership
02-06-96 - 11-08-96	Arnhem	M. Moderne Kunst-M. Modern Art	Lam de Wolf Textile Installation
03-06-96 - 25-08-96	Apeldoorn	Van Reekum Museum	Just Arrived
04-06-96 - 22-09-96	Groningen	Groninger Museum	Highlights of the V.O.C. Collection
07-06-96 - 24-11-96	Amsterdam	Joods Historisch M. - Jewish Hist. M.	Civil Equality
08-06-96 - 29-09-96	Amsterdam	Rijksmuseum	Dutch Weapons from Russia
08-06-96 - 25-08-96	Amsterdam	Stedelijk Museum M. of Modern Art	Gerrit Komrij's Selections
08-06-96 - 08-09-96	Den Haag-The Hague	Haags Gemeentemuseum	Ruud Kuijer
08-06-96 - 08-09-96	Den Haag-The Hague	Haags Gemeentemuseum	Ossip
08-06-96 - 18-08-96	Rotterdam	Kunsthal Rotterdam	Manifesta I, European Art Event
08-06-96 -15-09-96	Rotterdam	Kunsthal Rotterdam	Surrealism from Dutch Collections
08-06-96 - 18-08-96	Rotterdam	Witte de With/Cont. Art	Manifesta 1
09-06-96 - 25-08-96	Rotterdam	M. Boymans-van Beuningen	Manifesta
09-06-96 - 25-08-96	Rotterdam	M. Boymans-van Beuningen	The Multiples of Lawrence Weiner
09-06-96 - 18-08-96	Rotterdam	M. Boymans-van Beuningen	Guest Curator, Hans Haacke
09-06-96 - 19-08-96	Rotterdam	Natuurmuseum Rotterdam	Manifesta I
09-06-96 - onwards	Rotterdam	Natuurmuseum Rotterdam	Biological Diversity
09-06-96 - onwards	Rotterdam	Natuurmuseum Rotterdam	Dr. A.B. Van Deinse's Collection
09-06-96 - 14-07-96	Laren	Singer Museum	Henk Wolvers Ceramics
11-06-96 - 18-08-96	Groningen	Groninger Museum	30 Years of Acquisitions
14-06-96 - 15-09-96	Den Haag-The Hague	Haags Gemeentemuseum	Traditional Gems - Modern Jewellery
14-06-96 - 15-08-96	Haarlem	Teylers Museum	Master Drawings
14-06-96 - onwards	Middelburg	Zeeuws Museum	Middelburg and the VOC
mid Jun 96-Sep 96	Den Haag-The Hague	Haags Historisch Museum	Count Floris V of Holland
15-06-96 - 01-09-96	Eindhoven	Stedelijk Van Abbemuseum	Jubilee Exhibition 2
21-06-96 - 02-09-96	Leeuwarden	Keramiekmuseum Princessehof	Johan van Loon
22-06-96 - 18-08-96	Amsterdam	Stedelijk Museum M. of Modern Art	Photographs from the M. Collection
22-06-96 - 01-09-96	Nijmegen	M. Commanderie van Sint-Jan	Omdat Dair In Die Kleijne Arme
23-06-96 - 18-08-96	Laren	Singer Museum	Sjoerd de Vries Paintings
29-06-96 - 25-08-96	Amsterdam	Stedelijk Museum M. of Modern Art	Under Capricorn
29-06-96 - 22-09-96	Arnhem	M. Moderne Kunst-M. Modern Art	Intimacy
29-06-96 - 01-09-96	Den Haag-The Hague	Het Paleis	Leon Spilliaert and M.C. Escher
29-06-96 - 11-08-96	Haarlem	Frans Halsmuseum/Verweyhal	Classic Moderns
29-06-96 - 20-10-96	Rotterdam	NAI Ned. Arch. instituut-Architecture	Dutch Interior
29-06-96 - 25-08-96	Zwolle	Stedelijk Museum Zwolle	Cats in the Visual Arts
30-06-96 - 25-08-96	Arnhem	M. Moderne Kunst-M. Modern Art	Walter Stevens
30-06-96 - 01-09-96	Groningen	Groninger Museum	Dick Bruna & Paul Huf
30-06-96 - 18-08-96	Laren	Singer Museum	Margot Zandstra Objects
Jul 96-Aug 96	Apeldoorn	Paleis Het Loo - Nationaal M.	A Royal View over the Garden
Jul 96-Aug 96	Enschede	Rijksmuseum Twenthe	Henry William Bunbury (1750-1811)
05-07-96 - 14-07-96	Apeldoorn	Paleis Het Loo - Nationaal M.	National Lathyrus Show (Sweet Peas)
06-07-96 - 01-09-96	Middelburg	Zeeuws Museum	Stills Photographic Works
07-07-96 - 15-09-96	Schiedam	Stedelijk Museum Schiedam	Summer Exhibition
12-07-96 - 15-09-96	Amsterdam	Stedelijk Museum M. of Modern Art	Cobra and the Stedelijk
13-07-96 - 08-09-96	Amsterdam	Stedelijk Museum M. of Modern Art	August Sander
13-07-96 - 06-10-96	Den Haag-The Hague	Haags Gemeentemuseum	French Masters from Moscow

Exhibitions in chronological order.

THE NETHERLANDS

DATE	CITY	MUSEUM	ARTIST/THEME
13·07·96 - 25·08·96	Haarlem	Frans Halsmuseum/Museum	Jun Kaneko Ceramic Objects
13·07·96 - 06·10·96	Leeuwarden	Fries Museum	Written in the Book
14·07·96 - 01·09·96	Amsterdam	De Nieuwe Kerk	Russian Summer
20·07·96 - 01·09·96	Arnhem	M. Moderne Kunst-M. Modern Art	Twan Janssen Solo
26·07·96 - 17·11·96	Amsterdam	Van Gogh Museum	In Living Colour
01·08·96 - 29·09·96	Rotterdam	NAI Ned. Arch. instituut-Architecture	Coast Wise Europe
10·08·96 - 27·10·96	Amsterdam	Rijksmuseum	The Great American Watercolour
10·08·96 - 10·11·96	Haarlem	Teylers Museum	Time and Life
10·08·96 - 17·11·96	Rotterdam	NAI Ned. Arch. instituut-Architecture	Real Space in Quick Times
22·08·96 - 27·10·96	Amsterdam	Amsterdam Historical Museum	Open House
24·08·96 - 27·10·96	Rotterdam	Kunsthal Rotterdam	Mary Ellen Mark
24·08·96 - 10·11·96	Rotterdam	Kunsthal Rotterdam	African Sculpture
24·08·96 - 03·11·96	Rotterdam	NAI Ned. Arch. instituut-Architecture	Ben Loerakker
25·08·96 - 20·10·96	Arnhem	M. Moderne Kunst-M. Modern Art	Piet Stockmans
25·08·96 - 03·11·96	Laren	Singer Museum	F. Hart Nibbrig (1866-1915)
31·08·96 - 31·08·96	Apeldoorn	Paleis Het Loo - Nationaal M.	Royal Fireworks
31·08·96 - 03·11·96	Haarlem	Frans Halsmuseum/Vleeshal	Pop-Up
31·08·96 - 27·10·96	Haarlem	Teylers Museum	History of a Haarlem Drawing Academy
31·08·96 - 27·10·96	Utrecht	Centraal Museum Utrecht	Collection of Contemporary Drawings
31·08·96 - 27·10·96	Utrecht	Centraal Museum Utrecht	Take 2 Contemporary Art
31·08·96 - 17·11·96	Utrecht	Museum Catharijneconvent	The Utrecht Psalter
Sep 96	Enschede	Rijksmuseum Twenthe	Pjotr Müller
Sep 96 - Jan 97	Leiden	Rijksm. van Oudheden M. Antiquities	Hands On
Sep 96	Schiedam	Stedelijk Museum Schiedam	Art Relay
07·09·96 - 27·10·96	Amsterdam	Stedelijk Museum M. of Modern Art	Marcus Lupertz
07·09·96 - 13·10·96	Nijmegen	M. Commanderie van Sint-Jan	Servie Janssen (1949)
07·09·96 - 17·11·96	Rotterdam	Kunsthal Rotterdam	The Erasmus Bridge
07·09·96 - 27·10·96	Rotterdam	Witte de With/Cont. Art	Tony Brown
08·09·96 - 17·11·96	Dordrecht	Dordrechts Museum	Robert Zandvliet
08·09·96 - 01·12·96	Rotterdam	M. Boymans-van Beuningen	Willem de Kooning
13·09·96 - Dec 96	Amsterdam	Joods Historisch M. - Jewish Hist. M.	Jules Chapon
14·09·96 - 10·11·96	Amsterdam	Stedelijk Museum M. of Modern Art	Art from Surinam 1977-1995
14·09·96 - 24·11·96	Eindhoven	Stedelijk Van Abbemuseum	Brabant 200 Years of History
14·09·96 - 24·11·96	's-Hertogenbosch	Noordbrabants Museum	The Muse as Driving Force
14·09·96 - 27·10·96	Leeuwarden	Fries Museum	Harmen Abma
15·09·96 - 17·11·96	Dordrecht	Dordrechts Museum	Masters of Dordrecht/19th Century
15·09·96 - 24·11·96	Haarlem	Frans Halsmuseum/Vleeshal	Earthly Paradises
mid Sep 96 - Nov 96	Den Haag-The Hague	Haags Historisch Museum	Art and History
mid Sep 96 - Nov 96	Den Haag-The Hague	Haags Historisch Museum	The Dollhouse of Lita de Ranitz
15·09·96 - 24·11·96	Schiedam	Stedelijk Museum Schiedam	Autumn Exhibition of Contemporary Art
20·09·96 - 25·11·96	Leeuwarden	Keramiekmuseum Princessehof	Ceramics from Morocco
20·09·96 - end Nov 96	Maastricht	Bonnefantenmuseum	Gary Hume
20·09·96 - 14·01·97	Middelburg	Zeeuws Museum	Contemporary Art
21·09·96 - 12·01·97	Amsterdam	Rijksmuseum	Jan Steen Painter and Storyteller
21·09·96 - 01·12·96	Den Haag-The Hague	Het Paleis	Princely Possessions
Autumn 96	Otterlo	Kröller-Müller Museum	Franz West Retrospective
Oct 96-Mar 97	Leiden	Rijksm. van Oudheden M. Antiquities	Double-Crossing
03·10·96 - 07·01·97	Amsterdam	Amsterdam Historical Museum	Fans and Lace
05·10·96 - 05·01·97	Amsterdam	Museum het Rembrandthuis	The Old Testament
05·10·96 - 12·01·97	Assen	Drents Museum	Iron Spoons
05·10·96 - 09·03·97	Rotterdam	Maritiem M. 'Prins Hendrik'	The Dockworker in Rotterdam
07·10·96 - 10·11·96	Laren	Singer Museum	Johnny Rolf Graphic Work
11·10·96 - May 97	Leiden	Rijksmuseum voor Volkenkunde	Veils
12·10·96 - Apr 97	Amsterdam	Ned. Scheepvaartmuseum A'dam	Trapped in Ice
12·10·96 - 13·01·97	Leiden	Stedelijk M. De Lakenhal	Jan van Goyen
13·10·96 - 17·11·96	Arnhem	M. Moderne Kunst-M. Modern Art	Biennale Gelderland 1996
13·10·96 - 07·01·97	Leeuwarden	Fries Museum	It Fires

Exhibitions in chronological order.

THE NETHERLANDS

DATE	CITY	MUSEUM	ARTIST/THEME
19·10·96 - 01·12·96	Nijmegen	M. Commanderie van Sint-Jan	Biennale Gelderland
19·10·96 - 1997	Rotterdam	NAI Ned. Arch. instituut-Architecture	Europan
25·10·96 - 02·04·97	Apeldoorn	Paleis Het Loo - Nationaal M.	Between two Thrones
27·10·96 - 06·01·97	Apeldoorn	Van Reekum Museum	Cees Andriessen The Graphic Work
Nov 96 - Aug 97	Amsterdam	Tropenmuseum	Amazonia
Nov 96 - Dec 96	Haarlem	Teylers Museum	Johan Sybo Sjollema (1900-1990)
02·11·96 - 02·02·97	Amsterdam	Rijksmuseum	Reflections on the Everyday
02·11·96 - 05·01·97	Rotterdam	Kunsthal Rotterdam	The Motorway
09·11·96 - 12·01·97	Arnhem	M. Moderne Kunst-M. Modern Art	Ri-Jeanne Cuppens
09·11·96 - 15·01·97	Rotterdam	Witte de With/Cont. Art	Frederick Kiesler
10·11·96 - 05·01·97	Rotterdam	M. Boymans-van Beuningen	Kees van Dongen 1897-1914
10·11·96 - 1997	Rotterdam	NAI Ned. Arch. instituut-Architecture	The Collection Gispen
16·11·96 - 05·01·97	Zwolle	Stedelijk Museum Zwolle	Late Medieval Manuscripts from Salland
17·11·96 - 05·01·97	Laren	Singer Museum	Graphics Now 7
18·11·96 - 20·11·96	Rotterdam	Kunsthal Rotterdam	The Art of Cooking
23·11·96 - Jan 97	Amsterdam	Stedelijk Museum M. of Modern Art	20th-Century Italian Art
24·11·96 - 23·02·97	Haarlem	Frans Halsmuseum/Verweyhal	Herman Kruyder
29·11·96 - 02·03·97	Amsterdam	Van Gogh Museum	Sir Lawrence Alma-Tadema
29·11·96 - 01·12·96	Schiedam	Stedelijk Museum Schiedam	Kunstwerkt Foundation Art Fair
30·11·96 - Feb 97	Arnhem	M. Moderne Kunst-M. Modern Art	The Faience Earthenware Factory
30·11·96 - 03·02·97	Dordrecht	Dordrechts Museum	Bea de Visser
Dec 96 - Feb 96	Den Haag-The Hague	Haags Historisch Museum	House of Orange and Romanovs
Dec 96 - Feb 97	Haarlem	Teylers Museum	Dutch Drawings of the 17th Century
Dec 96 - Jan 97	Schiedam	Stedelijk Museum Schiedam	Historical Christmas Exhibition
Dec 96 - onwards	Schiedam	Stedelijk Museum Schiedam	Historical Exhibition
Dec 96 - onwards	Utrecht	Museum Catharijneconvent	Russian Popular Prints and Drawings
06·12·96 - 23·02·97	Rotterdam	Kunsthal Rotterdam	Sea in Sight
07·12·96 - Feb 97	Rotterdam	NAI Ned. Arch. instituut-Architecture	The Netherlands Goes to School
12·12·96 - 10·03·97	's-Hertogenbosch	Noordbrabants Museum	Jewish Culture in North Brabant
14·12·96 - 16·02·97	Den Haag-The Hague	Het Paleis	Suze Robertson
14·12·96 - 09·02·97	Haarlem	Frans Halsmuseum/Vleeshal	Kunst zij ons Doel
15·12·96 - 15·04·97	Amsterdam	Amsterdam Historical Museum	Czar Peter The Great and Holland
mid Dec 96-end Feb 97	Leeuwarden	Keramiekmuseum Princessehof	Modern Ceramics - two exhibitions
17·12·96 - 13·04·97	Amsterdam	De Nieuwe Kerk	Russian Winter
22·12·96 - 16·02·97	Rotterdam	M. Boymans-van Beuningen	Praise of the High Seas
Jan 97 - Mar 97	Rotterdam	Witte de With/Cont. Art	Tacita Dean and Gerco de Ruyter
19·01·97 - 16·03·97	Laren	Singer Museum	Reimond Kimpe (1885-1970)
Feb 97 - Mar 97	Arnhem	M. Moderne Kunst-M. Modern Art	Barbara Broekman
Feb 97 - Apr 97	Haarlem	Teylers Museum	Leonard Springer (1855-1940)
01·03·97 - 01·06·97	Den Haag-The Hague	Haags Gemeentemuseum	German Expressionism
01·03·97 - 11·05·97	Den Haag-The Hague	Haags Gemeentemuseum	The Golden Age in Denmark
Mar 97 - Apr 97	Den Haag-The Hague	Haags Historisch Museum	Pieter de Swart (1709-1773)
Spring 97	Middelburg	Zeeuws Museum	Reimond Kimpe (1885-1970)
Spring 97	Rotterdam	NAI Ned. Arch. instituut-Architecture	Michel De Klerk
22·03·97 - Spring 97	Apeldoorn	Van Reekum Museum	Nicolas Dings Drawings
22·03·97 - 01·06·97	Utrecht	Museum Catharijneconvent	Preachers
28·03·97 - 08·06·97	's-Hertogenbosch	Noordbrabants Museum	Children's Culture
28·03·97 - 14·09·97	Rotterdam	Maritiem M. 'Prins Hendrik'	Ships for the Environment
01·04·97 - 20·06·97	Laren	Singer Museum	Henri le Sidaner Drawings
22·04·97 - Jun 97	Amsterdam	De Nieuwe Kerk	World Press Photo

Exhibitions in chronological order.

SWITZERLAND

DATE	CITY	MUSEUM	ARTIST/THEME
until 30·05·96	Genève - Geneva	Petit Palais, M. d'Art Moderne	'Montmartre Vivant'
24·02·96 - 19·05·96	Solothurn	Kunstmuseum Solothurn	Ben Vautier
24·02·96 - 27·05·96	Vevey	Swiss Camera Museum	Dominique Derisbourg
10·03·96 - 12·05·96	Basel - Basle	Kunsthalle Basel	Beat Klein
10·03·96 - 12·05·96	Basel - Basle	Kunsthalle Basel	N. Araki, L. Clark, T. Struth, C. Williams
10·03·96 - 12·05·96	Basel - Basle	Kunsthalle Basel	Michel Majerus
15·03·96 - 19·05·96	Zürich	Kunsthaus Zürich	Erotika
15·03·96 - 02·06·96	Zürich	The Swiss National Museum	Those Who Can Get A Job Work!
27·03·96 - 02·06·96	Bern	Kunstmuseum Bern	John Webber (1751-1793)
28·03·96 - 15·06·96	Genève - Geneva	Centre d' Art Contemp. de Genève	Katia Bassanini
29·03·96 - 02·06·96	Bern	Kunstmuseum Bern	Drawing is Seeing
30·03·96 - 19·05·96	Aarau	Aargauer Kunsthaus	Ingeborg Lüscher
30·03·96 - 09·06·96	Aarau	Aargauer Kunsthaus	Works from the Collection
30·03·96 - 19·05·96	La Chaux-de-Fonds	Musée des Beaux-Arts	Christian Lindow 1945-1990
04·04·96 - 14·07·96	Zürich	Kunsthaus Zürich	Ancient China
04·04·96 - 04·07·96	Zürich	M. Rietberg / Villa Wesendonck	Mandate of Heaven
12·04·96 - 23·06·96	Zürich	Kunsthaus Zürich	Hans Danuser
12·04·96 - 09·06·96	Zürich	Konstruktive und Konkrete Kunst	Dadamaine 'I fatti della vita'
12·04·96 - 27·10·96	Zürich	Konstruktive und Konkrete Kunst	Work Groups
14·04·96 - 09·06·96	Aarau	Aargauer Kunsthaus	Jan Hubertus
18·04·96 - 06·10·96	Genève - Geneva	Musée d'Art et d'Histoire	The Alps as Seen by Geneva Romantics
19·04·96 - 14·07·96	Genève - Geneva	Musée d'Art et d'Histoire	Bronze and Gold
26·04·96 - 28·07·96	Genève - Geneva	Musée Rath	Rodolphe Töpffer (1799-1846)
27·04·96 - 11·08·96	Basel - Basle	Kunstmuseum	Canto d'Amore
28·04·96 - 23·06·96	Basel - Basle	Antikenmuseum Basel und Ludwig	Pandora
May 96-mid Jun96	Genève - Geneva	Gravure Contemporaine	Kristin Oppenheim (USA)
May 96	Lugano	M. Cantonale d'Arte	Collection M. Cantonale d'Arte
08·05·96 - 01·09·96	Genève - Geneva	Centre d' Art Contemp. de Genève	Ingeborg Luescher
15·05·96 - 01·09·96	Genève - Geneva	Centre d' Art Contemp. de Genève	Pipilotti Rist
15·05·96 - 22·09·96	Lausanne	M. Cantonal des Beaux-Arts	Aristide Maillo
18·05·96 - 25·08·96	Basel - Basle	Kunstmuseum	Engraving - Etching - Aquatint
24·05·96 - 27·10·96	Zürich	M. Rietberg/Haus zum Kiel	Keris Handles f.t. Malayan Archipelago
01·06·96 - 29·09·96	Basel - Basle	Museum für Gegenwartskunst	FremdKörper-Foreign Bodies
Jun 96 - Sep 96	Bern	Bernisches Historisches Museum	Pharaonic and Coptic Burial Treasures
Jun 96	Lugano	M. Cantonale d'Arte	Video Art
01·06·96 - 31·08·96	Genève - Geneva	Ariana	Dutch Majolica
02·06·96 - 11·08·96	Aarau	Aargauer Kunsthaus	Jan Schoonhoven
02·06·96 - 01·09·96	Zug	Kunsthaus Zug	Tadashi Kawamata
02·06·96 - 01·09·96	Zug	Kunsthaus Zug	Richard Tuttle
06·06·96 - 08·09·96	Genève - Geneva	Cabinet des Estampes	Only in Geneva
07·06·96 - 31·12·96	Genève - Geneva	Maison Tavel	Rodolphe Töpffer
07·06·96 - 31·12·96	Genève - Geneva	Maison Tavel	The Alps in Detail
07·06·96 - 18·08·96	Zürich	Kunsthaus Zürich	Inez van Lamsweerde
08·06·96 - 13·10·96	Vevey	Swiss Camera Museum	The World in Three Dimensions
09·06·96 - 25·08·96	Basel - Basle	Kunsthalle Basel	F. West, E. Krasinski, J. Rhodes
14·06·96 - Spring 97	Genève - Geneva	M. Histoire Sciences Villa Bartholoni	Anatomical Models
15·06·96 - 22·09·96	Solothurn	Kunstmuseum Solothurn	Friendships and Artistic Sense
15·06·96 - 22·09·96	Solothurn	Kunstmuseum Solothurn	Art from Africa, Asia and America
15·06·96 - 22·09·96	Solothurn	Kunstmuseum Solothurn	The Müller Family's Photographs
19·06·96 - 18·08·96	Bern	Kunstmuseum Bern	Life, a Dream Ernst Kreidolf
21·06·96 - 18·08·96	Zürich	Konstruktive und Konkrete Kunst	Hartmut Böhm
22·06·96 - 25·08·96	La Chaux-de-Fonds	Musée des Beaux-Arts	Three Painters' Collections
23·06·96 - 08·09·96	Aarau	Aargauer Kunsthaus	Robert Müller
28·06·96 - 28·09·96	Genève - Geneva	Gravure Contemporaine	Four Artists Books and Exhibitions
05·07·96 - 03·11·96	Zürich	Kunsthaus Zürich	Peter Fischli/David Weiss
19·07·96 - 27·10·96	Zürich	The Swiss National Museum	Art of Sound
23·08·96 - 10·11·96	Zürich	Kunsthaus Zürich	In Artificial Light

Exhibitions in chronological order.

SWITZERLAND

DATE	CITY	MUSEUM	ARTIST/THEME
24·08·96 - 17·11·96	Aarau	Aargauer Kunsthaus	Works from the Aargau Art Collection
30·08·96 - 27·10·96	Zürich	Kunsthaus Zürich	Pierrick Sorin
30·08·96 - 27·10·96	Zürich	Konstruktive und Konkrete Kunst	Florin Granwehr 'Stand der Lage'
07·09·96 - 10·11·96	Basel - Basle	Kunstmuseum	Watercolours
08·09·96 - 17·11·96	Lugano	M. Cantonale d'Arte	Odilon Redon
13·09·96 - 05·01·97	Genève - Geneva	Musée Rath	Dieter Roth
15·09·96 - 03·11·96	Basel - Basle	Kunsthalle Basel	Liz Larner, Zoe Leonard
15·09·96 - 03·11·96	Zug	Kunsthaus Zug	Heinz Gappmayr Text Images
20·09·96 - early 1997	Genève - Geneva	Musée d'Art et d'Histoire	The Episcopate of Geneva
26·09·96 - 03·11·96	Genève - Geneva	Cabinet des Estampes	Hors Scène II
28·09·96 - 17·11·96	Aarau	Aargauer Kunsthaus	Carmen Perrin
28·09·96 - 19·01·97	Basel - Basle	Kunstmuseum	Put into Light II
28·09·96 - 10·11·96	La Chaux-de-Fonds	Musée des Beaux-Arts	François Morellet
06·10·96 - 08·12·96	Lausanne	M. Cantonal des Beaux-Arts	Thomas Huber Paintings 1990-1995
mid Oct 96-Dec 96	Genève - Geneva	Gravure Contemporaine	Heimo Zobernig Book and Exhibition
19·10·96 - end Jan 97	Vevey	Swiss Camera Museum	Carlo Ponti, Image Wizard
26·10·96 - Mar 97	Basel - Basle	Museum für Gegenwartskunst	Dan Graham/Andrea Zittel
Nov 96 - Jan 97	Genève - Geneva	Centre d' Art Contemp. de Genève	Winners of the Swiss Federal Grants
03·11·96 - 30·03·97	Zürich	M. Rietberg / Villa Wesendonck	Sican
08·11·96 - 05·01·97	Zürich	Kunsthaus Zürich	Marianne Olsen/Walter Siegfried
08·11·96 - 12·01·97	Zürich	Kunsthaus Zürich	Hans Baumgartner
08·11·96 - 19·01·97	Zürich	Konstruktive und konkrete Kunst	The Colour WHITE From Zero to Today
19·11·96 - 15·02·97	Genève - Geneva	Ariana	Setsuko Nagasawa
23·11·96 - 26·01·97	Basel - Basle	Kunstmuseum	Russian Avant-Garde
24·11·96 - 11·01·97	Basel - Basle	Kunsthalle Basel	Annual Exhibition of Basle Artists
28·11·96 - 19·01·97	Genève - Geneva	Cabinet des Estampes	Robert Müller Prints 1983-1995
29·11·96 - 02·03·97	Zürich	M. Rietberg / Haus zum Kiel	Côte d'Ivoire
30·11·96 - 05·01·97	La Chaux-de-Fonds	Musée des Beaux-Arts	Young Painters
Dec 96 - Mar 97	Bern	Bernisches Historisches Museum	Stained Glass Designs/Armorial Glass
06·12·96 - 23·02·97	Zürich	Kunsthaus Zürich	Austria in a Net of Roses
07·12·96 - 12·01·97	Aarau	Aargauer Kunsthaus	Annual Exhibition of Aargau Artists
12·12·96 - 28·04·97	Genève - Geneva	Musée d'Art et d'Histoire	Greek, Melchite and Russian Icons
14·12·96 - 09·03·97	Basel - Basle	Kunstmuseum	Anne-Marie and Ernst Vischer-Wadler
Jan 97 - Apr 97	Genève - Geneva	Musée d'Art et d'Histoire	Fragments of Italiote Vases
Feb 97 - May 97I	Genève - Geneva	Centre d' Art Contemp. de Genève	Italian Art Today
20·03·97 - 13·07·97	Basel - Basle	Antikenmuseum Basel und Ludwig	Egypt Moments of Eternity